ANEURIN BEVAN

A BIOGRAPHY

MICHAEL FOOT

Aneurin Bevan

A BIOGRAPHY

Volume Two: 1945–1960

LONDON
DAVIS-POYNTER
1973

FIRST PUBLISHED IN 1973 BY
DAVIS-POYNTER LIMITED
20 GARRICK STREET LONDON WC2E 9BJ

ISBN 0 7067 0089 9

PRINTED IN GREAT BRITAIN BY
EBENEZER BAYLIS & SON LIMITED
THE TRINITY PRESS, WORCESTER, AND LONDON

To
JILL
without whose love and guidance
this book could never have been
completed,
and to the people of
TREDEGAR, EBBW VALE,
RHYMNEY and ABERTYSSWG

CONTENTS

PREFACE   *page* 11

1   1945   17

2   Minister of Housing: 1945–1947   60

3   Minister of Health I: The Making of the Health
        Service 1945–1946   102

4   Minister of Health II: The Making of the Health
        Service 1946–1948   139

5   Steel: 1947–1948   219

6   'Vermin': 1948   237

7   The Mixed Economy: 1948–1950   257

8   The Clash: 1950–1951   283

9   The Bevanites I: 1951–1952   350

10 The Bevanites II: 1953   388

11 The Bevanites III: 1954   424

12 The Arctic Volcano: January 1955–April 1955   453

13 The Unknown Factor: 1955–1956   485

14 Suez: 1956–1957   516

15 The Bomb: 1957   549

16 The Meretricious Society: 1958–1960   585

17 1960   654

INDEX   661

ILLUSTRATIONS

Frontispiece

The following pictures are to be found between pages 336–337

1 My (the author's) favourite photo. *Michael Peto*

2 Operation Sabotage by David Low. *Evening Standard*

3 With Tito in Brioni, 1952

4 With Pandit Jawaharlal Nehru. *Punjab Photo Service*

5 It's A Drive for Unity and Goodwill by Vicky. *News Chronicle*

6 Cutting the Patient in Half by Vicky. *News Chronicle*

7 With Jennie and Vaughan Griffiths. *Daily Herald*

8 Guess Who by Giles, 1952. *Daily Express*

9 One Way Only by Vicky. *News Chronicle*

10 Portrait by Vicky

11 With Mendès-France and Pietro Nenni. *Cartier-Bresson*

12 One of the last pictures

PREFACE

In this book – as in the earlier volume of the same biography published several years ago – I seek to describe the political values which Aneurin Bevan sustained throughout his life and the major political battles in which he engaged. That, I am sure, is what he would have wished anyone writing about him to do.

The earlier volume carried the record from his birth, on 15 November 1897, in Tredegar, in the Welsh county of Monmouthshire, until the moment when he took his place, as Minister of Health, in the Labour Cabinet of 1945. The present volume covers the period from that date until his death in 1960. The two volumes are intended to form a single whole, yet the dividing line between them is sharp, the problems set by each period for the biographer are strangely different (or at least I have found them so), and each volume is also intended to be understandable on its own.

As with the previous volume, Jennie Lee has given me invaluable assistance and guidance, but for this second volume my dependence on her knowledge has been even more continuous and essential. That statement might give rise to misunderstanding. It might be thought or inferred that she may have been the more tempted to impose limitations on what I wished to write. Nothing of the sort has occurred. I have had no dispute with her about any view or judgment I wished to express. Partly that situation has arisen from our general identity of political outlook, but it continued to prevail even in dealing with those occasions when differences between us momentarily emerged. Of course, the responsibility for any errors or mistaken views in the final verdict printed is mine, not hers.

To several others who helped me with the first volume, I must express my thanks again; members of Aneurin Bevan's family in Tredegar; Archie Lush, his closest friend dating back to the 1920s: Donald Bruce, who was Aneurin Bevan's Parliamentary Private Secretary between 1945 and 1950, and the late Will Griffiths, who succeeded him in that post; to two of my closest friends in the House of Commons, Tom Driberg, who once again kindly agreed to read the proofs and corrected many errors, and Ian Mikardo who assisted in the same arduous task, and, above all, Elizabeth Thomas whose general surveillance over every aspect of the book's publication has been indispensable; and to Una Cooze, my secretary, who has greatly eased the work involved and without whom publication at the agreed date could never have been achieved.

Several Members of Parliament in addition to those just mentioned, some civil servants who served at the Ministry of Health, and some of the doctors who participated in the making of the National Health Service have assisted me in different ways which, I trust, appear properly recognized in the text or the footnotes. But three other special debts must be further acknowledged.

For the period between 1951 and 1959, I have had the immeasurable advantage of reading the as yet unpublished diaries of Dick Crossman. He has allowed me to read, and to quote, and to compare my own recollections with his, in a manner for which the word generous seems to be wretchedly inadequate. He has allowed me to study diary entries which he himself had never scrutinized since the particular weeks in which they were written. I am sure the appetites of readers will be whetted for the full Crossman diaries which will take a most notable place in our political literature. But perhaps I should underline here the point which may later appear superfluous: Crossman is not responsible in any sense for my judgments, and vice versa.

Readers of the later sections of the book will also be able to see how much I owe to two other of Nye's closest friends among journalists, and lest this last category may be thought to qualify the intimacy, let the impression be at once removed. Geoffrey Goodman and K. S. Karol held Nye's friendship as Socialists as well as journalists, and each of them learned by experience how warm and overwhelming that friendship could be.

In addition to these personal debts I must make particular acknowledgment also of the advantage I have had in reading the unpublished diaries of Hugh Dalton, now in the library of the London School of Economics. Some of the passages from that diary which Dalton himself decided *not* to publish speak to us now, I believe, with a thunderous significance.

As in the first volume, the most necessary published sources on which I have drawn are Aneurin Bevan's parliamentary and public speeches, his own book, *In Place of Fear*, his own journalism, and the files of *Tribune*. The other main books quoted and used are indicated in the footnotes. One difficulty for the period between 1945 and 1951 is that I could not have had access to the Cabinet minutes for the time, but I hope the implications and the limits of this restriction are also sufficiently indicated in the text.

Perhaps I may be permitted a word also on the form of chronology I have adopted. Partly owing to this lack of access to the Cabinet documents and, more still, because of the desirability of telling the story of the establishment of the National Health Service as a consecutive whole, Chapters Two, Three, Four and Five, in a sense, overlap one another. But thereafter, I trust, the more regular narrative pattern which was followed in Volume One is resumed.

One problem of nomenclature has perpetually baffled me, but the system I have adopted, I trust, will not be found too irritating for the reader. Since this book is primarily a record of political and public events and controversies, almost always I refer to 'Bevan'. But sometimes the context seemed to forbid this necessary formality. So then, in some circumstances, I call him 'Nye', as most of us did. And sometimes the name is spelt 'Ni'. That was the spelling used by Jennie and his most intimate friends in Tredegar.

May 1973   MICHAEL FOOT

ANEURIN BEVAN

1

1945

The candidates were not men but principles.
—THOMAS PAINE[1]

NO SOCIALIST who saw it will forget the blissful dawn of July 1945. The great war in Europe had ended; the lesser war in Asia might be ending soon. This background to the scene in Britain naturally deepened the sense of release and breath-taking opportunity. And those who had served the British Labour movement for generations, renewing their faith after each disaster, in 1919, 1926 and 1931, had their own special cause for exultation. When the scale of the Labour Party's victory became known on the night of 26 July, bonfires were lit, people danced in the streets, and young and old crowded into halls all over the country to acclaim their elected standard bearers:

> *Men met each other with erected look,*
> *The steps were higher that they took;*
> *Friends to congratulate their friends made haste,*
> *And long inveterate foes saluted as they passed*[2]

Varying elements and expectations combined to make the Labour Party, but one theme united them as never before. Eyes were fixed on the promise of a new society. Suddenly the vision of the Socialist pioneers had been given substance and historic impetus by the radical political ferment of wartime.

Moreover, the victory had been won against all odds and orthodox prophecies; in particular, against the popularity of the most powerful war leader in British history. Winston Churchill had sought to emulate the Lloyd George of 1918; he had revived every

[1] *Rights of Man.*
[2] *Threnodia Augustalis* by John Dryden.

17

well-tried trick of the electoral game, mobilised every engine of publicity, and beat the patriotic drum in the Conservative cause. But somehow the performance looked old-fashioned and fustian. Many observers noted how thoughtfully the British people went to the polls. 'The national newspapers,' wrote Aneurin Bevan, in his last article for *Tribune* before his appointment as Minister of Health in the new administration, 'have become so accustomed to writing up personalities in place of principles that they have completely lost touch with the people. They persuaded themselves that when they wrote Churchill into their headlines they wrote him on the people's heart'.[1]

Bevan's own verdict on the result summarised his perception of the national instinct which he had long sought to impress upon others. His persistent accusation against the Labour Party leadership since 1940 – indeed since much earlier – was that it had underestimated its national support and been content to play the role of servitors. Now at last the Labour Party could stand erect. 'The significance of the election,' Bevan wrote in that same *Tribune* article, 'is that the British people have voted deliberately and consciously for a new world, both at home and abroad. In fact they have proved more courageous and far-sighted than their leaders. They had turned their backs on Churchill and his Tory values before their national leaders had realized that they had done so. The General Election was not an argument with the issue in doubt until all sides were heard. It was the registration of a change which had occurred in Britain before the war began. This fact enabled the people to withstand the assault on their emotions. For the first time in our history we have an electorate, adult and responsible, knowing what it wants, with some notion of the difficulties involved in attempting it, and ready to pay the price for the effort.' Allowing for post-election euphoria, the boast was just. Tories might protest otherwise, but the British people had not been swept off their feet by extravagant pledges. Long before 1945, at every available by-election, the electors had shown the same deliberate demand for change, and the goodwill behind the new Government lasted for years afterwards. The vote for a new world was no mere millennial illusion. Rather, despite all the excitement of the hour, it was a

[1] *Tribune* 3 August 1945.

sober judgment on how the national energy displayed in war could be turned to the work of peace; the very discipline of war could be used to buttress the necessary planning for the future. This, with the determination not to permit the disorder, misery and mass unemployment which had followed the 1918 armistice, was the central appeal Labour had made to the nation. If ever in British history, the 1945 election was a victory for clear political principles and ideas, defined with reasonable accuracy in the Party manifesto *Let Us Face the Future*, presented to the pre-election Party Conference at Blackpool.

When the House of Commons first met, Labour M.P.s, two-thirds of them Members for the first time, celebrated the occasion by singing the *Red Flag*. Tories were horrified, and the officials of the House went on with the ceremony, much as a polite host continues the conversation after his guest has upset the soup. Mr Herbert Morrison, the new Leader of the House, professed himself 'mildly disturbed . . . These youngsters still had to absorb the atmosphere of the House. But I recognized that it was largely first-day high spirits'.[1] Yet the spirit was sustained well beyond the first day. Through many subsequent months, the debating chamber was crammed while long queues of visitors waited to see the spectacle. Each Minister in turn introducing great reforms could be assured of a packed House. Hugh Dalton waved the Party manifesto in the face of the spluttering Tories. 'We are the masters now' was allegedly the bloodcurdling cry of one well-breeched champion of the sansculottes, Sir Hartley Shawcross.[2] M.P.s' postbags were bigger than ever before. Most new Members were reporting every month or more frequently to their constituency organizations. The whole place tingled with energy and youth. Overnight, Parliament – even the moribund institution elected in 1935, where Aneurin Bevan had often found himself fighting alone or in the company of a handful of fellow rebels – had become unmistakably the great national forum.

For Aneurin Bevan the transformation was especially sweet. He,

[1] *An Autobiography* by Herbert Morrison (Odhams, 1960), p. 251.
[2] Now Lord Shawcross. In fact he had said something rather different but the point was scarcely noted until Anthony Howard sought to investigate the matter in *Age of Austerity* (Hodder & Stoughton, 1963).

more forthrightly than anyone else, had prophesied that the Tories
would collapse into a period of insignificance, that Churchill himself would be reduced to mortal dimensions. He, without rival,
embodied the hopes of the most ardent Labour Party workers. The
old pre-1945 Parliamentary Party had never elected him to anything. A bare fifteen months before he had been saved from expulsion from the Party altogether by the narrowest of margins. Now,
at the age of forty-seven, he was the youngest member of the
Cabinet, charged with the responsibility of dealing with some of
the Government's most urgent domestic tasks in the very office he
would have picked for himself. His bitterest enemies foretold early
disaster. The demagogue would soon be exposed; how long could
it be before that loud mouth betrayed him? Others cynically remarked that the Prime Minister could not afford to leave so savage
a tongue unmuzzled on the back benches; cunningly he had been
given the most awkward of assignments. Bevan himself had never
thought in terms of office. The customary reckonings of politicians
were truly foreign to his nature and, in any case, his feuds with his
own Party dating back to 1930 and his tempestuous fights against
the wartime Coalition made the possibility seem infinitely remote.
But now, contrary to all expectation, it had happened. No mercy
would be shown him, either by Tories or his own Party, if he failed.
If he succeeded, every political prize would come within his reach.
It would be beyond human nature if he did not mark the
heights and depths surrounding the exposed precipice he had now
scaled.

Yet Bevan's distaste for personal calculation was no pose. No one
who witnessed what entranced him in conversation, in argument,
in books, in theoretical debate, could doubt that truth. His most
constant and genuine interest was the way the world was going or
would go or should go and what would happen to those whose
aspirations he claimed to make articulate and wished to make effective. As in the early days when he argued with his father or his
friend Archie Lush on their long marches across the mountains
round Tredegar, so in 1945 he placed his ambitions in a collectivist
context.

He was a democratic Socialist, and the 1945 victory meant that
the creed of democratic Socialism was facing its supreme test.

Stated thus, the assertion was no more than the platitude of every
Labour Party platform orator at the time. But Bevan meant something more intricate and fateful. His Socialism was rooted in
Marxism; whatever modifications he had made in the doctrine, a
belief in the class struggle stayed unshaken. Marxism taught him
that society must be changed swiftly, intrepidly, fundamentally, if
the transformation was not to be overturned by counter-revolution.
His own temperamental impatience fed the same thought, but its
mainspring was a Marxist estimate of the character of the class
enemy.

Often he lamented: 'The Tories are soft on the outside and hard
on the inside whereas we're hard on the outside but soft inside.'
This insight contrasted with the outward semblance. The same
Tories who could display such beguiling manners towards opponents in the House of Commons Smoking Room would band together and strike remorselessly in a crisis. Socialists, on the other
hand, who often showed themselves prickly and inflexible in personal dealings, would panic and surrender at the extreme moment
of challenge. All Bevan's own experience sustained his theory.
Labour's original sin was that it was reverential and deferential.
How many working-class leaders had curtsied to Tory dominance
and how many more had striven to mimic ruling-class fashions?
The deadly weakness could be exorcised only by a most deliberate
act of will. The brave new world could not be established without
bravery. Even a British revolution could not be made with rose-
water. Such phraseology about revolutions and counter-revolutions
might seem irrelevant to British conditions, but the reality embedded in it was still true. If British or parliamentary conventions
imposed limitations on the pace and scale of the change, it was
nonetheless necessary that the progressive forces should be continuously on the offensive. This was the cardinal requirement, and
the refusal of democratic Socialists to acknowledge it had so often
made them craven and contemptible.

Yet the democracy in Bevan's Socialism was no less vibrant than
his hard Marxist analysis of how ruthless the contest might be. All
his own experience – in the pre-war struggles for the unemployed,
within the unions, within the Labour Party, against the Churchill
Coalition – fortified his hatred of oligarchy and irresponsible

authority. Liberal economics had been exposed as sterile and self-defeating but the liberal virtues, protecting the right to heresy and free debate, retained an eternal validity. On the need for Socialists to capture the central state power Bevan took the orthodox Marxist view; any lesser ambition should be condemned as deceptive or *frivolous* – a favourite word in his vast vocabulary of scorn – for it involved leaving decisive weapons in the hands of the enemy. But on the issue of how Socialists should use and distribute the power once gained he dismissed the orthodox Communists as philosophically arid or illiterate.

'The purpose of getting power,' he often repeated, 'is to be able to give it away.' Democracy was both an end and a means. It was no outworn, bourgeois pretence, but the most sophisticated method of government, the potentialities of which had hardly been scratched. A continuous democratic process was essential for human dignity in modern societies. The Marxist theory of the state was inescapable, but the liberal criticism of it would re-emerge. Somehow a synthesis must be devised. What adequate checks could there be on exorbitant power but thriving democratic institutions? Once destroyed, how could those institutions ever be restored? And if they could be used to secure fundamental changes by persuasion and argument instead of force and bloodshed, how much more beneficent and enduring the victory could be? No nation had ever accomplished the feat; Britain, and perhaps only Britain, could set the example. Here the British democratic tradition, deriving from the Levellers and the Chartists, was grafted onto Bevan's Marxism. It could make him at times into a boastful or at least a passionate patriot, summoning to his aid forgotten voices from English and, more particularly, Welsh history.

Thus, by a quite different theoretical road than others had travelled before him, Bevan had become a convinced champion of Parliament as an institution.[1] He would accept neither the whole-

---

[1] It should not be forgotten that originally, in the 1920s, Bevan's views had been strongly syndicalist – see Volume I, Chapter 3. It was the failure of the trade union leadership which turned his mind to parliamentary action. There, in Parliament, he could speak to the people over the heads of the trade union bosses, among others. Suddenly, as an M.P., his voice was heard.

sale rejection of parliamentary methods occasionally prevalent on
the Left nor the more qualified criticism of those who sought to use
them while never abating their cynical derision. Yet he had certainly not, as Carlyle said of Gladstone, 'gone irrecoverably into
House of Commons shape'. He had studied the instrument much
more sceptically than the bulk of the Labour Party, and the language in which he stated his conviction showed how far removed
was his idea of the institution from that which appears in the textbooks. 'The issue in a capitalist democracy resolves itself into this:
either poverty will use democracy to win the struggle against property, or property, in fear of poverty, will destroy democracy . . .
The function of parliamentary democracy, under universal franchise, historically considered, is to expose wealth-privilege to the
attack of the people. It is a sword pointed at the heart of property-
power. The arena where the issues are joined is Parliament.'[1]

Could the sword be driven home? *Would* the sword be driven
home? Bevan knew all the restraints and perils – how the apparatus
of the Commons was weighted against the pressure for change,
how the House of Lords retained an immense reservoir of power
which property could still invoke, how the very style of parliamentary eloquence 'slurs and mutes the deep antagonisms which
exist in society'. Parliamentary action offered Socialists no guarantee of success; rather, the chance of success might be no more than
slender. Bare wisdom demanded that this fact should be recognized. 'The Socialist dare not invoke the authority of Parliament in
meeting economic difficulties unless he is prepared to exhaust its
possibilities. If he does not, if he acts nervelessly, without vigour,
ingenuity and self-confidence, then it is upon him and his that the
consequences will alight. He will have played his last card and lost,
and, in the loss, parliamentary institutions themselves will be
engulfed. Boldness in words must be matched by boldness in deeds
or the result will be universal *malaise*, a debilitation of the public
will, and a deep lassitude spreading throughout all the organs of
administration. Audacity is the mood that should prevail among
Socialists as they apply the full armament of democratic values to
the problems of the times.' These words appeared in Bevan's book,
In Place of Fear, published in 1952. But the early chapters had

[1] *In Place of Fear* by Aneurin Bevan (Heinemann, 1952), p. 5.

been drafted in 1944 and 1945 and they represented a political testament which he had formed in the 1929 Parliament and never wished to dilute throughout the rest of his life.

The sword was unsheathed in 1945. The interaction between poverty, property and democracy, which was Bevan's individual elaboration of the Marxist prophecy, had to be played out on a climacteric scale. He was one of the many who had expounded the dream of a new society which a Labour Government would seek to introduce. He was one of a very few with a clearly-defined philosophy of what the transfer of power must mean and what hazards it would encounter. Other adversaries of the new Government might arise, from the circumstances of the age, from famine-threatened Europe, from Russia, from America; who could tell? But one inescapable enemy was here at home. The Party of property was wounded, but not killed, and still had at its bidding all the main agencies of mass propaganda. Would his fellow Cabinet Ministers show the necessary nerve and stomach for the fight? Nothing that he had ever thought or said about them suggested that they would suddenly emerge as men capable of conducting an unprecedented democratic revolution. However, the war and the electoral victory, so shattering and complete, had given a fresh momentum to politics. In such a climate, Lilliputians might grow to Brobdignagian stature.

Within the new Government the rancours of the past were quickly buried. The comradeship of the election and the victory produced emollient effects, and few jealousies were reopened in the disposition of offices. Rumour hinted that some friends of Herbert Morrison had wished to intervene on his behalf before Clement Attlee was summoned to Buckingham Palace as the new Prime Minister. But the manoeuvre, if it was ever started, was quite ineffective and left no trace except a nasty taste in the mouth of Ernest Bevin. Attlee's leadership was undisputed. At the outset he chose three others as his closest associates, wielding final power – Ernest Bevin, Foreign Secretary, Hugh Dalton, Chancellor of the Exchequer, and Herbert Morrison, Leader of the House of Commons. Soon a fourth, Stafford Cripps, President of the Board of Trade, was knocking on this inner door. And just occasionally, the

80-year-old Lord Addison, Leader of the Labour Party in the House of Lords, slipped in at Attlee's special invitation – much to the annoyance of Bevan who was still kept outside. Cripps had been Bevan's chief political friend and ally in the thirties, but the old intimacy had not been sustained in the last years of the war. With Attlee, Bevin and Morrison, Bevan had, at one time or another, fought bitter, rasping, near-mortal duels. So in the 1945 Cabinet, as so often before in his political life, he looked a lonely figure. Yet the old quarrels were truly forgotten and, during the months and years that followed, both he and his chief colleagues made reappraisals of one anothers' characters.

When Attlee summoned Bevan to Downing Street to make the appointment, the words of the leader were characteristically laconic. 'I made it clear,' says Attlee, 'he was starting with me with a clean sheet.' Then the prospect was embroidered. 'You are the youngest member of the Cabinet. Now it's up to you. The more you can learn the better.'[1] And one thing Bevan did learn – a new, inter-mittent respect for Attlee himself. Before 1939 and since, Bevan had frequently been driven to desperation by what he construed as Attlee's total incapacity to devise or seize an initiative – his refusal to seek out new ways for the overthrow of Chamberlain, his accept-ance of a status of utter subordination to Churchill, his sheer, unshiftable, contented immobility. Had not this same Attlee believed right up till the moment when the votes were counted, despite the great Leftward swing of the times, that the Tories would still 'pull it off'? He was the beneficiary of a victory he had done little to contrive and his mask of insensibility did not sud-denly drop in 1945. He remained ill-at-ease on the platform or in Parliament, often giving an exhibition of feebleness or reducing great matters to the most meagre aspect. But, of course, there was another Attlee and Bevan now began to see him at work. His light shone best under a bushel. Behind the scenes, his sharp, cryptic manner assisted the despatch of business within both the Cabinet and the whole administration. Generally he allowed his Ministers to get on with their own jobs unmolested, and Bevan made the most of the dispensation. When he needed Cabinet backing for his own biggest decisions, he soon learnt to appreciate Attlee's leading

[1] Article in the *Observer*, 21 October 1962, by Lord Attlee.

virtue. The mind, however unadventurous, was usually open and unprejudiced; a case presented with close argument and detailed facts had a good chance of winning on its merits. On all the matters affecting his own department, Bevan went to the Cabinet well briefed. Attlee could be won as an ally.

Sometimes, in an effusive mood, Bevan would concede that Attlee brought the same virtue to the governance of his Party. As the controversies about the proper speed of advance and between Right and Left re-emerged, Attlee at least had the advantage that he was associated with no faction. 'It's very dangerous to be the centre of a small circle,' he once said himself[1] and the rule was generally preserved; only Ernest Bevin had a special access to and influence upon 'the little man'. Perhaps a sphinx was the only emblem which *could* lead the Labour Party. If he gave no wink to the Left, the same stony reproach was bestowed on the Right. Attlee did hold the balance between the two. He appointed Bevan to his office in defiance of all the hierarchical expectations within the Parliamentary Party, and backed him thereafter for his competence. Others who might have expected protection owing to their Party status were ruthlessly removed. The centre of gravity within the Parliamentary Party had moved Leftwards with the election and Attlee moved with it. Once in the Smoking Room Attlee joined Bevan and a few associates. 'What will you have, sir?' asked the waiter. 'A small sherry, please,' said the abstemious Attlee. 'Sweet or dry?' persisted the waiter. 'Medium, of course,' insisted Bevan, before Attlee could speak for himself. Considering the usual balance of forces within the Party, the designation was intended more as a compliment than an insult.

'The key to his [Attlee's] character lies, I think,' wrote one who knew him best in those years, 'in the fact that he is a true solitary. He requires less than most men the support of others. He will listen, he will consider their points of view, but once he has decided on the course to be followed he is completely sustained by his own inner strength.'[2] The sentences contain one essential strand of the truth. Attlee was the Prime Minister whom nobody knew. He bore

[1] *A Prime Minister Remembers* by Francis Williams (Heinemann, 1961), p. 83.

[2] *The Triple Challenge* by Francis Williams (Longmans, 1948) p. 60.

his immense individual burden with an amazing, almost carefree, fortitude. He made many great decisions, especially in those early years – in rallying the United States to help avert world-wide famine, over India, in the organization of his Government. But few, if any, members of his Cabinet would have accepted the picture of a lofty and lonely eminence exuding his carefully husbanded vitality and sagacity by some impalpable process throughout his whole administration. He gave no hint that he understood the need to sustain the allegiance of the nation; communication between him and the public was to be conducted by telepathy. He never seemed to realize that the engine of government must be refuelled with popular support and Party enthusiasm, or at least he regarded the work of stoker as too menial for himself to engage in. When one Minister after another – Shinwell, Cripps, Bevan, Strachey – became the targets of bitter, malignant hostility from the Tory Opposition and press, Attlee would never use his prestige to assist them; rather his withdrawal and silence became more marked. Was this caution or skilful calculation? Or was it a less worthy preference for not becoming bespattered in the hurly-burly of the political battle? Never once did he summon his Ministers together for a free, uninhibited discussion of the grand strategy of his Government. The conduct of business, the exchange of ideas, was kept rigorously within the formal precincts of Whitehall and Westminster. 'It was quite impossible,' wrote Morrison, 'to approach near enough to get inside his mind and to know what he was really thinking, at any rate what he would be thinking in a few days.'[1] True, Morrison had his own particular grouse against the man who had beaten him for the leadership. But Dalton and Cripps, with increasing irritation, even Bevin occasionally, made the same complaint. Was it a wiry toughness or just lack of imagination which kept Attlee cool to the point of obliviousness in a crisis? No one has ever unravelled the riddle.

Bevan made the attempt, so far as conditions would permit. Attlee, after all, had shown towards him in 1945 a conspicuous act of magnanimity, and the promise of a start with a clean sheet was honourably fulfilled. There were moments when the association between the two men trembled on the edge of a warmer friendship,

[1] *An Autobiography* by Herbert Morrison, p. 295.

and much might have developed differently in the Labour Party if
the chasm had been crossed. But just as suddenly the moments
passed. Attlee would stress the need for teamwork in some excruciating, cricketing metaphor, or he would seek to rally the Parliamentary Party with the moral uplift of a public school speech day.
Affinities with Bevan could be ruptured in a matter of seconds by
these prissy exhibitions. Attlee could reek of the suburban middle-
class values which Bevan detested. And often Bevan could become
as outraged as Morrison by Attlee's inscrutability. The difference
was that, whereas Morrison nursed his resentments, Bevan could
roar with laughter. 'You want to know Attlee,' he would cry to
assembled guests when the conversation had turned to this topic
after a good dinner at his home. 'We'll show you. Read Hazlitt's
essay on Pitt. Make a few cuts to exclude the tributes to the man's
eloquence and the cap fits perfectly.' Then he would take down
from his shelf the volume which I had given him and relish each
word.

'The character of Mr Pitt was, perhaps, one of the most singular
that ever existed. With few talents, and fewer virtues, he acquired
and preserved in one of the most trying situations and in spite of all
opposition, the highest reputation for the possession of every moral
excellence . . . This he did (strange as it appears) by a negation
(together with the common virtues) of the common vices of human
nature . . . Having no strong feelings, no distinct perceptions, his
mind having no link, as it were, to connect it with the world of
external nature, every subject presented to him nothing more than
a *tabula rasa* on which he was at liberty to lay whatever colouring
of language he pleased; having no general principles, no comprehensive view of things, no moral habits of thinking, no system of
action, there was nothing to hinder him from pursuing any particular purpose, by any means that offered; having never any plan,
he could not be convicted of inconsistency, and his own pride and
obstinacy were the only rules of his conduct. Having no insight
into human nature, no sympathy with the passions of men, or
apprehension of their real designs, he seemed perfectly insensible
to the consequences of things, and would believe nothing until it
actually happened. The fog and haze in which he saw everything
communicated itself to others; and the total indistinctness and

uncertainty of his own ideas tended to confound the perceptions of his hearers more effectually than the most ingenious misrepresentations could have done.'[1] So the recital could continue, page after page, and as the night wore on the fantasy of Attlee's leadership could provoke still wilder merriment. Only the bovine English could have brought forth such a Mirabeau to guide the beginnings of their Revolution. Here was no Lenin leading the masses but rather Labour's Lord Liverpool, the Arch-Mediocrity delineated by Disraeli: 'He was peremptory on small questions, and the great ones he left open.' Disraeli, it was happily agreed at last, had outdone even Hazlitt.

These caricatures may seem especially grotesque to those who, unconsciously perhaps, have grown accustomed to a quite different picture of the man often regarded as the most successful of Labour leaders. A model Prime Minister, an incorruptible Walpole, an assiduous, painstaking Melbourne, an unflamboyant Palmerston; a firm master of his Party, keeping the ranks united while he remained in charge and only condemned to watch their disarray once he departed; lacking Churchill's grand manner, but his superior at the council table where Churchill talked too freely; a man of few words but each precisely chosen; and a leader of men who picked and controlled his Cabinet as carefully as his words. Such is the paragon with which the nation later became increasingly familiar. What a Prime Minister should be and what a Prime Minister should do was elaborated in a vast spate of articles by Lord Attlee himself (in his later retirement laconicism edged towards garrulity) and the resulting composite all-purpose Premier bears a striking likeness to what Lord Attlee must have thought himself to be. The dazzling self-portrait has been approved almost without demur. Yet those who lived through the years after 1945 cannot suppress doubts. Who would regard the memoirs of St Helena as the authentic record of the Napoleonic Empire – especially if they were written by a Napoleon who had outlived most of his Marshals? There is a danger that the Attlee verdicts on Dalton, Morrison, Bevin, Cripps, Bevan and the others will be accepted as final. Yet all these, with the single conceivable exception of Bevin, would object. For them, the enigma grew ever more incomprehensible

Political Essays by William Hazlitt.

with the years. Each in a different way was battered and bruised by the ordeal of politics whereas Attlee seemed immune, almost disinterested. They might be embroiled in a dispute which had half the nation by the ears. No word, nothing more than a nod in the corridor, would come from their leader. The captain of the team resembled more a reasonably impartial umpire. Often he had become so solitary that no one knew he was there.

Still, at the outset particularly, the remoteness of the Prime Minister did have its advantages. Bevan, new to a government department, was both surprised and gratified to discover how free he was left to make his own plans. The occasion of his first rebuke from Downing Street left him all the more dumbfounded. In January 1946, he was summoned to a royal banquet at St James's Palace where he became the first man in history to attend such a function in a navy blue lounge suit. The invitation, issued by the Lord Steward, bore in the left-hand bottom corner: 'Dress, Dinner Jacket. Day dress. Service uniform.' Permission to wear day dress had been included to accommodate some guests from abroad, but no one except Bevan availed himself of the provision. Bevan had never worn a dinner jacket in his life and since he regarded it as the livery of the ruling class he did not want to start. Must he spend precious clothing coupons or resort to Moss Bros for the purpose of making himself look foolish? This would be for him the acme of *vulgarity* – another of his favourite words. He resolved to set a new fashion or rather to sustain the old fashion of the Wales of his youth. Of course the newspapers made a sensation of it, but at the banquet itself hardly an eyebrow was raised.

More comic was the hitherto unrecorded sequel which Jennie Lee recalls. Attlee, it seemed, more than the monarch or the Lord Steward, was the man most gravely offended. He took Bevan aside after a Cabinet meeting to express his displeasure, accompanied with entreaties that the solecism should not be repeated. As the next royal occasion approached, representations from Downing Street were renewed. At last Bevan considered yielding; most grudgingly he had come to the conclusion that it was not worth mounting the barricades for a suit. He had discussed the situation with Jennie who recollects saying that 'it seems impossible for the Attlees of this world to understand just what we do and why we do

it in our own way'. Nye, Jennie continues, would not go to the
lengths of being fitted, less still would he submit to wearing hired
clothes. 'So I crossed Sloane Square to Peter Jones who at that
time had a men's department on the ground floor and who had
had his measurements and selected a suit.' A few days later, however, she had a chance meeting with Mrs Attlee in the corridor of
the House of Commons. Mrs Attlee had heard from her husband
that Nye had reluctantly agreed to stifle his prejudices. But the
barbed pleasure with which she gleefully announced that she
could not wait to see Nye in a dinner jacket was too much for
Jennie, and for Nye too when he heard the report. He would
go to Buckingham Palace in his Sunday best which should be
good enough for anyone. And the new dinner jacket hung for
ever, unused, in his cupboard, a permanent emblem of the imperfect sympathy prevailing between the new Prime Minister and his
Minister of Health.

Altered relationships with the other main figures in the Government played their part in shaping the new life on which Bevan was
embarked. Ernest Bevin, the roughest and most formidable of his
Labour opponents in pre-war and Coalition days, never became a
friend, but the two men saw one another in a new setting and
wished to avoid fresh collisions if they could.[1] Bevin, it seems, had
been greatly struck by an incident which had occurred when he
was still Minister of Labour and when Bevan had come on a deputation to protest against some aspect of Bevin's manpower policy.
The deputation's criticisms were at first delivered in a manner
which Bevin found quite unimpressive. ' "It was just words," he
said, "it hadn't any guts to it. They made up their minds without
looking at the evidence and they wouldn't be satisfied with what
was possible – only with what sounded high-falutin." Then, after
the quarrel had raged for some time, Bevan threw back his head and
laughed. "Chuck it, boys," he said. "He's too downy a bird for us

---

[1] A famous story is often told of Bevin and Bevan. Someone is supposed
to have said to Bevin: 'Nye is his own worst enemy,' to which Bevin
retorted: 'Not while I'm alive, he ain't.' However, Bevin is also alleged to
have made the same brilliant retort about Morrison, Shinwell and others.
Probably, once he had made it he recited it about all of them. It has been
impossible to determine who was the original victim.

to pull that particular wool over his eyes. I'll tell him what we really must have. And I'll show you how you can give it to us, Bevin, and why you ought to." "And he did," said Bevin. "He told the others to keep quiet and put up a case that I could meet and had to meet. And I said to myself: There's some stuffin' in that fellow. He's got sense as well as blarney. Me and him can do business".'[1]

Bevin made the claim that he had persuaded Attlee to put Bevan in charge of housing. Attlee denied it. It was Ernest Bevin's way to imagine that the universe was kept moving not solely by his major excursions in policy but hardly less by the hints and half-hints of wisdom dropped casually in his ceaseless monologue. The egotism was gargantuan, yet oddly inoffensive, almost endearing. Partly it was an expression of his working-class arrogance, his confidence that his own class had the right and capacity to rule – rare qualities which Bevan certainly found attractive and sadly needed in a Labour administration where it was jokingly supposed that education at Attlee's Haileybury or some lesser public school was the surest passport to office. On the domestic disputes in which Bevan was involved he found that Bevin, like Attlee, could be secured as an ally, or at least kept neutral. In fact, often enough, Bevin *was* Attlee. It would be folly to overlook the powerful authority of this composite figure.

Yet within a few months, even weeks after the formation of the Government, Ernest Bevin was plunged into his long, intractable dispute with the Soviet Union which cast its shadow across the whole foreign scene in the years following 1945. The interests of Britain and Russia seemed to jostle and conflict at one point after another – in Persia, Greece, Poland, Germany and elsewhere. And since Bevin developed as his policy for dealing with the situation one which bore a striking likeness to that of the Churchill Coalition in its dying months, and since Bevan had been Churchill's principal critic, early clashes between the two might have been expected. Yet Bevan would not accept the conventional criticisms of Ernest Bevin's foreign policy which soon stirred on the Left wing of the Labour Party, and his reticence was not due to an unwillingness to face a fight in the Cabinet in which he knew he could muster little

---

[1] *The Triple Challenge* by Francis Williams, p. 137.

support. His criticism of the 'great power' politics of the latter period of the war had been directed at Stalin as well as Churchill. Other nations, the smaller nations, had a right to breathe and might reveal a surer wisdom than their towering masters. Britain herself, now the chief of the smaller nations rather than the third of the giants, had her own individual contribution to make to the world, and the fact that in the early months Soviet hostility was directed more against Britain even than against America suggested that the Communists might be reverting to their old line of selecting social democracy as their paramount enemy. Moreover, other features in Stalin's post-war policy could arouse in Bevan nothing but loathing. He would not condone or excuse the savage persecution of social democrats and peasant parties in Eastern Europe, and the apparent desire of Stalin to condemn the Germans to eternal penury offended against every principle of international Socialism and humanity – especially at a moment when Germany was starving and when the effort to stave off famine and epidemics in Europe was imposing the gravest handicaps on Britain's own recovery. Bevan had many individual doubts about the Government's handling of these issues, but he would not see Bevin butchered to make a Stalin holiday. Incidentally, he would have cut his own political throat if he had tried and he had no intention of obliging those who wished to see him finally achieve the feat.

What he refused to do was to suppress his fascination with the wide post-war scene and his eagerness to influence it. He was always determined to look on the world with his own eyes, and his junior status in the Cabinet could not put a curb on his tongue. Many of Bevin's individual responses to events could be defended but, to Bevan, his general vision seemed cramped and blinkered. Right from those first months Bevan found himself out of sympathy with the twin fears that seemed to govern and, in his judgment, to warp British policy, as approved by Bevin-Attlee, the Foreign Office and the Tory Opposition led by Churchill. The first strand in this orthodox doctrine sought to define Soviet policy; so potently aggressive was it considered to be that, given half a chance, Soviet legions would sweep across Europe to the Channel. Bevan always believed this fear was a figment. Soviet policy, however barbaric in its implementation, was defensive in its purpose. Stalin

2

was no gambler. The idea that his war-weary countrymen and his war-shaken economy could suddenly be impelled into a course of the wildest adventure could not appeal to anyone who had studied the facts of the immediate case or the facts of Soviet history.

It was the second fear, however, which distorted British policy more seriously. To hold the Russians in check it was supposed to be necessary to have American support, and the spectre with which Ernest Bevin constantly alarmed the Cabinet was that the Americans would withdraw into isolation once more, as they had done after 1918. Their helter-skelter demobilization after 1945 gave substance to the argument, but Bevan was never impressed. He was convinced that the Americans had come to Europe and the other continents to stay (he had been saying exactly that since about 1943[1]), and the new presence would not be found wholly advantageous. They would bring with them their own national interests, purposes, political methods and philosophy. Was it contended that these were identical with Britain's? No Socialist could sustain the proposition. Democratic Socialism, if it had any virility, would have serious arguments to settle with the Americans no less than with the Russians. Since the Americans were as aggressively capitalist as the Russians were aggressively Communist, this conclusion could be deduced from first principles.

But Bevan could make no headway with these formulations. The new Labour Cabinet, under Attlee's chairmanship, had little inclination, little patience and, to do it more credit, little time to spare for Bevan's theorising. He, in turn, waited (as we shall see) for the moments when he might be able to relate theory to the practical choices in which alone his practical colleagues were interested. His mind worked the opposite way from theirs, and he never ceased to lament that the outlawed discussions on more long-distant aims might have saved much trouble and even time in the end. Of course, the expediencies of political life, especially in the realm of foreign policy, must be permitted to modify principle. Bevan was no purist, objecting to all taint of compromise; he knew that to be a recipe for impotence. Yet allegiance to principle was the safeguard against losing one's way altogether and no worthwhile guiding principle could be constructed from a series of modifications.

[1] Volume I, pp. 434–9.

The chronic failing of politicians was to live from week to week and hand to mouth. The empiricists could easily flounder. That was the plight in which Bevin soon found himself over another great issue – Palestine – and even he could not claim that all the trouble there was due to the Russians jogging his elbow. The truth was that the new Foreign Secretary who boasted of his pragmatical commonsense placed himself at the mercy of his permanent officials. He looked so masterful and paraded his personal authority; but precisely because *he* scorned theory and principle, others were able to impose *their* theories and principles upon him. Once when Aneurin Bevan saw Ernest Bevin enmeshed in makeshifts he commented: 'He's a big bumble bee caught in a web and he thinks he's the spider.'[1]

This last remark was made to an appreciative Hugh Dalton whose ear was always cocked to receive mischievous comment about his colleagues as his tongue was restless in repeating it. When Dalton was friendly it was hard not to join the mirth provoked by those stentorian confidences. ('What a pity!' said Seymour Cocks when Dalton was not appointed Foreign Secretary. '*That* would have put an end to secret diplomacy.') Dalton on the crest of the wave – and in the first two years after 1945 he rode higher than any other Minister – had the panache which the Government so much needed. His spirit of aggression against the Tories satisfied the most exacting standards. The song in his heart was no egotistical solo; it swelled to a Socialist anthem. Even if Bevan, in charge of one of the chief spending departments, had not his own good reasons for securing a firm alliance with the Chancellor of the Exchequer, he could hardly fail to respond to such a display of extrovert gusto.

Dalton recorded in his diary, quite early in the Government's life: 'Bevan and I are on very good terms just now. I find him much brighter than most of them. We shouted at each other across the Cabinet table last week. He had been speaking at some length about Germany and reparations. I said, "I have *studied* this question. I don't just ooze a lot of flabby generalities". The P.M. then closured this exchange. Bevan and I looked thunder at each other for about thirty seconds. Then grins broke through. I scribbled

[1] *High Tide and After* by Hugh Dalton (Muller, 1962), p. 129.

him a note saying, "As half a real Welshman, born in Glamorgan, to a real half Welshman, born in Monmouth, we must allow for these poor Saxons failing to understand our Celtic high spirits". He wrote back, quick as a flash, "As one bastard to another, I accept your apology".[1] Dalton, although born in Neath, was about as Welsh as Oliver Cromwell, whom, however, Bevan was often eager to claim as a compatriot. He was never quite prepared to grant the same rare distinction to Dalton. The unholy alliance between the two so speedily signed and ratified still had an escape clause. Dalton 'down' could be a very different man from Dalton 'up', and Dalton as an enemy could soon efface any memory that he had ever been a friend. If fierce internal battles ever broke out afresh, if it came to a crisis, who could tell where Dalton would be? He might resume the other stance which he appeared to think suited his brash cunning – a cloven hoof in both camps. Yet in 1945 and 1946 all such memories or premonitions were banished. Dalton at the Treasury provided the resources and no small part of the drive behind Labour's great reforming measures. It is the achievement that can never be taken from him.

One other bond brought Dalton and Bevan together – the omnipresent, omnivorous, ever-vigilant, ever-meddling Herbert Morrison. Bevan did not, as Morrison supposes, 'on occasion conceive a feeling of hatred for me'.[2] Morrison, Bevan would often agree, had his uses. He would give and take. Reconciliations between the two were almost as frequent as their rows. If Attlee kept himself too remote from Party considerations, Morrison more than made good the deficiency. *Hatred* would be too strong a term; an irrepressible irritation would be a more accurate description of the emotion he aroused among many of his colleagues. Morrison's way of working offended all Bevan's instincts. He positively enjoyed committees and welcomed their proliferation, especially if he was appointed or self-appointed as chairman, as he frequently was. Then, if he failed to get his way at one encounter, he would seek a replay elsewhere. A contest with Morrison was rarely a knock-out competition; the struggle for points went on until the end of the season. He was also an incurable snapper-up of unconsidered

[1] *High Tide and After* by Hugh Dalton, p. 129.
[2] *An Autobiography* by Herbert Morrison, p. 263.

trifles. Bevan called him 'the Cockney sparrow', pecking for crumbs wherever he could find them.

Partly these harsh judgments arose from the nature of the case. For Morrison was Leader of the House, Lord President of the Council, Deputy Prime Minister, in Dalton's words 'a sort of informal Boss of the Home Front, interfering with everybody and everything'. He had some title to invade other people's preserves, especially Bevan's. He regarded himself as the champion of the local authorities whom Bevan was soon accused of treating roughly. Conflict was inevitable. In most of Bevan's early arguments affecting his own department, Morrison was his chief critic. Yet when Bevan discovered that the ebullient Dalton and the long-suffering Stafford Cripps shared his annoyance, Morrison's opposition could be borne. 'A man cannot be too careful,' said Oscar Wilde, 'in the choice of his enemies.' But, again, *enemy* is too fierce a word. It was rather that the constant buzz of intrigue and manipulation which surrounded Morrison's activities, the patent display of his anxiety lest someone might be out-smarting him, was wearing on the nerves. And yet, oddly, this same Morrison has written an autobiography in which a gnawing ambition for higher office or a wider Whitehall empire and a taste for the darker corners of the political workshop are attributed to almost everyone but himself. Others might stoop to conquer, but never he. The world has had to await this remarkable volume for the soul of Labour's Don Quixote to be unbosomed. In 1945 no glimpse of such profundities was available.

Attlee had in fact picked Morrison for the job he could do best. The art of leading the House of Commons may not be so vastly different from that of managing a Party; at least the two functions overlap. And yet the most successful Leaders of the House – Stanley Baldwin, for instance – have seemed to make a virtue out of a certain indolence, a readiness to let the curious moods of the place seep in through the pores. Morrison never had that; probably, in view of Labour's huge legislative programme, the luxury could not be afforded. Morrison lived politics, ate politics, dreamt politics, devoured statistics for breakfast and Cabinet papers late into the night. He was the great planner before there was any real planning machine in existence and while he himself barely recognized the necessity for creating one. His substitute for a guiding hand or a real grip was a finger in every pie. Objection from the other cooks was understandable.

Of all the leading Ministers, Stafford Cripps was the only one with whom Bevan had had close political association in the past. From about 1942 onwards this intimacy had faded. Cripps clearly had been unable to express even tacit sympathy with Bevan's criticism of the Coalition, and Bevan in turn felt that Cripps had forfeited some political influence by his readiness to accept subordinate administrative office under Churchill. Moreover, the post-war Cripps was a different man from the pre-war Cripps. His sojourn in the Soviet Union as ambassador had profoundly altered his political outlook; the Marxist veneer which had once supplied a crude cover for his Christian Socialism was now removed. But Cripps did retain his political glamour as a public man of irreproachable, independent rectitude, and his air of commanding authority marked him out from the start both in the Cabinet and the Commons as one who would play an increasingly dominant part in the administration. Owing to their old friendship, he and Bevan could talk to one another in a different language than they used to others; it was through Cripps, for example, that Bevan urged successfully that George Strauss, the third in the triumvirate expelled from the Party in 1939, should be given office.

The rest of the Cabinet noted the special relationship between Cripps and Bevan and were inclined also to misunderstand its significance. 'Nye was, of course, a very attractive character but very difficult,' Attlee has written. 'It was to the credit of Stafford Cripps that he kept Nye running in a straight and narrow path of loyalty for five years.'[1] Attlee has also written: 'Nye was much attached to Stafford, who could talk to him like an uncle. He always had a great respect for what he said and Stafford could argue him out of his attitudes and get him to see the whole picture.'[2] Such scenes do not sound probable. Maybe the impression derives more from what Cripps told Attlee he had told Bevan. Morrison gives a countervailing and possibly more perspicacious judgement. 'Nye Bevan,' he says, 'was able to persuade that brilliant Crippsian mind, so insuperable in a court of law or at a conference, to take second

[1] Article in the *Evening Standard* by Lord Attlee, 12 February 1962.
[2] *A Prime Minister Remembers* by Francis Williams, p. 249.

thoughts. This was the reason why Bevan got away with more and more money for his beloved health schemes in the 1945–50 Government.'[1] The truth was that the inner relationship between the two men, even in the thirties when the ostensible signs suggested otherwise, had never been that of leader and follower. Bevan never acknowledged a political uncle in his life. The two men always talked as equals. What Bevan admired in Cripps, apart from his prodigious brain-power, was his political cleanness, his courage, his sense of urgency, his utter contempt for the petty ways of politics, his resolve to grapple with the most intractable problems. True, Cripps could also behave as if he had just strolled down from Sinai and would expound what was written on the tablets of stone for the benefit of Aaron and the others who might not otherwise be able to understand. True also he not merely despised the worshippers of the golden calf but had more than his share of the rich man's lofty unawareness of the mundane anxieties that afflict other people – this combined with a burning idealistic determination to do all in his power to banish poverty from the face of the earth. He could infuriate Bevan as much as the others but Bevan had appreciated long before the others Cripps's true mettle. It was certainly important, in the first years after 1945, that the long-standing mutual respect could be reawakened.

So Bevan was not as isolated in the Attlee Cabinet as at first glance might appear. Old antagonisms had abated; new personal responses and alliances had not been formed. And there were several others around the table who were either ready to support Bevan's particular schemes or looked to him for backing in their own departmental measures – for example, Arthur Greenwood, charged with a general survey over the social services, a man whose kindness and geniality had always prevented political quarrels with Bevan from developing into personal bitterness; Ellen Wilkinson at the Ministry of Education who had been an occasional ally on the Left in the thirties and whom Bevan sought to sustain against Morrison in her fight to fulfil Labour's pledge to raise the school-leaving age; or Emanuel Shinwell at the Ministry of Fuel. Shinwell and Bevan had often been bracketed together by the newspapers as natural Left-wing confederates. They were the two

[1] *An Autobiography* by Herbert Morrison, p. 271.

leading members of the Cabinet uncommitted to the projected
Coalition policies for the post-war world. Churchill himself had
many old scores to pay off for their hostility to the wartime
administration. They had been entrusted with the most perilous of
the domestic tasks of the Government – whether deliberately only
Attlee could know. The assumption of the journalists had some
basis. But, in fact, the relationship between the two had always
been cool, if not cold. Each had always been wary about the other;
often they found themselves thrown together, but almost as often
they had veered away from a political companionship. All these
varying shades in the association of Bevan with his principal colleagues have their significance in his story. But some governing
features of the general political situation were more important. The
new Government was incomparably stronger in personnel and
public backing than the Labour Governments of 1924 and 1929.
An eagerness to carry through Labour's declared programme infused the Cabinet no less than the Parliamentary Party. A sense of
purpose supplied the cement for a true unity.

Aneurin Bevan's entry into the Ministry of Health was naturally
watched with curiosity and some alarm by his civil servants. What
would the wild man do? His first act was to sink into the too-well-
upholstered leather chair provided for the Minister. 'This won't
do,' he said sweetly, 'it drains all the blood from the head and
explains a lot about my predecessors.' The chair was changed.
After a few weeks some of the top civil servants were also changed.
But any fears of a boorish intruder vanished. He was positively
gentle. The one place where he schooled his temper most successfully was within his ministerial department. The gentleness was
not some opening gambit; it persisted. His officials saw a side of
him which many opponents and colleagues never suspected was
there at all.

Always throughout his life he had a congenital distaste for ring-
ing bells to summon somebody. It was not that he did not want
service – he liked the best – but something in the habit offended
his notion of good manners towards those who could not complain.
So he would walk to the outer office and ask for Mr Blank, or stroll
along the passage and invade his officials in their own rooms. Noth-

ing was further from his purpose than a false informality; rather, he could be almost stiffly correct. Rarely, if ever, did he bring his permanent officials back to his home. The point was that he liked to settle as much business as possible by discussion and contention, exploiting to the full his outstanding gift for near word-perfect recollection of what he had heard said. His hyper-sensitive ear saved reams of paper. When a major decision had to be taken, and especially in the early weeks and months at the Ministry, his method was to invite his officials, separately or together, to state their case. He listened with barely an interruption; then he probed; then he pressed again to ensure that no potential difficulties had been held back in reserve. As in open debate, he preferred to concentrate upon the strongest argument which might be used against him, leaving the weaker ones to fall by the wayside. Then when he understood the full mind of his official, he spent lavish time attempting to make equally sure that the official knew his. Thus he illustrated in practice the importance he always attached to first principles, and thus the principles of action were settled and the chances of misinterpretation of what he wanted were reduced to the minimum.

Sir John Wrigley, Deputy-Secretary in charge of the housing programme, who described the process to me, said that at first it could be unnerving. Bevan could recall what he had heard at previous conversations much better than anything he had read. But the time and trouble saved eventually was invaluable. Bevan, says Sir John, relieved himself of an enormous amount of 'case' work with which other Ministers sometimes found themselves smothered. The officials whose trust he had gained and to whom it was given knew clearly the doctrine he wanted applied and were left free to apply it without much interference. Sir John Hawton, who had been Deputy-Secretary in charge of the post-war plans on the health side of the Ministry since 1942, gives the same testimony. He himself had become a strong advocate of a free and comprehensive Health Service, and Bevan's arrival was a thrilling and uncovenanted blessing. Both testify that he was an easy master, considerate but exciting, and the same verdict was passed by many others. 'He sold himself to the Ministry within a fortnight,' said Sir Wilson Jameson, Chief Medical Officer of Health at the time.

2*

'I never heard any senior civil servant speak anything but good of
him,' confirmed Sir Alan Saunders, who worked in the Ministry
for several years on the housing programme, and who adds: 'He
was especially good at priorities – at the conferences where much
of the work was done. And he never forgot anything he was told; it
often came out verbatim three weeks later or more.' He had never
had the machinery of a department in his hands before and he drove
it with as much accomplishment and pride as the fast motor cars he
delighted in. Power and speed suited him.

For almost the whole period at the Ministry of Health his Permanent Secretary was Sir William Douglas, and perhaps the
curiously good relations between the two owed something to the
odd method of his appointment. Archie Lush happened to be staying at their home at Cliveden Place at the time and Bevan naturally
broached his anxieties; he had three unknown names to choose
from as Permanent Secretary and had not the foggiest notion how
to tackle the novel problem. 'What about that old bugger from
Rhymney?' he asked – the person in question, the most famous son
of Rhymney in Nye's constituency, being Dr Thomas Jones, the
éminence grise of Lloyd George and Baldwin. So Archie was
immediately despatched to the Athenaeum to seek his advice, and
Tom Jones was overjoyed to be granted this whiff of the secret
power he had wielded in previous decades. How soon was the
answer needed? Tomorrow, insisted Archie, and next day Tom
Jones had prepared an extensive report on all three candidates.
'Well, what does it say?' asked Nye. Archie was cautious; he had
not had sufficient chance to examine the elaborate foolscap pages
written in pencil. 'Well, who does he come down in favour of?'
Eventually Archie answered: 'Well, I think Sir William Douglas.'
And why? So Archie replied, more to ward off too close a scrutiny
or to keep the conversation going: 'Well, I think he comes to the
conclusion that Sir William Douglas has all the qualities which are
exactly the opposite of the Minister's.' 'Good,' said Nye; 'we'll
have *him*. We can't have *two* Ministers of Health.' Sir William had
previously been at the Ministry of Supply and was appointed temporarily to the post in 1945. A natural Conservative, near to the
retiring age, nothing had ever horrified him more than the idea of
being transferred to serve such a Minister. 'What do you think of

that man, Bevan?' asked a professional friend, John Buchan, a
few days after his appointment. 'I think he's a terrible fellow,'
replied Douglas, 'I'll never forgive him for all those attacks on
Churchill during the war. I made it clear that I would carry on
only for three months until they'd got someone else.' A few months
later John Buchan asked the same question. 'What are you driving
at?' replied Douglas, with some amazement. 'He's the best
Minister I ever worked for. I've made it clear that while Bevan's
there, I'll stay.' (He kept his word, resigning a few months after
Bevan's own resignation in 1951, and he died shortly afterwards.)
Sir William, like Bevan, gave Sir John Wrigley and Sir John
Hawton their heads; he himself was the skilled expert in the manipulation of the civil service machine. 'You are my fixer, usually for
immoral purposes,' Bevan would say to him, and Sir William
treasured the compliment as if he had been unexpectedly canonized
by the College of Cardinals.

Courtesy, banter and flattery were all used without scruple to
consolidate the enthusiasm of his officials. The fullest respect must
be shown to his Under-Secretary, Charles Key, and his Parliamentary Private Secretary, Donald Bruce. They were *elected* persons and the officials must never forget it. That law was firmly
established from the start. For the rest, those who worked for him
were treated as if they were members of a chosen race. The great
blusterer never shouted at them; the great demagogue never pan-
dered to obstreperous deputations of M.P.s. Indeed, the officials
sometimes trembled to see him use his blistering tongue in the
Commons or elsewhere on those who dared question the proficiency and zeal of the Ministry of Health. All these were manners
and mannerisms likely to enlist loyalty, but by themselves they
were not the prime cause of the devotion he inspired. More important was the fact that within months, or even weeks, he raised the
whole standing of the Ministry of Health within the Whitehall
hierarchy. During the war the Ministry had inevitably been pushed
into the shadows: who could recite the names of the wartime
Ministers of Health? Even the poor relation, the Ministry of
Works, had come up in the world more since Churchill had
appointed two of his cronies in turn – Lord Portal and Duncan
Sandys – to the office and put Sandys into the Cabinet when the

Minister of Health was still left out. The Ministry of Health had fears that more and more of its housing functions might be stripped from it. Then suddenly all was changed. Cinderella was taken to the ball by the youngest and most aggressive prince in the new administration. Sisters from the Ministry of Works or even more formidable and uglier ones from the Treasury could flash their green eyes in vain. In the Cabinet and in Cabinet committees, the Ministry of Health knew that its case would never go by default. That Bevan's effect in his department was electric and lasting is vouched for by a legion of witnesses. He soon had at his command a new weapon as sharp as his prowess in debate.

His own daily routine was transformed by Cabinet office. All his life the graph of his vitality, starting slowly in the morning, had mounted highest at night. As a boy he had stayed up reading to all hours and then tumbled out of bed, cursing, or occasionally returned to his sleep. In his forty-seven years the habit had become ingrained. Deep into the night he would pursue his talk or his reading. All plans or pleasures were arranged on the inspiration of the moment, like speeches in the House of Commons. Spontaneity and sudden adventures seemed essential to his zest. But now, by a mammoth exertion, the pattern was changed. He ate more hearty breakfasts during his five years at the Ministry than in the rest of his adult life put together. He left 23 Cliveden Place sharp at the same time every morning and returned at night laden, not with the fascinating philosophical treatise he would have brought home in triumph before, but with Cabinet papers, or, worse still – those portable prison gates – blue books and white papers. Only at the few weekends when he was not compelled to tour the country could he find time to satisfy his craving for the long, rich evenings required to fathom all the secrets of the universe. Often he chafed beneath the discipline; considering his natural bent, the feat was that he bore it at all. For late at night he might still be condemning himself to solitary confinement in the small top bedroom he retreated to on occasions when he had to face the purgatory of reading without delight, masticating the statistical straw which some politicians find ambrosial. Late one night he called to Jennie to bring a second bulging briefcase to him. 'No,' she said, 'one you may have but taking two to bed is positively immoral.'

1945 also brought a big and unforeseen change in Jennie Lee's life. In the early years of the war she had severed her links with the Independent Labour Party and in 1944 she made her peace with the Labour Party itself and was adopted as Labour candidate for the mining constituency of Cannock in the Midlands. So at the 1945 election she returned to the House of Commons after an interval of fourteen years. In the 1929–31 Parliament she had been a leading figure on the Left – because of her youth, her sex, and the spectacular by-election in which she was returned, better known in those days than Bevan himself. One of her old I.L.P. colleagues – George Buchanan – had been given office as Minister of Pensions with the new Government. James Maxton, in his one speech in the new Parliament before his death, bestowed a generous, if qualified, blessing on the new administration. At one of the first meetings of the Parliamentary Party it was proposed by Herbert Morrison and generally approved that the Standing Orders, imposing a rigid Party discipline, should be suspended; so even that old bone of contention was buried along with the hatchets. Jennie Lee had every incentive to resume her own independent parliamentary course. She and Nye had left their beloved country home in Berkshire to return to London precisely because they felt the move necessary to prepare for forthcoming political battles. Jennie Lee's mother and father were installed at 23 Cliveden Place as the guardians and managers of the home. To live in London at all was for Nye an affliction; but everything that tenderness and skill could do to mitigate the penance was done. Here was a secure and joyous base from which both could operate.

Yet within a few weeks of Nye's appointment to the Cabinet Jennie found herself moving towards a far-reaching personal decision to subdue her own strong and never-abandoned feminist instincts. It was not made in a moment, and with her temperament it was far from easy. She was coming to see Nye as the greatest creative intelligence in her world; but she also saw him as a guileless knight-errant, quite unequipped with the impregnable suit of armour which the outside world supposed that he wore. She knew what he had suffered in the wartime engagements with Churchill and the Labour leaders, wounds which he would only confess and uncover at home, and she sensed that more severe trials lay ahead. The strains of the 1945–50 period would have been intolerable if she had not accepted the necessity of subordinating her mind and interests to his. In the first years of their marriage when they were young enough to feel indestructible, Jennie had often gone off on lecture tours to America and elsewhere but later Nye could not bear to have her away so long. As he grew more burdened publicly, he became more dependent privately. The trust and love between them strengthened and deepened. Nye's gaiety and laughter, his varying spasms of activity and brooding, could make other politicians who led regular, careworn lives regard him as irresponsible. But how furiously he would repudiate the accusation. *Frivolity* was *his* charge against them; what could be more frivolous than to arouse political emotions without the courage to raise heaven and hell to see them satisfied? His political aims were never playthings; had they been, he could not have lived with himself – or with Jennie. And now, more than ever, he was in earnest. She shared the mood exactly. They did not make speeches in private to one another; Nye indeed believed that much in any private relationship was best left not too explicit. What was happening to them was scarcely discussed, but henceforward their lives were changed. All the burdens of public life – in his case, because of the role of chief-bogyman in which he was cast, far more severe than for most – fell upon his shoulders. But they fell remorselessly upon Jennie's too. 'I was not such a fool', she says, 'as not to see it was worthwhile. I reconciled myself to the strains because he was my alter ego. We were never at any time conflicting egos. He was doing what I wanted done infinitely better than I could have done it.'

Perpetually it is necessary to mark the contrast between the public and the private man. Naturally Jennie saw more than anyone else of the ways in which he needed to renew himself for the ardours of the time. But it was also true that, politically speaking, he was enfranchised, exhilarated, buoyant. One of his faculties was that he could become totally absorbed in what he was doing – in reading a book, listening to music, playing billiards, arguing about Nietzsche, digging a ditch, bringing his bottle of wine to precisely the right temperature, or cooking his elaborate version of *poulet en casserole*. Nothing else mattered but the business in hand. To sustain such absorption for longer periods and longer purposes normally calls for different qualities, but he acquired them with less agony than might have been expected. The chance of performing a clear, constructive task came as a marvellous healing balm. Any idea that he merely loved words for their own sake was utterly to misconceive what he used them for. He agreed with Montaigne: 'Fie on the eloquence that leaves us craving itself, not things!' The verb, he often said, is more important than the noun. Despite all his fascination with ideas and dreams, the deed was the accomplishment to which he gave the place of honour. 'Be ye conscious possessors,' his old mentor, José Rodo, had written, 'of the blessed power you contain within yourselves. But do you never forget that this power is no more exempt than other virtuous impulses from weakening and disappearing if it be not carried into action.' Nye had never forgotten. The bane and horror of his early manhood had been that his own people in South Wales had won the ostensible power to act, had voted by huge majorities for revolutionary action, and yet had seen their aspirations made abortive by sluggish, bamboozled England. Wales had been accorded the democratic privilege to go on talking. How deliciously it was done, but what a mockery those lilting perorations could become; good for the next world, not this! His own role before and during the war could be justified as an unavoidable preparation for future action, but not otherwise. A mere parliamentary career could be an obscenity; a perpetual promise never redeemed.

Now the testing moment had come, and he was much more stimulated than awe-struck. Yet, apart altogether from his own doubts about the capacity of his colleagues to respond to the summons and whatever objective justification there may have been for them, those who knew him best – Jennie, above all – had a reason for wondering what would befall which had little to do with the plain question of his competence to perform a work he had never done before. The most individual feature of his mental outlook and character was that he refused to conform to reality but expected reality to conform to him. When in private life circumstances were disagreeable he turned a blind eye or started some fresh pursuit; often – was it luck or intuition? – the awkward situation dissolved. It was often a mistake, he contended, to face tough or near-insoluble problems; they should be outflanked. He hated to see a harrowing film at the cinema and would leave, with Archie Lush, saying: 'Come on, boy, we've had enough of our withers being wrung'. He had an ideal conception of personal relations and if something distasteful happened to upset them, he could pretend that it hadn't. A most serried array of facts was required to upset one of his precious theories. Not many people knew it or could believe it, but his innocence could be child-like. And of course, this romantic aspect of his mind, inherited from his father, was reflected in his politics. He saw what should be and was impatient to grasp it, whatever the intervening obstacles. Conditions which others regarded as the harsh, inexorable features of the case he dismissed as absurdities and found it intolerable that others would not with equal assurance do the same. Describing the reading of his own youth, he once put his finger on the point: 'I went to the moon with H. G. Wells and it was the outside world that seemed unreal.'

This was Bevan's individualism, and it was much more than a streak in his nature; it was almost the whole man. When he was not thinking originally, or at least extending existing ideas into some fresh undiscovered field, he could be utterly bored. Of course the ideas were derived from his reading and experience, but somehow the results looked more like inspirations than deductions. 'The bees plunder the flowers here and there,' wrote Montaigne, 'but afterwards they make of them honey, which is all theirs; it is no longer thyme or marjoram. Even so with the pieces borrowed from others; he will transform and blend them to make a work that is all his own, to wit, his judgment.' This was Bevan's way of making his reading and thinking his own. He treasured his individual judgment; he had an anarchical pride which resented all authority. And here was the source of the genius he brought to politics, his power to see aspects of the future which no one else saw, his capacity to vault ahead of his plodding companions. Yet his delight in these mental adventures was so extreme and perpetual that he might have been thought to be unfitted for politics altogether. He should have been a poet; political parties only chain such spirits. Challenged on the point, he might have replied with Trotsky that individualism has its progressive characteristics: 'The working class has suffered not from the excess but from an atrophy of individualism.'[1] True, no doubt, but look what happened to Trotsky! And he at least had the advantage of acting on a stage of limitless turmoil where a man larger than life might not look quite so out of place. The mood of 1945 in Britain was novel and adventurous, but political operations were still constricted within unbroken contexts and conventions. The room for manœuvre was not so spacious, the stage circumscribed by austere facts. What could happen to such a man as Aneurin Bevan when, in high ministerial office, he and the real world collided?

The paradox was that the romantic was also a Marxist, that the most untameable individualist in Labour history had an abiding love for the Labour movement which spoke in the name of the British working class. This devotion bordered on humility. Such a claim would have sounded laughable to his fellow members of the 1945 Cabinet or the multitudes of others who had heard him berate the leaders and the led in every branch of the movement for their treacheries and stupidities and docility. Could such unbending pride *ever* be humble? Yet he was. This was the profound reason why, in the thirties and forties, he had always been a reluctant rebel. Unlike so many others – the Attlees, the Crippses, the Gaitskells and many more – he had not 'joined' the Labour movement. He was born in it and had grown with it. He could never sever himself from it and still breathe. Despite his persistent, aching need for refreshment in the fields of literature or the countryside or with strange companions completely divorced from his brand of politics, the Labour Party was his life. Time and again, hurt or humiliated or outraged, he bowed to its collective voice. However furious the quarrel, he knew that he always would in the end. For a refusal to do so would be a denial of his own truth. The deed required an instrument and in Britain that instrument was the Labour Party. Moreover this instrument had a history, interwoven with the struggles and tears and triumphs of his own people and the land of his fathers. Touched by his romantic wand, the political party, for all its intrigues and inadequacies, could be transformed into a shining crusade.

Thus, for Bevan, the excitement of 1945 had an added flavour. His individual and communal loyalties, each so strong, were no

[1] *Trotsky The Prophet Unarmed* by Isaac Deutscher (Oxford), p. 190.

longer at war, as they had been almost continuously since 1929. The harmony might be precarious, but to preserve it, he mustered, in a manner which most people thought quite beyond his power, those qualities of patience, self-discipline and calculation most offensive to his nature. As for his dear, reverential, deferential Labour Party which angered him, baited him, outlawed him but would never set him free, might it not at such a delirious moment in history at last aspire to the Promethean quality of daring?

A cloud much bigger than a man's hand darkened the bright morning.

Everyone knew vaguely that Britain would face a severe problem in her foreign trade and balance of payments when peace came; only those at the centre could guess its dimensions. Britain had fought longer than any other country except Germany. She had mobilized for war more fully than any other, Germany included, drastically cutting her own export trade to assist the purpose. She had survived economically only by selling foreign assets, piling up heavy debts to a host of different countries and accepting the provisions of the Lend-Lease Agreement with the United States which enabled her to receive imports without payment. 'The day the war ended,' Winston Churchill had said to a leading American politician in 1944, 'the country would be bankrupt, and the returning soldiers would have little to come back to.' The figures went far to substantiate the prophecy. In 1945 external aid of one form or another enabled Britain to overspend on her foreign account by about £2,000 million. The Treasury made the most optimistic reckoning of how speedily this drain could be stopped, how imports could be regulated and exports increased. Their estimate was that, if all went well, equilibrium in the nation's balance of payments could be established by 1949, the fourth year of peace. In the meantime a fresh deficit of £1,700 million would have been incurred in the years 1946, 1947 and 1948, apart from the deficit for 1945 which was not included in that sum. And this left out of the picture also the huge aggregate of wartime indebtedness to allies and neutrals amounting to £3,355 million.

However, these daunting totals had not been allowed to spread dismay or despair, even amongst the experts. Many discussions had taken place between the British and Americans about how post-war currency and trade relationships should be developed and several more or less firm agreements had been reached. These had been blessed, indeed partly devised, by the chief British expert, Lord Keynes. He had a vision of Keynesian techniques of economic expansion being introduced and operated over a large part of the globe by a magnificent Anglo-American financial and economic concordat. Less had been done to discuss the more precise and pressing question of Britain's inevitable post-war difficulties, yet immediately after the election in July steps were taken to repair the omission. Two of the leading American Treasury experts, Mr W. Clayton and Mr E. G. Collado, in Europe at the time on other business, were invited to London at the beginning of August for a conference with Keynes and the British Ministers where the question of assistance for Britain could be broached in a cool and informal atmosphere. Clayton and Collado responded with sympathy, but some caution. Before the American Government could be persuaded to consider the prospect, greater clarification would have to be reached about the post-war policies which the British Government intended to follow. Specifically this meant three things: Britain's sterling balances – her wartime debts to other nations – must be kept separate, since the United States could not be expected to make payments to Britain which would merely be passed on to others; there must be arrangements for making sterling convertible at an early date; there must be guarantees that Britain would be non-discriminatory in her commercial practices. The second and third of these requirements had figured in all the previous discussions with the Americans conducted by Keynes. They had become in effect a principal American war aim; for the advantage the Americans saw in the Anglo-American concordat was the establishment of a free trade world on the most august liberal principles. Keynes himself was not inclined to offer stubborn opposition to these requests. He was fully familiar with the American outlook and felt that a liberal response from Britain was essential to bring his great scheme to fruition. Other British representatives at that conference may have been more alarmed by the perils of a harassed post-war Britain being plunged too soon into a world of convertible currencies and non-discriminatory trade. But no matter. Differences between all those at the conference were questions of shade and emphasis. The approach was tentative and the discussions continued.

Those London talks began over August Bank Holiday weekend. On 14 August the war with Japan ended. On Sunday 19 August, Mr Collado, after some sightseeing, was having tea in a Cambridge teashop. There he heard on the radio the report of an announcement made in Washington that Lend-Lease had been stopped, and that henceforth Britain would have to pay for all supplies, including those in the pipeline. Mr Collado caught the next train back to London and hastened to the American Embassy where he was joined by an equally dumbfounded Mr Clayton. Yes, the incredible news was true. President Truman had signed an order cancelling all outstanding contracts for Lend-Lease and discontinuing all Lend-Lease operations. 'This very heavy blow,' wrote Hugh Dalton, 'was struck at us without warning and without discussion. We had expected at least some tapering-off of Lend-Lease over the first few years of peace. But now we faced, not war any more, only total economic ruin.'[1] The Labour Government had been in office for barely three weeks.

From that day in August 1945 until early December when a Loan Agreement was signed with the United States Government and accepted by the British House of Commons, the negotiations in Washington dominated the mind of the British Cabinet. Many other momentous issues crowded for attention, but none could compete with this in starkness and urgency. The question was how the British people were to be fed and British factories supplied with raw materials. If no loan was forthcoming as a substitute for Lend-Lease, the nation would have to endure a period of harsher austerity than it had known in the war. Worse still, all the Government's plans for reconstruction would have to be reshaped on a much less ambitious basis. The British Ministers, it may seem, had no choice; they were beggars and must take any terms offered. And yet there were a number of occasions when Dalton, the whole Government, even Lord Keynes himself, did consider breaking off the negotiations and facing the bleak alternative. Aneurin Bevan played a full part in the Cabinet debate. His voice, with Shinwell's,

[1] *High Tide and After* by Hugh Dalton, p. 68.

was the strongest raised in criticism of the American demands. No hint of his dissension became known at the time, but the controversy behind the scenes was clearly one of major proportions.

President Truman had acted apparently without the slightest comprehension of what he had done and how serious was 'the body blow', to quote Attlee, which he had dealt to Britain. Yet once the first stinging impact had passed (and once goods in the pipeline were excluded from the edict) the damage did not seem irreparable. Lord Keynes, after all, knew the American financial experts better than anyone, and he was optimistic. He believed that he could get £1,500 million as a free gift or an interest free loan from the United States Government. That would be almost enough, on the Treasury's reckoning, to fill the gap until 1949. 'When I listen to Lord Keynes talking,' said Ernest Bevin, 'I seem to hear those coins jingling in my pocket; but I am not so sure that they are really there.'[1] Keynes also believed that he could get the money without 'strings'. His idea was to explain Britain's needs, to fix a provisional figure for the loan and only later to discuss the general conditions affecting world trade which the Americans might seek to impose. Why he should have taken this view is not clear, particularly in the light of the representations already made by the two friendly emissaries, Clayton and Collado. Probably the answer is that he knew how irrefragable, on grounds of equity and common sense, was the fully documented plea which Britain could present. Lord Keynes was sent to Washington as Britain's chief negotiator at the beginning of September. 'His (opening) discourse lasted for three days,' writes his biographer. 'It was the pure gold of perfect English prose, describing a situation of vast complexity with the lucidity and good arrangement that only a master mind could have achieved.'[2]

Never was there such an advocate; never was there such a case. Yet what happened in the next three months was a steady British retreat from one last ditch to another. Any notion of a gift or an interest-free loan had to be abandoned. One by one the American 'strings' were drawn tighter. Occasionally Keynes 'hit the ceiling'

[1] *A Prime Minister Remembers* by Francis Williams, p. 132.
[2] *The Life of John Maynard Keynes* by R. F. Harrod (Pelican, 1972), p. 713.

in protest.[1] The Cabinet at home felt itself being subjected to well-nigh insupportable pressures. 'We fought inch by inch throughout the negotiations,' says Attlee. Towards the end a new emissary, Sir Edward Bridges, Permanent Secretary to the Treasury, was sent to Washington to test whether the terms secured by Keynes, both for the Loan itself and its awkward accompaniments, were the best obtainable. Sir Edward had little difficulty in confirming that they were. The figure eventually fixed, even with a Canadian loan made available on the same terms, brought the total line of credit to £1,250 million – a sum which fell far short of the minimum originally estimated to be necessary by the Treasury. More serious, however, were the conditions attached. To help further the American dream of early convertibility (and indeed for the purpose of breaking up the sterling area which the Americans regarded as a giant discriminatory practice) Britain was required to give undertakings about the speed and resolution she would show in settling – that is, attempting to cancel – her accumulated sterling balances. This was one of the issues on which Keynes 'hit the ceiling'. He made his protest against an unwarrantable interference with the affairs of the Commonwealth. But the Americans were adamant; in effect, he was compelled to yield. And more nerve-racking still was the American pressure on the direct issue of convertibility. Under the Bretton Woods Agreements which formed part of the grandiose Anglo-American concordat negotiated by Keynes during the war, a five-year transitional period was envisaged before full convertibility could be established. Now the Americans demanded – and secured – an undertaking that sterling should be made convertible within a year of the coming into effect of the Loan. This was the point on which the negotiations most nearly collapsed; Dalton was at one moment preparing his speech for the Commons announcing the break.[2] In the last hours a few flimsy safeguards were devised – for example, it was agreed that the date of convertibility might be postponed after consultation. The major result remained. Britain got much less money than she had hoped for, on terms which she regarded as unworkable.

Keynes had done his brilliant best. Doubtless no better settle-

---

[1] *The Life of John Maynard Keynes* by R. F. Harrod, p. 717.
[2] *High Tide and After* by Hugh Dalton, pp. 82–4.

ment *was* available at the time. That much is proved by the long anxious months during which the American administration fought a desperate uphill fight to secure Congress approval of the Loan. American public opinion understood Britain's necessities no better than Truman had done in August. Paraded before Senate committees week after week was the spectacle of a wily, sponging, Socialist Britain attempting to outwit the open-hearted, open-pursed Americans and steal their legitimate markets by indefensible trading practices learnt from Dr Schacht or inherited from Lord North. Every other member of the British Cabinet was naturally as outraged as Bevan by this wretched misrepresentation to which no open retort could be made without injuring the hope of getting the money. None of them liked their appalling predicament. But what could be done? The alternative always looked more appalling still. How was it possible for Bevan to continue his protests and to sustain his opposition – as he and Shinwell did – until the end? Keynes commented frequently on the lack of comprehension displayed by rebellious Ministers. The Cabinet, he wrote to Lord Halifax, British Ambassador in Washington, on 1 January 1946, was 'a poor, weak thing'[1] – a surprising remark to be made by one loyal servant of the new administration to another. But clearly Keynes's disdain must have been directed primarily against those, like Bevan, who argued that some other course was possible.

Some comment must be offered, not because Bevan's protest influenced events but rather because this was the first big dispute he had with his colleagues in the new Government and because it went to the heart of other disputes which came later. Bevan's case was not that more skilful negotiation could have produced a different outcome, although he, like his colleagues, was misled by Keynes's original optimism. Nor did he argue that Britain could afford to do without the Loan; as a Minister in charge of a great spending department he had a special interest in getting it. His immediate argument was that if negotiations were broken off the result need not be so dire; they could be reopened at a later date more advantageously. No doubt the interval for Britain would be perilous and harsh. But the nation could be rallied for the trial. As the months passed the American judgment of their own interest

[1] *The Life of John Maynard Keynes* by R. F. Harrod, p. 733.

would alter. American sentiment and American business would begin better to appreciate how intimate was their concern with the economic revival of Western Europe. Once that happened a post-war settlement could be made on a more hopeful and enduring basis. Of course, no one can tell what would have happened if this heroic choice had been made. But it is pardonable to recall that the Marshall Plan of 1948 did produce the wiser American approach which Britain and Europe so sorely needed in 1945 and 1946. The course prescribed by Bevan might have encouraged an earlier departure from the barren doctrines which dictated the Loan settlement.

These elaborate hypotheses cannot be proved. Bevan and the few other recalcitrants in the Cabinet had against them the formid-able weight of expert opinion and the natural desire of the Govern-ment to avoid the incalculable risks involved in a rejection of the Loan. Yet whatever may be thought about the possibility of any other course, no doubt is possible about one source of Bevan's hostility to the whole settlement. He would not acknowledge Keynes as the great economic prophet of the new age. He had never been prepared to accept Keynes's analysis as a substitute for a fuller Socialist criticism of capitalist society, and he had never been convinced that Keynesian techniques would be adequate to cure the disease. Now Keynes, for all his toughness and skill in negotiation, had revealed how much he was attracted by a con-siderable part of the American case; he was reverting in part to his earliest liberalism. Yet was it really conceivable that the checks and spurs required by Keynes's doctrines, which individual Govern-ments had never shown the wit to apply within their individual territories, would suddenly be applied over a much wider inter-national field by a beneficent, far-seeing American administration? Washington at that moment was not giving an attractive foretaste of wisdom. Bevan feared that if ever the world was launched on the free trade flood, which both the Americans and Keynes envisaged, Socialist Britain would be swamped in the process. It was an illu-sion to suppose that a Cobdenite-Keynesian paradise was just round the corner. Yet that was the supposition on which the experts had worked, the Americans naively, the British with cautious ambivalence.

Moreover, one part of the settlement exposed the fallacy – and the vice – of the new liberal economics. For what was the significance of the American obsession with Britain's sterling balances? Of course, it would be highly convenient for Britain if those balances were 'adjusted' which was the new word for 'defaulted upon'. But the nations who were owed the money also had rights. Some of them were among the most wretchedly poverty-stricken in the world. One of them was India who had been brought into the war on Britain's decree and with whom Britain would soon be seeking the most far-reaching political settlement of the epoch. For Britain to be told that she must brusquely repudiate her debts to such a country to suit American theory was surely a piece of insolence unsurpassed in all history. Here was the richest nation in the world seeking to dictate, behind their backs and with not even a pretence of consultation, how some of the poorest nations should be treated. Never did a money-lender seek to exert his power more rawly. The new liberalism took no more account of rich and poor among nations than the old liberalism was concerned with rich and poor within individual states. All must make obeisance before the new gods – convertibility and non-discrimination – just as in the twenties and thirties the people had been required to bend the knee to balanced budgets and the gold standard. Bevan indeed sought an older historical analogy. He compared the Agreement of 1945 with the Combination Laws of 1799 and 1800; they too, in the sacred name of free competition, purported to impose the same rules on masters and men. Of course, Britain in her extremity would be compelled to reach accommodations with the nations which held the sterling balances. But that she should be hustled and hectored into doing so by all-powerful America (with the approval of all the orthodox economists) – and all in the name of the splendid new liberal dream – was offensive beyond words. Keynes might think that he had conjured the class war out of existence. But here he and his fellow liberal economists on both sides of the Atlantic were content to wage it afresh on a global scale.

Such thoughts might be considered too fanciful to influence hard-headed negotiations between great states. Yet the same realistic experts resolved to turn a blind eye to the hardest fact of all. Bevan argued that the clause requiring Britain to make sterling convertible within a year of the Loan coming into operation was an absurdity; it was free trade run mad and would end in catastrophe. The claim was not original. Keynes had thought much the same at the beginning of the negotiations, but as the weeks wore on his opposition faded; for him it was not solely a question of bowing to American inflexibility; he was sympathetic to the American aim and gradually persuaded himself that it might be practical. Attlee and Dalton apparently believed right to the end that the condition could never be fulfilled. 'We knew the convertibility clause was quite impossible,' divulged Attlee some twenty years later.[1] Dalton committed his 'secret reflection' to his diary on the night the House of Lords had approved the Agreement. 'It is quite certain,' he wrote, 'that the conditions will have to be revised long before AD 2001 and that, even in the next year or two, circumstances may require a large revision, which might even be "unilateral".'[2] But these secret fears had to be kept secret. It was impossible to explain, much less to emphasize, the dangers to the British public. That would have ruptured any chance of the Loan Agreement passing through Congress. The grand new edifice of Anglo-American co-operation had to be constructed on a deception.

Despite his anger and forebodings, Bevan never considered resignation on the issue. The arguments for accepting the Loan were too powerful; a break-up of the Government so early in its life would have provoked nothing but muddle and disillusion; he himself would have been branded, with much justice, as one who had run away from the challenges of his own Department. Indeed he might have been tempted to sit silent and let the inner clique of leading Ministers make their own decision. No young Minister, suddenly attaining high office, ever had a better excuse for confining his Cabinet contributions to his own direct responsibilities. He knew that he must prove himself master of his own house before he could exert real influence outside it. But silence on the great issues would be pusillanimous as well as uncharacteristic. From the outset he chose to participate to the full in attempting to shape the policies which would decide the whole fate of the Government.

The first great debate in the Cabinet left an indelible mark on

---

[1] *A Prime Minister Remembers* by Francis Williams, p. 134.
[2] *High Tide and After* by Hugh Dalton, p. 89.

his mind. The policies of the United States could inflict great injury upon Britain. There was no evidence of a deliberate design to strangle British Socialism at birth – liberal America would certainly have disavowed any such aim – but the outward, palpable expression of the inner compulsions of American society had its own menacing logic. The British champions of private adventure, who were already extolling the United States as the model and decrying Labour Britain as a pensioner of American capitalism, could not be expected to understand. But Socialists should.

2

MINISTER OF HOUSING
1945–1947

A habitat planned so as to form a continuous background to a delicately graded scale of human feelings and values is the prime requisite of a cultivated life.—LEWIS MUMFORD[1]

IN HIS first big speech in the new Parliament Aneurin Bevan stamped himself as a principal figure in the Government and a principal target of Opposition attack. The occasion was a motion moved from the Tory front bench on 17 October 1945, viewing 'with grave apprehension the existing shortage of houses in both urban and rural areas'. The new Government could hardly have removed the shortage in ten or eleven weeks; any criticism must lie against others. So Bevan congratulated the Opposition on their courage and public spirit; 'only a very grave concern for the public weal could have inspired them to put down a motion on a subject so embarrassing to themselves'. Then he surveyed, amid much mockery of his opponents, past housing policies, the prospect for the future and the principles which would guide him.

Several newspapers compared the performance with those of the young Lloyd George in the Liberal Government of 1906. 'He dominated the House,' wrote the *News of the World* political correspondent, 'not merely by superb oratorical mastery, but by the warmth of his personality and imaginative approach to the dry problems of bricks and mortar.' 'Only an Act of Congress can stop him reaching Number 10,' said another commentator. Not all the tributes were in this strain. Lord Kemsley's *Sunday Times* detected 'revolutionary turbulence' in Bevan's reference to speculative builders, and called upon Attlee to impose discipline. 'A Minister who kicks over the traces in the House is a danger to the Govern-

[1] *The Culture of Cities* by Lewis Mumford (Secker & Warburg, 1938).

ment and a fomenter of trouble for his party in the country.'
Another observer, Harold Nicolson, wondered whether the Labour
Party would overcome its inveterate jealousy of younger men. (The
average age of the new Cabinet was well over sixty.) What would
they do with 'this young flapper' still in his forties? Compared
with the others he was 'like an eagle in a hen coop'. Clearly he had
made a new impact. 'If he now builds the houses,' wrote Hannen
Swaffer, 'he is in direct line for the Premiership. If he does not, he
is for the high jump.'

One other observer, as outraged as Lord Kemsley, found these
speculations absurd or galling. Winston Churchill had been absent
from the Commons on 17 October, but he noted every sentence
Bevan had uttered. Almost everything the new Government said
or did opened afresh the wound of his electoral defeat. Here was a
moment when, as he said, the nation, 'exhausted and overburdened
in a fearful degree', should have been spared 'deep-seated organic
changes'; instead some members of the Government had raised
'this great schism of militant Socialism'. Churchill's rumbling fury
was directed against many other Ministers too – only Attlee himself was acquitted of having sought to 'embitter and inflame our
proceedings' – but when it exploded into the first official Vote of
Censure in December, Bevan was marked down as the chief cul-
prit. Cripps, Dalton and Morrison were scoffed at; Bevan was the
victim of a full-length Churchillian philippic, ending with the
famous words: 'I say today that unless the right hon. Gentleman
changes his policy and methods and moves without the slightest
delay, he will be as great a curse to his country in time of peace as
he was a squalid nuisance in time of war.'[1]

---

[1] *Hansard* Vol. 416 Col. 2544. Bevan's own account of the earlier origin
of the phrase was given in a contribution he made to *Churchill by his
Contemporaries* (Hodder & Stoughton, 1956), p. 60: 'To oppose him
[Churchill] on a question of fact brought out the very worst in him. The
harshest epithet he applied to me during the war was when in my capacity
as spokesman for the back-benchers' Tanks Committee—an official and
bipartisan body with access to official information, and with a specifically
critical task to perform – I had to present some unpalatable facts to him in
front of the House. He called me a "squalid nuisance". He never said anything he meant more than that. By confronting him with the facts of the
matter I had sunk to the lowest depths.'

The phrase – 'a squalid nuisance' – was gleefully taken up by the Tory newspapers. Subsequent comment on the Bevan-Churchill parliamentary duel endowed it with a haze of grandeur and even chivalry. But in 1945 and the months that followed the focus was sharper and truer. Deliberately from the outset, Churchill made the destruction of Bevan's reputation a primary purpose of the Tory Opposition. He had many old scores of his own to settle, and to drive a wedge between Bevan and his colleagues, to brand him as an incompetent demagogue, was an obvious Tory tactic. Yet there was something more; a flavour of venom and intensity was added to the assault. Nothing could be further from the truth than that Churchill approached the contest with a touch of an old man's magnanimity and humour. He believed, and said, that the country was being thrust into 'party antagonism, as bitter as anything I have seen in my long life of political conflict'.[1] He saw Bevan as the evil genius who had conjured this spirit into being. Above all he believed Bevan was vulnerable; if he could be destroyed, the blow to the whole Government might be fatal. Nothing that invective could inflict must be spared to achieve that grand objective. The gibe about the 'squalid nuisance' hurt Bevan as it was intended to hurt. From that December debate onwards, he knew, if he had ever doubted it, that he could expect no mercy. Churchill, at rare intervals, would make a faint, gracious acknowledgement of the patriotism of his old Coalition partners. Such courtesies were never shown to, or reciprocated by, Bevan. These two combatants fought with cold steel.

Yet no weapons of debate could settle the outcome of this particular battle; the state of the battlefield – the real nature and scale of the housing problem – would be much more decisive, and here the circumstances favoured Churchill. Bevan *was* vulnerable; so much was glaringly apparent. The housing shortages caused more anguish and frustration than any other of the nation's manifold post-war problems; all over the country the need was desperate and every M.P. and every local councillor was being besieged by the endless queue of the homeless. According to Churchill in that December debate, a remedy should not be beyond the compass of goodwill and reasonable organization to achieve. Bevan, he said,

[1] *Hansard* Vol. 416 Col. 2534.

had inherited 'a rich legacy of achievement and preparation'; he had squandered it 'with a profligacy which has rarely been equalled by a Minister who has still to make a reputation'. One part of that legacy was 'a highly developed house-building machine and the network of well-equipped manufacturing industries which support it and are almost inextricably interwoven with it' – by that, Churchill meant Britain's pre-war building industry which, he inferred, could be speedily reassembled to perform the long-term task. More specifically, Bevan's predecessor had announced in the spring of 1945 his proposals for providing permanent and temporary houses. All this was set in train; the Coalition had decided to 'enlist the help of all house building agencies of every kind'; why was Bevan not content to put these beneficent schemes into operation? Instead, 'swayed by partisan spite and prejudice and by the hope of exploiting these vices to suit his own personal political ambitions', he had decided to 'chill and check free-enterprise house-building which had always provided the bulk of the nation's houses'.[1] And let none of Bevan's colleagues object that unimagined obstacles had suddenly arisen to cumber their path. Had they not all made prophecies at the time of the election? Ernest Bevin had promised 'five million homes in quick time'. Stafford Cripps had allegedly claimed that 'housing can be dealt with in a fortnight'. Arthur Greenwood had dismissed the Coalition figures as 'chicken feed'. Thus Churchill in the censure debate on 6 December 1945, and the Tory benches roared their derisive approval in a style they had never previously been able to capture since the calamity in July. 'The Minister of Health,' said Churchill, 'has already allowed four months of excellent building weather to slip away.' And so it seemed. At that date fewer than one thousand houses and ten thousand temporary houses had been completed since hostilities ended.

Herbert Morrison, replying to Churchill in the censure debate,

---

[1] One of Churchill's favourite romanticisms was to talk of 'the cottage homes' of the English people. A relevant comment on the pre-war programme is given by Derek Barton in his book *A Hope for Housing?* (Mayflower Books, 1963): 'Considering it dispassionately (if one can), it is difficult to describe the pre-war three to one predominance of private enterprise in providing houses as successful in anything but quantity. A lot of the houses were sub-standard, a lot were only of minimum standard, a lot are ugly beyond belief.'

skilfully sidestepped the attack on Bevan. ('Did Herbert rise to the occasion?' Bevan was asked by Harold Wilson that night. 'No,' he replied, 'he reduced it to his own level and then rode it.') Bevan himself, taunted Churchill, was not allowed out of 'his dug-out' by his comrades. Morrison was frequently interrupted by Lord Winterton, the cantankerous father of the House. 'Houses. H–O–U–S–E–S,' cried the noble Lord. 'I was asking how many houses.' For the first and last time in his life Lord Winterton spoke for the masses. The same cry mounted all over the country until it appeared that, with little need of aid from Churchill's diatribes, the new Lloyd George might be overwhelmed in the flood.

It was in this atmosphere that Bevan had to devise a housing policy. So it is necessary to examine the facts: what was the problem of 1945 and what did he do?

Churchill's great pre-war 'house-building machine' had one spectacular merit – it did eventually produce houses at the rate of roughly 350,000 a year, an achievement of sheer quantity un-exampled either in Britain or anywhere else in the world, and since unfettered private enterprise was primarily responsible, the Tories naturally boasted about it. Yet the figures by themselves conceal features of the situation which made any comparison with Britain's housing problem in 1945 quite inapposite. It was not until 1933 – some fifteen years after the end of another war which left a des-perate housing shortage – that private money poured lavishly into house-building. Before that date, high interest rates and building costs and the attraction of other outlets for capital made investment in housing unprofitable. In short, the building boom of the thirties was largely the product of general slump. Labour was plentiful, wages were low, the cost of building materials had dropped, interest rates were depressed. Only in these conditions did the machine begin to function. Earlier, the attempts to start a housing drive had petered out, and in the early twenties in particular the chief burden was carried by local authorities. Oddly, although Churchill did not know it, the complete inter-war experience pointed a moral exactly opposite to the one he wished to illustrate.

Moreover, even when the high rate of building was attained, the bulk of the new houses were built for the middle classes and for sale and certainly not for those whose housing conditions were most wretched. In the whole period between the two wars, only one out of every fifteen new houses was to clear slums or relieve over-crowding. Bevan did not exaggerate when he said that 'the housing problem for the lower income groups in this country has not been solved since the industrial revolution'.[1] Churchill's house-building machine, even if it could have been dramatically reconstituted, was never designed to serve the whole nation. And, of course, in 1945, the machine with all its vaunted well-equipped, interwoven supporting industries, was scattered over the four corners of the earth. Not merely such large numbers of building workers but also multitudes of those who produced building materials were in the armed forces. The pre-war building force of well over a million men had fallen to less than 350,000. Many of these had been sucked into southern England where the ravages of bombing attacks had been most severe[2]; many of them were old and feeble or too young to have learnt their trade. In wartime conditions most building contracts had been placed on a 'cost-plus' basis which was notoriously inefficient. To gather a building force was an obvious first necessity, but the idea that it should or could be regrouped to serve an industry of the pre-war pattern had never been contemplated, to do them credit, by the post-war planners in Churchill's own Coalition.

Britain had had twelve and a half million houses in 1939. Nearly one of every three of these was damaged in the war and those undamaged had mostly gone six years without repairs. Two hundred and eight thousand houses had been totally destroyed, 250,000 were made uninhabitable, 250,000 more had been seriously mauled. Since 1939 160,000 houses had been completed, but that tiny figure was almost counterbalanced by 50,000 requisitioned and converted for non-residential use. In short, the population of Britain was squeezed into some 700,000 fewer houses than the country had possessed six years before and no one knew precisely how gross was the unsatisfied pre-war demand even for the barest shelter and comfort. No one knew, further, that in the three

[1] *Hansard* Vol. 414 Col. 1219.
[2] *Housing Policy since the War* by D. V. Donnison (Codicote Press, 1960).

3

post-war years there would be 11 per cent more marriages and 33 per cent more births than in the three pre-war years. And less still was it realized that full employment and new expectations would increase the numbers of people demanding separate houses far beyond anything which the figures themselves indicated.

These longer and less palpable calculations were pardonably excluded from the reckonings of Ministry of Health officials. The more limited estimates were sufficiently challenging. However, during the period of the caretaker Government, in March 1945, the Ministry had published what Churchill called a 'programme' and what the Ministry itself preferred to call 'objectives' or 'targets'. The aim should be to produce three to four million houses in the ten or twelve years after the war; that total would imply a rate of building comparable with the thirties, but included within it was an allocation of 500,000 for slum clearance and the relief of over-crowding, a more ambitious figure than had ever been envisaged before. Immediately it was hoped that 300,000 permanent houses, built or building, would be provided in the first two years after the armistice with Germany and this would be augmented by some 200,000 prefabricated temporary houses. Finally, it was estimated – and here the reckoning became oddly exact – that 750,000 new houses would be needed 'to afford a separate dwelling for every family desiring to have one'.[1] Taking these last two estimates together, the mountainous problems began to look more manageable.

Confronted with all these figures in the first debate on 17 October, Bevan talked of 'crystal gazing'. Whether he considered them too high or too low was not clear; his main purpose was to explain that they did not constitute anything deserving to be dignified with the title of 'a programme'. 'No solid basis whatsoever' existed for the calculations, and it was better that they should not be paraded. Yet one figure did stick in his own mind. If it was approximately correct that 750,000 houses could give every family a separate home, even if an allowance was made for a 25 per cent error, the problem *was* manageable. All his life Bevan hated and distrusted statistics; always he sought to guard himself from being ensnared by them. Yet numbers were important, and it was impossible to

[1] Cmd. 6609.

suppress the consoling hope which the crystal gazers had bequeathed to him. On the test of his critics, the job *could* be done.

It remains to consider the more definable part of Bevan's inheritance, the actual preparations made before July 1945 for the postwar period. The best publicized aspect of this work was what Churchill had called 'the military operation' of manufacturing prefabricated or emergency houses. As long before as March 1944 he had described in a broadcast how his friend Lord Portal at the Ministry of Works was 'working wonders': 'I hope we may have up to half a million of these [prefabs], and for this purpose not only plans, but actual preparations are being made on a nation-wide scale. Factories are being assigned, the necessary set-up is being made ready, materials are being earmarked . . .' Unfortunately the Portal house was to be made of steel. The project would have involved devoting all the nation's steel supply to this purpose, leaving nothing at all for all the rest of the nation's needs. So that particular house had to be abandoned with only two prototypes completed. None the less a variation of the idea had prospered. In 1944 orders had been placed for 100,000 prefabs to be made of less exotic materials. Inevitable delays occurred in the actual production and by 1945 the estimated price of the house had risen from £600 to £1,000 but the order was raised to 150,000. Bevan contemptuously said that he wished the whole scheme had never been started. But he could not neglect the first-aid offered. Here was something – orders, if not houses – which he did receive from his predecessors.

They had also made a start with arrangements for permanent building. An Act had been passed extending the pre-war provision of subsidies for slum clearance to cover new houses generally. Local authorities had been authorized to acquire land for some 250,000 houses, the lay-outs for nearly half these had been approved and some sites had been prepared. Since the building of a house took roughly six months from the clearance of the site to its final construction these preparations had made possible the thousand-odd houses completed by the end of December 1945. More importantly, plans had been worked out for increasing the numbers of building apprentices and for attempting to ensure that building workers were given priority in demobilization. Yet no one

– except the romantic or fiercely partisan Churchill – claimed that
a considered plan was ready. The abrupt ending of the Japanese
war, the sudden stoppage of Lend-Lease and other unforeseeable
factors had in any case transformed the perspective. Inevitably, the
housing legacy left to Bevan was settled by events rather than by
previous Ministers in office. Not merely British experience after
1918, but experience all over the world had shown that the con-
vergence of all the circumstances required for a big house-building
drive was a rarity. To build good houses for poor people on a huge
scale was something that had never been accomplished in modern
industrial societies. Often, as in the Britain of the thirties, the spur
had come from the slackness of the economy as a whole. After
1945, the instruments for a house-building programme had to be
assembled virtually from scratch and it had to be inserted into an
economy where all the hundred and one materials required were
scarce and insistently needed for other purposes. Yet the situation
had one advantage to set against all the disadvantages. Except in
the case of the temporary houses, no irrevocable decisions had been
taken. Bevan could make his own plan and could be judged on his
own performance, not someone else's.

So what did he do? A preliminary recital must be given of palliative measures taken in the early months either to relieve the immediate suffering or to protect and assist his long-term purposes. He
was in command of a besieged city and the ramparts must be held
while the counter-offensive was prepared. 'This winter we have to
bite on iron,' he told the Commons in October. Priority was given
to the repair of unoccupied war-damaged dwellings; some 60,000
houses were brought back into occupation in 1945. Local authorities were instructed to requisition unoccupied premises (77,000
were taken over by November) or to derequisition others which
had been used for non-residential purposes. The conversion of
homes to offices, insidiously starting in some areas, was banned
except with local authority approval. The 'cost-plus' system of contracting was ended. A 'share your house' appeal was made to the
good nature of the public, steps being taken to remove any legal
obstacles and to install sinks and cookers so that different families
might have separate kitchens; despite mockery from sections of the
press an appreciable contribution was made by these means to the

total of housing space. A Rent Act was rushed through, strengthening the control over furnished tenancies and establishing rent tribunals in many areas. A strict licensing system was enforced over all but the most minor forms of repairs in an effort, only partially successful, to prevent the building labour force seeping away into work less urgent than the equipment of fresh homes. All these devices together might compare pitiably with the need, but without them distress would have been the more intolerable and it would not have been possible to find homes for 116,229 families, which was the total reached by the end of January 1946.

Several of the other first measures adopted had a long-term as well as a short-term aim. A drive was made, led by Bevan on the Cabinet Committee responsible for all building operations, to curtail ruthlessly the vast variety of housing components; the style of lavatory seats, for example, was cut from fifty to two. The operation of the Rural Workers' Housing Acts which gave subsidies for repairs was suspended ('callously discarded', according to Churchill), since it was feared that no new building in the countryside would ever get started while this counter-enticement was present. The procedure whereby local authorities could acquire land (which previously took as long as four to nine months) was speeded up by lifting the requirement for public inquiries and hearings, thus removing the impediment of protracted negotiations with landlords ('a form of control we are going to remove,' said Bevan to the Tories who were protesting that 'controls' were the cause of all the trouble). Land was not the problem, said the Opposition; the local authorities had more than enough sites ready and the spiteful Land Acquisition Act was superfluous. But Bevan was able to show that whereas some authorities had all the land immediately needed, others were being held to ransom. He cited a prize example from his own constituency where 'some of the valleys are so narrow that even the rivers have to run on their sides' and where his old enemy, the Tredegar Iron and Coal Company, had refused to release a site for a new factory. 'It is an area,' said Bevan, 'from which the landlord has sucked riches for the last hundred years. It has created millionaires and now part of it has been rendered derelict. The orange is almost dry. The sites are the possession of the colliery owners, but, like vultures, they will not desert the carrion for fear

there might be the slightest bit of nutriment left.' Similar pleasantries were exchanged when another Bill provided for £100 million
to finance the temporary housing programme. The Opposition
wanted better parliamentary checks to control this 'fabulous sum'.
Bevan marvelled that the Tories had the nerve to question the
money spent on this programme, since all their own calculations
about its cost had gone so monstrously awry: 'It does not lie in the
mouths of the Opposition to talk about commercial probity. They
should be silent about it; otherwise some other putrefying corpses
will be exhumed.' Despite these skirmishes, Bevan was granted all
the legislative powers he asked for, usually with Tory acquiescence.

His greatest anxiety in those months was one which no legislation or departmental circular could remove. 'I can confess,' he told
the Commons on 17 October, 'that the whole House and the whole
nation are mastered by the rate of demobilization.' This was a hint,
but no more than a hint, of the controversy raging behind the
scenes. At the Ministry of Labour in the Coalition Government,
Ernest Bevin had drawn up a demobilization scheme designed to
avoid a repetition of the inequity and chaos which had followed the
1918 armistice. He took a legitimate pride in the arrangements
whereby the exodus from the forces was to be conducted smoothly
and without favouritism; those who were oldest or had served
longest would be released first, wherever they might be stationed;
exemptions from this rule were to be permitted only on grounds
of exceptional national need. After the election Bevin stayed as
guardian of his child on the Cabinet's manpower committee and
his vigilance increased when Churchill embarked on a reckless
campaign to speed up the process of demobilization in a manner
which would have torn the whole scheme to tatters. 'Bring the boys
home, the quicker the better. The Americans are doing so [in a
style which President Truman later described as 'frenzied']; why
not us?' It sounded easy, but the demagogic cry would have involved a gross breach of faith with servicemen all over the world,
particularly in the Far East, and the risk of widespread mutinies.
Bevan agreed with his colleagues that any 'grave departure' from
Bevin's plan would be fatal, but wanted a more flexible interpretation of the priority of release given to essential workers. Skilled
craftsmen were being brought home as fast as shipping would per-

mit, but not the workers needed in the building industries; brick-layers, for example, but not brickmakers. Bevan battered at Bevin's door; other Ministers, with their own urgent requirements, battered there too, which did not help Bevan. In November, the controversy came near to an explosion. Bevin protested to Attlee about the pressures to which he was being subjected, invoking the effective blunderbuss of a threatened resignation to get his way. He had a powerful case but it was not improved by the suggestion that the Minister of Health did not have one too. Bevin confessed himself unhappy about this 'housing equipment problem'. The materials should be produced with less labour and 'in any case the houses are not up yet and there is time to move in this equipment business ready for output as the houses go up'.[1] This was a curious revelation of Bevin's thoughts about how houses should be built. Shortage of materials, in fact, continued to impose the most serious limitation on the building of houses long after the stringent winter of 1945. Since two good claims were in conflict and since Churchill tried to extract the last ounce of mischief from the predicament, the demobilization dispute was awkward and tantalizing. Yet Bevin and Bevan together did achieve one notable victory. By May 1946 the building force had been restored to well over a million and the Government's aim was that 60 per cent of this total should be allocated to housing. Shortage of labour, especially in the many industries making materials where standards were low, still gave Bevan many headaches; but on the actual building sites this was rarely the worst problem.

All or almost all the steps listed so far would have had to be taken, with varying degrees of boldness, by any Minister of Health after 1945. The Opposition might demur, but could not do much more. The clampdown on less essential building and repair work, enforced by a licensing system and tightened by fresh enactments in 1946, was the most irksome measure. It could not fail to breed a large black market and provoke Opposition raillery. Bevan and his colleagues were accused of being more eager to stop people doing things than to encourage initiative. But the gibe won no favour with the homeless; if they had seen inessential building going ahead with government sanction there would have been housing

[1] *A Prime Minister Remembers* by Francis Williams, p. 126.

riots. These lesser issues, however, controversial or not, do not touch the distinctive choices of Bevan's administration. Within a few months of taking office, on some matters in the first weeks, he made a few decisions which governed the whole of his housing policy.

What was to be the instrument for executing the housing programme? That was the most crucial question. Right from the start, Bevan placed almost the entire responsibility, under his direction, on the 1,700-odd local authorities, county boroughs, and urban and rural district councils. They were charged with drawing up their own programmes, preparing the sites, making the contracts with private builders or establishing direct labour departments, fixing the rents, allocating the tenants and supervising the estates thereafter. Compared with pre-war, this marked a revolutionary change. Previously, house-building had been left in the main to the operation of the free market, to speculative builders building for profit; now, even when a small proportion of houses was to be built for sale (one in five was the suggestion at the outset), permits had to be secured from the local authority. The nation soon became so familiar with the method that the boldness and simplicity of the original choice were forgotten. Yet at the time other alternatives or variations were canvassed. Some experts, including Labour spokesmen, had suggested that a separate Ministry of Housing should be established. Bevan argued that, in view of the powers he possessed, the spirit if not the letter of that promise had been fulfilled. However, some advocates of a separate Ministry had assumed that the new department would act directly in some fields without subordinate agencies, and that notion Bevan had killed. Similarly, he scotched the ambitions of the Ministry of Works which during the war had become an embryo Ministry of Housing on its own. It had placed the order for the temporary houses; it ran a special repair service which became after the war a mobile labour squad, despatched to areas where exceptional assistance was required. Bevan did not scorn this help, but there were some inside the Ministry of Works, with backing outside, who thought this apparatus should be developed into a mammoth Housing Corporation capable of operating, no doubt alongside the local authorities, on a big scale over the whole country. Such a grandiose conception would have attracted the headlines in the newspapers but Bevan was convinced it would not build the houses. The giant would be musclebound. Moreover, he became suspicious of the Ministry of Works; rightly or wrongly, he felt its officials were too much at the mercy of big business, the big building contractors and – whisper it not at Transport House – the building trade unions. Better to let local pressures cut these potential dictators down to size. Local councillors had one qualification for being charged with the responsibility which could make good any deficiencies in expert knowledge: they spoke for the homeless and needed their votes. Housing cried aloud for a *democratic* organization.

The most vocal challenge to this decision came from the Tories. Why not use *all* agencies instead of *one*; why not unleash the private builders as well as the local authorities? The plea was plausible, but Bevan's answer to it went to the root of his case. One reason, the social reason, for selecting the local authorities as the instrument was that only through them could houses be supplied to those in greatest need: otherwise, the private builders and private pockets would be selecting the tenants or house-owners. But there was another reason, a practical reason, which he believed to be equally valid: 'It is that, if we are to have any correspondence between the size of the building force on the sites and the actual provision of the material coming forward to the sites from the industries, there must be some planning. If we are to plan we have to plan with plannable instruments, and the speculative builder, by his very nature, is not a plannable instrument.' In fact, unknown to Churchill and the Tories, most of the housing experts at the Ministry of Health had been moving along undoctrinaire paths towards this same conclusion before Bevan arrived on the scene. The post-1918 experience, the likely conditions of scarcity, the tough struggle to obtain precious labour and materials and the will to use them sanely all pointed to the local authorities as the necessary chief instrument. Bevan's civil servants welcomed his Socialist approach as hard-headed realism. They or the previous Minister had also decided to sugar the pill for private enterprise by a provision that the same subsidies for local government housing were to be made available for the small total of houses built for sale. Bevan transferred this proposition from the pigeon-hole to the waste-paper

3*

basket without a moment's hesitation; was it really sensible, when local authorities were to be called upon to perform a great new task, to encourage private industry with government money to turn aside from assisting them? Bevan's civil servants did not trouble to press the argument. When complaints were raised in the Commons about his brusque dismissal of this pet scheme of the private builders, his contempt knew no bounds. 'The only remedy the Tories have for every problem,' he said, 'is to enable private enterprise to suck at the teats of the State.'

Yet many besides the Tories questioned the wisdom of Bevan's main choice even though they had no obvious alternative to offer. Could the local authorities perform the huge new functions now thrust upon them? Might they not just sink beneath the burden? Where would they get the technical staff and advice? If some of the big and progressive authorities could be expected to succeed, what about the others? How much could be hoped for from the small authorities, particularly in the rural areas, which had never undertaken this type of work before? Bevan was proposing the biggest enlargement of local government activity, in degree if not in kind, in the history of local government; would the new machine really work? These were legitimate doubts. Theoretically, his decision might seem right, well-nigh inevitable. But many who were not hostile to his intentions feared that the instrument would break in his hands. Bevan's answer and his department's answer was to embark on a great drive to enlist the enthusiasm of the local authorities or, in some instances, to release the pent-up desire for action already prevailing. He himself and his leading officials toured the country to explain the programme and hear local representations. Local government offices were bombarded with circulars covering every aspect of house-building. Sometimes they were driven dizzy in the turmoil; the newspapers could easily paint a picture of hectic confusion. But having offered his supremely confident prophecy about the efficiency of his instrument, Bevan worked overtime to make the prophecy come true. It was an old Marxist stratagem.

Another ingredient was needed for success, apart from administrative enthusiasm. To start on the job, money was hardly less important than the tools. Bevan's predecessors had already extracted from the Treasury a rate of subsidy higher than anything known in pre-war days, and Dalton had been most helpful with interim assistance in the autumn of 1945. But Bevan's conferences with local authorities convinced him that only a comprehensive financial settlement could give the programme the necessary impetus. A Housing (Financial and Miscellaneous Provisions) Bill was presented for Second Reading on 6 March 1946, and Bevan invited Charles Key, his Under-Secretary and a local government expert in his own right, to make the opening speech. Charlie Key's pride and pleasure burst forth in his opening sentence: 'There is no greater social problem facing the people of this country today than housing, and at no time have there been placed before the House financial proposals for tackling that problem more generous in amount, more consistent in principle or more complete in character than those embodied in this Bill.' Local authorities, he said, would welcome the proposals as being 'in excess not only of their wildest expectations but even of their highest hopes'.

These hyperboles were not unmerited. The existing subsidy on a standard three-bedroom house, granted on a forty-year basis, was £5 10s. from the national exchequer and £2 15s. from local rates. The new Bill lengthened the period from forty to sixty years and raised the subsidy to £16 10s. from the exchequer and £5 10s. from the local rates – thus altering the pre-war proportions of national and local contributions from two to one to three to one. This was the major substantial alteration, but a host of others was added to deal with special cases. Higher subsidies were proposed to cover houses for agricultural workers, houses in county districts where the rent-paying capacity of tenants was abnormally low, the provision of flats bearing high site costs, the provision of lifts in the flats, houses built in areas threatened by mining subsidence or where the rateable value was especially low and, finally, the extra cost of prefabricated permanent houses for which the Government was placing orders. No such far-ranging and meticulous effort had ever been made to use subsidies as a spur over the whole field of housing policy. Bevan's own officials felt at first that he was being too ambitious about what might be obtained from the Treasury. They argued that it would be wiser to concentrate on the demand for higher subsidies without raising the issue of an altered proportion between national and local contributions – an innovation likely to offend the Treasury's most tender susceptibilities about financial purity and precedent. 'No,' said Bevan cheerfully when Sir John Wrigley departed to open negotiations with the Treasury officials, 'tell them we want three to one.' Sir John did as he was instructed but was met, as he expected, with a sharp, almost supercilious, refusal. Bevan thereafter must have had private talks with Dalton. Sir John was advised to reopen the question with all the blandness he could muster. 'My Minister,' he said at the next meeting of the Committee, 'still thinks that the figure of three to one would be appropriate.' 'And my Minister agrees,' replied the Treasury official. Sir John was too polite to show signs of triumph. But Joshua must have felt the same sensation of delighted amazement when the walls of Jericho fell.

The choice of instrument, the money, above all the pitifully inadequate total of new houses actually built – these were the leading topics of debate inside the Commons and outside during 1945 and 1946. More and more Bevan considered that the discussion was distorted. Why was so much public interest concentrated on the local authorities, the building contractors, the building workers, and their alleged delinquencies? True, there was nothing streamlined in the sprawling private building with its vast proliferation of tiny firms and their varied, archaic methods. But a Hercules who tried to clear that Augean stable first would have no energy or time left to build houses. And the real constriction was elsewhere – in the innumerable industries serving the builders on the site. A house was at the end of the production line, not the beginning. Ideally, it would have been agreeable – the actual process of building would have been much swifter and less costly – if the whole operation could have been suspended until adequate stocks of materials were accumulated. Ideally, too, a few profitable years could have been devoted to the complicated legal task of breaking down the monopolistic and restrictive practices with which these industries were riddled. But he could not wait. What he did do, with considerable effect, was to use his public instrument to impose prescribed standards for materials and components on private interests, to ensure that the specifications of the British Standards Institution were made compulsory in local government housing.

Thus some element of order was introduced into the previous confusion. But he could not divert the flow of materials merely to suit the needs of his Ministry. So many other Ministers and industries were competing. At varying times, steel, cast-iron, bricks, timber, always timber, were desperately scarce. During the first months, Bevan spent more time and nervous energy on the committees concerned with these products, fighting for his share of the available pool and searching for expedients to enlarge the pool, than in any other pursuit. What drove him near to frenzy was to cross from Whitehall, where the great issue was, say, softwood and its shortage across the planet, to Westminster where Tory M.P.s wearily recited their criticisms of local authorities and the Minister who had placed so much faith in them. Could the point never be grasped? The chosen instrument could use much more than industry and imports could supply.

Yet amid all these pressures and long before the houses were going up in any number, Bevan found time to refresh himself – and to make some of his bravest departures – in a field where many Ministers of Housing at such a time might never have entered. What sort of houses, how should they look, what would they be like to live in and where should they be built? The last of these questions fell more properly within the province of the Ministry of Town and Country Planning, but Bevan invaded it whenever he could. He had the good fortune to be on excellent terms with the Minister of Planning, Lewis Silkin, who, if he had been a lesser man, might have resented the intrusions of the Minister of Health. But they had common aims and interests. And the other questions about how the houses were to be built offered a perennial fascination. To escape from the businessmen and the politicians into the company of the architects was a benediction in itself.

In his first housing speech Bevan thought aloud on these themes. He protested against the whole pre-war system of building; it produced 'castrated communities'. The arrangement whereby the speculative builders built for one income group and the local authorities for another was 'a wholly evil thing from a civilized point of view, condemned by anyone who had paid the slightest attention to civics and eugenics; a monstrous infliction upon the essential psychological and biological one-ness of the community'.

Local authorities had been left to provide 'twilight villages' whereas the speculative builders were responsible for 'the fretful fronts stretching along the great roads out of London', belonging to what he understood was called 'the marzipan period'. The local authorities could never do worse and, given the chance of architectural diversification, they should do much better. Sound social needs, as much as aesthetics, should point in that direction. 'After all, you know, a man wants three houses in his lifetime: one when he gets married, one when the family is growing up, and one when he is old; but very few of us can afford one.' A much wider embrace of municipal ownership could offer a tentative solution to these complexities. By the same reasoning, local authorities should strive to find hospitality for all age groups on their estates. 'I hope that the old people will not be asked to live in colonies of their own – they do not want to look out of their windows on endless processions of the funerals of their friends; they also want to look at processions of perambulators . . . The full life should see the unfolding of a multi-coloured panorama before the eyes of every citizen every day.'

These are extracts from what Bevan said in 1945. A similar selection could be made from almost every speech he delivered on housing. Hardly ever did Opposition speakers trouble to follow him on to this territory; no doubt their excuse would be that numbers and costs were too urgent. But Bevan refused to allow the issues of quality and variety to be submerged. In another of his Housing Bills he removed the 'ridiculous inhibition' incorporated in pre-war Housing Acts that public provision should be made only for 'the housing of the working classes'. 'We should try,' he said, 'to introduce in our modern villages and towns what was always the lovely feature of English and Welsh villages, where the doctor, the grocer, the butcher and the farm labourer all lived in the same street. I believe that is essential for the full life of a citizen . . . to see the living tapestry of a mixed community.' And often, especially when pre-war figures or costs were cited, he lashed out against what had been done in those years. He was not prepared to count in any total all the 'silly little bungalows' built before the war: 'builders made a fortune in putting them up, and fortunes are now being made in holding them up.' Of course it put up costs to forbid local authorities or anyone else stringing houses along the highways, but how many lives had been lost because no sufficiently strong regulations forbad this infamy before: 'children cannot obey the normal impulses of childhood without being murdered by the results of speculative builders'. Opposition speakers tended to greet these outbursts with a smile; had ribbon development Acts never been heard of before 1945? Yes, retorted Bevan, 'a little grass verge between the road and the houses; that is all'. The apparent lack of interest shown by the Tories in quality was an exposure of their class bias; *they* did not live in such houses. Bevan's passionate concern came from his love of beauty but also from a deep sense of the dignity of his own class. 'I believe,' he said, 'that if we scamp our work at present we shall never be forgiven. Because of the low standards tolerated, if not imposed, by the Ministry before the war, there are today all over the landscape ugly houses poking their stupid noses into the air because they are too high for their width.' Why should ugliness be thought good for *his* people?

One part of Bevan's interest in this aspect of housing policy derived from his strong visual sense, a faculty rare in politicians, particularly Welsh ones. Perhaps a too formal or rigid education, the routine which buries schoolboys' eyes in textbooks, helps to kill visual curiosity. Anyhow Bevan was never maimed in this manner, and he would gladly attribute the freshness with which he saw what was happening all around him to his early rejection of all educational authority, to his diligent self-education. He never moved anywhere without looking – at the use or misuse of the countryside, at the way towns and cities had been built, at the pictures on the walls of every house he entered. He was almost as much at home with painters as with poets, and never allowed anyone working in his department to relapse into the delusion that building houses was solely a question of economics or business. People had to live in them.

Many of these exhortations and reproofs fell on stony ground. Many of his hopes were disappointed and for an obvious reason: the interests of speed often conflicted with those of wise siting, and in those years speed was bound to win the day. Yet within the ambit where Bevan's writ ran, he applied his principle in practice: he insisted on good standards for the houses themselves. Prior to the war, the minimum size of a three-bedroom house had been fixed at 750 square feet. A Ministry of Housing manual in 1944 had cautiously recommended 800/900 square feet. At the same time an independent committee presided over by the Earl of Dudley had proposed 900 square feet (plus 50 square feet for storage). Bevan at once plumped for the Dudley formula and encouraged local authorities to do even better (which many did). The distinctions may sound trivial, but they soon became topics of controversy. Could not something be saved by abandoning Bevan's insistence on an upstairs lavatory? Could not more be saved, without reducing the actual living space, by making the passageways narrower, the larders fewer, the walls thinner? Could not more houses be built if these minor adjustments were permitted? The answer was plain; they could. But from 1945 to 1950 Bevan, the alleged demagogue, refused to increase the number of houses he could claim to have built by yielding to the demand. To cut standards, he insisted, was 'the coward's way out'. It would be 'a cruel thing to do. After all, people will have to live in and among these houses for many years. Enough damage has already been done to the face of England by irresponsible people. If we have to wait a little longer, that will be far better than doing ugly things now and regretting them for the rest of our lives.' Moreover, if one concession was made, how many more would be extorted? Nothing made him angrier than the attack on his housing standards, particularly when it came from those who would faint from claustrophobia in 900 square feet. And, to anticipate the story, nothing made him sadder than when his successor as Housing Minister, Hugh Dalton, surrendered to the clamour. Bevan, said Dalton, had been 'a tremendous Tory'[1] on the momentous issue of the upstairs lavatory; his whole attitude to standards was something near a phobia. Yet the breaches made by Dalton were widened by Dalton's successors. One of the oddities of Britain's post-war housing history is that the best houses were built in the first five years when the stringency was greatest, and that only after this most testing period was the great post-war opportunity lost to forbid the re-growth of giant working-class ghettoes. Fortunately, standards have not been universally depressed to the level encouraged by the Ministry in London after 1951, but,

[1] *High Tide and After* by Hugh Dalton, p. 358.

for that, the credit is due to local authorities who acquired better habits in those first ambitious years.[1]

The same approach influenced Bevan's attitude to prefabricated building. He had always criticized the *temporary* prefab programme – although he did not refrain from including the figures in his housing returns. These 'rabbit hutches', as he occasionally called them much to the annoyance of the many satisfied tenants, used up sites, materials and labour which could better have been devoted to permanent building. But the prefabrication of *permanent* houses was an idea deserving continued experiment, despite some protests of the building unions and their heavier cost compared with conventional building. Bevan gave much personal encouragement to the inventors, and in the spring of 1946 settled on two types – the British Steel House and the Airey House, a construction of precast concrete. Neither of these was exactly a thing of beauty but they were not eyesores – in the case of the Airey House, Bevan went to see for himself and told the contractors they would only get the order when they had devised a decent sliding roof. Later that year production was started on ten other non-traditional types, and a further type of semi-prefabrication and much the most attractive – the Cornish unit – won Bevan's unqualified approval. (He wanted to get one of his own and plant it in some distant countryside beyond the reach of Cabinet despatch-riders.) Altogether, permanent prefabrication added 10,000 houses to the total built during Bevan's period of office and an additional 170,000 thereafter. However, the cost was high and in the 1950s a decision was lamely made to bring the programme to a halt.[2]

Another adventure on a lesser scale illustrates his interest. After many preliminary rebuffs he at last succeeded in persuading the Treasury – once Cripps who had the same interest had arrived there – to provide a special subsidy for the reimbursement of

[1] One epitaph on the whole episode may be taken from the Parker Morris Committee which reported to the Government in 1961: 'Where for reasons of economic stability there may have to be a choice between standards and numbers built, we think that in future it should not be standards that are sacrificed.'

[2] Here, too, however, there was to be a later epitaph. For in the 1960s efforts were renewed to start afresh the programme for industrialized building.

authorities who found building in their own local stone more expensive than bricks. Of all the monuments left behind him, the lovely post-war cottages in the Cotswolds, suited to the surrounding countryside, were among those of which he was proudest. And the delight was increased when in some places – as with the stone terraces in Bath – the authorities paid heed to the ceaseless war he waged against the over-emphasis on semi-detached houses. 'The middle class in England,' he said, 'has always been the source of social ugliness, inflicting on us appalling architecture, so that many of our housing estates look like railway sidings. In future we should arrange houses in groups of four, six or ten where they suit each other.' Often when he preached these sermons all over the country the congregations were impatient. But he never stopped. 'We don't want a country of East Ends and West Ends, with all the petty snobberies this involves. That was one of the evil legacies of the Victorian era.' No one and nothing could prevent him peering into the future. 'While we shall be judged for a year or two by the *number* of houses we build,' he told a conference of rural authorities in May, 1946, 'we shall be judged in ten years' time by the *type* of houses we build.'

Yet the numbers mattered so much – for the homeless, his Party, and himself. During the early years, much to the annoyance of the Opposition, he refused to make public the target he was aiming at year by year. The Tories called this cowardice; he considered it elementary cunning. If he fixed the total too high and failed to reach it, he would have handed a weapon to his opponents; if he fixed it too low, he would be derided for complacency. The point was sound, but could hardly prevail against taunts from the Opposition, and much worse, the housing queues which seemed always to be getting longer, not shorter. In the summer and autumn of 1946, the ugly situation was dramatized by 'the squatters'. In many parts of the country, mothers and fathers, carrying their children and family belongings, invaded huts which had not been derequisitioned by the local authorities, and set up improvised homes of their own. The idea was adopted by Communists in London who organized 'the Great Sunday Squat' in an empty block of flats in Kensington. The Government feared widespread disorder. Eviction orders were served on the London squatters, most of whom

were scrambled into hostels. Elsewhere the squatters were sometimes victorious, retaining their primitive conquests with the backing of local public opinion. The alarm subsided. An outbreak of
direct action which could have spread like a prairie fire was kept in
check, and one reason why the Government could reassert its
authority undoubtedly was that it was thought to be acting fairly
in its general policy; houses were to go to the neediest first. Without that safeguard, a mass movement of lawless rage against the
housing shortage could have swept through many cities, disrupting
altogether any fair system of allocation.

Bevan sympathised with the squatters, but he could not allow
them to take command. For multitudes the problem was urgent,
but strangely, also, the multitudes were not getting less but growing. Was it not clear that full employment, fuller wage packets, the
fact that people were now being encouraged to *demand* a house of
their own, were multiplying his difficulties? 'Dissatisfaction with
the Government,' he said in an interview at the end of 1946, 'is the
real dynamic of democracy, the elemental force of political action.
How on earth can people be satisfied when the lack of houses is
such a fertile source of human misery?' Then, as was usual with
him, his own eloquence opened wider vistas. 'A society in which the
people's wants do not exceed their possessions is not a Socialist
society. That sort of satisfaction is not Socialism, it is senility.' But
sometimes he was enraged; the dynamic of democracy could become too importunate. And more and more he took refuge in the
estimate, made by his predecessor, of the 750,000 houses required
to give every family a separate house. In October 1946, Churchill
returned to the attack. 'The amount of needless suffering his
[Bevan's] prejudices have caused cannot be measured. There is,
however, a certain poetic justice in the fact that the most mischievous political mouth in wartime has become, in peace, the
most remarkable administrative failure.' Bevan replied with a
tirade against 'a wicked man'. But he added: 'I give you this
promise: that by the next general election there will be no housing
shortage as far as the mass of the British people are concerned.'[1]

---

[1] *Manchester Guardian* 10 October 1946. The same pledge was repeated
in only slightly varying forms throughout the year.

The 750,000 houses would be built and, after that, the task would start of pulling down the ugly houses built by the Tories and building beautiful cities and towns.

The severities of that 1946 winter were no less fierce than those of the year before. We were still biting on iron. Most local authorities were doing their job too well; their orders had outrun the supply of materials and those who had to be restrained naturally put the blame on Bevan. In London special labour difficulties arose. 'You can't find out what happens to the building force,' he said; 'it hides itself; if this had really been a military operation I could shoot a few builders.' 'Where *are* all the people I need for my programme?' he once asked in exasperation at the Cabinet. Attlee had the answer: 'Looking for houses, Nye.' That October a drive was conducted to finish the houses already completed up to eaves' level before too many others were started. One night Bevan stormed into the Smoking Room from a meeting of the Cabinet. Throwing back his head he lamented: 'It's like the Tower of Babel.' 'Yes, I understand,' said Seymour Cocks, 'they couldn't get the roof on either.'

Did the policy work?

To judge by the Tory attack, relentlessly sustained throughout the whole Parliament, Churchill had chosen his ground shrewdly. Neither he nor his subordinates had reason to repent the bitter prophecies of Bevan's failure made in 1945. In the House of Commons itself a long list of Tory spokesmen on housing – Henry Willink, R. S. Hudson, Harry Crookshank, Walter Elliot, David Maxwell Fyfe, Derek Walker-Smith – were dialectically massacred by Bevan. They would never answer his reiterated question: would they abandon his determination to provide houses for those in greatest need first, and, if not, what other instrument but his could they use for the purpose? Churchill kept clear of the direct controversy; never once did he face Bevan in a housing debate. But in the country outside the niceties of debate went unnoticed and the Tory newspapers pilloried the Minister of Health in a style to satisfy Churchill. Every hold-up, every obstacle, every muddle was magnified in screaming headlines. A miasma of doubt and discontent about Bevan's methods was easily spread. It would have been excited without the aid of Tory malevolence. For, of course, the truth was that the 750,000 estimate – the original calculation of the Ministry – was a monstrous underestimate. It made no allowance for the huge weight of past neglect, the spectacular post-war increase in the marriage rate and the birth-rate; above all, the vast submerged demand for better housing which post-war conditions brought to the surface.[1] The housing shortage which Bevan promised to cure in his term of office is not cured today. Tory propagandists thought they had in his pledge a blunt instrument with which he could be hammered to his political grave.

Yet this mistaken prophecy, by itself, was pardonable. Even if he had discovered that the official figures reflected so poorly the full gravity of the housing shortage, he might have been tempted, especially in the early years, not to blazon the fact abroad too brutally. The task to be undertaken would have been made to look so formidable that the nation might have quailed before it. No: a plainer condemnation of Bevan's policy derives from another source. At the Blackpool Conference of the Conservative Party in 1950, when the Labour housing programme was running at the rate of just over 200,000 houses a year, the floor forced on the platform a demand for the target of 300,000 houses a year. Within two years, under Harold Macmillan's direction at the Ministry of Housing, the figure was attained. Against this achievement, and the reflection it casts on Bevan's performance, no effective answer may seem possible. Macmillan's success compared with Bevan's failure is now enshrined in the mythology of the Conservative

---

[1] Derek Barton writes in his excellent book *A Hope for Housing?* (Mayflower, 1963): 'Twenty years after the first world war the supply of dwellings (regardless of quality) had almost caught up with the total number of families, but even the 1951 census showed the excess of households over houses to be almost the same as in the depression year of 1931. And today [1963], eighteen years after the end of the war, we are still estimating the deficiency in millions, and the scale of the operation proves to be bigger than it was ten years ago. "The political promise of 'a separate dwelling for every family which deserves to have one'," J. B. Cullingworth points out, "involves the provision of two or even three dwellings for every one that would have been required fifty years ago".'

Party, and historians accept it with the suave docility of *Daily Telegraph* leader-writers.[1]

Yet there is a solid, some may feel an overwhelming, answer to the indictment. The events which supply it are vital to the record of Bevan's career as a Minister, his relations with his colleagues, and the fate of the Labour Government itself. One symptom of those events is revealed in the housing figures. During the whole period of the Labour Government a total of one and a half million of additional units of accommodation were provided.[2] More than a million of these were new permanent houses; the rest was made up of temporary prefabs, conversions and the repair of war-damaged houses, all absorbing materials and labour which could otherwise have been used for permanent building. This achievement was no small one in the first years after the war when the country was also engaged in a big factory-building programme. It far surpassed anything achieved in Britain after 1918 or in most other countries after 1945. Incidentally, the target of 750,000, supposed to be sufficient to provide every family with a separate house, was achieved in the autumn of 1948. Some defence of Bevan's policy could be left to rest on this recital alone. A nation should be able to do better seven or ten years after a great war than three or five years after. Yet if this was all that could be said, some part of the charge would also stand. Macmillan achieved a rate of house-building spectacularly better than Bevan's, and Bevan certainly never regarded Macmillan as a man capable of working miracles. However, figures during Bevan's period of office show something else of deeper significance; the graph of new building rose to its peak in 1948 and then declined. In 1946 the number of new houses completed was 55,400; in 1947, 139,690; in 1948, 227,616. With the contributions from other forms of building the total in 1948 was 284,230. Thus, three years after the war, the Government was within striking distance of 300,000. If the natural expansion had been maintained,

[1] For example, Henry Pelling in *A Short History of the Labour Party*, writes: 'Bevan was less successful in dealing with housing, however, for although he encouraged construction by local authorities for cheap letting, and kept a tight rein on private building, he did not achieve the target of 200,000 houses annually which the Government had promised.'

[2] These and the subsequent figures are taken from Herbert Ashworth's *Housing in Great Britain* (Thomas Skinner, 1957).

it is certain that that figure would have been passed in 1949. (The magic total would have been all the more readily attainable if Bevan had agreed to cut standards[1] and the proportion of three-bedroomed to smaller houses, as his successors did, or if he had been able or willing to curtail the huge war-damage programme which was estimated to be the equivalent of 100,000 new houses.) The essential fact is that in the midst of its term of office, the Government deliberately cut and henceforth confined the housing programme. Bevan's house-building instrument was not permitted to produce the results of which it was buoyantly capable. Moreover, he had to keep silent then and thereafter, at least in public, about the causes of the change in policy. The agony he endured needs no emphasis. But, of course, he was not alone in his trials. The blow to the housing programme was part of a larger crisis, which must now be examined.[2]

[1] Derek Barton writes in *A Hope for Housing?*: 'Such a house [that is the People's House built under the Tory Government's specifications] needed only about nine-tenths of the materials required by the houses Labour had been building, so that 300,000 of them could be built with roughly the materials required for 270,000 of the slightly bigger ones.'

[2] No one so far as I know has attempted before to examine the truth about Bevan's housing policy, both the reasons for the high figure of 280,000 houses built in 1948 and the curtailments later. Meantime, plentiful comments have been published which appear to vindicate the Conservative propaganda of the time. For example, Harold Macmillan wrote in *Tides of Fortune* (Macmillan), p. 66: 'He [Bevan] failed over his housing policy for the simple reason that the Ministry over which he presided was too wide in its responsibilities . . . When I succeeded him in Housing, I found how wrong the so-called experts of the Treasury and of the Ministry had been about the potentialities of the building industry when given encouragement and freedom.' And then again, on page 374: 'Yet his advisers had persuaded even so determined a man as Aneurin Bevan that 200,000 was the absolute maximum at which it would be reasonable to aim.' These misapprehensions cannot be allowed to stand. They libel the civil servants of the old Ministry of Health no less than Bevan. It is not the case that Bevan's advisers in his own Ministry ever argued that 200,000 was a maximum figure or anything like it; rather they were proud of having already achieved a much larger figure three years after the war. Nor is it the case that the Treasury policy was based on an estimate of the building industry's potentialities. Bevan would never have tolerated such a claim. What happened was that the Treasury laid down a figure for the capital investment programme which in turn savagely cut the existing housing programme.

1947 was the year of Labour's travail. It began with the coldest winter since 1880, snow, frost, storms and floods following one another like the afflictions of Job, an acute coal shortage, a breakdown in transport and shipping, and a fuel crisis which brought great stretches of British industry to a standstill for three weeks – incidentally imposing fresh checks on the supply of building materials for housing. The shock left its wounds and tremors everywhere – on the economy, in the Cabinet, throughout the country and the Labour movement. Never did the Labour Government recover its first dashing confidence. Dalton and Cripps pinned much of the blame on Shinwell and sought to persuade Attlee to remove him. Attlee was unconvinced, but it was clear that there had been a breakdown in planning as well as everything else and that a much stricter system was needed. At first Attlee considered giving greater powers over the domestic field to Herbert Morrison, but Dalton and Cripps shuddered at the prospect. Was not Morrison already supposed to be the great planner? Had he not claimed at the Party Conference in 1946: 'The Government is rapidly building up an overall planning organization . . . The real problem of statesmanship in the field of industry and economics is to see the trouble coming and to prevent ourselves getting into the smash.' Yet one smash had come and, as the country clambered out of it, another seemed in the making. In any case, Morrison fell ill, struck down by thrombosis for several weeks.

Governing the whole mood of desperation inside the Government was the knowledge that the American and Canadian loans were being spent faster than any one had foreseen – partly because rocketing American prices had reduced the value of the loans and partly because the recovery in production and exports was too slow. At the beginning of the year Dalton sent stern warnings to Attlee and the Cabinet and cast around for ways to ward off the peril. The most unconscionable drain on the nation's resources was the huge sums which had to be provided, often in dollars, for the armed forces still maintained all over the world. 'What shall it profit Britain,' wrote Dalton in a fierce note to the Prime Minister, which came near to threatening resignation, 'to have 1,500,000 men in the Forces and Supply, and to be spending nearly £1,000 millions on them, if we come an economic cropper two years hence?'[1] He talked of the danger of another and worse 1931 collapse and yet complained that he had met with 'a blank wall' from Attlee. The unshakable realities of the personal combinations in the Cabinet emerged. Defence expenditure was a reflection of foreign policy; foreign policy was in the hands of Ernest Bevin and in any dispute Attlee would infallibly side with Bevin and the Defence Ministers against all comers. Moreover, in that bleak spring of 1947, Attlee and Bevin had to face a towering challenge on the international front. Attlee had to dismiss one Viceroy of India, find another, and fix the date for Britain's departure from India. Bevin made the decision that the British Government could no longer support the regimes in Greece and Turkey and wished to time his withdrawal at the precise moment when he could secure American willingness to take over the burden. These were fantastic problems for a Government to have to solve while the country was plunging towards bankruptcy. Bevin would not be hustled by Dalton, and Attlee had other reasons, apart from personal sympathies, for backing Bevin.

Much less excusable was the full support which Attlee gave to Bevin's Palestine policy which ended in total fiasco. There 100,000 British troops became engaged in a hopeless war with the Jews. Bevin had never attempted to follow the pro-Zionist policy enunciated by the Labour Party before 1945, but had nothing to put in its place but blind, harsh repression. Since it was plain that Arab and Jew would never agree, a partition of the twice-promised land became the only honourable, workable alternative. This was the course strongly urged by Dalton, Bevan and others. But Bevin was adamant; having given an awkward pledge to 'eat his hat' if he himself did not solve the problem, he seemed determined to let no one else try. On this issue Bevan contemplated resignation; 'I advised him,' says Dalton, 'not to be too quick off the mark.'[2] Bevan also backed Dalton on the more general issue of defence expenditure and overseas commitments. Bevin's rigid command over the whole range of the Government's policy afflicted the work

[1] *High Tide and After* by Hugh Dalton, pp. 194–8.
[2] *High Tide and After* by Hugh Dalton, p. 199.

of other Ministers less defensibly than it had done in the first demobilization disputes of 1945 and 1946.

The malaise at the top produced reverberations on the back benches. In October 1946 an amendment critical of Bevin's foreign policy had been moved by R. H. S. Crossman in the debate on the King's Speech. Crossman had also returned from Palestine (he had been a member of the Anglo-American Commission which had produced a report, rejected out of hand by Bevin) with a devastating critique of Bevin's policy there. In the spring of 1947 a number of back benchers had made their activities more formal. They started what they called a 'Keep Left' group, and in April produced a pamphlet[1] which sounded the alarm about the course the Government was pursuing. One part of the criticism was aimed at what was considered to be Bevin's excessively anti-Russian, pro-American policy; the main peremptory theme was to stress that drastic measures must be introduced to ward off the menace presented by the exhaustion of the American Loan. Several of the specific proposals resembled those which restive members of the Cabinet had been urging vainly on Attlee-Bevin. The 'Keep Left' M.P.s suggested that a Minister of Economic Affairs should be installed to organize and direct a real planning machine – Dalton and Cripps had been urging that this step must be taken, if necessary over Morrison's dead body. They backed to the hilt the demand for a much swifter demobilization on lines which almost paraphrased Dalton's private remonstrance to Attlee. They called for immediate savings in imports – many of which were enforced that autumn. They insisted that the condition of the American Loan settlement whereby sterling should be made convertible on 15 July was utterly unworkable and that the clause in the settlement which permitted convertibility to be postponed, in exceptional circumstances, should at once be invoked. Here as yet they found no support in the highest circles. The most inexplicable feature of the whole situation, unexplained still, is how the Cabinet

---

[1] The signatories of the pamphlet were R. H. S. Crossman, Michael Foot, Ian Mikardo, Geoffrey Bing, Donald Bruce, Harold Davies, Leslie Hale, Fred Lee, Benn W. Levy, R. W. G. Mackay, J. P. W. Mallalieu, Ernest R. Millington, Stephen Swingler, George Wigg and Woodrow Wyatt.

relinquished all control over this fateful decision to the Treasury, accepting from that department a view about the practicability of the step which, as Dalton admits, was 'quite irrational'.

Apart from this item, much that appeared in *Keep Left* looked like a direct leakage from the Cabinet controversies. But it was not. No liaison between the Left on the back benches and the rebellious Ministers existed. Dalton had a hand-picked Finance Group to whom he sometimes vouchsafed his troubles, but none of them believed in taking the controversies openly to the Party. Bevan was even more isolated; he scrupulously refused to discuss Cabinet matters even with his most intimate friends. And Bevin was easily able to pulverize his open critics. At the Party Conference at Whitsun 1947, he sank without trace all the disputes about demobilization and defence expenditure with a broadside against those who had 'stabbed him in the back' during the previous October. At this Conference Aneurin Bevan was re-elected at the top of the list to the Party's National Executive by the constituency parties. Thanks partly no doubt to Churchill's assaults upon him he remained the hero of the rank-and-file. But he too had his rebuffs; a spokesman of the building unions was openly hostile and a resolution demanding that the Government should take immediate steps to abolish tied cottages in the rural areas was narrowly carried, despite his pleadings. The whole Conference was fretful and fearful. 'We are in a dark patch just now,' concluded Morrison, 'but we have our plan, we have our purpose ... we shall win through to a better day.'

The purpose may have been clear, but there was no real plan and the Government stumbled forward into its greatest crisis, with Attlee's hold on the reins becoming so feeble that he was almost unhorsed. At a series of meetings at the end of the session an effort was made to rally a dejected Party. But the accents of the leader were plaintive and halting; he could not draw together the strands of policy and weave them into coherence; rather he preferred to call on each Minister in turn to answer for his own responsibilities. During these critical weeks, moreover, the rumour spread that the Government's commitment to nationalize iron and steel was to be abandoned in deference to protests from the steel interests, and suddenly this issue surged to the forefront as the test of the Government's determination not to be bullied by its political opponents.[1] Dalton perhaps understood most clearly what the economic situation required; he had introduced a strong anti-inflationary Budget and still gave much of his old impression of mastery; behind the scenes he was fighting for the cuts in imports and the armed services which alone could bring immediate relief and he showed no weakness about steel. But at this fatal moment, almost overnight, he emerged more as the architect of disaster than the possible saviour. On 15 July, sterling was made convertible according to the Anglo-American contract. The storm did not break immediately. But after a six weeks' trial, in the middle of August, the experiment had to be called off. Many of the last millions of the American Loan – 700 million dollars in one month – had been squandered in the most inept manœuvre ever executed by a brilliant economist and the Treasury brains trust. Dalton confessed himself 'humiliated'; as a political power he was destroyed. The unhappy event later that November, when he most punctiliously insisted on resigning following a quite innocent but foolish leakage of a budget secret to a journalist, was doubtless a sequel to those weeks of mid-August madness. ('Anyone could see for some time,' said Bevan later, 'that Dalton was under such strain that something was bound to happen. There is no immaculate conception of disaster.')[2]

Yet before he departed Dalton had engaged in the most elaborate, the most excusable and the most abortive intrigue of his career. From July until October, he, Cripps, Morrison and Bevin tentatively discussed with one another whether Attlee could be removed from the Premiership and replaced by Bevin. The essence of the whole matter was: could the four come together? If so, the deed would be done. The answer was they could not. Cripps was the most eager and active in the plot: if Bevin was unwilling to take the Premiership, he was ready himself. Dalton, both before and after the convertibility fiasco, eagerly abetted Cripps. Morrison had his own alternative preference for the highest post. Bevin came down fiercely against the whole idea at the end, although not quite so fiercely at the beginning, if Dalton is to be believed. Bevin would not 'do a Lloyd George' on his 'little man'. The decision did much

[1] See below, Chapter 5.
[2] Quoted by Francis Williams in *The Triple Challenge*.

credit to Bevin's approach to politics. He preferred power to the trappings of office. And, with Attlee there, he had the power already. Furthermore, during those particular months, Bevin was engaged in the most considerable feat of his Foreign Secretaryship. In June, General Marshall, the United States Secretary of State, made a speech at Harvard in which he hinted that the United States might be willing to give aid to Europe on a new, more fruitful and far-reaching basis. Bevin saw at once the potentialities of the declaration, worked to foster them, and doubtless wanted no distraction, such as a change of government in London might interpose.

Yet the whole intrigue was not entirely profitless. Attlee might bear the chief responsibility for the general disarray of his administration but he still showed his coolness and quality in dealing with men. He seemed to bear no grudge against Cripps and gracefully bowed to the new, alternative reorganization which Cripps proposed – that he (Cripps) should be appointed Minister of Economic Affairs, with full command over the home front. And when Dalton left the Exchequer, Cripps took his place. The Government would make a new start under a partially new regime.

Bevan himself played no part in these particular personal conflicts. The first – and the last – he heard of the proposal for replacing Attlee was at what Jennie Lee calls 'one of Stafford's high-minded teas'. The occasion occurred in the early days of August. Aneurin and Jennie had everything ready for starting their holiday and Aneurin was frantically impatient to get off, when they received an urgent request to call upon Cripps and Lady Cripps that afternoon. The terms of the invitation made refusal impossible and when the four assembled at Cripps's flat in Whitehall Court, Cripps broached his ideas in a manner which showed that he believed the fate of the Government to be at stake. It was imperative that Attlee should step down from the Premiership and make way for Bevin or himself. Cripps gave an account of his soundings so far – the names included some of the most 'loyal' members of the Party – and sought to enlist Bevan's support. But Bevan was wary and unpersuaded. He, like the others, had been increasingly critical of Attlee but he could restrain his enthusiasm for the substitution of Bevin and thought Cripps's own chances were much more remote than he realized. Bevan's short reply was that he was against 'palace revolutions'; it would be wiser for all Cabinet ministers who felt disturbed to concentrate on the policy changes they desired. So Bevan departed on his holiday and when he returned the climax had passed.

But the crisis of 1947 had brought for him a denouement bitter beyond words – the cut in the housing programme. Earlier that year, in June, July and August, as the danger mounted, many voices had been raised, outside the Government as well as within it, urging that the real source of the nation's economic troubles was the much too ambitious programme of capital investment which government policy had allowed. 'We must accept the need for curtailing capital expenditure on long-term capital projects – housing, schools, hospitals,' said Sir Clive Baillieu, President of the Federation of British Industries. Several newspapers – notably *The Times*, the *Economist*, and the *Manchester Guardian* – directing their attention to housing, struck a note very different from that of Bevan's earlier critics. 'The main issue now,' said the *Guardian*, 'is not whether we are building as many houses as we could, but whether we can afford to go on trying to build as many as we are doing.' Lord Woolton took up the cry: 'I ask in these days of over-full employment for the postponement of all works of a public nature, and for the discouragement of all capital expenditure, whether by Government or private industry.' Bevan, in a housing debate in July, had set his face against these demands. 'I resist the suggestion that it is necessary for us to reduce our housing programme. I believe that if we did that, we would greatly jeopardize national progress.' Yet he was called back from his holiday to the critical Cabinet meetings summoned to deal with the wreckage left by convertibility and the mounting threat to the balance of payments. The whole atmosphere was one of suffocating necessity. Before the convertibility climax one programme of cuts and austerities was announced; food imports from dollar areas were curtailed, the basic petrol ration was reduced by a third, miners were to work a half-hour longer. Three days after the climax, other rigours were added: the meat ration was cut, foreign travel allowances were stopped, the basic petrol ration was abolished. In the days that followed, a saving on housing also figured on the Treasury list of essential measures. Partly the purpose was to make possible a reduction on general capital construction and partly to reduce dollar expenditure on timber. The changes could not produce results at once; the effect on the number of houses built in 1948 might be small. But for 1949 it was calculated that the number of houses completed would be reduced to 140,000.

Short of resignation, Bevan had no remedy, and that remedy was barred. Had he left the Government at that moment, the whole administration might have tottered and he himself would have been blackened as the administrative failure Churchill had always denounced – this on the eve of the year when his programme was to produce the high total of 280,000 houses. Clearly, resignation would have been folly. Moreover, he believed that the full cuts would never be carried through – and they never were. In 1949, 217,000 houses were built instead of the 140,000 forecast by Cripps in October 1947. Thereafter the figure was maintained at round about the 200,000 mark. Bevan never ceased to rail against what he called 'the whistle-blowing' planning of the Treasury experts in manipulation of capital investment programmes. They thought when they moved figures on charts, men moved too; 'they thought a building worker in Liverpool became a cowman in Kent'. So the full rigour of the 1947 Treasury edict was never imposed. Its results were nonetheless heartbreaking for Bevan and his officials – and the homeless. All the schemes, which were working well, for the training of building workers and the recruitment of apprentices, suffered a severe setback.[1] Henceforth, Bevan's instrument for house-building had to be used in reverse; instead of stimulating the laggard authorities into action, it became a main function of the Ministry to stop local authorities building too much. The rueful comment of Sir John Wrigley to his Minister indicated how painful was the consequence for those who had struggled so hard to make

[1] An indication of the effect of the 1947 cuts is given in Richard A. Sabatino's book *Housing in Great Britain* 1945–9 (Arnold Foundation Studies, 1956), p. 31. 'These cuts caused a retrenchment in the planned housing programme and crippled the careful plans which had been made for (a) the recruitment of apprentices and the training of adults to provide the labour required by the housing programme and (b) the controlled expansion of the productive capacity of the building materials industries in a manner designed to meet the needs of the housing programme '

the instrument effective. 'If we build more than 200,000 houses,' said Sir John, 'I'll be sacked by the Chancellor, and if I build less, I'll be sacked by you.'[1] The instrument was working with uncanny precision. After the 284,230 houses built in 1948, the figures for 1949, 1950 and 1951 were 217,240, 210,258 and 204,117 respectively.

Looking back, the decision about housing taken in the autumn of 1947 emerges as one of the most politically fateful in the Government's period of office. If it had been possible to avoid fixing the limitation on the potentialities of the programme, the Conservative Opposition would have been deprived of an argument which they deployed with immense effect. No one would have been able to level the foolish charge that whereas Bevan succeeded with the Health Service he had failed with housing. At the time, however, the nature of the decision was masked.

One reason was that the injury to the housing programme was only part of a whole grim series of austerity measures which looked unavoidable. Another reason, as we have seen, was that the full severity of the cut, originally announced by Stafford Cripps when Parliament reassembled in October 1947, was mitigated. Indeed, in the following weeks Bevan seemed to have won a complete last-minute reprieve in the Cabinet. Speaking on 18 December, Cripps replied to critics who were insisting that housing should be further cut and that Bevan had succeeded in 'torpedoing' his plan for the restriction of capital investment. Cripps did not directly repudiate this last accusation, but argued instead that timber was the only real limiting factor; the Government was not reducing the housing programme 'more than the materials compelled us to do'. Bevan was glad to embrace this argument himself. He wished to remove, so far as he was able, the disillusion which a more general reduction of the programme would spread throughout the country, particularly among building workers. He was proud of what had been achieved by technical innovation in vastly reducing the amount of softwood needed in each house and he hoped that, if the dollar situation eased, the cut could be restored. The third obvious reason for the concealment of the reality was that the cut did not take

[1] In conversation with the author.

effect for many months; the Opposition did not challenge another housing debate until the following July and then their attack turned more on the cost of building than on numbers. On this score, too, Bevan believed that he had a good reply. Costs had risen sharply; no one could deny the charge. His own hopes and forecasts that costs would eventually fall and that the subsidies could be reduced had gone completely awry. But the costs of everything had increased and, since the price of houses had gone up less than the materials used in house-building, the new attack was not so damaging. He could welcome the diversion in the terms of the debate. The overwhelming fact was that, since by 1948 the housing programme was producing houses in big numbers, the most intensive pressure on the Ministry of Health was somewhat relieved. The full political consequence of the 1947 decision and of further similar decisions came later and will be treated later.

Then also, as the winter of 1947 approached, other events lightened the darkness which had so nearly engulfed the whole Government that summer. Cripps at the Treasury, however distasteful his individual measures might be, showed that a new grip had been fastened on the levers of administration. The prospect that General Marshall's speech might be translated to a plan lifted the threat to Britain's balance of payments. Finally, 1948 was to be the year when the Labour Government would bring into operation its reforms covering the whole field of social security. The Acts of Parliament incorporating these plans had already been passed; James Griffiths had introduced the National Insurance Act and the Industrial Injuries Act, Bevan himself had introduced the National Health Service Act and was at that moment engaged in his final negotiations with the doctors – to be described in the next chapters. He also introduced in successive weeks in November two other major Bills. Neither compared in importance with his work on housing and health, but they were each measures which in pre-war Parliaments might have been regarded as principal legislative proposals for a full session.

The first – the National Assistance Bill – brought to an end, amid barely a whisper of controversy, a whole tumultuous epoch of British social history. For centuries the harshest ignominies inflicted on British citizens were associated with the Poor Law.

4

Every few decades almost, since the days of Queen Elizabeth I, fierce controversies had stirred against the pitifully inadequate, haphazard system of outdoor relief for indigent people or the inhuman conditions in which they were crowded into workhouses. Bevan himself had played a foremost part in the last of these great revolts – the fight in the thirties against the family Means Test and all its kindred degradations. Now his National Assistance Bill, incorporating the proposals of the Beveridge Report and extending enactments made in the war, ended the old Poor Law, decreed that the workhouses should go, and provided a new system of relief for all those – estimated at about 450,000 at the time – whose needs would not be covered by the other security measures. The disbursement of the money for these persons was made a national responsibility, to be discharged by a National Assistance Board operating scales approved by Parliament; where administrative care and welfare were needed in institutions, responsibility was placed on the local authorities. Bevan, in his Second Reading speech, referred to special provisions made for the blind, the deaf, other handicapped persons and those suffering from pulmonary tuberculosis. Hitherto, those encouraged to give up their jobs to undergo treatment for tuberculosis were entitled to grants so long as their condition was considered incurable; thereafter the grant ceased. The Bill made an end of this 'cruel affliction'. Much the biggest category of persons affected by the Bill, however, were the old. Here, too, Bevan's sympathies derived from his pre-war experience. The old and the defenceless had always been the chief victims of the indignities and harshness of the Means Test. In most of his housing speeches as Minister he had paid special attention to old people's needs. He welcomed the fact that many more people in their old age were able to continue living in their own homes, welcomed the fact that many were staying at work longer, and urged that local authorities should provide houses for the old, not in separate precincts, but interspersed throughout the new estates. Even so, for many, something more would be needed and 'a great departure' was proposed. The workhouses would go; instead, the welfare authorities would be encouraged to provide special homes or residential hostels catering for some twenty-five to thirty persons. This should be the optimum size; 'bigness is the enemy of humanity. That is the reason why the metropolis is such a bad place to live in'. Such plans, said Bevan, were easy to state, but difficult to execute. But despite all the difficulties, the start would be made. Certainly he did not underrate the immensity of the task. By 1970 old people would be one in five of the population. 'It is a staggering figure; indeed it can be said that in some respects the proper care and welfare of the aged is the peculiar problem of modern society.'[1]

Bevan's other major 1947 Bill also awakened ancient memories. One of his complaints of the thirties was that the system of exchequer aid for local authorities left those authorities with the smallest resources in rateable value to carry the heaviest burdens; the poor kept the poor. He naturally wished to alter those arrangements, and in any case the many new adjustments in the respective financial burdens borne by central and local government resulting from the security programme or nationalization measures made imperative a new apportionment between the two. Bevan's Local Government Bill had an easy passage, although he himself admitted that only a senior wrangler could comprehend the more complicated parts of it.[2] South Wales and the other old distressed areas were appreciative; 'the fact that the Welsh counties receive assistance,' he said, 'is a purely arithmetical relationship, and not an *a priori* principle'; it merely underlined how unfairly Wales had been treated before. The same measure made it mandatory for the first time for local authorities to pay councillors for lost time if they applied. The Tories still objected; they would have left individual councils free to decide whether they would make the provision. But Bevan insisted that his proposal was essential for the vitality of democratic government. He had no fear of grave financial scandals. All the payments would have to be made public. The councillor's 'neighbours can check him, and I know of no more bitter auditor than local gossip'.

Some measure re-ordering local government finance would have had to be introduced by any Government at the time. The payment of councillors had long been advocated by the Labour Party and an overwhelming case for it had been made by a committee which Bevan had appointed. But he added his own distinctive

[1] *Hansard* Vol. 444 Cols. 1603–1613.
[2] *Hansard* Vol. 444 Cols. 988–1009.

touch to the Bill. Councils were empowered for the first time to levy a rate up to sixpence to help in the establishment or maintenance of theatres, concert halls, dance halls, bands or orchestras. He could not expect much use to be made at once of this new facility but he believed that the Local Government Act 1948 might be remembered for this clause when most of its other provisions were forgotten or superseded. 'Some day,' he wrote, 'under the impulse of collective action, we shall enfranchise the artists, by giving them our public buildings to work upon, our bridges, our housing estates, our offices, our industrial canteens, our factories and the municipal buildings where we house our civic authorities. It is tiresome to listen to the diatribes of some modern art critics who bemoan the passing of the rich patron as though this must mean the decline of art, whereas it could mean its emancipation if the artists were restored to their proper relationship with civic life.' Popes, kings, dukes and princes had had general revenues at their disposal; that was public rather than private patronage, an illustration of the power of collective action. Had such sources not been available, 'Leonardo da Vinci and Michelangelo would have died largely inarticulate'.[1] And had it not been for Bevan's Section 132 of the Local Government Bill, the Liverpool Philharmonic Orchestra is among the bodies which would never have survived.

Apart from the major Bills, he also introduced several minor ones (altogether between August 1945 and January 1951 he was responsible for 23 Acts of Parliament), and sometimes his particular interest was provoked by these measures, as for instance with the Births and Deaths Registration Bill of 1947 which provided for a shortened birth certificate without mention of parentage, thereby helping to protect the 'illegitimate' child. He referred to the matter in these terms: 'If we can prevent injustice to one person we ought to do so. There is an old English roundelay which runs as follows:

> *One is one and all alone*
> *And evermore shall be so.*

It varies in different parts of the country, but it is very old, and it shows how deeply sympathetic mankind is towards the isolated individual.'

[1] *In Place of Fear* by Aneurin Bevan, p. 51.

1947, then, for all its political tempests and blizzards, had its softer moments. Even amid the clatter of parish pumps on the Committee Stage of the Local Government Bill, Bevan found some release. His Tory opponent, Walter Elliot, pictured him stopping his ears against all entreaties 'like Ulysses of old with the sirens'. Bevan intervened at once: 'I can readily imagine myself,' he said, 'in the role of Ulysses, but I cannot imagine the right hon. Gentleman in the role of a siren.'

3

MINISTER OF HEALTH (1)
The Making of the Health Service
1945–1946

What is now proved was once only imagined.
—WILLIAM BLAKE

ON THE DAY when the results of the 1945 general election were being declared, the British Medical Association was holding its Annual Representative Meeting in the Great Hall in Tavistock Square, the B.M.A. Headquarters. Debates were interrupted with the latest electoral bulletins, and when the news came through that Sir William Beveridge, Liberal M.P. for Berwick, had been defeated, some delegates broke into a cheer which the *British Medical Journal* preferred later to dismiss as a gasp of astonishment. Thanks to his advocacy of a comprehensive national health service in the famous Beveridge report, Sir William had won his place in the doctors' gallery of bogymen. Other tremors at that meeting showed that the doctors felt themselves being impelled across strange frontiers into an unknown land. 'I have spent a lot of time,' said one eminent Harley Street surgeon, 'seeing doctors with bleeding duodenal ulcers caused by worry about being under the State.' The scene illustrated the collective neurosis afflicting the most articulate section of the British Medical Association even before it was confronted with the apparition of Aneurin Bevan at the Ministry of Health.

During the next three years the argument was dramatized by the newspapers in sharp personal terms. 'Bevan versus the B.M.A.' fitted neatly into the headlines and summarized the simplicities of propaganda on both sides. Winston Churchill inferred that it was Bevan's contumacy which had imported bitterness and suspicion into what might otherwise have been a smooth development of a project prepared in the days of his Coalition. A spurious validity

was given to the claim by the fact that the other social reform measures inherited from the Coalition – the National Insurance
Scheme, the Industrial Injuries Scheme, the Family Allowances
Scheme, and the National Assistance Scheme – were passed through
Parliament with all-party concurrence, if not enthusiasm. And the
Churchillian assault produced a natural response. Bevan's trial of
strength with the B.M.A. was seen as the test of the Government's
will. Such was the outward appearance of events, and from the
press reports of the time the story might be told exclusively in these
terms. But more elaborate explanations are required. Not merely
could the duodenal ulcers be diagnosed *before* ever Bevan appeared
at the bedside. His dealings with the doctors were influenced by
his private personality, so little understood by his enemies.

On the doctors' side, opposition to the form of national health
service proposed by Bevan was compounded of many elements. At
best, it derived from a deeply entrenched belief that almost any
system of State control over medicine would destroy the doctors'
clinical freedom. They wanted to preserve the sacred relationship
between doctor and patient; the intervention of the State, they
imagined, would compel service to a new master. Since this lofty
thesis implied a defence of the existing method whereby doctors
secured their incomes, the taunts of cynics and Socialists were
inevitable. Yet the fear was genuine. Many doctors did feel that
they were fighting a noble battle in defence of their Hippocratic
oath. Some of them may have been actuated by political hostility;
yet this impulse too was rarely predominant. Much the strongest
bent in the medical mind was a non-political conservatism, a revulsion against all change, a habit of intellectual isolation which
enabled them to magnify any proposals for reform into a totalitarian
nightmare. Nothing good could ever come from the meddling of
outsiders. No bridge was desired between the world of politics and
the world of medicine, and any who dared seek a way across from
one side to the other must be suspected of wickedness or treachery.
Finally, with these other emotions went a powerful streak of professional arrogance. What politician of any party was capable of
instructing the doctors how to perform their high, mysterious,
dedicated mission? 'A doctor,' Lord Moran explained to me with
sly self-mockery, 'prescribes his pills and potions and expects the

patient to take them, if necessary three times a day, without demur and in perfect assurance. That the patient, particularly a politician, should cavil and tell the doctor what to do is an insufferable presumption.'

Aneurin Bevan himself would have made an excellent diagnostician.[1] His political antennae which worked so sensitively at great public meetings could operate no less in private gatherings. He soon realized that no simple treatment would succeed with so obstinate and frail a neuropath as the medical profession, and yet it maybe doubted how much the methods he used were so deliberate. His political aim governed his thinking and the task in which he was engaged enabled him to illustrate the three strongest strands which interwove perpetually in his political creed – his detestation of a class-ridden society, his belief in the collectivist cure, and his dream (he would never dare call it a certainty) that democratic processes and democratic vigour, intrepidly unleashed, could accomplish revolutionary ends.

The *cri-de-coeur* of the doctors against the menace of State action came strangely from a profession the majority of whose members had to perform their work with primitive facilities for shockingly low salaries. If their ideal was truly one of service, was not the State offering to step forward as an indispensable ally? Why should the alliance be spurned? Fundamentally, the unspoken answer was a class answer. Many of the spectacular triumphs of British medicine had been won in private practice and in the best voluntary hospitals where leading specialists treated patients who, for the most part, could afford to pay. The mystique was handed down from the top to the rest of the profession. How melancholy it would be if these standards were debased, if the vanguard was prevented from making its dashing conquests because a whole army must advance with it. This appeal might be presented respectably in clinical terms, but did it not involve the claim that the chosen few must have a right to health denied to the rest of the community? Moreover, it clashed with the reality of modern industrial societies.

---

[1] Author's note: He cured or at least helped cure me of acute eczema, where most doctors had failed. Having discussed the symptoms, he felt that Vitamin C, supplied by ultra-violet ray, would assist, and next day he came round with the machine.

The most spectacular triumphs of all had been achieved by quite other means; by Public Health Acts, by sanitary inspectors, by Medical Officers of Health, by proper drainage systems, by the provision of water supplies; in short, by collective action. Private enterprise offered no remedies over this wide territory; it merely purloined an illegitimate credit for having tolerated within the society it dominated innovations stemming from a quite different order of values. 'Capitalism,' wrote Bevan, 'proudly displays medals won in the battles it has lost.'[1] The same stricture was prompted by many of the discoveries which had revolutionized surgery and the treatment of disease. 'They were made by men and women,' wrote Bevan, 'whose work was inspired by values that have nothing to do with the rapacious bustle of the Stock Exchange: Pasteur, Simpson, Jenner, Lister, Semelweiss, Fleming, Domagk, Roentgen – the list is endless. Few of these would have described themselves as Socialists, but they can hardly be considered representative types of the Competitive Society.'

Thus, in extracting the true principle of success from the past and applying it to the future, and reaching out for the ideal of a classless society in the field of health, the new summons was to carry the power of collective action into the domain of curative medicine. Condemning the old he wrote: 'No society can legitimately call itself civilized if a sick person is denied medical aid because of lack of means.' Heralding the new, he added: 'Society becomes more wholesome, more serene, and spiritually healthier, if it knows that its citizens have at the back of their consciousness the knowledge that not only themselves, but all their fellows, have access, when ill, to the best that medical skill can provide.' *Serenity* was one of his favourite words. It meant something richer and more enduring than merely *security*. He had always searched for it himself and he presumed others wanted it too. His enthusiasm for removing ill-health from the frenzied arena of money-making was closely associated with his belief that people have a craving for a design in society, a settled, serene sense of order, not imposed, but co-operatively established.

Today the existence of the National Health Service is taken for

[1] *In Place of Fear*, p. 74.
4 *

granted. Yet the extraordinary nature of the commission with which Bevan was charged must be emphasized: it was nothing less than to persuade the most conservative and respected profession in the country to accept and operate the Labour Government's most intrinsically Socialist proposition.

To assess his achievement it is necessary first to scrutinize the legacy which he inherited at the Ministry of Health and the nature of that curious institution, the British Medical Association, with which his own fate was now embroiled.

During the twenties and the thirties vague proposals for the establishment of 'a General Medical Service for the Nation' were put forward, notably by the British Medical Association itself. Ever since National Health Insurance had been introduced by Lloyd George in 1913, after a famous struggle with the doctors, the nation had had its embryo public service. Eventually about two-thirds of the doctors in practice joined the scheme and about a third of the average practitioner's income came from this source. Registration of doctors to perform certain services for panel patients who paid for their treatment partly with their insurance premiums had not, as the profession feared, destroyed their freedom. The State *had* intervened and the heavens had not fallen. Moreover, in many parts of the country, notably in Bevan's home-town of Tredegar, workers had banded together in friendly societies of one form or another to provide for themselves and their families medical aid beyond the bare facilities available to panel patients. They paid by weekly subscription for medical attention in hospital from consultants and specialists, and the doctors did not complain that they had lost status. The medical profession, or the bulk of it, became converts to the national scheme and sought an extension of it. Deficiencies were glaring. Wives and dependants were excluded altogether; the benefits obtainable were severely restricted; an income limit for participation was imposed – in 1942 it was fixed at £420 a year.

For the mass of the population serious illness could still come as a calamitous financial blow. Money, or the lack of it, was the real barrier between doctor and patient. The distribution of doctors throughout the country bore no relation to need; for example, there were only half as many doctors per head in South Wales as in London. Moreover, these defects in the provision of medical care by individual doctors were matched by the haphazard organization of other services. Hospitals begged for money; hostility prevailed between those maintained by charitable bodies and local authorities, and within the so-called voluntary system itself the great teaching hospitals tended to stand aloof from the British Hospitals Association which feebly sought to execute a coordinated policy; and above all no comprehensive arrangement for building hospitals where they were most wanted had ever been contemplated, much less imposed. Local authorities struggled to provide a variety of other services in institutions and outside – for the chronic sick, for the mentally sick, for the treatment of various infectious diseases, for maternal and child welfare. Here was another embryo public service, which had started to grow in isolation. Many doctors failed to appreciate the work done by local authorities, sometimes regarding them more as rivals than as allies.

A few idealists had proposed a radical cure. In 1933 the Socialist Medical Association formulated its programme for a 'Socialized Medical Service'. They wished to lift the financial burden from the individual altogether and to combine all services in a national plan. But they spoke only for a tiny, derided minority. Most of the inter-war suggestions for improvement envisaged no more than a development of National Health Insurance coupled with diffident measures of coordination. The words 'National Health Service', occasionally whispered, had not begun to acquire their modern connotation.

It was the experience of war which gave sharper definition to these aims. Not merely was the State forced to intervene, through an Emergency Medical Scheme, to maintain hospitals hitherto dependent on charity and to subsidize other services. A spur was given to future ideas of planning. In 1940 the B.M.A. invited all the other leading medical institutions to join with it in setting up a Medical Planning Commission, and its Draft Interim Report,[1] published in May 1942, went beyond anything previously conceived by the doctors outside the Socialist Medical Association.

A brand new structure of administration to cover all civilian

[1] *British Medical Journal* 1942 i, 743.

medical and auxiliary services was outlined, comprising a central authority, either in the form of a government department or a corporation responsible through a Minister to Parliament, and a whole hierarchy of regional and local units of administration. Briefly, the Ministry of Health was to be a reality instead of a name. The acknowledged aim, even if its implications were not faced, was to provide 'a State scheme of medical service . . . in effect for about 90 per cent of the population'.

Hospital management was to be overhauled. All the surveys of wartime had shown that there was no real hospital 'system' at all. No coordination existed either between the two main groups of hospitals – the 1,000-odd voluntary and the 2,000-odd municipal hospitals – or within the groups themselves. Half of the municipal hospitals and half the voluntary hospitals had a capacity of less than 50 beds; only 100 voluntary hospitals and 250 municipal hospitals had more than 200 beds. The great teaching hospitals which had established the reputation of the voluntary hospitals numbered only 30 – thirteen in London, seven in the rest of England, nine in Scotland and one in Wales. The machinery available was absurdly inadequate. Major surgery was often performed by men without surgical training and the training of physicians might be no better. Of the 150,000 beds in the municipal hospitals, 78,000 were general beds – that is, not for infectious diseases and serious ailments. Of these 78,000 again, one-third were in public assistance institutions, providing little more than food and shelter in a near-Dickensian environment. Vast areas had no hospitals at all. Many doctors gave their services on an entirely voluntary basis in the time they could spare from their private practices. Many hospitals had no means of securing the specialists they required. Money for capital investment was not forthcoming. No one who looked at the facts could doubt that drastic measures were needed. The Medical Planning Commission proposed a complete reorganization, with the region as the chief hospital administrative unit. Consultants and specialists would be recruited on an orderly basis and paid a proper salary.

Even more surprising were the changes proposed for general practitioners who formed the bulk and backbone of the profession. Apart from, or in addition to, money paid them by the State for the

numbers of panel patients they might treat, they got their livelihood by quite arbitrary charges made to private patients. Many
doctors were ready or forced to play Robin Hood, helping their
poorer patients at the expense of the richer. All or almost all had
been able to establish themselves only by buying a practice from
an older doctor or making some payment for a partnership. This
was the time-honoured system of private practice which, it had
once been feared, Lloyd George's innovations would injure. And
yet the Medical Planning Commission now proposed to transform
it beyond recognition. 'Greater efficiency and economy would be
secured and less expense incurred,' it said, 'if groups of practitioners would cooperate to conduct a single centre.' Whether
practising at centres or individually, the greater part of the doctor's
remuneration should henceforth come from public funds. The sale
and purchase of practices by doctors within the scheme should
cease. General practitioners should henceforth get their income
from three sources: apart from their private fees they should receive a basic salary with special additions for special qualifications
and a capitation fee related to the numbers of persons and families
on their lists.

Finally, at every level of administration in the new structure,
elaborate provisions were proposed for professional representation.
The doctors could not conceal their syndicalist tastes; they wanted
a tight control over their own trade. Yet the Medical Planning
Commission's report did represent an imaginative breakthrough.
It was the boldest document ever issued by the British Medical
Association. Its principal draughtsman was Dr Charles Hill, at that
time the B.M.A.'s Deputy Secretary.

Oddly, in the light of what happened later, the Draft Interim
Report was not at once denounced by medical diehards, although
many who never regarded themselves as such viewed the proposed
rupture of the old methods with distaste and anxiety. The doctors
were brooding amongst themselves; maybe they hardly expected
to be overheard or that anyone would take their advice literally.
No one was definitely proposing *when* anything should be *done*.
But at the end of 1942 and the beginning of 1943, the first intrusion
occurred. Sir William Beveridge produced his report covering the
whole range of social security and recommending as one of its main

features 'a national service for the prevention and cure of disease and disability'. Insofar as it contained any detail under this heading, it was largely based on the Medical Planning Commission's recommendations. But this obvious fact went unremarked by most of the doctors. Instead, when the House of Commons approved the Beveridge Report and when the Government outlined what most people considered a tardy and indefinite timetable for consultations and eventual legislation, the *British Medical Journal* protested that Ministers were moving too speedily. No step forward should be taken, said the B.M.A., until a Royal Commission had examined the subject; everyone knew how elephantine was the period of gestation required by such bodies. A nonplussed and apologetic Mr Ernest Brown, then Minister of Health, was summoned before one meeting of B.M.A. delegates and called upon to explain the tentative consideration then allegedly being given at the Ministry to the notion of a wholetime salaried service.

In 1943 Mr Brown was succeeded as Minister of Health by Mr Henry Willink who continued the preparatory work required to give administrative form to the aspiration expressed in the Beveridge Report. In February 1944 he produced his White Paper entitled *A National Health Service*. The scheme aimed to provide comprehensive medical services free of charge to all who wished to use them. No patient or doctor would be forced to join; private practice, it was assumed, would continue on a substantial scale. Central responsibility for the direction of the Service would rest with the Minister, advised by expert professional bodies.

It is not necessary to list the full details, but reference must be made to the arrangements for the hospital and general practitioners' service. The planning of hospitals over regional areas was to be entrusted to Joint Boards of grouped local authorities who would take over the ownership of all municipal institutions. The voluntary hospitals could make their own choice whether they came into the Service or stayed out or preferred a half-way status whereby they would receive public funds in return for a partial submission to the authority of the Joint Boards. Thus, the voluntary system was to be preserved while a form of negative control was instituted in the general practitioner service. Emphasis was laid on the desirability of group practice in health centres provided and equipped by the

local authorities. Individual practice would continue side by side
with the new service. Doctors in health centres would be paid on a
salary basis; doctors practising individually would be paid by
capitation fee under contract to a Central Medical Board, set up by
the Minister but largely composed of doctors. This Central Medical Board would also have as one of its main functions the duty to
secure a fairer distribution of doctors throughout the country by
forbidding entry into over-doctored areas. The question of abolish-
ing one existing factor influencing distribution – the sale and purchase of practices – was left over for discussion with the profession.

Altogether, the Willink White Paper commanded wholehearted
approval in the House of Commons. The chief parliamentary question was not 'whether' but 'when'. The Labour Opposition was
deeply suspicious about the Government's intentions about timing,
but this impatience meant that they were not inclined to cavil too
much at the details of the plan itself. Tories, it seemed, bestowed
their unqualified blessing in the belief that no one was proposing
to do anything soon. Politically it was unwise to defy the mood of
the hour.

But some of the doctors thought differently. Their anxieties
changed to panic. Blood-curdling charges of deception and dictatorship shrieked from the correspondence columns of the *British
Medical Journal*. 'The ultimate intention,' declared one writer, 'is
brilliantly camouflaged. Underlying the subtle phrases of the White
Paper is the mailed fist of bureaucratic control carefully wrapped
up in the velvet glove of political diplomacy.' The editor of the
Journal, himself an independent power within the innermost
B.M.A. councils, came near to concurring with this extreme judgment. 'If this interpretation is correct,' he commented, 'it is useless
to deny that there is trouble ahead.' He apparently believed that
'the unmistakable direction' in which the Government was moving
was 'towards the institution of a whole-time salaried medical service'. If the proposals went through it was hard to see how 'private
practice as we know it today can survive as much more than a
shadow of itself'.

Thenceforward the leaders of the B.M.A. captured or inspired
the mood of the vocal rank-and-file. They produced a Draft Statement of Policy opposing the White Paper in general and most of its

provisions *seriatim*; this show of resistance, despite many less hostile voices within the profession, was sufficient to force a retreat in Whitehall.

A few weeks later the amenable Mr Willink – like the amenable Mr Brown before him – embarked on 'discussions' with the doctors which to outside observers and to the doctors' leaders themselves looked more like negotiations. Concessions were 'agreed', or at least more closely considered, governing the structure of the Service, the pace at which health centres should be introduced and, most specifically of all, the tender question of the sale of practices. When the reports of these conversations filtered through to the public, Labour M.P.s accused the Minister of betraying the principles of the White Paper behind the back of Parliament. Willink denied the charge; he had made no 'commitments'. Perhaps he was the victim of a misconception by the doctors' leaders. They chose to see themselves, not as mere advisers to the Government, but more as high contracting parties. And the further oddity was that the doctors themselves had embarked upon the discussions on the understanding, formally approved at one of their Special Representative Meetings, that the major questions should not be agreed or even discussed until the administrative detail had won acceptance on all sides. The doctors' leaders, it seemed, were skilfully getting the best of both worlds. Their own contributions to the exchanges were purely exploratory and committed them to nothing; but any item suggested by the Minister which met with their approval was quickly elevated to a firm assurance. And whatever the truth about Willink's concessions and denials, a softening of tempers at Tavistock Square was noticeable. Willink, the author of the outrageous White Paper, was obviously eager to appease.

But had not the doctors' leaders been too clever? The fashion of the time was to demand a 'comprehensive 100 per cent Service'; 'comprehensiveness' was the chief feature of the Beveridge Report as a whole and the doctors did not wish to swim too strongly against the tide. But, for the doctors, 'the 100 per cent issue', as they called it, had a special meaning which did not apply to other parts of the social security programme. Ever since the twenties the doctors had been willing to accept – and even to advocate the extension of – public provision for the poorer members of the community provided they were left free to practise privately among those who could afford to pay. It was at very best a 90 per cent Service that they were prepared to accept without too much heart-searching. Once they formally acknowledged the 100 per cent principle, as they did at a Special Representative Meeting in May 1945, they were committed to radical change. Henceforth they would be over-whelmingly dependent for their incomes on public funds, and from that fact a whole series of logical and far-reaching developments must follow. At that 1945 meeting the Association gracefully acknowledged that 'the 100 per cent issue was one for Parliament to decide'. A few among the diehards muttered accusations of betrayal and by the time of the Annual Meeting in July the mutter-ings had grown considerably louder. This acceptance of a major principle by the B.M.A. leadership at the very moment when they were engaged in such obstinate and successful discussion over details with the Minister is hard to fathom. The most plausible explanation seems to be that neither Willink nor the B.M.A. leaders recognized the full implications of a comprehensive Service, coupled with the fact that Willink had made it evident that the doctors would not have imposed upon them anything they did not want. Summing up the debate at the May meeting, Dr Guy Dain, the Chairman of the B.M.A. Council, said: 'Those who have spoken in favour of a 90 per cent Service appear really to be in favour of no Service at all.' Confusion was excusable. Even though it was at this meeting that the B.M.A. made its historic decision in favour of a 100 per cent medical service, it was by no means clear what kind of Service Dr Dain and his colleagues did want or would be ready to accept. They were committed to the ideal but to none of the measures required to secure it, not even those outlined in the Medical Planning Commission's Report three years earlier. Almost all of those proposals had been repudiated or diluted at subsequent authoritative meetings of the British Medical Association. And Dr Charles Hill, the putative father of that Report and now elevated from Deputy-Secretary to Secretary of the B.M.A., had rarely been heard speaking a word in defence of his infant prodigy.

Such was the stage which discussions between the Government and the profession had reached when Aneurin Bevan was appointed Minister of Health. One other element in the situation must be noted. At the Blackpool Conference of the Labour Party in 1945, just prior to the election, a resolution moved by the spokesman of the Socialist Medical Association calling for a return to the principles of the Willink White Paper and emphasizing what were considered to be its more radical features had been passed unanimously. The resolution had been drafted before it was known that Labour's final breach with the Coalition was to be announced; it was, therefore, directed more to the Government of the day and against Willink's alleged betrayals in negotiation with the doctors than to the kind of service which a Labour Government should consider. Previously, most of Labour's medical experts, led by the prominent members of the Socialist Medical Association, had favoured making the profession into a full-time, salaried, pensionable service and this view had been reaffirmed in an official Party statement published in April 1943. At Blackpool, however, the Party had been more eager to express its suspicions of a doctors' plot, abetted by Willink and designed to disrupt the whole dream of a National Health Service. This may help to explain the generally uncritical enthusiasm for the original Willink plan; if the B.M.A. was against it, it must be good.

So what was this body – the British Medical Association – which had exerted such sway over Bevan's two ministerial predecessors? In the popular supposition, it always appeared stubborn and unbending. Yet, as we have seen, it could also be agile when necessity required. Some attempt must be made to examine its political bone-structure.

At first sight, the B.M.A. leaders, headed by Dr Guy Dain, chairman of the B.M.A. Council, and Dr Charles Hill, Secretary of the Association, wielded power with few trammels. The Association had some 75 to 80 per cent of all doctors practising in the country within its membership. It was wealthy and fully equipped with an office machinery capable of communicating with the whole country. Despite the multiplicity of other bodies in which doctors were organized (notably the more ancient, restricted and professionally eminent institutions such as the three Royal Colleges of Physicians, Surgeons and Obstetricians) the B.M.A., representing predominantly but by no means exclusively the general practitioners, had long established itself as the all-embracing, most effective organization. One illustration of this fact was the composition of the Negotiating Committee set up to conduct the discussions with the Ministry about the proposed National Health Service. B.M.A. nominees kept an assured majority on this Committee and, considering the varieties of opinion likely to be displayed among the other nominees, if any signs of rebellion against B.M.A. policy might appear, the majority was overwhelming.[1] A whole range of different interests and outlooks was evident in the Association; young and old doctors, specialists and general practitioners, those working in poorer and richer districts, the salaried and the non-salaried had their divergent ideas. All these factors might have been expected to push or relinquish immense authority into the hands of those directing the organization from the centre. The built-in tendencies towards oligarchy look formidable. Both Dr Guy Dain and Dr Charles Hill had long experience within the Association. They, or the small executive which they might be expected to influence or dominate, seemed to hold the reins.

Yet the appearance was startlingly deceptive. For the B.M.A. cannot be compared with other apparently comparable bodies. It was not a trade union; to the doctors the word was anathema. It was not concerned solely with the protection of professional status and standards; rather, in its infancy it had been much more dedicated to the dissemination of medical knowledge. Gradually its primary interest became political pressure; but that fact, if made explicit, was always furiously denied. Sidney and Beatrice Webb had once described it as 'one of the most highly developed and most efficient of all British professional organizations', then adding, as if to clinch the point, that its 'complicated constitution' included 'all the devices of advanced democracy'. The proliferation of these devices and the knowledge that they were all kept in working order offer the key to the whole apparatus.

[1] The National Health Service Negotiating Committee consisted of sixteen representatives of the B.M.A., three from the Royal College of Physicians, three from the Royal College of Surgeons, two from the Royal College of Obstetricians, three from the Royal Scottish Medical Corporation, two from the Society of Medical Officers of Health, one from the Medical Women's Federation and one from the Society of Apothecaries – a sixteen to fifteen majority for the B.M.A. See *Pressure Group Politics* by Harry Eckstein (George Allen & Unwin, 1960).

Under the B.M.A. constitution, final authority rested with the Representative Body, a great mass assembly normally called together for a few days at the Annual Representative Meeting and empowered to make 'decisions of the Association' only by a two-thirds majority. Subordinate to this was a Council constituted of some seventy members, meeting roughly six or seven times a year, some members being appointed ex-officio and the bulk elected by the Divisions throughout the country. Both of these excessively large bodies, it might be supposed, would be unable to transact much detailed work; doctors are busy men. Power *must* have resided with the permanent officials. But the fact belied the natural supposition. Under the Council, there was no constituted executive. The chairman and secretary had to exert their influence by continuous argument in the vast number of individual comittees appointed to deal with separate matters and before the Council and the Representative Body. Even the *British Medical Journal*, the main means of communication between leaders and followers, was not under the leaders' control; the powerful and opinionated editor demanded and obtained full editorial freedom.

During the years of crisis – and that meant the whole of the Bevan era – both the Council and even the Representative Body were jealously summoned by the active members of the Association much more frequently than the constitution required. And added to these resorts was the right of either the leaders or the led to demand plebiscites and questionnaires addressed to the whole membership. The leaders might be outbid or rebuked by the Council; the Council in turn might suffer the same experience at the hands of the Representative Body; on some occasions the Representative Body found itself hamstrung by the results of a referendum. And in the Great Hall in Tavistock Square (still not 'great' enough to hold all the delegates and with no proper microphone) where the mass meetings were held, a final, rare feature was evident – what may be called a democracy among resolutions. No one resolution could be composited with another. When the platform sought to produce some degree of order from the chaos by settling an agenda in advance, the rank-and-file were not slow to suspect skulduggery. Rebels or would-be alternative leaders could always feel for some new lever in a democratic machine seemingly constructed by Dr Strabismus.

'We were spokesmen, not leaders,' said Dr Hill more temperately.[1] 'I had none of the power of a general secretary of a trade union. Always we entered negotiations with no power to negotiate without reference.' Certainly no trade union leader would have wished to conduct detailed negotiations beneath the glare of publicity, within the profession, decreed by the B.M.A. constitution. However, Dr Hill's claim cannot be taken to mean that the B.M.A. leadership reflected with mathematical accuracy the views of the whole membership; the response to the 1944 questionnaire showed plainly that it did not. What the leadership did often reflect, sometimes with a pallor which raised the cry of foul play, was the militant outbursts which swept all before them at meetings of the Representative Body.[2] There, the respectable, stiff-jointed B.M.A. was capable of the most staggering contortions.

It is wiser to abandon all anatomical metaphors. For a parallel with the manner in which the B.M.A. was compelled to transact its affairs, it may be more enlightening to recall the year 1793 in revolutionary France. None of the leaders then could afford to be long outpaced by more extreme orators; they had to speak almost every day in the Convention and be re-elected every month. This last democratic refinement had somehow been overlooked by those who framed the B.M.A. constitution. But they had ensured that if the British people were ever to have a national health service, its detailed provisions must be filtered through the fine mesh of mass meetings in Tavistock Square.

'I usually met its [the B.M.A.'s] representatives,' wrote Bevan,

[1] In conversation with the author. Later he became Lord Hill.

[2] Professor Harry Eckstein, of Harvard University who wrote *The English National Health Service* (Harvard Press, 1969), might not have agreed with Aneurin Bevan's strictures on the type of doctor who exercised excessive sway over the B.M.A. But he does much to explain the phenomenon. 'To exert weight in medical politics,' he writes, 'one must have a certain amount of money and, above all, time. The work-load of a middle-class practice and the income derived from secure consultant status are eminently suited to participation in medical politics. "Representative" bodies are therefore inevitably weighted in favour of age, affluence, private practice and the suburb.'

'when they had come hot from a conference at which the wildest speeches had been made. My trade union experience had taught me to distinguish between the atmosphere of the mass demonstration and the quite different mood of the negotiating table. I was therefore able to discount a great deal of what had been said from the rostrum.'[1] It was unlucky for the B.M.A. that in their greatest crisis they confronted a man who had studied the art of demagogy – and scorned it.

The first problem Bevan had to settle after his arrival at the Ministry was a simple one: should he renew the discussions or negotiations, whichever they might be, with the B.M.A. where Willink had left off? The answer could not be in doubt, although some of the doctors' leaders were later to object that the choice he made was gratuitously offensive. No one in the previous Parliament had protested more vigorously than Bevan that precise negotiations with outside bodies about major legislative measures subverted the authority of the House of Commons; it meant that a Minister came before M.P.s with his hands tied, unable to accept amendments. Negotiations about particular regulations or about terms of service or consultations designed to secure general advice from outside bodies were in a different category, and these he would be prepared to undertake at a later stage. In fact a mass of evidence had been already accumulated at the Ministry about what the doctors felt. Moreover, Bevan quickly concluded not merely that the supposed results of the secret Willink discussions were unsatisfactory but that the White Paper itself was in certain vital respects unworkable.

As he turned to the task, many in his department and elsewhere were startled by the first contrast between the menacing fiction and the real man. By equipping him with horns and a tail during the period of his wartime battles with Churchill, the yellow journalists had done him a favour. Many came to scoff or be shocked and went away mesmerized. This was certainly the effect when he made his 'maiden' speech before members of the profession at a dinner of the Royal Medico-Psychological Association a few weeks after his appointment. Not one of his thirteen predecessors, remarked the *British Medical Journal*, had started as he did. He told the assembled

[1] *In Place of Fear* by Aneurin Bevan, p. 87.

company that his officials had prepared three separate speeches for him – there they were on the table, all beautifully typewritten – but he had resolved to make his own indiscretions. 'Thereupon,' reported the *Journal*, 'Mr Bevan spoke without a note for half an hour – one of the most candid, disarming and engaging speeches we have ever listened to from a Minister. Could this really be the stormy figure from Ebbw Vale?' He announced that he intended to hold his office for five years, a record achieved by no previous Minister of Health, adding hastily lest this note might cause alarm: 'I believe myself to be a good doctor. I have got a therapy – that is the right word, isn't it?' Then he teased them again, insisting that he wanted their help, 'for after all, gentlemen, you are the experts, while I, I am a comparative virgin'. Whereupon Dr Dain intervened with a protest that this comparative condition was unknown to medical science. However, before the occasion dissolved in geniality, Bevan went out of his way to touch upon the heart of the doctors' apprehensions. 'I know,' he said, 'that the doctors feel anxious lest there should close upon them a national machine which would obliterate their individuality. They need have no fear, no fear at all. I conceive it the function of the Ministry of Health to provide the medical profession with the best and most modern apparatus of medicine and to enable them freely to use it, in accordance with their training, for the benefit of the people of the country. Every doctor must be free to use that apparatus without interference from secular organizations. The individual citizen must be free to choose his doctor and the doctor must be able to treat his patient in conditions of inviolable privacy.'

The same mild and magic accent worked on the members of the B.M.A. Council. Their first meeting with the Minister took place at a fork luncheon where no detailed business was intended to be transacted. 'We expected to see a vulgar agitator,' said Dr Roland Cockshut,[1] one of the leading spokesmen on the B.M.A. Council who was to play a considerable part in all that followed, 'we had screwed up our nerves to face the worst. We might have been going to meet Adolf Hitler. However, the first thing I noticed was that the fiend was beautifully dressed.' Then came the speech; 'we were quite surprised,' added Dr Cockshut, 'to discover he talked

---

[1] In conversation with the author.

English'. Modestly disclaiming any medical knowledge, he professed his eagerness to learn. Again he refused to read the speech prepared for him by his civil servants, this time on the grounds that he did not wish to give a false impression of omniscience. Somehow he managed to expound his constitutional dilemma about the negotiations in a manner which made his own case appear so irrefragable that no one but a political ignoramus would question it. Playfully he placed himself at the mercy of those better informed than himself; yet was it not true – dare he ask for enlightenment? – that even within the medical profession itself there were faintly varying shades of opinion about what he should do? 'I suspect as much,' he said, with no more than a hinted lapse in his diffidence; 'I have my spies.' When questions followed he seemed ready to stay the whole afternoon to answer them. His audience noted that, unlike most other Ministers, he never turned to the civil servants for guidance. The amateur talked like a man who had been avidly curious about medical science all his life. Somehow he even steered the questions into fields far removed from the legislation he was preparing; to trespass there, after the explanation he had given, would be an unpardonable constitutional solecism. At the end he was given an ovation. One of his strongest critics described him as 'obviously clever and charming, with the cherubic outlook and manner of a boy'. Some who were present on that occasion, according to one observer, woke up the next morning to ask themselves: 'What the hell were we doing, cheering him yesterday?' The *British Medical Journal* issued a stern warning: 'Behind this disarming front there is probably a very combative spirit. The Welsh Aneurin from whom Mr Bevan takes his name was both a bard and a warrior.' And at the subsequent Council meeting the more sceptical executed what in the actor's vocabulary is called a 'double-take'. What was it he had said? *He had his spies.* What could he mean?

He did have his spies. While striving at those first meetings to allay the doctors' fears, he explored and exploited the political ramifications of the profession with mischievous zeal and delight, but also, as contentions developed, with a settled purpose. He studied the varying susceptibilities of the specialists and the general practitioners. He made his own estimate of the personality and resolution of the men with whom he had to deal. And his quickly acquired interest in all medical matters was no artifice. His curiosity was genuine and incessant and he clutched at every chance to argue with doctors of every rank about their most earnest or secret enthusiasms.

The impression left by Bevan on some of the leading figures in the doctors' world illustrates how wide of the mark was the vision conjured up by the Tory newspapers at the time of an arrogant or clumsy novice buffeted in seas which he had not troubled to chart in advance. The record of those impressions, compiled chiefly from recollections of the persons concerned years later, necessarily anticipates the later narrative. But the immediate impact was considerable, and the deductions Bevan drew from these first meetings greatly influenced all that was to follow. What *were* the real fears of the doctors? How could their services be enlisted? What would the profession do in the end? Bevan's own answers to these questions shaped his measure and his actions. He backed his own judgment from the start and clung to it even when the flood of opposition rose to a torrent.

Dr Guy Dain, chairman of the B.M.A. Council, was (and remained at the age of ninety-one when I saw him) a miniature bundle of energy, bristling with determination to wrest every advantage he could for his beloved B.M.A., responsive to the gusts of feeling which blew from the Representative Body, passionately concerned above all else to keep his army united whether behind him, beside him or in front of him. Ever since the meeting with Ernest Brown in 1943 and the report of 'that old blighter Beveridge' he had become convinced that the Ministry of Health was conspiring to turn doctors into civil servants. The threat would be carried out only over his diminutive dead body. 'Responsibility is the salt of life' was his maxim. (When he received a knighthood he got it translated, *onus salet vitam*.) He saw himself fighting to hold the pass at a medical Thermopylae. His meetings with Bevan were confined to the formal occasions. Early in the proceedings an invitation from Sir William Douglas to discuss matters privately at the Ministry was refused on the excuse that any conversation must be reported in detail to his Council. Only later did he discover that some among his colleagues had not shown the same excessive scruple. But Dr Dain made no accusation of ignorance or intrigue against Bevan. 'He knew his subject,' said Dain, 'in a very short time. He was extremely efficient. In all my forty years of dealing with Ministers he was the only one who ever argued, never referring to his staff, always having the answer himself. All that really mattered we settled with him. He knew what he wanted and so did we.' Sometimes during the later stages, voices were raised in anger around the negotiating table; sometimes Bevan hit back or hit first. 'But Dr Dain is never rude to me,' said Bevan, and Dr Dain prized the tribute.

Dr Charles Hill and Dr Dain concerted most of their moves together – not quite all, as we shall see. Like Dain, Hill's chief concern was to keep his army together, although he believed that the manœuvre sometimes required more cunning and calculation than the others realized. 'We were children in politics,' he told me, recapturing his lost innocence with the kind of effort which detracts from total conviction. '*All* politicians,' he insists, 'were suspect to the doctors, and we had none of the intimate connections with the Opposition leaders which many at the time supposed.' Certainly, in his view, Bevan dispelled from the outset any belief that he wanted to treat the doctors' opinions brusquely. The discussions continued in 'a more reasonable tone' than the outside world considered possible.[1] Occasionally patience broke and tempers flared. Occasionally, Bevan's sensitivity failed to span the gulf

---

[1] These comments were made to me by Lord Hill in conversations in 1964, and doubtless it was accurate to talk of 'the reasonable tone' in which many of the discussions were conducted. But Lord Hill has since given his version of the whole episode in his book, *Both Sides of the Hill*, (Heinemann, 1964), p. 94, and his muted record of events, in my judgment, falsifies the atmosphere of the time and the reality of the dispute which led to the making of the Health Service. However Lord Hill has given a notable verdict on Bevan's methods as a negotiator: 'Charming and sympathetic at one moment, he could be hotly indignant at the next. In a flash he could spot a point or detect a flaw in an argument, without waiting, or wanting to wait, for a speaker to finish. He would purr or pounce according to his mood. Gaily argumentative in debate, he preferred giving it to taking it – but so do we all. If a suggestion was unacceptable to him, he said so, at once, never using the comforting formula that the matter would be considered when he really rejected it. I do not remember any occasion on which he said one thing and meant another – this was part of the trouble at certain moments.'

between these two distant worlds. A witticism designed to smooth might hurt instead. The doctors wanted every protection which pedantry could devise and were always ready to escape from immediate business to consider afresh the spectral fears haunting the profession.

However the private courtesies might be sustained, Dr Dain and Dr Hill were soon to lead – or follow – their army into open public conflict with the Minister. Less formal and more subtle were the relations Bevan established in other significant quarters. No special insight was needed to discover that the profession was *not* united; it was evident, for example, that the sympathy prevailing between the Royal Colleges and the B.M.A. was far from perfect. Pride, jealousy and divergent interests prevented them from acting always in concert, even though the Royal Colleges were represented on the Negotiating Committee and were supposedly committed to the same agreed objectives. Bevan sought in turn the advice of the Presidents of the Royal Colleges. When at first they demurred, he urged them to remember their obligations to the Crown. Could the custodians of the Royal Colleges refrain from assisting the King's Minister? The discussions, of course, were innocent. No one was committed to anything. The Minister left no conceivable room for doubt that he intended to make up his own mind. And the three Presidents differed in temperament and outlook. Each required special attention. *This* doctor-patient relationship (which was which was too tender a matter to be broached) must certainly be kept sacred.

One of the three, Sir Alfred Webb-Johnson (later Lord Webb-Johnson), the President of the Royal College of Surgeons, approached Bevan first a few weeks after he had assumed office. The idea was that the new, inexperienced Minister should be introduced to and examined by several of the most eminent members of the profession on an informal occasion. Who could tell? The gauche demagogue might be softened and overawed, if not actually tamed. Unhappily for the doctors, the place chosen for the meeting was a private room at the Café Royal, one of Bevan's pre-war haunts. He naturally strode in as if he owned the establishment, remarked that it was not quite what it had been when he, Oscar Wilde before him and others had made it famous, and, when the company sat down to dinner, ordered an especially large plate of oysters. 'When I was a nipper,' he said, 'we could buy that lot for a few pence; then the price went up when Mayfair thought they were aphrodisiacs.' The confrontation did not quite achieve its purpose; it was Harley Street which went away impressed. But the understanding between Bevan and Sir Alfred was important. Sir Alfred somehow managed to retain the full confidence of the B.M.A. leaders while keeping open his line of communication with the Minister; no 'spy', if the word can be used in an entirely honourable sense, could be more well-placed and valuable.

Mr Eardley Holland, President of the Royal College of Obstetricians and Gynaecologists, was the second of the Royal triumvirate, although he never established with Bevan the intimacy of the others. Once when a group of the doctors' negotiators, including the Presidents of the Royal Colleges, had spent a long morning considering the maternity services, Dr Holland spoke at considerable length, and, by way of explaining his wordiness, turned to Bevan and said: 'You see, Minister, this is a matter of great importance to me, for I am responsible for all the pregnant women in the country.' 'You're boasting,' interrupted Bevan, but the joke left no scar. Mr Holland too could usually be relied upon to favour a softening of the rigours of controversy between the negotiating parties. But more powerful, august and ancient than either of these bodies was the Royal College of Physicians, presided over by Lord Moran. He was elected to the office for the unprecedented period of nine years in succession, each year during the later period beating off the challenge of his rival, Lord Horder, a growling conscientious objector to almost any national health service in any form whatever.

Lord Moran claims that he made his own initial advance to Bevan. Since he was nicknamed 'Corkscrew Charlie' in B.M.A. circles, they would not be surprised at the revelation. 'The Service was inevitable,' he said, 'so it at once became important, if the doctors were to have any say in things, that Bevan, as Minister of Health, should look upon them as allies and seek their advice. I felt that we should have a much greater say in things if we could establish a friendly approach to the Minister, for he had a way of dividing up the world into those who were for him and those who were

against him.' Bevan was willing. At first he may have been suspicious of 'the prima donnas' of the profession, as he politely
greeted Lord Moran at the first meeting. But soon any sense of
reserve or formality faded. 'If he looked upon you as a friend,'
continued Lord Moran, 'things began to happen, for he had great
power in his Party. If you could convince him, it was not necessary
to bother about anyone else, for, unlike most Ministers, he himself
made all the decisions that mattered. He would listen to what you
had to say, and when you had done, give his decision. Nor would
he change his mind a few days later because his civil servants had
intervened . . . Bevan was a man apart. I would go to him with
some measure, bent on converting him. He would come to the heart
of my case almost before I had put it to him, and then, when it was out
of the way, he would abruptly change the subject. Perhaps he would
launch into a disquisition on the mechanism of pain, remarkable in
its detailed accuracy. Conversation was meat and drink to him.'

Lord Moran put his finger on one secret of Bevan's conversa-
tional magnetism. 'Most Ministers,' he said, 'talk to you as if they
were thinking of something else. But not Bevan. He applied his
mind to the matter in hand as if he had been wrestling with it for
days. He never appeared tired, never mentally lazy. He was a rare
phenomenon, always ready for new mental adventures.'[1] Clearly the
Minister and the President of the Royal College of Physicians
established an accord. Maybe Moran *had* converted the Minister.
Or maybe the B.M.A. army had lost a field marshal.

To Moran, Bevan appeared primarily as a rare combination of
thinker and orator. Added to these qualities were his power of
independent decision and 'an aristocratic contempt for the consequences'. He was prepared to back his own judgment against the
world's. But, added Moran, 'I would not call him a great administrator. He hated the detail too much. He would go away and try
out my arguments on someone else. That was how he got his
information – by talking to people. He could not be bothered to
study documents. His critics among the doctors complained that he
would not sit down and think out their problems. That was not his
way.' Such was certainly one impression which Bevan gave – the
charge that he refused to do his 'homework' recurred throughout

[1] In conversation with the author.

his life. But the assessment was still not accurate. Certainly he had an uncanny way of learning much more by the ear than is normal, and he thought the method could save much time and labour. But he also knew that on some occasions he must not rely on his gift of osmosis and this was clearly proved in his transactions with the doctors. Lord Moran's evidence on this point conflicts with that of Dr Roland Cockshut, already quoted as one of the most aggressive figures on the B.M.A. Council, who was involved in the negotiations from the beginning to the end. 'Bevan,' says Dr Cockshut, 'had the finest intellect I ever met. From the outset, we were startled by the calibre of his mind. We had been living with this subject for years. For years we had been puzzling and arguing about what a health service would involve for the profession. The amount of written material was gargantuan. Yet suddenly Bevan appeared before us, apparently grasping every detail. He certainly knew his own Bill backwards.' And Dr Cockshut recalls how the charm mixed with the expertise. Even while other B.M.A. leaders suspected that 'the swells' were nobbling him on the backstairs, he managed to let them infer that the obstinate, hard-worked, under-paid general practitioners retained a tender place in his heart. At one meeting dispute broke out because the consultants and specia-lists were still excluded from the disciplinary provisions to be applied to the G.P.s. 'What?', asked Bevan, shocked and yet sympathetic, 'would you have me discipline the prima donnas?'

'Generally speaking,' wrote the great Lord Halifax, 'a trowel is a more effectual instrument than a pencil for flattery.' Bevan could wield the trowel with good results even when his victims were fully conscious of what he was doing. But gradually, almost impercept-ibly, he resorted to sharper weapons. As in debate, so on less public occasions, he knew the advantage of seizing the initiative. 'Mr Bevan,' wrote the *British Medical Journal*, 'is one of those who can say infuriating things in such a way that his audience, after a gasp of astonishment, ends by laughing and applauding.' He told one audience, largely representative of the hospitals, that patients some-times took longer to recover from the hospitals than from the cause that sent them there; seemingly his audience enjoyed the seriously intended joke. He opened fire on the Chartered Society of Physio-therapists by telling them that the sex breakdown of their member-

ship depressed him; of their 15,000 members only one thousand were men; they were in danger of becoming a matriarchy.
How the matriarchs cheered! He launched at the same meeting
into an elaborate (and undisputed) criticism of the way some members of the medical profession gave easement from the incidental
by-products of rheumatic diseases without paying proper attention
to their removal. And when some hecklers in the hall tried to bring
the discussion back to the hoary question of the abolition of the
sale of practices, he stuck to his theme. 'I am more concerned about
the fate of millions,' he said, 'than I am about the physiotherapists
themselves.' Despite this final shot, the physiotherapists, like other
sections of the profession, were bewildered by the press headlines.
Could the man be such a monster when he displayed this perceptive appreciation of the superior art of physiotherapy?

The treatment was varied to suit emissaries from religious bodies.
A delegation of Christian Scientists were subjected to a meticulous
philosophical cross-examination about what, if anything, they
understood by the word 'sickness'. When finally he had extracted
the confession that it signified nothing definable at all, he asked in
return for a detailed memorandum on how he could persuade the
Cabinet to allocate hard cash for the purpose of liberating the
human race from these gossamer chains. When greeting the Archbishop of Canterbury he cheerfully assumed a new guise as the
Gideon of the Free Churches: 'I'm a Welsh Baptist myself,' he
said. As the interview was ending, after the Anglican pleas had
been pitched in too High Church a tone for his taste, he concluded: 'You leave it to me, I'll look after the Protestants.' The
Roman Catholics showed more stamina and subtlety. Bevan was
not inclined to add a dispute about birth control to the other
impediments his Health Service must surmount; he knew
time was needed for more education on the subject. He managed
to avert the religious controversy upon which health schemes
have foundered in other lands, and Cardinal Griffin in return
secured the dispensation he sought for Catholic hospitals – but not
before he had been shaken by the most startling elucidation of the
revolutionary implications contained in Pope Leo XIII's *Rerum
Novarum*.

Sometimes, then and later, the doctors' leaders complained that

Bevan, preoccupied with housing problems and all his other duties, had not devoted sufficient time during this period to their concerns. The accusation was hopelessly inapposite. For it was during these first crowded months in office when the whole weight of the new department and Cabinet responsibility fell upon his shoulders that he made most of the critical decisions determining the shape of Britain's National Health Service. He was hammering out the arguments with his civil servants, analysing the hospital surveys, picking the best medical brains he could find, and producing his own synthesis of a solution which he believed would survive all the attacks he knew would be made upon it. In November 1945, a few sensational leakages occurred in the press, suggesting that the Minister was making serious departures from the Willink plan. Angry questions were posed by the Opposition; it was notable perhaps that the first shots in the battle were fired from that quarter and not from Tavistock Square. Dr Hill wrote to him politely asking what were his intentions, and Bevan replied that he would be happy to meet the representatives of the profession before he finally decided what proposals he would present to Parliament. So, while the Minister prepared his legislation, the B.M.A.'s Negotiating Committee drew up a list of 'Seven Principles' which they held must be fulfilled, if the proposed Health Service was to be satisfactory to the profession. One: No full-time salaried service for general practitioners. Two: Freedom to practise without state interference. Three: Freedom of choice by doctor and patient in general practice. Four: Freedom to practise anywhere. Five: Right of every practitioner to take part in the service. Six: Planned hospital service, based on teaching hospitals. Seven: Adequate medical representation on the administrative bodies. Here was a formidable list of negative or professional requirements, but no system of arithmetic could make it add up to a national health service.

Bevan's order of priorities naturally differed from those in the mind of the doctors. Apart from urgent administrative problems to be overcome if the facilities for a health service were to be kept in being at all,[1] he had to fight and win on other battlefields –

[1] One of Bevan's first actions in this field announced by him in Parliament on 8 November 1945, was to produce a Charter for Nurses. The plan

notably in the Cabinet – before he could face the B.M.A. Since he never intended to interfere with the doctors' clinical freedom and since he included generous provisions to meet their fears in his first draft proposals, he never believed that his plan would founder on this rock. The making of the plan itself was a more considerable enterprise. During the debate on the King's Speech in August 1945, Herbert Morrison, Lord Privy Seal and Leader of the House of Commons, had said: 'We must go back to the beginning. We must go back to the White Paper, which is what my right hon. Friend, the Minister of Health, proposes to do'. At that date the statement may have been accurate. Many years later – and just occasionally while the National Health Service Bill was being debated in 1946 – the claim was made that it was an all-party measure, the work of many hands before 1945. In a limited sense this was true; the stage reached when Bevan took office has been defined. But he also transformed the scheme and his changes became the focal point of conflict in the ensuing two years. What he did and why he did it must be examined.

The Socialist purpose of the National Health Service Bill was plainly stated in the first Clause of the Bill. It deserves to be recited, since the aim was often blurred in the subsequent controversy:

---

had been drawn up in association with the Ministry of Labour and a variety of other organizations and was designed to assist an immediate recruiting drive for nurses, midwives and domestic workers in hospitals. Improved salaries and training facilities figured most prominently in the plan. But the codes of conditions to be maintained in every hospital, later to be brought into the Health Service, looked further ahead and sought to end the maternalistic exploitation of nurses and hospital workers which had prevailed, almost unchallenged, for generations. A 96-hour fortnight for nurses was laid down as the proper standard 'to be brought into universal operation for hospital nurses as soon as circumstances permit'. This was also to be accompanied by a considerable liberalization of all the fussy rules governing a nurse's off-duty time and all her rights both within and outside hospital. For the first time a national joint council was formed to formulate agreed terms of service for domestic and non-nursing staff. 'The Government are to be congratulated,' wrote the *Lancet*, 'both on the codes and on their success in winning agreement on them.' They incorporated, none too swiftly, recommendations made by the *Lancet* Commission on Nursing in 1932.

5

[CLAUSE (I)] (I) It shall be the duty of the Minister of Health to promote the establishment in England and Wales (a separate Bill on almost precisely the same lines was produced for Scotland) of a comprehensive health service designed to secure improvement in the physical and mental health of the people of England and Wales and the prevention, diagnosis and treatment of illness, and for that purpose to provide or secure the effective provision of services in accordance with the following provisions of this Act.

(2) The services so provided shall be free of charge, except where any provision of this Act expressly provides for the making and recovery of charges.

Critics of the measure, both in the Tory Opposition and the medical profession, pretended to accept this purpose without demur. Bevan's constant retort was that they did not accept its implications. They dared not oppose the end but they strove to sabotage the means. In particular, orthodox spokesmen of the profession and their political backers never seemed ready to acknowledge the vast advantages *for the medical profession itself* which the broad purpose of his measure implied. The point was best put by the *Lancet* which, on this aspect of the debate, gave persistent support to Bevan. 'The truth is,' it wrote in an editorial, 'that the doctor-patient relationship in its modern form needs improvement rather than preservation: it can never be wholly satisfactory while the doctor (as someone has put it) is not only a friend in need but also a friend in need of his patient's money; nor while there is competition rather than co-operation between him and his colleagues. Though the views of our predecessors in Elysium must always be a little uncertain, we fancy that Hippocrates and Galen might be pleased rather than distressed to hear that their successors in this country were no longer vying with one another for the means of supporting wife and family.'

Once the Minister was given the paramount duty described in Clause (I), he had also to be given the power to fulfil it. The authority of the Ministry of Health was bound to become immense. Willink's plans had always fought shy of this seemingly logical consequence. Fearing perhaps the dangers of excessive centralization, he had sought to shift responsibility from the centre to the periphery. When the profession protested that this would mean the municipalization of medicine, which they hated more than any alternative, he had devised a compromise which restored some of the apparent power to the centre while blunting the instruments to wield it. Both voluntary and local authority hospitals would be left in their existing ownership and the planning bodies to be set up at area and regional level would become solely advisory. All the various 'interests' were thereby mollified, since nothing could be too rapidly or drastically changed. 'Mr Aneurin Bevan, a man in more of a hurry,' wrote the *Lancet*, 'proposes bolder action.' The Minister *must* have the power to perform the duty laid upon him. This was Bevan's first assault upon the ambiguities left by Willink.

Of all the instruments through which the power was to be exerted, his most far-reaching innovation affected the hospitals. 'At our very first full discussion,' I was told by Sir John Hawton, who was Deputy Secretary in charge of health matters at the Ministry throughout most of the period, 'Bevan put his finger on the hospital arrangements devised by Willink as the gravest weakness. And, of course, he was right. They would never have worked. I came away that night with instructions to work out a new plan on the new basis he proposed.' Bevan restated his defence of this major decision frequently throughout the debates that followed. 'The trouble with the Willink scheme,' he said (in a Committee Stage debate), 'was that he ran away from so many vested interests that in the end he had no scheme at all. He could not deal with the voluntary hospitals because they were too powerful. He could not deal with the local authorities because they were also too powerful. All he did was try and decant into local authorities functions they were incapable of carrying out.' Instead, Bevan himself proposed an expropriation of all hospitals, while leaving the teaching hospitals a separate status, a special control over their endowments and a special method of nomination of their Boards of Governors. Here indeed was one of Bevan's crucial decisions, for only by attracting the best and most prestigious medical brains into the service could he hope to make it *universal*, covering the whole or nearly the whole population. This was the key to so much else he had to keep in mind – outflanking the B.M.A., enlisting public support, averting Left-wing attack, winning over the Cabinet. But, of course, the arrangements for the teaching hospitals and all the special sensitivities involved in them must not upset the plan as a whole. Authority over the hospital system, for both planning and supervision, would thus in Bevan's plan be delegated to fourteen regional boards appointed by the Ministry and through them to the local management committees. All the tenderness towards local vested interests shown in the Willink plan was abandoned. Bevan had little patience with those who defended small hospitals on grounds of intimacy and local patriotism. 'Although I am not my-self a devotee of bigness for bigness' sake,' he said, 'I would rather be kept alive in the efficient if cold altruism of a large hospital than expire in a gush of warm sympathy in a small one.'

The plan, of course, was concerned not only with bricks and mortar and not only with the assembly of hospital equipment. A foremost commitment of the new service – the biggest proposed advance on the old National Health Insurance system – was the guarantee of specialist and consultant treatment. Willink's White Paper had left vague how and on what terms a sufficient number of specialists were to be recruited into the hospitals. To secure the proper distribution of man-power might prove even more baffling than the attempt to spread physical assets more evenly. Lord Moran recalls a conversation he had with Bevan at that time:

Bevan: I find the efficiency of the hospitals varies enormously. How can that be put right?

Moran: You will only get one standard of excellence when every hospital has a first-rate consultant staff. At present the con-sultants are all crowded together in the large centres of popula-tion. You've got to decentralize them.

Bevan: That's all very well, but how are you going to get a man to leave his teaching hospital and go into the periphery? [He grinned] You wouldn't like it if I began to direct labour.

Moran: Oh, they'll go if they get an interesting job and if their financial future is secured by a proper salary.

Bevan (after a long pause): Only the State could pay those salaries. This would mean the nationalization of hospitals.

No one, as Willink often protested, had ever suggested this solution. The nationalization of the hospitals had not figured in any of the widely various permutations of central, regional and local control suggested at various times by the B.M.A. or the Ministry. 'This fancy of the Minister,' said Willink, 'this idiosyncrasy of the Minister – because no one ever thought of it before him – will destroy so much in this country that we value.' Sir Harold Webbe, Conservative M.P. for the Abbey division of Westminster and Conservative leader on the London County Council, called it 'a hotch-potch of political prejudice, political idealism, and a very large measure of intuition'. It is difficult today to recall the widespread sense of shock which the plan aroused, but the reason is evident. By the same stroke Bevan was challenging two of the most powerful and respected vested interests in the country. None of the B.M.A. leaders had ever imagined that any Minister of Health would dare lay a finger on the established regime of the local authorities – particularly, those at County Hall in London. None of the reformers had envisaged so complete a transfer of the voluntary hospitals to State ownership; even the Socialist Medical Association had not included this demand in its resolution at the 1945 Labour Party Conference. Yet Bevan concluded that the two challenges must be made if he was to secure a functional unity in the new hospital service. Existing local government areas had no relevance to the need for hospitals. If he had to wait for a reform of local government, the National Health Service would have to be held up for a generation. On the other hand, there could be no defence, except an inexcusable sentimentality, for taking over the municipal hospitals while excluding the voluntary hospitals. The case was overwhelming on its organizational merits. 'A patchwork quilt of local paternalism,' he said, 'is the enemy of intelligent planning. Warm gushes of self-indulgent emotion are an unreliable source of driving power in the field of health organization. The benefactor tends also to become a petty tyrant, not only willing his cash but sending his instructions along with it.'[1] And he believed this practical case was sustained by other considerations; a moral principle had more appeal for him than sentiment. 'It is repugnant to a civilized community,' he said, 'for hospitals to have to rely

[1] *In Place of Fear* by Aneurin Bevan, p. 79.

upon private charity . . . I have always felt a shudder of repulsion when I have seen nurses and sisters who ought to be at their work, and students who ought to be at theirs, going about the streets collecting money for the hospitals.'

His biggest battle on this issue – the most crucial in the whole fight for the Health Service, even though it was fought behind closed doors – occurred in the Cabinet. County Hall had a powerful friend there in the person of Herbert Morrison; indeed most of the members of the Labour Government, including Bevan himself, had been reared in local government. They did not like to see the transfer of local government powers to non-elected, appointed bodies such as Bevan's regional boards. On democratic grounds their plea had great force; Bevan himself, as we shall see, looked forward to the time when either a reform of local government or some other arrangement would restore the process of election which his system denied. But this distant hope could not ease the dilemma in 1945. If he had succumbed to Morrison's pressure, if he had yielded to the temptingly phrased suggestion, in Hugh Dalton's words, 'to proceed by stages, spread over years, and not by one bold stroke',[1] a much less ambitious, second-best service is all that could have emerged. If the Minister was to perform his duty under the Act, if the hospital service was to be co-ordinated and planned in any real sense of those terms, if the specialists were to be recruited into the new combined service on a sufficient scale – that is, if there was to be a National Health Service at all – the nettle had to be grasped.

Bevan persuaded the Cabinet, not without leaving some hard feelings; for years afterwards Morrison, in unwitting tribute, might refer to 'Nye's precious Health Service'. Bevan also persuaded a regretful Lord Latham, at that time leader of the Labour Party on the L.C.C. Storms broke out at County Hall. 'How long,' said Sir Harold Webbe, 'has all the wisdom on this matter resided with that ridiculous theorist who swaggers at the Ministry of Health? He is so full of his own importance that he is prepared to pit his knowledge against the accumulated experience of this Council which is to be butchered to make a Welshman's holiday.' These cries of parochial anguish were soon to be drowned by a more furious and possibly less legitimate din raised in other quarters. But they help

[1] *High Tide and After* by Hugh Dalton, p. 106.

to stress how awkward was the assignment Bevan undertook when he cast aside the previously prepared hospital plans and devised his own. By no other means, as he saw it, could he establish one of the Rights of Man – the right of a sick person to a hospital bed.

A second instrument which Bevan required at his disposal was the service which only the general practitioner could perform. Here he did not so much make innovations as select from the various methods which had figured, sometimes only tentatively, in previous discussions, welding them into a system fair to doctor and patient alike. In that sense the proposals were a compromise, as some of his Left-wing critics complained. But the concessions, as he believed, would not jeopardize the pledge made to the patients; they were legitimately demanded by doctors who wished to serve their patients. He rejected the idea that doctors should be in direct contract either to the Ministry of Health or the local authorities; they would instead be employed by local executive councils, half of the representatives on which would be professional. Moreover, if a local executive council refused to employ a doctor he would have a right of appeal to a tribunal before he also exercised, if he wished, a further right of appeal to the Minister. This was an addition to the rights which panel doctors had had under the old National Health Insurance; the procedure should help to give the necessary assurance that the Minister who wished to have the power to provide a service did not seek illicit power over the conduct of the doctor. As for method of payment, he rejected the idea of a full-time salaried service. This laid him open to the accusation that, in deference to the doctors, he had set aside the ideal system long advocated by Socialists. But the criticism was neatly parried. He could not see how, under a full-time salaried service, the doctor's right to refuse a patient and – the other side of the same coin – the patient's right to choose a doctor could be properly protected. At least the problem was not easily soluble; the doctors' objection on this score had some merit. But Bevan desperately wanted the patient to have the free choice of doctor. He saw it as the best safeguard against poor service from the general practitioner, and if the doctors so passionately wanted it too he was ready to oblige them without any doctrinaire qualms. Instead of a full-time salaried service, therefore, he proposed the combination of a small

basic salary (say £300) plus capitation fees according to the numbers on the doctor's list.

In return for these arrangements, so advantageous to the profession and so advisable anyhow, it was not asking much that the
doctors should help to correct the maldistribution of general practitioners throughout the country which every inquiry had uncovered
as a basic impediment to any national scheme. These further measures, too, Bevan believed, would be in the long-term interest of
the profession; immediately they could help the young doctor. The
twofold proposals for achieving this purpose were adapted from
those discarded by Willink. A negative control preventing doctors
starting up in areas where doctors were not really needed should be
exercised by a Medical Practices Committee. The buying and selling of practices should be stopped within the Service, compensation being paid to cover the investment and expectation of those
already practising. Together, these ideas for enlisting the general
practitioner into the Service constituted, in Willink's eyes, a further
'disastrous' change introduced by Bevan.

Two other instruments completed the armoury which the Minister hoped to have at his command – first, the establishment of
health centres, and second, an enlargement of the various other
services performed by local authorities. Backing for health centres
had figured in the report of the Medical Planning Commission;
experiments with them had been favoured by Willink. Bevan's Bill
imposed a duty on local authorities to provide them. Of course,
physical shortages would limit the pace at which they could be
forthcoming; but 'their creation will be encouraged in every possible way'. Similarly, options were turned into duties for the local
authorities in such matters as the care of nursing and expectant
mothers, the provision of health visitors, home nursing and the
ambulance service. Thus Bevan argued that, although the local
authorities were to lose control over their hospitals, many other
avenues were being opened where their responsibility would be
expanded. He was conscious at the start that the whole scheme
would be criticized because of the division of responsibility which
it enforced between local and national authorities. The only other
conceivable and no doubt tidier remedies would have been to
make either the local or the national responsibility complete and

all-embracing; neither, he believed, would have been tolerable or workable. The necessary division, he insisted, involved no true contradiction – 'Day is joined to night by twilight, but nobody has suggested that it is a contradiction in nature.'

One other criticism he anticipated. He was not, of course, out-lawing the private practice of medicine; any doctor or patient would be free to stay outside the scheme if he wished. Certainly he did not think it feasible or desirable to impose his system on the individual by force. What he did hope to secure was a scheme so advantageous to patient and doctor that both would join freely and both would insist on imposing a single standard of treatment for rich and poor. This was the central aim, the final Socialist test by which his achievement would stand or fall. Yet he did make one major deliberate departure from the principle which, as he admit-ted, had caused him more anxiety and heart-searching than any other provision in the Bill. He agreed that specialists should be allowed to have fee-paying patients in hospitals. The risk was obvious, but the representatives of the Royal Colleges of Physicians and Surgeons had told him that without this concession some specialists would encourage the establishment of private nursing homes. To get the specialists into the hospitals and to keep them there as regularly as possible was crucial to the whole enterprise. He bowed to the necessity before he had ever opened consultations with the B.M.A.

Such then were the choices Bevan made in the autumn and winter of 1945 in preparing his Bill. He had the help of a Social Service Committee of the Cabinet, presided over by Arthur Green-wood, but the strong support of one other member of the Cabinet, Hugh Dalton, the Chancellor of the Exchequer, was indispensable. Bevan's demands in the interests of the National Health Service were heavy and importunate. First, he had always been suspicious of the insurance principle applied to the social services; all too easily the insurance contribution could merely become a poll-tax capable of the most obnoxious manipulation by the Treasury. That such an all-embracing scheme as the National Health Service should be financed by insurance payments he regarded as a bureau-cratic absurdity; the most straightforward way to pay for the Service would be out of taxation. This presumably had been

5*

recognized in the Willink plan, although the details had not been divulged. Bevan was eager that every penny should come from that source or at least if, according to Treasury book-keeping, some part of the money collected in insurance contributions was allocated to the Health Service, the arrangement must be temporary. This he secured in the main; only about one-twentieth out of the total came from the insurance fund. And of course the general figure, as he blithely told Dalton, was bound to be guesswork. The true provision for a free health service must depend on the behaviour of the public, and the only way to discover it must be to permit the public to behave! A year's practical working of the scheme would be needed to discover the cost with real accuracy. Finally, to complete the Bill, Bevan was proposing to include dental, ophthalmic and hearing services within the scheme from the first day, and for the first time, moreover, treatment for mental health was to be integrated – and therefore paid for – along with physical treatment. 'The separation of mental from physical treatment is a survival from primitive conceptions and is a source of endless cruelty and neglect.'[1] Under the Willink plan most of these additions were to be made piecemeal over a period and Morrison continually urged the same caution. Bevan argued that the psychological and political advantages of introducing the whole Service at the same time were overwhelming. If each section of the Service was to be delayed until the facilities were proved to be available, the drive to provide them would be lost and an argument would be presented for dismembering many other parts of the Service. Dalton agreed. He and Bevan had had quarrels in the past and were to have more in the future. But during these months they established an excellent understanding. After Bevan, Dalton was the chief architect of the National Health Service.

However, the Bevan-Dalton compact on the question of cash and the publication of the Bill itself did not settle the matter. Churchill, the Conservative Party, the B.M.A., Dr Hill and some sceptics in the Cabinet were still convinced that the egregious Minister of Health was the most vulnerable member of the Administration. He could still be beaten, and he nearly was.

[1] *In Place of Fear*, p. 182.

4

MINISTER OF HEALTH (II)
The Making of the Health Service
1946–1948

I do not think there has been anything like it since the days when Daniel went into the lion's den. I was on the dissecting table for hours, but I can assure you they treated me with the same civility as the lions treated my illustrious predecessor.—DAVID LLOYD GEORGE[1]

AN OUTLINE of the proposals for a National Health Service worked out by Aneurin Bevan during his first months of office was presented to the B.M.A. and other bodies in the first weeks of January 1946. These were the 'consultations' he had promised. Altogether during the period he had twenty conferences with doctors, pharmacists, nurses and midwives, and the representatives of the voluntary hospitals, local authorities, insurance committees and kindred organizations. His officials held several more. At this meeting with the B.M.A. leaders (according to one unfriendly witness, Lord Horder), he merely told them what he intended to do, pledged them to secrecy, and showed them on their way. The *British Medical Journal* complained that doctors were being 'gagged'. Bevan, it was said, had received them like a Victorian capitalist dealing with a deputation of employees. Such leakages appeared to confirm the expected pattern already fixed in the public mind. Quickly the Opposition in the House of Commons drew the deduction that the doctors were lining up in a solid phalanx against the Bevan plan, and that plentiful political capital could be extracted from the clash.

[1] Speech made by Lloyd George at a public meeting in Birmingham, 1911, describing his recent meeting with a Special Representative Meeting of the British Medical Association.—Quoted in *Doctors' Commons* (Heinemann).

But the truth was not so crude. 'We assembled at that first meeting,' said Dr Cockshut, 'expecting that our beautiful profession was to be hung, drawn and quartered. Instead, we were reprieved. It was the most dramatic moment I can ever remember. On one point after another – control by the local authorities, the free choice of patient and doctor, clinical freedom – the Minister had accepted what we were demanding before we had had the opportunity of asking for it. We were jubilant and stunned.'[1] The unexpected proposals confronted the doctors with unexpected choices. They had been mobilizing on a battlefield where no battle was to be fought.

An informal but crucial meeting of the B.M.A. Council occurred immediately after the Minister's departure. Imaginative leadership could have directed the negotiations into channels quite different from those actually followed. The B.M.A. leaders could have reasserted in convincing accents their desire to see a national health service, welcomed the constructive nature of the Minister's approach, and resolved to confine their criticism to detail. That in broad terms was the line of action which some spokesmen of the specialists, notably Lord Moran, recommended. They, after all, had got most of what they wanted – a special status for teaching hospitals, pay-beds, the continuance of private practice, the prospect of good salaries. Yet the very enthusiasm for the scheme displayed in this quarter revived fissures and suspicions. Others were unable or unwilling to escape from the prison of their past propaganda. They smelt trickery somewhere. Was it still true that the Minister had insisted on the abolition of the sale of practices? What real guarantees had been given that the basic salary could not be augmented by his edict until a full-time salaried service was instituted? Was it really credible that Bevan, of all people, had abandoned this declared aim of the Labour Party? And added to these points of doubt were considerations of medical politics. What shouts of betrayal would be heard at the Representative Body if the Council appeared before it as the apologists of the Minister? How incongruous such a soft note would appear in comparison with the screech of political controversy outside! At first it had seemed that there might be a landslide of opinion favouring the Minister; but gradually the old fears re-emerged in their old monstrous shapes.

[1] In conversation with the author.

Called upon to gauge the spirit of the meeting, Dr Hill put his emphasis on the resolution with which the B.M.A. must fight those provisions in the scheme to which they still objected. Moran was furious; he accused Hill of churlish folly and for long afterwards cultivated his resentment. 'In those days,' wrote Hill,[1] 'I had some difficulty in understanding the working of Lord Moran's subtlety.' But a battle between Moran and Hill awakened ancient loyalties. 'If Charles's head was going to roll,' said Dr Cockshut,[2] 'we were not going to allow it to be cut off by Moran.' Cheerfully he boasted: 'I then slaughtered Moran.' (Lord Moran himself cannot recollect the execution.) Was it not true that the specialists had received favoured treatment? Of course they wanted to call off the struggle now that their own booty was safe. Moreover what was to be lost by a show of resistance? If the B.M.A.'s sense of relief became too evident, they could expect little public support. Lord Moran might seduce his Royal College. The same art was unknown at Tavistock Square.

The ambivalent attitude of the Council was translated into a massive report, ready for circulation on 'B-day', as the doctors now apprehensively described the moment when Bevan's proposals would be made public. This was not an open declaration of war but less still was it an offer of peaceful negotiation. The B.M.A. leaders reckoned that the posture of qualified belligerence gave them the best chance of extorting further concessions. But the strategy had its perils; it could incite others to prepare for a more stubborn stand than the leaders themselves had originally intended. Not a whisper escaped to the outside public about the immediate reaction of the Council to the Bevan plan. Instead newspapers reported that the doctors were mobilizing; the B.M.A. was to ask all its members to guarantee £25 each to a Defence Fund. ' "No future for us in Britain" – DOCTORS TURN TO EMPIRE', ran headlines in the *Daily Express*. When 'B-day' came both Dr Dain and Dr Hill insisted that the proposals 'could lead sooner rather than later to doctors becoming a branch of the Civil Service'. In an article in the *Daily Mail* Dr Hill declared: '50,000 DOCTORS SAY "THE PLAN WON'T WORK".' 'Battle orders', according to the *Mail*, had been

[1] *Both Sides of the Hill* by Lord Hill, p. 91.
[2] In conversation with the author.

issued. Area conferences and meetings were to be organized all over
the country. 'There is nothing phoney about this campaign,' said
Dr Dain; 'we are in deadly earnest. This is the most serious thing
that has ever happened to doctors.' 'This is the most critical phase
in the history of the profession,' echoed Dr Hill. 'If every doctor or
most doctors refused to take service under the Act,' added Dr
Solomon Wand, an influential member of the Council, 'then the
Act cannot be worked.' Tory newspapers and Tory politicians
took their cue from these pronouncements to unleash an attack on
the plan in general and the Minister in particular.[1] And correspondents in the *British Medical Journal*, who for weeks past had
been needling the B.M.A. leaders for their lack of energy and
courage, soon showed that the medical capacity for invective out-
did that of journalists and politicians. 'I have examined the Bill,'
wrote one of them, Dr Alfred Cox, a highly respected figure who
had been medical secretary of the B.M.A. at the time of the pre-
1914 controversy, 'and it looks to me uncommonly like the first
step, and a big one, towards National Socialism as practised in
Germany. The medical service there was early put under the

---

[1] Here are a few of the interpretations which Tory newspapers gave to
the doctors' case:

Daily Express : 'They [the doctors] bitterly resent the attempt to manœuvre
them into becoming civil servants. They ask: "What have we done to
deserve this?" They sense a reflection on their calling . . .'
Evening Standard: 'Where fees are pooled, how long will it be before
patients become subject to the same inhuman system . . . As a fact the
Bill is a first step towards the full-time employment of doctors as State
servants.'
Daily Sketch: 'This Bill is the apotheosis of red tape. It threatens the
independence of the general practitioner. The doctors have a justifiable
dread of becoming salaried government servants.'
The Scotsman: 'It is not likely that a vast State scheme will be long in
operation without bringing about radical changes in the personal relationship between doctors and patients and without circumscribing the independence of practitioners in professional matters.'
Sunday Chronicle: 'Is one man entitled to antagonize the majority of a
medical profession which firmly believes that so complete an autocracy
must lower the standards of our present health service? Can one man –
however well-intentioned – avoid the mediocrity that must follow the
regimentation of our doctors into the ranks of our Civil Service?'

dictatorship of a "Medical Fuehrer". This Bill will establish the
Minister of Health in that capacity.'

Bevan was astonished by these outbursts. They bore no relation
to what he still described as his 'extremely agreeable meeting' with
the B.M.A. Council. He felt the whole campaign was factitious,
something malevolently contrived by an interaction between the
Tory newspapers and a few medical politicians. Later he was
accused of having an obsession about the motives of his opponents.
If obsession it was, its origin is worth noting. The public atmosphere in which the whole subsequent debate was to be conducted
had been fatally determined, and the choice had been made by the
doctors themselves, or at least by leaders who felt they must reflect
the ardour of the B.M.A.'s more active members. A familiar fable
of the French Revolution tells how a dejected figure was discovered
trailing through the streets of Paris in the wake of a cat-calling
rabble. 'Why do you follow that mob?' asked a passer-by. 'I've got
to,' said the figure, 'I'm its leader.' The medical politicians were
much too respectable to be described as a mob. Dr Dain and Dr
Hill managed to conceal their dejection. But the fable is still
apposite.

'AN UNFAVOURABLE DIAGNOSIS'; this was the marvellously meiotic
verdict of *The Times* on the doctors' reaction to the plan. An element of caution could be detected in some of the leaders' own
speeches. When Dr Hill went to Wimbledon Town Hall to address
a thousand doctors at his first meeting after the publication of the
plan he did not excite the same full-throated cheers as those who
denounced Bevan as 'a dictator' and 'an autocrat'. 'This Bill,' said
one speaker, who stole the show, 'is strongly suggestive of the
Hitlerite regime now being destroyed in Germany.' Another
described the hospital proposals as 'the greatest seizure of property
since Henry VIII confiscated the monasteries'. During the next
week or two Dr Hill still appeared to be damping down the first
burst of unqualified opposition. The Bill, he said, early in April of
1946, 'is not the result of negotiation with the profession; it is
the Minister's own Bill, and he seems to want to hurry it through
its Second Reading before the country has time to consider it fully.
It has some merits; the profession approves the marriage of the
two hospital systems, however much we criticize the transfer of

ownership as superfluous'. Challenged on this point, by a rare well-wisher of the scheme who succeeded in infiltrating into these raucous assemblies, he argued: 'We should beware lest our gratitude on points of administration obscures our general dislike of the proposition which would lead to the conversion of the profession into a salaried branch of government.' Even more direct was the question: 'What can we do as a profession?' The answer was not as thunderous as some might have expected. 'We should clear our own minds,' said Dr Hill, 'define our criticism and formulate our constructive proposals. Never has the profession stood in greater need of leadership and unity. The B.M.A. will provide the leadership; and the unity must come from the ranks of the profession.' Asked what would happen if the Bill in its final form was unacceptable, he sidestepped. The profession could win, 'if you mean business'. The truth was that Dr Dain and Dr Hill were deeply conscious of what had happened between 1911 and 1913. Then, the doctors, led by the B.M.A., had pledged themselves to boycott the National Health Insurance Scheme, while individual doctors signed up on the Government's forms. The B.M.A. itself had been well-nigh broken in the process.

Bevan knew that story too. He made no response to provocation, coolly announcing that he was quite content with the Bill's reception. Breaches were already beginning to appear in the doctors' ranks. Mr Henry Souttar, a former President of the B.M.A., called the Bill 'an exceedingly good' one. Lord Moran in the House of Lords initiated a debate in which he applauded the Minister's 'great political courage' and deplored the distortion of the real argument. 'Meetings are being held all over the country,' he said, 'and they are having put before them, not the considered views of people who have been following this thing on negotiating committees, but in many cases just slogans, and great harm is being done.' Lord Moran was violently repudiated by Lord Horder. However, even this attempt of the prima donnas to scratch each other's eyes out attracted little attention. The Tory newspapers had made up their minds; it was to be a fight to the death between Bevan, the bully, and the heroic, liberty-loving medical profession, a cry too tempting for the Tory leaders to spurn. And soon, with exaggerated grimaces and protestations, the doctors were performing the barn-

storming role allotted to them. Oddly, it was not to be the flamboyant politician but the members of a learned profession who were
to be most guilty of over-acting.

A three-day debate on the Second Reading of the Bill began on
30 April. 'This,' reported the parliamentary correspondent of the
Manchester Guardian,[1] 'was Bevan's day. He had a big House and
a most flattering reception from the Government benches, and an
hour and a quarter later he sat down to salvo after salvo of cheers
from the same quarter. And he deserved it . . . The speech was
masterful yet conciliatory, cogent and persuasive . . . He had a
manuscript, but why Heaven knows. He completely ignored it.
Here was a real Parliamentarian acting on the House through living
speech . . . He held the close attention of the House throughout.
Not for a moment did it relax . . . In the main his speech was
directed to explaining and justifying his proposals in respect of the
three main instruments of the new service . . . It all went to show
that he had approached his problem with greater breadth of mind
than many of his critics have allowed.'

Most of the speech was delivered in this emollient, thoughtful
vein. Then, in the last few minutes, he conjured up his old fire to
consume the two strongly critical amendments on the Order Paper.
One, in the name of Sir Henry Morris-Jones, Liberal National
M.P. for Denbigh, complained that the Minister had had no consultations with the profession. The real complaint, said Bevan, was
that he had refused to *negotiate* before Parliament had been informed. 'I protested against this [prior negotiations] when I was a
Private Member. I protested bitterly and I am not prepared,
strange though it may seem, to do something as a Minister which
as a Private Member I thought wrong . . . The House of Commons

---

[1] The same correspondent recalled a telling incident from the thirties:
'One night after dinner in 1933, Mr Baldwin [as he then was], was loung-
ing on the Treasury Bench beside a colleague. Sir Stafford Cripps was
addressing the House. He was then devotedly helping George Lansbury
to lead the Labour half-hundred against the first National Government.
"Some of our people," remarked Baldwin to his colleague, "think Cripps
is the most dangerous man on that side. They are wrong; the most
dangerous man over there is behind him." It was Mr Aneurin Bevan.
Mr Baldwin meant, of course, dangerous to the Tories . . . Mr Bevan hates
not Tories but Toryism to the depths of his soul.'

must assert its supremacy, and not allow itself to be dictated to by anybody, no matter how powerful and how strong he may be.' But consultations of course were different. They had taken place over a wide field and had produced a considerable sum of agreement. 'The opposition to the Bill is not as strong as it was thought it would be. On the contrary, there is a considerable support for this measure among the doctors themselves. I myself have been rather aggrieved by some of the statements made. They have misrepresented the proposals to a very large extent, but as the proposals become known to the medical profession, they will appreciate them because nothing should please a good doctor more than to realize that, in future, neither he nor his patient will have any financial anxiety arising out of illness.' More apparently formidable was the amendment of the official Tory Opposition condemning several main provisions of the Bill.[1] Bevan permitted himself little more than a glance at the particular charge that, in taking over the voluntary hospitals, he was diverting charitable funds to purposes not intended by the donors. 'Do hon. Members suggest,' he asked, 'that the intelligent planning of the modern world must be prevented by the endowments of the dead? Are we to consider the dead more than the living? Are the patients in our hospitals to be sacrificed to a consideration of that sort?' At this a voice interrupted: 'Henry VIII did it.' 'He was a good King, too,' replied Bevan with a flash of Welsh chauvinism. For the rest, he hardly troubled to treat the Opposition amendment seriously. The whole House and the whole country, he concluded, should take pride in a Bill which 'will place this country in the forefront of all countries of the world in medical services'.

The appeal won no response. Tory front-bench opposition to the Bill was entrusted to Mr Henry Willink, the former Minister of Health, and Mr Richard Law (later Lord Coleraine). Willink was

[1] The Tory Amendment read as follows: 'That this House, while wishing to establish a comprehensive health service, declines to give a Second Reading to a Bill which prejudices the patient's right to an independent family doctor, which retards the development of the hospital services by destroying local ownership, and gravely menaces all charitable foundations by diverting to purposes other than those intended by the donors the trust funds of the voluntary hospitals; and which weakens the responsibility of local authorities without planning the health service as a whole.'

well versed in the subject and petulantly eager to defend his own White Paper. Richard Law had no similar qualifications. He viewed the whole phenomenon of a Labour Government with more lugubrious distaste than any of his colleagues. He had the rugged features and testy contrariness, although not the eloquence, of a major prophet; compared with him Jeremiah was a riotous old roué, with a devilish sense of fun. Called upon to rend Bevan and brand him as the arch-persecutor of the doctors, he showed that he had the will but none of the necessary weapons. The scene of tumult provoked by his opening sentences set the temper of many of the debates on the Health Service.

Bevan's speech, said Law, was 'utterly unconvincing and disingenuous'. He had cast aside the opportunity to introduce a measure approved on all sides. Instead he had brought to the House 'proposals which are in fact feared and distrusted by the great majority of those who will be called upon to make them effective . . . It is surely most extraordinary that the right hon. Gentleman, the Minister of Health, who has absolutely no administrative experience of a great government department, and who has no great knowledge, either practical or theoretical, of the very important subject matter with which his Bill is dealing, should have set his own intuition and judgment against all those best informed in the medical profession and in the hospital service outside the House'. Law started to reel off the list of organizations which had made their criticisms when Bevan interrupted: 'Have the Royal Colleges placed anything on record against the Bill?' Law stumbled on. He thought they had; among them, the Royal College of Obstetricians had said, 'if my memory serves me right, that the Minister's proposals are likely to lead to a great increase in maternal mortality'. At this uproar broke loose. Mr Law's memory had *not* served him right. He struggled for a foothold on firmer ground, but recovery was impossible.

Law and Willink together made a fivefold attack. Bevan, they said, was preparing the way for a full-time salaried service; he was threatening the patient-doctor relationship; he was undermining local government; he was wantonly wrecking the voluntary hospital system. Above all – and here they were well on the mark – he had abandoned many of the precepts of the Willink White Paper. Both

came armed with quotations from Bevan's colleagues, notably
Herbert Morrison, committing the Government to the previous
plan. 'What is this baleful influence of the Minister of Health,'
asked Willink, 'which has overthrown the judgment of those so
far more experienced?' The question might open wounds among
those sitting beside him, but Bevan himself remained immune. The
more Willink denounced him as an innovator, the more he welcomed the label. And the more Willink pressed, the more Bevan
vainly pressed in turn that Willink should recite the details of his
own plan. The Second Reading was carried by 359 votes to 172.
And Bevan had won the argument as well as the vote.

While the Commons was holding this debate, however, the
Representative Body of the B.M.A. was assembling in Tavistock
Square for what many described in advance as the most important
meeting in the history of the Association. Copies of *Hansard* were
distributed among the delegates, but Bevan's eloquence was not
likely to win any converts there. Most of the 300 delegates came
mandated from their divisions. Dr Dain quickly set the tone with
the charge that the Bill put the Minister in the position of 'a complete dictator'. Bevan, he said, often talked of divisions within the
profession. Let him dare act on that assumption. We shall go back
to him, said Dr Dain, and tell him: 'You want a good service, we
want a good service; you want the doctors, we *have* the doctors.'
The boast looked true. On the first day, by thumping majorities,
any mild voice of dissent was silenced, and one by one large holes
were knocked in the whole fabric of the scheme. State ownership
of the hospitals was defeated by 210 votes to 29. Any idea of control
over the areas where doctors should practice was defeated by 214
votes to 2. The proposal to combine a basic salary with capitation
fees was defeated by 209 votes to 9. A resolution 'that this meeting
regards as essential to the freedom of patients and the profession
the right to buy and sell practices as at present' provoked the
liveliest debate. The mover saw in Bevan's sinister objection to the
system 'a levelling operation, a clearing of the ground for the erec-
tion of that glittering edifice of a Socialist dream – a whole-time
State salaried service'. No sobering influence could dispel the nightmare. 'We shall become West Indian slaves,' said Dr Cockshut;
'they had complete security – subject only to two disadvantages.

They could not own property and they could not move from their plantations. That is what will happen to the medical profession.' The resolution was passed by 229 votes to 13. Another motion suggesting that the matter might at least be 'investigated' was thrown out without even a vote.

Next day the meeting passed judgment on the Bill as a whole. Only by a hair's breadth was a proposal sidestepped which pledged the rejection of all aspects of the measure 'in their entirety'. Instead, a resolution was passed, with only two dissentients, which, 'while agreeing on the need for improvement in and coordination of existing medical services', disapproved of the methods proposed in the National Health Service to achieve these ends. Dr Linwald, of the City of London, greatly daring, had suggested an amendment welcoming the Bill as 'an important step' towards a comprehensive service. Dr Cockshut ridiculed the fainthearts. 'Some speakers,' he said, 'have asked for leadership. The profession has got leadership. What it wants now is troops, a united army. The City of London amendment is a big one. The City is a big place, a humming beehive by day, and at night left to the cats, the caretakers and the Socialist Medical Association. The City motion describes the Bill as an important step. Well, I suppose it is; it turns the medical profession from a great profession into an inferior branch of technology. But if this is a step, what is the goal? The Bill can be written in two lines: "I hereby take powers to do what I like about the medical service of the country – (signed) Nye Bevan, *fuehrer*".' Dr Cockshut clearly had the meeting in the palm of his hand. Only five votes were mustered for the City of London resolution. Never, said one speaker after another, had they known the Association so united and resolved. And the Association, insisted one member of the Council in reply to taunts from the Commons, *did* represent the profession. It had 51,508 members out of the total of 54,369 active doctors in the country, whereas the Socialist Medical Association, 'according to their organ *The Times*', had only 1,800.

The debate in Tavistock Square had a palpable effect on the B.M.A. leaders. Abandoned in deference to the fevers of the Representative Body, or at least gravely impaired, was the original strategy of concentrating on the three or four major amendments in the scheme which the leaders desired to extract from the Minister. Gone was any idea of working out a scale of priorities about which of these amendments should be regarded as the more vital. At one moment the chief grievance seemed to be the proposed abolition of the sale of practices, at another the basic salary. Many much lesser issues were allowed to intrude. But all issues were now amalgamated into one – an attack on the huge potential powers of the Minister. This was the Aaron's rod which ate up all the serpents. The new strategy suited the Tory politicians; after all it was Bevan's head they wanted. Yet there was little coordination between the doctors' leaders and the Tory front bench. Mr Richard Law's gaffes in the Commons made the B.M.A. squirm. No one dared mention again the threat to the mothers of the nation, and both Law and the other Tory spokesmen tended to concentrate their fiercest fire against the takeover of the voluntary hospitals. Here was the clearest breach with the Coalition White Paper and one which was thought to offend most deeply against local interest and pride. Had not Sir Bernard Docker, chairman of the Hospital Association, spoken of the 'mass murder' of the hospitals? Yet the B.M.A. leaders knew that this was their weakest ground. Secretly they much preferred Bevan's plans to Willink's; several of the specialists, and not only Lord Moran, had said as much openly. Here, despite the big votes at the Representative Body, was the exact point on which it would be most difficult to sustain the unity of the profession. The same difficulty, in a lesser degree, applied to some of the other arguments. On each of the individual complaints the Minister had a case backed by authoritative medical opinion. Once the debate on detail started, might not the profession find itself at a disadvantage? Why not respond to the desires of the Representative Body and deliver the attack on a broad front against the whole conglomeration of objectionable changes, symbolized in the inordinate powers which the Minister of Health was arrogating to himself? The course along which the B.M.A. leaders found themselves impelled by the momentum of debate meant challenging the principle which the Minister refused to discuss, much less negotiate. He *must* have the power to discharge the duties laid upon him by the first clause of the Bill.

Thus, after the debates in May, Parliament and the profession

seemed set for a head-on collision. Many were alarmed. The resolutions passed by the Representative Body taken together, said the
Lancet, would wreck the Bill. 'In the coming weeks of discussions,
in committee and outside, the Minister must show himself ready to
consider all reasonable objections, remembering that Oliver Cromwell held that "what we gain in a free way is better than thrice so
much in a forced way, and will be the more truly ours and pos-
terity's". On their side the representatives of the profession, in
visiting Whitehall, should spare a thought perhaps for Charles I.'

So grand an historical analogy is excellent, but the contest also
resembled a game of poker. Whose nerve was the stronger? Assuming they could keep the profession united – the first consideration
in all their manœuvres – Dr Dain and Dr Hill felt they had one
major asset. They were in no hurry, but the Minister was – he had
to get through his Bill and prepare for its administration. But
Bevan also drew some comfort from the way events had developed.
The more violently the B.M.A. protested, the more he could quell
Left-wing suspicions that he had already conceded too much and
the more he could mobilize support in Parliament and the country.
This he believed was essential, for in the subsequent months anxious Morrisonian voices were often raised in the Cabinet. How *was*
the deadlock to be resolved? No one knew. Often Bevan came home
at night exhilarated and hopeful after a meeting with the Negotiating Committee or with one of his medical spies. Sometimes he
returned depressed after a wretched rearguard action which he had
been compelled to execute in Downing Street. Meantime he curbed
his tongue and temper at his meetings with the doctors in a manner
he had never in his life before wished to achieve. An explosion
would only have given verisimilitude to the Tory headlines. At the
next meeting of the Representative Body Dr Cockshut showed that
he had taken the measure of his opponent. 'Mr Bevan,' he said, 'is a
charming and brilliant man, strongly convinced about the ends he
has in view, though perhaps not careful enough of the means whereby he gains them. He is no village tyrant, but a big man on a big
errand. If the profession is going to stand in his way, as I hope it
will, it means a very grave decision. Mr Bevan will stick to his guns;
we must stick to ours.'

Bevan did stick to his guns, during May, June and July of 1946, when the Bill was passed through its Committee stage, but his manner belied his resolution. Some disputes with his own followers were interpolated, but the major argument was with Willink and the Tory lawyers recruited to assist him. 'I know there is a great deal of apprehension among members of the medical profession as a whole,' said Bevan, 'but unfortunately, those who show the apprehension have not read the Bill.' His main purpose still was to soothe. A selection from his almost daily interventions during the sittings on the Committee stage may illustrate the claim.

The fear of Bevan's critics on his own side was that the opportunities left for private practice would be so wide that a double standard of treatment would remain, that the best standard would never be incorporated in the National Health Service itself. Partly for this reason some of them still favoured the whole-time salaried service which aroused such alarm among the doctors. Bevan himself had seemed to reveal some sympathy for this view. Explaining the rejection of the idea on the Second Reading he had said: 'I do not believe that the medical profession is ripe for it,' and then a day or two later, when challenged he had interjected: 'There is all the difference in the world between plucking fruit when it is ripe and plucking it when it is green.' But too much significance was attached to the remark, and in the Committee, he was more deliberate in defence of his arrangement. His contention was that his 'ingenious compromise' of a capitation fee combined with a basic salary was not a concession; the choice had been made on grounds of principle. 'I found it difficult,' he said, 'to reconcile the free choice of doctors with complete abolition of capitation.' To put general practitioners on a fully salaried basis would have meant allocating doctors to patients and patients to doctors, and that would have produced an unhealthy relationship. He did admit, however, that his acceptance of the idea that specialists could have pay-beds for some of their patients was a concession. It was a direct departure from principle introduced only for the purpose of encouraging specialists to come into the Service and preventing them from setting up their private nursing homes. The system could be tolerated only so long as fee payment remained the exception and the rights of other patients were not prejudiced. He never sought to disguise the possibilities of abuse and agreed that remedies might have to be sought later. Much the strongest of his replies both to his own critical supporters and to his opponents, who vainly pleaded for a whole series of further concessions to those engaged in private practice, was that both underrated how comprehensive would be the number of doctors and patients entering the Service once it was shown to have at its disposal the best apparatus and facilities. The fear of his supporters and the hope of his opponents was that some 20, 30 or even 40 per cent of the patients and doctors would stay outside the scheme. Bevan was much more optimistic; the number of people staying out would be 'negligible, insignificant'. He argued that the appeal of the Service itself and subsequent vigilance must be relied upon to exorcise the survival or renewed growth of a double standard striking at the very heart of the Bill.

With the Tories the first clash centred on the transfer of hospital ownership. Willink's plan, which Bevan had completely overthrown – 'I willingly accept the accusation' – was, said Bevan, 'a hopelessly impracticable compromise based not upon functional considerations but merely upon a desire to conciliate conflicting interests. I have determined that what we must keep before us all the time is the welfare of the patient, the individual citizen, and not the vested interest of corporate bodies'. To leave the hospital authorities independent would be to rob the Minister of his responsibility – 'how can the State enter into contract with a citizen to render service through an autonomous body?' Moreover, Bevan was not prepared to concede that the acquisition of this final responsibility at the centre would mean less protection for the individual at the periphery. 'A great deal has been said in many places,' he said, 'about the advantages of local responsibility. To whom are the voluntary hospitals responsible? If any complaint is made, what authority is able to be approached by the complainant? Scarcely anybody at all. In future there will be the house committee, the management committee, the regional board, and, what is very important, there will be the responsibility of the Minister to Parliament. In my experience, which now extends over a great many years, the most sensitive instrument in this country for bringing about effective administration is the Question on the Order Paper of the House of Commons.' This was the application of the doctrine which Bevan

adumbrated so consistently in the Parliament of the thirties. He did
not wish to shelter behind or relinquish any of his authority to a
public board. The place for Ministers to be responsible was across
the floor of the House of Commons. His aim was to make his
administration 'more human than that which exists in many hospitals now. Many of them are a cross between a barracks and a
prison.' On the whole issue of the hospitals Bevan could afford to
treat his opponents with polite patronage. They did not realize how
secretly 'delighted' most of the people engaged in the work were to
find the financial burdens removed from their shoulders. And
when the Tory lawyers sought to engulf him in legal complexities
about the transfer of the endowments of the voluntary hospitals, he
refused to succumb. The patients mattered more than the
donors. What he really deserved was 'effusive thanks'. He never
quite got them. But the hospital debate did fade from the fore-
ground.

On the Committee Stage, therefore, the principal disputes once
again revolved around the proposed conditions of employment for
general practitioners. The payment of *any* basic salary, insisted one
Tory, meant that doctors would become servants of the State.
'That argument is used over and over again as if it were a self-
evident truth,' retorted Bevan. 'But how does it become a fact when
doctors are, under the Bill, in contract with local executives on
which half the representation is professional?' What he was trying
to do, partly through the basic salary, was 'to destroy the worst
features of the old panel system'. The comedy was that thirty years
before Tories had fought against the institution of the system they
now thought sacrosanct. 'Now,' he said, 'the unlimited panel system has almost mystic virtues. It has acquired in the passage of
years a sort of' – and it was at just such moments that his stutter
would come to his assistance '. . . a sort of n-nimbus. But it was not a
n-nimbus in 1911 – it was horns. Hon. Members opposite always
discover the merits of any plan of their political opponents twenty-
five years after it is established.'

The same belated conversion, he prophesied, would occur over
the hotly disputed issue of the abolition of the sale of practices.
Here too he claimed to have been generous; the figure of £66
million for compensation had been agreed with the profession,

even though they were still opposing the principle. No more concessions, said, Bevan, were possible – 'If I did offer any, the most
surprised people would be the doctors, who would regard it as
evidence, not of softening of the heart, but of the brain'. Nor would
he budge on the issue, which now came more to the fore, of the
form of discipline to be exerted over doctors in the Service. Bevan's
plan offered more protection for the individual doctor than that
which existed under the National Health Insurance Scheme. Under
the Bill, a doctor against whom complaints were made had the right
to appeal first to a committee on which doctors had half the representation, next to a tribunal, and finally to the Minister himself.
But the doctors and the Tories demanded that there should be a
further appeal to the High Court. 'We cannot admit,' said Bevan,
'that the Courts should have the final decision about whether a
doctor had been a good servant to the people. If we said that, why
should not others claim it – miners and railwaymen, for example?'
Such a procedure would involve 'a real judicial sabotage of the
social services'. His strong words on this topic drew from the Tories
the charge that the Minister was 'back in his old style of vehemence'.

Such an accusation was almost an admission. Hardly ever were
voices or tempers raised in the Committee debates. 'His agility and
flexibility,' wrote the *Lancet*, 'won the admiration of all beholders.
He gave on occasion the soft answer which turneth away controversy and on others the swift retort that is out almost before the
critic has finished speaking.' One of the most knowledgeable of his
Labour critics, Sir Frederick Messer, M.P. for Tottenham, marvelled at the performance. Not merely had Bevan shown 'scintil-
lating and dialectical brilliance' in dealing with the Tory lawyers;
'as one who disagreed with him at the beginning on some things
and at the finish agreed with him on most, I think his outstanding
success was the way he applied the anaesthetic to supporters on his
own side, making them believe in things they had opposed almost
all their lives'. Certainly Bevan had much success in his novel
endeavour of reducing the temperature. The natural parliamentary sequel would have been a sedate Third Reading in which
the Opposition reiterated its criticism but gracefully accepted the
will of the majority. By normal parliamentary convention the fight
would have been over.

But the political circumstances of the time were far from normal. Churchill, in command of Opposition strategy, flogged his wearying subordinates into fresh belligerence, and his backers in Fleet Street needed no incitement. Most of the newspapers did not trouble to report the Committee proceedings; the delicacies of debate there did not suit their portrait of an angry Bevan thwarted in his totalitarian ambitions. And the B.M.A. continued to supply them with pretexts. At another rip-roaring session of the Representative Body in July all the major hostile resolutions of May were reaffirmed. Once a binding resolution had been passed by that assembly, it was difficult, if not impossible, to reverse it or escape from it. Any brave soul who suggested such a course was liable to be branded as a quisling or a coward. So, almost without the leadership being forced to take any positive initiative, the B.M.A. crossed the frontier from protest to action.

The new precise question put to the meeting was: should the Negotiating Committee refuse to negotiate with the Minister on the Regulations under the Bill and should the B.M.A. seek further to fortify its authority by securing an answer to the same question by a referendum of the whole membership? Overwhelmingly the answer to both questions was 'Yes'. Despite some confusion about the exact timing and form of the referendum, little doubt was possible about the response from the membership which the B.M.A. leaders desired or felt impelled to desire. The Council was instructed to make the necessary preparations. One reason perhaps why the Representative Body resorted to this extreme course was that the Royal Colleges were making their divergent attitudes to the Bill more explicit. A few weeks earlier Sir Alfred Webb-Johnson had described the Bill as 'bold and statesmanlike' and the Royal College of Physicians had actually passed a resolution generally favourable to the whole measure – 'a turning point', as their decision was hopefully described by the *Lancet*. If no clear trumpet was sounded, the army might indeed become a rabble. More obstinately than before the B.M.A. took its stand against the Bill.

This meeting of the Representative Body coincided with the Third Reading debate in the House of Commons. Bevan was incensed by the action of the Tory Opposition in putting down an amendment for the Bill's rejection in terms even fiercer than those employed on the Second Reading.[1] One Tory objective might be to encourage the House of Lords to emasculate the measure. Even if that was not the purpose, the Tory leaders were certainly associating themselves with the extremist position adopted by the Representative Body. For the first time in the controversy Bevan decided to counter-attack. The country, he said, was astonished at the action of Churchill and his colleagues. Their aim obviously was 'to incite the medical profession as much as possible. It is an astonishing thing to me that the leaders of the doctors have now identified themselves in a spirit of partisanship with the Conservative Party. That is what has happened, because the spokesmen of some elements of the medical profession have now become the most reactionary politicians in Great Britain . . . We know that some Hon. Members got into their brains at the very start a number of *a priori* objections to this scheme and from first to last they have been incapable of examining it and understanding what it is. Their minds have been hopelessly prejudiced by headlines in some of the worst newspapers in Britain'. He rounded on those who still talked of his attack on the voluntary principle and the liberty of the doctor. 'The only voluntary part of the hospital service destroyed by the Bill,' he said, 'is the necessity to sell flags and to collect money. Hon. Members opposite, as they represent the party of property, always imagine that the only voluntary act which has any sanctity behind it is the writing out of a cheque.' Still more direct was his retort to those who argued about the hospital endowments. 'The real reason for the bitterness of Hon. Members opposite,' he said, 'is because this is taking away from them one of their chief sources of social and political patronage. It is notorious in the world of medicine that doctors, first-class

---

[1] According to parliamentary custom, an Opposition votes against the Third Reading of a Bill only when it is rootedly opposed to the whole principle of the measure. The Tory amendment to the Third Reading read as follows: 'That this House, while welcoming a comprehensive health service, declines to give a Third Reading to a Bill which discourages voluntary effort and association; mutilates the structure of local government; dangerously increases ministerial power and patronage; appropriates trust funds and benefactions in contempt of the wishes of donors and subscribers; and undermines the freedom and independence of the medical profession to the detriment of the nation.'

people, first-class surgeons, gynaecologists and general physicians have from time to time to desert the practice of their profession in order to seduce millionaires to provide money for teaching medicine.' Quite a number of people, he continued, who sat in the House of Lords got there because of their hospital benefactions, and now those who defended such a system for financing hospitals were eager to keep the endowments tied to bricks and mortar and deny them to the patient. As for the liberty of the doctor, he repudiated the Tory charges utterly. Under his Bill, the doctors would be 'the most protected profession in the country'. No interference whatever was made with the professional conduct of the doctor. The idea of a basic salary had been proposed for honourable reasons. 'Why should the young doctor have to seek the assistance of a usurer before he could practise?' Finally, he prophesied that the vast bulk of the medical profession would decide to work the Act wholeheartedly, despite all the clamour. 'Now that we are reaching the conclusion, let me hope that the echoes of controversy will die down and that what will reach our ears will not be the declamations of partisans, but the whispers and piteous appeals of sick people all over the country, of the weak and distressed, who are reaching out their hands to this House of Commons to give them succour.' But again the Tories voted against the Bill. On 26 July 1946 the Third Reading was carried by 261 votes to 113.

During the next few months many fresh voices were raised. Mr Eardley Holland, President of the Royal College of Obstetricians, appealed to all sides to get round a table. Professor Johnstone Jervis, President of the Society of Medical Officers of Health, described the Bill as 'incontestably the greatest thing that had ever been done in social medicine in any age and country'. In a questionnaire conducted among the ten thousand students at medical schools throughout the country, a good majority expressed their willingness to work the Service and in particular approved the idea of a basic salary. The new mood seemed to exert some influence on the House of Lords which started to examine the Bill in October. Their Lordships could not agree with the medical students about the needs of young doctors. They inserted a clause (later removed in the Commons) forbidding the payment of a basic salary; but this was the only attempted alteration. The Lords debates were chiefly

notable for a renewed round in the all-in wrestling match between
Lord Moran and Lord Horder. 'Much of the criticism which this
Bill has provoked,' bewailed Lord Moran, 'has seemed to me to be
tethered to the earth; it has never become airborne, and it has been
totally lacking in idealism. The politicians have made their debating points, and too many of the doctors have merely expressed their
fears and prejudices. It has been left to the Minister to generate the
momentum that overcomes obstacles and to enlist the strenuous
support of ardent minds.' Lord Moran believed that, despite all the
controversy, the medical profession would join to make the Service
work. But he could not mollify Lord Horder. Horder admitted that
the Minister has 'courage, enthusiasm, a nimble mind and I
believe a conscientious belief that these proposals are in the best
interests of the community. I think that the Minister will go far,
but in what direction I am unable to say.' The trouble was that his
measure threatened 'the nationalization of medicine with a dead
level as the final goal. I see no escape from this unthinkable state of
affairs except through the medium of a black market in doctoring
and my mind boggles at the thought of its probable immensity.'
Further edge was added to the controversy between possibly the
two best-known figures in the medical profession by the annual
contest for the Presidency of the Royal College of Physicians. Just
at this time Lord Moran scraped home with his narrowest majority
– six.

During that summer and autumn of 1946, Bevan gave the
impression that he had few qualms about the general outcome.
An independent committee, presided over by Sir William Spens,
had reported on the salaries, or rather fees (the B.M.A., said
Bevan, suffered from 'a terminological sensitivity') to be paid to
doctors under the new scheme. The Minister had at once accepted
what everyone acknowledged to be generous terms, assuring most
doctors better incomes in real terms than anything they had known
in pre-war days. Bevan had also agreed, after an original refusal, to
increase immediately the capitation fee paid under the existing
panel system; this was hailed by the doctors as a climb-down, but
Bevan cheerfully declared that he was not worried about prestige.
He told a dinner of the British Orthopaedic Association that his
relations with the B.M.A. were getting more cordial every week

and expatiated on how much he had enjoyed his dealings with the profession. How refreshing he found the harmony among doctors contrasted with the acrimony among politicians. Each branch of medicine, he had noticed, was eager to acknowledge the superiority of the others; how eagerly they all joined to serve the same altruistic cause. 'Members of the Royal College of Physicians emerge flushed with enthusiasm for the Royal College of Surgeons; specialists are concerned for the general practitioners, and general practitioners for the specialists; and all found their blessed unity under the umbrella of the B.M.A. The most eloquent politicians in Great Britain are to be found in the medical profession. Indeed, I've been learning quite a few tricks in the last year or two, and I hope to use them for the benefit of the medical profession.' At a meeting with medical students, he was, as the *British Medical Journal* reported, 'boisterously confident'. 'I have always,' he said, 'regarded the British Medical Students' Association as more important than the B.M.A., because you and I will have to live together when some of those presiding over the B.M.A. will be in a position to require your services.' He noted gratefully that the medical students had voted in favour of the basic salary. Around this question had arisen all the charges about 'state slaves', 'mere civil servants', 'regimented doctors', 'Bevan boys'. 'It is really all nonsense, you know,' he added. The whole scheme was much more popular than people supposed; many who opposed it in public were more favourable in private. It was backed by the great municipal authorities, by the best elements on the specialist side of the profession, by those who knew most about the voluntary hospitals, by the vast majority of the public, by Parliament. 'All we have to do now is to win the British Medical Association.' This was his last appeal before the measure became law. On 6 November 1946 the National Health Service Bill received the Royal Assent.

Yet the B.M.A. was committed to the course laid down by its Representative Body in May and June. No power in heaven or earth, it seemed, could divert that tide. And as the time for the proposed referendum approached, it became evident that the B.M.A. leaders were not content merely to allow the profession to choose for themselves. That, as they laid their hands on their democratic hearts, was what they claimed to be doing. But a genuine unguided free choice might leave the Association evenly or almost evenly divided. So, increasingly, the leaders exerted themselves to secure an adverse vote against negotiation with the Minister. Some drew comfort from the retreat which Bevan had executed on the issue of the panel doctors' capitation fee. At the Annual Conference of Panel Committees in October, Dr Cockshut hailed that victory as a prelude to further victories: 'Some people say that we must not kick a man when he is down. Why not? He's still breathing, isn't he?' Dr Dain at the same conference was hardly less militant. He cited the example of Australia where, as he claimed, a Socialist design for a medical service had become a dead letter because the profession refused to work it. 'We are in a strong position,' he said; 'if you want to stand by your principles, you will vote against discussion of regulations with the Minister.' These clamant appeals were coupled with assurances that the doctors did not intend to strike; if the referendum opposed negotiations on the existing Act and if the Minister then refused to change his Act in deference to the doctors' demand, the care of the sick could still continue outside the Service. 'It is not fair or true,' said Dr Hill, 'to say that the referendum is somehow "seditious", that the B.M.A. is "challenging the authority of Parliament" by organizing it. We are not faced in this country, thank God, with the alternative of signing on the dotted line or going to prison, the choice (let us say) between "Bevan or Belsen".' That was true enough. But a vote *for* negotiations would certainly appear disloyal to the B.M.A. leadership.[1] '*The independence of medicine is at stake*' – that was the final, hectoring sentence in the document, setting out the B.M.A.'s view, sent out with the referendum forms.

Many eminent participants and observers were critical of the way in which the full weight of the B.M.A. was being thrown against the Act. Sir Alfred Webb-Johnson appealed for the negotiations to be permitted. Mr Henry Souttar, the former President of the B.M.A., expressed his intense disappointment that his Association was refusing to assist 'the great conception of a universal

[1] *B.M.J.* Supplement, 11 January: 'One obvious feature of the doctors' vote is that while "Yes" involved no obligation, "No" was more than an expression of opinion: it was an undertaking to refuse, if so advised, to enter the new Service.'

6

medical service for the nation'. He hoped that the doctors would 'refuse to be led into an untenable situation which could only bring discredit on us all'. *The Times* noted that in the B.M.A. document nothing but a few grudging words were said in favour of any part of the Act; Dr Dain and his colleagues were repeating the folly of 1911. Even some of the B.M.A.'s strongest supporters in the Tory press deserted. 'The B.M.A. leaders,' wrote the *Evening Standard*, 'should have the honesty to acknowledge that the fight is over. By persisting in stubborn faction they will forfeit the sympathy and respect of the people.' None of these warnings could alter the mood aroused by the previous propaganda of the B.M.A. leaders and their final appeal for professional unity.

Nearly 80 per cent of the doctors voted in the referendum. Of the total 54 per cent voted against negotiations and 46 per cent for. Of the general practitioners 64 per cent voted against. A breakdown of the figures showed that service doctors and younger doctors were more favourable to the scheme. The *British Medical Journal* wrung its hands over the outcome. All the trouble was held to be due to 'the one-man decision' not to negotiate with the profession in the first place; 'it is for the Minister to find a way out of the impasse'. The *Lancet* blamed the B.M.A. leaders; 'a situation has been allowed to develop in which the B.M.A. finds itself standing bravely, on untenable ground, with little more than half its force mustered'. 'The B.M.A.,' said Dr Dain, 'is a democratic body and in the light of these figures the Council has no mandate to negotiate.' His own solution was clear. Nothing but a wholesale amendment of the Act would suffice. He had made his demands before the referendum and he reiterated them afterwards. 'We want,' he said, 'to put into the Act the right of every doctor to come in, and the right of appeal to the courts from the Minister's decision to take him out of the Service; we want removed from the Act the State ownership of hospitals, the embargo on the buying and selling of practices, all direction of general practitioners, and the salary element in general practitioners' remunerations; we want altered the procedure of election on the councils and committees so that we may nominate our own representatives instead of the Minister choosing them all, and in that way we may curb dictatorship in the Service.' Dr Dain had no doubt that the refusal to negotiate and the insistence on his demands would be overwhelmingly backed at the Special Meeting of the Representative Body fixed for the end of January. Bevan's comment, made within a few hours after the publication of the referendum figures, was that he hoped 'wiser counsel' would prevail before 'the final decision' was taken. Meantime he had 'a clear duty' to proceed with plans for fulfilling the will of Parliament.

Deadlock seemed complete. Undoubtedly, if the Representative Body had met in January, as was proposed, without any change in the situation, tempers would have been inflamed still further. A huge task of administration had to be carried through if the Act was to come into operation on the proposed date in April or July 1948. The whole work would have to be done without the co-operation of the main body representing the profession. Alarm at this prospect produced a flurry of activity behind the scenes. At the centre of it was Sir Alfred Webb-Johnson, President of the Royal College of Surgeons. He had talks with Bevan who encouraged moves towards conciliation. Sir Alfred then approached Dr Hill on the same private basis. If the Minister was ready to make a conciliatory gesture, how could the opportunity be created? Would a letter from himself (Sir Alfred) to the *British Medical Journal*, appealing for a compromise, be effective? Hill was doubtful, even hostile. He wanted the deadlock broken, but suspected the proposed means of breaking it. The President had no power to commit even his own College. Relations between the B.M.A. and the Royal Colleges were still uneasy; an apparent usurpation of the B.M.A.'s title to speak for the whole profession was certain to be resented. On the other hand, Hill had not opposed all efforts to find a way out. Sir Alfred discussed the problem with his fellow Presidents, Lord Moran and Mr William Gilliatt who had now succeeded Mr Eardley Holland as President of the Royal College of Obstetricians. They favoured a more formal initiative, and the result was an exchange of letters between the three Presidents and the Minister, published in the first days of January of 1947, much to the fury of Dr Hill and the B.M.A. intransigents.

The aim of the three Presidents was to remove a fear – that entry into discussions with the Minister by the doctors would imply approval and acceptance of the Act – and to seek clarification on four main points: the method of remuneration, the right of appeal, the control over the liberty of movement of general practitioners and the rights of specialists to continue independent practice. Bevan responded at once. The fear, he said, was groundless: 'Every doctor will have to decide for himself when the proper time comes whether or not he should take part in the new Service, and the profession as a whole will be free to determine their views on the Service when they know what it is to be. The resumption of discussions now would not prejudice these eventual decisions.' He promised to meet any views of the profession which did not conflict with the principles of the Act. He was quite ready to discuss the basic salary, and insisted that he was not interfering with the civic rights of doctors or their freedom or movement; 'there is no power to direct a doctor to go anywhere or do anything'. Above all, he insisted: 'It is a basic principle of the new Service that there should be no interference with clinical freedom of any doctor – specialist or general practitioner.'

This reply, framed in the friendliest of terms, was accepted by most of the press as an olive branch. Dr Dain and the other B.M.A. leaders were still sceptical and aggrieved. The Minister had promised to negotiate 'within the framework of the Act'; what the B.M.A. wanted was wholesale changes in the Act. But the manoeuvre had confronted the B.M.A. Council with an awkward dilemma. If they persisted in their refusal to negotiate they would be branded as wreckers; if they agreed to negotiate, they might be torn to pieces by the Representative Body. Eventually a compromise resolution was devised. The original resolution proposed to be put before the Representative Body was abandoned and in its place was substituted an agreement to meet the Minister for discussions, 'provided that such discussions are comprehensive in their scope and that the possibility that they may lead to further legislation is not excluded'; thereafter a fresh plebiscite would be taken on the issue of entering the Service. The decision was reached only after much heart-searching. 'We are being manoeuvred outside our present strong position,' said Dr Cockshut, 'by forces outside the Association.' He condemned 'the unilateral action' of the Presidents of the Royal Colleges and hoped that such conduct would not be repeated.

Dismay at the 'defeatism' of the Royal Colleges was expressed by one speaker after another at the Representative Body and even more violently in the columns of the *British Medical Journal*. 'It would serve little purpose,' wrote the *Journal* itself, 'to ignore the fact that the action of the Presidents has caused disquiet. Perhaps the chief reason for this is a general feeling that medico-political action is best taken by the organization whose job it is – namely, the British Medical Association. The Royal Colleges are primarily academic institutions and the Presidents are elected to them because of their qualities as heads of such institutions. For them to enter the medico-political fray except as individuals is thought by many to place their Colleges in a false position.' 'The letters between the Presidents and the Minister get us nowhere,' wrote one of the *B.M.J.*'s correspondents more explicitly. 'The Act . . . was forced through Parliament in this form by Mr Aneurin Bevan. It gives him more absolute authority than any man in peace has had since Cromwell. He can, on the plea of national health, prohibit beards or make cremation compulsory, and is answerable to nobody but Parliament.'[1] In short, the three Presidents had been guilty of sabotage and the trick was the more galling because it had worked. After many such outbursts, the Representative Body felt compelled to authorize its Negotiating Committee to enter what one Council member called 'the spider's web'.

Momentarily, indeed throughout most of the year 1947, the great controversy appeared to the outside world to have died. Bevan proceeded with his administrative plans, defining the regional areas

---

[1] It is tempting to quote many more extracts from similar letters and articles in the *British Medical Journal*. The mood of the doctors at the time cannot be understood unless it is appreciated that they were being bombarded every week, in the authoritative organ of the B.M.A., with the extreme interpretations of the Act. For example, on 18 January 1946, the *Journal* published, in eight closely printed columns and with evident approval, a lecture on 'some constitutional and medical issues' involved in the Act which Reginald T. Payne M.S., M.D., F.R.C.S., had given to a special meeting of the Royal College of Surgeons some weeks before. 'If the Bill is operated,' he had said, 'no patient or doctor will ever feel safe from interference by some ministerial edict or regulation, and no independent institution connected with medicine will feel safe from interference, expropriation, or dissolution. The Minister's spies will be everywhere and suspicion and intrigue will rule.'

and making appointments to the regional and local bodies. Meantime, the Minister's officials and the B.M.A. were talking. Six separate negotiating committees were established to discuss different aspects of the Service. Every detail was microscopically examined. The main purpose was to discuss the regulations under the Act but at the first meeting, to suit the B.M.A.'s demand, the Minister had agreed that an amendment of the Act would not be excluded. After all the discussions, the main Negotiating Committee would make a co-ordinated statement of the findings of the various sub-committees. It was hard to believe that an accommodation could not be reached after all these exertions.

A study of the proceedings at the B.M.A.'s Annual Representative Meeting in July might have prompted other thoughts. The *British Medical Journal* reported a general uneasiness about the negotiations and Dr Dain spoke in slightly defensive accents. He realized that the resolution authorizing negotiation, passed at the previous meeting, had not been expressed in forceful enough terms for the taste of many. But they need have no fear. 'We have stuck to our principles,' he said. 'We have not made concessions or retreated at any point from the position we had taken up. [*Applause*] The attitude of the members of the Committee has been that they are instructed by you and that they are there to see that your views are maintained ... The Negotiating Committee is not involved in any sort of compromise.' These assurances were insufficient to prevent the moving of a critical resolution, calling for an end of secrecy and readiness for a 'showdown'. There may be 'subversive elements on the Negotiating Committee', said Dr Goodman of Newcastle; 'the passing of this resolution will be a sign that we refuse to eat the crumbs which fall from the table of the Minister'. Was it certain that the B.M.A. leaders – even the most aggressive of them like Dr Cockshut – were not being jockeyed into betrayal of the profession on the 1912–13 pattern? Dr Cockshut confessed that he had had his own original misgivings. But 'as a member of the Negotiating Committee I tell you that nothing has been given away'. Let the Representative Body be patient for a little longer. 'Over and over again,' said Mr Lawrence Abel, another member of the Committee, 'it has been said that if certain points were not conceded there will be no Service. Dr Dain has been a rock, stronger than ever in these negotiations.' The Newcastle resolution was superfluous. 'What has happened,' said Dr Dain himself, 'is that we have been preparing the field on which the contest is to take place; as soon as we have the full details we will publish them; and then the profession can marshal its battalions for the formation of its opinion and the taking of a new plebiscite.'

Clearly the 1947 negotiations were conducted under a misapprehension. Bevan believed that the documents governing the tone of the discussions should be the exchange of letters with the Presidents of the Royal Colleges. Dr Dain and his cohorts had other ideas. The only tangible result of the exchanges was a massive statement of the Negotiating Committee's case running to several thousands of words and condemning the whole Act as 'unacceptable'. Twelve points were listed where modification was needed, 'in most cases by amendment of the Act'. If these requirements were conceded, a major fresh piece of legislation would be required. Not merely would it have been impossible to introduce the Service in July 1948, as proposed; the National Health Service would have been transformed into a very different organism. The powers of the Minister would have been curtailed; the attraction of the Service for the patient would have been reduced; nothing approaching the 100 per cent participation in one medical Service would have been attainable. On all the major questions in dispute – the control over the distribution of doctors, the buying and selling of practices, the form of remuneration, the appeal to the courts, the Minister's 'monopoly' of hospitals – he was required to reverse the settled opinion which he had sustained throughout the debates in Parliament, and many secondary alterations were thrown in as makeweight. The demand was for unconditional surrender. Even if Bevan had ever contemplated such a course, which indeed he had not, it was politically barred to him. He would have incited his Left-wing back-bench critics whom he had hitherto successfully 'anaesthetized', and he would have played into the hands of his Cabinet critics who would justly complain of having been led to such a humiliating denouement. Even so, his steadiness did require nerve. Many in the Cabinet and in the House of Commons were shaking their heads in trepidation. Morrisonian mutterings of 'I told you so' began to filter through the lobbies despite the tight-

lipped discretion of Morrison himself. What *would* happen on 5 July
if the doctors refused to serve? If this single measure in Labour's
social security programme brought confusion and chaos, might not
public sympathy – so easily influenced by the Tory newspapers –
turn against the intransigent Minister of Health?

The two meetings which Bevan held with the Negotiating Committee at the beginning of December – on the first day to discuss
the case of general practitioners and on the second that of consultants – were the most stormy he ever had with the doctors. Dr
Dain said at the time that Bevan was 'rude, blustering and threatening' on the first morning and then 'smooth and amiable' on the
second. 'When,' said Dr Hill, 'we met the Minister – I think I had
better draw a veil over his demeanour in the discussion on the
general practitioner phase – a strange blandness and friendly accommodation came over him as he came to the hospital and consultant
aspects of his reply. I wonder if he hopes to divide the general
practitioners and the consultants in the dispute that lies ahead.' A
third witness, Dr Solomon Wand, was more specific in his charges.
'Mr Bevan threatened us and raved at us,' he divulged to the press
at the time. 'He waved his finger in the air and said that if, as a
result of anything the profession did, the number of patients who
signed on was much less than 95 per cent, he would make serious
reductions in capitation fees. He threatened us on the question of
compensation. When we resented that threat he ordered one member out of the room, but that member did not go.'

These brief and tendentious contemporary reports must be elaborated with the assistance of the recollections of those who participated. In the original expectation of Bevan and his Ministry officials
this December meeting was to mark the culmination of the negotiations; the work of the subsidiary committees was to be preparatory
for it. Gradually throughout the summer and the autumn this hope
faded; it vanished altogether when the Negotiating Committee
produced its document, not merely assembling its case, but dismissing the Act as 'unacceptable'. Bevan drew the conclusion that
'the Negotiating Committee on its side was never in a position to
negotiate . . . Every important provision in the Act had been rejected by the Negotiating Committee before negotiations were
concluded'. His first question at the meeting, therefore, was to ask

whether the document represented the final word of the B.M.A. To this, he received from Dr Dain a blunt 'Yes'. Thereupon he did explode and the convulsion continued for several minutes. The subsequent silence was ended by Sir Alfred Webb-Johnson who asked him, in quiet, clinical tones, whether he felt better. Apparently he did. For the confrontation which might have ended there then went on for several hours. The *British Medical Journal*, the least friendly observer, reported that Bevan treated the committee to 'a brilliant exhibition of dialectical skill'. If there was to be a fight, the opportunity for impressing prospective opponents was not to be missed. One temptation, too obvious to be resisted, was to cultivate the divergence between the consultants and the general practitioners. For the rest, his tactic was more novel. He invited Dr Dain to expatiate on his final word and when the recital was over insisted that all the suggested amendments listed by the Negotiating Committee added up to a repudiation of the Act itself. Very well; how would it be if he scrapped it and started all over again? The new measure might appeal, at least to some sections of the profession, much less than the old; some concessions might have to be withdrawn. This was his 'threat', delivered for the purpose of making the ungrateful count their blessings. Thereafter he launched into a philosophical disquisition on the nature of political power. If there was to be a national health service at all, power to administer it must reside somewhere. No Parliament could surrender that power to the profession. It might be dispersed among many bodies, notably the local authorities. Did the doctors want *that*? It was better, in their interests no less than in the nation's, that everyone should know and see who wielded the authority. Then everyone would know where to make his representations and exert his influence. The open exercise of power, the banishment of all surreptitious, irresponsible manipulations, was what he meant by democracy. When the speech was over, Dr Dain intervened. 'That,' he said, 'is just a clever misrepresentation.' 'It couldn't have been so clever,' retorted Bevan, beaming sweetly to the rest of the company, 'if the Chairman spotted it so quickly.' Everyone enjoyed the joke, Dr Dain doing his best to make the enjoyment unanimous.

At the end of these happy asperities, Bevan agreed to give his

6*

reply in writing. Not merely did he insist on retaining the general structure of the measure. He also rejected a second alternative – the offer of an Amending Act designed to secure clearer definition on some of the disputed points. Amending legislation, he agreed, might be desirable in the light of experience, but he had not been convinced by the discussions of the need to get Parliament to alter its intentions. What he did offer were continued 'adjustments within the framework of the Act' to be made as discussion proceeded. The Minister's case was stated in two documents – one an official reply to the Negotiating Committee's memorandum and the second a more popular version, seeking to set at rest the fears of the doctors, which he hoped would be circulated to B.M.A. members when a new plebiscite was conducted. 'Hardly any major step to better social services,' he wrote, 'has provoked more misstatements and misunderstandings than the National Health Service Act . . .' He sought to remove the misunderstandings and still invited the profession's constructive partnership in launching the enterprise.

The Times attacked Bevan's decision to send the Negotiating Committee away empty-handed as 'a crowning misjudgment'. And later, many looked back to these December meetings, arguing that if Bevan had chosen to display a more accommodating spirit, the crisis of the next few months could have been avoided. Little warrant for the claim appears; indeed, if Bevan had decided then to make a retreat, it is certain that the B.M.A. would have been encouraged by the display of weakness to press their attack. The contrasted comments made at the time by the Lancet and the British Medical Journal show that the alleged 'brusqueness' of the Minister was not the cause of the trouble. The B.M.A. wanted a different Act and still believed they could get it. 'Mr Aneurin Bevan,' wrote the Lancet, 'is a controversial figure who attracts accusations. He is accused of deceiving the Negotiating Committee in that he was never really prepared to submit an Amending Bill to Parliament before the Act was tried. He is accused of using a politician's guile to divide the profession, because he seems to listen more readily to the spokesmen of the specialists than to the spokesmen of the general practitioners. He is accused of a failure in political wisdom because when he feels sure of his position, he does not allow his opponents to capture those minor trophies without which they cannot confidently appear at home. An outstanding parliamentarian, the Minister may in fact have faults as a negotiator. Two things, however, must be said in his favour; he has already been proved right in his bold solution of the almost insoluble problem of the hospitals; and he has also – on paper at least – been consistently conciliatory and reasonable in his pronouncements of the past year.' The *British Medical Journal*'s estimate of the situation at that same moment showed it was not interested in minor trophies. 'The conflict between Mr Bevan and the profession centres round one fundamental principle, and no assurance or gloss of interpretation from him can alter this fact. The National Health Service Act commends itself to the political party in power because it leads unmistakably to the eventual establishment of a whole-time State medical service . . .' What the profession would be voting about in the forthcoming plebiscite was 'their continued existence as a body of free men'.

Such was the mighty theme into which the B.M.A. leaders felt that all the complex issues could be woven. In fairness to them, it may be admitted that they could quote the past statements of the Labour Party spokesmen favouring a whole-time salaried service and Bevan's own remark about the difference between plucking fruit when it was ripe and when it was green. On the other hand, he had given the doctors the most specific guarantees forbidding what they feared. The profession argued that the combined use of many of the instruments Bevan intended to employ would spell their slavery. Yet the merit or purpose of each of these instruments severally – the basic salary, the control of distribution, the abolition of the sale of practices, the health centres – had at one time or another been acknowledged by the profession itself in the years of previous controversy. His proposals for hospital organization, as he well knew, were eagerly, if secretly, approved. Opportunity for the profession to participate in the conduct of the Service throughout its whole structure had been extensively assured. When a plan of this character, comprising so many recognitions of the claims of the profession, was condemned as a challenge to medical freedom, a frontal clash could no longer be shirked. Such 'freedom' was the enemy of any national health service worth the name. No guile could succeed at that hour.

So the fight was on. It started with a huge mass meeting of doctors in the Great Hall of B.M.A. House on New Year's Day 1948,
presided over by Dr Cockshut and addressed by Dr Hill. Dr
Cockshut repeated the assurance that nothing had been given away
in the past months; 'we have reached the stage now when the future
of medicine is at stake'. Dr Hill surveyed each item in turn, regret-
ted that a stronger line had not been taken on the ownership of the
hospitals, but brought the argument back to the central charge.
'The events of recent months have made it absolutely clear that
these proposals mean and are intended to mean a whole-time
salaried service under the State. And I have no doubt in my mind
that our profession would be right to reject this thing by an overwhelming negative vote in the plebiscite shortly to be taken. This
is the last chance to do so. If we do have to enter the Service in its
present form, life will still go on, but medical practice will have
changed its character. There will be lost to the profession and the
public a form of practice which by its emphasis on the individual,
by its insistence on the doctor-patient relationship, by its human
yet efficient character, has been a credit to this country. These will
be lost and lost for ever unless the profession forgets its past differences, learns a new loyalty, and stands with firmness for its
principles. It is *now or never* for the profession to which we belong.'
Dr Dain a few days later in Wimbledon Town Hall was no less
heroic. Often, he said, Bevan had mentioned to him that the views
of the profession were divided. 'When he said it the first time I
thought he was just being funny; the second time I attributed it to
mere repetition; but when he said it a third time I decided that he
was afraid we were not so divided as he liked to suggest . . . For my
part I hope that the consultants and specialists will have nothing to
do with the Service until the proper amendments have been put
into the Act . . . I see no reason why we should not have 100 per
cent disapproval [in the plebiscite] . . . Will Mr Bevan try to
implement his scheme, whether the doctors are in or not? Well, Mr
Bevan is very determined. He has told the dentists that he will start
a Service on 5 July, dentists or no dentists. Are such expressions
more than hot air? . . . I say that the new Service is entirely unsuit-
able, entirely improper for us to accept, and we shall endeavour to
persuade our colleagues to vote against accepting any Service under

the Act in its present form. The B.M.A., so far as I have any influence, and the Representative Body will most certainly stand firm for that position. This is a demand for action and the action is up to you.'

Some of these professions of unity may have been a little over-strident. The *British Medical Journal* made a nervous appeal to consultants urging them not to be enticed by the baits so 'cynically dangled' before them. Elaborate explanations were made to show that there was no parallel with 1913. This time there would be no mass desertion. At the Special Representative Meeting on 8 January, special precautions were taken. The vote in the new plebiscite was to be more than a pious expression of opinion. The profession was to be asked directly whether it would accept service under the Act. If a majority refused and if that majority included 13,000 general practitioners (out of a total of 20,500), the B.M.A. leaders would advise the whole profession not to serve. A 'solemn declaration' was passed, without a dissentient voice, by the Representative Body stating that the Act in its present form 'is so grossly at variance with the essential principles of our profession that it should be rejected absolutely by all practitioners'.

Controversy now became violent and public. A brief selection from the vast outpouring of opinion at the time is needed to illustrate the climate in which the doctors were called upon to vote. Lord Horder summoned consultants 'to cry halt to the mad march of totalitarianism'. Dr Cockshut, in a letter to *The Times*, said that Bevan's 'implacable intention' was to impose 'servitude' on the profession. The doctors, he said, were equally implacable; 'confronted by a plain threat to the independence of medicine, fortified by our deepest instincts and guided by our traditions, we know where our duty lies'. The B.M.A. Council's message to every doctor stated that 'the issue is not one of money or compensation but of the intellectual freedom and integrity of a great profession'. And the *British Medical Journal*, week after week, used all its authority to muster the biggest adverse vote in the plebiscite. A leading article on 17 January, headed 'WHY BE FEARFUL?' spelt out more bluntly than ever before what the editor thought the battle was about and what resistance was expected to achieve. 'In its present form the Act is the first and irrevocable step towards a whole-time

State Medical Service (not "Health" Service). If doctors are convinced that this is so and if they hold fast to the centuries-old detestation of State medicine – then the "Noes" will have it . . . The Association will advise general practitioners not to enter the Service only if the number who say "No" is sufficient to defeat Mr Bevan. This number must be large enough on 31 January and remain large enough until 5 July. Faced by what will probably be overwhelming opposition, Mr Bevan will choose between postponing the appointed day or adhering to it. If he postpones it, the compensation and other issues will also be postponed, and National Health Insurance will continue. If he does not postpone it, he will be unable to operate his Service because he will not have the manpower. Again, he is defeated. He must in that case come to terms with the medical profession, terms which will have to be acceptable to those who have voted "No". The strength of the profession will lie in the size of the majority against the Act . . . If the "Noes" are in the sufficient majority medical men will be asked to form small security groups in each division. They will be asked to enter into bonds with one another, and thus keep firm their "Noes" . . . Five hundred years ago Medicine had to free itself from the dictatorship of authority – the authority of Galen. This freedom was won by men who thought fearlessly. Today we are faced with that recurring historical phenomenon – the dictatorship of the State.'

Bevan, on his side, felt that the time had come to mass his own forces in the open. The *Lancet* put to him a series of questions. The answers were mildly phrased, but to a final question then being advanced in some quarters as a possible escape from the impasse – why should the general practitioner service not be postponed until some semblance of agreement had been reached? – he replied firmly: 'Why should the people wait longer? The Minister will give them the Service on 5 July'. In a speech at Pontypridd he appealed to the doctors not to be misled by slogans and distortions. 'The Health Act will start on 5 July; that is the will of Parliament, and Parliament, after all, is still the supreme authority in Britain.'

Bevan also took another step – barely precedented in modern parliamentary history – to ensure that Parliament should speak again. He secured the Cabinet's approval for a further debate in which the Government's determination to introduce the Act on the appointed day would be solemnly reaffirmed.[1] Increasingly throughout his parliamentary career he had grown jealous of every outside influence which sought, or was permitted, to impair the status of Parliament. A Labour Government, above all others, had a supreme interest in asserting the doctrine in its most immaculate form. In the House of Commons, Labour wielded power quite unmatched in the board rooms and controlling institutions of the great industries outside. If it quailed before the B.M.A., what chance would there be of survival against the steelmasters or the Federation of British Industries? At this point his dispute with the doctors merged with his larger political ideas about the proper rights of the people's elected representatives. When Tory opponents tended to dismiss this talk as grandiloquent humbug, he regarded their readiness to see Parliament demeaned as renewed proof that they were skin-deep democrats; they had never wanted so much power assembled within the walls of Westminster since they wished to continue exercising the real power outside.

The circumstances surrounding the new doctors' plebiscite forced this issue to the front of the stage. Certainly, all doctors had the right to choose whether they would enter the Service; that had always been conceded. The leaders of the profession were entitled to learn the detailed opinion of their followers. But they were also using every influence at their disposal, including, as Bevan believed, massive misrepresentation of the meaning of the Act, to secure the verdict they desired and, furthermore, to secure undertakings that *all* doctors would refuse to enter the Service if a sufficient number expressed their hostility to it. The third question asked on the plebiscite forms could be construed to mean: 'Are you

[1] The Government resolution put down for debate on 9 February 1948 read as follows: 'That this House takes note that the appointed day for the National Health Service has been fixed for 5 July; welcomes the coming into force on that date of this measure which offers to all sections of the community comprehensive medical care and treatment and lays for the first time a sound foundation for the health of the people; and is satisfied that the conditions under which all the professions concerned are invited to participate are generous and fully in accord with their traditional freedom and dignity'.

prepared to put yourselves in the B.M.A.'s hands in trying to break
this scheme and defy the will of Parliament?'[1] This may be considered a legitimate construction. But Bevan embroidered the
charge. Each doctor had to sign his name on the voting paper with
his address and professional particulars. 'This House may well
feel,' replied Bevan to a question in the Commons, 'that this procedure is a long way removed from the secret ballot and the workings of democracy as we know it in this country – [*loud Socialist
cheers and Opposition counter-cheers*] – and it is bound to cast
doubt on the validity of the result. [*Opposition cries of "Oh"*].'
To this accusation the B.M.A. leaders had an effective retort; for
it did appear that the doctors' signatures were required only to
comply with the necessities of a postal ballot. Dr Dain, in a letter
to *The Times* almost a column long, recapitulated the B.M.A.'s
arguments against the Minister. During the negotiations he was
alleged to have 'treated the representatives of a not unworthy profession with that contemptuous derision of which he is a master'.
The charge about the ballot means that 'there are no depths of
innuendo and imputation to which Mr Bevan will not stoop'.
Nonetheless, Bevan's major charge remained unaffected. The clear
aim of the B.M.A. leaders *was* to make an Act of Parliament unworkable. Much else besides the National Health Service would
depend on whether they succeeded.

And Parliament, in Bevan's eyes, was not only a prize to be defended; it was a weapon to be used. Normally, a Minister has no
interest to provoke violent conflict in the Commons; the lower the
temperature, the swifter the passage of legislation. But Bevan, in
office as in Opposition, wanted to keep Parliament as the great
forum of the nation. It could and should be used positively to
retain the initiative in the hands of a reforming administration.
Immediately, his purpose was to impale the Opposition on the
horns of a dilemma. Was it their contention that the deadlock was

---

[1] The undertaking read thus: 'I agree to abide by the decision of the
majority and undertake not to enter the Service if the answers to part B
reveal a majority against undertaking to enter the Service as defined in
paragraph 4 of the preamble and if so advised by the British Medical
Association.'

due to his own bad manners, his ineptitude as a negotiator, his unwillingness to offer a few more comparatively minor concessions? This was their easiest line of argument, at that moment being fully paraded in the Tory newspapers. Yet if they were content with it, what became of the B.M.A.'s grand indictment of the whole measure as an outrageous assault on medical freedom? Bevan could be the gainer either way. If the issue in the debate was kept narrow, the Tories would have to abandon the major claims of the doctors and he could later confront the B.M.A. with the disheartening news that their allies had no stomach for the fight. If, however, the Tory leaders made the second choice, they would become accomplices in the attempt to sabotage an Act of Parliament. The whole future of the Labour Government would be staked on the outcome, but, if there was to be a challenge, what better ground could be chosen? He would use the House of Commons to rally his backers in Parliament and the country, to cow the B.M.A. and the Tory Opposition, and to suppress any last-minute signs of faintheartedness in the Cabinet. The risk was that he himself might be out-manœuvred in debate.

In fact, his speech on 9 February was one of the most coruscating he had ever delivered. Mr David Eccles (later Lord Eccles), his most forthright critic later in the debate, talked of his 'Jacobin eloquence', and the epithet was apt. He expounded his whole case more forcefully than ever before and pilloried the B.M.A. leaders – 'a small body of spokesmen who have consistently misled the great profession to which they are supposed to belong . . . raucous-voiced people . . . politically poisoned'. He used in turn every art at his command, and the great majority behind him rocked with laughter or yelled their delighted enthusiasm. Danton himself could not have done better. Indeed no one can guess how Danton could have adapted his style to the British House of Commons where the speaker knows that nearly half his audience comes to mock or to sneer. Printed words can never even distantly reflect the power of great debating, Bevan's least of all, but it is only by extensive quotation of at least a few of his speeches that an indication may be given of how he might achieve his effects by a mixture of logical detail and emotional passion. Here, almost verbatim, is what he said:

I would like to make one personal reference. It has been suggested that one of the reasons why the medical profession are so stirred up at the moment is because of personal deficiencies of my own. I am very conscious of these. They are very great. Absence of introspection was never regarded as part of a Celtic equipment; therefore I am very conscious of my limitations. But it can hardly be suggested that conflict between the British Medical Association and the Minister of the day is a consequence of any deficiencies that I possess, because we have never been able yet to appoint a Minister of Health with whom the B.M.A. agreed. My distinguished fellow countryman had quite a little difficulty with them. He was a Liberal, and they found him anathema. Then there was Mr Ernest Brown who was a Liberal National, whatever that might mean, representing a Scottish constituency. They found him abominable. As for Mr Willink, a Conservative representing an English constituency, they found him intolerable.

I am a Welshman, a Socialist representing a Welsh constituency, and they find me even more impossible. Yet we are to assume that one of the reasons why the doctors are taking up this attitude is because of unreasonableness on my part. It is a quality which I appear to share in common with every Minister of Health whom the British Medical Association have met. If I may be allowed to make a facetious digression, they remind me of a famous argument between Chesterton and Belloc. They were arguing about the cause of drunkenness, and they decided to apply the principles of pure logic. They met one night and they drank nothing but whisky and water, and they got drunk. They met the next evening and drank nothing but brandy and water, and they got drunk. They met the third night and drank nothing but gin and water, and again they got drunk. They decided that as the constant factor was water it was obviously responsible – a conclusion which was probably most agreeable to Bacchic circles.

I think we can dismiss at once the suggestion that the disagreements with the medical profession are a consequence of the personal qualification or disqualification of the Minister concerned, and I have made reference to it now only in order that I might call attention to the sort of propaganda which seems to be recurrent in British politics where issues of principle are vulgarly personalized. It is becoming almost impossible for the citizens of Great Britain to see the differences of political principle through the smoke of personal misrepresentation. That is one of the reasons, but the least important reason, why the Government thought it necessary to have this debate this afternoon.

It has been suggested by the spokesmen of the B.M.A. that we have not negotiated with them sufficiently, that if we had only been more approachable things would have been different. But there were long negotiations with Mr Brown and long negotiations with Mr Willink, and on every occasion the B.M.A. rejected the advances made. I have met them on numerous occasions. I have met the Negotiating Committee itself eight times, three times before the Bill was introduced and – I hope this will not be brought against me – most irregularly I met them three times whilst the Bill was before the Committee. I consider this was somewhat of a sin against constitutional practice because I do not believe a Minister ought to be running two committees at the same time, one in the House of Commons and the other outside. I did it in order to give them every opportunity of stating their case.

Since the Act, I have met them twice, and since August 1945, the officials of my Department have met representatives of the Negotiating Committee twenty-eight times. There have been continuous discussions, so microscopic that I am almost weary of the issues involved because they have been so much investigated. But the Negotiating Committee on its side was never in a position to negotiate. It had received from its own committees, at its own request, instructions not to negotiate. Indeed – and I would like the House to note this – when I met members of the Negotiating Committee in December of last year for a two-day discussion, I was presented with a printed circular which they had themselves caused to be printed rejecting the Act before the final negotiations had taken place. All the main features of the Act are contained in that document; not merely remuneration, not merely basic salary, not merely the appeal to the courts, but every important provision in the Act had been rejected by the Negotiating Committee before negotiations were concluded.

I called the attention of the chairman of the Negotiating Committee to that fact and asked him what was the use of two days' negotiations when one side had already decided to reject the whole scheme. The answer was that they had already made up their minds.

Mr Wilson Harris (Cambridge University): Have they rejected the whole of the hospitals section of the Act?

Mr Bevan: The hospitals section is included in the rest. This document is in the Library for hon. Members to look at – it rejects the sections dealing with distribution, buying and selling of practices, remuneration, right of appeal to the courts, midwifery, the administrative bodies, public hospitals, hospital accommodation for private patients, facilities for diagnosis, statutory health committees, public health service, representation of the profession on the administrative bodies.

We are not now dealing with a body which is seeking to bring about the modification of principles in what they consider to be the legitimate interest of the members of the medical profession. We are dealing with a body organizing wholesale resistance to the implementation of an Act of Parliament.

Futhermore, and I would like the House to note this, they had already rejected the Act before they knew the terms of renumeration for the general practitioner. They had not been told by me officially whether or not there would be a basic salary. They had not been told at this stage what was to be the scale of renumeration and, when they go around the country at the present time saying that one of the main causes of their decision is the basic salary, it should be remembered that they had decided to reject the Act before they knew there would be a basic salary in the remuneration.

In fact the whole thing begins to look more like a squalid political conspiracy than the representations of an honoured and learned profession and, I say this deliberately, when the bulk of the doctors in the country learn the extent to which their interests have been misrepresented by some of their spokesmen, they will turn on those spokesmen. In fact, one of the weaknesses of the

B.M.A.'s present position is that they mustered their forces on the field by misrepresenting the nature of the call and when the facts are known their forces will disperse.

There are four main issues on which the B.M.A. say they join issue. They say, in the first place, that they cannot accept the abolition of the sale and purchase of practices. The abolition of the sale and purchase of practices was recommended by the profession's own health commission. They voted for the abolition in their own plebiscite and all I have done, and all the Government and the House have done, is to put in the Act recommendations about this step on the best medical information. We regard it as being inconsistent with a civilized community and with a reasonable health service for patients to be bought and sold over their heads. When I am told that all they desire is that patients should have the best medical treatment, how can that be argued when a doctor succeeds to another doctor's panel not on account of personal qualifications but on the size of his purse? How can it reasonably be argued that there is any effective free choice of doctors when the doctors negotiate the terms between themselves and the patient knows nothing at all about it? This system exists in no other country in the world. It is a blot upon our medical system.

I ask the Opposition whether they accept or do not accept the abolition of the sale and purchase of practices. We should like to know. We should like the Opposition to tell us – because I think that these matters ought to be made quite clear – whether they are in favour of doctors being able to buy and sell their panels in the public service. It is very necessary that we should know. It is very necessary that we should know the body of opinion behind this practice so that we can estimate what it is worth. One of the main reasons why we are having this debate today is not merely in order that the Government can clear up their position, but that the Opposition shall have the opportunity of making their position clear, too. After all, the second body of importance next to the Government is the Opposition, and I do not think that the nation ought to be denied the counsel of the Opposition in this matter. There cannot be, as far as we are concerned, any question at all that a health service which we consider to be reputable must not retain the buying and selling of private practices.

The doctors have said that their second objection – indeed, many of them said that this is the one thing that is offending them – is that they will not accept a basic salary as part of their remuneration. The first time that a full-time salaried practitioner service was put before the medical profession was in 1943, in the days of the Coalition Government. It came from Mr Ernest Brown. I hope the Opposition will note that. This principle, to which such exception is taken, which is supposed to reveal such Socialist partisanship, which is supposed to embody such regimentation, did not come from a Socialist Minister of Health but from a Government composed of Conservatives, Socialists and Liberals, and was put forward by a National Liberal. And I rejected it; I thought it contained too much of the element of regimentation.

There were some hon. Members on this side of the House who expressed the view that competition for patients on panels had the effect of degrading the standards of the service, and that, consequently, it was much better to have a full-time salaried service. It was argued out on the Committee stage and on the Second and Third Readings, and it was decided that that was not what we were going to do. But what I made clear during the passage of the Bill was that young doctors ought to have the opportunity of living decently whilst they were building up their practices. At the moment, the only way in which a doctor can get into general practice is either by becoming an assistant to a principal, and accepting very important limitations when he takes up his work, or by borrowing sums of money and, therefore, for the first fifteen to twenty years of his professional life, loading himself with debt, so that when he is approaching his patients, he is not in the state of mind in which a doctor ought to be.

We not only desire in this scheme to relieve patients of financial anxiety; we desire to relieve the doctors of financial anxiety when he approaches his patients. It is one of the most deplorable features of the existing system that young doctors, when they go into practice – and they are by no means boys, but men of twenty-four to thirty years of age, with young families to feed and educate and clothe and look after – just at that time when the young doctors ought to be freest of financial burdens, they have financial burdens put upon them. We consider, therefore, that a salary, only of £300 – but, nevertheless, a salary of £6 a week – plus what he can get from capitation fees, would be a financial support for the young doctor whilst he is building up his practice.

Mr Lipson (Cheltenham): Would the right hon. Gentleman deal with the proposal that the basic salary should be optional, and paid only to those doctors who ask for it and not to those who do not want it?

Mr Bevan: It would make administrative practice extremely complicated, because we should then have to pay two capitation rates, a higher one for doctors not receiving salary and a lower one for the doctors receiving it.

Mr Lipson: I would suggest the same capitation fee, but not giving the basic salary to those who do not ask for it.

Mr Bevan: My hon. Friend is dealing with the point I was just about to meet. It is perfectly true that if a general practitioner believes that this element of basic salary is repugnant, and by its very existence makes him into a State salaried servant, he need not take it. He can give it back. The Chancellor of the Exchequer would be delighted. It will be of interest to see how many general practitioners find this so dishonourable to the traditions of the profession, so besmirched by the element of regimentation that they will hand it back as though it were poison. There is nothing at all to prevent a general practitioner from handing it back if he likes. But it would be a most complicated arrangement if we had two capitation fees running simultaneously in the Service . . .

Another argument we have heard advanced is that the partnership agreements will be rendered very difficult and that it is hard to see what the Act means when partnership agreements remain after the Act has come into operation. The mind of the general practitioner has been confused by the B.M.A. propaganda in this respect; but there is natural anxiety among general practitioners as to what is the effect of the Act upon partnership agreements. In order to try to clear it up I have decided, with the co-operation

of the Attorney-General and the Lord Chancellor, to appoint a
legal committee to inquire into it and to recommend what they
consider should be done. It is a most unusual proceeding. As a
general rule, when Parliament passes a Bill and it becomes law, it
is left for the courts to construe it. However, if any further light
can be thrown on this matter, if competent legal opinion can find
any way in which those Sections of the Act can be clarified, I
shall be perfectly prepared to recommend the Government to
have an Amending Bill for that part of the Act to make clear
where the general practitioners stand.

The other thing to which the B.M.A. takes serious objection
is what they consider to be the removal of their legal rights. Here
the misrepresentation has reached really staggering proportions.
It has been said that a doctor has had taken away from him his
right of appeal to the courts against unlawful dismissal. That is
entirely untrue. A doctor will have exactly the same right of
appeal to the courts against unlawful dismissal as any other
citizen in the country. It has never been challenged during the
whole of my negotiations with the representatives of the profession. They have never been able to show any part of the Act
which takes away from the doctors those legal rights. But some of
them want to go further than that. They want to have the right of
appeal to the courts against dismissal from the Service on the
ground of misconduct or neglect.

I want the House fully to appreciate the significance of what is
being asked. It is perfectly competent to go to the courts against
a Minister on the ground that he has unlawfully removed any
doctor from the Service. That remains. It is an entirely different
matter if they want to take the Minister – whoever he might be –
to the courts on the ground that he has acted wisely or unwisely,
because whether a Minister has acted wisely or unwisely is for
this House to determine, not the courts. If a doctor has the right
to go to the courts to ask the courts to arbitrate, not on the law,
but on the merits, how can that right be denied to anybody else –
to the teachers, to the railwaymen, the miners, everybody, in
both public and private service?

Under this reasoning, if there were this right to go to the
courts of law, appealing not on the ground that the doctor has

been unlawfully dismissed, but on the ground that he has been wrongfully dismissed in the terms of his contract, what would be the situation? The relationship of the judiciary to the legislature would be completely revolutionized. Day by day the courts would be arbitrating on a thousand and one matters on which they are utterly incompetent to judge. The courts are competent to judge law and to construe the statutes; but the courts are not competent to say whether a foreman ought to get rid of a workman or a workman ought to dismiss an employer – because the converse is always the case, and under conditions of full employment it is as easy for the workman to dismiss the employer as for the employer to dismiss the workman. But if the B.M.A. had their way, if this queer constitutional doctrine were accepted, both would be tied together by an Act and by the courts. We should find ourselves in an entirely impossible situation. Therefore, we decided it was constitutionally impossible to give the doctors this concession.

However, when the Act was being drawn up and the protection of the doctor being considered, I gave this point special attention. I would have the House realize that, under the existing National Health Insurance Act, protection for the doctor is merely an appeal to the Minister. It is only that. The local insurance committee reports the doctor to the Minister; the Minister makes an inquiry, and the doctor is upheld or removed. That is the existing situation. That was the situation as it was left by my predecessor. Mr Willink, in his scheme, had left the position under the new Health Service exactly the same as it is now; but I, of my own volition, decided that that protection for the doctor was not sufficient, on the ground that the new Health Service would be universal and that removal from the National Service of the future would carry heavier penalties than removal from the National Health Insurance Act scheme. So I decided to put a tribunal in between the local executive council and the Minister.

The present position, therefore, is that under the scheme the general practitioners are in contract with the local executive council, on which they have seven direct representatives – I emphasize, seven direct representatives – not appointed by the Minister, but elected by the doctors in the locality themselves.

That is the first body to discuss the behaviour of a doctor. If, after examination, that body decides that a doctor ought to be removed, they report it to the Minister. At that stage the Minister can do nothing. All he can do is to refer it to this tribunal, the chairman of which is appointed by the Lord Chancellor, and on which there is another doctor and a layman. If that tribunal decides that the doctor should be retained, the Minister can do nothing at all about it, and the doctor is retained.

The Minister is brought into the picture only where the doctor himself invokes the Minister against the decision of the tribunal. The Minister can then order another inquiry, public or private, as the doctor requires, with witnesses if need be, and with all the apparatus of full investigation; and the Minister can then decide whether or not the contention of the doctor should be upheld. There is no professional body in Great Britain or the world where more protection exists than that. The fact is I am myself beginning to wonder whether the public is sufficiently protected under machinery of that sort. Certainly no doctor could claim that he is not adequately protected in those circumstances.

Let me ask this question, which I hope the doctors will read tomorrow; what would be the consequence of the sort of protection for which their so-called spokesmen are asking? Compare it with this. Suppose that we did find it constitutionally practicable – which we do not – to give the doctor the right of appeal to the courts in these circumstances. Consider what a weapon of tyranny that would put in the hands of the Minister. Because remember, not only would the doctor have the right of appeal to the courts, but the Minister, being responsible to the House, would himself have the right of appeal to the courts for the removal of a doctor. In such circumstances any Minister would have very considerable powers of intimidation over the doctor, because he could take a doctor to the courts, force the man to undergo all the odium of publicity, to have his conduct examined, newspapers reporting it, all the circumstances of the case revealed to everybody, and his professional reputation besmirched.

The fact is that, if the medical profession could be given what they are demanding, then in six months' time they would be cursing the people who asked for it. In fact, in this matter lay people like ourselves have acted with a far greater sense of responsibility in protecting the doctor than their own professional representatives. Those are the main facts on which the doctors are at present making their complaint.

Mr Paget (Northampton): There has been great misrepresentation on this. Is the position that a doctor can bring an action for wrongful dismissal, precisely as any other citizen can, and that everything in the Act is additional protection, enjoyed by the doctor but by nobody else?

Mr Bevan: Yes, that is absolutely correct. In fact, the doctor can go to the courts, as I understand it – my right hon. Friend the Attorney-General sits beside me, and he can correct me or otherwise if he wishes – on the ground that this tribunal or the Minister has not carried out the statute, or has prejudiced the case by the way in which it has been handled by the tribunal, or otherwise. There is adequate protection at every stage.

These are the four main grounds upon which the doctors have been alleging their opposition to entrance into the Service. I apologize for keeping the House so long, but this is a matter of very great importance, and I am desperately anxious to get the medical profession into the scheme, enthusiastically and harmoniously, and I deplore the atmosphere which has been created in the last six months. I would point out to the House that so anxious was I not to take part in these polemics that I made no public speech of any sort until the meetings in January, when the B.M.A. decided to reject the Act. Although, for between six months and a year, meetings have been held all over the country and the most extravagant things have been said, I nevertheless took the view that it would be better for me to say nothing at all at that stage, or I might have added to the acrimony rather than reduced it. Therefore, I made no statements of any sort. It may be that the miseducation of the doctors is partly my responsibility, and that if I had not left their education solely to those who are supposed to speak on their behalf, they might now know a little more than they do about the Act.

It may be said by the right hon. Gentleman the Member for Saffron Walden [Mr R. A. Butler], when he replies, more in sorrow than in anger, 'Well, now, cannot we get together? Is it not possible, at this late hour, for some concession to be made to assuage the high feeling and try to bring about greater harmony between the Government and the doctors?' The Opposition might want to put themselves into the position of 'honest broker' – a position, historically, very difficult for them to occupy; but it might appear to them to be congenial in these circumstances to take up that position. But that would be to assume that there have been no concessions made to the medical profession, and that we should start off once more negotiating and making concessions. I want to point out to hon. Members in all parts of the House that these negotiations have been a long series of concessions from us, and not one from the medical profession – not a single one. Indeed, one member of the Negotiating Committee boasted that during these negotiations they had not yielded a single inch.

Consider what we have done. Consider the long record of concessions we have made. First of all, in the hospital services we have accorded paid bed blocks to specialists, where they are able to charge private fees. (*Hon. Members:* Shame) We have accorded, in addition to those fees for those beds which will have a ceiling, a limited number of beds in the hospitals where there is no ceiling at all. (*Hon. Members:* Why?) I agree at once that these are very serious things, and that, unless properly controlled, we can have a two-tier system in which it will be thought that members of the general public will be having worse treatment than those who are able to pay. That is a very grave danger, and it is a very serious and substantial concession made to the medical profession. We have also conceded that general practitioners and specialists can have private patients. That was repugnant to many of my hon. Friends. They hated it, because they said at once that we can have, if we are not careful, a revival of the old Poor Law system, under which the man who does not pay does not get the same treatment as the man who does.

This kind of propaganda contains the possibility of developing that atmosphere. I would warn hon. Members opposite that it is not only the British working class, the lower income groups, which stands to benefit by a free health service. Consider very seriously the tradition of the professional classes. Consider that

social class which is called the 'middle class'. Their entrance into
the scheme, and their having a free doctor and a free hospital
service, is emancipation for many of them. There is nothing that
destroys the family budget of the professional worker more than
heavy hospital bills and doctors' bills. There is no doubt about
that at all, and if hon. Members do not know it, they are really
living in another world. I know of middle-class families who are
mortgaging their future and their children's future because of
heavy surgeons' bills and doctors' bills. Therefore, it is absolutely
vital, not only for the physical good health of the community,
but in the interests of all social groups, that they should all be put
in the system on 5 July and that there should not be some in and
some out of the scheme. That is why I deplore the letter today in
The Times from a distinguished orthopaedist, who talked about
private practice as though it should be the glory of the profession.
What should be the glory of the profession is that a doctor should
be able to meet his patients with no financial anxiety.

I now come to the Amendment on the Paper, and may I say at
once that the Government are prepared to add the Amendment to
this Motion? I think that the language of the Amendment
reflects the political sagacity of the Opposition. They are not
anxious to enter the tilting yard led by such doubtful leaders as
the B.M.A. They wish to avoid the tourney, and are prepared to
stand on one side and gather up whatever spoils may come to
them. If hon. Members look at the Amendment, they will see
that it is one to which all Members of the House can subscribe.
It 'declines to prejudice in any way the right of individuals in all
the professions concerned to express their opinions freely,
according to their traditions, and in the interest of their patients,
upon the terms and conditions of service under the proposed
National Health Scheme.' Who disagrees with that? A more
innocuous collection of bromides I have never heard of or seen.

And here it may be permissible to interpolate the report in the
News Chronicle at the time of what had happened when Bevan
reached this part in his speech. *Hansard* alone, alas, cannot express
it: 'I have not in years heard such a roar of laughter in the House of
Commons . . . With an adroit switch from exposition of the

Government case he came to the Opposition's Amendment, the sting of which, as the Minister pointed out, was that it left out the last part of the Government resolution. With a wave of the hand Bevan observed blandly: "I say at once that the Government is prepared to add the Amendment to the resolution . . ." The perfect stymie first jerked the House, then convulsed it. Laughter petered away, then as even the Opposition saw the way the joke had been turned on them, it roared up again. Added Bevan: "A more innocent collection of bromides . . ." That was the end, What else he had to say was drowned as effectively as the Amendment.'

But he was not quite finished:

If Members opposite think there is anything in the Act which interferes with the freedom of choice, they should say so; we should hear it. If they think there is anything in the Act, scheme, or terms of remuneration, which prejudices the doctor-patient relationship, we should hear it. So far, we have not. We do not object, and never have objected, to the doctors expressing their opinions freely; we do not object to the B.M.A. recommending their doctors not to take service under this scheme. What we do take serious objection to is to organized sabotage of an Act of Parliament. We desire to know from the Opposition whether they support that. Do they support the B.M.A. organizing resistance on 5 July, because I would warn them that the beginning of that road might look very pleasant but the end would be exceedingly unpleasant, not only for us but for Members opposite. (*An hon. Member:* Is that a threat?) It must be clear to everybody that if there is one thing we must assert, it is the sovereignty of Parliament over any section of the community. We have not yet made B.M.A. House into another revising Chamber. We have never accepted the position that this House can be dictated to by any section of the community.

We do concur in the right of any section of the community to try to persuade the House of Commons to change its mind. That is perfectly sound. The position we are taking up is that the B.M.A. have exceeded their just constitutional limitations, and that the best thing they can do now is to put on record their opinion that while they may disagree with the Act in this or that

particular, or in general if they wish, nevertheless they will
loyally accept the decision of Parliament and continue to agitate
for such revisions as they think proper. That is the right position
for any section of the community to take up.

May I say this in conclusion? I think it is a sad reflection that
this great Act, to which every Party has made its contribution, in
which every section of the community is vitally interested,
should have so stormy a birth. I should have thought, and we all
hoped, that the possibilities contained in this Act would have
excited the medical profession, that they would have realized
that we are setting their feet on a new path entirely, that
we ought to take pride in the fact that, despite our financial
and economic anxieties, we are still able to do the most
civilized thing in the world – put the welfare of the sick
in front of every other consideration. I, therefore, deplore
the fact that the best elements in the profession have been thrust
on one side by the medical politicians, who are not really concerned about the welfare of the people or of their own profession,
but are seeking to fish in these troubled waters. I hope the House
will not hesitate to tell the British Medical Association that we
look forward to this Act starting on 5 July, and that we expect
the medical profession to take their proper part in it because we
are satisfied that there is nothing in it that any doctor should be
otherwise than proud to acknowledge.

Bevan, reported the *Manchester Guardian*, 'sat down at the end
of this speech to one of those long, sustained cheers that Parties in
the House of Commons reserve for an unusual gladiatorial triumph'.
It was some minutes before the debate could proceed, and thereafter Opposition speakers wavered in response to the baffling choice
he had presented. Would they enter the tilting yard at the B.M.A.'s
behest? Clearly, their original decision was not to do so; the mild-
ness of the Opposition amendment was one sign of their attitude,
the choice of the supposed Tory reformer, Mr R. A. Butler, as the
first Opposition spokesman, another. He concentrated his criticisms on the conduct of the Minister, discarded several of the
doctors' claims – for example, on the sale of practices and the
appeal to the courts – as no longer sustainable, and offered himself,

despite Bevan's prophylactic warnings, as the honest broker. This was too thin a diet for the benches behind him. Sir Ernest Graham-Little, one of the doctors' spokesmen, alleged that many young doctors were leaving the country and were thus resorting to the only available remedy. And Mr David Eccles spoke in the authentic accent of the general revolt against the Government which the Tories were seeking to engineer outside. Some time in the autumn, he claimed, Bevan had deliberately made up his mind to pick a quarrel:

I do not think we can understand why the opposition of the doctors to the Minister has increased unless we see the Minister's recent obstinacy as one of a series of blows delivered by this Government against the middle class. Houses are not to be built for sale; the purchasing power of professional incomes goes steadily down – (*An hon. Member*: So does everybody else's) – the basic petrol ration is abolished; university seats in this House are to disappear; and now there is talk of a capital levy which will hit those people for whom the Secretary of State for War does not care a 'tinker's cuss'. All this looks like a concerted attack upon the middle class . . . So it happens that the Minister of Health, by his brutal tactics, has roused 40,000 British men and women to defend the freedom of action and the freedom of conscience of all their fellow citizens . . . If the Minister is determined to fight, we on these benches will not leave the doctors to fight alone.

Here was the call for which they were waiting at Tavistock Square. Yet even before it reached them the bugle note had become muffled. Mr Richard Law, the chief casualty of the Second Reading debate in 1946, made the closing speech for the Opposition. He finished more plaintively. Would not the Minister make one concession, just one? [*Cries from hon. Members*: Which one?] 'If the Minister could give way on one thing – any one thing – he might find that he had broken the log-jam.' Then Parliament gave its verdict. The Government resolution was carried by 337 votes to 178, and Bevan had the best of both worlds. The Tories had been manœuvred into voting against the most exciting and popular of the Government's measures a bare four months before it was to be introduced. Even so and despite Mr Eccles's Bourbon eloquence, the doctors could mark how fickle their backers were likely to be. Only on rare occasions do specific debates in the House of Commons dictate the course of events. That on 9 February was one of these exceptions. Parliament could see that it was not Bevan's nerve which was fraying, and Dr Charles Hill, listening in the gallery, could see it too.

It was at this time also that Bevan had to take a critical decision in his department. Some urged upon him that he should make plans for an improvised service after 5 July in case the bulk of the doctors did stay out. Prudence might argue in favour of the idea, but the disadvantage was that if the B.M.A. leaders got wind of it their morale and determination would be fortified. Bevan adhered to the view which he held throughout the three years of controversy. The doctors *would* come in. Every move by the Government must be based on that assumption.

The drama in the House of Commons naturally heightened public interest in the result of the new plebiscite. If Bevan had ever hoped, as one by-product of the debate, that the doctors themselves could be influenced in his favour, he was sharply disappointed. On an 84 per cent poll the voting showed a nine to one majority against the Act in its existing form. Altogether, 40,814 votes were cast against the Act and only 4,734 for. The number of general practitioners voting against acceptance of the Service was 17,037. For the B.M.A. leaders this looked like an unqualified triumph. 'The result of the plebiscite,' wrote the *Manchester Guardian* Political Correspondent, 'has been a shock to the Government and has caused dismay among members of the House . . . There is already some doubt among Labour Members about the prudence of Mr Bevan's handling of the matter in the debate last week. The view has been put today that Mr Bevan spoilt a good case by his polemics.' But Bevan's will did not waver. On the same night as the results became known, a terse statement was issued from the Ministry of Health. 'The Act,' it said 'will come into operation on 5 July in accordance with Parliament's decision.'

Most commentators at the time dismissed this claim as bravado. Dr Roland Cockshut declared bluntly in a radio debate that the

7

service would definitely not start on the scheduled day. 'Let me ask,' he insisted, 'how you propose to work the medical service without doctors. You can't bring in the troops or anything like that.' The most partisan sections of the Conservative press gloated that the Government as a whole had suffered a near-mortal injury. 'The doctors' stand,' wrote Candidus in the *Daily Sketch*, 'is the first effective revolt of the professional classes against Socialist tyranny . . . There is nothing that Bevan or any other Socialist can do about it in the shape of Hitlerian coercion . . . Even if we had the means at our disposal to carry out the scheme, I should still applaud the doctors' resistance. I should applaud it because the State medical service is part of the Socialist plot to convert Great Britain into a National Socialist economy.' Some papers – the *Glasgow Herald* and the *Observer* – called for Bevan's resignation. Others pleaded for the appointment of third-party mediators.

The *British Medical Journal* naturally welcomed the result of the voting as a vindication of the profession and its leaders against all Bevan's charges. But a note of hysteria was also detectable. It now directed special attention to the right of appeal – the very issue on which Butler had confessed Bevan's case to be strongest. 'Whatever may be the constitutional niceties of the right of appeal to the courts against dismissal in the National Health Service,' it wrote, 'many, we believe, are gravely disquieted by the fact that in a State medical service available to the whole community a man's life and career may be ruined by the decision of a tribunal of three men of whom only one has a legal training . . . In future the Ministry of Health will be able to get rid of what it will regard as an unsatisfactory servant, and that servant will then have no alternative but to emigrate or to try and gain a livelihood in another occupation for which he has not been trained. This power of the State over an individual highly and lengthily trained to do one kind of work is indeed alarming in its enormity.' A flood of resolutions poured in from B.M.A. branches denouncing the Minister, and demanding that the Association should act upon the plebiscite results. Only a few feeble voices dared plead for the reopening of negotiations.

The B.M.A. Council, however, was less ebullient than its followers in the country or its backers in the press. One reason, it seems, was that the Commons debate had made its impact there.

At the first Council meeting after the plebiscite a member, Dr F. Gray, said that on reading *Hansard* he had reached one inescapable conclusion: the profession could not rely on *any* political party. Dr Dain replied that he had always sought to avoid party politics, urged that the plebiscite should be left to make its impression on the public mind, and secured approval for a resolution milder than that passed in January before the plebiscite had ever taken place. At the meeting of the Representative Body – to be held on 17 March – a call was to be made for such changes in the Act 'as are necessary to maintain the integrity of medicine and to prevent doctors being turned into State servants'. The Representative Body was therefore 'to express the hope that the Government will make it possible for the profession to co-operate by making such changes, and states its view that it is not in the best interests of the public and of medicine for members of the profession to enter the Service until such changes are made'. Both the terms of this resolution and the delay in summoning the Representative Body were interpreted by some diehards as signs of weakness in the leadership.

Bevan himself appeared unperturbed. A different kind of plebiscite had passed a different verdict. The Gallup Poll had asked the general public the simple question: What is your main feeling, that the new Health Service is a good or a bad thing? Sixty-nine per cent said 'good', 13 per cent 'bad', 7 per cent 'neither' and 19 per cent 'don't know'.[1] In public, Bevan turned aside from the dispute with the B.M.A. to the larger prospects of the scheme. 'After 5 July,' he said at the annual meeting of the Institute of Almoners on 12 March,

the Minister of Health will be the whipping-boy for the Health Service in Parliament. Every time a maid kicks over a bucket of slops in a ward an agonized wail will go through Whitehall.

[1] The same Gallup Poll asked the question of those who claimed to know what the Bevan-B.M.A. dispute was about: In the main, would you say your sympathies are with the doctors or against the doctors? The replies were 30 per cent 'with the doctors', 28 per cent 'against doctors', 6 per cent, 'don't know'. Among the well-to-do there was a four to one majority supporting the B.M.A. while the attitude of the poorer groups was mainly against the doctors.

After the new Service is introduced there will be a cacophony of complaints. The newspapers will be full of them. I am sure some doctors will make some irate speeches. The Order Paper of the House of Commons will be filled with questions. For a while it will appear that everything is going wrong. As a matter of fact, everything will be going right, because people will be able effectively to complain. They complain now but nobody heeds them. What the Health Act will do after 5 July is to put a megaphone in the mouth of every complainant, so that he will be heard all over the country. As the months go on and the limelight of publicity is brought to bear upon every aspect of the Health Service, for a while it will be almost intolerable. But this public scrutiny will have a medicinal effect . . . The Health Service is being launched in stormy waters, but then the launching of any big ship causes considerable water displacement. It is hopeless to expect such a service to be started without controversy. But it will be a very great revolution. It is being watched by every country in the world. There will come over here a stream of visitors to find out how it works and how its difficulties are being resolved. We shall of course find from time to time that alterations and adjustments have to be made. We are not ridden by doctrine; we are a nation very largely of visionary empiricists, able to adjust things where necessary, and between us we shall have a standard of health service that will be the envy and admiration of the world.

No signs of readjustment were evident at the meeting of the Special Representative Body on 17 March. 'The Representative Body,' reported the *British Medical Journal,* 'was in a decisive mood and inclined to think that the Council's recommendation was not worded in strong enough terms.' Lord Horder set the tone in an opening speech. 'We believe,' he said, 'that the Association regards the points at issue, as we regard them, not as bargaining points, but signs of the doctor being a free man to practise his science and art in his patients' best interest . . . We must not yield on any of the points which, collectively and individually, spell the doctors' freedom.' A few resolutions specifying particular demands on which the leaders should insist were turned down on the grounds that they were either embraced in the Council's resolution or would weaken the Council's hands. When one heretic suggested that negotiations should be opened and concessions made, provided an Amending Act was passed to ensure that a whole-time salaried service would not be introduced, the proposition was condemned as 'a frightful exposition of appeasement' with hardly a hand raised in its favour. Several resolutions were passed reinforcing the impression that the B.M.A. would not yield an inch. One instructed the Council to draw up an alternative health scheme of its own. Another warned the Government that the introduction of the scheme would lead to 'a state of chaos'. A third condemned the possibility of intervention by 'Quislings'. Yet an-another revealed that the whole attack of the B.M.A. was being broadened. Many delegates chose to believe that the Minister was on the run, and that there were other reasons, apart from the continuing dispute, why the Service could not be introduced. A resolution from Guildford ran as follows: 'That in view of the recent plebiscite result . . . the Representative Body, whilst agreeing with a comprehensive health service available to everyone, requests that it should be postponed until the necessary hospitals and other facilities have been built and equipped, and the personnel for a complete service have been trained.' Guildford merely echoed Dr Dain. 'The Minister's power in this Act is absolute,' he said. That was the core of the doctors' case. But Dr Dain had also come near to assuming that the Service was unworkable, doctors or no doctors. 'This Act,' he said, 'is a paper service and nothing more. [*Applause*] The people who have been promised a free-for-all service available to everybody are going to be very greatly disappointed. The Service will not and cannot be there on 5 July or any reasonably approximate date. A wise Government would have thought it the proper way to start such a Service by stages. I hope we shall not lend ourselves to any idea that the Service can be properly implemented by the given date. The failure of the Service must recoil on the people who produced it well knowing that it was impossible to implement it.' [Applause]

Once more Dr Dain had placed himself at the head of his army. The Council's policy was overwhelmingly approved and, to sustain the leaders, two final resolutions were passed. One, put through in private session, established an Independence Fund to finance the profession's activities,[1] and another from Doncaster slipped through as members were departing: it pledged support for the Council 'in any action it may take'. The Independence Fund, backed with 'an initial contribution' of £400,000 from one of the doctors' trusts, would, according to the Chairman, Dr Gregg, 'provide the sinews of war for the conduct of the campaign'. It was linked with warnings that the Government would soon be issuing leaflets describing the detailed terms of the Service to patients and doctors, and promises that other leaflets and a handbook for the guidance of practitioners would be distributed from B.M.A. headquarters in a matter of days.

Bevan was still unperturbed. 'I am sorry,' he told the dinner of the Women's Public Health Officers' Association, the day after the Special Meeting at Tavistock Square, 'that the new Health Service is being launched rather stormily. I would have liked to see the Act come into operation on 5 July – and I still believe it will – with the enthusiastic co-operation of the whole medical service. There has been some little misunderstanding which I am sure will be cleared up. We are going ahead with our preparations, the machinery is being established, and the whole mighty fabric of the new scheme is slowly being woven before our eyes. I believe that 1948 will be regarded as a year of emancipation for many poor people in this country who are suffering pain.' A few days later – on 2 April – the Ministry of Health issued the details of the duties which would be required of doctors and dentists accepting service and the steps patients must take to place their names on doctors' lists.

Outwardly, as the stage was set for the climax, there was no glint of reconciliation. The Minister and the B.M.A. were stolidly glaring at one another. Some of the newspapers – headed by Lord Kemsley's chain – prophesied chaos with ill-suppressed satisfaction. 'OUT-PATIENT QUEUES MAY SWAMP HOSPITALS', ran one headline in the *Empire News*. 'Only one person in three,' it said, 'is expected to get free doctoring under the Government's health

---

[1] This was a serious error, for the fund met with an extremely poor response and the fact was not lost on Dr Hill. In his memoirs, he harps on the incident: 'The modest success of the fighting fund was a chastening reminder that some hands are more active in applause than in signing cheques.'

scheme due to start on 5 July. 'STATE HEALTH SERVICE UNLIKELY
ON 5 JULY', ran another headline in the *Daily Graphic* on 5 April.
That same issue of the *Graphic* carried a report that a move
towards compromise had been made by Lord Moran, President
of the Royal College of Physicians. But the *Graphic* was convinced that nothing of significance had occurred. 'It is felt,' it
said, 'that the onus rests on the Government to put forward some
new formula to meet all the doctors' demands or else their scheme
will break down completely. The view is held in many quarters
that so long as Mr Bevan remains at the Ministry of Health
no settlement can be reached.' Conceivably the *Graphic*'s reports
were influenced by the spirit in which most of the delegates to
the Representative Body returned to their districts. Many of
them started organizing what they called Local Independence
Groups designed to persuade doctors to band together in mutual
undertakings for concerted action while they awaited further instructions from headquarters.

But in fact, ever since the plebiscite, Bevan had reopened
his private lines of communication with the prima donnas. On this
occasion Lord Moran was the chief intermediary, but Sir Alfred
Webb-Johnson and Mr William Gilliatt, President of the Royal
College of Obstetricians, were also at some stage parties to the plot.
The first concrete result, kept remarkably secret for some days, was
a resolution passed at the Comitia of the Royal College of Physicians
on 22 March urging that the Minister should make clear, in an
Amending Act, that a whole-time service would not be introduced
by Regulation and that all Regulations affecting the Service should
be subject to a special procedure. Mr Gilliatt backed the resolution
in full, while Sir Alfred Webb-Johnson gave his support with the
proviso that the suggested legislation 'would not by itself be sufficient to secure the willing co-operation of all branches of the profession'. Immediately, when the Royal College's resolution was
made public in the first days of April, a welcoming response came
from many quarters. 'The Government is pleased with the intervention,' reported the *Manchester Guardian*, '. . . it has cleared
away many hazards by dwelling on one major issue – whether
doctors in the Health Service are to become whole-time salaried
officials or not. It has moreover chosen an issue on which Mr Bevan

could satisfy the profession without budging an inch from his position. He has been as specific as a Minister could be, short of putting a clause in a Bill, in asserting that neither he nor the Government intends the basic salary to be the thin end of the wedge.' The proposal, said *The Times*, 'would go a long way towards meeting the demands of the B.M.A.' A spokesman of the B.M.A. itself (could it have been Dr Hill or, rather, could it have been anyone else?) welcomed the move as 'a step forward' – adding hastily: 'But it does not by any means go the whole way to meet the doctors' objections.' Considering that the Representative Body had specifically rejected a proposal in precisely the same terms as Lord Moran's, he could hardly say less. The remarkable fact was that he had said so much.

Dr Dain stepped in to stop the rot. 'I should be failing in my duty,' he wrote in a letter to *The Times*, 'if I did not make it clear that this single change, suggested by many and now repeated by the Royal College of Physicians, would not be regarded by the profession as sufficient and satisfactory.' Dr Dain was naturally piqued that the initiative seemed to be out of his hands. He was at pains to emphasize that Lord Moran had said nothing new. A cryptic final paragraph added that contacts between the Minister and the profession need not be 'circuitous'. 'Corkscrew Charlie' was at his manœuvres again. But no time was allowed for the Representative Body or even the *British Medical Journal* correspondents to unmask the Royal Quislings. Dr Dain's letter appeared on the morning of 7 April and that afternoon Bevan transformed the situation in the House of Commons. He and his officials had always reckoned that an eleventh-hour rapprochement with the doctors must be sought – especially as so much they were asking for he had never intended to withhold. Made too soon the move would be interpreted as weakness or dismissed as worthless. Delayed too long, the benefits would be squandered. Lord Moran's intervention, partly contrived in the Ministry, offered the exact moment.

Bevan's new statement was framed in the most moderate and uncontroversial terms. 'I have been trying,' he said, 'to determine for myself what it is that is really and sincerely worrying the doctors.' He had come to the conclusion that 'the unease and restlessness' derived from 'some instinctive fear – shared by many well-meaning men and women – that, although the Act does not propose it, and although the Government have themselves denied it, the real objective is a full-time salaried State medical service. It is this fundamental point which I want now to tackle once and for all.' The Royal College of Physicians had made 'the most useful suggestion' that the point should be made statutorily clear and the Government accepted it 'most cordially'. Already it had been promised that new legislation would be introduced, if necessary, to clarify any disputed legal point about particular agreements. A new provision forbidding the establishment of a full-time salaried service could be brought in at the same time. Moreover, Bevan offered a further alteration in the scheme to fortify the assurance. His plan for the £300 basic salary had always been envisaged as a method of helping the young doctor. He would be quite prepared to agree – and this would require no fresh legislation – that after three years every doctor would have the choice whether he wished the basic salary to continue or whether he preferred to be paid entirely by capitation fees. He also repeated – what had been repeated many times before – that there was no intention to interfere with the doctor's right to express himself in speech or writing with absolute freedom and that the chairman to preside over the appeal tribunal under the Act would be a lawyer appointed by the Lord Chancellor. Altogether, he hoped that his announcement would 'finally free doctors from any fears that they are to be turned in some way into "salaried civil servants" '. In the House of Commons and the House of Lords the statement was welcomed on all sides. Lord Moran claimed that the Minister had 'boldly met the doctors' main fears', and deserved to be rewarded 'by the loyal support of all reasonable members of the profession'.

Dr Dain and his colleagues were now confronted with their most painful decision. The main proposal of the Royal College of Physicians, accepted by the Minister, had been specifically condemned as 'appeasement' at the last meeting of the Representative Body; Dr Dain himself had underlined his dissatisfaction in his letter to *The Times*. Moreover there were fresh signs of irritation at the intervention of Lord Moran and his fellow Presidents; had they not repeated their trick of January 1947 with even more devastating results? The innermost fear of the doctors' leaders –

7*

that their army might become divided and confused – had suddenly acquired new menace. Public sympathy had swung sharply
in favour of the Minister; it could only be countered if the B.M.A.
responded with a comparable spirit of conciliation. After the first
meeting of Dr Dain and his closest associates on 8 April the news
leaked out that they favoured a new plebiscite. On the same day
they drew up a fourteen-point questionnaire to the Minister to
which he replied four days later. In reality, the exchange carried
the matter no further than Bevan's statement to the Commons. On
12 April he had a meeting, not with the full Negotiating Committee, but with a B.M.A. deputation, consisting of Dr Dain and Dr
Hill and four other leading B.M.A. figures. The discussion was
polite and indecisive. Confusion in the B.M.A. leadership was
reflected in the *British Medical Journal* of 17 April. Considerable
space was devoted to a defence of the intervention by the Royal
College of Physicians. 'It would be undignified,' said the editorial,
'to indulge in a squabble for priority for a suggestion that has been
fairly widely mooted, and in a country where freedom of opinion
is held dearly it would be, to say the least of it, paradoxical to challenge the right of any organization to state its opinion on a matter
that is the concern of everyone.' In other words, Lord Moran had
been exercising his right to write and speak freely on which the
B.M.A. had so adamantly insisted. The defence of the meddling
Presidents was not to the taste of Dr Dain. A bare four weeks before
he had seemed to have his army unitedly behind him. Suddenly he
was stabbed in the back. Even the *British Medical Journal* was
faltering in its allegiance.

The awkward debate was resumed at a meeting of the full B.M.A.
Council, hastily summoned by telegram for 15 April. This was the
most crucial Council meeting in the Council's history, and, significantly, it is one of the few *not* reported in the columns of the
British Medical Journal. Dispute still prevails about what really
happened, but the main outlines appear. A fierce debate took place
about whether the situation had changed sufficiently to justify a
new plebiscite and whether this step could be taken without calling
a further meeting of the Representative Body. Dr Dain was persuaded to reverse his judgment of a few days before; he had in any
case always been dubious about the second plebiscite, believing

with much justice that the mere decision to hold it would be tantamount to an admission that the Council wanted a reversal of the
previous verdict. However, Dr Dain's leadership was, in effect,
challenged. Strong pressure from those favouring the new plebiscite ensured that Dr Hill should be heard, and he turned the meeting. A few days earlier he had addressed a meeting of the Insurance
Acts Committee, a body of some fifty members representing all
insurance practitioners, whether members of the B.M.A. or not.
There each member had been called upon to answer the specific
question: has the proposed Amending Bill altered the attitude of
practitioners towards entry into the Service? All but a handful
replied that it had. This decision supported reports received from
throughout the country that the mood was changing. Even doctors
who backed the past policy of the Council had indicated that they
personally would be joining the Service. The old spectre which had
never been absent from the leaders' mind was now reviving – the
danger that the pre-1913 history might be repeated. After Dr Hill's
speech, on a show of hands, a small majority favoured a new plebiscite. Yet clearly the battle had been evenly contested. For it was
also agreed that the plebiscite form should be accompanied by a
memorandum containing the words: 'Bearing in mind that what
we have secured falls short of what we sought, the Council's view
is that, while progress has been made to that end, the freedoms of
the profession are not sufficiently safeguarded.' Dr Dain's worst
fear had become real. Not merely was his army in disarray. Division had penetrated the High Command.

How serious was the split among the B.M.A. leaders was exposed
in the next few days. While the new plebiscite forms were being
despatched over the weekend of 18–19 April a cacophony of contradictory medical voices filled the air. Clearly there was no common assumption about what had actually been decided at the secret
Council meeting on 15 April. Dr Dain believed that the fight was
still on. At a meeting at Shrewsbury on 18 April he first secured the
passage of a resolution condemning the Minister's concessions as
insufficient and then elaborated the theme with strong fighting
words. 'If you deal with this plebiscite as you did with the last,' he
said, 'we can obtain everything necessary for the freedom of the
patients and ourselves before we go into this Service. We are ready

to see this campaign right through. We have all the material ready. You have the opportunity of standing fast in the position you took up at the last plebiscite.' Some criticism was forthcoming about the failure of the Council to reassemble the Representative Body before ordering the new plebiscite. Dr Dain's fighting mood was quite capable of parrying the charge. 'If we have the necessary majority,' he said, 'there will be no need to call the representative meeting because the deal will be off.' No fresh negotiations would be initiated until the Minister came to heel.

This stirring call was quickly taken up in other quarters. Twenty-six members of the Council and the Representative Body drew up a letter to be sent to the *British Medical Journal*, urging continued resistance 'so that no one can take our freedom from us'. Lord Horder carried a meeting of the Marylebone division of the B.M.A. in the same sense and issued a fervent appeal to the public and all members of the profession. 'The Minister,' he wrote, 'remains all-powerful . . . I would say this to the public: If you nationalize and regiment doctors you take a retrograde step both in the advance and in the service of medicine. To the doctors I would say: Give the same answer to the present plebiscite that you did to the last, for the conditions have not changed in respect of any of the fundamental points at issue. Do not be outwitted by the expert in political manœuvre. Be loyal to your patients, for whom alone you follow your high calling.' Others were horrified by these appeals. 'Whereas last time,' wrote the *Lancet*, 'the B.M.A. Council was really asking for a mandate to negotiate from strength, its chairman declares that it is now asking for a mandate to fight. If the profession follows this lead there are to be no more negotiations . . . All idea of compromise having been rejected, a campaign will be undertaken which is intended to oblige Parliament to accept "everything we think necessary" – a campaign which must be resisted by everyone who cares for constitutional government . . . Dr Dain's call to arms is as wrong as it is rash.'

Often the *Lancet* had been a lone voice in the medical press advocating courses of conciliation. But now behind the scenes powerful allies transferred to its side. The Shrewsbury speech alarmed several of the other members of the B.M.A. Council, including Dr Hill. Dr Dain was accused of speaking in a manner unauthorized by the Council meeting. Under pressure he retracted, first in a statement to the press and later in a letter to the *British Medical Journal* published on 24 April. His speech, he said, seemed to have caused 'some misunderstanding'. He wished to make it clear that he departed in no way from 'the careful and balanced statement' issued by the Council. 'The Minister of Health's concessions present us with a changed situation which makes the new plebiscite necessary. I would urge that it is the duty of every doctor to make up his own mind on the facts, and to decide whether Mr Bevan's concessions go far enough to safeguard the essential freedoms of the practising doctor.' This letter in fact marked the end of the battle.

Dr Dain and the *British Medical Journal* had changed from belligerence to neutrality. The Shrewsbury speech was not even reported in its columns. Instead the note became defensive. 'At all costs we must strive to preserve our unity and agree to differ, if differ we must, in a spirit of tolerance . . . We must, too, remind ourselves that the B.M.A. has declared its "whole-hearted desire" for a comprehensive medical service available to everyone in Britain.' The *Journal* sought to save something from the wreckage by reviving the new theme discovered at the last Representative Body meeting. 'The Edinburgh division of the B.M.A. on Sunday reminded us too of the need for "warning the public that the full range of service will not be available for many years to come". On this point the public has been misled by ill-informed publicists and it will need repeated correction.' Dr Dain struck the same note. The Minister, he said in a speech at Birmingham at the beginning of May, had gone 'only a little way' towards meeting the doctors. 'To jump straight into a Service of this magnitude is asking for trouble. We have not enough beds, nurses or doctors to run it properly . . . It is unwise to start this Service suddenly and completely on 5 July. We shall gain a great deal if it is postponed for six months.'

That muffled call to arms was delivered on the night before the new plebiscite results became known. Next day the B.M.A. Council met to consider them. A majority – 25,842 to 14,620 – still expressed disapproval of the Act. But this was not the essential figure. On the question of entering the Service, some 7,000 general practitioners had changed their minds and another 2,000 had not troubled to vote. A bare majority was still opposed to entering the Service, but among general practitioners the number expressing this view was 9,588 – a figure falling far short of the 13,000 which the B.M.A. Council had agreed upon as the total needed if all doctors were to be advised to stay out. For seven hours the Council studied the results and debated what should be their reaction. Then at last the choice could no longer be postponed. Provided the Minister was prepared to continue negotiations on the terms of the Amending Act and other issues, the Council recommended that doctors should join the Service. A resolution to this effect would be placed before a meeting of the Representative Body. The plebiscite results forbad any other course. 'To organize collective action on such an insecure basis,' wrote the *British Medical Journal* on 8 May, 'would be disastrous whatever the merits of the case.' Even so the *Journal*, like Dr Dain, still clutched at its last straw. 'Mr Bevan,' said the same editorial, 'has very few bricks at his disposal to build his new house, and the foundations of it even are still in the main only architect's plans. We foresee endless confusion in the administration of this new Service, and foresee too, that the public will express their disappointment in no uncertain manner.'

The reaction to the Council's decision in the next few weeks cast a glare of illumination on the whole campaign conducted by the B.M.A. leaders ever since the publication of the Beveridge Report in 1942. Some of these leaders had always believed in their hearts, whatever their show of resistance, that some form of national health service and, later, Bevan's plan in broad outline would come into operation. They could quote phrases from their policy statements paying lip-service to the ideal of a comprehensive service. But this was not the impression that their propaganda had purveyed and they themselves had become the victims of it. Multitudes of doctors had swallowed whole the charge that the all-powerful Minister was engaged in a dastardly attack on medical freedom. They had plentiful excuse. It was too fanciful to suppose now that the offer of an Amending Bill which left untouched so many of their complaints had transformed the situation. A flood of letters poured into the *British Medical Journal* complaining of the Minister's trickery and the B.M.A.'s betrayal. The 'colossal and fundamental mistake,' said one, was that the leaders had ever dabbled with the notion of a 100 per cent service. 'If we agree to work an all-in compulsory scheme like the Health Act,' said another, 'we shall sell out to Communism. I have voted "No" and I mean to vote "No" as consistently as Mr Molotov.' Even some of these who concurred with the Council's view did so with furious lamentations. 'The monster about to be born,' wrote another, 'seems capable of creating great misery. Since we do not possess the power of superfecundation all we can do is to palliate the Minister's evil potentialities.' Similar stridency was evident in the controversy outside the medical press. The Rev. Irving Bulman, Vicar of St Gabriel's, Cricklewood, called the Act 'the new health swindle'. 'If you are going to be ill, be ill now,' he told some of his parishioners, 'because Heaven knows what will happen to you if you don't. If you leave it till after 5 July you will probably make a job for me. This is what the Socialists call planning, but some of us call it the new lunacy. See what we have been brought to by a set of political tomtits.' And the belief that the fight was still on was not the view merely of a few freaks. Lord Horder made it clear that he would carry the struggle to the Representative Body. 'Up till a few weeks ago,' he said, 'we had the ball at our feet and I can tell you from my own observation that the Minister's anxiety was very great . . . Then, unfortunately, the ball was passed to the other side, by whom I don't know. I think we have, I hope only for a time, been outwitted by a political manœuvre.'

Confronted with these signs of open defiance against the Council's leadership, the leaders gradually devised a new tactic. Bevan's concessions, they averred, particularly the latest one, were immense and far-reaching. This hardly accorded with Dr Dain's final claim, on the eve of the plebiscite, that he had gone 'only a little way', or even with the official statement circulated at the time. Much play was made with the verdict in the *Economist*: 'Undoubtedly the doctors have won a big victory, for Mr Bevan does not easily climb down to the extent that he has done.' The *British Medical Journal* produced an elaborate editorial on this text entitled: 'What we have gained.' The whole battle was retraced back to the Beveridge Report. Every improvement, from the doctors' point of view, on the schemes drawn up by Ernest Brown and Henry Willink were represented as triumphs extorted from a recalcitrant Ministry of Health by the tenacity and unity of the B.M.A. Yet all these 'concessions' of any significance were incorporated in Bevan's original Bill and the Amending Bill merely proposed to give legislative form to pledges he had given of his own volition on the Second Reading and the Committee stage. Bevan himself and his Ministry officials regarded the Amending Bill as no more than a move which could help save the face of the B.M.A. leaders.[1] It gave away nothing which it had not always been intended to give. For the B.M.A., their new tactic had two merits. Not only did it help to rescue their prestige. It offered the only hope of preventing the army from being scattered.

Much the most influential intervention, backing the Council's view, came from Dr Alfred Cox, 'the Nestor of medical politics', as the *British Medical Journal* described him – the same Dr Cox who had denounced Bevan's Bill as 'National Socialism' and Bevan as a 'Medical Fuehrer' in March 1946. In a letter to the *Journal* he recalled the pre-1913 struggle in which he had participated, explaining how doctors had flocked to join the panel because they felt the concessions made by the Government satisfactory, while the leaders were still denouncing the scheme as unworkable and unacceptable. A quite unnecessary humiliation had been courted. 'Is history to repeat itself?' he asked. Was the B.M.A. in the same position of not knowing when it had won? 'I do not think that we have won a big victory,' he added candidly, 'because we have failed to hold what to my mind would be the chief security against a whole-time salaried service – namely the right of private property in the goodwill of medical practices.' But to continue any fight on this issue would be 'to fly in the face of what is possible'. The doctors had no friends left on this issue in any of the political parties and the press. 'A very considerable number of general practitioners (to my amazement) do not think it worth fighting for.' The numbers prepared

---

[1] Perhaps the most remarkable testimony to the manner in which Bevan had negotiated was given by Dr Talbot Rogers who was a member of the Negotiating Committee throughout. At a lecture given to the Royal Society of Medicine on 30 June 1971, he said: 'It is my contention that Mr Bevan, in spite of his claiming comparative virginity, knew all along what he wanted and the concessions he was willing to make in order to get it.'

for such a fight were just not enough. 'As an old medical politician, loving a good fight,' he concluded, 'I have never seen any good in refusing to face facts and in continuing to try to get the unattainable.' So the only course was to accept the verdict of the plebiscite 'ungrudgingly', not to 'fritter away' the power and prestige of the Association, and to enter the Service as unitedly as possible. Dr Cox's letter detected and guided the new prevailing mood, but it could not stop the outbursts from many others denouncing the 'abject surrender' or demanding the postponement of the appointed day.

Bewilderment and recrimination welled up and overflowed at the special meeting of the Representative Body on 28 May; at moments it appeared that the decision of the leaders was in jeopardy. A long series of resolutions critical of the Council had been sent in by the divisions and the morning began with an hour-long wrangle about how many of these should be taken before the Council's own recommendations. Fierce demands were made and rejected that the voting of individual Council members at the fateful 15 April meeting should be published. The first tough resolution condemned the calling of the new plebiscite as premature, prejudicial to the results and improper without the recall of the Representative Body. This was carried by 167 votes to 148. The snub to the Council added fresh intensity to the main debate which followed about entry into the Service. If the leaders could be defeated once, why not again? But in fact Dr Dain and his Council colleagues gradually reasserted their control. He skirted round the prickly question of his Shrewsbury speech. 'I was taken seriously to task about it [loud cries of, "by whom?"] by members of the Council.' He elaborated and extolled the concessions achieved, slightly weakening the effect by the admission: 'I was never so disappointed in my life as I was when the figures of the April plebiscite came in.' One after another the Council members sought to resist a clamour from the floor threatening to leave the Association leaderless and distracted. The redoubtable Dr Cockshut, who had failed to win support for the Council's policy in his own division of Hendon by a single vote, hurled himself into the fray, bravely arguing that the demand for opposition to the Minister's proposals about the sale of practices must at last be abandoned. 'If you enter a fight with the Government and lose, you lose everything. Anybody who advises you to

continue the fight will be lacking in a sense of responsibility.' Dr
Dain himself warmed to his task. The safeguards required, he said,
had been effectively secured. By the Amending Bill, the Association had gained 'the greatest victory against the Government'.
More eloquent still, however, were the latest figures he read out
about the numbers of doctors actually joining the Service. Right up
till a day or two before, the B.M.A. had been advising doctors and
patients that there was no urgency in signing the forms sent out by
the Ministry of Health. Yet among general practitioners already
26 per cent in England, 37 per cent in Wales and 36 per cent in
Scotland had joined. Clearly within a matter of weeks or even days
a majority of practitioners – not to mention patients – would have
flocked into the Service. The Representative Body, it seemed, did
not represent the doctors – most of them were not even troubling
to wait until that august assembly had passed its verdict. There was
little more to be said. The recommendations of the Council were
carried by large majorities. A vote of no confidence in the Council
leaders was crushed. As the afternoon session wore on the hall
emptied and some fifty of the most critical resolutions were counted
out for lack of a quorum. At last the doctors, as Lenin said of the
Russian armies in 1917, were voting with their feet.

A final forlorn effort was made to revive the controversy at the
Annual Representative Meeting in June. The diehards who had so
often carried all before them at these gatherings attempted to set
up a Commission of Inquiry into the conduct of the profession's
case throughout the critical weeks of 1948. When the proposal
seemed to be defeated on a show of hands, the platform ignored the
cries for a count and hastened on to the next business. Both the
platform and the floor knew what had happened without any
inquiry. The simple truth was that the Council *had* usurped the
authority of the Representative Body at their meeting of 15 April.
They had overthrown the specific decisions of the Representative
Body in March, resolved on the 'premature' plebiscite, gagged
their obstreperous chairman and bowed to the inevitable. It was
the only way they could be sure of muffling the raucous voices
which they themselves had once been so ready to excite and to
heed.

Yet, if the real fight was over, a few signs of rebellion still flickered. Throughout the weeks of June the dazed diehards of the B.M.A. continued to probe the mystery of the Council's volte-face and what one *B.M.J.* correspondent called 'the strangling of free speech in what I have hitherto thought to be a democratic body'. Sir Frederick Menzies launched an imposing correspondence in *The Times* favouring a postponement of the Service since it was 'quite impossible' for the Minister to provide the facilities required. Many other eminent authorities rushed to his support. Sir Lancelot Barrington-Ward, Surgeon to the King, thought the whole idea 'magnificent', but protested: 'They are in too much of a hurry about it.' Dr Dain, to his credit, would not be a party to these last distractions. On 18 June he wrote to *The Times*, making his grand gesture. Inevitably, he said, there would be difficulties and deficiencies at the outset, but, the decision having been reached, 'the profession will do its utmost to make the new Service a resounding success'. Lord Horder at once protested. How dared Dr Dain make such assertions when, at the last meeting of the Representative Body, a resolution had been passed demanding that 'the public be informed' of the grave shortage of personnel and equipment which must prevent the Government carrying out their pledges? Lord Horder, backed by the Marylebone division of the B.M.A., invited doctors to write him their views on the B.M.A.'s conduct. He and his friends would consult to see whether a new and more vigilant body could be established to assist those who did not join the Service. Dr Reginald Hale-White, his chief backer, insisted that the plan was not a last-minute attempt to sabotage the Act. 'The truth is that nothing is really ready. Nor will it be ready for two or three years. We are a nucleus of people who are trying to point out that the Government has sold the public a pup.'

Bevan killed the talk of postponement stone dead. 'It is stupid nonsense,' he told a meeting of nurses at the beginning of June. 'We never will have all we need. Expectation will always exceed capacity. If there is a shortage of doctors on 5 July, when the cash relationship between doctors and patients will disappear, it is very much more important that the doctors who are in short supply should spend their time looking after patients who really need to be looked after than that they should be looking after a lot of hypochondriacs who can afford to pay. I shall try to go about disguised after 5 July. Any mistake that is made I shall have to bleed for. I shall be going about like Saint Sebastian pierced by a thousand javelins.'

As throughout the whole controversy, the most remarkable contrast was the Bevan of the headlines who might be pardoned for imagining himself as Saint Sebastian and the Bevan who dealt directly with those who would have to organize and operate the new Service. Once all the other arrangements had been fixed, he called a meeting in London of all the people whom he had appointed to serve on the fourteen new Regional Hospital Boards. 'There must have been over three hundred of us gathered at that meeting, doctors, dentists, nurses, county councillors, voluntary hospital governors, all with experience of the considerable troubles besetting the hospitals and with no very clear idea of their future' – the scene stuck in the memory of Dr Talbot Rogers who sat beside the other gladiators, like Dr Dain and Dr Cockshut, on the Negotiating Committee throughout the whole affair:[1]

The Minister came onto the platform, flanked by all his senior civil servants. He said how grateful he was to us that we had each been able to accept his invitation to take part in the great adventure of building a new health service . . . He spoke pertinently for twenty minutes. He then stood up to questions for a further three-quarters of an hour. They were informed and searching questions from people who knew their hospitals and their problems. He answered every question quickly and spontaneously; he did not refer to a single one of his advisers; occasionally he would say he had no answer for that question – that was one of the matters he had chosen us to resolve – and on the few occasions he had to say this, it was the right answer. We, all of us, came away from that meeting impressed by the Minister's mastery of his subject, and persuaded that here was a man who knew exactly what he was doing.

The Minister's own last word was addressed to the National Association of Maternity and Child Welfare Centres on 25 June.

[1] Extract from the Wander lecture given by Dr Talbot Rogers at the Royal Society of Medicine 30 June 1971.

'The new Health Service,' he said, 'has been having a most uneasy gestation and a very turbulent birth, but all prodigies behave like that . . . This Service must always be changing, growing and improving; it must always appear to be inadequate. This is the answer I make to some of the Jeremiahs and defeatists who have said: "Why start this Service when we are so short of so many things?" '

So the great day came – 5 July 1948. On the day itself three-quarters of the population had signed up with doctors under the scheme. Two months later, 39,500,000 people, or 93 per cent were enrolled in it. A few months later again the figure had risen to 97 per cent where it has been stabilized ever since. The overwhelming bulk of the middle class had joined with the working class; all the prophecies of boycott and disaster were confounded at the outset. More than 20,000 general practitioners, about 90 per cent, partici-pated from the scheme's inception. Of course there were deficien-cies and difficulties, but there was no 'endless confusion' as foretold by the *British Medical Journal* a bare two months before. The Select Committee on Estimates passed its general verdict on the first year of operations. 'The scheme,' it said, 'is settling down with surprisingly little friction.'

Bevan's own personal relations with the B.M.A. were soon re-stored to the happier terms which had prevailed in 1945 and 1946; the old sardonic exchanges were renewed. In the newly recovered atmosphere of relaxation one B.M.A. leader asked him: 'What, Mr Bevan, is your long-term prospect and hope for members of the profession?' He replied: 'A high incidence of unemployment.'

But he did not always have the last word. One evening the regular inhabitants sat in our Smoking Room corner, and the conversation turned on the remark allegedly made by Seymour Cocks, the wit-tiest of the company. It was he without doubt, most of us thought, who had once, in the thirties, described Sir John Simon as 'the worst Foreign Secretary since Ethelred the Unready'. But Nye teasingly disputed the claim and accused Seymour of plagiarism. 'Never mind about that,' said Seymour, with a smile sweeter even than Nye's own, 'at any rate no one disputes that you're the best Minister of Health since Willink.'

Some political disputes associated with the National Health Service, particularly with its finances, belong to later chapters of this book. Within the Service itself developments have occurred which Aneurin Bevan directly opposed or deplored. Other developments which he hoped to see – for example, the establishment of health centres – have never come to fruition on the scale he envisaged. His aim was to make the best standards of medical treatment universal throughout the country; the ideal is still far from fulfilment. He himself was always ready to suggest proposals for the reform of his own administration, especially to make it more democratic.[1] Yet when all these qualifications are accepted, the major achievement remains. The prodigy has lived and the furious controversies of the 1945–48 epoch have died. The general idea of the Service devised by Bevan stands intact while the forebodings of his opponents are forgotten. Few victories in politics have ever been so conclusive. A postscript, anticipating the sequence of years, may be permissible.

The Service won national approval, immediate and lasting. In the general elections of 1950 and 1951 the Labour Party presented it as the greatest of the Labour Government's measures of social reconstruction. Conservative propagandists offered an alternative historical theory. While striving to expunge from the public memory the record of votes cast by Conservative M.P.s against the Second and Third Readings of the Bill, and the final vote on 9 February 1948 against the implementation of the Act five months later, they sought to restore the Service to its status as an all-Party achievement. Indeed a too casual reading of Conservative Central Office hand-outs might suggest that the National Health Service was a war-time brain-child of Sir Winston Churchill, successfully delivered despite the clumsy and callous midwifery of Aneurin Bevan.

In May 1953, the then Conservative Minister of Health, Mr Iain Macleod, appointed a Committee, presided over by Professor

---

[1] How Bevan believed that 'election is a better principle than selection' and why he believed this principle must eventually be applied to the Health Service he described in *In Place of Fear*, p. 91. But he also believed that the achievement of this aim must be dependent on the reform of local government, and this aim he described most fully in an article for *The Municipal Journal*, published on 12 March 1954. See page 266.

Guillebaud, to review the present and prospective cost of the Service and 'to advise how, in view of the burdens on the Exchequer, a rising charge upon it can be avoided while providing for the maintenance of an adequate Service'. Many, including Bevan himself, regarded this as a partisan resort designed to expose and isolate the Service as the most extravagant feature of the Welfare State and one which any prudent government must curb or curtail. But when the Committee reported to Parliament in January 1956, all such hopes or fears were confounded. Few institutions in this country – certainly few private industries – have ever been subjected to such a detailed scrutiny as that which the Guillebaud Committee undertook into the Health Service. At the end all the widely publicized charges or suspicions of financial laxity were repudiated.[1] But that was not all. The impartial investigators bestowed a barely qualified blessing on the whole organization. 'We believe,' they wrote, as their main conclusion,

that the structure of the National Health Service laid down in the Acts of 1946 and 1947 was framed broadly on sound lines having regard to the historical pattern of the medical and social services of the country. It is very true that it suffers from many defects as a result of the division of functions between different authorities, and that there is a lack of co-ordination between the different parts of the Service. But the framers of the Acts of 1946 and 1947 had not the advantage of a clean slate; they had to take account of the basic realities of the situation as it had evolved. It is also true that even now, after seven years of operation, the Service works much better in practice than it looks on paper . . . We are strongly of the opinion that it would be altogether premature at the present time to propose any fundamental change in the structure of the National Health Service.

[1] Extracts of the following nature from the Report (Cmd 9663) could easily be multiplied: 'It may come as a surprise to many to find that the National Health Service has absorbed a decreasing proportion of the country's resources since the year 1949–50 – i.e., the first full year of the Service' (para. 21). 'The widespread popular belief that there has been an increase of vast proportions in both the money cost and the real cost of the National Health Service is not borne out by the figures . . .' (para. 23).

Similar tributes continued to come from other independent quarters. Much the most exhaustive American survey of the Service was that conducted by Dr Almont Lindsay, professor of history in Mary Washington College of the University of Virginia and published in January 1963.[1] He traced the results of many of the 1945–48 controversies, showing how considerable had been the achievements in the co-ordination of the hospitals, the better distribution of doctors, the expansion of the services provided by local authorities, and the protection of the doctor's freedom and the enhancement of his status and opportunities. He examined every aspect of the Service in the utmost detail and passed his verdict:

> While the National Health Service is something magnificent in scope and almost breathtaking in its implications, certainly ten or twelve years hardly permits a definitive judgment. As a growing evolutionary program it will be reappraised from time to time. With its origins deeply imbedded in the past, the Service is giving good performance in spite of blemishes. In the light of past accomplishments and future goals, the Health Service cannot very well be excluded from any list of notable achievements of the twentieth century. So much has it become part of the British way of life, it is difficult for the average Englishman to imagine what it would be like without those services that have contributed so much to his physical and mental well-being.

More notable even than these outside judgments was the later verdict of the medical profession. When Aneurin Bevan died in July 1960, the editor of the *British Medical Journal* (the same formidable controversialist who had been in charge of the paper between 1945 and 1948) paid tribute to 'the imagination and flexibility' of 'the most brilliant Minister of Health this country has ever had . . . When he became Minister of Health in 1945, Mr Bevan made it his business to understand, so far as he could, just what kind of a profession the medical profession was. He visited hospitals and research units and discussed the problems of a health service with many individual doctors and groups of doctors. But we

[1] *Socialized Medicine in England and Wales. The National Health Service 1948–1961* (Oxford University Press).

doubt whether he really understood the professional mind and the professional man. For him the National Health Service was at the very centre of politics, and we believe that most medical men would think that that is not the place for a profession practising an art and pursuing a science.' On the establishment of the Service the *British Medical Journal* had its own individual assessment which it supposed would win a subsequent, wider acceptance. 'The historian who will be able to view these events dispassionately in the future,' it wrote, 'may come to the conclusion that after 1911 the principal architect of the National Health Service was the medical profession itself.'

One historian, or rather autobiographer, who would not make the claim in quite those terms, Dr Hill, writing his memoirs as Lord Hill in the year 1964, was ready to acknowledge: 'Whatever the flaws in the Service today, nothing can detract from the greatness of the unified hospital plan', and he knew who was the author. 'The most imaginative feature of Aneurin Bevan's proposals was the fusion of voluntary and local authority hospitals into one national co-ordinated hospital scheme. He exhibited rare courage . . .' And the same Lord Hill even prepared to concede victory on another front. 'Whether the abolition of the ownership of medical practices has, in fact, reduced the clinical independence of general practitioners in the Service, I find it difficult to say. My guess is that it has not . . .'[1]

Another medical opinion was even more generous and comprehensive. In 1958 all the medical institutions of the nation, headed by the Royal Colleges and backed by the B.M.A., appointed a Medical Services Review Committee presided over by Sir Arthur Porritt, to examine the whole working of the Service. Its conclusions, published in 1962, were too muted to cause much stir. The concept of a national health service was held to be sound. 'No other country,' it said, 'has attempted to provide organized medical care on so comprehensive a scale as Britain.' The 'most unfortunate aspect of the first fourteen years' of the experiment was that 'the health services of the country have been used for electioneering propaganda and become the subject of party friction'. Yet some interest may attach to the authoritative view of this body on the

[1] *Both Sides of the Hill* by Charles Hill, p. 99.

vexed question of clinical freedom. 'When the National Health Service came into being,' it said, 'fears were expressed about possible effects upon the general practitioner's clinical independence. At that time much emphasis was laid by the profession on the need to preserve the doctor's freedom. So far as we can judge these fears expressed in 1948 have so far proved to have been largely unfounded.'

The Porritt Committee's Report was reviewed in the *Daily Telegraph* on 2 November 1962 by Sir Henry Willink. 'Having presented to Parliament in February 1944 the Coalition Government's outline of the Service then envisaged,' he wrote, 'I have been intensely interested in this review of the outcome of that great wartime project.' Sir Henry continued more modestly: 'It was not my privilege to introduce the resultant legislation, but it is true to say that except in one respect, there was no fundamental departure from the wartime scheme.' And what could that exception be? 'This is an opportunity for me to admit that in my view the Labour Government was right when it undertook the daunting step of taking over 1,334 voluntary and 1,771 municipal hospitals.'

Sir Henry's magnanimity, however, had limits. His review did not mention the name of Aneurin Bevan. Possibly he had an excuse; it was not mentioned either in the Porritt Committee's 'review of the Medical Services of Great Britain', not even in the 'Historical Background' with which the bulky treatise opened. Thus, as the *British Medical Journal* so perspicaciously foresaw, the historians could rewrite history. Future generations may learn that Aneurin Bevan did not make the National Health Service; he inherited it from that much underrated social visionary Sir Henry Willink. After all, did not Jesuit scholars in the nineteenth century teach children in their schools that Napoleon was a general employed by Louis XVII?

5

STEEL

1947–1948

A matter of business . . . not really a party political matter at all.
—HERBERT MORRISON in 1946[1]

ALL GOVERNMENTS, particularly those that aspire to be Left-wing, need momentum as well as poise and toughness; they must grapple with the crises which crowd upon them but they should also know where they want to go. It says much for the inspiration of the 1945–50 Government, and for the vitality of the Labour movement which sustained it, that amid all the hurricanes, domestic and foreign, which blew Ministers off course, they still had energy enough to argue about their Socialist aims. 1947 was the year of trial, starting with the fuel crisis in the coldest of Februaries and mounting to the convertibility crisis in August which in turn brought the cuts in the capital investment programme and all the consequent injury to so many hopes. Any nerve could weaken in the face of this catalogue of disaster. Yet all through this same year one of the major controversies behind the scenes, occasionally emerging into the House of Commons and outside, centred upon what might be considered, and some did consider, an irrelevant, distant Socialist commitment – the undertaking contained in *Let Us Face the Future* to nationalize the steel industry. Aneurin Bevan was more passionately attached to this item in the Party programme than any other member of the Cabinet, and, despite his overwhelming preoccupations at the Ministry of Health, he was ready to do battle for it, as if in defence of his own child.

Not merely did his interest derive from the fact that he had

[1] Quoted in Duncan Burn, *The Steel Industry 1939–1959* (Cambridge University Press, 1961), p. 291.

219

within his constituency the most modern and famous steel works in the country; rather it was that the experience of Ebbw Vale illustrated the nature of capitalist crisis in Britain, offered the classic proof why competitive industrialism could never be expected to solve the nation's problems. Ebbw Vale and steel became part of the texture of Aneurin Bevan's Socialist thinking and gave it an appropriate hardness. Never had he forgotten the interview he had in the early thirties with Neville Chamberlain's expert on policy for the old distressed areas when, in his first years as a young M.P., he had been fighting for the reopening of the steel works in Ebbw Vale, and when indeed half the working population of the town was without a job. The appalling answer from the expert concerned not only Ebbw Vale and the common excuse that a narrow valley twenty miles from the coast was not the best site for a steel works. Much more shattering was the assertion that Britain was already producing 'enough' steel; for the foreseeable future, the market could consume no more. That was what Bevan had been solemnly told as the last word in the conventional wisdom of the time. At that date Britain was consuming ten to eleven million tons of steel a year whereas if we had been using steel at the same rate per head of the population as the United States, it would have been necessary to raise the figure to nineteen million tons at least. Such was the ingrained defeatism of the leaders of British industry in the 1920s and 1930s; those were the decades when industrial hegemony was yielded to the United States. Bevan would never forget the lesson. 'We had failed to realize,' he wrote, 'that in Britain at least the propulsions of private economic adventure had lost their force.'[1]

But Ebbw Vale taught other more specific lessons. Despite entrepreneurial caution in the higher reaches of the steel industry, despite opposition from great far-seeing financial houses in the City, the works were reopened, and despite early setbacks, they prospered and made an essential contribution to the nation's steel requirements in the second world war. No one who had learnt about the technical requirements of a modern steel plant from Sir William Firth,[2] the man to whose independent vision Ebbw Vale owed its reawakening, was likely to be impressed by the claims of

[1] *In Place of Fear*, p. 72.
[2] See Volume I, p. 216.

the other steelmakers and their accountants, 'the pirates who pushed us on the rocks and boarded us', according to Sir William.[1] When, in the first months after 1945, in preparation for their resolute campaign against nationalization, the steelmakers started to spread the sedulous tale about their efficiency, their forethought, their readiness to serve the nation, Bevan could not listen with patience. Before the war, Britain's shortage of steel had only been concealed by slump. During the war, we had been so short of steel that precious lives had to be risked to bring imports across the Atlantic. After the war, the shortage of steel imposed one of the most severe limitations on the pace of the nation's recovery. True, during the last days of the Churchill wartime Government, the industry had produced what some called a 'deathbed repentance' plan proposing an expenditure of £168 million over a period of seven and a half years and designed to raise capacity by 1951 to a total of sixteen million tons. But Bevan was not impressed. Even though the sixteen million target would involve a vast expansion, it would still not be enough to supply a fully-employed Britain. Moreover, even on the industry's own reckoning, half the capital required for the programme was expected to come from the Government. The industry's attempts to raise capital from private sources soon proved conspicuously unsuccessful. So why, urged Bevan whenever the topic was broached, should the Labour Government have any second thoughts about its steel commitment? At first everyone seemed to concur, especially the men who mattered, Dalton, Cripps and Bevin in particular. Indeed the assumption of the whole Labour Cabinet was that steel nationalization would proceed at the proper time, and meanwhile many more urgent matters clamoured for attention.

But there was a special question about steel nationalization which soon dovetailed into the kindred questions about the Government's intention and will. Since the industry could not be taken over at once, since the Bill for the purpose must follow others in the legislative programme, how was it to be conducted in the interim? How was the necessary development to be pushed ahead without delay? What degrees of co-operation could be expected from leaders of the

[1] Quoted in *The Nationalisation of Steel* by George W. Ross (Mac-Gibbon & Kee, 1965), the best account of the steel controversy.

industry under suspended sentence of takeover? John Wilmot, the
Minister in charge at the Ministry of Supply, did his best to answer
these awkward inquiries and he worked under the critical surveillance of Herbert Morrison who had opposed the inclusion of steel in
Labour's nationalization programme ever since the Party Conference in 1944 had carried the Mikardo resolution to this effect against
his will. Morrison naturally saw all the difficulties of the post-war
period as a vindication of his foresight. Nonetheless, the Cabinet
did make a formal decision reaffirming the commitment in March
and April of 1946, an announcement to the same effect was made to
the House of Commons on 17 April 1946, and, despite a finely-
staged Churchillian uproar, the Labour majority in the House of
Commons gave its fresh backing to the policy in May. A *modus
vivendi* between the Government and the steelmasters was reached
in the establishment of an Iron and Steel Board in September.
Meantime, Wilmot went ahead with the preparation of his nationalization Bill which, in its main outline and despite some growth in
the opposition within the Cabinet, was formally approved by them
in April 1947. Given all the other distractions, no one could truly
say that the Government had been laggard or craven. If the Bill
could be introduced in the autumn session of 1947, good time was
available to see the measure through.

But one man in the Cabinet would never admit defeat for his
own predilections while there were still avenues to be explored and
stones to be turned. The drive to proceed with the measure in the
circumstances of 1947 offended against Morrison's deepest conviction of what Labour's proper strategy should be. When, therefore, Attlee invited him to undertake private discussions with Sir
Andrew Duncan, chairman of the British Iron and Steel Federation, to see whether the *modus vivendi* of the previous September
could be translated into a more enduring compromise, Morrison
was happy to oblige. The mission suited his nature exactly. Sir
Andrew had made the original approach to Attlee. Attlee's choice
of Morrison as the emissary is the proof – apart from Morrison's
uncorroborated testimony – that Attlee himself favoured the
search for a compromise. And, lo and behold, Morrison and
Duncan lost no time in patching up an acceptable formula. 'I got
the Federation,' wrote Morrison with staggering naivety in his

memoirs,[1] 'to the point that there should be an Iron and Steel Board with extensive powers including the power, subject to Parliament, to take over unsatisfactory undertakings . . . The Board would take over Steel House, a considerable concession.' Others might define the transaction as Steel House taking over the Board and with it the policy of the Government. But Attlee, according to Morrison, 'appeared to be very pleased', and promised to support the hybrid or 'halfway house' measure which these confabulations had devised. A change in Attlee's attitude could tip the balance in a wavering Cabinet.

Rumours of a compromise reached Bevan and he resolved to take his stand, in public, on the decision reached by the Cabinet in April. So far, he told a May Day celebration of the National Union of Quarrymen at Blaenau Festiniog, what the Government had done in the field of nationalization had been fairly orthodox; 'but when it sets about nationalizing the steel industry, then the band will begin to play. Suggestions will be made that some parts of the industry are efficient and satisfactory and so should be left alone, but I am opposed to the Government taking over the cripples and leaving the good things to private ownership.' A few weeks later at Morpeth he made the clear prophecy that the Government would nationalize the steel industry in the coming parliamentary session, and started to envisage what difficulties and enticements might arise if the House of Lords stood in the way. 'Steel is a great monopoly, and we cannot trust the manufacture of steel to the steel masters who in the past have made large profits by not making steel. If the House of Lords, as the last refuge of ignorant reaction in Britain, stands in the way, we shall take whatever steps are needed to set aside this power. It may not be entirely necessary to shut it up. We do not always do things like that in this country. We might leave them the toy and take away the sword.' At another meeting he took credit for the squeals of protest from many quarters which seemed to overwhelm the Government. 'Democracy means that if you hurt people they have the right to squeal. But when you hear the squeals you must carefully find out who is squealing. If the right people are squealing then we are doing the job properly . . . There is a biblical phrase: *Act so that thy enemy shall be aware of thee.* So

[1] *An Autobiography* by Herbert Morrison, p. 296.

far we have been all right and here is the whole delusion of coalition
or national co-operation. You cannot focus the full national will on
the main evils of society, because in a coalition there are people who
benefit from the very evils themselves.' These speeches were addressed to the movement outside and to his colleagues round the
Cabinet table, some of whom resented them the more since he was
expressing the official Party policy. Or rather, everything was
official except the two emphatic words: *next session*. That was
Bevan pushing to see whether the door was closed, and getting
ready, if need be, to kick it open.

In the last heated days of July and the first weeks of August 1947,
while the Ministers were drifting through the convertibility crisis
and the whole standing of the Administration was shaken as never
before, steel seemed mystically to emerge as the test of the Government's will over the whole range of policy. Some Ministers, headed
by Morrison himself, preferred to believe that the whole ferment
was a Bevan plot; who else cared about steel as he did and why did
the backbenchers, now bombarding the newspapers and every
Minister they could button-hole in the corridors, talk in accents so
like Bevan's own? But Morrison's mistake – and Attlee's – was to
imagine that most of the Party felt on this subject as tepidly as
themselves. Attlee's grip on the Party just at that moment seemed
more feeble than at any other period in his twenty-two-year
tenure of the leadership. At a series of hectic Party meetings he
seemed even more petulant and peremptory than usual and more
than once Morrison had to step in to his rescue. Precious little
detail of what had actually happened in the Cabinet trickled across
to Parliament, although the general atmosphere felt explosive. At
one of the early Cabinet meetings, when the results of the Morrison
manœuvres were reported, Bevan threatened to resign if the full
Bill for steel nationalization was not presented. Morrison later
claimed that only two other Cabinet Members supported Bevan's
opposition to the hybrid measure, but that Attlee withheld his
promised backing for it with the words: 'It looks as if the scheme is
unacceptable'. Presumably Cripps and Dalton were the two others
who opposed Morrison; Dalton was also considering resignation,
although both he and Cripps were seemingly more concerned about
Attlee's palsied leadership in general than about the specific issue

of steel. And, in the result, although the Cabinet rejected the Morrison scheme, he had his grain of compensation. The Cabinet was not committed to the major Bill in the next session: the matter of timing was still left open and Morrison lived to manœuvre another day. At the critical Party meeting a few days later he needed all his skills and gave a virtuoso performance. By now the Parliamentary Party was fully aroused. A resolution was moved demanding the full nationalization of the steel industry within the coming session, and it was backed by a petition signed by the overwhelming majority of Labour M.P.s outside the administration. If the resolution was defeated, so some of his Cabinet colleagues assumed, Bevan would carry out his resignation threat. On the other hand, if the resolution was carried, it would look like a hectoring instruction from the Party Meeting to a half-hearted humiliated Cabinet, and speaking for the divided Cabinet was the arch-Right-winger Morrison who never liked to occupy openly too Right-wing a stance before the Parliamentary Party in a Left-wing mood. How to take into his reckoning in the same twenty-minute speech all these varying pressures, emotions and ambitions: such is the rare accomplishment required by the Party manager. At the end of the stifling morning, when the chairman was just about to put the resolution, some unknown man of destiny, uninspired even, so far as we knew, by Morrison himself, moved the previous question which was carried amid scenes of total confusion – some Cabinet Ministers voting one way and some the other – by 81 votes to 77, with 90 abstentions. No one could tell who had won the day. Yet one conclusion was evident even in that harsh summer when the members of the Parliamentary Labour Party limped away to recuperate from the most shattering scene of political disarray which most of them had ever witnessed. A clear call about steel could have rallied and united the Party, but a temporarily paralysed leadership had shown itself incapable of giving it. The private approach to Sir Andrew Duncan and its sequel had come within a hair's-breadth of removing the immovable, insensible Attlee.

During that summer Dalton and Cripps tried to carry through their own clumsy plan to change the leadership and the corridors and tearooms thundered to the loyalist tread of George Brown and Patrick Gordon Walker engaged in the same contrivance. Bevan, as

8

we have seen, would not participate[1] but he did also figure in the disposal by Dalton of the offices which were not his to dispose. 'Cripps and I,' Dalton wrote,[2] 'wanted to give Bevan full scope in what should be a key office in the next chapter of Labour Government. There was much to be said for making him Minister of Supply with an urgent mandate to nationalize iron and steel. Both Cripps and I were keen to see this done, but Attlee was less keen, and Morrison wasn't keen at all. So this promising transfer could not be effected.' But Dalton, it seems, was so eager for the move that he renewed it later, after the anti-Attlee manœuvre had collapsed. Attlee did make suggestions to Bevan that he should go to either the Ministry of Supply or the Board of Trade but Bevan, in the midst of his negotiations with the doctors and grappling with (and still resisting) the proposed capital investment cut in his housing programme, had no wish to leave the Ministry of Health. On steel, he and Dalton had always been staunch allies. Dalton's solicitude and admiration for his most adventurous Cabinet colleague were certainly genuine. But Dalton could also make Bevan shudder at the ghoulish zest with which he launched himself and others into a new intrigue – particularly if the proffered victim happened to be one of his large menagerie of *bêtes-noires*, such as Morrison or Shinwell. A curious altruistic twist ran through Dalton's ambition. He thought little of self, was most eager to see his young acolytes promoted, was content if his Party antagonists of the moment could be trampled or shouted down in the process.

For Bevan, the affair was a victory but one which was qualified, even soured, by the struggle which led to it. Steel nationalization was to go forward; the hybrid solution had been killed; but any chance of passing the measure in the 1947–48 session would have to be forfeited. It was partly on the ground of the time needed for the major measure that Morrison had argued for the hybrid, and any new Minister taking over from Wilmot would be likely to favour more time to complete his proposals, which is what George Strauss, the new Minister, did. Moreover, postponement of the Steel Bill would mean introducing before it, in 1947, the accompanying Parliamentary Bill required to deprive the House of Lords of its

[1] See page 93.
[2] *High Tide and After* by Hugh Dalton, p. 246.

delaying powers; otherwise, once the 1945 Parliament was embarked on its two last sessions, the effective power to influence the date of the next election would have been yielded to the House of Lords. All these were additional reasons, in Bevan's view, why the Steel Bill should have been expedited. His concept of parliamentary strategy, contrasting so sharply with Morrison's, told in the same sense. This was the way to hold the initiative, to prove the Government's good faith to its followers in both Parliament and the country. Why should he have to fight so strenuously, even to the point of threatening resignation, in order to sustain a commitment already established and understood on all sides?

Still, it *was* a victory. Central to the whole of Bevan's thinking on these questions of Party strategy was his confidence that the next election could be won, that the Labour Government would therefore have longer than the five-year span of one Parliament to bring its projects to fruition. The postponement of the Steel Bill's introduction, although thoroughly undesirable, need not be fatal. Moreover, he could draw solace from the sudden upsurge of militancy within the Parliamentary Party and the manner in which the impetus from it was directed towards the Socialist goal of public ownership. When, at the beginning of the 1948 session, the Bill was eventually presented, a correct moral was drawn and one not altogether unpalatable to Bevan. The Steel Bill, said *The Times* (on 5 September 1948), 'is primarily a sop, a ransom paid to radical insistence . . . to the shrewd and successful demagogy of Mr Bevan'. It was introduced, confirmed the *Manchester Guardian*, 'to satisfy the yearning of the Left wing'. The decision, wrote the *Economist* in more alarmist terms (6 November 1948) 'was made because a handful of Ministers . . . have established a moral ascendancy over the majority of their colleagues . . . The introduction of the Steel Bill is the clearest example west of the Iron Curtain of the way in which a minority within a minority can achieve its aims'.[1]

The demagogue himself spoke in terms which showed how inextricably the argument about steel interwove with the rest of his political philosophy. Speaking in his constituency at Cwm he put his case in a manner which drew outcries of protest in London.

[1] Quoted in *The Labour Government and British Industry 1945-51* by A. A. Rogov and P. Shore (Blackwell's, 1954).

'The steelmakers,' he said, 'are strong and rich. Against them the people on their side have nothing but the courage of the ordinary man and woman. But I feel sure they will succeed. If and when they do, they will show by their example and the intelligent use of the ballot box that parliamentary democracy can overcome the powerful use of money by the steel barons. Such a victory will be a beacon to mankind throughout the world. On the other hand, should money-power triumph over parliamentary democracy, then those responsible may, in the end, be proving something they do not wish to prove.' Altogether an outrageous distortion, screamed the *Evening Standard* among others; yet the subtlety of the last sentence had apparently escaped the London leader-writers. It was the restatement in modern terms of the old famous exchange in Putney Church between Oliver Cromwell and Thomas Rainborough. 'If they that have no goods and chattels make the laws equally with them that hath,' said Cromwell, 'they will make laws to take away the property of them that hath.' 'And if it be,' retorted Rainborough, 'that all Englishmen cannot be free and some Englishmen have property, then you have said it, My Lord General, not me.'[1]

Some of Bevan's colleagues thought he had an obsession about steel. He could make it obtrude into discussions where at first thought it appeared to have no appositeness whatever. For example he kept on asking in season and out of season: 'How much steel do the Russians produce?' Few of his fellow politicians, none of the nation's military advisers seemed to bother to find out until he rammed home the implication. Yet he thought that question decisive. A nation producing barely 30 million tons a year, if indeed the Russians had reached that total, which had to service a population of 200 million was unlikely to launch an aggressive, full-scale war against allies with an annual production of some 120 million tons, and a potential of 180 million. Later, as we shall see, this potent argument was to help shape the whole of Bevan's individual attitude to foreign affairs. In June and July of 1948 – quite unknown and unsuspected by anyone outside the Cabinet room at the time – it was one factor in his mind prompting him to advocate

---

[1] *The Putney Debates.*

a course which provoked much amazement and even alarm among his Cabinet colleagues.

The issue was: how should Britain meet the Soviet challenge in Berlin? How should the British Government, along with the Governments of the United States and France, deal with the situation which suddenly arose when the Russians clamped down a blockade around the city, thus threatening to prevent the British, the Americans and the French from exercising their responsibilities under the quadripartite control of the city and to hold the beleaguered people of Berlin at their mercy? This presented the sharpest and potentially most menacing dilemma which the Labour Cabinet had known since 1945, and they had to face it at a time when most of the bravest hopes for reconstruction in post-war Europe had been blighted in a manner few had forseen.

The Continent was war-weary; across great stretches of it, especially in Germany, people were near starvation-point and were only rescued by the much-begrudged bounty of austerity-ridden Britain; and yet, insanely, one event after another threatened to thrust the nations back into war or at least into the crushing absurdity of fresh mobilizations and renewed ruinous military expenditure. In February, the Communists seized plenary power in Prague, and the shiver of fright and horror was certainly not confined to Central Europe. Everyone knew how events in that far-away country could shape the affairs of the whole planet. In Germany, the Soviet authorities blocked every proposal for settlement among the occupying powers. Tito's Yugoslavia was expelled from the Cominform, and there were even fears that, after a differing pattern, the subjection of Prague might be repeated in Belgrade. Response from the West was swift and far-reaching. A new Pact to ward off what some considered the imminent danger of aggression was signed in Brussels, and in Washington the necessary constitutional dispositions were made to make it an Atlantic Pact. And agreements were hastily and secretly reached, but without any formalities or conditions, whereby American bases, equipped with the atomic weapon, were established on British soil. Bevan, it appears, did not oppose or cavil at any of these measures in which the British Government participated. If he had, he would have been swept aside; the currents were moving much too strongly to permit any opposition. He may have had doubts about the first Western ripostes of 1948, but there is no evidence that he broached them. Not that he was a great admirer of Ernest Bevin's handling of foreign affairs, particularly in Germany. Indeed he had long been a bitter critic of the so-called 'dismantling' policy conducted in the zone for which Britain was responsible whereby factories were put out of business on the pretext of preventing the recrudescence of German militarism but in reality to appease the Russians and the Americans at the same time. The Russians demanded crude reparations; the Americans still retained remnants of the Morganthau plan for converting Germany into a pastoral country. Bevan from the start opposed these fatuities; partly because he was on record during the war in opposing a policy of vengeance, partly because he saw what fresh burdens these measures would impose on the British people as well as the Germans, partly because he was horrified at the injury which a British Labour Government might inflict on the German Socialists struggling to rebuild their fortunes in the country at large and in Berlin. So Bevan was no Bevinite on any definition whatever. He had long been growling his discontent against a policy towards Germany which he believed to be lacking in humanity and political imagination. But when all these events culminated in the Berlin blockade, when the Soviet leaders delivered so frontal a challenge, he favoured the boldest retort. He believed bold action would end the crisis most swiftly and he believed, moreover, that no risk of war was involved. The argument in London and in Washington was how Berlin was to be sustained; could it be done by an airlift? The difficulties looked prodigious and were certainly novel. But the alternative of sending through a force on land, covered by tanks, would mean risking a direct clash with the Russians. Yet this was the alternative Bevan preferred and argued for powerfully in the Cabinet. He was convinced that the Russians were as war-weary as everyone else, and, once their challenge was rebuffed, would take no action which risked war. He knew they had not got enough steel. As it happened, the airlift surpassed all expectations, even of its authors. Berlin was saved, and Bevan's assumptions were never tested. But many round that Cabinet table must have been freshly impressed by the assurance with which its youngest and most talkative member would not only expatiate on his theories but recommend action.

He was equally active behind the scenes on another aspect of German policy which had been uppermost in his thinking ever since the armistice and indeed long before. Just as steel was vital for Britain and for the determination of Soviet policy, no less might it be the arbiter of what kind of Germany would re-emerge from the ashes of defeat. What was to happen to the German coal and steel industry of the Ruhr, the great interlocking network dominated by half a dozen giant vertical combines, the Vereinigte Stahlwerke, Krupp, Mannesmann, Hoesch, Kloechnev and Gute Hoffnungshuette? Apart from owning almost the whole of the German steel industry, those six combines had owned before the war about 40 per cent of the Ruhr coal, as well as iron ore mines, limestone quarries, rolling mills, trading companies and engineering works. Ernest Bevin had assured the House of Commons in October 1946: 'It is the intention of the British Government that Germany's heavy industry shall be nationalized.' But no sufficient action accompanied those words, despite the fact that the bulk of the industry concerned happened to be in the British Zone. The Foreign Office doubtless believed they must act in collaboration with the Americans who preferred a policy of trust-breaking or 'demonopolization'. In any case, this excuse for inaction was fortified by the plausible argument that the Germans themselves must be responsible for the necessary action, that elections would soon take place there which would give electoral backing to the necessary measures. But Bevan could not be persuaded, as is shown by the letter he eventually wrote to Attlee on 4 November, and the conversation he had with Bevin a day later.

4th November 1948

My dear Clem,

GERMAN INDUSTRIAL TRUSTEESHIP SCHEME

I have had a hurried glance at the note prepared by the Foreign Secretary on the above. There has been no opportunity of seeing the actual text of the statement on future ownership. I appreciate the progress made in persuading the U.S. Government to modify their original position. I am, however, unhappy at the likely outcome of the action proposed.

Under the proposed law it appears that the German Government will be able gradually to dispose of the industries concerned if they are so minded.

The West German Government will be the first to have been elected since the early 1930s. It is bound to feel itself under the tutelage of the occupying powers and exposed to pressure from their business interests, particularly as the first Government is likely to be Right-wing.

In the event the industries are likely to be handed back to private ownership. Inevitably the West German Government would be strongly influenced by the new owners. While we find it necessary to protect ourselves from the steel interests, the West German Government may be without any such protection.

If these industries do pass into private ownership, the pacification of Europe will be made more difficult and agreement with East Germany hard to secure.

I would urge, if action has not gone too far, that some provision should be inserted in the new law to the effect that no transfer to private ownership will be permitted within five years of the passage of the Act. Such a provision would enable the new West German Government to consolidate its position.

Now that the present U.S. Government is to enjoy a new term of office, I think it worth while to test their reactions to this proposal before any further step is taken.

You may wish to call a special Cabinet but, in any event, I must place my views on record.

Yours sincerely,

ANEURIN BEVAN

Note on Foreign Secretary: *Future of German Industry*:

I met the Foreign Secretary, Mr Bevin, and Lord Henderson at 12 o'clock on Friday 5 November 1948 at the Foreign Office. The meeting was arranged following a telephone message from the Prime Minister who asked me to see the Foreign Secretary to discuss a letter I had written on the future of German industry.

The Foreign Secretary said that he had had a long tussle with the Americans to prevent them setting up conditions favourable to the private ownership of German industry. He had, however, finally persuaded them to agree that the fate of German industry ought to be settled by a freely elected West German Government and it would be both improper and unwise to fetter the action of that Government.

Mr Bevin said that the psychology of American businessmen, and particularly the bankers, was changing and they were unlikely to press for private ownership. They were moving away from the private control of industry even in America itself, though they would probably not call their aims Socialist, preferring to describe them as comparable with the T.V.A. Both Mr Bevin and Lord Henderson agreed that the West German Government, when elected, was unlikely to be of a political complexion hostile to public ownership of industry. Both of them stressed strongly that neither from the American nor the German side was there danger of my apprehensions being realized. They assured me that I could safely rest in the belief that a West German Government would, of its own initiative, wish for public ownership of key industries, particularly steel and coal.

I dictate this note for the record as I fear what may happen. I have already written of my doubts separately to the Prime Minister, and I need not repeat them here.

5 November 1948

This is not the place to examine the subsequent developments of the German coal and steel industries. Perhaps the development of the European Coal and Steel Community in some degree falsifies some of Bevan's fears, but the revival of the Krupp empire underlines what danger might have been averted if his warnings had been heeded.

Certainly Bevan's interest never waned in European affairs and German affairs – and particularly in what happened in those countries internally, in their domestic politics, which he believed would shape their external politics. He regarded the defeat of the German Social Democrats under the brave and independent Dr Kurt Schumacher in the first election in August 1949 as one of the

8*

blackest days in the history of post-war Europe. Undoubtedly the dismantling policy coupled with the feebleness of any Socialist initiative had contributed to the catastrophe. The interest of the Continent required a Socialist Germany, and as, in one after another of the European states, the Left suffered setbacks, failing to sustain the high expectations of 1945, Bevan attributed much of the failure to the total lack of interest of the Foreign Office in these aspects of foreign policy – to Ernest Bevin.[1] On one occasion – in October 1949, when the news came through to a meeting that the Socialists had actually won an election in Norway – he startled an Executive sub-committee with the comment: 'Oh, dear, what's gone wrong with Ernie's foreign policy there?' But such explosions were rare. All the conditions of the time dictated that he had to fight inside the machine. He was deeply committed to help ensure that the Labour Government succeeded, and he gave his whole energy to the task.

One scene during the spring of 1948 presented in microcosm the hopes and anxieties which possessed his mind as they did that of the Labour movement generally. He had a message for his friends and another for his enemies but it was not easy to deliver them both in the same speech. It seemed necessary almost to compress them into a single sentence, if his meaning was not to be bowdlerized. He was more than ever awakened to the problem of how a democratic government could enlist the enthusiasm of the people long enough to carry through great Socialist or reforming measures – especially when most of the means of communication were in the hands of the sworn opponents of Socialism. At the Scarborough Conference of the Party he used his opportunity to explore afresh this whole question, and he had unwittingly ensured himself in advance full attention from the newspapers. Speaking at the traditional Sunday

[1] Many German Social Democrats at that time thought the British Foreign Office was actively working for the victory of their opponents, the Christian Democrats, and that Ernest Bevin was carried along with them. The Social Democrats were often then characterised as the 'British' Party and the Christian Democrats as the 'American' Party. A few days before polling day in the German elections, Bevin made a tough 'anti-German' speech, along the lines of 'we in Britain don't forget what we suffered at the hands of the Germans'. Many Social Democrats believed that speech had lost them a huge number of votes.

pre-Conference rally he reiterated his theme: 'whether political democracy in Britain is sufficiently self-disciplined, sufficiently mature, sufficiently sophisticated and imaginative to be able to bring about the profound changes necessary without full revolution'. And then he added, for makeweight: 'Why should we who are responsible for clearing up the muddle of a century of capitalism allow ourselves to be scared by headlines in the press, the most prostituted press in the world, most of it owned by a gang of millionaires?'

Two days later, when he rose to make his main speech at the Conference, with the newspapers poised for their revenge, he was ready tactfully to explain how 'modern publicity put a megaphone in the mouth of a fool'; how the enemies of Socialism were 'trying to surround us in a cocoon of defeatism'; how the whole elaborate and wretched attempt to portray the British post-war economic achievement as a failure was a wretched distortion. 'The fact of the matter is that this nation in the last three years has been rescued from economic disaster by the productive capacities of the principles of Socialism . . . I say to the editors of the newspapers of Great Britain, who dig coal so industriously with their pens, that had it not been for the application of Socialist principles to mining last year many of them now would be out of a job . . . Let us take steel. Never was there a better example of the virtues of Socialism, because the workers in the steel industry are producing steel in the hope of Socialism, and the employers for fear of Socialism.' The facts about Britain's productive achievement were overwhelming, and yet it was still not enough. For one thing, 'the Marshall plan itself is absolutely essential in order to maintain full production in this country. If we did not have Marshall Aid, unemployment in this country would at once be raised to one or one and a half millions. We are deeply grateful to the generous inspiration that lay behind that great plan, but nevertheless we do not want this country to depend upon the charity of any nation in the world. We want independence. We do not like living on the aid given by any other nation. That is the reason why this Conference and this country has to lay the greatest possible emphasis at this time upon increasing our productive capacities in every way . . .' It was a serious summons, and yet it was also a joyous repudiation of the weary

Conservative picture of a nation so undernourished by austere rations that it was too weak even to work. 'Look at the starvelings on the sands outside,' he pleaded at last. 'As I have walked through the streets of Scarborough, I have seen a good many vinegary-faced women making acid comments on the Labour Party delegates at the Labour Party Conference, and they were all very well-dressed and very well-nourished.'

On the Tuesday morning, Bevan had been elected head of the poll in the elections for the Constituency Party Section of the National Executive. On that morning he was acclaimed with laughter and cheers. And on the Friday the same Conference carried a resolution *against* the advice of the same Bevan and demanded that the Government should introduce legislation to abolish the tied cottage. 'It is quite impossible,' Bevan had said, 'for a Conference of a thousand people, even if it is constitutionally proper, to determine the order in which the Parliamentary Labour Party and the Government introduces legislation into the House of Commons. It is for the Conference to lay down the policies of the Parliamentary Party, and for the Parliamentary Party to interpret those policies in the light of the Parliamentary system.' But Conference swept aside that plea, even from its hero of the hour.

Scarborough came almost midway in the life of the 1945 Parliament, just under three years since the last election, just over two years before the next one. For all the agonies and setbacks of the period, there was still a world to win. That was still his firm conviction.

6

'VERMIN'

1948

If the Tories give a man a bad name, must the Whigs hang him?
—WILLIAM HAZLITT

'THE DAY IS HERE', proclaimed the *Daily Mirror* in its best stentorian manner on the Monday morning of 5 July 1948, and on that day the Labour Government's great social security measures, headed by the National Health Service, came into operation. Amid so much other bleak news, here was certainly a theme for celebration, and on the night of 4 July the Prime Minister delivered a national broadcast which included a few words of graceful tribute to all political parties for the contributions made to the development of Britain's social services. On that same Sunday Aneurin Bevan spoke at the great rally held every year by the Labour Party in the north at Belle Vue, Manchester. He felt that Attlee's generosity to the other political parties was excessive and drew attention to the point when the statement was shown to him. Still, he had his own special reasons for a sense of release. He could set the achievement of the National Health Service in an historical context somewhat different from Attlee's and at the same time bend more of his mind to the topic which Attlee appeared to neglect altogether – the Government's general political strategy.

'The eyes of the world are turning to Great Britain. We now have the moral leadership of the world and before many years we shall have people coming here as to a modern Mecca, learning from us in the twentieth century as they learned from us in the seventeenth century.' These were the words from Bevan's Belle Vue peroration selected by the *Manchester Guardian* as the keynote of the speech, and they may sound far removed from party recriminations about ration cuts, the balance of payments and disinflationary budgets. But Bevan, as usual, had led to his climax by credible, imperceptible degrees. He had presented an elaborate moral defence of the Health Service, paying his tribute to those who had served the voluntary hospitals in the past, but insisting, 'private charity can never be a substitute for organized justice'. This led naturally to more spacious applications of the doctrine. Every choice between awkward alternatives in the allocation of scarce resources posed moral questions. Labour demanded that the weak should be succoured first, but Churchill preferred a free-for-all; so 'what is Toryism but organized spivvery?' But before the end he struck a practical and topical note about the Government's next steps: 'In 1950 we shall face you again with all our programme carried out. And when I say all, I mean all. I mean *steel* is going to be added.' The challenge would involve a great struggle; every obstacle would be put across the Government's path, including 'the old battered carcass' of the House of Lords.

Undoubtedly it was these last references which Bevan considered political dynamite. For the rest, he mixed his moral philosophy and his lash for the Tories in a way which the audience at least found inoffensive. At one point, contrasting Labour's social programme with the memories of his own youth on the Means Test, he added: 'That is why no amount of cajolery can eradicate from my heart a deep burning hatred for the Tory Party that inflicted those experiences on me. So far as I am concerned they are lower than vermin. They condemned millions of first-class people to semi-starvation. I warn young men and women: don't listen to the seduction of Lord Woolton. He is a very good salesman. If you are selling shoddy stuff, you have to have a good salesman. The Tories are pouring out money in propaganda of all sorts and are hoping by this organized, sustained mass suggestion to eradicate all memory of what we went through. But I warn you, they have not changed – if they have, they are slightly worse than they were.'

That night he had quite an argument with Hugh Delargy, at the time M.P. for one of the Manchester constituencies (later M.P. for Thurrock), who had become one of his closest friends and most fervent admirers but who often undertook the risky assignment of telling his hero what he preferred not to hear. A word of criticism could on occasion unloose cascades of raillery and abuse. Bevan was astonished to be told that the Belle Vue reference to vermin might get him into trouble. 'Nonsense, boy', he said. (All his friends were 'boy,' according to the Welsh mannerism, no matter how old they were.) 'People will only have to read the report to know what I was referring to.' In Wales, Tories were something to be stamped out, politically speaking, of course; like snakes or, yes, vermin; what term could be more appropriate? No one could complain of that. And next morning, 5 July, the newspapers seemed to bear out his judgment. 'MR BEVAN'S BITTER ATTACK ON CONSERVATIVES. No "Free for all" Policy under Labour,' ran the headlines over the longest report in the *Manchester Guardian*. 'BEVAN: my burning hatred for the Tories', was the headline in an early edition of the *Daily Express*, changed in a later edition to 'BEVAN: I HATE THE TORIES': not, it might be thought, a sensational confession. Only one newspaper picked on the fatal word. *The Times* headline read: 'Mr Bevan's "Burning Hatred". Attack on Tory "vermin" '. And possibly it was this nose for news of a *Times* sub-editor, so much more discriminating than that of his yellower rivals, which unloosed the storm. Bevan himself was quite oblivious: why was Delargy always discovering bogys under the bed? He spent that Monday visiting hospitals in Lancashire and nothing marred the geniality of the occasion. No one, he said, could accuse him of political bias in selecting those to run the new service; the 'universal measure of disagreement' he had achieved was proof of his complete impartiality. That night he stayed in Manchester to see the first showing of a Theatre Workshop production – Ewan MacColl's *The Other Animals*. Next day he returned to London to attend the annual meeting of the National Institute of the Deaf, where the new hearing aid provided and produced by the new National Health Service was on display. Nothing made him prouder than the entirely fresh departure in care for the deaf made while he was Minister of Health. Hearing specialists and aural technicians were brought together to devise an instrument for mass production and they invented one costing a tenth of the commercial product. In the next few months and years, assistance was provided for tens of thousands of deaf people who had never been able to afford any hearing aid before.

But the deaf were not news; 'vermin' were – even if the

newspapers were not the first to pounce. On the Monday night, Capt. Gammans, Tory M.P. for Hornsey, called Bevan 'the Conservatives' best propagandist; even in a moment of crisis Socialism will still only appeal to class hatred and inferiority complex'. Lord Reading in the House of Lords said he had never read a more deplorable speech. By Thursday the *Daily Express* claimed to be inundated with protests. On Friday an exchange of letters between Mr Lionel Heald K.C. and Bevan was made public. Mr Heald protested that he had recently agreed to continue service as governor of the Middlesex Hospital; but since he was also a Conservative, did the Minister want his services? Bevan replied as quietly as he could; regretting that remarks made upon a political platform had been taken so much amiss, but insisting that of course the Health Service required the assistance of all, irrespective of party. That night other hands went to work. Someone daubed across the outside of Bevan's house at 23 Cliveden Place the inscription in huge black letters: 'VERMIN VILLA – HOME OF A LOUD-MOUTHED RAT'. At last, one week after the notorious speech had been delivered, the newspapers began to extract the full measure of political profit from it.

Under the title 'Vermin', Lord Kemsley's *Sunday Times* wrote: 'Tories are "lower than vermin" said Mr Aneurin Bevan . . . nothing said at a political meeting for a long time has been more talked about or will be longer remembered'. 'We do not ask,' wrote the *Observer*, 'that democratic argument should lack vigour or even invective; but to attack policy is not to insult persons. Free and frank speaking is quite different from the irresponsible falsehoods and disgusting abuse recently flung by various members of the Cabinet at Mr Churchill, the middle class, and now at every member of the Conservative Party . . . These dirty missiles may not harm the actual target but they foul the whole air through which they pass. They cause the ordinary citizen to despise politics, and to make politics contemptible is not just a trifling breach of manners. It is a crime against a democratic society.' The *Sunday Dispatch* epitomized the case in one mammoth headline: 'THE MAN WHO HATES 8,093,858 PEOPLE' – that being the total who had voted Conservative at the 1945 election. Useless to argue that the phrase could bear other interpretations; that the demons Bevan might have had in mind were the Means Test inquisitors of his youth or their lineal political descendants who greeted, with such niggardly applause and such miserly care for the cost, the prospective human triumphs of the National Health Service; the meaning had now become fixed for ever in British political mythology.

During that awkward week Bevan received from 10 Downing Street an envelope marked 'Strictly Personal' within another envelope sealed thus: 'To be opened by the Minister only. No action till he calls for his secret papers'. Inside Attlee scrawled in a barely decipherable hand:

My dear Aneurin,

I have received a great deal of criticism of the passage in your speech in which you describe the Conservatives as vermin, including a good deal from our own Party.

It was, I think, singularly ill-timed. It had been agreed that we wished to give the new Social Security Scheme as good a send-off as possible and to this end I made a *non*-polemical broadcast. Your speech cut right across this. I have myself done as much as I could to point out the injustice of the attacks made upon you for your handling of the doctors, pointing out the difficulties experienced by your predecessors of various political colours in dealing with the profession. You had won a victory in obtaining their tardy co-operation, but these unfortunate remarks enable the doctors to stage a comeback and have given the general public the impression that there was more in their case than they had supposed.

This is, I think, a great pity because without doing any good it has drawn attention away from the excellent work you have done over the Health Bill. Please, be a bit more careful in your own interest.

Yours ever,

CLEM

The rebuke, if rebuke there had to be, could hardly have been framed more delicately, and after his first irritation that Attlee had accepted the criticism of his Belle Vue utterances without asking him about them first, Bevan bore no grudge. His general relations with his leader at this time were growing more affectionate. But he never ceased to be amazed at Attlee's apparent belief that the war with the Tories could be fought without battles, without wounds, or even without bruises. It was not merely that the leader's trumpet gave an uncertain sound. Months would pass without the waiting army of Labour being roused by so much as a squeak.

Another leader had different views on the requirements and opportunities of political warfare – Winston Churchill. He brooded for a few days while Bevan seemed to be successfully dismissing the incident with a few playful asides – at Holyhead, for example, boasting that Welshmen rather than 'the bovine and phlegmatic Anglo Saxons' were needed to push through great reforms. At a dinner given in his honour by the Monmouthshire County Council (which Lord Raglan, Lord Lieutenant of the County, refused in his verminian capacity to attend), he said that he had never regarded himself as a politician but more as 'a projectile discharged from the Welsh valleys'. In a full-dress Commons debate on housing, the word was muttered, but never daringly thrown down like a gauntlet. The Cabinet, said Lord Woolton in a speech in the country, were 'frightened of Mr Aneurin Bevan', and maybe some others were too. But not Churchill. Having held his fire for a few days, he launched his counter-attack, not in a casual outburst but in a speech in the country in which every sentence was sharpened and polished. The National Health Service, he said, had been 'marred and prejudiced in its initiation by the clumsy and ill-natured hands of the Minister of Health to whom it was confided. Needless antagonisms have been raised largely by bad manners . . . with the medical profession, and the whole process of imposing this new contribution has been rendered more painful by the spirit of spite and class hatred of which Aneurin Bevan has made himself the expression . . . He has chosen this very moment to speak of at least half the British nation as lower than vermin . . . We speak of the Minister of Health but ought we not rather to say the Minister of Disease, for is not morbid hatred a form of mental disease . . . and indeed a highly infectious form? Indeed I can think of no better step to signalize the inauguration of the National Health Service than that a person who so obviously needs psychiatric attention should be among the first of its patients . . .'

The thrusts struck hard as they were intended to: 'Minister of Disease' was no gentle piece of mockery; its purpose was to kill. But Bevan replied in terms which somehow dissuaded Churchill from pursuing this theme in their continuing vendetta. The reply was delivered at 'the big meeting' of the Durham Miners' Gala, the great carnival of the working class where the names of the previous speakers, dating back to 1880, tell of a tradition of the English people which Churchill never knew: Peter Lee, Prince Kropotkin, Charles Bradlaugh, Michael Davitt, Keir Hardie, Bob Smillie, Tom Mann, A. J. Cook; a splendid array. No one speaking at Durham can banish from his consciousness the records of the class struggle recited on the banners carried proudly through the streets. Here was a good arena for replying to Tory Britain.

'When I speak of Tories,' Bevan began, 'I mean the small bodies of people who, whenever they have the chance, have manipulated the political influence of the country for the benefit of the privileged few.' So much for the 'vermin' label; everyone ought to have known what he meant. Then he turned to the main charge: 'I want to spend a little time comparing what Churchill did when he had the power in peacetime with what we have done . . . In 1926 when Churchill was Chancellor of the Exchequer – one of the most disastrous Chancellors of the Exchequer in British history – the infant mortality rate was seventy in a thousand. In 1946 it was forty-three, last year it was better than that again, and the first half of this year is better still. In 1926, 2,092 mothers died in childbirth. In 1946, 1,205 died. Now who ought to be called the Minister of Disease? I am keeping the mothers and children alive but he half-starved them to death. He has the impudence to call me Minister of Disease when every vital statistic by which the health and progress of the population can be measured is infinitely better now under the provision of a common miner than it was then under the supervision of an aristocrat. I know if you took the vital statistics of the aristocrats they were as well off then as now. He looked after them all right. I am not concerned about that. I am concerned about our own people.' And that indeed was the drumbeat in Bevan's oratory. He could not and would not expunge from his memory 'the story of 1926 and of the Tory barbarism of that time'. Churchill did so readily and even boasted of it. 'It is,' continued Bevan, 'a queer definition of a gentleman, one who is able to forgive and forget the wrongs done to other people. I am prepared to forget and forgive the wrongs that were done to me. I am not prepared to forget and forgive the wrongs done to my people. We need twenty years of power to transfer the citadels of capitalism from the hands of a few people to the control of the nation. Only after twenty years can we afford to be polite. Then maybe I won't have enough energy to be rude, but while we have the energy, let us be rude to the right people.' These last words may have stirred fresh tremors of loathing in respectable middle-class homes. But at Durham they were delivered with the sweetest of smiles in the softest of accents, once the fifty-thousand-odd audience had been reduced to the required anticipatory hush. Being rude to the right people was a highly honoured tradition among miners. Having been scorched by the invective, they now basked in the raillery. Those picnic dinners had never been tastier on as perfect a day as Durham had ever known.

The contrast between the Bevan of the headlines and Bevan on the platform and, more still, with the man himself must figure prominently in this story. It influenced his whole attitude to the outside world. Whatever else he was, he was not a rasping, uncouth demagogue. Yet this was the portrait which stared at him from most of the front pages. Even when his actual words were accurately reported, the total added up to a monstrous lie. The phenomenon deserves some scrutiny.

Once – but only once as far as I can discover – Bevan attempted to analyse the art of speaking, and, characteristically, he abandoned the effort. The explanation of his reticence is given, maybe, in the opening words he wrote on the topic. 'At the heart of genius is mystery. If this were not so, then the secret of genius could be uncovered and made accessible to all. Thus genius is beyond science, for science is concerned with behaviour that repeats itself with sufficient frequency to establish a pattern which we call laws. A scientific law is therefore nothing more or less than a description of events that can be predicted beforehand. The essence of genius consists in the fact that it contains a plus factor not amenable to prediction. This seems a long way from a discussion about oratory.

But it is not really so. The genuine orator, like his peers in the other arts, cannot be predicted. He produces his results unexpectedly – quite often as much to himself as to his audience. If this were not so, then he could convey to others the mechanism of his achievements. But I have never met an orator whose advice to others was worth listening to. It usually consisted of a number of turgid, often pompous and almost always empty generalizations which can be read in most handbooks for public speakers. These handbooks, by the way, are a menace to those who want to learn how to speak in public. They emphasize the need for clear enunciation. This is important but by no means overriding. The example of Winston Churchill at once springs to mind. He slurs his sibilants in a fashion now familiar throughout the world. It might be said that he would be an even better speaker if he did not. I doubt it. It lends colour, and a certain uniqueness to his speech. It does more than that, and to it I attach the utmost importance. It imparts a naturalness and a sense of spontaneity to his utterances which would be wholly lacking if he produced his words with impeccable clarity. This quality of spontaneity and immediacy is the very kernel of effective speech. It induces in the audience a disposition to give themselves to the speaker because their surrender has not been obviously and carefully prepared beforehand.'

Then, in this unpublished piece, Bevan digressed to discuss the role of the actor. 'The political speaker,' he insisted, 'is in an entirely different category. Many of his listeners will have turned up to listen to him in an attitude either of scepticism or of wariness or at least of open-mindedness. Of course there is always the core of partisans either for or against the point of view of the speaker. But his main task is to deal with the unconvinced. He has no hopes of success unless he can establish common ground between himself and his listeners. If he is a genuine orator, he will convey an impression of naturalness. He will share the perplexities and anxieties, the hopes and misgivings of those who are listening to him. This is as important whether he is addressing the House of Commons or a meeting of villagers. He must establish an ascendancy through the medium of equality. His audience will never give their minds to him if he appears alien either by manner, matter or by the remoteness of his illustrations. If he is strange there will be no intimacy, and intimacy based on mutual sympathy is the essence of successful advocacy. He must therefore belong to those whom he is trying to persuade; belong in the profoundest sense of the term. No amount of other qualities will suffice if that is lacking. I have known distinguished members of the House of Commons who appeared to possess all the qualities necessary to successful advocacy but because they lacked the warmth that comes from sympathetic sincerity, they failed. Sir John Simon, as he then was, illustrates this. He had everything except one thing. Nobody believed he believed.'

And there, maybe as he approached the heart of the mystery, he turned aside to deplore the displacement of the political meeting by the radio and television, both potentially an apparatus of dictatorship. Then he abandoned the effort altogether. Perhaps he was trespassing too near forbidden ground. Certainly he found any extensive discussion of how a speaker produced his effects abhorrent and indecent. Greatly daring, let us tread further or at least enlist the aid of one who has come near to the heart of the mystery. 'We are apt to forget,' wrote Bagehot, 'that oratory is an imaginative art . . . Now it seems to be a law of the imagination that it only works in a mind of stillness. The noise and crush of life jar it . . . The rarity of great political oratory arises in a great measure from this circumstance. Only those engaged in the jar of life have the material for it; only those withdrawn into a brooding imagination have the faculty for it.'[1]

Still, however elusive the secret, it is not so difficult to tabulate some of its effects. Bevan on the platform and in debate wrought an alchemy before our eyes. He could mix fire with ice. He could evoke dreams and the boldest aspirations, yet the purpose always was to use the motive force thus generated to help forward the business in hand. He unleashed the imagination yet still wanted it tethered to the earth where the immediate enemy must be fought. 'Oh! the brave music of a *distant* drum!' was a quotation he scornfully applied to those – how well he knew them in Wales – who wanted to escape from awkward present conflicts altogether. He himself was often accused of letting words run away with him, yet few speakers who have been called orators have indulged less in

[1] *Biographical Studies* by Walter Bagehot.

rhetoric and rodomontade. At his best, he was never strident; most others seemed hurried and hoarse beside him. He hated grandiloquence: instead, the bulk of his speeches was an intricate, intellectual elaboration, interspersed with paradox and irony. He made the application of Socialist theories sound like commonsense, and he could weave theories from mundane facts. He presented arguments emotionally and emotions argumentatively. An illustration is offered in one of his most frequently quoted aphorisms: 'the language of priorities is the religion of Socialism.' Many of his hearers were just beginning to learn the meaning of priorities; they were startled and gratified to learn that the novelty was all part of the purest political milk they had sucked in at their mothers' breasts. Thus the noblest nostalgic sentiments of a movement born as a protest against injustice were recruited to make justified and tolerable the harsh, essential self-denials of a Labour Government in office. Bevan gave the impression of having brooded long on the issues at stake, yet the impact of his conclusions was produced also by their electrifying spontaneity, coupled with the suggestion that such effects could only be achieved by the joint enterprise of those who spoke and those who listened. The flattering semblance contained its grain of truth. He thought on his feet continuously, searching not only for the words but also for the ideas or for the formulation of the ideas which would express them most clearly and enlist the fullest sympathy. The habit had been learnt in his stuttering adolescence, and to the end the stutter would reappear when he needed to refer to written or printed documents. He resented all obstacles, including often interruptions, which impaired the flow of communion with his audience. And one result, contrary to the common supposition, was that every speech exacted a huge expenditure of nervous vitality. He could spare himself the weary toil of detailed preparation. But for hours before an important occasion he was tense almost to breaking point, and the delivery of the speech itself became an act of creation, a trial when success or failure would turn on the hazard and exertions of the moment.

The method had obvious snares and pitfalls. Of course his themes were deeply pondered, many of the actual phrases premeditated. But he could not stand sentinel over every sentence, lest it escape without the proper restraints and qualifying clauses of an official White Paper. Such caution would affront the English language itself. A speech was not an essay; to suppose that each paragraph could be presented with its final polish was to mistake the whole art. A speech was not a sculpture to be unveiled in its conclusive shape; it must be cut and chiselled in the sight of the audience, false emphases being corrected and the full effect being achieved only by the long accumulated effort. So much too depended on the inflections and the pauses. The fresh and original contributions to political debate contained in a Bevan speech were marked out by his unconscious skill in timing; on the other hand, casual asides or hyperboles, not intended seriously or literally, were kept in proper proportion by a shade in the voice or a flicker of a smile. Indeed, a drop in his voice was one peculiar method he employed to subdue hecklers; he could have them straining their ears to catch what he had to say.

For this variety of reasons, Aneurin Bevan on the platform was *unreportable*. Even if his speeches had been reproduced verbatim, the impression would have been false, and the passages reproduced in these pages can offer, alas, no more than the palest reflection of that blazing light. As it was, many of the newspapers were searching for a few sensational sentences which might have no relevance in his major disquisitions, and when he read them in the headlines next morning he found it impossible to believe that the distortion was not due to malice. He had several other additional reasons for quarrelling with the newspapers. He detested, as an obscenity in itself and a new hazard in public life, the invasion of a public man's privacy in which newspaper reporters thought themselves entitled to engage. He abhorred the growing practice whereby all issues of principle were discussed in terms of persons. And these objections merged into the larger question of what protections a democratically elected government could properly seek against irresponsible press power. One of the unavoidable economic tasks of the Labour Government was to restrict consumption in the interests of the export trade and investment for the future. In the post-war circumstances the effort was painful and unpopular enough anyhow; but might it not be a delusion to suppose that the feat could be accomplished at all in the face of a blaring or subtle newspaper campaign of denigration suggesting that every shortage and every sacrifice of immediate rewards was the result of ministerial incompetence? These questions about the role of the press Bevan shared with others; he was by no means the only victim of the skilful manner in which the Tory newspapers directed their fire on one selected member of the Cabinet after another. But in his case there was a special reason why his quarrel with the press should become an obsession. No one who heard him could deny the quality of his artistry. He was the greatest master of the spoken word in British politics in this century, second only, if second at all, to Lloyd George. Yet the newspapers so easily and brutally translated him into a blusterer. Bevan comforted himself that they would not be believed. The vast audiences which now jammed every meeting where he went – who came to see the horns and a tail with their own eyes – would be angered at the deception practised upon them. Partly he owed his swiftly growing reputation as the most controversial and magnetic figure in the Government to his newspaper enemies. But the attacks still hurt. A politician compelled to watch his character assassinated week by week could hardly be blamed if he saw something deeply evil in the mechanism that contrived it.

Echoes of 'the vermin speech' drilled in Bevan's ears for months, even years, afterwards until the 1950 election and beyond. Adult members of Conservative Associations founded Vermin Clubs, pinned Vermin badges on their breasts, or invaded Bevan's meetings with the chant 'vermin, vermin'. Herbert Morrison, in the semi-privacy of a Parliamentary Labour Party meeting, wished that some opponent had applied the remark to the Labour Party. Harold Laski guessed that it was worth two million votes to the Tories. If the claim was true, the one casual word was responsible for deciding in advance the outcome of the 1950 election and with it the subsequent course of British politics. Who will accept this historical judgment – which, however, Morrison was still gravely repeating in his autobiography twelve years later? It is surely much nearer the mark to realize that the episode was not the cause but the symptom of the bitter post-1945 frustration, the diseased fury, suffered by sections of the British middle class. They hated all the shortages, privations, controls and restrictions retained from the war period or introduced by the new Government and, in particular, all those they were required to bear in common with the rest of the community. They were told by their leaders that these afflictions were superfluous; all were imposed by the class hatred of the Socialists. This was the stock-in-trade of Tory propaganda, and no one preached it more fervently or appeared to believe it more faithfully than Winston Churchill. Treatises have been written to prove how the Tory recovery after 1945 was due to Lord Woolton's salesmanship, R. A. Butler's work in the backroom or other abstruse arts; but none of them must be allowed to snatch the garland from the greatest demagogue of the century. The Socialists, said Churchill, had broken the mainspring of the nation's productive system; they were wantonly extravagant; they piled ever more insupportable burdens on the backs of the taxpayer; and, worst of all, spite and malice inspired their persecutions. Soon after the 1945 election, Churchill had singled out Bevan as the arch-aggressor in this shameful war, and all the alleged harrying of doctors, dentists, houseowners and would-be houseowners, the professional backbone of the nation, 'the vermin', could be cited to confirm the charge. After Churchill's invocations, it is not surprising that the Belle Vue speech stirred such anger.

The expression of it sometimes took a form more offensive than Vermin Clubs. Stacks of foul letters and parcels were pushed through the letter box of 23 Cliveden Place. This had happened before the Belle Vue speech, but the volume and variety were now increased. At this time, regularly, Jennie would creep down early to dispose of the worst, at least those containing excrement, before Nye or a young secretary they shared could see them; she did not want him saddened at the beginning of a hard day's work by this vomiting of the political underworld. At the same time Nye wanted to prevent Jennie knowing about the worst attacks on him. One early morning she found him engaged at the letter box on the same errand as herself. The English middle class *did* have their revenge for the vermin gaffe.

Even some of Nye's and Jennie's closest friends were inclined to criticize them on the grounds of being too sensitive about newspaper importunities and intrusions, and, looking back from this more polite age, it may not be easy to recall the atmosphere of those

times. Another incident may help to illustrate the tension of 'the
vermin days'. Nye used to enjoy walking by the Thames late at
night, and Jennie noticed, without much remarking on the point,
that he had acquired a big walking stick to take with him. One
night he pressed her most earnestly to walk with him and she was
not eager, since she never shared his taste for midnight London
expeditions. But when at last he had persuaded her he told what
had happened the night before. Walking down one Chelsea street
towards the Embankment he had been accosted by a prostitute,
and at that precise moment the press bulbs flashed and an attempt
was made to take a picture. He swept the intruder away with his
walking stick, but was not eager to run the same risk again. It was
not pleasant to be perpetually vulnerable as public enemy number
one.

For Churchill, there was at least the excuse that he had stumbled
on a poetic truth, the distinction between Bevan and his colleagues.
Bevan did not in fact regard all Tories as vermin and never
imagined that he had called them such; ever since his Tredegar
days he had been prepared to argue with them and bewitch them
individually, even to wine and dine with them if they offered good
enough meals and sufficiently uninhibited talk. But his tastes never
changed his conviction that the class conflict retained its central
place in politics. He may not have subscribed in 1948 to the absolute letter of the 1848 doctrine that 'the history of all hitherto existing society is the history of class struggle'. History itself had
modified the *Communist Manifesto*, and if it had not, Bevan would
have been quite prepared himself to undertake the necessary revision. No one could be more scornful about those who paraded
slogans as ideas. But nothing altered the fact that the determination
of the Tories to recapture complete power in the British state
would be relentless and inflexible. No respect for traditional
courtesies would appease them. No willingness on the part of
Labour to proceed cautiously with its policies would soften Tory
antagonism; it would merely invite contempt. Labour must keep
on the offensive. In the remaining months of 1948 and throughout
1949 Bevan showed, in his department, on the National Executive
of the Labour Party, in the Cabinet, in Parliament and in the
country at large how he believed this strategy could be followed.

Some of his exertions led to disputes with his colleagues, but it was not the case as some have written that Labour's élan had been dissipated in 1947 or even earlier. At any rate that was not Bevan's view. He retained his belief in a new Labour victory.

Within his own department, 1948 registered some substantial achievements, and at the end of a housing debate in July, the first the Opposition had dared ask for for months, he could afford to become almost benign. The programme represented 'a vast job of social co-operation and could not have been accomplished except by all kinds of people in all walks of life'. The provocation was too blatant; Opposition members cried: 'Vermin'. 'Yes,' replied Bevan, 'I do not put it beyond them to promote themselves in time.' In September the total of houses built since the war passed the now notorious Coalition Government target of 750,000. Of course it was true, said Bevan, that the figure was 'exceedingly conservative'. Hundreds of thousands of families were still without a separate home. The experts had, among other miscalculations, 'underrated the matrimonial enthusiasm' of the British people. Still, here was one milestone passed, and Bevan hoped that, with the pressure suitably applied at the right moment, the 1947 cuts could be restored altogether. Curiously, it was developments within the Health Service which at that moment promised the more serious political repercussions. By September, 92 to 93 per cent of the public had signed up with the Service and fresh signatures were coming in at the rate of some 150,000 a week; no one had foreseen that the 100 per cent figure would be approached so swiftly. Head-lines in the newspapers reported a tremendous rush for spectacles. ('Why should the editors complain?' asked Bevan. 'My only mis-giving is that practically everyone will be able to read the nonsense they write about the Act.') He himself made several appeals that the Service should not be abused, and warned that the nation's maturity was being tested. He could not repress his enthusiasm for long. 'Why is Churchill so misanthropic? Why doesn't he step down out of his car now and again? Visitors who come to this country say they have never seen finer babies. The prams are full. It shows that the sap is moving in the old oak still.' But the dif-ferent items, the babies, the dentures, the wigs (for six months the total figure for them was £36,500 but the headlines made it sound

more like £300 millions) and the rest piled up a huge t⟨
had argued with canny foresight that no worthwhile estin⟨
Service's cost could be given until there had been practic⟨
ence of its working; here he, not his critics, was the tr⟨
matist. But the demand was exceeding anything he had dre⟨ ⟩ or.
All through the autumn and winter of 1948 he was arguing with the
Treasury and in the jealous testimony of Herbert Morrison
'got away with more and more money for his beloved health
schemes . . .'[1]

Then, in the early days of February 1949, the news broke. Supplementary Estimates for a total of no less than £221 million –
£52 million of them for the Health Service – were to be required.
Huge headlines in the press forecast a political crisis; in particular,
the Health Service might collapse beneath the weight of such
extravagance.[2] Churchill, for one, took these charges at their face
value, and at the earliest opportunity demanded of Morrison, the
Leader of the House of Commons, three days to debate 'an event
without precedent in time of peace . . . the most wild miscalculations . . . an enormous addition to the burdens of the nation . . . the
grossest carelessness . . .' He had stirred what he had doubtless
intended, a parliamentary uproar, and above it all, quite out of
order, could be heard the taunt of Bevan from the Treasury bench:

[1] *An Autobiography* by Herbert Morrison, p. 271.
[2] A small irritant which could infuriate Bevan more than the larger ones
was provided at this period when Mr Peter Thorneycroft, at that time
Tory M.P. for Monmouth, introduced a Private Member's Bill, called the
Analgesia in Childbirth Bill, which purported to propose measures to
assist in providing the facilities to secure painless childbirth. Much capital
was attempted to be made from this by the Tories at a by-election in St
Pancras at the time, protesting that this Charter for Mothers had been
blocked by the monster Bevan. But in fact all the powers for dealing with
local authorities and hospitals which the Bill proposed to allocate to the
Minister were already available to him under the National Health Service;
the powers were so well used that the number of midwives being trained
was increasing much faster than ever before; and under his Act the fully
trained service for midwives would be provided two years earlier than
Thorneycroft was envisaging. Bevan had some excuse for regarding the
Thorneycroft Bill as a stunt designed to assist a surreptitious attack on the
Health Service, and he was the more enraged when some Labour Members were apparently deceived by the Thorneycroft manœuvre.

'Hear, hear. Let the Opposition come along.' Churchill flushed, told Bevan to control his touchiness, and suggested that a Vote of Censure might be required to deal with the Government's 'gross financial mismanagement'. But when the next week came there was no censure and no Churchill. It is a revealing truth that never once in that Parliament did Churchill choose to fight Bevan on his own ground of housing or health, two topics on which he could be extremely eloquent at a safer distance. Instead when the great day came the Saint George drafted to slay the Dragon was Mr Ralph Assheton, the mildest-mannered of the Tory team. 'The right hon. Gentleman', said Bevan, 'has generally a most amiable presence, but it is always a foolish spectacle for a weak man to use strong adjectives.' One by one the others were flicked aside. Then, with silence established, Bevan defended his Health Service from this fresh assault, and extracted the last ounce of political profit from the exercise. 'I could, of course, have emerged from this examination perfectly clear of any charges of arithmetic inexactitude. All I need have done was to have failed as an administrator to have emerged successfully as an arithmetician. And why? Who suspected before 5 July last that in six months, before the end of 1948, these figures would have emerged? Who would have said that we would have in the Service many more general practitioners than we ourselves thought would have come in? Who would have suspected that 95 per cent of the population would have registered with general practitioners by the end of the year? Who would have said that by now even in the most obdurate of all the professions, the dental profession, we should have got 92 per cent of the dentists in? As these people came into the Service, naturally the expenditure went up. But that mounting expenditure was an admission of an administrative success, because if they had not come in I would not have had a deficit: I would have had a surplus, and I would then be praised by the Opposition for being a financial success and a failure as a Minister of Health. It is just because all these services expanded so quickly, so harmoniously, and so fruitfully that we find ourselves with this deficit.' Of course the Service cost money. But was there not some compensation in the relief provided for 'the vast amount of inarticulate misery and pain' uncovered by the Service? 'Why do not right hon. Gentlemen opposite start ceasing to be so sour? Why is it that as the health of the population goes up, their spirit goes down? The Tory Party used to represent themselves as a jocund Party. (*Hon. Members:* What?) They cannot understand English now. I will give them a clue: "How jocund did they drive their teams afield". However, that has all gone now. Pale and miserable lot, instead of welcoming every increase in the health of the nation, the buoyancy of the nation, and the vitality of the nation, they groan at it. They hate it because they think it spells electoral defeat. I have sympathized with hon. Members opposite this evening because they have had a really difficult task. They began by attacking this scheme. Especially in 1947, their hopes were raised because they thought that the economic difficulties into which the country was getting over the balance of payments would result in the jettisoning of the health scheme . . . They always hoped that it would be shipwrecked in the initial difficulties of launching . . . They conspired with some of the most reactionary elements in the medical profession . . . I met with pressure in the House and every Thursday I was pressed as to why I did not come to an agreement with the dentists and why I did not come to an agreement with the doctors. Instead of supporting Ministers in the negotiations with the professions, the Conservative Party organized itself into a series of pressure lobbies in the press, pressure lobbies all over the country against every single thing. What they are saying to the country is "We were never against it. It is quite true that we voted against it, it is quite true that we agitated against it, it is quite true that we plotted against it, but we were really in favour of it all the time".' Experience had brought wisdom. Would the Tories vote against the Supplementary Estimates for the Health Service as in 1946 they had voted against the Second and Third Readings of the Health Service Bill? Not likely. When the vote was called, the Tory benches sat silent.

The most hopeless task of a Bevan biographer is the attempt to describe his victories in debate. This was certainly one of them. Somehow the countless millions so scandalously squandered, according to Churchill's accusation, were reduced to – and the words were stuttered out as if by a man making a generous concession to his enemies – 'an arithmetic inexactitude'. And who but Bevan, when the Tory front bench was looking at its

most bedraggled, would have thought of calling them *jocund*?
Who else would have crowned the gentlemen of England with
Gray's *Elegy*? The very blow by which the Tories hoped to
destroy him had been used to destroy them. It was a kind of
rhetorical jujitsu.

7

THE MIXED ECONOMY
1948-1950

The Central Committee assured the party that by holding the 'commanding heights' of large-scale industry, the state would in any event be able to control the national economy.—ISAAC DEUTSCHER[1]

Long ago Aristotle discovered that every human community is a community of diverse aspirations.—MILOVAN DJILAS[2]

URING THE autumn and winter of 1948 and the early months of 1949 much of Aneurin Bevan's time was absorbed by the business of the Labour Party's National Executive where the immediate task was to frame a new election programme and a new legislative programme for what was confidently hoped would be another five years of power. The process involved passing judgment on the post-1945 experience and reassessing the future prospects. Wittingly or, more in accordance with Labour's customary practice, unwittingly, the Party was forced to redefine its general outlook. Did it still claim to be a Socialist party and, if so, what did the word mean? How many features of the new society had been truly established; how many more were needed to secure the fundamental change which Labour had traditionally demanded; how long was to be the period of transition; and did the leaders wish to travel this road at all? More overtly than before, Herbert Morrison emerged as the leading advocate of one doctrine and Bevan of another, and the resulting clash over principles shaped the Labour Party of the fifties and the sixties. Then, and even more later, the newspapers suggested that a bitter personal antagonism prompted Bevan's fight with Morrison over policy, and Bevan

[1] *The Prophet Armed* (Oxford, 1959).
[2] *The Unperfect Society* (Methuen, 1959).

9

never tired of insisting that this was proof of their political illiteracy or malice. Almost precisely the reverse was true. To the disputes with Morrison in the Cabinet over steel or the cost of the Health Service was now added a profound argument about political faith and philosophy. Thus were opened some old wounds which after 1945 had started to heal.

Morrison at the Party Conference in June 1948 had first spoken the word which was taken to epitomize the controversy. 'Whilst in the next programme, it will be right – and I can promise you that the Executive will do it – to give proper consideration to further propositions for public ownership, do not ignore the need, not merely for considering further public ownership, but for allowing Ministers to *consolidate* . . .' Thenceforward Morrison directed his inexhaustible energies to ensure that the consolidation of past achievements should dominate Labour's thinking: here was the best way to make the nationalization measures already taken administratively successful, to liberate the parliamentary timetable for other less controversial measures, to dissipate middle-class resentments, to hook the floating voter. Bevan on the other hand wanted the swiftest possible drive forward to establish the pre-eminence of the publicly-owned sector of the economy. The two views may appear flatly irreconcilable, but practical political requirements removed at least that appearance. Morrison knew that the Party would insist on some fresh measures of public ownership, never stated a theoretical opposition to such developments, and indeed found it wiser to eschew theory altogether. Bevan had reached the firm theoretical conclusion which he held for the rest of his life. It marked a notable departure from orthodox Marxism, and might offend the purity of some of his Left-wing associates but as usual he saw no reason for reticence in stating his opinion. To define the next stage was the urgent requirement, but it helped greatly – it was only fair and the opposite of demagogic – to know and say what would be the later destination. 'The kind of society which we envisage, and which we shall have to live in, will be a mixed society, a mixed economy, in which all the essential instruments of planning are in the hands of the State, in which the characteristic form of employment will be by the community in one form or another, but where we shall have for a very long time the light cavalry of private competitive industry.' This was his formulation to the Labour Party Conference at Blackpool in 1949, and when he dealt with the same question in his own book a few years later he did no more than underline it. 'It is clear to the serious student of modern politics that a mixed economy is what most people of the West would prefer. The victory of Socialism need not be universal to be decisive. I have no patience with those Socialists, so-called, who in practice would socialize nothing, whilst in theory they threaten the whole of private property. They are the purists and therefore barren. It is neither prudent nor does it accord with our conception of the future, that all forms of private property should live under perpetual threat. In almost all types of human society different forms of property have lived side by side without fatal consequences either for society or for one of them. But it is a requisite of social stability that one type of property ownership should dominate. In the society of the future it should be public property. Private property should yield to the point where social purposes and a decent order of priorities form an easily discernible pattern of life.'[1] Clearly in 1948 this was a distant aim. Nothing was to be lost and everything was to be gained by stating it. It was an acceptance of reality. It made possible an honourable compromise between Left and Right of the Party. It neatly defined the double task which the National Executive had to undertake in 1948 – to plan the expansion of the public sector and to face the challenge which most Socialists had dodged of what was to be done in the meantime with the private sector.

Morrison was chairman of the Executive's Policy and Publicity Committee, its Election Campaign Committee and its two sub-committees on nationalized industries, one on their administration and the other concerned with future projects. He collected chair-manships as other men may collect stamps. Bevan meanwhile, at one of the earliest meetings of the Home Policy Commit-tee, delivered a brilliant disquisition on how the Party was play-ing into the hands of the Tories by permitting too much scrutiny to be concentrated on the nationalized industries and their alleged

[1] *In Place of Fear*, p. 118.

failures; why should the searchlight not be switched onto the manifold deficiencies of *private* industry? He was promptly appointed
chairman of the sub-committee to examine this hitherto uncharted
region of Labour policy. The division of labour looked so ideally
fitted to keep Bevan busy in a sideroad while Morrison blocked the
main advance that it is hard to believe it was not devised for that
purpose. Moreover, Bevan had another disadvantage. He wanted a
clear commitment to a fresh range of nationalization measures but
sometimes wavered about the best way to get it. By temperament
he favoured stating the case in the broadest terms. Public ownership was needed for particular reasons in particular industries, but
much more in order to ensure that 'effective social and economic
power passes from one order of society to another'. However, too
vague an undertaking might be perilous. It could leave the
Morrisonians uncommitted to anything. Rooted in Bevan's mind
was the knowledge of how tense had been the struggle to keep steel
nationalization on the Government's agenda and how unavailing
his insistence would have been if it had not been for the precise
words about steel in the Party manifesto *Let Us Face the Future*.
Bevan therefore could not object to the method proposed of drawing up what came to be called a 'shopping list', a list of the next
industries to be taken over, and yet this procedure played into the
hands of the anti-nationalizers; they could invoke arguments and
interests against each individual proposal and hope to ensure at the
end that the whole programme was severely limited.

The Executive, its sub-committees and its research department
did in fact conduct a comprehensive survey of one industry after
another. Two of the biggest tussles centred on chemicals and shipbuilding. Bevan and his supporters urged that the Imperial Chemical Industries should figure at the head of the nationalization list,
partly because of its near or potential monopoly position in the
industry but chiefly in view of the vastly increasing role which
chemicals must play in a modern industrial society. The proposal
was voted down, partly owing to the opposition of the trade union
representatives with members in I.C.I. A similar fate befell most
other major proposals, although in the case of shipbuilding the
possibility of action was at least kept open. In the end only four
items – sugar, cement, meat-slaughtering and water, two of them

near monopolies and one an obvious public utility – slipped through
the Morrison sieve; these and one other – the nationalization of
industrial assurance, and it was upon this last proposal that the
Executive debate concentrated more and more. Industrial assurance was the system by which the sixpences, shillings and half-
crowns of the public were collected for death benefits and other
contingencies, but these weekly collections were big business,
headed by the Prudential Assurance Company, valued then at £32
million. The proposal was to take over all these aspects of the insurance companies and convert them into a public service. Here
was no minor proposal. At one stroke Labour could extend the
public control of investment and round off its great social service
measures. For Bevan too the chance of having the Prudential head
on a charger added to the attraction; he had some old scores to pay
off, dating back to the pre-war days when they had preferred to
invest in Poland than South Wales.

Week after week on the Executive, the great debate on the issue
proceeded and the exchange began to follow a pattern.[1] James
Griffiths, the Minister of National Insurance, would present the
overwhelming case for removing private profit from this sphere
altogether. Even the normally jaded Executive would be shaken
and moved. Bevan naturally would back him. Then Morrison would
warily reply. Of course, he knew the strength of the case, but other
considerations must be weighed. Electorally the project could be
damaging, since the insurance agents could be turned into doorstep
canvassers for the Tories. Inside the movement there might be
trouble since the Co-op were engaged in the industrial assurance
business; was this the moment to offend *them*? Were there not
aspects of the matter which deserved full examination and could
they not be referred to a committee (of which he was doubtless to
be chairman)? The discussion would sway back and forth, and at
last Dalton, normally a strong enthusiast for public ownership and
no enthusiast at all for Morrison, would throw all his weight into
the scales *against* the proposal. 'Votes, votes, votes,' he would
boom; that was all that counted, and Morrison's case was made.

[1] Author's note: Having been elected to the Executive at the 1948
Conference, these debates on Industrial Assurance were my first introduction to Executive discussions.

And yet time after time Griffiths and Bevan carried the day, and the Executive went to Blackpool in June 1949 committed to win overwhelming support for the proposition that industrial insurance should be taken into full public ownership. The victory had been arduously won. After leaving one of these meetings, walking to the House of Commons from Smith Square, Bevan, limp with exertion, would stop to express his amazement at the proceedings. 'It is a form of torture unknown to the ancients,' he would say, 'to be compelled on the last Wednesday of every month to convert the leaders of the Labour Party afresh to the most elementary principles of the Party; to be compelled to fight every inch of the way to recapture territory occupied by Beveridge.' Then he would stop again a few yards further on and his stutter would return: 'Now I can sympathise with that fellow S-S-Sisyphus and his bl-bl-bloody boulder.' One of the veins which the world rarely suspected in him was his innocence. He could be perpetually astonished when other people's minds did not work like his own. Once a principle was accepted, the rest should follow; it should not be eaten away by persistent, plodding, empirical second thoughts. Often, for him, to bend his mind to the world of so-called practical politics was a physical agony.

Compared with the titanic struggle over industrial assurance, Bevan's sub-committee on the working of private enterprise seemed to be conducted by ordinary mortals. Yet here, as he told the Blackpool Conference, the Party was 'breaking fresh ground . . . we have to restate the relationship between the public and private sector'. He warmed to the task: 'At the same time that we are advancing on the public sector as fast as we can, we want to replenish and revitalize the private sector.' One way to tackle the job was to deal with the monopolies, cartels, trusts and price rings which throttled private enterprise. 'We have given our attention to setting the private sector free. We have taken Mr Churchill's advice! We are pointing out to the nation that part of the private sector is suffering grievously from exploitation by some other part of the private sector.' Some of these restrictions could be dealt with by referring cases to the Restrictive Practices Commission; already 'three candidates for liberty' had been presented to it, and more would follow. But much wider powers of intervention were needed to enable the State to compete with private firms in some industries instead of taking over all of them, to provide state factories or equipment which could be rented out to private entrepreneurs, to provide small manufacturers with better access to finance. Partly, no doubt, this part of the programme had won Bevan's backing because of its advantages in the field of propaganda; it did help to direct criticism at private enterprise. But it also represented his attitude to a whole range of matters. Often the State could provide the equipment while the individual provided the enterprise. That could be an intelligent partnership. Only the 'parasitical money-lenders', thus deprived of their profits, need complain.

Altogether, Bevan's speech at the Blackpool Conference in June 1949 showed a virility which goes ill with the notion of a Government on its knees before its enemies. Much of the preceding debate had turned on the deficiencies of the industries already nationalized and naturally this was a constant theme of the Tory newspapers. Bevan set his face against any mood of pessimism. Mistakes had been made, alterations there must be, but without too much breast-beating. The real achievement was enormous. 'We must be able to improve on what we have done, without at the same time having to say what we did was wrong; otherwise all reform would begin at the penitential form.' Then he elaborated his views on public ownership and the mixed society. But it was the peroration which stayed most in the mind. Some had complained that Labour's out-look was too materialistic, that the vision was lacking. 'I would point out,' said Bevan, 'that in some way or another the conception of religious dedication must find concrete expression, and I say that never in the history of mankind have the best ideas found more concrete expression than they have in the programme that we are carrying out. "Suffer the little children to come unto me" is not now something which is said only from the pulpit. We have woven it into the warp and woof of our national life, and we have made the claims of the children come first. What is national planning but an insistence that human beings shall make ethical choices on a national scale? . . . The language of priorities is the religion of Socialism. We have accepted over the last four years that the first claims upon the national product shall be decided nationally and they have been those of the women, the children and the old people.

What is that except using economic planning in order to serve a moral purpose?' Therefore, concluded Bevan, 'this great movement had the right to raise its head high and look at the stars'. Given another five years of office, it could not only raise material standards but build a society of which Britons everywhere could be proud.

At Blackpool the speech won rapturous applause, and even his enemies, in Fleet Street and outside it, were compelled to acknowledge its skill and authority. His standing in the Labour Party had never been stronger and many who witnessed the scene at the Blackpool Winter Gardens saw him then as the inevitable future leader. A sense of outrage, however, was still expressed from one quarter, prompted by the reference to 'Suffer the little children'. Politicians, said the Archbishop of Canterbury, should not in their speeches quote 'the words of the New Testament and especially the words of our Lord. Such quotations are out of place and cause discomfort and distress.' The stricture suggested that Archbishop Fisher was poorly acquainted with British history. He might have known that English reformers, radicals and revolutionaries, had been using the language of the Bible as if it belonged to them and the English people, not the bishops, ever since John Ball had first raised the standard of Socialism on English soil. Since then a host of others, from the Levellers to the Chartists, from John Bunyan to Keir Hardie, had wielded the same weapon to drive the money-changers from the temple, and the Tolpuddle martyrs, Bible-quoters almost to a man, had doubtless 'caused discomfort and distress' to Lord Melbourne's Christian administration. Was rejoicing in biblical terms to be forbidden now that politicians were practising what churchmen had sometimes preached? No. This time Bevan had gone too far. He had compared himself to Christ which was held to be scarcely less reprehensible than calling the Tories 'vermin'.

But archbishops apart, Bevan's Blackpool speech does pose essential questions about his political character and his Socialism. Was the display of optimism about the achievements and potentialities of the Government justified, or was it no more than the desperate cry of a cheer-leader? Can the demagogy, if such it was, be excused? What was his private verdict on the administration? Was he making behind the scenes a more perceptive analysis of the Government's deficiencies and the obstacles across its path? Some Socialist critics have written as if it was plain to all but the most myopic that Labour had lost any sense of direction long before 1949. From the Conservative Opposition came the mounting charge that the country was being led to economic disaster. The Labour Party Conference was held in June; by September the Government was forced to devalue the pound, and a series of fresh economy measures, some of them directly affecting the Ministry of Health, followed. Clearly the Government's calculations were belied, and the measures forced down its throat must impair its electoral chances.

The answer to the questions about Bevan's politics will be correct only if it reflects the extreme individuality of his opinions. Certainly they cannot be fitted into any simple category laid down by the Left-wing critics at the time or historians since. He had his own unique combination of criticisms and judgments. First of all, his outlook was influenced by what he considered to be the renewed evidence of the oldest vice of the Labour leadership: its inveterate, incorrigible timidity. A touch of boldness could have paid rich dividends. Specifically, the Steel Bill could have been brought in a year earlier, Churchill's campaign in the country could have been countered more robustly, a new and more extensive nationalization programme could have been presented without apology. Other complaints called in question the Government's wisdom, its imaginative capacity, more than its nerve. Bigger and swifter defence cuts, such as Dalton had pressed for and Bevin had blocked, could have released some of the extra resources urgently required for housing, investment and other civilian necessities. True, the Government was right (in Bevan's firm estimate) to resist the pressures of the Soviet Union; however, that necessity made it all the more desirable to pursue policies likely to enlist Socialist support in Central Europe, the Middle East and elsewhere, but Bevin did the exact opposite. Moreover Bevan found himself thrust into deeper conflict with Cripps at the Exchequer. Added to the normal hostility between a great spending department and the Chancellor went Bevan's growing suspicion of Treasury planning. Book-keeping records of the capital investment programme, indeed the convention of annual Budgets, gave the Treasury planners the idea that

9*

when they moved figures from one column to another physical resources could be adjusted as easily. More and more he complained that the Treasury had neither the means nor the will to plan in a Socialist sense. The real planning of the Government was confined to, or at least was most effective in, those areas where it commanded the instruments of planning – in the nationalized sector, in local government, wherever Government finance could exert its direct influence. And finally, after Blackpool, Bevan found himself caught in the gruelling combat with Morrison on the National Executive. Morrison proposed and secured the appointment of a new sub-committee to examine the plan for industrial assurance. Gradually, for the outright nationalization of industrial insurance, a suggestion for 'mutualization' was substituted. Morrison's persistence and vigilance had worn down all rivals. He was White-hall's greatest exponent of what might be called 'murder by committee'.

These various grounds of dispute covered a wide territory, and throughout the spring and summer of 1949 Bevan became increasingly conscious of his disagreement with his colleagues. He did indeed argue with himself, with Jennie and a few others about the possibility of resigning from the Government. The argument ran thus: The Steel Bill, the last major public ownership measure to which the Government was committed,[1] would soon be on the

---

[1] One other major measure, although not exactly to be defined as one affecting the issue of public ownership, which Bevan would have liked to have seen carried through as the next major project of his own Ministry was a reform of local government. He knew there was no immediate political advantage to be gained by it and probably he did not press the matter strongly in the Cabinet. But he did believe such a development was essential if the Health Service and indeed many other services were to be made properly democratic and responsive to public pressure. He had a scheme worked out in considerable detail, and especially for those who deplore the managerial and bureaucratic aspects of the local government reform measures put through in the early 1970s, Bevan's much more truly democratic approach to the problem must have a strong appeal. His scheme never saw the light of day; it was left in the pigeon-holes of the old Ministry of Health. But when Bevan wrote a major article on the subject for *The Municipal Journal* on 12 March 1954, he clearly drew on the ideas which he had helped to formulate in 1948 and 1949. He envisaged all-purpose authorities which would cover the whole country but he envisaged also

Statute Book, even if the appointed day for the take-over was post-poned until after the coming election. It would be possible for Bevan to resign, not on any specific issue of dispute with the rest of the Cabinet, but on the claim that, with the Steel Bill complete, he wished to devote himself to a campaign of what he called 'Socialist education' in the country. Of course, the Tory newspapers would represent his decision as evidence of a hopeless split in the Party. But the charge could be refuted at the huge meetings he would undoubtedly attract and which could be used for the twin purposes of challenging the Tory offensive with the full-blooded counter-offensive required and exerting Left-wing pressure from outside instead of within the Party leadership. The idea had much merit. It might have enabled Bevan to embark upon the task which he believed was so necessary – a great effort to renew the Socialist energies of the Party – without stirring the bitter personal antagon-isms which later followed his resignation in 1951. But wise or not, the serious consideration he gave to the idea was overtaken by events. As the decision about devaluation came nearer, it was evident that the Government as a whole would be under much hotter fire from the Opposition and that rearguard actions might have to be fought by his own Ministry to protect the Health Service and the housing programme. Resignation at that hour would have looked more like desertion.

Amid his disputes with his colleagues, Bevan could never forget that the Tory enemy could overhear them. Morrison, Bevin, Cripps and the others might infuriate him as he doubtless infuriated them, but his irritation and anger were drowned by the flood of Churchil-lian invective. Churchill, in Bevan's judgment, was using his immense authority and eloquence to propagate a great lie. He was

---

that they would be smaller and more truly local than the so-called unitary authorities of later schemes. Except in the great cities, these new all-purpose authorities – some 235 or 240 would be needed to cover the whole country – would serve populations ranging from 50,000 to 100,000 and yet the bulk of the population would be within ten miles of the civic centre. Of course, the chief casualty of his scheme would have been the county council, but that, for him, was an attraction. 'Those of us,' he wrote in that 1954 article, 'who have experience of country and district administration can be in no doubt as to which is local government in all the essential meanings we attach to the term.'

telling the British people that they were being starved, strangled, suffocated by Socialist planning when the truth was that the moderate doses of the medicine so far applied were achieving spectacular results. The facts about Britain's recovery did not need to be stated in reticent tones; by every test the achievement was considerable. The country was healthier and happier, the economy fundamentally stronger, than Bevan had ever known in his lifetime. The banishment of the scourge of unemployment, the new life brought to the old distressed areas, were transforming the England and, more particularly, the Wales of his youth. For Churchill, these changes could be no more than figures in blue books, if he could understand them or if anyone troubled to tell him; for Bevan, they were the first reality of politics, something he could smell by walking down Commercial Street in Tredegar or crossing the mountain to the booming Ebbw Vale steelworks. His own eyes and ears and instinct told him more than any statistics, but there were also plenty of statistics on his side. So, mixed with his anxieties and criticisms about the immediate past and the future went a genuine pride and buoyancy. The Blackpool speech was not demagogy. The word was intended to be a deed; to help forward the immediate work in hand; to give the Labour Party the necessary resilience and resonance to fight off the Tory attack and prepare for victory at the coming election. His moods could vary in a way which neither his followers nor critics could predict. When the Government appeared to be emerging from its difficulties, his criticisms would also emerge. When the Government was driven into a corner, he would rush to its defence. He allowed himself the luxury of criticising his colleagues but could lambast anyone else who did the same.

Bevan preferred his own gauge of the nation's well-being, but other tests confirmed the verdict. Despite the shrieking from the Tories about all manner of shortages, it was legitimate to boast in the early months of 1949 of the nation's economic recovery. 1948 had been a good year. Exports and production were climbing upwards well above pre-war levels; investment was strong, and the balance of payments gap had been closed. But then in the middle of 1949 came a quite unforeseen setback. It was not that Socialist administration had engineered a catastrophe, although some commentators in the United States appeared to take Churchill's perorations seriously. 'UTOPIA ON THE ROCKS', ran screaming headlines advertising a Scripps-Howard series on the new Britain. 'How Millions of our Money have been Poured Down the Drain of Political Exploitation – How Crippling Taxes and Soaring Living Costs, Resulting from High Wages and Low Production, are bringing the British People to their Knees...' In fact, the sterling area's dollar gap had widened suddenly and alarmingly owing to a recession in the United States. Here was the post-war world's first taste of a phenomenon to become common: when Wall Street sneezed, the whole of Western Europe caught a cold. The development uncovered the reality which several economists had foreseen but which was not easy to meet face to face – that the dollar-sterling exchange rate could no longer be sustained at the level fixed before the war. Britain was pushed inexorably towards devaluation, by United States financial opinion, by speculators who saw it coming, by an intelligent if belated estimate of the alternatives. At least these are the discoveries of hindsight. At the time Cripps and his Treasury advisers struggled hard to escape the decision. Cripps committed himself even more rigidly than convention might require to insisting that he would not devalue before he actually did, and the discomfiture of the Ministers looked the more serious. Naturally enough, the Tories saw the event as a crushing vindication of their whole case against the Government. Parliament was recalled for a special three day session in September in an atmosphere of crisis. Churchill was on the warpath, and had some right to feel this was his moment for the kill. No one could suppose that the Government's huge majority would evaporate, but a moral victory should certainly be won.

Famous House of Commons occasions, heralded by much publicity, usually subside into boredom, but the 'devaluation' debate of September 1949 was the greatest of the 1945 Parliament. For a moment, the historic nation-wide clash between the Parties – something quite different from routine parliamentary tit-for-tat – was compressed into that forum. At the centre of the stage stood Stafford Cripps, the dominating figure of the time; by sheer intellectual force and moral authority he seemed to be recreating the Labour Party in his own upright, forbidding image. But by now he was a wounded man. Devaluation was a blow to his heart, and he

was outraged by the charge, pressed particularly by Churchill, that
his personal honour was stained, following his previous repeated
assertions that the step was not intended. According to the brilliant
sneer of the Tory M.P., Nigel Birch, he came into the House with
a look of 'injured guilt' on his face. However, Cripps's opening
speech was acknowledged on all sides to be as masterly as ever and
thereafter a high standard was sustained. Several of the best de-
baters in that Parliament on both sides – Oliver Stanley, Dick
Crossman, Robert Boothby, Quintin Hogg, David Eccles, Sydney
Silverman, Ian Mikardo – grappled with one another on the real
issues which did divide the Parties. The coming election, said
Churchill, 'will be fought out with more fundamental divergences
at every grade and in every part of our society than have been
known in our lifetime'. This was no Tweedledum-Tweedledee contest, and the mood filled every corner of the Chamber. A young and
little-known figure recently appointed President of the Board of
Trade, Harold Wilson, gave the first hint the Commons had
seen that he might wish to abandon his civil service brief and
engage in the wider political argument.[1] And Attlee, at the end,
replying to Churchill ('His only suggestion is "Vote for Me". It is
1945 all over again'), was caustic and almost ferocious. The wasp
could sting.

Yet by common consent the real duel was between Churchill and
Bevan. For this direct conflict between the two, the House had had
to wait for four years; Churchill had chosen not to trespass on
Bevan's territory of health and housing and Bevan's jealous colleagues had previously insisted that he should not be allowed to
stray outside it. At least he could not complain now that the battlefield was constricted. For Churchill charged that the Government
had 'played the party game with national stakes in a manner which
no other Government I can remember in my long life or read about
in modern history have ever done'; that they had brought the

[1] Some years had still to pass before Mr Wilson acquired his later reputation. But on 21 October 1949, a note in Ian Mikardo's column in *Tribune*
recorded this report from the proceedings of a trade union branch in
London: '*Annual Dinner*. There was a discussion on speakers to be
invited and entertainment to be provided at the dinner. Bro. S. urged
that no political bias should influence the choice. It was decided to have a
conjuror. Mr Harold Wilson was proposed . . .'

country 'to the verge of national and international bankruptcy'; that nothing less was at stake than 'all the slowly gathered treasures, customs, qualities, and traditions of the ancient and famous British state'. It was Churchill at his electioneering best, gay and sombre by turns, sounding the alarm until it deafened, exerting his unfailing powers to the limit to secure the sweetest prize he had ever striven for and which now seemed so nearly within his reach – revenge for 1945. Churchill seemed to hurl the whole of his political experience into the scales, but then Bevan did the same. Against the ancient customs of the famous British state, Bevan rallied another Britain. On no other occasion in British history did two such articulate spokesmen of the two nations confront one another in single combat. Members seemed to have a premonition of what was to come and they crowded into the Chamber for the last day of the debate, expectant and excited.

Bevan began softly, as always. Of course, the Government benches were grateful for 'the full-throated abandonment'of Churchill's speech the day before; it enabled them to reply in kind, to explain the phenomenon which so much puzzled foreigners – how the British people, said to be 'undernourished, fatigued and down-and-out still struggled to the polling booths to vote for Government candidates at every by-election. 'I welcome this opportunity,' said Bevan, 'of pricking the bloated bladder of lies with the p-p-poniard of truth.' The House exploded with laughter; only Churchill did not seem to enjoy the joke. He rose to protest that only recently the ruling had been given that the word 'lies' was as much to be ruled out of order as 'liar', but the Speaker parried the charge that Bevan had been referring so directly to Churchill himself. 'No,' confirmed Bevan, 'I was referring to the almost Goebbelesque system of mass suggestion' which had been evolved to persuade the British people and other nations that Britain's plight was desperate. Then he proceeded to stutter out the figures, in rebuttal of 'the flatulent generalities' of the day before, which proved the extent of Britain's recovery both compared with pre-war terms and the post-war achievements of other nations. The recital was lightened by a flow of wit, mostly at Churchill's expense. He is 'a very great stylist . . . A reason why he moves so gracefully across the pages is because he carries a light weight of fact'. Of course, all the figures were comparative; 'they only have meaning in comparison with members of the same family. Even the effulgence of the right hon. Gentleman is not his own personal endowment: it reflects the twilight around him'. Bevan was indeed able to prove that on every legitimate test – exports, output per man, dependence on dollar imports – post-war Britain had done better than the European nations which Churchill had paraded as examples for our emulation. The mountain of facts was huge, and was fully visible and accepted by foreign observers. That placed in a light all the more sinister Churchill's rhetoric and the bitterness left by his thwarted ambitions of 1945. Did he not realize what damage he was doing to Britain? Would it not be better if, before tarnishing his reputation further, he retired from public life? By now, any lightness in the mood induced by Bevan's wit was dispelled by his ferocity. The record of fact and Churchillian distortion was related directly to the immediate debate. Bevan asserted his own belief, whatever the Chancellor of the Exchequer or anyone else might think, that the studied denigration of past months had contributed powerfully to the exchange crisis. Churchill and his friends had been led on by 'the most vicious campaign of misrepresentation that British newspapers have ever indulged in' and had continued the indulgence when the newspapers were beginning to show signs of contrition. 'I cannot understand why Tories should behave in this way. Other nationals do not denigrate their own country abroad. I have not heard Italians doing it. The only people in the world who have used this present situation to undermine the credit of their own country have been the British Tories. They do not care what was the effect upon the fortunes of their own country, so long as they could reap some Party glory.'

Thus the Tories were stripped of their patriotic colours which they normally flaunted with such arrogance. Parliamentary tempers had been raised to the highest pitch. The speech could have ended there and been hailed as a customary Bevan broadside. But amazingly, almost musingly, he turned aside to other themes. Churchill, he said, had invited the House to show its historical sense. Several of his supporters had done the same, among them Sir Robert Boothby who had even dared to foretell what a Tory Government might achieve. Bevan picked out his old parliamentary companion of the 1930s, as if inviting his companionship on a special journey. Why had he joined the prophets? 'Why read the crystal when he can read the book?' Boothby interrupted and Bevan was able to turn the tables once more. Part of the history he wished to recall was the peacetime achievement of Churchill as Chancellor of the Exchequer. He had before him Boothby's account of the return to the Gold Standard in 1926 and he came to the sentence in which Boothby had said: 'The best Mr Churchill can say about it was that we were shackled to reality.' At that Bevan paused, looked round the House and with a gesture of the head to Churchill and what looked like a wink to everyone else, dropped his voice to an incredulous whisper and repeated the words: '*shackled to reality*'. At once, all eyes turned upon the dishevelled, romantic figure on the Tory front bench, and the whole place dissolved in one mighty gasp of good humour. Churchill's face, a few seconds before all scowls and venom, reflected the scene. It was a perilous moment. The brilliant touch of comedy could have reduced the speech to a charade.

But Bevan talked on, even more softly still. He might almost have been reminiscing to a band of cronies in the Smoking Room. Gradually Churchill himself, abandoning any effort to sustain the pretence of nonchalant resignation, became riveted. For Bevan was intermingling with his attack on the present-day Tory performance his recollection – and Churchill's – of earlier performances. 'The right hon. Gentleman thinks that he is the Leader of the Conservative Party. He is not. He is their decoy ... The Conservative Party have always tried to find a false face ... If he capitalizes the reputation he still has to get them, the Conservative Party, once more back to office, he will not be in office long himself. They will fling him aside like a soiled glove ... Does he not remember that although he was himself one of the most brilliant parliamentarians of the day, a crowd of mediocrities kept him out of office for nine years ... that in the war years ... it was the Labour Party that virtually made him Prime Minister?'

Banished for the moment was the shadow of the 1949 crisis. Instead the misery and the grandeur of English history in the twentieth century, of 1926 and 1940, was paraded before us, and amid it all one unforgettable spectacle too often forgotten – Lloyd George and Churchill, the two men of the century, unsurpassed in

gifts and genius but kept out of office by the very persons responsible for 'undermining the industrial fabric of Great Britain'. But
why should he rely on his own memory? Confronting his old
opponent face to face, almost embracing him, he read out the words
which Churchill himself had used in 1938: 'When I think of the
fair hopes of a long peace which still lay before Europe at the
beginning of 1933 when Herr Hitler first obtained power, and of
all the opportunities of arresting the growth of the Nazi power
which have been neglected or squandered, I cannot believe that a
parallel exists in the whole course of history. So far as this country
is concerned the responsibility must rest with those who have the
undisputed control of our political affairs. They neither prevented
Germany from rearming, nor did they rearm ourselves in time.
They quarrelled with Italy without saving Ethiopia. They exploited
and discredited the vast institution of the League of Nations, and
they neglected to make alliances and combinations which might
have repaired previous errors, and thus they left us in the hour of
trial without adequate national defence or effective international
security.'[1] Contemptuously and angrily, in the tone which Churchill himself had once used, Bevan finished the quotation and
struck. 'Those are the people Churchill will lead back to power.
There they are. Those are the guilty men – all of them' – and he
swept his arm over the Opposition bench as in the years gone
by Lloyd George had swept *his* arm. 'I almost believed at that
moment', wrote the most perceptive reporter of the scene, 'that
Winston was going to abstain on his own Amendment. There have
been attempts, since the debate, to write off Bevan's speech. It did
not deal directly with devaluation. It was too violent. It did not get
the country anywhere in its hour of crisis. That is what they say.
But no one who heard it and saw it – no one in the packed galleries,
no Member in the House, not Winston, nor the Guilty Men, nor
the Chaplain leaning intently behind the Bar – no one will ever
forget it. It hauled down Winston's election flag and trampled on it.
It cut the already shaky ground from under Winston's feet. And as
for his followers, his confederates, his masters, or whatever they
might rightly be called in the Tory Party, Bevan not merely pressed

[1] *Hansard* 5 October 1938 Vol. 339 Col. 366–7.

their noses to the brimstone but hurled them over the abyss into the everlasting bonfire.'[1]

The logic of that speech, which feels as compulsively valid today as it did to many at the time, was that a general election should have been fought forthwith, say in October or November of 1949. Bevan strongly and persistently pressed the case on Attlee, and, as far as these indelicacies could be mentioned there, in the Cabinet. *Tribune* launched the debate in the press with a special article on 30 September and was promptly accused of engaging in some conspiracy with Ministers of the Crown. The charge was disavowed, but some inkling of the mood at Cliveden Place may have wafted to Fleet Street. One reason in particular would have been approved by Bevan, then locked in one of his major contests with the Treasury on behalf of his department. 'Already,' wrote *Tribune*, 'civil servants are well-known to be suffering from that peculiar form of suspended animation which afflicts them when a general election is in the offing . . . The higher the civil servant, the worse the disease. So many of the top-ranking officials are ingrained with a Tory consciousness that, in the hope or belief of a Tory victory, they recommend action opposed to the spirit of the Government . . . Hence the pressure on the Government from its official advisers to make cuts in the social services before the Washington talks.' Indeed there were plenty of other good reasons for the election, particularly as every leader on the Labour side never doubted that Labour would win with a substantial majority. Bagehot said – *Tribune* reminded its readers on 14 October – that the final authority in the British constitution was a newly-elected House of Commons. It was such commanding authority which the Labour Government needed in the aftermath of devaluation, and if it had been sought and secured in that autumn the whole post-war history of Britain could have been beneficially transformed. When Attlee, to kill the widespread speculation, made the announcement in the middle of October that there would be no election that year, *Tribune* characterized it as 'a serious mistake'. Bevan confided his misgivings to his friends but still believed that the error could be repaired. He

[1] J. P. W. Mallalieu, M.P. in his weekly 'Westminster Commentary' in *Tribune*, 7 October 1949.

had his own fifteen-year plan which he disclosed at a speech in Tredegar. 'During the next five years we shall begin to reap the advantages of what we have sown. Then we shall want another five to consolidate. Then, when everything is foolproof, you can risk a Tory Government.'

However, some other matters required more urgent attention. Devaluation spread fresh fears about the perils of inflation; every department was required to cut its programme of expenditure, and Bevan, not for the first or the last time, found his own department subjected to a double assault. The announcement of these measures made by the Prime Minister in October included a £35 million cut in housing investment, which would reduce the total built by 25,000 a year and a proposal for imposing a shilling charge on prescriptions under the Health Service.

Something of the battle behind the scenes may be indicated by the letter which Bevan sent to the Prime Minister on 21 October:

My dear Prime Minister,

The more I reflect on the conclusions of this morning's Cabinet Meeting, the more convinced I am that they are ill-balanced. You will recollect that the earlier decisions about economies in capital and budgetary expenditure were all subject to the complete picture being revealed. When I agreed that it might be possible to cut the housing programme by 25,000 houses per year, leaving the local government housing programme substantially untouched, it was always on the assumption that the reduction in defence expenditure would also be of the order of magnitude which would have justified the reduction in houses.

It, however, emerges in the final issue that the defence expenditure is only going to be cut on the administrative side, and even that in a full year to no more than £30 million out of something of the order of an expenditure of £800 million. When the two figures are put into juxtaposition, that is to say £40 to £50 million social services and £30 million on the already gorged and swollen defence estimates, I am afraid the result will be painful in the extreme.

Furthermore, a reduction in housing expenditure cannot be

justified on the basis of the existing national emergency. Housing makes its own peculiar and essential contribution to economic revival. It has been agreed all through our discussions in the last few weeks that the increase in the export of goods and services following devaluation will change the pattern of labour in the country and, therefore, more, not less, mobility in the labour force will be required. A reduction in the number of new houses will not decrease but rather increase the rigidity of the existing pattern and consequently make it more difficult to bring about a redeployment of the labour force.

So, both from the political and economic points of view, I must impress upon you that I regard the decision to reduce the size of the housing programme as not being justified. Even at this late hour I suggest that we modify our plans accordingly.

I am sending copies of this letter to the Lord President of the Council, the Secretary of State for Foreign Affairs, the Chancellor of the Exchequer and the Minister of Defence.

Seemingly the appeal was of no avail. Attlee still made the announcement, including the housing cuts and including the prescription charge. How, while Bevan remained Minister of Health, neither of them was actually imposed is another story, to be resumed after the appeal to the polls.

Churchill described the 1950 general election as 'demure', and subsequent commentators have too readily accepted his opinion. For Churchill himself it may have been. He was paraded from one great mass meeting to another, where his elaborately prepared orations were delivered to devout and enthusiastic audiences from platforms draped in the Union Jack. Normally no questions were allowed; mostly only Conservative ticket-holders were admitted to these faintly Edwardian, Elgaresque occasions. For once in his life at least, Churchill had at his command the panoply of a Party machine; it makes for convenience and comfort. Bevan had no such facilities. His own Party managers, headed by Herbert Morrison, were engaged in the task of pretending he did not exist. Deliberately kept off the radio and out of the main centres, it was hoped that any fresh indiscretion from him would not be too widely publicized. Transport House shuddered every night at the news which might come from some distant marginal outpost, such as Oldham or Devonport, where the man who, it was thought, could lose the election with a single false step walked his tight-rope twice or thrice nightly. Half Fleet Street followed him around to be present at the drop. With the later intrusion of television, the 1950 election (together with 1951) was probably the last in British history when the platform dominated a campaign, and Bevan was, by now, incomparably the biggest platform draw in the country. He believed in the arena as fervently as Gladstone or John Bright; only here was the choice of weapons not weighted in favour of privilege, conformity and wealth. Some caution is needed, however, in interpreting the records available. What actually happened on the platform and what most of the London press reported next morning seemed to be events occurring in two distinct hemispheres.

According to newspaper headlines, Bevan's progress through the country left behind a trail of tumult and class fury. Almost everywhere he was greeted with chants of 'Vermin, vermin', and if the overture was somehow omitted at the start of a meeting, it would be sure to assist the uproar at the end. Editors were eager for new Bevanite morsels of abuse to chew upon, and their reporters, or more likely, their sub-editors did their best to supply them until the old portrait of a loud-mouthed, irascible demagogue began to acquire a credible outline once more. 'Bevan Calls Woman a Virago', said the *Western Mail* (7 February). 'Bevan talks of civil war again', said the *Birmingham Gazette* (7 February). 'Bevan Booed by Crowd Outside Hall', said the *Western Morning News* (20 February). 'Churchill Starved the Babies – Bevan', said the *Daily Mail* (4 February). Actually the shrill-voiced virago of Bury, as Bevan did indeed call her, would have strained the patience of saints. Nothing can be more disturbing to a speaker than a steady, inane, hen-like cluck, but Bevan did his best to woo even her, until finally he felt constrained to say: 'There was an old medieval priest who said that the three worst things in life were a false friend, meat cooked twice and a cackling woman.' As for the menace of civil war, the old 1945 Laski scare which Bevan had allegedly unleashed once more, the explanation was simple. He had been telling his Socialist friends that it was better to take over industries by paying compensation than by risking bloodshed. But who cared?

Bevan, the ruthless cut-throat, snarled from every cartoon and headline.

I recall his visit to Devonport during that campaign; we were never likely to forget it. For days before, the prospect of his coming had given a tingling, mounting excitement to the contest. Friend and foe wanted to see for themselves how truly inhuman the monster might be. The hall was jammed long before the scheduled time with great crowds overflowing outside. For a moment, when Bevan started to speak, there were the customary chants and catcalls. But everything had to be hushed to hear him at all. There was no hint of any ranting; he was all sweetness and light. Within a few minutes he made a bargain with his Tory hecklers. He would put their case for them and they could tell him whether he had done it adequately. He then proceeded to state the case for laissez-faire economics with scruple, discrimination, almost affectionate artistry. Richard Cobden would have applauded. Devonport Conservatives were amazed at the intellectual sophistication of their argument; Devonport Socialists were caught by a palpitating fear that their hero might have carried things a little too far. Had he been fair? Yes, no one could deny it. He had applied the Bevan maxims for debate; seize the enemies' stronghold; once capture that and all other outposts will fall in the same assault; fail there, and no lesser victories will avail. Then he proceeded, with general assent, to dismantle the whole elaborate structure, almost brick by brick, with the audience so captivated by the delicacy of the performance that they could not tell what transformation was being worked upon them. He would turn to translate his theory into practical terms of coal, housing, steel. Steel, in particular, which Bevan sought to make a principal issue in the election, provided him with his classic illustration. Churchill should have learnt a little more by now of these industrial matters of which he was so profoundly ignorant. During the war he and his friend, Lord Portal, had planned to produce a steel house – 500,000 of them, it was said, would soon be rolling off the production belt. Yet only two had ever actually been seen, one the prototype and the other a model put on display for the troops in Berlin. Why? *Because there was not enough steel.* And there was *still not enough steel.* Steel was the matrix of modern industry. Britain needed more. Plymouth needed more; steel for the houses and hospitals and new factories her people were still crying out for. And thus he returned to the matter in hand, the election. Even outside the hall where the speech had been relayed to waiting thousands the boos and catcalls were eventually subdued. Many who had come to jeer went away amazed. They had seen him display one of his chief faculties – the capacity to raise the level of national debate.

During the last few days of the campaign he returned to the warmth of his own constituency and to the traditional eve-of-poll meeting on Waunpound, the mountain between Ebbw Vale and Tredegar. An election campaign can stir the emotions of a participant to a pitch of intensity quite unappreciated by the casual observer, and for Bevan the 1950 election must have been especially testing. Every night he was addressing huge and, for the most part, ecstatically enthusiastic audiences and every morning he awoke to find himself a kind of national butt, half-boor, half-buffoon. The vermin charge drilled in his ears; he had already referred to it in his Election Address. 'I have been accused, perhaps with justice,' he wrote in the message for the Ebbw Vale electors, 'that I am too intensely aware of the grim experiences we have endured together, and that I have allowed the memory of them to embitter my judgment. So passionately have I resented the unmerited privations to which we were subjected in the years between the two wars, that I have sometimes expressed myself in language that may have appeared crude and harsh to those who were fortunate enough to escape our experiences. All I will say about that is that it is a virtue to forgive wrongs done to oneself; it is a poverty of spirit to forgive the wrongs done to others.' In the same message, he stressed one of his other constant themes. Principles, not personalities, were the issues in the election. 'We consider it to be an insult to the intelligence of our people to ask them to trust the wisdom of any one individual, no matter how eminent or revered. The insistence on the supremacy of one personality, I regard as unwholesome in a democracy. It denies the dignity of the individual citizen and undermines the responsibility of each of us for the policy which should govern the nation.' His hatred of the Churchill cult touched the roots of his democratic faith. Back in his own constituency, he could at last allow his tensions to relax. 'In the last few years,' he told them, describing the pleasantries of his tour, 'I have been represented as an ogre, as a man animated by hate and malice. I think the Tories came along to my meetings expecting to see someone with sabre teeth, a dagger at his side, and wearing a red sash. I noticed expressions of surprise flitting across their faces when there appeared on the platform a comparatively mild-mannered individual – not too bad-looking, perhaps – not hand-some, perhaps – but not hideous either.'

Bevan, like most of the other Labour Ministers, believed the Labour Government would be returned with a sizeable, certainly a workable majority. He had a deep faith, part mystic, part Marxist, in the virtue and efficacy of universal suffrage. If the issues were fairly presented, he could not imagine that the mass of working people would fail to recognize their interests, just as they did in Ebbw Vale. Despite all the weaknesses, hesitations and timidities of the Labour Government, he saw the choice in 1950 as a clear one. The people would use their quite recently acquired weapon of the franchise to carry a stage further, if Labour had the will and courage, the peaceful transfer of the ownership of the nation's wealth from the few to the many, in fulfilment of the prophecy and the programme outlined by Thomas Rainborough and the Level-lers before Cromwell and his generals in Putney Church three centuries before.

Just before the 1945 election he had recalled 'that most memor-able debate in British history', and five years later his faith had not abated. 'The three elements,' he had written, 'are now present: democracy, property and poverty. There is no rest between them; rather a ceaseless struggle and ferment . . . There is no com-promise possible between these three discordant forces. They are the solvent of the nations and societies which refuse to yield to their logic . . . They are the imperative of politics, and those who ignore them have neither a sense of direction nor an abiding purpose to fulfil. They speak across the centuries the wisdom of Thomas Rainborough: Either poverty must use democracy to destroy the power of property, or property, in fear of poverty, will destroy democracy.'[1]

[1] *Why Not Trust the Tories?* by Aneurin Bevan (Gollancz, 1944), p. 88.

This was the level on which Bevan believed that the Socialist argument of the 1950s should be presented and the battle could be won. It was a shattering blow when the election results declared on 2 February cut Labour's overall majority from 152 to 6, and drove Labour's timorous leaders even more readily on to the defensive.

8

THE CLASH

1950-1951

Though man may endure his ordeal like Sisyphus, the time must come
for him to revolt like Prometheus, before his powers are exhausted by
the ordeal.—MILOVAN DJILAS[1]

WHEN the newspapers of the early 1950s drew the picture
of a grotesque Caliban, diseased with hatred and ambition, the portrait did reflect the view of a considerable
section of the public. Somehow Aneurin Bevan attracted and unleashed the pent-up furies of the time. It was no mere petty
resentment against the offensive language he had used; a whole
threatened class seemed to hurl their frustrations and fears in his
face. With unconscious discernment they saw him as a revolutionary figure who *would* change society if he could; who would
strip them of their profits and privileges and enthrone in their place
his beloved working class. Such nightmares or dreams still looked
real in 1950.

Bevan himself was perpetually tantalized and tortured by the
possibilities. He saw the stubborn strength of the Labour movement and how much it could achieve if audaciously led; certainly
nothing could ever be done in defiance or contempt of it. Then he
would be confronted afresh with the timorous, stunted imagination
of the Party leadership – their pussy-footing campaign of 1950 was
just the latest example – and he was driven, not so much to despair
or reckless protest, although both moods occasionally prevailed,
but rather to cleanse himself, to expiate his guilt at encouraging
men and women to put faith in such leaders, by redefining the
great democratic argument and re-galvanizing the forces which
gave these men their authority. What was happening in the Soviet

[1] *The Unperfect Society* (Methuen 1969).

283

world enormously strengthened his belief in the democratic Socialist case; democracy in Britain had the chance to make revolutionary changes without the horrors and distortions inseparable from the resort to force and bloodshed. And yet how often that democratic retort to the Soviet challenge was debased, and how little it was understood that to achieve fundamental social change by democratic means was a most delicate and original enterprise, likely to be accomplished only in the first instance in Britain with her unique combined tradition of working-class power and parliamentary representation, and therefore how momentous for all mankind was the responsibility which British Labour carried. Sometimes he drew sustenance from the vitality of the great working-class audiences he saw all around, and sometimes he was enraged at his incapacity to respond adequately to their ambitions. For years now he had imposed upon himself an uncongenial restraint. 'No one knows,' he said to Jennie more than once, 'the violence that is in me.' 1950 and 1951 were to give some hint of those volcanic secretions.

The newspaper reader of the time was prepared for all eventualities. Every available circumstance of Bevan's public and private life was ransacked for clues and gossip. During the election campaign, a favourite rumour was that he intended a post-election *putsch* to unseat Attlee and Co., and a few days after polling-day, when he failed to attend a Cabinet meeting, shrieking headlines pictured him sulking in some tent which, however, reporters could not locate. It is necessary to emphasize repeatedly how he strove to lift the debate high above these levels. Writing in *Tribune* just before the campaign started,[1] he sought to escape from 'the incidental noises' which would soon obtrude. Indeed he was eager as ever to stress how dangerous it was for Socialists to neglect theoretical thinking. 'If the grand design in which we are involved is hidden from us or even blurred we shall falter, hesitate or perhaps even lose our way ... More than ever we need lamps for our feet or we shall stumble.'

Thus he wrote and spoke in a tone employed by no other politician of the period. Even such issues as full employment, the social services, and the more rational distribution of industry, he described as subordinate. They only pointed to a solution; the solution itself

[1] *Tribune*, 3 February 1950.

'demands a restatement of the relations between the individual and society'. Modern industrial society meant that the framework of the past was broken, that 'the individual is adrift on endless and turbulent seas', that somehow a new compass and chart must be found for him, and that nothing less than this philosophic requirement was the true meaning of Socialism. And first he applied his theory to the Communist states, offering an analysis in sharp contrast with the stark pro-Communist or anti-Communist diatribes of the day: 'The techniques of modern industrial civilization call for an educated, trained population which in turn demands full political status . . . Here is the yeast that is fermenting internal relations in the Soviet Union. You cannot educate a man to be a trained technician inside a factory and ask him to accept the status of a political robot outside . . . a totalitarian state or a one-party state is a persistent contradiction with the needs of a thriving industrial community.' Gradually these truths would become comprehended, and the older nations which had carried through their programme of industrialization amid appalling privations and a denial of political liberty should show some patience and understanding. Not that anything justified the barbarities committed in Eastern Europe. The Communist leaders should know better – 'history shouts louder in their ears than it did in ours'. But the world should take some encouragement from the fact: 'The richer the furniture of civilization, the more incompatible with it is the armament of dictatorship.'

However, others besides the Communists needed to learn the lessons of modern industrial society. 'Economic anarchy, the arbitrary decisions of the market place, are as senseless and oppressive to the worker in the factory as the edicts of political dictatorship. He cannot understand why there should be a plan inside the factory and planlessness outside. It does not make sense to him that planned operations in his work should be described as efficiency while chaos everywhere else should be called freedom.' All the hazards of a system dominated by 'private economic adventure' would not be tolerated by those who saw that the economic structure could be planned and reasonably predictable. But a conclusion followed which was only dimly recognized. 'If all the factors of production both human and material are fully deployed, then any

addition to the total of production or change in its direction immediately gives rise to the question: What goes where? Who is to be
the beneficiary or loser by the change? This was the question that
laissez-faire liberalism never had to answer – except in a narrow
budgetary sense – for it allowed human values to emerge from the
sum total of human scramblings. The liberal never knew what
kind of society he intended until he had, in fact, made it. If we, on
the other hand, accept the obligation of planning the direction of
economic activity, then we accept with it the burden of deciding
who and what must first be served. In short, we determine the order
of priorities. It would be fatal for a Socialist to underestimate the
importance of this. Before the industrial revolution the order of
priorities in society was decided by tradition, rank, usage and the
edict of princes, kings and potentates. With the industrial revolution the burden of deciding was abandoned to the niggling of the
market and the compulsions of greed. Now, the people, through
their representative institutions, must choose between a number of
competing claims, and when that happens we have left the lower
levels of economic planning and are treading the uplands of moral
decision. This is the complete answer to those who think Socialism
is merely a matter of appetite. On the contrary, it is the first time
in human history that mankind will have accepted the obligation of
free collective moral choice as the ultimate arbiter in social affairs.
This, in truth, is the People's Coming of Age.'

But those brave expectations had been shattered by the election
results. It did appear that Labour was reduced to a state of parliamentary impotence, and Churchill knew how to fortify the impression. Moreover, how could damaging inquests within the Party
into so unexpected a near-defeat be avoided? The familiar story
told by observers since is of a tired, squabbling, exhausted bunch
of men who eighteen months later surrendered their seals of office
almost eagerly: Labour had finished its programme, lost the will to
govern, yearned only for the soft pastures of opposition. But that
was not the mood of the participants at the time. Outsiders should
never underrate how weary bones and downcast spirits may be
sustained by the penicillin of office. And some of the circumstances
of the setback forbad defeatism. Labour still had thirteen million
votes, more than had been cast for any other political party in

British history. A fractional swing back could give another five-year period of power; the people's coming of age was postponed, but not indefinitely. Bevan certainly was motivated by no political death-wish, but he did find himself thrust into a more complex party contest. Real divergences of policy and principle emerged more sharply than ever about the way Labour should seek escape from the deadlock, but they came to be expressed in clashes of personality. The men at the top had lived together five years in oppressive proximity. Nerves and temperaments jarred. And both the Conservative Opposition and the newspapers eagerly translated all these varying pressures and counter-pressures into a daily melodrama of personal rivalry and ambition.

Herbert Morrison easily convinced himself, as politicians will, that events had confirmed his previous convictions. He set to work with his usual subterranean tenacity to fashion the kind of Party he had always wanted. Good, tidy, efficient administration was his cure for all the ills man is heir to, and the prescription must be applied in particular to the industries already nationalized instead of adding to their number. Morrison believed he could turn into complete victory the long rearguard action he had fought on the National Executive over the previous three years against an extension of public ownership. Moreover he prided himself as the greatest of electioneers and felt that one cause of the electoral setback was the manner in which the Party Secretary, Morgan Phillips, had been permitted to elbow him away from the centre of the Transport House stage. And Morrison was more persuaded than anyone that the 'vermin' cry had disrupted all his own sedate wooing of the middle class. Inevitably, Morrison and Bevan re-emerged as rivals, and Morrison had a discovery to feed his animosity. It was at this period that he would carry round in his breast pocket, to be produced as clinching evidence when Bevan's 'ambition' was the topic of conversation, an extract from the famous speech[1] in which Bevan had described how he pursued power from the local Council, to the County Council, to the House of Commons, only to see its coat-tails disappearing round the door. The speech, delivered at the time in Bevan's most playful tone, was in

[1] Delivered in the House of Commons and referred to in Volume I, p. 84 (*Hansard*, Vol. 395, 15 September 1943).

fact, of course, a commentary with a Socialist moral on the nature of political and economic democracy. Morrison interpreted it as a confession of naked careerism.[1] And the irony was that at that moment more than ever one of Morrison's spurs was his particular personal ambition which he could hardly stop himself blurting out even to political strangers. 'Fair play for Herbert' – as Nye himself might say when the barb came from someone else instead of himself – Morrison was no careerist; his devotion to the Party he had served all his life was deep and genuine. His trouble was a total absorption in the minutiae of politics, an engrossing parochialism with a restless ego at the centre of it. He was a soft-hearted, suburban Stalin, for ever suspecting others of the conspiracies in which he was engaged himself. After the 1950 near-fiasco Morrison felt the doodling Attlee should make way for his obvious successor. He had a case.

The post-election argument about the Party's future strategy was supposed to be brought to a climax at a joint weekend meeting in May of the Cabinet and the National Executive held appropriately in the salubrious draughts of Beatrice Webb House, Dorking. Indeed, most of the newspapers agreed on Monday that the conference had been what the *Daily Express* called 'a peak triumph for Mr Herbert Morrison'. But the truth was more tentative. Morrison, as chairman of the Party's Campaign Committee, had opened the discussion with an elaborate report designed to transform the tone of the Party's national appeal. Public ownership was to be pushed into the shadows; all the particular nationalization proposals in the 1950 programme were to be dropped; their place was to be taken by a 'New Model' ten points and a new definition of Socialism itself. The ten points, as it happened, had already been achieved, almost in their entirety, while the new definition consisted of the rousing tautology: 'Socialism means the assertion of social responsibility for matters which are properly of social concern'. But no matter; tactically, if not philosophically, Morrison

---

[1] How Morrison would carry the cutting round with him is reported by his close friend, Leslie Hunter, in *The Road to Brighton Pier* (Arthur Barker, 1959), p. 25. Morrison recited the same Bevan story with the same misapprehension of its meaning in his own *Autobiography* and again, after Bevan's death, in the last article he wrote in the *Spectator*.

threatened to carry all before him. He had reconnoitred the ground well and prepared his forces in advance; those were the days when the big unions looked to the political leaders for guidance and Morrison seemed to be the man who was giving it. But, after his first hour of victory, events took an unexpected and unreported turn. Late into the night a 'stop-Morrison' resistance movement was started, and one which had considerable significance for the future. The three leaders of it were Bevan, Morgan Phillips and Sam Watson from Durham, a formidable combination, three ex-miners who could in extremity renew the old comradeship of the pits. Next day they mustered enough strength to prove that the Morrison 'consolidation' thesis could only be forced through at the cost of bitter Party disunity. Dorking ended in deadlock, and Morrison turned, as was his custom, to renew the contest else-where. His tireless, burrowing diligence could extort an unwilling respect, and it is hard, looking back, not to sympathize with his gnawing sense of injustice. Throughout the Dorking proceedings, and indeed through the whole ideological dispute, Attlee sat silent. If Morrison had won, Attlee would have concurred. While Morrison fought, he never lifted a finger to assist him. 'I didn't realize that the poor little man was full of seething ambition,' said Attlee years later.[1] It is hard to say whether that pitiless last word tells more of the unhappiness of Morrison or the insensibility of Attlee.

The National Executive was not the only arena where the leader resolutely refused to lead. During those same months a concurrent struggle proceeded in Whitehall. Attlee had no obligation to inter-vene directly. But what surprises is his complete lack of interest – as revealed in his repeated recollections of those days – in the origins of an argument which settled the fate of his administration. For Bevan, fresh departures in an intricate debate proceeded in his own department and his own mind. Being responsible for two of the Government's expenditure programmes, health and housing, and being passionately determined to get more for both, he had sometimes to calculate where pressure could be relaxed, where a compromise must be made, to secure a gain or prevent a break-through elsewhere. He had to fight on two fronts, and hence grew

[1] Clement Attlee in the *Granada Historical Records Interview* (Panther, 1967), p. 53).

the rumour that he was much less interested in housing than in his precious Health Service or, alternatively, that he had betrayed the principle of the Health Service by putting on the Statute Book an Act containing a clause which authorized the imposition of prescription charges without actually imposing them. He manœuvred. No other course but resignation was available. Theoretically one other mitigation of the situation was possible: responsibility for health and housing might be divided, thus relaxing at least the double pressure concentrated upon his own department. But that remedy could hardly appeal to Bevan at the precise moment when so much of Tory fire was directed against him, and it would have meant slicing in half a department which had served him so faithfully and which he had helped to make into one of the most powerful in post-war Whitehall. And, after all, whom was the two-front war against? The enemy was the Treasury. Doubtless the Treasury experts were discharging to the best of their ability, in the new age of peacetime inflation, the essential duty of controlling the nation's finances, and doubtless part of Bevan's hostility derived from the normal antagonism between spending departments and the Exchequer. But his criticism cut deeper and ranged wider. And piquancy was added to the situation by the fact that the Chancellor who spoke in the Treasury's precise, authoritative terms was Bevan's closest associate in the Labour hierarchy, Stafford Cripps. Attlee thought Cripps kept Bevan under his thumb. Morrison thought Bevan twisted Cripps's arm. Both were wrong. The old association had always been respectful but never intimate, and during these months it was strained to the limit.

An open crisis was only narrowly averted within days of the 1950 election. Several newspapers suggested, or rather shrieked, that Bevan and Attlee had quarrelled about the disposition of offices, that Bevan wanted to be moved from the Ministry of Health to higher things, and that he had refused to attend a Cabinet meeting in order to express his displeasure. In fact he was sick for a few days, but he soon returned to ward off a double assault, one from the Tories and the other from his Cabinet colleagues. Eager to exploit their electoral gains and in an atmosphere in which no one knew how long the Government majority of six could last, the Tories put down two votes of censure on successive days, against Bevan in particular. He was there to deal with them in what Capt. Walter Elliot described as 'his usual rude health'.

One motion deplored 'the continuing decline in the number of new houses built each year', and since the housing shortage had been a principal issue at the election and since the capital investment cuts of the previous October, following devaluation, had proposed to reduce the annual rate of building from 200,000 to 175,000, this appeared to be the flank where Bevan was most vulnerable. But he consumed his opponents in what *The Times* described as 'a display of verbal pyrotechnics'. Partly the feat was due to the error of his opponents in suggesting a reduction in housing standards as one way to increase the numbers built. Nothing could make Bevan more righteously furious. 'If for nothing else, I will go down in history as a barrier between the beauty of Britain and the speculative builder who has done so much to destroy it.' His denunciation of 'the marzipan period of architecture' distracted attention from the capital investment cuts, and of course too much open debate on those figures could have been awkward. Bevan was convinced that the cut to 175,000 would never be executed. That was one of his private Whitehall fights and the less he said about it publicly the better.

Much more serious from Bevan's point of view was the renewed opportunity for attack upon the Health Service offered by supplementary estimates of nearly £100 million which his department required. Apart even from their hatred of Bevan and the Service he had shaped, this, for the Tories, touched the nerve-centre of politics. The whole Government were a bunch of spendthrifts and Bevan was the arch-offender. Health Service finance was completely out of control and no recovery could be expected for the whole national economy until this flow of blood was staunched.[1] In the actual debate Cripps replied valiantly to this attack, adopting Bevan's own defence – the Health Service was new and its exact cost could not be estimated until the behaviour patterns of the public were known. Of course, a financial 'ceiling' for the Service

---

[1] It may be asked: what was the truth about the Opposition's charge of Health Service finance being out of control? The Guillebaud Report of 1956 (Cmd. 9663) – alas, too late to assist Bevan in 1950 – put these accusations in their proper perspective. See p. 215.

would have to be established and observed. Cripps emphasized the word two or three times, but it is doubtful if the Opposition knew how closely they were fingering one of the Government's tenderest joints. Only in the last few minutes of the debate was a hint given. Mr Osbert Peake persisted with the question: would Bevan say what had happened to the one-shilling prescription charge, announced by the Prime Minister in the previous October and calculated to save £10 million? Bevan would not. He parried the blow, while claiming a few more victims for his pyrotechnics.

But in fact Health Service finance had become a big issue in the Cabinet, and it figured there prominently during those two days of the Commons debate. On 14 March, Bevan wrote to Attlee:

My dear Clem,

As I told you, Morrison, Cripps and Gaitskell this morning, I do not agree with the minutes of yesterday's Cabinet as they relate to the National Health Service. No firm decision was taken about a statement in the House this afternoon. I do not, however, want to press this point as it has been overtaken by our discussion this morning.

I wish to emphasize that I have no recollection of any decision having been taken in the form in which it is recorded at Conclusion (ii) to Minute 3, 'Agreed to resume at a later date their discussion of the finances of the National Health Service'. I do hope that I can have a little peace to get on with my proper work without this continual nibbling, and I must give notice that I intend at the next meeting of the Cabinet to challenge this Conclusion.

Alas, exactly what occurred when the Conclusion was challenged will be unknown until the Cabinet papers are made public in the year 1980. But the letter gives a whiff of the sulphurous atmosphere behind the scenes. Bevan kept few letters; his complete carelessness in preserving records to protect his reputation – almost unique in a modern politician – was part of his endearing lack of self-consciousness; but he did occasionally stuff an original or a copy in his pocket, presumably for reference in future political controversy, and this, significantly, was one of them.

For more than a year there had been talk in Whitehall about various forms of charges on the Health Service. The Treasury detested the idea of a *free* Service, free to the patient, as being opposed to every canon of sound finance, and returned to the theme with unyielding dourness. Cripps broached the subject in his 1949 Budget statement; charges had been considered but a further period of experiment was conceded. That was one of Bevan's first victories in the long campaign, but the price he had to pay for it was a clause in the National Health Service (Amendment) Act, 1949 which authorized a one-shilling prescription charge to be imposed, if a fair and workable scheme could be devised. The measure attracted little attention at the time, although a few speakers, led by Dr Somerville Hastings and Dr Santo Jeger of the Socialist Medical Association, warned that a dangerous precedent was being set. Bevan welcomed the warnings and doubtless hoped that they would be heard in other quarters.[1] He never believed that there could be a fair and workable system for prescription charges. But more sinister, in his estimation, were the other proposals for charges which could be endlessly extended to undermine the whole principle of the Service. And it was not only the Treasury which did not appreciate the principle. ' "Nye is getting away with murder," was the general feeling of my colleagues,' wrote Morrison. 'It was not so much a selfish attitude to the problems of his fellow Ministers as Bevan's unquestioning regard for dogma. The original plan was that the medical services should provide everybody with everything needed for nothing, and nothing must alter that.'[2] Confronted with this hostility, he had to accept the strict tone of Cripps's reference to the Service in his 1950 Budget statement in April: 'We must now regard the period of initiation as passed so that there

---

[1] The brief debate and the vote on the subject took place on 9 December 1949 (*Hansard*, Vol. 470). Bevan, in the course of the debate, said: 'I have been asked a number of questions as to how I propose to use this power. I say frankly that if I could give the answer there is no excuse for my not having the regulation ready. I do not myself yet know all the answers. I am not myself displeased that we have had this discussion this morning. I am not displeased that hon. Members have been brought up against the administrative difficulties of carrying out principles which many people have so glibly proposed.'

[2] *An Autobiography* by Herbert Morrison, p. 267.

is no excuse for exceeding the estimates in the coming twelve months . . . Any expansion in part of the Service must be met by economies, or, if necessary, by contraction in others . . . Should present powers of control be insufficient, an Amending Act will be introduced.' This section of the speech might be seen as a Cripps memorandum to Bevan, delivered in public to add to its solemnity. But the charges, including the prescription charges, had been stopped, and Bevan lived to threaten to resign another day.

The crisis had almost come then, and perhaps was only avoided through the good offices of a go-between, Harold Wilson. One weekend at Buscot Park, Lord Faringdon's home in Berkshire, Wilson heard Bevan make the declaration that he would resign if the plan for charges went ahead. So he made it his mission to see Cripps and plead that no sacrilegious hands should be laid on Bevan's 'Ark of the Covenant'. Then in turn he pleaded with Bevan to be gentler with Cripps who was already suffering from physical affliction. The corner was turned, a compromise arranged. In return for the abandonment of the charges Bevan would accept the ceiling and accept further what he regarded as a barely sufferable indignity, the surveillance of Health Service finances by a special weekly Cabinet Committee, presided over by the Prime Minister. 'That night,' Jennie recalls, 'he came home white with passion.' It was on this Committee that Bevan had his first close contact with Cripps's recently appointed Minister of State, Hugh Gaitskell, and the mutual impression was unfavourable. Gaitskell made his mark on Bevan's political horizon as the pedantic spokesman of the Treasury's most arid doctrines, and nothing of his experience in government had encouraged him to suffer economists gladly.

Less belligerently at first, Bevan and Gaitskell had been meeting for months past at the Thursday night dinners which Cripps held with the Ministers associated especially with economic departments. This was Cripps's substitute for the informal consultations which Attlee abjured or found distasteful. Bevan attended these gatherings rather as a long-standing political friend and he certainly approved of meetings between Cabinet colleagues where the give-and-take of discussion could be completely private and uninhibited. But Gaitskell insisted on pressing the health charges argument, in season and out of season. 'It became a mission or an obsession with him,' says Harold Wilson.[1] Much else on the political arena became obscured by the fierce controversy it could provoke. For Bevan, according to another witness at those dinners, John Strachey,[2] would give Gaitskell a verbal lashing, and Gaitskell would reply with cold silence or a dry, factual contradiction. Walking away with Bevan one night, Strachey asked him why he was doing it: 'Why,' he asked, 'are you going out of your way to make a rift between yourself and one of the really considerable men of the Government?' 'Considerable?' Bevan replied, 'But he's nothing, nothing, nothing!' The conversation sounds authentic, even if doubts must remain about who was the aggressor in what was to prove a lengthy and famous war. Why, one wonders, however, did not the precise issue which provoked these onslaughts stick in Strachey's memory? 'I tried to explain to Bevan,' continues Strachey, 'that the quiet, rather slight man who sat opposite him had "a will like a dividing spear". I might have saved my breath for all the effect I had on Bevan. I talked the thing over with Stafford Cripps, and with that curious fatalism about personal relations which he often exhibited, Stafford shrugged his shoulders and said there was nothing to be done.' But to Bevan the matter was not one of personal relations: it was concerned with policies, principles, political themes. He pictured several of his Cabinet colleagues, now assisted by this glorified civil servant, banded together, contentedly it seemed, to undermine the greatest Socialist achievement of the Labour Government. He noted not the will and courage but the other aspects of Gaitskellism: the parched political imagination, the pedantic insistence on lesser truths in the presence of great ones.

So he exploded. But curiously the reverberations were not heard or felt outside the smallest circle. What angered Bevan especially was that Gaitskell continued to pursue his campaign for health charges even after the compromise of March 1950. So, at the end of June 1950, he wrote to Cripps to say that he would be going to no more Thursday dinners, and received in return the following scribbled reply:

[1] In conversation with the author.
[2] John Strachey in an obituary notice on Hugh Gaitskell in the *Sunday Times Weekly Review*, 20 January 1963. The words here attributed to Bevan may be accurate, but they should not be taken as his final verdict on Gaitskell.

Personal and Private
My dear Ni,

I have your note of June 29th.

Would it not have been more friendly to have stated your real reason for giving up our weekly meetings at dinner?

I am sorry that you feel that way about it.

STAFFORD

To which Bevan replied more deliberately:

Private and Confidential
My dear Stafford,

Thank your for your note, though I must say I was rather surprised at its acerbity.

If you will consult your colleagues who have been dining together you will find that I have on a number of occasions recently expressed the view that these dinners were outliving their usefulness. There really must be a good reason for a dinner every Thursday, particularly as it usually comes at the end of an exhausting day. However, you are right in your assumption that I finally made up my mind on this question because of something that happened recently.

I have made it clear to you, the Prime Minister, and Gaitskell that I consider the imposition of charges on any part of the Health Service raises issues of such seriousness and fundamental importance that I could never agree to it. If it were decided by the Government to impose them, my resignation would automatically follow. Despite this, spokesmen of the Treasury and you have not hesitated to press this so-called solution upon the Government. But surely it must be apparent to you that it can hardly create friendly relations if, in spite of the knowledge of how seriously I regard this question, you continue to press it. I am not such a hypocrite that I can pretend to have amiable discourses with people who are entirely indifferent to my most strongly held opinions.

I have thought it better that I should no longer attend the dinners rather than that I should try to suppress opinions on a matter of so fundamental a character.

I am very sorry, because our personal association has been so long and I think of public benefit. But really you must not go on treating every issue as of the same importance. Some go too near the bone and this is one.

I would not have written at such length had it not happened that at the Prime Minister's meeting last Wednesday, under what I consider to have been unjustifiable needling, I gave way to an outburst of resentment.

Yours sincerely,

ANEURIN

The letter which started this exchange is lost, but its terms can be guessed. No guesswork is needed about the significance of what is revealed. It is evident that through many months, *before* the 1950 election and in the months immediately following, Bevan was fighting a battle in the Cabinet in defence of the Health Service, with few allies.

One customary way for a Prime Minister to alleviate such tensions in a Cabinet is to shuffle his Ministers to fresh departments, and there is little doubt that this expedient was discussed at various moments throughout 1950, but the details are obscure. The misleading newspaper story, immediately after the election, was that Bevan demanded 'promotion' from the Ministry of Health and was aggrieved when Attlee refused it. Dalton suggested to Attlee that Bevan should become Colonial Secretary: he himself was to take over a remodelled Housing, Local Government and Planning Department from which the Ministry of Health would be severed. But Dalton told Attlee that he would only accept this rearrangement if Bevan favoured it, and he understood at the time that Bevan demurred. Morrison said, according to Dalton, that 'Bevan has made a mess of the Ministry of Health, and should be made to stay there and clean it up'. The touch of malice rings true, but not the inference that Attlee was ever influenced by it.[1]

What certainly did happen is that Bevan urged on Attlee a general reconstruction of the Government not so much in terms of personalities as of administrative coherence. Maybe the idea was

[1] *High Tide and After* by Hugh Dalton, p. 350.
10*

first mooted in the weeks after the election but it was certainly
revived, in more forceful and comprehensive terms, months later
and partly as a result of the conflicts within the Cabinet and the
National Executive. The starting-point of the idea was the Ministry
of Health where, in the long run, the logic could not be denied that
health and housing should be kept apart, but Bevan's scheme
envisaged a whole series of rearrangements and concentrations.
Clearly there was a case for putting all the responsibility for local
government, planning and building in every form under one head,
and clearly the old Ministry of Health with its vastly extended
health functions could not undertake this aggrandisement. Similar
redefinitions of function were required in the Ministry of Health,
Labour, and National Insurance. But clearly also the splitting of
Bevan's own department would be an extremely painful operation,
and if it did happen he would wish to move elsewhere; to make that
calculation was not exactly a proof of inordinate ambition.

Bevan indeed that summer, for all his worries and alleged tan-
trums, was full of zest and curiosity. He was no weary Titan bowed
down by the cares of office, much as he hated the grind of intrigue,
much as he feared for the Labour Party's future. Asceticism, in his
book, did not make men dutiful and wise; it made them skinny and
miserable and unfit to instruct their fellow men about anything.
Equally to be deplored were intellectual ascetics, content to pursue
a single line of knowledge to the inevitable dead end. His favourites
had always been the encyclopaedic lovers of life: Renaissance men
or Thomas Jefferson (greatly helped by a Welsh grandfather) or
Jack London (greatly helped by a Welsh mother) or Stendhal (*Le
Rouge et le Noir* was a favourite book) or H. G. Wells or Lewis
Mumford. One sign of his catholic taste was his lust to get out of
London, to get the dirt of Westminster out of his pores, to absorb
himself utterly in some new occupation. One glorious weekend that
summer, I recall, we (that is, Nye, Jennie, my wife and myself)
went to Stratford and saw John Gielgud's Lear and Peggy Ashcroft's Rosalind, and late into the night the bogyman instructed a
captivated and astounded audience of theatre directors, headed by
Anthony Quayle and his wife, Dorothy Hyson, on the fatuities and
misapprehensions of Shakespearean critics. Next day we took a
boat on the Avon, and I can still recall the castigation he gave me

for having mastered the decadent, bourgeois art of punting. 'Raillery is the finest part of conversation,' said Swift, and Bevan could exemplify better than anyone what he meant. It was more than playfulness or badinage; it was a kind of non-stop satire designed for the occasion. All his genius was momentarily at the service of the immediate company, and lavished without a care. He could live for the moment. 'Anyone can be a millionaire for five minutes,' he would say, as we embarked on some scandalous extravagance, prompted by his utterly uncalculating generosity. Morrison and Gaitskell, even the hideous news from Korea just coming through, were a million miles away. No one who knew those days and nights will ever forget. The champagne never tasted so good in any other company. And that was just one of the moments of unqualified delight: Stratford in August 1950, when the creature was supposed to be grubbing in some labyrinth of malice, plot and counter-plot.

However, as we return to London in this story, it is necessary to anticipate one important event. Korea transformed the political and world scene and certainly transformed Bevan's relationship with his colleagues. But one later incident that year fits better into the present context.

In July Stafford Cripps fell ill and in October he resigned as Chancellor and Hugh Gaitskell was appointed in his place. Bevan was staggered by the news; but not, as so many of the biographers have guessed, because he had been grooming himself for the office or had even considered himself as the likely candidate. True, both Cripps and even Attlee had at one time or another dropped hints that he might be Cripps's successor, but his deep objection to Gaitskell's appointment was not personal, and derived from another source altogether. Political leaders in a democracy, particularly in the Labour movement, should *represent* something and somebody; they must speak for the major sections of the movement. But Gaitskell – in Bevan's estimation – represented nothing, unless it was the civil service-cum-middle class which was already vastly over-represented at Westminster and had no business to wrest the leadership from the working class. Moreover, just prior to this appointment, at the Labour Party Conference in Margate, Bevan had done his best to repair some of the wounds inflicted in the internal battles of the spring and summer and in private he had had the opportunity of renewing his proposals for the overhaul of the administration. Gaitskell's appointment, and even more perhaps the equanimity which Attlee showed in making it, came as a severe jolt.

Bevan did not believe in concealing his feelings; two days later he wrote to Attlee:

My dear Prime Minister,

You will recollect that during our discussion a short while ago we agreed that I should let you have a private note setting out my views on some changes which could be made in the structure of the Government. I was proceeding to do this when I heard to my consternation and astonishment of the resignation of Cripps and the appointment of Gaitskell.

I am sure you will agree that it is impossible to give advice and counsel about Government policy when only a part at a time is disclosed to me, so that I have no means of knowing the relevance of my advice to the whole of your policy. I have no complaint that you have not thought it prudent or wise to consult me before reaching your decision, but you will, I hope, appreciate that it is only possible to be of service in an atmosphere of candour and trust.

I feel bound to tell you that for my part I think the appointment of Gaitskell to be a great mistake. I should have thought myself that it was essential to find out whether the holder of this great office would commend himself to the main elements and currents of opinion in the Party. After all, the policies which he will have to propound and carry out are bound to have the most profound and important repercussions throughout the movement.

This decision must necessarily change my attitude to the new office which you suggested for me and, therefore, before your mind is finally made up I should like the opportunity of a few words with you.

ANEURIN

To which Attlee replied:

My dear Nye,

I have your letter. I am sorry you have not let me have the note with regard to the changes of structure, as I do not see that the other matters to which you refer really affect this point.

I should, of course, be glad to have a talk with you, though I do not think that your views are shared by many people.

Yours ever,

CLEM

Bevan did have what he called later 'a tremendous row' with Attlee over the Gaitskell appointment and the failure at that propitious moment to reconstruct the Government more ambitiously. Immediately, too, his own attitude to a new office was implicated. Attlee offered him the Ministry of Labour but he was not greatly tempted, and part of his reluctance in moving from the Ministry of Health – despite the fact that he himself had urged the necessary reorganization – arose from his fear of a new attack on the Health Service. These suspicions would have been fortified if he had known what some of his colleagues were saying behind his back. Dalton, the father-confessor and father-promoter of Gaitskell, was rubbing his eloquent hands with glee over the advancement of his protégé. 'Nye is being very difficult and behaving very badly,' he wrote in his diary on 30 October, and he reported also how Morrison 'couldn't make out why the P.M. is afraid of him [Bevan].' According to Morrison (as reported by Dalton), 'the P.M. should say: "Labour or out". Then if he resigned he would do himself much harm.'[1] A Morrison-Dalton combination to damn Bevan was a grisly, bizarre development. However, all these other weighty matters in the autumn of 1950 were swamped by the Korean avalanche.

The tribulations of the 1945–51 Labour Government started with one Anglo-American crisis and ended with another. That forgotten feature of the history of the time, too often overshadowed by the cold war with the Soviet Union or the domestic war with the Tories, is essential to its understanding. Britain and the United States had common interests all over the world, and the paramount feature of

[1] Hugh Dalton, unpublished diaries.

the Bevin-Attlee foreign policy was to insist upon them *at all costs*, in the phrase Churchill applied in the same context. But Aneurin Bevan had been sceptical about these claims ever since the Lend-Lease rupture of 1945. It was not that he denied the frequent common interest which needed to be sustained: Marshall Aid had made possible the economic recovery of Europe and Truman's Point Four programme could be no less invaluable in the war against world poverty. To call him anti-American, as many did, was a crude distortion. But he was dubious about the American title to world leadership, so sycophantically accorded by the worshippers of power in the post-1945 epoch. American society was too unpredictable and violent, its reaction to events often clumsy and hysterical. American capitalism had developed aspects which seemed to belie the Marxist prophecy but it was not transformed. All the more necessary was it for Britain to retain and exercise her independence of judgment and action. Great Britain (he always used the 'great' long after most others had abandoned it) still had her own individual role to perform, and Anglo-American relations should not be defined in black and white colours, but were subject to endless shades and variations.

When, at the end of June 1950, President Truman made a swift decision to oppose the aggression of the North Koreans against the South and appealed to the United Nations to back the same cause, British support was instantaneous and unqualified. No word of dissent was raised in the Cabinet, and few in Parliament or outside. All the available evidence suggested that it was a case of plain aggression, even though no one took the precaution of asking the North Koreans to state their view. Indisputably, large forces, equipped with Russian tanks, had crossed the frontier of the 38th parallel which divided North from South and had penetrated deeply. To demand their withdrawal, and to mobilize resistance when they refused, was a perfectly defensible act of collective security, in full accord with the United Nations Charter. Indeed, towards the end of September, it did appear that the feat had been achieved: that what was so lamentably not done, in Manchuria in 1931, in Abyssinia in 1935, and in Spain in 1936, had been accomplished in Korea in 1950. Collective action had worked; aggression had been repelled; General MacArthur and his armies, acting under the authority of the Security Council, had succeeded in throwing the North Koreans back across the 38th parallel. It was one of the great opportunities in post-war history; the forces of peace could have sought a negotiated settlement from a legitimate position of strength. And a few voices pleaded in that sense; Jawaharlal Nehru insisted that the failure to seize that moment would plant 'the seeds of a mighty conflict'.

But nations and peoples rarely approach a hot crisis with clinical wisdom, and Truman's America was in no mood to do so. Fear and hatred and ignorance of the real world combined to spread an atmosphere of near-hysteria. Stalin was thought to be directing from the Kremlin a world-wide and brilliantly successful conspiracy, of which the latest stupendous example was the revolution in China, the most savage rebuff to American pride and power since Pearl Harbour. Senator McCarthy was already filling the air and the headlines with his accusations of treachery in high places. With astonishing certainty – this applied on both sides of the Atlantic – it was assumed that the precise order for the Korean attack had come from Moscow. And General MacArthur, dizzy with success at his first swift victories, had a programme of his own, a vast dream of reversing the verdict in China and rolling back the tide of world Communism from East to West. In the first days of the Korean war, he gave orders – on instruction from the United States Government, not the United Nations – for the American fleet to provide protection for the counter-revolutionary forces of Chiang Kai-shek on Formosa, and within a few days he and Chiang were engaged in eager consultation. And when the United Nations armies reached the 38th parallel in September, MacArthur scorned any idea of stopping there. He was authorized to cross the frontier, and perhaps the deadly step was unavoidable and excusable: no American President could have agreed that the North Koreans should be permitted to regroup for a counter-attack with impunity. But MacArthur carried the interpretation of his authority much further. He pressed relentlessly forward, demanding unconditional surrender and brushing aside all suggestions or signs or warnings that the Chinese might be forced to intervene in battles so near their own borders. Early in November 'a fresh enemy force' was reported on the battlefield and for a breathless week or two something like a diplomatic lull was interposed. There was talk of a buffer strip along the Manchurian border, of an approach towards the negotiating table; a delegate from Peking arrived in New York to put the Communist Government's case at the Security Council. And that same day MacArthur launched two encircling movements towards the Yalu river in what he himself called a 'home-by-Christmas' offensive and what others construed as outrageous provocation. Two days later Chinese regular forces retaliated in strength, and the Korean conflict was transformed from a police action into one of the most hideous wars in human records – in the end four million dead and wounded, twenty million refugees, a country laid in ruins, north and south. But still MacArthur had his immediate remedy; bomb the Chinese mainland, blockade the Chinese coast, and let Chiang off the leash. However, by now, at the thirteenth hour almost, Washington was starting to appreciate the nature of the menace from its headstrong Commander. A general war against China had never been the Truman administration's aim: that would be, in General Bradley's famous phrase, 'the wrong war, at the wrong time, in the wrong place, against the wrong enemy'. Yet these glimmers of strategic sense were often concealed from outside observation. Within a few days of the realization that the world was plunging into a new conflict of incalculable dimensions came the news – from a Truman press conference – that use of the atom bomb was being considered. Wild apprehension about American intentions swept across the planet; the British House of Commons was plunged into what the United States London Embassy described as 'the most serious, anxious and responsible debate on foreign affairs since the Labour Party came to power in 1945', and Attlee made sudden plans to fly to Washington, as the newspapers put it, 'to stop a third world war'.

It is necessary to recall the flavour of those times, and especially that moment of desperation, in order to judge fairly the role of all the various combatants in the particular controversy which soon engulfed Britain. American policy could – and so nearly did – push the world into war. That made a case for plain speaking and tough diplomacy; but it also made a case for Britain keeping such diplomatic leverage as she did possess in Washington. Ernest Bevin at the British Foreign Office had in fact recognized the new Chinese

Government a few months before the outbreak of the war, and in the first weeks, he opposed, albeit behind the scenes, the American moves about Formosa and Chiang. He did not swallow the crude American propaganda that the new China was a mere Moscow pawn. Moreover, the chiefs of staff were giving the most serious warnings about the danger of getting involved in a war with China.[1] So Britain did adopt a distinctive attitude and one which might retain links with India and other Asian countries and thereby eventually pave the way to negotiation. On the other hand, Bevin, no less than his American counterparts, accepted quite uncritically the idea that orders for the Korean aggression had been given in Moscow, and he drew the same moral that similar orders might soon be given for similar action against defenceless Europe. The newly-founded North Atlantic Treaty Organization must be equipped with military power at top speed. That was the most urgent and direct British interest, infinitely more important than any manœuvres on the Manchurian border. It was at this time that the figure of 175 Russian divisions, poised in the East ready to strike towards the Channel ports, gained prominence – Emanuel Shinwell, the Defence Minister, first used it in a debate in July. And it was at this time too – on a sudden suggestion of Mr Dean Acheson at a meeting of Foreign Ministers in Washington in September – that a proposal to enlist German military support against the Soviet menace was approved in principle. 'Unthinkable' had been the word used by Ernest Bevin to describe any suggestion of German rearmament a bare five months before. The speed with which he and the British Cabinet were 'bulldozed'[2] over this particular item is proof of the general state of alarm. However, amazingly, comparatively little stir was provoked at the time by these first thoughts on the unthinkable proposition. More urgent necessities clamoured for attention: in particular, the British rearmament programme which suddenly threatened, as if by some form of pressure cooking, to bring all the pre-Korean issues more swiftly to the boil.

Aneurin Bevan's governing thought about the Far Eastern scene – it derived from the most formative period of his political youth when he had witnessed the Churchillian attempt to strangle the

[1] Hugh Dalton, unpublished diaries.
[2] Hugh Dalton, unpublished diaries.

Soviet revolution of 1917 in its cradle – was that the Western powers had a primary responsibility not to repeat against revolutionary China the crime they had perpetrated against revolutionary Russia. No measure could be placed on the evil consequences which had flowed for all mankind from the wars of intervention and the long, unrelenting ostracism of the Soviet Union. That brand of Churchillism had helped to breed Stalinism; it had contributed to making a nationalist caricature of a great international doctrine; the thought of the same monstrous error being re-enacted on the same world-wide stage was too tragic to contemplate. From the moment Mao's armies seized power in Peking, right through the fifties, this was one of Bevan's most constant themes. Moreover he was convinced – quite a prophecy to make in those far-off days – that China was not and would not be Russia's natural ally. She would find her own independent path. So it followed that one major purpose of Western statesmanship must be to foster these tendencies, not for the crude purpose of driving a wedge between China and Russia, but rather to shorten, by every available means of trade and restrained diplomacy, the ice-age of China's intensive industrialization, when the coldest winds might blow westwards. It followed also, of course, that he was adamantly opposed to the MacArthurite adventures. Certainly he was not alone in the British Cabinet in that opposition – Dalton was a strong ally and Bevin himself, in Dalton's words, was 'quite good and cautious on China'[1]–but none of the others set the issue in the same spacious historical framework.

Bevan had a second governing conviction, even more distinctive, and strictly related to the Korean-war period. Deep in his political intelligence – and quite contrary to the orthodox judgment about the 175 posed Russian divisions – was a belief, unshakable by the panic of the age, that the Russians did not intend large-scale military adventures, that the march across Europe was *not* a possibility, much less a likelihood. The Korean aggression might be a Russian probing operation. Tito's Yugoslavia might be threatened, for ideological reasons primarily, and must be suitably protected. Precautions must also be taken elsewhere; N.A.T.O., as a defensive organization, could help to soothe nerves on both sides of the Iron Curtain. But, fundamentally, Stalin's Russia was a conservative

[1] Hugh Dalton, unpublished diaries.

power which had already extended its European frontiers further
westward than her ideological authority warranted. And where was
the evidence that the Russian leadership was prepared for the risks
of world military conquest or, in the later Churchillian version of
the proposition, that they were only checked by the American atom
bomb? Bevan got the chance at some Cabinet committee to put his
old question to the Chiefs of Staff. How much steel have the
Russians got, he insisted; perhaps the military realists would find
out. Were the Russians leaders, commanding an annual production
of less than 30 million tons and who thought more in terms of
industrial power than any other ruling clique in history, to hurl
themselves against an alliance commanding 140 million tons?
Nothing could persuade him that the major premise of Western
policy was sound. And it might be as dangerous to over-estimate
the strength of an enemy as to under-estimate it; the over-
estimate of Mussolini's strength in 1935 and of Hitler's in 1938 had
contributed to the diplomatic paralysis which led to catastrophe.

So Bevan approached the task of Western rearmament in a frame
of mind very different from that of his Cabinet colleagues. In the
prevailing atmosphere some rearmament was inevitable but it must
be executed on a scale which did not undermine the nation's economy and at a pace which did not feed the general hysteria, and
how difficult that qualified exertion would be was soon evident.
Britain's defence budget for the period ahead, for 1950–51, was
already considerable – Bevan, as we have seen, had already called
these particular estimates 'gorged and swollen', less than twelve
months earlier;[1] they were fixed at £700 million or 7·5 per cent of
the national income, and this total included £100 million only
recently added to help meet Britain's new N.A.T.O. commitments.
A debate on this last addition was taking place in the House of
Commons when the urgent appeal came from Washington for more
and much more, and a request too, almost a summons, that the
answer should be forthcoming in ten days. The British Government kept the deadline. Within this absurdly short time a new
three-year programme was devised and announced, adding no less
than £1,100 million to the figures previously envisaged and proposing an expenditure over the three years of £3,400 million. Only

[1] See letter on page 276.

one condition was attached; to make the programme feasible, direct
assistance for Britain's balance of payments would be required
from the United States – and that, it was understood, was agreed –
to a figure of some £500 million. Britain had certainly shown herself
a responsive ally, and further confirmation was offered when
Parliament heard the details at a special session in September.
Forces pay would be increased; the conscription period would be
extended; above all, a swift increase in arms production was envisaged; it would be necessary to increase the total programme of
£3,400 million to £3,600 million. This, said Attlee, is 'the maximum
we can do by expanding and using to the full our industrial capacity
without resorting to the drastic expedients of a war economy'. But
Bevan already had serious doubts whether so big a programme
could be inserted into the economy without causing the most serious
social consequences, and he could not help being fascinated to see
how speedily the parsimonious Treasury would vote money for
arms, but for nothing else. During the Cabinet meetings in August
he strongly underlined his doubt and dissent and found himself
embroiled in an argument with Sir Norman Brook, secretary of the
Cabinet, about the way in which Cabinet minutes were kept. Bevan
wanted his 'opposition' recorded, but Sir Norman replied that so
strong a term would raise the question of collective Cabinet responsibility, of resignation. Bevan had not reached that point, but he
had moved towards it. With deepening misgivings he accepted the
£3,600 million programme. But no doubt was possible about his
increasing alarm at the conduct of the American administration,
and not merely the free rein given to MacArthur in Korea; the
reckless tempo of American rearmament, the way they intended to
pile the new productive burden on the existing economy without
any attempt to impose priorities or discipline, threatened runaway
inflation and a vast material shortage for the rest of the Western
world. He was indignant too at the peremptory manner in which
American demands were presented in London. And yet the greater
the risk that United States policy would take the world over the
edge, the greater the need for Britain to be able to impose a restraining hand. Attlee's flight to Washington was a proof of the value of
the alliance and of the hazards of breaking it. Certainly one of those
in the Cabinet who had pressed most strongly the plea which was

also coming from back-bench M.P.s was Bevan; indeed the original initiative may have come from him.[1]

The mythology of Attlee's Washington visit tells how he strode into the President's room in the White House, put the atomic maniacs in their place, prepared the way for the dismissal of Mac-Arthur, and generally restored the proper balance in the Anglo-American alliance. Considering the temperaments of the two men the tale always sounded improbable, and there was indeed little talk at that meeting of the atom bomb. Truman claimed that his remarks on that subject had been vastly misrepresented, and clearly Attlee accepted the explanation in advance. However, the meeting did cover the whole range of world policy, and the testimony of Truman's memoirs is there to show that Attlee's was a most formidable performance: a major achievement of his premiership. Confronted with the military and diplomatic chiefs of the greatest power on earth, each smarting from shattering defeats at the hands of the upstart Chinese and all the more unlikely to tolerate criticism, Attlee nonetheless succeeded in presenting a more sophisticated argument about China and Asian opinion than Truman seemed to be receiving from his own advisers and thereby powerfully reinforced the case for limiting the war. To say that he tipped the balance against MacArthurite adventurism would be excessive and unprovable. But the British weight in the scales counted and the trust established between the two men gave Attlee the chance to argue another day. During one of their informal exchanges, according to Truman, they discussed some of their domestic political problems and 'Attlee spoke of the opposition from some of his own Labour Party leaders, especially Aneurin Bevan, and his group, and the trouble they gave him'.[2] Evidently Bevan's criticisms had

[1] Hugh Dalton, unpublished diaries. The entry for 30 November read as follows: 'Nye and I spoke. He said he had told Clem he ought to fly out to U.S. to see Truman . . . I said I didn't like this [situation]. Dalton then wrote a letter to Clem [supporting Bevan's advice].'

[2] *Years of Trial and Hope* by Harry S. Truman (Hodder & Stoughton, 1956), p. 434. It is unlikely that Attlee in fact made any reference to Bevan's 'group', particularly as at that stage no such thing existed. Probably the reference was provoked by the reports leaking out of London, just prior to Attlee's visit, about Bevan's growing restlessness about the scale of the rearmament campaign.

impinged on Attlee's political consciousness which was not always so sensitive.

However, Attlee returned to London in something like triumph; if he had not stopped a war, he had at least lowered the diplomatic temperature. But a price had to be paid for his accord with the President. Item One in their communiqué stated that 'the military capabilities' of the two countries 'should be increased as rapidly as possible', and it soon became clear that the Americans did not regard even the £3,600 million programme as a fulfilment of that promise. All through the last weeks of that hectic December and the first weeks of January, argument proceeded back and forth across the Atlantic and back and forth between the Cabinet and the Government's military advisers, and the latest demand was for a £6,000 million defence programme to be compressed into the same three years. And all the while, intensifying the pressure, came the news from Korea of the devastatingly successful Chinese retaliation against MacArthur. At the Washington meeting Truman had argued from the outset that if the Chinese counter-attack became so successful that they in turn crossed the 38th parallel, immediate steps must be taken to brand them as the aggressor. Attlee had turned aside the suggestion, fearing it would make abortive his effort to search for a basis of negotiation. The issue had been successfully sidestepped in the communiqué. But nothing could withstand the icy blast from Korea. It swept across the United States where 'branding the aggressor' became a kind of national battle-cry, and it penetrated into the innermost conflicts of the British Cabinet.

The complex of dilemmas touched Bevan more closely than his colleagues, for at this moment they were translated into an invidious personal form. Attlee now renewed the proposal that he should move to the Ministry of Labour, and the choice would have been painful enough if it had not come at the height of the international crisis. Doubtless all Ministers who contemplate resignation have to consider whether their influence can best be exerted inside or outside an administration; but rarely can that test have been presented in more awkward circumstances. British policy both in the field of arms and diplomacy had to be accommodated to American policy: that was the requirement of the alliance, and that the alliance itself was required was freshly indicated in the fierce pressures which the Soviet Government was exerting on Tito's Yugoslavia. Bevan favoured a guarantee for Yugoslavia precisely because he believed it could stop a war. But he was more and more alarmed by the general course of American policy, more and more dubious about the efficacy of whispered diplomatic restraints. Passionately he wanted to do what no one had ever really stopped him doing all his life: to define in public his individual attitude to the greatest world themes. But now he was gagged by ministerial inhibitions. He had something to say which no one else could say in the same way, and it was not conceit which persuaded him that large numbers of people in many lands might listen. On the other hand, to surrender direct opportunity to shape events at a Ministry especially involved in the conduct of the economy and the rearmament programme; would not that be desertion? Immediately it might concede victory to those elements in the Cabinet whose views on American policy were so much less astringent than his own; it might just tip the balance the wrong way, even in Washington. And one particular factor which undoubtedly weighed with him was the unresolved controversy about the branding of China as the aggressor. American pressure to secure British support for this proposition at the United Nations mounted relentlessly all through January. One frantic and frenetic note on the subject followed another. But there was also strong opposition in the Cabinet, led by Bevan and backed by many Governments in the Commonwealth, India in particular: 'to brand China,' said Nehru, would be 'to bolt and bar the door to a peaceful settlement in the Far East'. On this issue at least, the Cabinet had ranged itself against the American appeal, and that might lead to an Anglo-American controversy of a different complexion. It was hardly the moment for resignation.

So Bevan wavered, and argued with himself and Jennie, and eventually accepted Attlee's offer. He did so on one condition; that there should be no fresh attack on the social services, no repudiation of the March 1950 compromise about the Health Service. Attlee seemed to agree and that appeared to remove one of Bevan's major fears of the previous autumn. Even so he still had qualms about the proposition. Never did a man comport himself less like his public portrait: the bitter, scheming, chip-on-the-shoulder

egotist. He yielded with a shrug and a curse and after his own preferred method of reflection which some called carelessness. He was
much more Hamlet than Coriolanus. Of all the explanations of
Bevan's actions during 1951, the most inapt is that popularized by
Dalton which sees Bevan driven by pique and personal rivalry,
resenting in particular Gaitskell's appointment as Chancellor in
October and thereafter searching for a pretext to stage a dramatic
exit from the Government. *Obscene* was Bevan's favourite word
for describing the notion that politicians might determine great
political issues according to personal advantage. If the Dalton interpretation contained even the slenderest thread of truth, Bevan
through these months (indeed through his life) must have been the
greatest actor since Garrick, on or off the stage, a kind of Machia-
velli of the emotions, always parading a false man to deceive his
wife, his loving mother-in-law, his friends. They in fact saw as the
reality the unaffected shrugs, the curses, the never-long-suppressed
gaiety, a positive lust to escape from politics to the loveliness and
freedom of his home or the mountains. He was open to the point of
innocence. There was indeed, although the word may sound
strange, a naivety about him. All genius is somehow naive. That
was something the Daltons and Morrisons could never comprehend.
So they searched for clues in their own hearts and practices.

In any case, January 1951 offered little scope for introspection
and little time for an appraisal by the new Minister of his new
department. At once he was enveloped in one test arising from the
Korean debates. How big was the British rearmament to be and
how fast could it be implemented? These were the questions tirelessly urged by the Americans. (Years later Attlee said: 'Pressure on
rearmament was very heavy from the United States. I think they
were inclined to press too hard.'[1]) The £6,000 million programme
over three years was the figure first proposed by the American
generals and backed by the British generals. But the Cabinet and
the defence departments scaled down the total to £4,700 million.
And yet even this lesser figure represented a £1,000 million increase
on the total approved as recently as September as the maximum
Britain could undertake without 'the drastic expedients of a war

[1] Attlee in an interview with Frank Barber, *News Chronicle*, 20 April
1959.

economy'; it would raise defence expenditure to 14 per cent of the national income; it would mean that the Government proposed to double the already considerable pre-Korean level of defence expenditure; and, at the same time, any suggestion of American assistance with Britain's balance of payments, virtually agreed in the previous summer, was abandoned. From the time when the heavier programme – the third increase since July – was first mooted in December, Bevan expressed his opposition to any commitment to such a figure and during the protracted arguments through the subsequent weeks, he found an ally in the young President of the Board of Trade, Harold Wilson. Both argued that a programme on this scale could not be realized; the physical resources were not there to meet it, apart even from the grave raw materials crisis then developing as a result of United States stockpiling. But the majority, with only these two dissenting, thought it right to specify and approve the precise figure. The only protection Bevan and Wilson were able to secure was the injection of the 'cautionary words', as Bevan called them later – 'the completion of the programme in full and in time is dependent on an adequate supply of materials, components and machine tools. In particular, our plans for expanding our capacity depend entirely upon the early provision of machine tools, many of which can only be obtained from abroad.' It was not much; but hairs must often be split to keep parties united.

Not so easy to conceal with a formula – although, oddly, the way in which the Cabinet was involved in this particular controversy never emerged in public[1] – was the fate of the 'brand China' resolution. China had in fact replied to the United Nations resolution demanding the withdrawal of all foreign troops by appropriate steps with a proposal of her own for a seven-power conference and the withdrawal of the U.S. Fleet from the Formosan straits. Asian countries argued that the reply was not a blank rejection; that the

[1] What happened in the Cabinet was somehow kept secret, but there was no doubt about the alarm in the country. Six Labour M.P.s – Dick Crossman, Barbara Castle, Ian Mikardo, Tom Williams, Marcus Lipton and myself – wrote a strong private letter to Attlee on 23 January, in which we said: 'It is impossible to exaggerate the strength of the feeling which exists in the constituencies about the proposal to brand China as an aggressor and to operate sanctions against her. We have never seen anything so strong since 1945 . . .'

door was open for the talks which might lead to a negotiated settlement. But the Americans would have none of it: nothing but the 'branding' resolution would offer balm to their mutilated pride. All the allies of the United States were bombarded with demands that they should concur; only three in Asia as it happens – the Philippines, Thailand and Formosa – did so. We have 'used the whole apparatus of the United Nations,' wrote Walter Lippman, 'to make a spectacular demonstration that Asia is not with us'.[1] Nor was the British Cabinet – until it performed an extraordinary somersault. Ernest Bevin was away ill and the voice of the Foreign Office in the Cabinet was momentarily muffled. Perhaps that is why Bevan had been able to carry his views at previous meetings. But he was soon faced with another protagonist of the American attitude who even took the extraordinary step of visiting the Foreign Office to recruit its clear support and formidable backing, expressed in what Dalton called 'an egregious paper', for a reversal of policy. The change had been induced, as Bevan thought, by an intrigue, and the result was that on 30 January the 'branding' resolution, slightly modified to placate those who feared it would imperil negotiations but still deeply offensive to the Chinese and most of Asia, was passed through the United Nations General Assembly with British backing. The man who had swayed the Cabinet was Hugh Gaitskell.

At the Cabinet meeting on 25 January opposition to the American resolution had seemed to be confirmed; the Cabinet had at last made up its mind. But Gaitskell was 'so much upset' that he went to see Attlee and said he would have 'to reconsider his position' if the decision was sustained. Next day, with the Foreign Office machine trundling into action alongside the Treasury, the decision was revised.[2] It was certainly a formidable event, and Gaitskell had revealed both his mettle and the strongest strand in his political outlook. No doubt is possible about the devoted fervour with which he gave allegiance, all his life, to the American alliance. More doubt may surround the question of how long the uncontrolled American mania to brand China sustained the senseless killing in Korea, or, more portentously, whether that was truly the moment when a

[1] Quoted in *The Cold War* by D. F. Fleming (Allen & Unwin, 1961), Vol. II, p. 632.
[2] Hugh Dalton, unpublished diaries.

reconciliation between China and the West was blocked. Certainly it added to the intensity of the Bevan-Gaitskell feud that Bevan had accepted his new post in an administration committed to oppose the American pressure only to find, once he had made the critical choice, that the policy had been reversed. He could not know that the deed had been done by a successful threat of resignation from his despised rival. 'It was all a battle for power; he knew it and so did I,' said Gaitskell years later.[1] It was, for Bevan, rather a complicated assessment of how principle could be applied in practice, how his own individual approach might make its imprint on the sharpening national and international crisis.

This is what he appeared to do, spectacularly, in his first major parliamentary intervention in his new office. Formally the speech was a defence of the £4,700 million arms programme announced by Attlee at the end of January, and Bevan confirmed his commitment at the end in words later to be much quoted: 'We shall carry it through; we shall fulfil our obligations to our friends and allies...' In debating terms it was another brilliant reply to a Churchillian vote of censure. But these and several other features were combined in a style more commanding than ever before. For here was the authentic voice of an independent British foreign policy suited to the time: one which appreciated the Soviet challenge but wished to see it defined in much more sophisticated terms than the anti-Communist crusaders employed; one which sought to sustain the Anglo-American alliance while abating its dangerous crudities and dogmatisms. It is ironic that the supposedly loud-mouthed demagogue spoke so much more softly than the Foreign Office or the State Department. 'For Heaven's sake, do not let us have so much bogyman talk,' he insisted, referring to 'those evil people in many parts of the world who are talking as if the third world war had already begun'. A true gauge of Soviet strength pointed to less frightening conclusions, and here Bevan elaborated his favourite argument about steel production which he had had with the Chiefs of Staff a few weeks before. And the Soviet Union also suffered from ideological weaknesses: 'Soviet thinking has not adjusted itself to the fact that the most revolutionary power in the world is

[1] Quoted in *The Gaitskell I Knew* by George Brown in the *Spectator*, 24 January 1964.

political democracy . . . As the Soviet Union pushes further West she gets more and more theoretical defeats.' Plentiful reasons existed for qualifying the picture of a would-be world-conquering state, immaculately strong, inordinately cunning, and winning nothing but victories, and deterred only from nameless aggressions, as Churchill loved to assert, by the American monopoly of the atom bomb. And the cause of peace must equally be protected from other hazards. 'We have seen in other places that a campaign for increased arms production is accompanied by a campaign of hatred and witch-hunting.' If rearmament were undertaken in a mood of haste and hysteria, the machine might soon be out of control. The great purpose, in Bevan's concluding words, must be 'to give mankind another breathing space'.

At such moments most national statesmen called upon to launch an unpopular arms drive would have been tempted to beat the war drum. Churchill would surely have done so, and such was the advice of the nation's defence advisers. Only a few days before the debate, John Strachey had produced at the Cabinet a War Office statement saying that war was 'possible in 1951, probable in 1952'.[1] Many of Bevan's Cabinet colleagues were convinced that the American judgment on events was correct, and that the British war preparations must be made to match the American tempo. But Bevan held to his own peculiar interpretation of the world-wide scene, and the miracle of that debate of 15 February 1951 was that he seemed to impose on his hearers his own imaginative will. 'Don't spoil a good speech now,' interrupted Churchill himself towards the end when Bevan was turning back for a moment to chide the Conservative front bench. It was an extraordinary tribute: a sign that the old man's vision could in the last resort embrace even his most detested adversary, but a sign too of the mastery which Bevan could now exert over the House of Commons. 'It was as good as Lloyd George at his best,' commented Chuter Ede, sometimes one of Bevan's critics. Few who heard that speech doubted that they were listening to a future Prime Minister, particularly when they recalled, if any did, that the debate had been most competently opened by a then-forgotten Hugh Gaitskell.

During the next few weeks there was danger that he might be

[1] Hugh Dalton, unpublished diaries.

drowned in the departmental vortex of the Ministry of Labour; perhaps that was the hope in some quarters. Apart from the additional tasks required by the rearmament programme, he was quickly involved in narrowly averted railway and electricity strikes and an angry dispute in the docks.[1] He had time too to prepare the abolition of the long-detested wartime regulation, Order 1305, which insisted upon a 21-day notice period before a strike could be legal, and to devise, or get devised for him, an elaborate, tentative, unpublicized plan for a national incomes policy, a 1951 foretaste of the late 1960s.[2] But despite these other preoccupations, the whole month of March and the first days of April were dominated by a behind-the-scenes debate in which the arms programme and the Chancellor of the Exchequer's forthcoming Budget, promised for 10 April, intermingled with a third reflection of the international crisis: a week-by-week, almost day-by-day intensification of the world-wide inflation and shortage of raw materials induced by the Korean war. Moreover, the saving clause he and Wilson had been able to extract about the speed and timing of the arms programme, underlined afresh in Bevan's speech of 15 February, clearly touched also the pre-Budgetary considerations about the action the Chancellor would need to take to deal with the scale of inflation and the levels of public expenditure. Bevan became more and more concerned as he discovered how determined was the Treasury to revive, in a more precise form than ever before, their year-old and two-year-old expedients for dealing with the cost of the Health Service and how eager and resolute the new Chancellor appeared to be to win outright victory where Cripps had been prepared to compromise. But Bevan could still hardly believe it: that the accumulated, concentrated crisis of the past few years was now upon him. After all, he had won this particular combat several times before. Quite

[1] See below p. 318.
[2] Apart from the documents on this subject left at the Ministry of Labour, Bevan discussed it at some length in *In Place of Fear*, Chapter 7. But he also qualified the view expressed there, for example in a *Tribune* article on 22 January 1955, where he wrote: 'Socialist planning demands planning instruments, and these are not present if industry is the domain of private economic adventure. Those who talk of a national wages policy under present conditions are misled by the temptation to find short cuts.'

specifically, even though he had taken the most scrupulous and successful pains to ensure that the information was not leaked to the press or M.P.s, he had warned Attlee, Cripps, Gaitskell and every other Cabinet colleague concerned that the imposition of charges on the Health Service would mean his resignation. That was not some sudden threat concocted in those mad March days; it dated back to 1949. And Bevan was legitimately confident that most colleagues did not want to see the disturbance which his departure would create, particularly when he had just undertaken fresh duties in sustaining government policy which no one else was qualified to fulfil half so well. What perhaps he underrated was the weakening of his own position in the Cabinet, if a final test should come, with the departure of Cripps, and the formidable combination of the rigid steel in Gaitskell's character when allied with Morrison's astute, unsleeping assiduity in every corner and corridor. Perhaps only Gaitskell and Morrison together foresaw – and invited – the April 1951 crisis.

It might be imagined that that Cabinet had plenty else to argue about: how to ward off the harrowing tactics of the Tories in the Commons; how to get the Steel Bill (miraculously passing its Second Reading with a majority of 10); how to stop a dock strike;[1]

[1] In 1963, a book called *The Braddocks* by Jack and Bessie Braddock (MacDonald) was published, extracts from which, with accompanying sensational headlines, were published in the Liverpool newspapers. Bessie Braddock's allegation was that, prior to the conspiracy trial initiated in February 1951 against seven dockers under the Conditions of Employment and National Arbitration Order 1305, she had attempted to persuade Bevan to ensure that warrants for the arrest of the dockers should not be issued since the strike was fading anyhow, that he had assured her the arrests would not be made, but that later she had been given a quite different account of what had occurred by Sir Hartley Shawcross, at that time Attorney-General; he, allegedly, had said that the arrests had in fact taken place after Bevan had told him that 'the strikers are on their knees, now is the time to strike them'. Such a story sounds monstrously improbable on the face of it, but it is necessary to repudiate it lest the absence of comment here might in any sense be taken as some sort of corroboration.

No one knew better than Bevan what might be the dangers for a Labour Government of the involvement of other Ministers in the decision about a prosecution which rested solely with the Attorney-General. Indeed during this affair he had occasion to repeat this warning to some of his fellow Ministers when there was a risk that the issue might be raised at a Party

how to manage Britain's rearmament programme; how to keep in
check the continuing American pressures in the Far East; how to
deal with the unthinkable question of German rearmament which
the Americans were also pressing (and where Gaitskell was also
complaining that Dalton's and Bevan's opposition 'was becoming
known'); and, finally, who was to succeed Ernest Bevin at the
Foreign Office, now that his health was so obviously failing and
even Attlee could hardly keep him there much longer. All these
interlocking items did not exhaust the list, and yet into it was
inserted the issue of health charges. At the Cabinet meeting on
22 March, according to Dalton's report in his unpublished diaries,
'it went according to plan'. Morrison in the chair, deputizing for
Attlee who was in hospital, announced that the Prime Minister
supported Gaitskell's proposals for a charge on teeth and spectacles
and hoped that the Cabinet would support them too. Ernest Bevin,
according to Gaitskell, had been 'squared' beforehand, and in any
case was too sleepy or tired to participate in the proceedings. Edith
Summerskill, Hilary Marquand, Hector McNeil, Daltonians all,
spoke for Gaitskell's proposition. Apart from Bevan, only Harold
Wilson opposed. James Griffiths demurred, asking for more time
for the whole matter to be reconsidered. Bevan, according to Dalton, made 'very heavy weather', and yet even in the records of this
prejudiced witness it is not clear what reply Gaitskell had to his
question. Why not take the £23 million – the annual sum to be
gained from the charges – off the rearmament estimates? 'We
knew,' said Bevan, 'we couldn't spend all the money we proposed.'
Why could the Cabinet not draw back from the crisis which seemed

---

meeting. But there were several discussions between Ministers which the
Attorney-General attended and by the time the warrants were actually
issued a considerable dispute took place between Bevan and Shawcross
which Shawcross reported to Attlee in a 'private and personal' letter dated
9 February. While that letter explained Shawcross's attitude to the whole
dispute, it also made clear that Bevan thought 'it would be a mistake to
introduce an emotional issue' and that Hector McNeil (at that time
Secretary of State for Scotland) 'said that he took an entirely opposite
view and thought that this was the moment to attack, the strikers were on
their knees and should be knocked out'. Clearly Bessie Braddock had got
the facts muddled to suit her hostility to Bevan, and this illustration
should be sufficient to discount her other references to him.

to be impending? But the Cabinet would not agree and Bevan warned that he might resign. Gaitskell in turn warned that he could not go on if he did not have satisfactory support from his colleagues. The deadlock was complete, and yet the final moment had not come. Budget day was three weeks hence, and an Easter holiday intervened. 'Nye looked very evil this morning,' wrote Dalton.

Ten days later, on the night of 3 April, he addressed a rowdy meeting in Bermondsey where the urgent topics uppermost in the minds of his audience concerned the forthcoming trial of the seven dockers and the projected revocation of Order 1305, but where all comers felt entitled to 'have a go' about anything.[1] At one point Bevan remarked, in response to an interruption: 'I will never be a member of a Government which makes charges on the National Health Service for the patient'. In Bermondsey, the words caused no stir: no one was surprised at so obvious a revelation, and most of the reporters there did not appreciate what had been said. But in the *News Chronicle* the next morning the sentence looked stark and significant, and soon the other papers followed the scent: was there truly a Cabinet crisis brewing? In the Treasury it looked like an open challenge. And that morning Harold Wilson bumped into an ebullient Hugh Dalton who had not seen the *Chronicle*. 'Nye won't resign,' said Dalton. 'Yes, he will; have you seen the speech?' answered Wilson.

Dalton was himself alarmed, and doubtless sensed the rising alarm among Labour M.P.s. He was now convinced that Bevan was not bluffing. So, as he describes in his book,[2] he sought him out, and had 'a long and friendly' talk (7 April), urging with all his con-

---

[1] Robert Mellish, M.P. for Bermondsey, has informed me of one of Bevan's retorts at the meeting which brought the house down. Many of the hecklers were members of the Housewives' League, asking questions and shouting protests about the meagreness of the meat ration. And on the morning of the meeting reports from the Argentine had told of the suppression of the Liberal newspaper, *La Prenza*, by the dictatorship in Buenos Aires. After the housewives had had their go at Bevan, he was asked what he thought of the suppression of *La Prenza*. He paused for a moment and replied: 'If I answered that truthfully, you wouldn't have any meat at all next week.'

[2] *High Tide and After* by Hugh Dalton, p. 367.

siderable powers the unwisdom of resignation in his (Bevan's) own interests and even more those of the Party and the Government. But what had driven Dalton to seek this meeting and to set out his case against the resignation in a letter next day was the hitherto unrecorded talk he had had with Gaitskell the day before.[1] Dalton presumably wanted to see whether any hint of a softer attitude could be detected in this quarter, and he did not have to wait long for an answer. Asked whether he had considered what might be the consequences of Bevan's resignation, Gaitskell replied that he had and accepted them. Dalton's unpublished diary continues: 'He was very firm and determined. He said he would not always be black-mailed and give way. If we did not stand up to him, Nye would do to our Party what Lloyd George had done to the Liberals. It would, he thought, do us good in the country to make a stand on this. Nye's influence was much exaggerated. When the case was put he would have very little support. He had himself accepted the pre-scription charge which was more objectionable than teeth and spectacles, and people would think little of these things against the background of the Budget. He wouldn't much mind if the charges were carried by Tory votes.' This last was a reference to the warn-ing Bevan himself had given at the Cabinet meeting that the Labour Government might find itself in the undignified position of only being able to carry through the offending Bill in the lobbies if the Tories connived with the Government, but the scorn with which the possibility was derided was only one symptom of Gait-skell's cold hostility. When Dalton mentioned that Strachey was considering resignation with Bevan and Harold Wilson, Gaitskell replied that 'we will be well rid of the three of them'. Even Dalton, who usually chronicled the views of his disciple with doting adula-tion, was shaken: 'I thought that H.G. thought too little of the Party and too much of the general mood of the electorate.' But here indeed Dalton was secretly in possession of one missing link in the drama, as it appeared to outsiders at the time: to some leading participants in it, the clash was positively welcome. If the Gaitskell attitude to Bevan, as expressed in this extraordinary outburst and as recorded only in Dalton's unpublished diaries, had been known

---

[1] Hugh Dalton, unpublished diaries.

at the time, the Party explosion would have been even more shattering.

When Dalton had his talk with Bevan two days later he was certainly treated to an uninhibited expression of Bevan's personal animosity towards Gaitskell, but there were plenty of political arguments as well which Dalton did not rehearse in his published memoirs and which indeed Bevan's opponents were at pains to argue that he had only fabricated later. That was always a falsehood. The personal arguments *and* the arguments about the Health Service *and* the arguments about the rearmament programme *and* indeed more general political arguments always blended inextricably in his mind, as they did when he talked to Dalton. Gaitskell, he said, had behaved like a second Snowden in his efforts to please the Treasury, 'when this whole Treasury business is out of date'. He had blindly accepted an impossible rearmament programme. He was wildly pro-American and anti-Russian. He was 'an amateur foreign secretary' – and here Bevan was appealing to the common Bevan-Dalton front on China which had existed only two months before. Gaitskell had tried to get Bevan's agreement to the charges a year before and had been successfully resisted. But both he and Attlee must have known that the proposition would involve a Cabinet crisis. He (Bevan) does clearly feel, recorded Dalton, that an effort is being made to drive him out. Dalton does not record that he attempted to disabuse Bevan of any such fanciful impression, and after his talk with Gaitskell two days before, he might have found it hard to make any nonchalant disavowal convincing. Dalton, after all, had not been performing the role of mediator. He talked to everyone and everyone talked to him, but in all his Leftward or Rightward lurches, he never moved far from the centre of gravity within the Party. Apart from his particular intimacy with Gaitskell, he looked to see who was likely to win any contest for power. Gaitskell was convincing; the Cabinet majority was overwhelming and unshakable.

So it appeared when the Cabinet met for most of the morning and most of the evening on Monday 9 April, the day before Budget Day. At some point in the long wrangle, according to Dalton, Bevan 'threatened to widen the issue to rearmament', but no one need have been surprised. That wider issue, with Bevan's attempted dissent, had figured in Cabinet debate since the previous September. But did not Gaitskell also widen the issue? If the health charges were not accepted, he was ready to put off the Budget, to resign and go quietly without recrimination, and Dalton felt that his colleagues were impressed by the nobility of such a gesture. Gaitskell also added the gratuitous provocation that, even if he could spare the £23 million saved by the charges, he would not use them to avoid their imposition and to relieve the crisis; he would rather use the money for further improvements in old age pensions. Could there be no possibility of a postponement? That at last was the plaintive question of George Tomlinson, Minister of Education, who had scarcely engaged in the discussions before. Again the answer was no. Bevan was very near to the actual resignation that night.[1]

But the conclusion of the matter was still not quite so sharply determined as some students of the period have supposed. Possibly Ernest Bevin had intervened with Attlee, after he had had apparently unavailing interviews with both Bevan and Gaitskell. At any rate when Bevan and Wilson that night went to St Mary's Hospital, Paddington, where Attlee was being treated, he did not give the impression of the unyielding upholder of Gaitskell's views, as Morrison so constantly suggested to the Cabinet. According to Harold Wilson's recollection, Attlee promised to speak to Gaitskell, indicating that he would advise him 'to be more reasonable', and the discussion then turned to the topic which increasingly became associated with the rest of the argument – it was mentioned in Dalton's letter to Bevan on 7 April: the question of when the election might be called. If it was to be called soon, say in June of that summer, how foolish to risk a Party split just before it. The point could cut two ways; it was a reason why Bevan should not resign but it was also a reason why the charges should not be imposed. The discussion at Attlee's bedside had an intelligent relevance. But when Gaitskell arrived that night Attlee's laconicisms were not so clear. Gaitskell is said to have reported that he and Bevan were in complete disagreement on the health charge issue, and that neither would give way, whereupon Attlee is alleged to have mumbled, 'in that case – must go!' 'Certainly,' said Gaitskell, thinking Attlee had

[1] Hugh Dalton, unpublished diaries.

said he must go. 'I said *he* must go,' which, as the reporter of this exchange rightly says, put a different complexion on it.[1] But something else had happened. A last-minute effort *had* been made to avert the crisis, and again Gaitskell had slammed the door. According to Gaitskell himself, Attlee – and even Morrison at one point – 'had had cold feet and wanted him to drop all mention of charges',[2] and in response he had left out one sentence from the Budget speech – the actual date when the charges were expected to come into operation. But more than that millimetre he would not budge. On the afternoon of 10 April he presented his Budget, including the proposal to save £13 million – £30 million in a full year – by imposing charges on spectacles and on dentures supplied under the Health Service. And glancing over his shoulder at the benches behind him he had seemed to underline his resolve: having made up his mind, he said, a Chancellor 'should stick to it and not be moved by pressure of any kind, however insidious or well-intentioned'. Bevan did not take his accustomed seat on the Treasury bench, but listened to this part of the speech from behind the Speaker's chair, with Jennie by his side. A muffled cry of 'shame' from her was the only hostile demonstration Gaitskell received that afternoon. The rest of the Party was holding its breath.

That night Bevan and Wilson returned to St Mary's Hospital for another discussion with Attlee, and it is evident the leader still believed some compromise was possible. He urged Bevan to attend the Party meeting scheduled for the next morning and make his own plea for postponement and forbearance. And that night advice, exhortation, warning, expressions of alarm, poured in from all sides:

April 10

Dear Nye,

All sorts of rumours exist about your position. None of us know the merits until we hear the Budget. But we know the Party's interests will only be saved if we *all* go into a general

---

[1] *Five Lives* by Frank Pakenham (now Lord Longford) (Hutchinson, 1964), p. 187.
[2] Hugh Dalton, unpublished diaries.

election *together*. Any fragmentary resignations will split the Party in the constituencies, and we shall be not only defeated in the election – but routed. In the Party's interest we urge you to wait until the Party meeting has expressed itself tomorrow.

Ever yours,
JIM CALLAGHAN
ALFRED ROBENS
MICHAEL STEWART
ARTHUR BLENKINSOP
FRED LEE

Dear Aneurin,

I know that you will not resent my writing to you because I feel so seriously anxious about your threat to resign over the proposed charges under the Health Service.

I hope, with all my soul, that you will not.

After all, the proposed charge for prescriptions involved the same principles and to resign over charges for false teeth and spectacles (involving identical principles) would seem small and altogether out of proportion.

As you know we sometimes differ but we do so openly and with sincere mutual regard – but do remember please your great powers and possibly great future and do not endanger them and the great things we stand for in these difficult times.

This is written with a full heart and with sincere affection, and entirely on my own.

Ever yours sincerely,
ADDISON

Westminster Hospital,
Budget Day.

My dear Nye,

Rumour reaches me here from visitors that you are threatening 'direct action' on the question of the Health Service. I do hope this is not true and I would beg you very earnestly not to pre-cipitate a crisis at this stage. The rumours may be based on

misunderstanding. But I thought I ought to drop you a line
and would, if need be, see you.

Yours ever

A.G. (Arthur Greenwood)

Don't do anything rash on that – it won't carry.

Yours,

DICK (Stokes)

Dear Nye,

The Budget is popular in the Parliamentary Party, even among
those who have indicated sympathy for your point of view. It
will be popular, though perhaps less so, in the Labour movement
in the country. If you resign now on the Budget there will be
amazement as well as anger among our colleagues, and the consequences to the Party which would in any circumstances be
extremely grave, will be catastrophic. Your own position, and the
views we share will be, for some time ahead, seriously com-
promised. The impending election will find us disunited, without
policy and with the reactionaries in full charge of the Party
machine which will be used unscrupulously against you and
those who stand with you. The result will be a debacle of 1931
proportions – and little or nothing gained.

If you could find some way of not making your resignation
public at this moment and on this issue, you would not lack the
opportunities in coming weeks – perhaps even days – to go out
on an issue to which millions of Labour supporters would rally
enthusiastically – the drive towards war, the absence of any
coherent foreign policy, the inflationary and anti-working class
character of our rearmament economies. The split on all this
would be just as big; we should still probably lose the election,
though not by so much; but three-quarters of the Labour movement would rally to you, and would hold the initiative and have
a good chance of capturing the machine. I beg you to think long
and earnestly before you throw away this tremendous opportunity which I believe to be close at hand.

The assurances I gave you this afternoon are in no way modified or withdrawn; but they do give me the right to address this last appeal to you.

JOHN FREEMAN[1]

Ni Darling,

Hugh Delargy was saying he hoped you would wait until after the Party meeting tomorrow but on reflection the Party meeting would certainly come down against you. I should think therefore it is better if you made your decision known before then.

JENNIE

Next day when the members of the Parliamentary Labour Party crowded into Committee Room 14, a fresh sensation added spice to the moment. The news, most welcome to all shades of the Labour Party, came from Washington of Truman's sacking of MacArthur. Morrison assured the meeting that he could not take 'the whole credit' for the happy event.[2] It was not the best time for a self-induced crisis in London. 'BEVAN GIVES WAY ON HEALTH CHARGES: NO RESIGNATION: FAILURE TO WIN SUPPORT IN PARTY' ran the headlines in the *Daily Telegraph*. But the reality was not so crude. Bevan did indeed say that, in deference to many appeals, headed by Attlee's, he would not resign, but that he would await events. He reproved Morrison who had sought to open a general debate on the merits of the issue, and concluded by expressing the hope that other parties to the dispute would show a concern for Party unity matching his own. Gaitskell bridled at what he considered a bitter thrust. What Bevan meant and what he later proposed was that the

---

[1] At that time John Freeman held the office of Under-Secretary at the Ministry of Supply, but, thanks to the extreme competence he had shown at the despatch box and elsewhere, he was clearly destined for early promotion. Dalton put himself in charge of these enticements, as he describes on pages 368-9 of his memoirs, *High Tide and After*, and much more elaborately in his unpublished diaries. With Bevan, as this letter indicates, Freeman had had some private talks, but they were not intimate political friends. Indeed, they never became quite that. Bevan later would describe Freeman as the most inscrutable of his Bevanite colleagues, 'the man from Saturn'.

[2] *The Best of Both Worlds* by Tom Driberg (Phoenix, 1953), p. 8.

actual legislation incorporating the charges might be deferred. Since a split in the Party did seem so imminent and menacing, must not each side contribute to the remedy?

And the free advice continued to pour in:

Dear Nye,

I've talked about the business again to some of my friends. Our unanimous view is that the Cabinet's decision must be accepted – and that no significant section of the Party will oppose it.

Neither do we think many of the constituency parties will oppose it.

Ever yours,
JIM CALLAGHAN

Perhaps Callaghan epitomized correctly the general opinion of the Parliamentary Party, Right, Centre and most of the Left. Shinwell got some backing in the tea room for his declaration, 'Some people must be made to toe the line'; he had momentarily become the most virulent anti-Bevanite. But neither of these views took account of the pro-Bevan attitude of masses of Socialists in the country on the one side or the moves which were still being made to avert the final breach on the other. No date had been fixed for the Second Reading of the Bill. So why not hold it back? Why not hold it back until after June when the Prime Minister was considering a general election? This was the plea that Bevan again made to the Cabinet on 12 April when he also repeated that he could never drag his feet through the lobbies to impose the charges. But the Cabinet, without yet fixing the date, still decided to go ahead. And Bevan was bombarded with still more advice and exhortation.

The agony was drawn out through interminable days and nights at Cliveden Place where friends called one after another mostly to encourage, urge, plead with him *not* to resign. Bevan himself had been within an inch of doing so on the night of 9 April and his own determination was backed by the few who knew him most intimately, Jennie among the foremost. Only she understood in full measure what wounds he had suffered in previous encounters with

his Cabinet colleagues and how fierce had been the tension in those
crises. No one but the combatants knew how long, stretching back
to 1949 or even to 1947, had been the campaign he had had to
wage, sometimes alone, to protect the sacred first principle of the
National Health Service, in particular against Morrisonian sabotage
and subterfuge. For the most part, the majority of Bevan's advisers
and would-be companions were more interested in the rearmament-
cum-foreign policy controversy – witness the cogent letter from
John Freeman quoted above – but few of them appreciated, until
those Cliveden Place discussions over the weekend of 15–16 April,
how long Bevan had fought, with few allies, on that front too. So
the argument swayed back and forth. One participant with expert
qualifications to explore the labyrinth was John Strachey, at that
time Minister of War. He sympathized with Bevan's views, noted
all his dilemmas and fawned – it is not too strong a word – on a
political courage he knew he was unable to match. He could writhe
so smoothly in endless, harmless coils, a cobra without a fang. For
he too, of course, came down *against* resignation. But Bevan could
be contra-suggestive. The sheer weight of opinion favouring one
opinion in the House of Commons could emphasise for him how
divorced it was from opinion outside. During that weekend, also,
Archie Lush arrived from Tredegar to stress how strongly opinion
there backed Bevan's Bermondsey declaration and its near-inexorable
consequences. And Bevan himself took his stand on the offer he
had made to the Party meeting. If the leadership of the Party
wanted to avoid the crisis, the gesture he had proposed could assist.
On the other hand no gesture, no move whatever, would merely
mean that he would have to face fresh humiliations, fresh setbacks
to his point of view, in the months ahead. But still the powerful
appeals in the opposite sense poured in – one from an old Communist friend, Wilfrid Macartney, on 19 April: 'Don't go into the
wilderness unless like Moses you can take the tribes with you, and
remember he was there for forty years.'

On 18 April he received another private letter from Attlee, the
first communication since the hospital meeting on the night of
10 April. Attlee could be pardoned if his whole mind was not given
to this correspondence. In the interval Ernest Bevin had died, and
Attlee felt the blow more than anyone else.

Private & Confidential   *April 18*
My dear Nye,

I gather that all went off well at the Party meeting and I am grateful to you for the line you took.

The death of Ernie has rather overshadowed these differences, and I hope that everyone will forget them.

I think that it is particularly essential that we should present a united front to the enemy. The next few weeks will be very tricky with the U.S.A. going haywire over MacArthur. Hope to be back at work by the end of next week.

All the best,

Yours ever,

CLEM

But Attlee must have been unaware or unappreciative of the decision made by his own Cabinet the day before. There it had been generally agreed that the Health Charges Bill would be introduced forthwith, although it did appear that some final clinching of the decision was left over until the next meeting on the Thursday. On this occasion, Bevan gave notice that if the date for the Second Reading of the Health Bill was announced, he would resign and he wanted that recorded in the minutes. Nothing was now left to chance. Morrison, Gaitskell, Chuter Ede and William Whiteley, the Chief Whip, went on another journey to the hospital bed, and when Dalton arrived a little later he was told that an ultimatum had been despatched. Allegedly, Attlee also called Bevan 'a green-eyed monster,'[1] although the term sounds more Daltonesque than Attleeite.

April 20

My dear Nye,

I have a report of yesterday's Cabinet meeting and of subsequent meetings of Ministers on the subject of dental and ophthalmic charges.

I understand that you have stated that, if there were a vote on the Second Reading of the Bill, you would be unable to go into

[1] Hugh Dalton, unpublished diaries.

the lobby with the Government. You have also made statements about resignation. You will, I am sure, realize that matters cannot be left like this.

Cabinet Ministers must accept collective responsibility for Government measures. Decisions of the Cabinet taken after full consideration must be supported by all.

I must, therefore, ask you to let me know how you stand in this matter. I have discussed the issues with you very fully.

I shall be glad to know today that you are prepared to carry out loyally the decisions of the Government.

Yours ever,
CLEM

Perhaps the peremptory tone of that letter owed something to another document ('A most wicked publication',[1] Dalton scrawled across his copy) brought to Attlee's attention by prominent headlines in the newspapers that day – the reports of an article appearing in that week's *Tribune* entitled 'A Dangerous Budget' and drawing comparisons between Gaitskell's performance as Chancellor in 1951 and Philip Snowden's in 1931. 'We have had to wait twenty years for a Labour Government to win such warm approval in Conservative quarters.' That charge indeed was undeniable, however unpalatable. But clearly Attlee was no more inclined for further argument than Bevan himself. That Friday night Bevan communicated with Wilson who happened to be away on a speaking engagement in East Anglia. 'I am resigning,' he said, 'they've introduced the Bill.' The question remained: how should the resignation letter state the issues and who would resign with him? Bevan despatched the letter at half-past two that Saturday afternoon and continued the discussion throughout the day. When Wilson and Freeman arrived at Cliveden Place next morning, Bevan indeed did his best to persuade them both not to resign: that, he argued, might be the right way to ensure that the inevitable clash over policy would inflict least damage on the Party. Freeman was inclined to concur, but not Wilson. Next day the letters were published.

[1] Hugh Dalton, unpublished diaries.

My dear Clem,

In previous conversations with you, and in my statements to the Cabinet, I have explained my objections to many features in the Budget. Having endeavoured, in vain, to secure modifications of these features, I feel I must ask you to accept my resignation.

The Budget, in my view, is wrongly conceived in that it fails to apportion fairly the burdens of expenditure as between different social classes. It is wrong because it is based upon a scale of military expenditure, in the coming year, which is physically unattainable, without grave extravagance in its spending.

It is wrong because it envisages rising prices as a means of reducing civilian consumption, with all the consequences of industrial disturbance involved.

It is wrong because it is the beginning of the destruction of those social services in which Labour has taken a special pride and which were giving to Britain the moral leadership of the world.

I am sure you will agree that it is always better that policies should be carried out by those who believe in them. It would be dishonourable of me to allow my name to be associated in the carrying out of policies which are repugnant to my conscience and contrary to my expressed opinion.

I am sorry that I feel it necessary to take this step after so many years of co-operation in a Government which has done so much for the cause of Labour and the progress of mankind.

I need hardly say that my adherence to the cause of Labour and Socialism is stronger than ever and that I believe that renewed efforts by all of us will result in another thrust towards the goal of our hopes.

As is customary, I shall explain my position in greater detail in my speech to the House of Commons.

May I conclude by wishing you a speedy return to health and vigour.

ANEURIN

To which Attlee replied:

My dear Nye,

I have your letter of today's date. I note that you have extended the area of disagreement with your colleagues a long way beyond the specific matter to which as I understood you had taken objection.

I had certainly gathered that if the proposal for imposing charges on dentures and spectacles were dropped, you would have been satisfied.

I much regret that you should feel it necessary to offer your resignation, but in these circumstances I have no option but to accept it. I note that you propose to make a statement in the House.

Thank you for the good work that you have done as a Member of the Government during these difficult years.

Thank you also for your good wishes for my health.

Yours ever,
CLEM

When Bevan rose next day to deliver his resignation speech parliamentary conditions were arctic; he did indeed resemble some primitive polar explorer setting off, in the face of blinding sleet and snow, on a wild, inexplicable adventure. He was almost alone. No newspaper that morning backed his stand. Some, like the *Daily Mirror*, had been whipped up by Morrison, not that much whipping was necessary, to destroy his character.[1] No shred of sympathy for him prevailed on the Tory benches; rather he had revived overnight all the fears and frenzies of the 'vermin' period. On the Labour side, the immediate overpowering alarm was that he had plotted or clumsily contrived the destruction of the rickety Labour Government and an electoral disaster of, conceivably, 1931 proportions. Even most of those reckoned as his friends were dubious

[1] The evidence is provided by Claud Morris who at that time worked on the *Mirror*, in the article he wrote in the *South Wales Voice* on 15 July 1960, at the time of Bevan's death. Morris described how, arriving at the *Mirror* office, he was told how Morrison had been on the phone to the editor, stressing the scandalous nature of Bevan's action and how it was all part of his 'power' mania, as illustrated by the quotation Morrison kept in his pocket. See pp. 287–88.

about or, more usually, bitterly critical of his tactics. Gone, irre-coverably it seemed, was the fulsome admiration he had extorted by his parliamentary triumph of a bare eight weeks before. And when he sat down forty-five minutes later not a touch of warmth alleviated the universal coldness. No single cheer greeted his perora-tion. And at once, in various quarters, the whole speech was pro-nounced a crime and a blunder, and, judged by the impact in those first freezing minutes when he left the Chamber, with only two or three of his friends following him, it certainly appeared that he had made a ruinous error, more than enough to wreck a career. Yet it was partly the quality of the speech which left his hearers gasping. It was not solely a work of calculation; no speech by Bevan could be. It was a deliberate political act, but it was also an explosion of the forces pent up within him over months, even years. Some of the phrases, and perhaps the least premeditated, lingered on in the political atmosphere throughout the 1950s and the 1960s and retain their force today. At every turn it had upon it the stamp of bold-ness, the audacity of a Danton. So an assembly accustomed to all the arts of appeasing eloquence, and Bevan among the foremost could use them when he wanted, was stunned.

The very construction of the speech helped produce the shock. For with the briefest acknowledgment to the courtesies which the House allows to resigning Ministers, Bevan plunged into the major questions of the arms drive of the Western powers and its end-less ramifications. He quoted from his February speech about the perils of a too feverish rearmament and quoted too the cautionary words about the timing of the programme inserted in Attlee's January declaration. Ministers, he asserted, had been aware for some time that raw materials, machine tools and components were not forthcoming, in sufficient quantities. Therefore 'the figures in the Budget for arms expenditure are based upon assumptions already invalidated. I want to make that quite clear to the House of Commons; the figures for expenditure on arms were already known to the Chancellor of the Exchequer to be unrealizable ... I begged over and over again that we should not put figures in the Budget on account of defence expenditure which would not be realized ...' Indeed the hectic scramble for raw materials, 'the lurchings of the American economy', were intensifying the dangers week by week,

almost daily. 'I therefore say with the full solemnity of the seriousness of what I am saying that the £4,700 million arms programme
is already dead. It cannot be achieved without irreparable damage
to the economy of Great Britain and the world.'

And truly, he insisted before his audience could get their breath
back, the damage was already extensive and immeasurable. Already
there was serious under-employment in British industry and the
chronic raw material shortage could only intensify it. Already there
was serious inflation and the Budget seemed to abandon any hope
of restraining it and instead envisaged a serious cut in the standard
of life of the British worker. At this the Tory Opposition mustered
a few 'Hear, hears', and Bevan turned on them: 'The Opposition
have no remedy for this at all. But there is a remedy *here*' – pointing to his own benches – 'if it is courageously applied, and the
Budget does not courageously apply it. The Budget has run away
from it. The Budget was hailed with pleasure in the City. It was a
remarkable Budget. It united the City, satisfied the Opposition and
disunited the Labour Party – all this because we have allowed ourselves to be dragged too far behind the wheels of American diplomacy.' It was at that precise second that the speech caught fire.
The Tories sneered when he had talked a few minutes before about
the Soviet weapons being more social and economic than military
and they sneered again now when he talked about the remarkable
reconstruction achieved in Britain and now threatened by the
anarchy of American competitive capitalism. But was not his warning of the perils of American diplomacy all too menacingly true?
And was that not why some hated to hear him say it? 'Nothing,'
said another observer of the British parliamentary scene, the
great Lord Halifax, 'has an uglier look than reason when it is not
on our side.' 'There is,' continued Bevan, 'only one hope for mankind, and that hope remains in this little island.' He would never
allow the Tories to purloin the patriotic argument.

And then he turned aside, almost musing. 'Over and over again
I have said that these figures of arms production are fantastically
wrong . . . that if we try to spend them we shall get less arms for
more money . . . we have to adjust our paper figures to physical
realities, and that is what the Exchequer has not done. May I be
permitted, in passing, to give a word of advice to my colleagues in

the Government?' For a brief moment it seemed that the sweet Aneurin had reasserted himself, and then, the next moment, the illusion vanished. 'Take economic planning away from the Treasury, they know nothing about it ... It has been perfectly obvious on several occasions that there are too many economists advising the Treasury, and now we have the added misfortune of having an economist in the Chancellor of the Exchequer himself.' It was the first gibe of the speech, and not, one might consider, a particularly vicious one; not certainly by the standards of abuse to which Bevan himself was accustomed. But Labour skins were so tender at that hour they could scarcely bear to be touched. Coupled with the passage that followed which explained how the Chancellor, to help pay for the rearmament programme, had filched another £100 million from the Insurance Fund, it won sympathy for Gaitskell. And yet some of his words had supplied the essential epitaph for a whole epoch of Labour government: *Take economic planning away from the Treasury. They know nothing about it.*

Only at the end did he come to the Health Service and it is necessary to quote the whole passage, for it was delivered to an accompaniment of boiling resentment and fury on the 'loyalist' Labour benches. The more deadly each thrust, the more unanswerable each question, the greater the response of impotent anger. An irresistible momentum carried him forward:

I now come to the National Health Service side of the matter. Let me say to my hon. Friends on these benches: you have been saying in the last fortnight or three weeks that I have been quarrelling about a triviality – spectacles and dentures. You may call it a triviality. I remember the triviality that started an avalanche in 1931. I remember it very well, and perhaps my hon. Friends would not mind my recounting it. There was a trade union group meeting upstairs. I was a member of it and went along. My good friend, 'Geordie' Buchanan, did not come along with me because he thought it was hopeless, and he proved to be a better prophet than I was. But I had more credulity in those days than I have got now. So I went along, and the first subject was an attack on the seasonal workers. That was the first order. I opposed it bitterly, and when I came out of the room my good

My (the author's) favourite photo-portrait – taken when Nye was 55.

OPERATION SABOTAGE

(*Above*). Nye and Jennie at Brioni, Yugoslavia, in the autumn of 1951. (See page 247.) Vladimir Dedijer is on Tito's left.

(*Right*). Nye with Jawaharlal Nehru on his visit to India in 1957.

'*It's a drive for unity and goodwill.*' – Vicky's view of the row with Deakin & Co. in July 1953.

'*But are you sure the best way to heal a rupture is cutting the patient in half, Dr. Edith?*' – Vicky's view of the Great Expulsion of 1955.

(*Above*). Jennie and Nye,
with young Vaughan,
son of his friend and
Parliamentary Private
Secretary, Will Griffiths.

(*Right*). '*Is HE here yet?*'
– Giles and the rest of
the nation, in October
1952, had no doubt who
he was.

"SOCIALISTS!"

Vicky's portrait, hitherto unpublished.

(*Above*). Nye talking Asheridge with Mendés-France and Nenni. (See page 616

(*Left*). One of the las
photographs – Nye in
his Brighton 1957
mood.

old friend George Lansbury attacked me for attacking the order. I said, 'George, you do not realize this is the beginning of the end. Once you start this there is no logical stopping point.'

The Chancellor of the Exchequer in this year's Budget proposes to reduce the Health expenditure by £13 million – only £13 million out of £4,000 million. (*Hon. Members:* '£400 million.') No, £4,000 million. He has taken £13 million out of the Budget total of £4,000 million. If he finds it necessary to mutilate, or begin to mutilate, the Health Service for £13 million out of £4,000 million, what will he do next year? Or are you next year going to take your stand on the upper denture? The lower half apparently does not matter, but the top half is sacrosanct. Is that right? If my hon. Friends are asked questions at meetings about what they will do next year, what will they say?

The Chancellor of the Exchequer is putting a ceiling on the Health Service. With rising prices the Health Service is squeezed between the artificial figure and the rising prices. What is to be squeezed out next year? Is it the upper half? When that has been squeezed out and the same principle holds good, what do you squeeze out the year after? Prescriptions? Hospital charges? Where do you stop? I have been accused of having agreed to a charge on prescriptions. That shows the danger of compromise. Because if it is pleaded against me that I agreed to the modification of the Health Service, then what will be pleaded against my right hon. Friends next year, and indeed what answer will they have if the vandals opposite come in? What answer? The Health Service will be like Lavinia – all the limbs cut off and eventually her tongue cut out too.

I should like to ask my right hon. and hon. Friends where are they going? (*Hon. Members:* Where are you going?) Where am I going? I am where I always was. Those who live their lives in mountainous and rugged countries are always afraid of avalanches, and they know that avalanches start with the movement of a very small stone. First, the stone starts on a ridge between two valleys – one valley desolate and the other valley populous. The pebble starts, but nobody bothers about the pebble until it gains way, and soon the whole valley is overwhelmed. That is how the avalanche starts, that is the logic of the present situation, and that is the logic my right hon. and hon. Friends cannot escape. Why, therefore, has it been done in this way?

After all, the National Health Service was something of which we were all very proud, and even the Opposition were beginning to be proud of it. It only had to last a few more years to become a part of our traditions, and traditionalists would have claimed the credit for all of it. Why should we throw it away? In the Chancellor's speech there was not one word of commendation for the Health Service – not one word. What is responsible for that?

Why has the cut been made? He cannot say, with an overall surplus of over £220 million, and a conventional surplus of £39 million, that he had to have the £13 million. That is the arithmetic of Bedlam. He cannot say that his arithmetic is so precise that he must have the £13 million, when last year the Treasury were £247 million out. Why? What is the cause of it? Why has it been done?

I have also been accused – and I think I am entitled to answer it – that I had already agreed to a certain charge. I speak to my right hon. Friends very frankly here. It seems to me sometimes that it is so difficult to make them see what lies ahead that you have to take them along by the hand and show them. The prescription charge I knew would never be made, because it was impracticable. (*Hon. Members:* 'Oh!') Well, it was never made.

I will tell my hon. Friends something else too. There was another policy – there was a proposed reduction of 25,000 on the housing programme, was there not? It was never made. It was necessary for me at that time to use what everybody always said were bad tactics upon my part – I had to manœuvre and I did manœuvre and saved the 25,000 houses and the prescription charge. I say, therefore, to my right hon. and hon. Friends, there is no justification for taking this line at all. There is no justification in the arithmetic, there is less justification in the economics and I beg my right hon. and hon. Friends to change their minds about it.

I say this in conclusion. There is only one hope for mankind – and that is democratic Socialism. There is only one Party in

Great Britain which can do it – and that is the Labour Party. But I ask them carefully to consider how far they are polluting the stream. We have gone a long way – a very long way – against great difficulties. Do not let us change directions now. Let us make it clear, quite clear, to the rest of the world that we stand where we stood, that we are not going to allow ourselves to be diverted from our path by the exigencies of the immediate situation. We shall do what is necessary to defend ourselves by arms, and not only with arms but with the spiritual resources of our people.[1]

This was the speech that stunned the House of Commons, and next morning the newspapers were eager to jeer. 'He made all the impact of a bust and broken bull-dozer' – *Daily Express*. 'He would leave Britain confronting a perilous world, armed with false teeth' – *Daily Sketch*. 'An Uncomradely Farewell' – *Daily Telegraph*. 'It is in Mr Bevan's personal attack on the Chancellor of the Exchequer,' wrote *The Times*, 'that the mood and motive of his departure from the Cabinet most clearly show themselves.' And the newspapers also picked up quickly the fierce comment that came from some quarters in the Labour Party – for example, Alderman Pigott, chairman of the Hereford Labour Party; he called the resignation 'an act of supreme treachery on the part of a man consumed with personal ambition to achieve the highest office'. More sombre and significant was the verdict from Mr Sam Watson, secretary of the Durham Miners and Bevan's old ally of Dorking days. 'The trade union movement,' ran the statement, 'has a traditional dislike of resignations when members cannot get their own way and a greater dislike when, following full opportunity for discussion, a majority decision is cast aside.'

This same atmosphere, like a blow across the face, greeted Bevan at his next ordeal. For, fearing the loss of their parliamentary majority that very week, the Party leaders called an emergency Party meeting for 9.30 on the Tuesday morning. As happens when such meetings are called irregularly, they are often held, not in the customary Committee Room 14 upstairs, but in the so-called Grand

[1] *Hansard* Vol. 487 Col. 34.

Committee Room in Westminster Hall, a gloomy Gothic penitentiary, where by some gruesome accident we were always condemned to assemble when 'hanging' matters were on the agenda. Theoretically, Party meetings were designed exactly for the purpose of ensuring that majority decisions were reached after free and fair discussion. But the process requires rules of debate; the right of minorities to be heard even to the point of tedium; the assurance that discussion will not be cut short as well as decisions imposed by packed majorities bound together by some interest remote from the debate itself. It was no accident that Bevan always preferred the freedom of the House of Commons Chamber to the suffocations of the ante-chamber; that he would go to the claustrophobic Party meetings like a man fearing to be strangled.

It must have been that 24 April meeting in 1951 which gave the Grand Committee Room its villainous reputation, starting from the moment when the normally moderate, middle-of-the-road Chuter Ede, then Leader of the House, spoke the most savage word. As one of the few who had been a member of the 1929-31 Parliament, he protested violently against the *Tribune* article of the weekend before with its reference in the same breath to Hugh Gaitskell and Philip Snowden. He replied in kind, with interest, the inference being that Aneurin Bevan might be another Mosley. From this sour moment the meeting never recovered, except for a few rollicking minutes of relief when Tom Proctor, M.P. for Eccles, a good-natured if slightly humourless Lancastrian, gave his version of events based on his ludicrous recollections of what Archie Lush had allegedly told him on a journey up from Newport. But Bevan was not amused. He freely offered the Government the relief about the voting lobbies they craved, all the more readily since it had never been part of his purpose to defeat them there. He would inflict no wanton injury on either the Government or the Labour movement. But his adversaries should consider what injury they were doing, how much they had forced him to endure, how he had to fight long and lone campaigns in defence of what should have been considered elementary Socialist principles, how he had been 'martyred'. The word dominated the meeting and was held by some to be an outrageous display of egotism. And the moment was not improved when the luckless Proctor intervened again, and Bevan flashed back: 'Shut up, bonehead.' The scene, compressed thus, sounds like a shouting match and nothing more. But it was not that: the essential business had been transacted; the Government's majority was safe for a few weeks or months; and Bevan had pressed his case, with no especially telling reply being offered save the simple and powerful reiteration: why had he agreed to the rearmament programme in January and said he would carry it through in February? And the answer to those questions, as we have seen, had a long history. Most Ministers who resign from governments find particularly awkward the task of defining when agreed policies become intolerable, and they are always told they should have gone sooner or stayed longer. Bevan was always ready to concede that he might have chosen an earlier occasion more advantageously to himself; frequently he had been near it. But this accusation came badly from those who accused him of a reckless disregard for the interests of the Party. He had stayed in the Government too long for his own comfort; he had made concessions, he had *manœuvred*, and that was now held to be the most heinous of his confessions. He had thought others might contribute to easing the crisis by making a concession to him, and there was that much justice in Attlee's surmise, in his letter, that if an accommodation had been reached about the health charges, he would have stayed. But Attlee, more than anyone, knew of the private remonstrances Bevan had made about the £4,700 million arms programme and was scarcely entitled to pretend that this was some last-minute fabrication. ('It padded it out a bit,' he said years later,[1] doggedly oblivious, it appears, of the record of the three previous months.) However, Gaitskell at least and Morrison, with only one lapse, had long since made up their minds that there should and could be no concession, and doubtless Bevan's style of resignation – at Bermondsey, in the House of Commons and the Grand Committee room – made any accommodation the more impossible. M.P.s streamed out of that meeting, aghast at what they had seen and marvelling only that a structure as fragile as their majority of six could still survive, having been blasted by such hurricanes. But how long *could* it stand?

[1] Quote by Frank Barber in an interview with Attlee, *News Chronicle*, 20 April 1959.

The answer is: much longer than could have been imagined or, rather, the development was not entirely out of accord with Bevan's own prognostication. He always dismissed the idea that his resignation would have dire consequences for the Party electorally and was more inclined to argue that it was the only way to revive the Party's fighting spirit and idealism. And as the weeks passed, tensions relaxed. Political life began anew without every feature of the landscape having been altered. Six months after the resignation, Labour won more votes at a general election than had ever been cast for any political party, before or since. No one will ever know whether Bevan lost more votes for Labour by the onslaughts on his colleagues, so heavily personalized in the newspapers, than he gained by the general invigoration of politics.

However, this anticipation of events must not be allowed to conceal the nature of the controversy in the months after the resignation, for the seeds of many future controversies were sown at this time. One development certainly was the sharpening of personal antagonisms. Bevan himself was accused then and thereafter of being activated by a furious personal hatred of Gaitskell. Not merely did he disown the charge; he despised it. No doubt he misunderstood how deep were the wounds his tongue could inflict and no doubt his opponents believed that he and his associates – particularly Jennie Lee and myself, the editors of the offending *Tribune* article of 18 April – were the aggressors in this contest. But any imbalance in these scales of invective was soon readjusted by Bevan's ex-fellow Ministers. 'It would have been better,' said Maurice Webb, Minister of Food, 'if he had had fewer sycophants around him. He has the faculty of shouting down people but if he had been able to shout down his friends he might not have found himself in the present position.' Sir Hartley Shawcross, once the leader of the sans-culottes[1] made his contribution: 'There are those on the extreme Left wing – some with outlooks soured and warped by the disappointment of personal ambitions, some highbrows educated beyond their means – who see in it [the Budget] an absence of the class-war ideals in which they have indoctrinated themselves.' Stanley Evans M.P. said that Bevan was leading 'an uneasy coalition of well-meaning emotionalists, rejects, frustrates, crackpots

[1] See p. 19.

and fellow-travellers, making Fred Karno's Army look like the
Brigade of Guards'. And some concentrated on Bevan himself.
The May edition of the *London News*, the monthly publication of
the London Labour Party – the hand and voice were those of
Herbert Morrison – talked of how he had put 'personal ambition
and personal interests' above those of the Party which must naturally resent 'a man who appears to take a pride in manœuvring
against his own colleagues in the Cabinet'. The same journal
printed the comradely gibe: 'Y'know, he had a dream last night –
thought he was General MacArthur.'

'Some say,' wrote another commentator, 'that he will now subside into the leadership of an anonymous clique of Left-wing adu-
lators, the Samson of the Smoking Room,'[1] and certainly Bevan's
friends – the term 'Bevanite' now first gained currency – were
thought to have played an especially sinister role in the resignation
crisis. But this was the purest fiction. For years, it had been the
habit of Bevan and several of his closest friends to appropriate and
monopolize one corner of the House of Commons Smoking Room
and the assumption in official quarters was that from this brilliantly
camouflaged conspiratorial HQ, agents were despatched on fur-
tive Morrisonian errands or dashing Daltonesque initiatives. But,
alas, it was only infrequently so; the conversation was much more
a general political debate in which, while he was a member of the
Government, Bevan might offer a subtle and elaborate defence of
some of the administration's most indefensible actions. In protecting
the Cabinet and its secrets, he was ultra-loyal and ultra-secretive;
no Privy Councillor ever respected his oath more faithfully,
and it was largely for this reason that, while he was in the
Government, no interchange occurred between him and any Left-
wing groups in Parliament. The Keep Left group had offered the
most consistent and coherent criticisms of government policy and
several of its lines of criticism had coincided with or overlapped
Bevan's in the Cabinet. But they and he had formulated their attitudes in a different language and a different political idiom, and
during the days of the projected resignations, several of the most
prominent in the group, notably R. H. S. Crossman, were strongly
opposed to the final decision. But once Bevan resigned, all other

[1] Article in *Y Cymro* by Goronwy Roberts, M.P., 3 August 1951.

Left-wing activities were swamped by it. And soon some steps were taken to give the Morrisonian nightmare a semblance of reality. It was necessary to engage in propaganda, to recruit, to organize, and a first result of this activity was the publication in July of a *Tribune* pamphlet called *One Way Only*. For days beforehand, the newspapers prophesied a new Bevan eruption against his ex-colleagues. When it appeared, they searched for the names and the vitriol. When they could find neither, they pronounced the whole document a 'damp squib', although several political fire brigades were mobilized to extinguish it.

Bevan wrote the introduction to *One Way Only*, and he also supplied the enlargement of vision which gave it its element of surprise and its virtue. At the meetings at which it was devised, it was on his insistence that the Bevanite arguments about world-wide rearmament and the raw materials crisis were presented against the background of what should be the only policy for Socialists – a ceaseless war against poverty, tyranny and social injustice wherever they might be found. That meant a far more ambitious approach than ever before to the idea of 'fair shares' between the rich and poor nations; but it also meant a positive alliance with the forces of social revolution and political freedom – as Britain had shown in her dealings with India and several of the other countries of Asia and Africa, but as she was palpably not showing at that very moment in her dealings with Persia where British Socialists 'had never examined in time the social implications of drawing enormous wealth and inflated profits from a backward area'. Others besides Bevan and his friends, of course, had argued this case before; but no political manifesto of the time had stated more bluntly that 'the social revolution in Asia, Africa and the Middle East is the dominant fact of the twentieth century'. Today the emphasis on the aching needs of underdeveloped continents may sound platitudinous; but in 1951 it offered a different priority from that accepted by most leaders of the West, 'blinded by their hysterical fear of Russian aggression'.

This was the second main theme of *One Way Only*, and the one which attracted the most furious displays of derision and counter-attack. 'Today the policies of the West are based on a gross over-estimate of Soviet strength and a cringing inferiority about Soviet political warfare' – the charge was based on one of Bevan's firmest instinctive convictions and one he elaborated over the years inside the Government and out of it. It was central to his whole outlook on the world of the late 1940s and the 1950s. It did not mean that he was against military provision and precaution – he was one of the foremost advocates of guarantees for Yugoslavia. It did not mean that he would approve or condone Soviet motives and methods. It did mean that he felt almost the beginning of wisdom must be a true estimate of the Soviet challenge and its nature: a complete rejection of the notion that 175 Soviet divisions (sometimes raised to 220 in the more hysterical intelligence reports) would soon be hurled westwards towards the Channel ports and that nothing stood across their path but the atom bomb. And once this wiser appreciation was accepted, it would be easier for the dangerous pressures of American policy to be resisted. *One Way Only* cited not only the excessive and impracticable rearmament which threatened to inflict such injury on Britain's economy but several other processes whereby the wiser first thoughts of Western leaders were overruled by United States pressure: the step-by-step endorsement of Chiang Kai-shek on Formosa with the implications of Western involvement in a renewed civil war in China; the Japanese Peace Treaty, forced to signature in defiance of the wishes not only of the Soviet Union but also of China and India who should surely have some say in shaping the future of Asia; above all, the reckless, ruthless pressure to secure German rearmament, despite the strong British objection expressed by Ernest Bevin as recently as March 1950. To prevent this folly 'should be one of the prime aims of British policy'.[1] Altogether, Britain's position, it was argued – in particular the presence of American bases on British soil – gave us the right to play a much bolder part in shaping the strategy of the alliance than we had yet exercised. That was the principal plea before the pamphlet elaborated the more familiar

---

[1] On receipt of his copy of *One Way Only*, James P. Warburg, an American friend, wrote to Bevan agreeing with most of it, but questioning where the pressure for German rearmament had come from. Bevan replied on 27 August 1951: 'You can accept it from me that it is American pressure, and American pressure alone, which has forced us to agree even now only in principle to German rearmament.'

case about the effect of the rearmament on Britain's own economy, the cost of living and the Health Service.

One Way Only was an essay in qualified judgments; 'all or nothing is a silly slogan,' wrote Bevan in the introduction; '. . . we fear the consequences if too much of our wealth and energies is canalized into the creation of a great war machine. The result must be a debilitation of the civil impulses of society and a declining reliance on reason, discussion and co-operation as the ultimate arbiters. It is not our view that we should deprive ourselves of the means of effective defence, for if we did, fear would supervene. But it is our view that the vast war machines to which the Western world is fast committing itself will obstruct and not open the paths to peace.' The tone sounds moderate enough, and it requires a huge effort of the imagination to realize that these accents were so much out of tune with the orthodoxy of the time. *One Way Only* was bitterly denounced as a near-treacherous document in Britain, as an imperialist war cry in Moscow, and a sinister charter for appeasement in Washington. It is perhaps no bad tribute to Bevan that he was branded as both anti-Russian and anti-American in the age of Stalin and McCarthy.

What he did set out to do in the months after the resignation – elaborate speeches in Ebbw Vale, Glasgow on May Day, and a host of other great meetings, more packed out than ever, are there to show it – was to execute the personal strategy he had often discussed when he so nearly resigned in 1950 or 1949 – to help re-educate the Party in some of the first principles of Socialism, and yet to sustain and further Labour's electoral chances. 'At the moment,' he said in Glasgow at the biggest May Day meeting for years, 'there is a great famine in India. People are dying inside the British Commonwealth for lack of food. Nehru has warned them that they may die by the millions – all because mankind has got the priorities wrong. We shall find people starving to death by the side of television sets if we are not careful. All the genius of modern science will enable us to see ourselves dying by starvation. Surely an intelligent civilization would see the table well supplied before the gadgets were there. That is why we are asking for a Socialist plan . . .' And that was Bevan in the aftermath of the resignation, once he had escaped from the oppressive Westminster corridors.

He thought indeed that the particular row he had had with the Chancellor and the Treasury about the scale of the rearmament programme would resolve itself; he had pronounced the programme dead, and so it was. Even on the Health Service charges a concession had at last been made – it had been conceded that the charge would not be permanent; it must be reviewed annually.

Meantime he and Jennie went off, in August, for a month-long much-needed holiday in Yugoslavia, and there to make new associations and friendships which would influence the rest of his life. He went in particular to Brioni where Marshal Tito, Prime Minister 'for the time being' as the Yugoslav Constitution said, entertained Ivan Ribar, President of the Praesidium, Aleksander Rankovic, Minister of the Interior, Edvard Kardelj, Minister for Foreign Affairs, Boris Kidrik, Chairman of the Planning Commission, Milovan Djilas, Minister without Portfolio, and Moshe Pijade, Vice President of the Praesidium. It sounds like a formal diplomatic occasion, but in fact they sat in a grey stone shelter on the beach, open to the sea on one side and furnished with plain wooden trestle tables and wooden forms, a kind of outdoor dining room but with the flavour, too, of a partisan company's headquarters. And that is what it truly was, a gathering of brothers-in-arms who had shared a heroic past and faced together a perilous present. Bevan was deeply impressed by the intimate, trusting spirit they revealed and also by the carefree, refreshing style in which they showed how Communists could argue with one another. He hurled himself into the debate with his customary lack of reticence and almost felt himself embraced by the same magic comradeship. He came away with indelible memories of the special quality of Yugoslav bravery, of their absolute resolve to resist Soviet encroachment, of the greatness of Tito, and with another possession more peculiar to Jennie and himself – an immediately established affinity with Milovan Djilas, who had acted as his host in his official residence in Belgrade. They spoke to one another as fellow romantics, fellow Marxists, fellow poets and men of the mountains who had somehow fallen from on high into the nether-world of politics.

Yugoslavia also offered one of those rare intervals of peace when he was able to write without the horrors of political life pressing upon him. Jennie gave him assistance with the book he had long been contemplating. He needed no one to supply ideas, but he was diffident about syntax and tended to write long sentences which Jennie would simplify. They were happily arguing about such minor matters when they were suddenly interrupted by Vladimir Dedijer, after Djilas the most intimate and sympathetic of his new Yugoslav friends. All his six foot six inches towered over Jennie and raising his arms high, he expressed his indignation: 'You must not destroy the fine feathers of his thought.' Back in London Bevan wrote a series of articles for the *Evening Standard* on his visit. 'As a regular reader' – wrote one typical of hundreds – 'I must ask leave to record my astonishment and disgust at your allowing the unspeakable, anti-British, anti-Empire and pro-Communist Bevan to publicize himself and his Moscow-trained Communist dictator friend Tito in a decent English newspaper.' He was truly back home with the subtleties of English politics.

A few days later (1 October) he received a letter from his new friend Milovan Djilas. A few extracts may help to prove how close was the intimacy already established. 'It is understandable that – in different countries under different conditions – identical or similar viewpoints are being born. Yet it is striking how ideas unite hitherto unknown people. I think that the personal relationship established between both of you and ourselves is only the beginning of something much more lasting and deeper, the beginning of that unbreakable link between people who through different methods and ways and even from different ideological positions truly fight for the freedom of men and peoples. Our last talk in Zagreb was, as Jennie obviously remarked, a little "rough". Yet it was the most fertile as far as understanding goes. In the future its theoretical results can be the basis of further discussions which do not have to be "rough" any more. Maybe the "roughness" could not be avoided if a clash of opinion was to produce a "spark" and if the opinion were to approach and crystallize mutually. This letter is meant for Jennie as much as for you. You are inseparable in our thoughts as you are inseparable in your lives and in the struggle you are leading. Yet she should not think we only see in her – a wise and independent – yet conjugal part of A. Bevan. Nothing could be more wrong.'

Election rumours came and went. Everyone agreed that it would scarcely be possible for the Labour Government with its flimsy majority of six to survive anything like a full term, but a fairly wide range of choice for the date still seemed available. Besides, Herbert Morrison, the arch-electioneer, was away in San Francisco, giving British assistance to the formulation of the Japanese Peace Treaty; an election announced without him would be a political blasphemy. Bevan himself lent a hand in writing the introduction to a sequel to *One Way Only*, in which he insisted that the resigning Ministers had 'refused to be irritated into personal polemics by the splenetic speeches and imputations of base motives to which they had been subjected from all sides . . . The problem for the movement is how to combine unity with vigorous thought and robust action. This is easy to say but not easy to achieve. It will call for tolerance and at the same time for candour. Herd cries are not enough if the herd is rushing to the precipice . . .'

However, Bevan and his pamphleteers, no less than Messrs Morrison and Shinwell who first heard the news on the radio on the *Queen Mary*, were startled by an unaccustomed initiative on the part of the Prime Minister. A statement was issued from Downing Street announcing that the general election would take place on 25 October. All concerned would have been even more startled if Attlee had explained his approach to the problem, as he did candidly years later.[1] 'It wasn't a sudden decision. One of the reasons I wanted it was because of the King. His health was bad and he was going off to Australia. It would have been unfair to allow a crisis, which might blow up at any time, while he was out of the country. He would have been worrying all the time whether something was going to happen.'[2]

[1] Interview with Frank Barber, *News Chronicle* 20 April 1959.
[2] Only once did I ever see Attlee emotionally affected in public and the occasions for doing so were frequent, dating back to an early morning in San Francisco in May 1945 when his Parliamentary Private Secretary, John Dugdale and I broke into his bedroom to tell him that the Second World War with Germany was over and that we would like a statement from him for the British Labour movement; then he just got back into bed. He was cool even when he spoke of Ernest Bevin whom he clearly loved. But when he spoke of George VI's death, tears were in his eyes and voice.

9

THE BEVANITES: I

1951–1952

It is perhaps a strange observation to make but I think you will find it to
be true, that a man of high ideals and exalted standards is apt to reserve
his chief bitterness of language for his own party, or to use it with more
satisfaction than he does with regard to his opponents. And the reason is
simple enough. The honour, the interest, the welfare of his own party
are part of himself; part of his being, his own life; and when, therefore,
he sees his party, as he thinks, playing false to him, then it is that he
pours over them the vials of his bitterest wrath.

　　　　　—LORD ROSEBERY, in his speech on Lord Salisbury, 1904

LABOUR almost *won* the 1951 election; it was a much
closer run thing than the battle of Waterloo. The Party
secured more votes than the Tories, more than the total
cast for any political party in British history, before or since. Only
the vagaries of the electoral system robbed Labour of a third successive victory and the pundits of all their profound judgments, to
be deduced from the change of government, about the impalpable
shifts in British opinion. If we reflect on wartime conditions of
austerity persisting six years after V.E. day – the meat ration was
still no more than eightpence a week – and on the formidable
propaganda onslaught which the Tory machine had been able
to mount, day in, day out, the voting figures testify to the in-
herent robustness of the British Labour movement. Two men
agreed on that, if on nothing else. Winston Churchill, in shaping
the policies of his new administration resolved to treat organized
labour with the tenderest circumspection. Aneurin Bevan believed

that the Labour army retained its strength almost intact on the battlefield; given a modicum of generalship all lost territory could be regained. No judgment on his conduct over the previous months is more misplaced than that which saw him languishing for the sour grapes of opposition. He wanted power: collective power for the Labour movement to which he was wedded, for better or for worse. That was the ruling passion of his political life, and those who misunderstood it, understood nothing.

As he himself believed, he had picked his course to serve that end, even through the tempestuous months of 1951. Often, before the resignation, he had argued that his action would help revive the movement rather than debilitate it, and in the following months he asserted that the claim had been confirmed. Once the election date was announced he made clear his desire to assist in drawing up an election manifesto on which all sections of the Party could agree, and at the pre-election Conference at Scarborough in October he was one of the National Executive sub-committee of four – Hugh Dalton, Sam Watson and Morgan Phillips were the others – who had little difficulty in reaching a reasonable formula. Even on the arms question – on which the Conference agenda was filled with numerous Bevanite resolutions – it was not found difficult to avoid a clash: approval of *some* rearmament was accepted without specifying any figure. 'I have been fighting Tories all my life, ever since I was a nipper,' he told the pre-Conference rally. It had never occurred to him to stop. The speech at the Conference itself was a masterly, unifying appeal, emphasizing at the end a theme his friends often heard him reiterate in private: 'We must avoid at all costs a repetition here of what has happened to continental Socialist movements. We must never carry doctrinaire differences to the point of schism; that is why our movement is based primarily on the industrial masses.' Of course this tone was partly inspired by the exigencies of the election, and why not? It was also an expression of his deep instinct that what Britain needed was a long period of resolute Labour government. In this spirit he threw himself into the subsequent election campaign, not omitting to urge in the last few days, in a rare burst of grandiloquence, that the Ebbw Vale results would be 'headlined all over the world'. He always awaited the declaration of his own figures with a feverish tension which could prostrate his Committee rooms. In 1951 he increased his majority by 28. No open enemy or candid friend could make much of that.

But, unsuspected by most observers at the time, the 1951 election and the Scarborough prelude to it did initiate a big change in his political fortunes. For it was on the night of Tuesday 2 October, in the St Nicholas Hotel at Scarborough, that the first step was taken to organize a 'Stop Bevan', or rather an 'Expel Bevan' movement. One irritant which had possibly helped to provoke this response was the publication just prior to the election announcement of a new *Tribune* pamphlet entitled *Going Our Way?*, a successor to *One Way Only*, in which trade union representatives were admonished for voting on the Executive, particularly on matters concerning the Gaitskell Budget, in a sense directly contrary to the declared wishes of their members. The criticisms had been mildly stated, however much they invited violent headlines; but here, for sure, Bevan and his coterie of journalist intellectuals were trespassing on holy ground. And a more shocking display of *lèse-majesté* followed. For at Scarborough, in the election for the Constituency Party Section of the National Executive, Bevan came out top easily as he had done on the previous four occasions, with an increased vote; more spectacular was the election of a fervent Bevan supporter, Barbara Castle, in second place. She had withdrawn from the Women's Section where the displeasure of the union leaders would have ensured her defeat and, snapping her fingers at them, had regained a much more secure Executive position at a single leap. Two other Bevanite supporters, Ian Mikardo and Tom Driberg, increased their vote substantially. Three ex-Ministers and anti-Bevanites, Herbert Morrison, Hugh Dalton and Jim Griffiths, saw their votes drop, and one longstanding Executive member, ex-Defence Minister Emanuel Shinwell, was removed altogether, and stormed out of the Conference in a rage. Another aspirant who did well, but not quite as well as expected, was one who appeared strangely disguised on the ballot paper as J. H. Wilson (a cunning piece of Transport House sabotage, said some). The writing was not merely on the wall but blazed across the Scarborough skies. Overwhelmingly the constituencies had expressed their confidence in the man who had been driven out of the Labour Cabinet. Given a quarter of a chance, the Party was going Bevanite.

This was the crisis which three men in particular resolved to face at the St Nicholas Hotel meeting. The ringleader was Arthur Deakin, general secretary of the Transport and General Workers' Union, a fierce, breezy, irascible, stout-hearted bison of a man who genuinely believed that any proposition he could force through his union executive must be the will of the people and more especially the will of Ernest Bevin whose requirements he had normally taken the precaution of finding out in advance. But Bevin was now dead, and Deakin lacked Bevin's redeeming powers of individual imaginative rumination. Leaders must be loyally followed; that was the Deakin dream of democracy, and with Bevin gone he cast around for a new god he could serve with the same restless devotion. Meantime the identity of the devil was plain enough. From Scarborough 1951 until the day of his death, Arthur Deakin was a man with a mission – to exterminate the infamous Bevan.

Two other leading trade union leaders backed him, according to their different lights, somewhat dimmer than Deakin's. One was William Lawther,[1] President of the National Union of Mineworkers, a much less intense and dedicated Right-winger. Once indeed he had had a quite lengthy flirtation with the Communists and he always took a pride in his knowledge of Marxist temptations and techniques. Long since, he had made up his mind to swim with the strongest tides, even giving the impression that he had helped to unleash them with his own bulky interventions. The other was Tom Williamson,[2] general secretary of the National Union of General and Municipal Workers Union, altogether a much milder, more introvert type, more an earnest civil servant than a trade union leader, who however reflected accurately enough the normally sedate industrial manners of his members. These three alone commanded at that time no fewer than two million out of the total union vote at a Labour Party Conference. Given the natural or impressionable allies they could muster among the other union delegations, they had a ready-made majority for almost any policy or course they prescribed. And on that Tuesday night, they and a few

[1] Later Sir William.
[2] Later Lord Williamson.
12

others of the less important trade union leaders resolved – once the general election was out of the way – not only to 'stop Bevan', but to crush the Bevanites, and one way to achieve that might be to alter the clause in the Party Constitution whereby – in a fit of weakness way back in 1937 – seven places on the Executive had been bestowed by the unions on the ungrateful constituency parties. The unions could use their whip-hand before matters got worse. That was the gist of the St Nicholas compact. But, alas, thanks to the presence among the conspirators of a mere novice – the sprightly Tom O'Brien of the National Association of Theatre and Kiné Employees, a fervent Roman Catholic and anti-Communist, but always the most refreshing companion for thirsty journalists – a garbled report of the affair leaked out into most newspapers. Several falsely charged with being parties to the plot – Robert Willis of the Compositors, Charles Geddes of the Post Office Workers, and Jack Tanner of the Engineers – indignantly repudiated the accusation, and both Bevan and the Bevanites left Scarborough in the naive belief that there had been little smoke and less fire. It had not occurred to them that to use the democracy of the Labour Party to nominate candidates for elective office who actually became elected might be construed as a criminal proceeding.

Soon, too, after the election, Bevan committed another offence which rankled, maybe, even more: in one of the major controversies arising from the Gaitskell Budget, he appeared to be vindicated. All through the summer and autumn of 1951 a complicated argument continued about the nature of the £4,700 million arms programme commitment, how it was qualified, whether it was being adhered to, whether Bevan's prophecies were being fulfilled or not. At first the Party leadership stood by the letter of the commitment: a National Executive document, *Our First Duty – Peace*, published in August, said that the programme 'represents what all consider *the minimum* required to deter aggression and so prevent a Third World War' and that 'the burden of rearmament, though heavy in its demands on raw materials and manpower can be carried by our economy without too much strain'. One of the main arguments of the offending pamphlet, *Going Our Way?*, was that the Labour Government itself had been compelled to retreat from the absolute budgetary commitments which had helped to force the resignations. A main retort of the Gaitskellites was that they were still protected by the very qualifying phrase in the original Attlee statement which Bevan had often emphasized. In September *Tribune* had carried the headline: 'HAS GAITSKELL JOINED THE BEVANITES?' and the taunt was based on remarkable reports of his visit to Washington where he was said to have 'created a deep impression with pleas for a more moderate defence drive that would avert the threat of a new financial crisis now facing Western Europe' and when an American official was reported to have complained, 'He is trying to take us half way to Bevan'. Then, for the few weeks of the election campaign itself, such surmises were suspended: neither the Tory nor the Labour leadership wished to see the rearmament debate forced to the centre of the stage. But after the election a new witness offered his evidence. Churchill, as the Prime Minister and the Minister of Defence, had been able to see the books, and in his first speech in a defence debate he announced, almost casually: 'We shall not, however, succeed in spending the £1,250 million this year' [the part of the £4,700 million allocated for the first year] 'and some of the late Government's programme must necessarily roll forward into a future year. The point was, I believe, made by the right hon. Gentleman for Ebbw Vale after his resignation . . .' And then, while the House took a few minutes to grasp the revelation, Churchill amiably explained that he meant no reproach to his predecessors; he more than anyone had seen many a munitions programme lag behind the estimates. But Bevan interrupted: did the statement mean that the whole three-year programme would be rolled forward? What was to be the new period for the full programme? Churchill parried the insistence with a smile about the 'instructive and animated' discussions among the Labour leaders soon to be expected, adding: 'I am not really wishing to embark on a debate with the right hon. Gentleman. I was giving him an honourable mention in despatches for having been right by accident', and then when Bevan sought to interrupt again: 'I was giving the right hon. Gentleman an honourable mention for having, it appears by accident, perhaps not from the best of motives, happened to be right'.[1]

[1] *Hansard* Vol. 494 Col. 2602.

No flout from Churchill, in the extensive record of their exchanges, infuriated Bevan more than that one. He had staked his political future on the point at issue – the most direct claim in his resignation speech had been the charge that the £4,700 million programme was 'already dead' – and all Churchill could offer was a jeer about unworthy motives and accidental wisdom. Certainly it was a staggering announcement, probably the first and the last in all history in which a Defence Minister explained – at a moment of soaring inflation, what's more – that the Service departments were not able to spend the money made available by a profligate Treasury. And the deduction Churchill himself drew was even more instructive: the lag in arms production, he said, 'will, of course, be helpful to the Chancellor of the Exchequer in his special problems'. In other words, the failure to spend the Service estimates allowed for would assist in providing a handsome surplus in the Budget, and what a world of reflection that reopened about the 1951 convulsions inside the Labour Party.

But one man at least was not impressed by the Churchill revelation. Invited by *Tribune* to comment upon it, Hugh Gaitskell wrote an elaborate reply, reiterating the qualifications about the programme; recalling Bevan's own 'less guarded' statement of February, 'we shall carry it out'; challenging again the Bevan claim that the supply departments had known the figures to be unrealizable even at the time of the Budget; arguing that if an easier Budget had been feasible, neither he nor the rest of the Parliamentary Labour Party had been at all certain that the Health Service should have priority. Never then or thereafter did there come from that quarter a single admission that the calculations of the Treasury had been erroneous, either too lax or too strict. All had been as infallibly and meticulously correct[1] as the Treasury could make it.

[1] Many independent commentators since have taken a different view. For example Samuel Brittan in his major work on the role of the Treasury *Steering the Economy* (Secker & Warburg, 1969, pp. 110–11): 'The most extraordinary episode in the Labour Government's history was the cavalier way in which it embarked upon an enormous rearmament programme at the time of Korea . . . The Treasury which is habitually pessimistic about the capacity of the economy to bear civilian programmes which are quite tiny by comparison, took the view that the nation would just *have* to afford this extra arms bill. Mr Gaitskell and his official advisers, who shared his

Bevan himself used the Churchill admission for a different purpose. Stepping on the same thin ice where in his resignation speech he was accused of having slithered most perilously, he returned – in a major Commons speech in February – to the reasons 'why I am not in favour of leaving economic planning to the Chancellor of the Exchequer. He is preoccupied with annual arithmetic, and not only that, for he is also preoccupied with recurrent crises; and then he comes along, like other Chancellors of the Exchequer' – at that an anticipatory hush and a few jeers came from both sides, expectant of a new 'personal' attack – 'Oh, yes, he is bound to get the figures right even if the facts are wrong. In this country we have an annual Budget. Every year the figures are totted up and every year they have to balance. Why? Because we are still carrying on, in an industrial community, the conventions of a pastoral society. Just because the harvest occurs every year, we must have an annual Budget, although in a modern society the annual crops are an insignificant proportion of total production, and no balance sheet today corresponds with the actual facts. That is the reason why my right hon. Friend' – again came the hush and a quieter jeer – 'I do not blame him for this; he was the inheritor of the convention, although he followed it with conspicuous enthusiasm – tried to push into one annual statement of account for 1951–52 machine tools which will not arrive until 1953. That is a fact, because the statement of accounts bears no relation at all to the rhythm of industrial production.' And then came one practical illustration after another of the same argument: of why planning should be taken from the Chancellor and given to an immediately-appointed Minister of Production:

---

devotion to the cause of Western defence, made the mistake of assuming that sufficiently strict budgetary planning, together with the reimposition of physical controls, would produce the raw materials, machine tools, and components required for an enormously enlarged defence programme . . . *The Bevanites proved right in the rearmament controversy – a fact which most politicians and civil servants often wanted to forget.'* (Author's italics, Brittan's economics.)

Joan Mitchell, the pro-Gaitskellite, mildly pro-Wilsonite, anti-Bevanite author of *Crisis in Britain, 1951* Secker & Warburg, (1951) p. 276, summarized the same point more demurely: 'Time was very much on the side of the Government's Bevanite critics. As we have seen, the rearmament programme was not carried out as planned.'

'I would not do it because the Chancellor of the Exchequer is not an extremely able man. We all know that he is, but the greatest possible ability cannot prevail against the myopia of the Treasury.' So the point was pressed home, without any personal assault whatever, and just to prove how objectively the argument might be applied, he enticed Churchill again to his aid. Did the Prime Minister agree with the statement made by his own Chancellor a few days before that one of the ways the 1952 books would be balanced would be by running down industrial stocks? Did he agree with that, as Minister of Defence? Churchill did indeed agree in all his various capacities, as a veritable Pooh Bah. Then, pounced Bevan, he was 'unfit for his office'; for did the Government truly intend in that year of supremely urgent rearmament, against a power said to be equipping itself with a vast new submarine fleet, to run down our stocks all for the purpose of balancing the Treasury's annual accounts? Either the rearmament could not be so imperative or the precise book-keeping was a dangerous fatuity. Bevan would gladly have it both ways; he had convicted Churchill of treason – due to ignorance of course: a sweet revenge for the charge that he himself had been patriotic by accident.

However, these outward parliamentary pleasantries were deceptive. Sections of the press and sections of the Parliamentary Labour Party showed a greater interest in what they construed as signs of a conspiracy behind the scenes. Since the opening of the new session the Bevanites had sought to organize themselves into a more effective parliamentary group. On the suggestion of Ian Mikardo and on the precedent of the Keep Left group, it was agreed to elect a regular chairman – Harold Wilson was the first – and to meet at a regular time in the parliamentary week: 1.30 on Mondays. None of those participating in these secret rites thought at the outset that they might be indulging in some scandalous Mau Mau activity – (none at least except the compulsive informer in our midst who reported our proceedings regularly to Hugh Dalton and thereby to the Whips).[1] Unofficial groups had existed in Parliament ever since the first Witenagemot, and the Bevanites of the early 1950s ima-

[1] His identity as Desmond Donnelly has been notorious for years but the full proof is contained in Dalton's unpublished diaries which record that the leakages to Dalton started on 30 November 1951.

gined they were following a more recent precedent set by others, notably the XYZ Club, which had been talking politics over exclusive dinner tables since its foundation by Douglas Jay and a few others in the early 1940s. No one, after all, had ever suggested that the Keep Left group should be outlawed. By January 1952 the new Bevanite arrangements were in full working order and the agenda was crowded – new and permanent charges on the Health Service, announced by R. A. Butler, the Tory Chancellor; the continuing debate over defence costs; fears that the new Government was abandoning the restraint which the Labour Government had sought to exercise on American policy in the Far East; the forthcoming Budget. On all these issues, the Bevanites, headed by Bevan himself, played a leading role in the Party meetings immediately after the Christmas recess.

But some ill-wishers saw these operations in a sinister light: 'BEVAN CRISIS WEEKEND. He has two plans to grab the Socialist leadership', ran the headlines in the *Sunday Express* on 3 February; a tale followed of how the plotters had been assembling at 23 Cliveden Place. It was all a fabrication and Bevan took the rare step of issuing a public denial: 'Mr Bevan's father-in-law, Mr Lee, has been since Saturday morning, lying desperately ill at Mr Bevan's home. The only persons visiting his house this weekend are friends of his family, relatives and doctors.' But no word of apology or withdrawal appeared in the *Daily* or *Sunday Express*, and a little while later, Arthur Deakin returned to the subject in a speech at Bristol. 'The trade unions,' he said, 'will not be misled by the *Tribune* group of politicians who seek a short cut to the leadership of the Party.' *Tribune* promptly asked him to explain why he seemed to popularize the tittle-tattle of the Tory press, but Deakin was characteristically unrepentant. *Tribune*, he said, was the medium for a dissident element; it was associated with people who had 'run away' from their responsibilities; the sole object of the whole exercise was the personal advancement of the unnamed, unspeakable Bevan. It is necessary to recall a few of these exchanges from the plethora which filled the current headlines. They were an essential ingredient of the hysteria of the time; the distorting mirror in which even practised performers marked the antics of their rivals.

Parliamentary tactics appeared prominently on the Bevanite agendas; hardly surprisingly since these had been the immemorial topic of Tea and Smoking Room and every congenial corridor for centuries. To the outsider their intricacies may seem boring or inscrutable; but to the insider the twists and turns involved may signify the will to fight, to obstruct, to construct, and thereby to point the way to the determination of the large questions of politics. The Labour Opposition of 1951 and 1952 was caught cruelly in the normal dilemmas of the predicament. Ex-Ministers were obsessed by the notion of defending their past policies and reputations. Doubtless the Bevanites were equally determined to defend theirs, but they had the advantage and interest of appealing to the future, and Bevan himself quickly aroused a response outside the strictly defined Bevanite group. Even if he had not been the outstanding parliamentary debater on the Labour benches, it would have been hard for him not to give the impression of wresting the initiative from the feeble grip of the official leaders. When Butler announced the new range of Health Service charges, it was naturally Bevan who could denounce them most savagely – although he did in fact take pains not to embarrass his colleagues: what Labour had done reluctantly, he insisted, the Tories did with relish and hatred of the whole conception of a free Health Service.[1] But no one could con-

---

[1] It was in one of these debates (on 27 March 1952, *Hansard*, Vol. 498) that Iain Macleod leapt to parliamentary fame with what was acclaimed at the time, and has been even more certainly established in parliamentary tradition, as a brilliant debating attack on Aneurin Bevan. Not merely did Macleod challenge Bevan on his own ground, the National Health Service; the story suggests that he drove a routed or at least discomfited Bevan from the Chamber altogether. But it was not quite like that. Bevan in his speech had in fact been doing his best to repair some of the divisions within the Labour Party on the subject of the charges being imposed. Of course, he was on difficult territory. The Tories were exploiting the breach which Labour had opened the year before, to impose still further charges on the Service; but Bevan did not wish to reopen that quarrel, especially since the Party was uniting behind him to oppose the new charges. Macleod, called to speak immediately after Bevan, started with the arresting statement that he intended 'to deal closely and with relish with the vulgar, crude and intemperate speech to which the House has listened'. Later he accused Bevan of 'going behind the back of his Cabinet and his leader to defraud the House of Commons'. Tories, and particularly Churchill on the

ceal the emerging contrasted temper of back-bench and front-bench opposition. It became evident even more strikingly in a debate on the Korean war, following a visit of Churchill to Washington, when it appeared that British policy had moved much closer to American policy just at the moment when American policy was being dragged much nearer, by a declaration of its Far Eastern plenipotentiary, John Foster Dulles, towards a world-wide anti-Communist crusade. Morrison led the attack on Churchill, Labour's Shadow Cabinet having devised a careful censure motion designed, after some pressure from Bevan at the Party meeting, to unite all sections of the Party. But Churchill retaliated with crushing effect. He brilliantly and scandalously revealed – in defiance of the rule which the Civil Service is normally supposed to enforce on incoming administrations about the activities of their predecessors – that Morrison and the previous Cabinet had on two specific occasions envisaged and accepted the idea, in certain eventualities, of counter-action and an enlarged war against China. It was a painful blow, and possibly Morrison never recovered from it: the dedicated tactician had been adroitly out-manœuvred. Strangely, it was left to Bevan to pick up the pieces, and he did so in a manner which illustrated afresh the stature of the different performers. For he did indeed come momentarily to Morrison's rescue: the House was forced to listen as he rebuked the Prime Minister for his constitutional impropriety – all the older M.P.s were well aware that Bevan knew ten times more about parliamentary procedure than

---

front bench, naturally pricked up their ears. Yet no one who reads the full exchange today – and less still those who heard it at the time – could believe that those accusations had been sustained in the rest of the speech. It certainly was packed with facts and figures, and it certainly did revive Tory spirits, and yet by the end Macleod was taunting the official Labour leaders and the rest of the Labour Party for 'a surrender to the views of the right hon. Member for Ebbw Vale'. He did that in the absence of Bevan for the reason that the debate and Macleod's speech had been interrupted at seven o'clock, and when it was resumed three hours later, since Macleod had already spoken for twenty-six minutes, Bevan assumed he had finished.

Over the years, Macleod and Bevan became friendly and Macleod acknowledged that once he was established in the Ministry of Health, he found little in the work which Bevan had done which he felt ought to be altered. He was certainly no innovator at that Ministry.

12*

Churchill; and gradually he restored the debate to the dominant world themes enumerated by Dulles.[1] Churchill, said Bevan, had inferred at the end of his speech that the vote of censure upon him was an attack on the United States – 'this shows how his ego now fills the whole cosmos'. But the world must escape from such 'juvenile polemics'; great nations were often divided on great issues of world policy, and intelligent people must be permitted to join the argument without being branded as anti-American or anti-British. The Churchill failure to comprehend the new trends in American policy and the failure of American policy to comprehend the true causes of revolutionary ferment in Asia and elsewhere might mean 'the end of what is described as bipartisan foreign policy in this country'. It was a speech which succeeded where Morrison had failed, uniting the parliamentary Opposition when it might have been left in utter disarray by the Churchill disclosures. But next morning some of the newspapers placed a more hackneyed interpretation on what had occurred. 'BEVAN'S BID FOR POWER. End of Bi-Partisan Foreign Policy Threatened,' said the *Daily Mail* headlines. The story underneath suggested that the National Executive, meeting that morning, might be called upon to settle the issue of the succession there and then.

Another choice before the Party could not be blurred and posed fresh tactical problems of the utmost complexity. What was to be done about the arms programme, now that the Tories were in charge of it? The year's defence estimates were published, proposing an increased expenditure of £500 million on the previous year. The total had, in effect, been approved in advance by the Labour Government as surely as it had become the chief target for Bevanite attack: so how could a split be avoided? The lobbies of the House of Commons do not offer the elaborate exits and entrances available at the maze of the Party Conference; there are only two of them and the Tories would certainly demand outright 'approval' of the largely-inherited White Paper. How could the challenge be dodged?

---

[1] As quoted by Bevan in *Hansard* 26 February, a report in *The Times* of 12 February had said: 'Mr Dulles, during a broadcast discussion last night, said that the U.S. must let all the Far East know that it would not stand idly by while any part of the world remained under the rule of either Communist or Fascist dictatorship.'

The Shadow Cabinet devised its own supremely imbecile solution. It proposed to accept the motion 'approving' the Defence White Paper, and then to add the rider: 'but has no confidence in the capacity of Her Majesty's present advisers to carry it out'. The formula had its comic aspect, bearing in mind the identities of the respective Ministers of Defence in the two administrations: replace the military novice, Viscount Alexander of Tunis, with the modern Carnot, Emanuel Shinwell, and the defence of the realm would be assured and Labour's just demands satisfied!

However, the formula had not been concocted carelessly or hastily. It was the work of several days of internal party wrangling. The Bevanites had taken the initiative. They presented, first in writing to the Parliamentary Committee and later to a full Party meeting, the terms of a reasoned amendment which could be pressed against the Government's White Paper. Of course, it was Bevanite in tone; it gave chapter and verse why the £4,700 million programme could not and should not be fully carried out in the conditions of 1952. But this proposal was not an ultimatum or at least it was not considered as such by the Bevanites. Conceivably it could pave the way for a compromise; probably it would increase 'Bevanite' support in the Party; at least it was an effort to find a method of circumventing the Party's impasse. But the Party leaders saw it all as a devilish piece of scheming, typical of Crossman who moved it at the Party meeting: his sponsorship of any project was enough by itself to stir Attlee's spleen. At the Party meeting, the Crossman proposal was voted down; the Shadow Cabinet's 'sham amendment', as *Tribune* called it, was adopted instead; and the meeting broke up in considerable confusion, no one being sure what, if anything, had been resolved about the Government's own motion demanding 'approval' of the White Paper. To clear up this substantial detail, a specific instruction was issued, signed by Attlee, Morrison and Whiteley, the Chief Opposition Whip, saying that the decision of the Party was to support the Party's amendment and abstain on the Government's motion. Nothing could be plainer. If the Attlee-Morrison-Whiteley instruction was obeyed, the Defence White Paper would be 'approved' without a dissenting voice, and the Bevanites would have been chastened, if not curbed.

So the Defence debate, which came on 5 March 1952, ended with two sensational votes. Bevan himself had not spoken – it was self-denial week, said Nigel Birch – but Crossman, now firmly in the fold or perhaps wielding a crook of his own, put the Bevanite case. Labour's amendment to the official Tory motion was defeated by 314 to 219, a majority of 95, in place of the normal majority of 20-odd, and when it came to the official government motion of approval, Bevan led 57 Labour Members of various shades and affiliations against it; 57 varieties of Bevanites, pacifists and long-standing critics of the Party leadership, a much larger number than anyone had expected. When the figure was read out the explosion was immediate, and thereafter for some time detonations continued daily.

Next morning the official *Daily Herald* rebuked the rebels in its most magisterial tone. 'This is a time for frankness. We must tell Mr Aneurin Bevan and his supporters that they have set out on a course which will harm the country and imperil the future of the Labour movement. They are now deliberately bent . . . on challenging the democratic decisions of the Parliamentary Labour Party, and advertising their antagonism to its elected leader, Mr Attlee . . . The Labour movement as a whole is becoming tired of this minority's egotism'. A day later Arthur Deakin stepped in; 'the present squabble,' he said, 'is not centred around any principle at all but rather around personalities'. And the Shadow Cabinet were already moving swiftly to the counter-assault. A Party meeting was called for the following week. By the weekend, it was reported that every rebel would be called upon to sign a recantation or at least an understanding that he would never indulge in such disloyalty again – on pain of expulsion, if he refused. It did indeed look as if the climax in the Bevanite crisis was near. Speaking in his constituency that weekend, Bevan was asked if he knew what the press meant by the headlines saying he 'must toe the line next week'? To which he replied: 'If that means a recantation of what we did, the answer is, we won't. If they say "Promise not to do it again", I cannot. If you think what you did was right, you cannot promise not to do what you think right again.' And then later: 'Is a Socialist in danger of being expelled from the Labour Party because he voted against the Tories?' Altogether it was a belligerent

Bevan, backed more enthusiastically than ever by his constituents, who returned to London to face an equally belligerent Attlee, backed by his Shadow Cabinet. But the desire to stand firm and a readiness to accept all the highly awkward consequences of expulsion were not exactly to be equated, and when the Bevanite group assembled in London, several voices, especially those of Harold Wilson, Barbara Castle, Dick Crossman and John Freeman urged a degree of caution which would not have found favour in Ebbw Vale.

The Party assembled for the most crowded meeting since the 'resignation' meeting of April 1951, and the scene was arranged to take place, by some punctiliously grim Providence, in the Westminster Hall Grand Committee Room. Attlee produced his resolution which many believed must lead to a deep Party division. It was not precisely a demand for recantation, but it was fierce enough; it required condemnation of the 57; the reimposition of the strict Standing Orders which had been in suspense – in the expectation of good behaviour – since 1945; and a signature by all members that the Standing Orders were accepted. The calculation was that once this resolution was forced through, most members would bow to it. Only Bevan and a handful of his most intimate followers would refuse and that would be the ideal solution. To expel fifty-seven, would disrupt the Party; to expel five or six might be its salvation. This was certainly the design of the chief 'expellers' in the Shadow Cabinet; it followed the advice often tendered by Arthur Deakin. Most members came to the meeting convinced that the Attlee recommendation would be carried; after all, when had the leadership ever failed to have its way on what was almost the equivalent of a vote of confidence? But within a few minutes it became apparent that an unexpected ferment was at work. M.P.s did sense that they were attending a meeting which might disrupt the Labour Party for generations, and some had come prepared with a plan to avert the catastrophe. Against Attlee's proposition, a group of 'middle-of-the-road' ex-Ministers, George Strauss, John Strachey and Kenneth Younger, carried by the astonishing majority of 162 to 73, a mediatory amendment which omitted all reference to the past and concentrated solely on the introduction of Standing Orders to safeguard the future. The debate was tense and bitter, but one man certainly swayed the outcome. Probably Tom O'Brien, M.P., was called by Attlee at the critical turn of the debate in the expectation that he would rally trade union M.P.s to the well-known Deakin line. But Tom just occasionally could escape from his leash. If the Party truly wished to destroy itself, he said, condemning the Attlee proposal, it should move *en masse* from the Committee Room to the neighbouring Westminster Hall where public executions could more fittingly be conducted. Then alongside the plaques for Charles I and William Wallace, might be placed another: 'On this spot the Labour Party committed suicide, aided and abetted by Clement Attlee and Aneurin Bevan.' After he had spoken, the pressure was on Attlee to withdraw his own motion in favour of the moderate amendment. That would have saved his face and the Party by the same belated gracious stroke. But Attlee curtly refused, thus fortifying the impression that the Right wing within the leadership had come to the meeting with the firm intention of forcing the split. It was a near shave and next day there was another nearer still when, at a meeting of the National Executive, outraged representatives of Deakin, Lawther and Williamson deplored the timorous discretion of the Parliamentary Party. But they too had to yield. Somehow the commonsense of the Party had prevailed against all odds and in the incongruous accent of 'one-speech O'Brien'.[1]

One aspect of the controversy showed no sign of subsiding. Persistently the newspapers described the debate in terms of 'Bevan versus Attlee, Bevan's grab for power'. 'If I disappeared tomorrow,' said Bevan in a weekend speech in Tredegar during the crisis, 'the same issues would still be there. It is time this obscene preoccupation with individual lives and careers gave way to a much more

---

[1] 'Among those whom I saw vote for extreme measures,' recorded Crossman in his diary, 'were Tony Crosland, Douglas Jay, Patrick Gordon Walker, Woodrow Wyatt, Roy Jenkins, as well as the whole Parliamentary Committee.' He continued: 'We certainly felt it was a triumph and celebrated it in the Smoking Room with Tom O'Brien. The fact is that, without Bevin to advise him, Attlee has completely misjudged the attitude of the unions, which realistically assess the strength of Bevanism in the rank-and-file. Attlee's support was almost exclusively middle-class in this meeting.'

dispassionate consideration of the facts.' And then he pressed his defamers more specifically: 'I challenge any journal or any responsible person to find a single statement or writing of mine to justify the statement that I want to be leader of the Labour Party.' No response came. But what was the truth? Could it really be that his personal ambitions were as modest as those words might imply? The final answer remained locked in his own heart, and of course it would be absurd if the possibility of his succession to the leadership had never crossed his mind, as it did the minds of enemies and friends, particularly in those years of the early 1950s when evidently a successor to Attlee would soon have to be chosen. He had every right and title to consider himself a candidate for the office. But what was false was the suggestion that all his moves, manœuvres, protests, resignations, attacks, were calculated, however ineptly, to further his personal advancement to the leadership: the Deakin-Dalton caricature. In all his intimate discussions with his friends, without any lapses whatever, he never indulged in the crime he alleged against the newspapers – the personalization of public events – in the sense of picturing himself as the hero. He remained faithful to the habit of his youth and upbringing; ambition was seen in class, not individual terms. He could be querulous, petulant and savage about his opponents just as he could be gay and bantering about them too. But about his political self he was utterly unegotistical: he was much too interested in the objective scene and all its tumultuous manifestations to become obsessed with his own personality. To think in terms of personal ambition was an offence against his most treasured theories. The claim may sound extraordinary, especially in view of the elaborate, ceaseless exertion of his enemies to prove that he was composed of ambition and almost nothing else. But his closest friends knew the truth. And just at the moment when the lies about him mounted to a new crescendo, he revealed himself, for those with eyes to see, in a new light.

For several years he had been trying to write a book about his political philosophy, and the departure from office gave him the opportunity to complete the task. It was no pot brought to the boil to capitalize a sudden fame. Several chapters – on his early life and experience in the pre-war Parliaments – had been written before he became a Minister in 1945.[1] Some were more hastily dictated soon after his resignation. Then he bundled together the old and new and took both away with him to Yugoslavia in the autumn of 1951, and, with Jennie's assistance, welded them into the volume *In Place of Fear* published by Heinemann in April 1952. It was an instantaneous publishing success. Huge publicity followed the press conference on the day of publication. Thousands of copies were sold. Translations were made into French, Italian, German and Spanish. Reviews and comment appeared in a mountainous stack of newspapers and periodicals. And yet from the bulk of this comment – there were notable exceptions such as John Strachey's review in the *Daily Herald* – the book would not be judged a political and literary success. No one would ever be fool enough to claim that Bevan wrote as well as he spoke; for in the second art he was pre-eminent, and in the first he was often awkward and inhibited and almost always his writing lacked two of the principal features of his speaking, the effervescent, all-pervasive humour and the driving momentum of argument. But these were not the reasons for the annoyance or the derision or the lack of generous apprecia-

[1] Not all the best passages in the pre-1945 draft were included in the final volume. For example, this one anticipating some of the controversies of the 1970s and illustrating Bevan's attitude to London and the provinces:

'The metropolitan mind is a suggestible, superficial, fickle mind. It is quick, facile, shallow and profoundly irresponsible. It mistakes slogans for principles and quackery for philosophy. It changes its sentiments with the slickness of the vaudeville stage which is its favourite form of entertainment. It has the warmth of impulse without sustained generosity. Every idea wins its attention but none its fealty. Its interest in public affairs is so tepid that only a small percentage trouble to vote at the national and municipal polls. On its fringes is suburbia which is emptied and filled each morning and night with the ebb and flow of the city, having no deep waters of its own. It is an aesthetic monstrosity, an ethical crime, an economic nightmare, and a physical treadmill.

'Social science has not yet decided what is the optimum limit for a town. For myself I should judge that the sight of the civic centre should be almost a daily experience of its citizens. Only in a community of such a size can the individual hope to identify himself with the corporate life of his fellows and take an intelligent interest in public affairs. There is no conflict between a wide cosmopolitanism and a rich local life. The one gives meaning and particularity to the other. It is not an accident that totalitarianism and centralism go together.'

tion which *In Place of Fear* elicited from so many of the official critics. It was more that so many of them felt puzzled, even cheated. This was not the man they expected to meet at all. The book is in fact packed with striking aphorisms and original reflections; it offers rather the notes for a political treatise than the treatise itself which Bevan wistfully hoped one day to have the leisure to write. But this was not the complaint of most of the complaining critics. Why did he not stick to the slogans and the rantings which the newspapers attributed to him? To imagine he could speak any other language was pretentious sophistry.

He was expected to write of the class war, nationalization, the Tories, capital levies, America, Communism and the cold war and all the typical clichés of political debate and the book covers all such topics, but almost always in unexpected contexts and often with tentative, unexpected conclusions. But he also wrote, and sometimes with even greater eagerness, of the need for more 'serenity in man's relations with society', of his passion to escape from 'the all-pervading restlessness', the impersonal character of the Great Society, and how such themes would come to dominate our future politics. Being an incorrigible individualist himself, he strove to reconcile his individualism and his collectivism. 'Not even the apparently enlightened principles of the "greatest good for the greatest number" can excuse indifference to individual suffering. There is no test for progress other than its impact on the individual.' Hazardous propositions indeed for a busy and ambitious Socialist politician to tackle just at the moment when he was supposed to be making off with the sceptre.

And from this discussion with himself about the nature of his political faith, at the moment when he was fighting with all his might on what some dismissed as marginal differences and fictitious issues, emerged his classic description of democratic Socialism, the most apt and memorable ever written. For the men of action sometimes say things better than the men of words, like Lincoln at Gettysburg. The idea was beyond the reach of the *In Place of Fear* critics:

The philosophy of democratic Socialism is essentially cool in temper. It sees society in its context with nature and is conscious of the limitations imposed by physical conditions. It sees the individual in his context with society and is therefore compassionate and tolerant. Because it knows that all political action must be a choice between a number of possible alternatives it eschews all absolute prescriptions and final decisions. Consequently it is not able to offer the thrill of the complete abandonment of private judgment, which is the allure of modern Soviet Communism and of Fascism, its running mate. Nor can it escape the burden of social choice so attractively suggested by those who believe in *laissez-faire* principles and in the automatism of the price system. It accepts the obligation to choose among different kinds of social action and in so doing to bear the pains of rejecting what is not practicable or less desirable.

Democratic Socialism is a child of modern society and so of relativist philosophy. It seeks the truth in any given situation, knowing all the time that if this be pushed too far it falls into error. It struggles against the evils that flow from private property, yet realizes that all forms of private property are not necessarily evil. Its chief enemy is vacillation, for it must achieve passion in action in the pursuit of qualified judgments. It must know how to enjoy the struggle, whilst recognizing that progress is not the elimination of struggle but rather a change in its terms.[1]

It was not easy to read those sentences and still to picture the boorish adventurer ready to trample his way to the top at any price.

One other strand running through *In Place of Fear* must be emphasized, since it merged strongly with the current debate in the Party. At the Bevanite meetings, as throughout earlier discussions on the National Executive, Bevan himself was always the foremost to insist that the demand for extended public ownership must retain its place at the head of any Socialist programme. Indeed he was shocked that anyone could think otherwise. A Socialism which did not envisage a transformation in property-owning and property-relationships would be one drained of all virility. And that was not some old-fashioned view sustained only by extremists. It was the accepted doctrine of the Party, and those who threatened it were

[1] *In Place of Fear*, p. 169.

the true disturbers of Party unity.[1] This had been Bevan's view about Morrison's 'consolidation' campaign a few years before, and in *In Place of Fear* he reiterated it. Effective social power must pass from one order of society to another. A continuous drive in that direction, conspicuous proof that the change was happening, was essential for the achievement of all other Socialist objectives and the removal of other social tensions – in the fields of taxation and wages policy. No Socialist should have any doubt about that governing proposition. But there were doubts which came to play an increasing part in the Bevanite argument of 1952, spread by what Bevan called the Fresh Thinkers. 'I use capitals,' he wrote in an article in *Tribune* on 13 June, 'to distinguish Fresh Thinking from the perfectly proper desire to keep our minds alert and adaptable. Perhaps a better term would be Socialist Revisionists. These are people who want to substitute novel remedies for the struggle for power in the State . . . Now that we are once again engaged in policy-making, it is essential that we should keep clear before us that one of the central principles of Socialism is the substitution of public for private ownership. There is no way round this.'

However, he was never dogmatic about the manner in which the substitution should take place. He never boggled at the term 'a mixed economy' and had thought that aspect of the controversy had been disposed of in 1949.[2] Many operations could and should be left in private hands: what was necessary was that the public form of ownership should become dominant. This view was aimed partly at the 'all-or-nothing' enthusiasts; but partly too it was aimed at the new brand of Morrisonianism: 'Let us have no detailed "shopping list" of industries to be nationalized, no exact pledges; that merely stirs unnecessary enmity. Let us rather say that we will take over all those industries which fail the nation. That could be much more far-reaching and revolutionary.' The plea was always fraudulent and both Bevan and Morrison knew it. And it was Bevan who consistently urged that the Party's attitude to public ownership should be comprehensively defined. He called

[1] Much Morrisonian and Gaitskellite nonsense on this subject has been disposed of for ever by Samuel H. Beer in his *Modern British Politics* (Faber, 1965).
[2] See Chapter 7, pp. 259–66.

the boards of the nationalized industries, because of their lack of public accountability, 'a constitutional outrage' and he told the Socialist Revisionists, in so far as their doubts about nationalization arose from administrative difficulties, that the remedy must be sought in 'probably a greater ruthlessness in the selection of our administrative agents and a wider application of the principle of industrial democracy'.[1]

So far from the truth was it, then, that a further provocation to the rapidly intensifying Party crisis of 1952 was the rigid reassertion of old and dying dogmas about nationalization by Bevan and the Bevanites. Bevan was among the first to accept the idea of 'a mixed economy'. He was among the most eager to accept manifold departures from the form of the old-style public corporation. But he was not prepared to abandon or debase the main argument for public ownership, and he became suspicious as he discovered that this was the course contemplated, but rarely stated openly. Here indeed was an act of aggression against the cohesion of the Party, against its whole purpose no less than its tradition.

It was likely that most members of the Party agreed with him. At the September meeting of the T.U.C. the rare event occurred – rare in those far-off days – of a resolution being carried against the wishes of the General Council. It called upon the Council to formulate proposals for 'the extension of social ownership to other industries and services, particularly those now subject to monopoly control', and for 'the democratization of the nationalized industries and services', so as to make possible 'the ultimate realization of full industrial democracy'.

On questions of policy – or, more accurately, general political attitudes – the Party in the country was certainly moving in Bevan's direction, but within the Parliamentary Party the possibilities of change, the very contours of debate, seemed much more confined. M.P.s had their own dominating preoccupations. At the Party meeting when the Standing Orders were formally reimposed, Charles Pannell, speaking for the most determined of the Right wing, gave one of the first indications that their real quarry was something which so far the Standing Orders did not touch at all – the existence of a special group within the Party, 'organized,

[1] *Tribune* 13 June 1952.

secret, with their own whips on', as Pannell alleged. In fact the
group was considerably less organized than outsiders imagined and
several insiders desired. What exact role the group should perform
and what relationship it should seek with the rest of the Party was a
perpetual subject of discussion within its own ranks. In the main,
Ian Mikardo and Dick Crossman were the protagonists favouring
a stronger, more tightly-knit group, while Bevan himself was more
sensitively aware of the soreness this might provoke within the rest
of the Party, and this disagreement impinged on another, the perpetual complaint that the group in general and Bevan in particular
was much too slow in embarking on the thorough task of devising
a complete new policy for the Left. These discussions continued all
through that year while a few of the newspapers gave the impression that Bevan, a mixture, say, of Cassius and Joseph Chamberlain, was engaged with his fellow conspirators in a relentless plot
against the leaders. Selections from Crossman's diary for the period
give a better guide to reality:

5 December 1951: The fact is that Bevanism and the Bevanites
seem much more important, well-organized and Machiavellian
to the rest of the Labour Party, and indeed to the U.S.A., than
than they do to us who are in it, who know that we are not
organized, that Aneurin can never be persuaded to have any consistent and coherent strategy, and that we have not even got the
beginnings of a coherent constructive policy.
17 December: Nye instinctively feels that detailed discussion
about recruitment of civil servants, organization of statistical
departments etc. is somehow not politics, which is concerned
with achieving power, with a very big and vague P. So far from
being a great strategist and organizer of cabals, Nye is an individualist, who, however, is an extraordinarily pleasant member of
a group. But the last thing he does is to lead it. He dominates its
discussions simply because he is fertile in ideas. But leadership
and organization are things he instinctively shrinks from.
28 January: Nye made a final appeal that we should not separate
ourselves off from the Party in any way. By this time I think some
people there felt that Nye didn't want to be a Bevanite at all . . .
He launched the most ferocious attack on the Right-wingers of

the Party who, he said, would certainly fail to make a proper Socialist policy. It was the group's duty to fight the Right wing . . . In the course of an hour he had come back full circle from an attack on sectarianism to an appeal for group action. Partly, no doubt, this was a tactical instinct. He had deflated the group too much early in the meeting and he felt need to revive it. But shrewd people like Barbara [Castle] were really very curious what exactly was up. Ian Mikardo was very angry indeed.

17 March: At our *New Statesman* lunch we had Aneurin Bevan; not much came of it, except that Aneurin, across the table, rebuked me lightly for stating that I would not mind if the Party stayed out of power for a few months in order to work out an agreed policy on the next stage of Socialism. 'It isn't a new policy we want,' said Aneurin, 'we've got one. What we want is the victory of one tendency in the Party over another.' This is typical Bevanism. He really hates policy-making, and thinks that is what you do when you are in power. Before that moment you worry about getting to power, and even that you don't worry about very much except by making speeches which help the tide along.

10 April: On Thursday morning there was a special meeting of the Bevanite group. Nye, who had not been attending group meetings for two or three weeks did what I expected. He indicated that he thought the group should cease to be exclusive, and a long discussion followed on how to retain cohesion and leadership for Bevanism and yet to avoid being a secret cabal inside the Parliamentary Party. Nye has never liked the cliqueiness of a closely-knit group. Moreover he always resents any idea of seriously thinking out policy. He instinctively rejects the *raison d'être* of the group, which is precisely to think out policy.

23 July: Nye never as a Cabinet Minister intrigued with outside groups. Indeed, the trouble was that, whereas Morrison, Shinwell, Dalton were busy organizing cliques, Nye was like a bear in his corner.

Yet, group or no group, as the Bevanites themselves argued, or leadership and no leadership, as the whole Party might argue, 1952 saw the most fretful and foetid spring and summer which most of us could recall. At the union conferences the critical issue was

Bevanism in one guise or another, and the vote often went against the desires of the Party leadership; the shopworkers, the engineers and the railwaymen all passed strong pro-Bevanite resolutions. At another gruesome meeting of the Parliamentary Party the panoply of pre-1945 Standing Orders was restored, after harshly closured debates. On the National Executive, despite the normally solid anti-Bevanite majority, the Bevanites secured what they considered to be a wisely restraining statement on the subject of German rearmament: there, too, military and American pressure favoured reckless courses which could jeopardize political settlements and which it was Labour's duty to resist. In the House of Commons, almost inevitably, the advantage passed into unofficial hands. The Bevanite backbenchers could move much more nimbly than the arthritic ex-Ministers. They had the guidance of the most know-ledgeable expert on parliamentary procedure in the place, Geoffrey Bing, and one after another issues were presented on which they had no front-bench inhibitions. Night after night they led the attack on the Government's health charges – 'a sham fight' by the official Party, muttered Morrison behind the scenes, as well he might.[1] Occasionally, such as when the Americans bombed instal-lations across the Yalu river without consulting Britain, a frontal attack on the Government was only pressed after back-bench insistence. It was particularly galling for the loyalists to feel them-selves led into the battle by the rebels and so often to have to acknowledge their superior generalship. On one happy occasion indeed, after the Bevanites at the Party meeting had persuaded the leadership to cast a vote in qualified opposition to the Govern-ment's plans for ratifying the treaties to permit German rearma-ment, the Right wing of the Party, eager to back the Government on this new issue coming more and more to the fore, found them-selves forced to vote with the majority, hoist with their own Stand-ing Orders petard. Crossman gave a jubilant diary report (1 August 1952) of how the victory had been gained: 'Everyone at the group was very pleased because Nye, at the Party meeting, had made a mellow speech, in which instead of calling Christopher Mayhew a pimp, as he called George Brown last week, he had

---

[1] *An Autobiography* by Herbert Morrison, p. 291.

laughed at him and got the whole of the rest of the Party laughing at him. I said this to Aneurin over a drink, and he replied characteristically: "Anyone can be good-tempered at the Party meeting when he is speaking for the majority. But no one in a minority has ever succeeded in keeping his temper." This is a profound truth, which the Right-wingers are now discovering.'

Bevan could indeed make his own friends tremble as well as the enemy. Once, in that perishing summer in the House of Commons, he destroyed one of his own speeches and inadvertently recruited another enemy for life when he turned on the diminutive Mrs Freda Corbet, the ultra-Right-wing Morrisonian M.P. for Peckham who was muttering some interruption, with the rebuke: 'What are you babbling about, woman?' But he could also be sweetly reasonable and that might fray tempers even more. Concluding a further speech on the arms programme, or the lack of it, on 30 July, he protested that he felt no rancour in proving himself right – 'After all, I can assure my hon. Friends that if they disagree with me I shall not try to get *them* expelled from the Party.' Then he turned, in the same sunny mood, to instruct Churchill on the manner in which he might beneficially reconstruct his Government. 'It is a very great mistake for our economic affairs to be managed by the Chancellor of the Exchequer . . . I am pleading that there shall be established in Great Britain a Minister for economic expansion . . . keeping a vigilant eye upon the future, not only tomorrow, not only to talk about what we are to do with a balance of payments crisis in 1952–1953 but how Great Britain is to face the economic crises of the next twenty-five years or more.' It was, he admitted, his King Charles's head. Everybody nodded, even approved, and did nothing about it.

But one other remark in that speech did stir sudden action. He had referred, as on so many previous occasions, to the precautionary words inserted in Attlee's famous rearmament statement of 29 January 1951. They had now become 'the sheet anchor' of some of those with whom he argued, but 'they were actually inserted in the Prime Minister's speech at my instance'. Next day, Attlee made a personal statement. Bevan, he said, 'no doubt through inadvertence', had made statements purporting to describe what had happened in the Labour Cabinet. It was a breach of a well-established rule which existed for the obvious reason of preserving confidence between colleagues. To affirm or deny the accuracy of the statement would be to repeat the error, but his silence could not be misconstrued. 'COMMONS REBUKE TO MR BEVAN. CONFIDENCE BROKEN, SAYS MR ATTLEE. SOCIALIST LEADERS IN OPEN CLASH', said the *Daily Telegraph* headlines next morning, and there was no doubt about Attlee's laconic ferocity.

Bevan could make no reply on that afternoon. Personal statements permitted by the Speaker in the Commons are not open to comment, and in any case Bevan had not received the belatedly despatched note informing him of Attlee's intention. He was astounded by the action, particularly because he had made the same illegitimate disclosure, if such it was, on several previous occasions. But the accusation had to be rebutted, and next day that task was well and duly done in what was, reported *The Times*, 'indeed a dignified performance'. Of course, said Bevan, he accepted the principle of collective Cabinet responsibility. 'But collective Cabinet responsibility breaks down just at the point that the collectivity breaks down, and that is when a Minister resigns.' Otherwise a Minister could not explain the reasons for his resignation. All the precedents were there to prove how other resigning Ministers had exercised the right just as he had done on precisely this point in his own resignation speech; '. . . and I hope I shall be exempted from any blemish which my right hon. Friend's statement yesterday may inadvertently have cast upon my reputation'. The whole incident might bear the title 'The inadvertence of Mr Attlee'. In the next few days a correspondence in *The Times* proved that other resigning Ministers had been a good deal more garrulous than Bevan in describing the prelude to their action, without being rebuked from any quarter.

But Attlee's rare move was a signal to those who had long been waiting for, or preparing for, an assault on Bevan and all his works and confederates. To whom must be accorded the credit of unleashing it, is a matter of some dispute. Some say that the first hand raised was that of George Brown, M.P. for Belper, who had been known to wield hatchets before – against Stafford Cripps in 1939 and Attlee himself in 1947. Others accord the palm to A. J. Cummings of the *News Cronicle* who, in an article printed with formidable deliberation on 5 August, accused Bevan of conducting 'a party within a party' with all the paraphernalia of whips, officers, secretaries.[1] Some of the intended sinister effect was diminished by the fact that side by side with the article appeared a Vicky cartoon, showing Churchill addressing his Cabinet, all of them with hairstyles like Bevan's, on the subject of cuts in the arms programme, with the caption underneath: 'There's no split in our Party. We're all Bevanites now.' Still Cummings did assert that the Bevan conspiracy went far beyond a straightforward attempt to win over official policy by democratic persuasion. Similar charges were made by George Brown in the *Daily Herald* and by R. R. Stokes, the Labour M.P. for Ipswich. 'One of the great difficulties of discussing inside the Labour Party such matters as German rearmament,' said Patrick Gordon Walker, M.P., 'is that we cannot consider the merits properly. We have to take account that there is a deliberately organized party within the Parliamentary Party.' Bevan, said Aidan Crawley, 'has come dangerously near to breaking his Privy Councillor's oath. It is the most deplorable thing he has done, and is bringing Party relations to a pretty pass.' A host of lesser and greater figures sustained the fury throughout the ensuing weeks in preparation for what certainly promised to be one of the most explosive Party Conferences in Labour's history. The Bevanites were accused of every form of machination, but Bevan himself had been away with John Mackie in Scotland where he gleefully caught his first salmon at the first attempt and then knocked his knee and was momentarily lame. 'Typically,' lamented Crossman, 'there has been no meeting of the Bevanite group or any attempt to devise strategy or tactics for Conference. Once again we are going to it, an army of innocents.' But that was not what the outside world saw. The final touch was supplied, on the eve of the Conference itself, by Hugh Cudlipp, of the *Sunday Pictorial* – quite unknown to Crossman – in a full front page article. 'END THE BEVAN MYTH' was the screaming headline and every twist of the typographer's black art was used to present the maniacal voice of a man whose 'arrogance, vanity and spleen' threatened the whole future

---

[1] His detailed charges were rebutted at the time but no withdrawal was forthcoming.

of the Labour movement. It was the nearest the Britain of the
1950s saw to a McCarthyite essay in character assassination.[1]

Morecambe was rowdy, convulsive, vulgar, splenetic; threatening
at moments to collapse into an irretrievable brawl. But it also had a
fierce human ebullience about it; much essential business was intelligently transacted; and the decisions reached could have pointed
the way to a new and fruitful compromise within the Party. Every
Labour Conference has a personality of its own – so unlike the
machine-fashioned products of the Tories; the ugly, raucous features of Morecambe were evident for all the world to see (and all
the newspapers to seize upon), but in the strident passion of those
who believed that they had a right to use their votes to change the
course of politics there was a true democratic vitality which it
should have been the business of leadership to cherish. Yet it
seemed that leaders and led alike were being swept along by events,
just as the blustering, driving wind of Morecambe itself herded
delegates off the promenade into the Conference hall with stream-
ing noses and screeching perorations. On the Monday afternoon,
when at most Conferences the gladiators are still content to polish
their lances or daggers, Deakin and Lawther found themselves in
the midst of a rough house. A resolution had been moved by a constituency party delegate from Salford, urging Conference support
for 'industrial action', if need be, to defeat the Tory Government.
Deakin had already made a major speech an hour earlier on a resolution about transport, but he trundled to the rostrum again to kill
this idea with a single hammer blow. 'I call the tune because I hold

---

[1] Crossman had been writing for the *Pictorial* for several months and
this particular article led to a conversation between Crossman and
Morrison, recorded in the diary:

'*29 September:* Herbert Morrison, whom I met on Sunday morning,
took me for a long walk during which we were photographed together. (He
said: "Will you lose votes?" and I said "Will you?", but the photograph
didn't appear.) Morrison said (referring to the article), "You are clever
enough to persuade the Editor to do that." I replied, "I am decent enough
not to spread the rumour that you did it." In fact the article, that is the
Sunday Pictorial article, enormously assisted the Bevanites, and the only
person it really damaged was me. Since a great number of Left-wing
delegates were, I think, shocked at the idea that I was writing for such a
paper.'

the money bags': that is not exactly what he said, or what the official report registers, but that is what it sounded like. A huge blast of booing and baying rent the air, and thereafter it was never far beneath the surface. When Lawther was interrupted by a heckler in the same debate, he made the retort immortally linked with his name: 'Shut your gob!' And when a card vote was taken, on the extreme Salford resolution, it mustered, 1,728,000 votes against the platform's 3,986,000. Later that afternoon Bevan was scheduled to answer for the Executive on an insignificant resolution on unemployment. 'I know I must be careful lest I make a controversial speech'; thus he walked like Agag into the argument, and managed by the end to flay the *Daily Mirror* for a renewed outburst that morning against the Party's nationalization commitments; to elaborate the case for Socialist planning; to explain 'how American industry is being kept in full spate by the biggest piece of public enterprise she has ever undertaken – a big arms programme'. At the end, he evoked not so much a standing as a shouting ovation.

Next morning the heavens fell. When the votes for the Executive were announced, Wilson and Crossman were on, and Morrison and Dalton were off. That was the sensation, greeted with round after round of cheering. And the figures were by any reckoning amazing. Bevan at the top, Castle, Driberg and Mikardo had all increased their votes substantially on the previous year. Only one non-Bevanite, Jim Griffiths, was left on the Constituency Section of the Executive. Hugh Gaitskell, standing for the first time, received little more than half the votes cast for Crossman and Mikardo. 'Half vague emotion, half Mikardo's cunning organization,' recorded Dalton.[1] Mikardo was for years afterwards regarded by the Right as the greatest magician since Mephistopheles. But a part of the truth was simpler. Little doubt was possible that the bulk of active workers in the constituency parties were Bevanites. 'It seems to me that this Conference is rapidly going mad,' said George Brown at the rostrum that afternoon. The defeat made the acolytes of the Labour Establishment smart, and one after another they came to the platform to counter-attack Bevan in particular – Denis Healey, Christopher Mayhew, Roy Jenkins. They might have been

---

[1] Hugh Dalton, unpublished diaries.

wiser to have followed the example of Herbert Morrison who re-captured the sympathy of the whole place with a valiant display of sportsmanship. And so might Arthur Deakin, scheduled that year by a sublime irony to carry the traditional 'fraternal greetings' from the trade unions to the Labour Party. He soon brushed aside the normal courtesies and turned to consider what he claimed most people were thinking, 'that there is a great struggle for the leader-ship going on'. Very well, organization would be countered by organization, and then battering on against the cries of those whom he later described as 'howling dervishes' he insisted: 'My sugges-tion is that such misunderstanding can only be disposed of by a complete abandonment on the part of this dissident element within our midst of the tactics they have so recently been employing. Let them get rid of their whips, dismiss their business managers, and conform to the party constitution. Let them cease the vicious attacks they have launched upon those with whom they disagree, abandon their vituperation, and the carping criticism which appears in *Tribune*.' At which juncture, the official report inscribes the word: 'Interruptions'. They were Vesuvian, and delegates stepped out for lunch as if over cascades of molten lava.

Inevitably these were the incidents which monopolized the front pages. But much else happened at Morecambe. One resolution reasserted the principle of a National Health Service free to the patient, which the T.U.C. Congress had also reasserted a month before. Another, also reaffirming what Congress had decided, instructed the Executive to prepare a list of further industries to be transferred to public ownership. A third, moved by John Mendel-son, representing the Hallam constituency party of Sheffield and endorsed by the Executive, bore a distinctly Bevanite flavour, and on 'the tortured question of rearmament' as Bevan called it, some-thing like a truce was achieved. A resolution from the Shop, Distributive and Allied Workers' Union calling for 'a re-examination and reduction of rearmament' was defeated – by 3,644,000 votes to 2,228,000, but no flat-footed approval of the £4,700 million pro-gramme was asked for or secured. In policy terms, Morecambe did mark a shift Leftwards, but it was by no means a rout from the Right-wing vantage point. The outcome could have been a new equipoise, a fresh balance between Left and Right. That is what

Bevan believed had occurred and what he strove to make the more feasible in his speech at the *Tribune* rally in the Winter Gardens on the Wednesday evening.

> Sometimes, [he said] I say what I mean so awkwardly that people get offended. But I say to my friends, Arthur Deakin and Will Lawther: it is all right, boys ('boy' was the surest proof of Bevanite endearment), we are the same kind of chaps. I say sincerely I would rather be attacked in the blunt language with which I am familiar than be surrounded by smoothies. We have always been a rough party. Some delegates imagine we have been witnessing a pretty rough house this week. Not a bit. I recall that Stafford Cripps once organized a rebel conference and I was one of the speakers. The rebellion was about more seats for the constituency parties. [*Loud laughter*]. When I heard Arthur Deakin being indignant at the Labour Party Conference now, it is nothing to what Ernest Bevin said about us then. We have to keep our sense of proportion about these things. Many of the harsh things that have been said this week will have been forgotten next week. In public life for every kiss you get two slaps, and the decisions of democratic votes are not declarations of individual worth. Those who are defeated are not defeated because they are not respected. We respect them all. We respect those who this week after many years of service receive what may appear to be a rebuff. That rebuff is not for them as individuals, nor is the acclaim for the successful acclaim for them as individuals. It is because large numbers of people can only select individuals on the basis of their representative capacity.

And then he spoke of the agreed resolutions, the genuine prospect of a reunited Party. That was Aneurin Bevan in an hour of victory; no sign of the arrogance and venom delineated by the *Sunday Pictorial* three days before.

The effective reply to Bevan's verdict on Morecambe was given four days later in a speech at Stalybridge delivered by Hugh Gaitskell. One part of it claimed with considerable exaggeration that the leadership had gained the day at the Conference on all the principal policy issues. But included too were the following sensational sentences: 'A most disturbing feature of the Conference was the number of resolutions and speeches which were Communist-inspired, based not even on the *Tribune* so much as the *Daily Worker* . . . I was told by some observers that about one-sixth of the constituency party delegates appear to be Communist or Communist-inspired. This figure may well be too high. But if it should be one-tenth, or even one-twentieth, it is a most shocking state of affairs to which the National Executive should give immediate attention.' And then, after a selective recital of some of the resolutions passed, 'which must be accepted by all loyal members of the Party', came the final thrust: 'It is time to end the attempt at mob rule by a group of frustrated journalists and restore the authority and leadership of the solid, sound, sensible majority of the movement.'[1]

It was a strange riposte to the situation from a performer normally so cool and meticulous: he had, after all, invited the suffrage of the Conference and been defeated in the contest. Moreover, neither the *Daily Mirror* nor Senator McCarthy himself had ever attempted a vaguer, more unprovable, and therefore more despicable smear. But the results were far-reaching. Stalybridge scotched the prospect of any post-Morecambe accommodation. It spread the sense of boiling outrage against the leadership throughout the Party. And it was the making of Hugh Gaitskell. Nothing at Morecambe had angered Arthur Deakin more than the manner in which, as he believed, Attlee had refused to lead the loyalists against the rebels. After Stalybridge, he knew he had found his man. Almost it might have been whispered (but no one did) Arthur Deakin was starting a rebellion of his own.

Back at Westminster it could not be doubted that the main and immediate objective of the Party leadership was the destruction of the Bevanite group, and the process of achieving it was quickly set in hand. Demands for the 'disbandment of privately organized factions' came from Morgan Phillips, the Party Secretary. Tom Williamson[2] wrote in his *Municipal Workers' Journal* of how 'a

---

[1] *The Times* 6 October 1952.

[2] William Lawther was away in the United States where in Cincinnati he described Bevan as 'a man with his feet in Moscow and his eyes on No. 10 Downing Street'.

disgruntled group of ambitious individuals have been organizing within the Party and have succeeded in organizing a recalcitrant faction . . . its ultimate objective is the usurpation of power'. Gaitskell in the *Spectator* varied the claim with a dark suggestion that 'there must be a new arrangement about the Left-wing press'. No one at the time outside the closest Gaitskellite circle could guess what this meant, but Dalton recorded:[1] '*Tribune*, H.G. thinks should be taken over. This is very wild.' The *Manchester Guardian*, which at that time could never refer to Bevan without sneering, called on the Labour leaders to crush the Bevanite cabal.[2] And Attlee himself eventually bowed: no party, he said, could tolerate another party within its ranks.

Bevan himself was bitterly affronted by these developments; not merely did he regard them as grossly unfair to himself and his

[1] Hugh Dalton, unpublished diaries.

[2] No newspaper, not even the *Daily Mirror*, conducted a more sustained attack on Bevan and Bevanism at this time than the *Manchester Guardian*, and, as David Ayerst explains in the official history of the paper, *Guardian* (Collins, 1971, p. 607), the assault on 'Mr Bevan and the hate-gospellers of his entourage' was inspired directly by A. P. Wadsworth the editor. Mr Ayerst suggests, somewhat defensively, that Wadsworth's 'emotional' rejection of Bevan was traceable to the 'vermin' speech, in which case it is a pity he had not appreciated better the report of his own reporter on that occasion (see p. 237). Wadsworth, it is said, conducted 'a personal feud' against Bevan, and on occasion this seemed to be backed by his brilliant parliamentary sketch writer, Harry Boardman. The antagonism broke all bounds in November 1952 when Boardman in a passing and gratuitous reference wrote: 'Besides Mr Bevan is only technically a member of the House of Commons. They have probably noted in Tredegar that he takes no part in the business of the House. He has been seen in the Chamber twice since . . . the House reassembled, and then only for a few fleeting moments . . .' On reading that, Bevan rang the *Guardian* office in London, spoke to the chief sub-editor, and demanded an immediate withdrawal in the most prominent position, at the same time accusing Boardman of a possible breach of privilege, and undoubted malice. In fact during the period in question Bevan had voted in nine out of fifteen divisions and any charge against him of poor attendance in the House was an absurdity. Wadsworth had to write what, for him, was an apology. Possibly a main reason for his disgruntlement was that at the elections of 1951 and 1955 he had recommended *Guardian* readers to vote Conservative, citing Bevan as one of his reasons. Significantly, in recounting this affair, Mr Ayerst reports that, with the coming of 1956, 'the paper could be itself again'.

friends; he felt they were deeply hostile to the proper functioning of Parliament. Never had it been true that the Bevanites had had whips and party managers and the paraphernalia of a party within a party; but every denial had been brushed aside. Group meetings were another matter; they were a normal feature of parliamentary activity. If other members of the Parliamentary Labour Party found the idea objectionable, they were invited to attend the meetings and discover for themselves how sinister these activities might be. One of the activities, enquirers were warned, was the organization of *Tribune* Brains Trusts up and down the country; to forbid them would be to interfere with a form of political agitation with a long and honourable tradition, such as was conducted by the Left Book Club of the 1930s or Blatchford's *Clarion* decades earlier. And was the idea to kill *Tribune*? Bevan at that time was the chief target of abuse from the whole British press, Right, Centre and supposedly Left – the *Guardian*, the *Mirror* and the *Herald*, no less than Tory newspapers. He might be excused his irritation when they protested because *Tribune* came to his defence and when Gaitskell demanded 'a rearrangement' to remove this anomaly. But – as Bevan wrote in *Tribune* on 17 October – 'the task of maintaining the unity of Labour falls primarily on the Left'. For the Right with its majority in the Parliamentary Party, so soon after Morecambe to defy the expressed will of the Left with its overwhelming majority among the constituency parties,[1] was a reckless act of disunity. It could have incited counter-defiance and the Party would have been shattered to fragments. As it was, in all the discussions with his closest associates after Morecambe, Bevan urged courses designed

---

[1] It was Bevan's view also at this time that several of the union leaders were quite unrepresentative of their members. His good friend, Wilfrid Paling, M.P. for Dearne Valley, wrote asking him to come and speak in Yorkshire and in the course of his reply he wrote: 'It really is saddening to think of the way in which the rank-and-file of the miners are now being misrepresented by their national leaders. Indeed, the gulf that separates some of the top trade union bureaucrats from the rank-and-file of the trade union movement is frightening. They don't appear to realize that it contains within it all the possibilities which have so far developed on the Continent. Unless some more intimate relationship can be established between rank-and-file opinion and official policy, nothing will prevent a wave of cynicism from engulfing the whole trade union movement.'

13

to ease relations with the Party as a whole and it was primarily on his initiative – against an opposition led by Ian Mikardo who feared the disintegration of the whole group – that the *Tribune* article made it clear that the group meetings would be open to all members of the Party. On Tuesday 21 October – Trafalgar Day – the first open meeting was held and the four first respectable new members proved to be Lord Strabolgi, Emrys Hughes, Norman Smith and John McKay.

But by now no appeal to precedent or what the Left considered the logic of the voting at Morecambe could count against the resolve of the leadership to crush Bevanism by formal bell, book and candle. At the Party meeting when Attlee moved the resolution calling for the immediate abandonment of all group organizations within the Party other than those officially recognized[1], several members did seem to favour the search for some rebuke less brusque. Bevan himself urged that everyone's face could be saved if the resolution, having been sufficiently aired, were now referred to the new Shadow Cabinet to be elected in the next few days. But Morrison, winding up the debate, would have none of that, and Attlee in the chair used his impartial power with flagrant and effective bias; when someone formally sought to move that the vote should be postponed, he leapt in with a mumbled closure. Effectively he had kept the middle-of-the-roaders out of the debate. Strachey and Strauss had been deprived of the chance of repeating their mediatory tactics of the previous spring, and the Attlee resolution, a vote of confidence, was carried by 188 votes to 51. The Bevanites condemned the reasoning which led to the vote but bowed to the conclusion. It was the second major contribution to Party unity which, in his belief, Bevan had made since Morecambe. And then came a third, in the Parliamentary Party elections a few days later at the beginning of the new session.

First, he stood against Morrison in the election for the Deputy Leadership, receiving 82 votes against Morrison's 194, but this contest was really no more than a gesture. The much more awk-

[1] Introduced at a meeting of the West African Students, just at this time as 'the one and only Aneurin Bevan', he said: 'I heaved a sigh of relief when you said that, because if there had been more of me, I would be declared an illegal association.'

ward question was whether he should stand for the Shadow Cabinet
and risk losing the parliamentary freedom which he had used so
fully during the previous twelve months. One of the criticisms of
him and his immediate associates, Wilson and Freeman, was that
they had refused to stand for the Shadow Cabinet in the previous
autumn. 'I can't do it right either way,' he told a meeting in
Tredegar, 'if I stand, I'm accused of ambition, if I don't, I'm
accused of irresponsibility.' In November 1952, when he and
Wilson and a few other Bevanites did stand, he came twelfth in the
ballot. Then, much to the Party's amazement, an alteration of the
rules was proposed in the middle of the election. The second six
out of the successful twelve would ballot again against any other
comers. Bevan almost withdrew; however, after much persuasion
he persisted and again secured the last place among the twelve
successful candidates. A list had been circulated of the twelve candidates which the Right had wished to see elected. Someone
showed it to Dalton who blurted out the fact to Crossman who in
turn recorded somewhat enviously in his diary how the Right had
disbanded the Bevanites but could still organize themselves. In any
case, with or without contrivance, the result was one the Right
would have chosen – one reluctant Bevanite among eleven opponents. Had he broken into the innermost citadel of Party power or
was he conveniently incarcerated by his own hand? Speculation in
the lobbies at the time veered towards the second alternative, and
Bevan by no means excluded it. It was hard, a bare five weeks after
the Morecambe triumph, to hear the prison gates clanging behind
him.

10

THE BEVANITES: II

1953

The most powerful nation in the world was also the most frightened.
—LEON TROTSKY[1]

A TERM IN Aneurin Bevan's political vocabulary which he liked to apply to some of the more subtle of his opponents was *a decoy*: according to the definition, a bird (or other animal) trained to lure others (usually of its own species) into a trap. He had used it about Churchill in the great 'devaluation' debate of 1949, and the irony was that, with his arrival in the Shadow Cabinet, it might become applicable to himself. He was aware of the peril, and often reflected in a manner which would have astonished critics, both to the Right and the Left, upon the dilemmas of a Left-wing rebel isolated in a Right-wing Cabinet or Shadow Cabinet. He was honour-bound to offer the best advice he could to his colleagues. Occasionally he might help to sway decisions in the direction he desired; but he always knew that, more probably, the agreed purpose would be injured by half-hearted execution or that he would assist in parrying legitimate criticism of the leadership. So why had he ever undertaken the invidious role? The answer mixed with the perennial dilemma about how difficult it was to whip the shambling, lethargic Labour Party into Socialist action and yet how impossible to devise a rival body for the purpose. Some of his closest friends had opposed his standing for the Shadow Cabinet; with him as leader of His Majesty's 'disloyal' Opposition, 1952 had been an exhilarating parliamentary year, and it could be argued that a continuance of these activities was needed to maximize support for Socialist causes in the country. On the

[1] Quoted in *The Prophet Outcast* by Isaac Deutscher (Oxford), p. 18.
388

other hand, a policy of exclusiveness inside Parliament would condemn the Party to the split which Bevan believed would be barren
and fatal, and meanwhile it should be possible instead to sustain
the growing strength of the Left outside Parliament without which
he knew no change inside would ever be accomplished. If any interpretation of his conduct could be sillier than that of the Deakins
who saw him as the ruthless, careless wrecker of Party unity, it was
the picture drawn at the other irascible extreme of the jaded warrior
deceived and satisfied by the trappings of Party leadership. No one
knew better than Bevan himself that he had gained not a laurel but
a yoke, and never did it cut into his shoulders more sharply than in
1953. But he could see no other way.

An indication of the side of his mind which his friends knew well
but which his enemies, and especially those in his own Party, could
not imagine existed, was given in January 1953, on a B.B.C. programme entitled *This I Believe*. 'Life would indeed be easy,' he
said,

if it were always clear what our duty is. Usually there is a conflict
of duties as there is of loyalties. In order to serve one, you often
have to abandon others. I remember a man saying to me in the
last war that he had no use for rebels. Then I asked him how he
would describe a German living in Germany and working for the
defeat of the Nazis. Judging by conventional standards, the man
was a rebel and a traitor. But judging in the wider context of
humanity he was a hero. All you can readily say here is that a man
ought not to betray his first loyalty, and the fact is that few people
do. The problem is one of deciding which is the first loyalty from
a number of competing ones. And the higher the intelligence, the
wider the knowledge, the keener the imagination, then the more
loyalties there will be competing for our allegiance, and of course,
the deeper the spiritual struggle involved in sorting them out . . .
If I am right in saying that what we have to do is decide from
among a number of almost equal claims, then the mood in which
we approach our fellow human beings should be one of tolerance,
for the slightest shift in the balance might have resulted in a different decision. If, furthermore, I am right in saying that the
search for the truth will result in a number of different answers

to the extent that the circumstances are different, then to tolerance must we add imagination so that we can understand why the other truth differs from ours. We should 'learn to sit where they sit'. I am now ready to answer the question. I believe imaginative tolerance to be among the foremost virtues of a civilized mind.

And this was the same Bevan who also inhabited such resorts as Morecambe and the Westminster Grand Committee Room, and knew that battles there had to be fought with a fierce, unrelenting zeal.

Organization was imperative too. Bevan detested the processes whereby it was done, the tedious committee meetings, the reading of papers and the rest, but he never denied the need – except, maybe when Crossmanite insistence on policy-making as the elixir of eternal political life stirred him to outbursts of contra-suggestive invective. Never certainly did he overcome his sense of outrage against Attlee and the rest for their suppression of the Bevanite group. Some other means of operation had to be devised: he was certainly not content that the Deakinites should meet in the St Ermin's Hotel or the Gaitskellites should assemble in their XYZ clubs while he and his friends were denied the right of association. One place they could meet was at the informal editorial conference which *Tribune* held every Monday. Bevan would come every third or fourth week and enliven the gathering with a cheerful tirade directed against his enemies on the Right of the Party or his friends on the Left, but more often with soaring ideas which could have kept a staff ten times as big as *Tribune*'s fully occupied. In the weeks after the banning of the group he was especially scornful of the rumours that the *Tribune* Brains Trusts were also to be banned by the Transport House inquisitors, acting on the instructions of the handful of Deakinite trade union leaders, 'the mandarins', as he called them. So plans were made to intensify these democratic activities. But there was also a need to retain some of the cohesiveness between action outside and inside Parliament which had been one of the main purposes of the group. So over the next few years a much attenuated Bevanite group – six members of the Executive, Bevan himself, Crossman, Driberg, Castle, Mikardo, Wilson, plus the journalists who kept contact with *Tribune* and the *New States-man*, Jennie Lee, John Freeman, J. P. W. Mallalieu and myself – assembled every Tuesday lunch-time, while Parliament was sitting, at Dick Crossman's house at 9 Vincent Square. It was not, as it had never been, 'a party within a party' but it was 'a group within a group' and undoubtedly over the years the Party's action in ban-ning the larger group in Parliament reduced its effectiveness. But this development was not apparent at those early Vincent Square meetings. As normally when Bevan was present, he would lift the debate from the rut of intrigue and gossip. One paramount con-cern, in that January of 1953, was the consequences likely to follow from the arrival of the Republican administration in the United States and the alarming pronouncements of John Foster Dulles; the other centred round the policy document on public ownership which the Party's National Executive had been charged to draw up at Morecambe. After considerable discussions with his fellow N.E.C. members, assisted by Thomas (now Lord) Balogh who had been the principal economic adviser of the Bevanite group, Bevan himself wrote an article for *Reynolds News* setting out the range of industries which he believed should be included in the new Party programme – they included all rented land, the chemical industry, the aircraft industry and sections of engineering – and the case was powerfully backed by a more elaborate article in the same sense from Harold Wilson, not always the most ruthlessly dedicated of nationalizers.[1]

But all these good resolutions for the New Year were suddenly

[1] Another sign of Bevan's private mind, that January, was given to Claude Bourdet, the French Socialist who at the Morecambe Conference had enlisted Bevan's support for a new journal he was starting in Paris. After consultations with the Party Secretary, Morgan Phillips, and in view of the difficulties he might cause with the official French Socialist Party through direct political association with Bourdet, he felt he must withdraw his previous acceptance; '. . . the situation for me at the moment is very delicate. We are, as you know, attempting to get through a new policy statement by the Labour Party in time for our Conference in the autumn. There are a number of very difficult and dangerous shallow waters through which we shall have to steer our little barque before it gets to harbour and, to continue the metaphor, I really don't want at this moment any sharp winds to blow either from the shore or the sea.'

disturbed, and in a manner no one had calculated. Based on little more than some minor procedural wrangles, a crop of stories had appeared in the Conservative newspapers suggesting that the National Executive of the Labour Party and the General Council of the T.U.C. were at loggerheads over policy. *Tribune* in its issue of 16 January purported to set the record straight. Under the head-line 'LABOUR-T.U.C. SPLIT: THE REAL STORY' it described how the strategy of the Churchill Government was indeed to woo the trade union leaders; how the mellifluent Sir Walter Monckton had been appointed Minister of Labour for the purpose; and how some trade union leaders – Deakin, Williamson, Lawther – had helped to encourage him in the seduction by the lack of enthusiasm they had shown for the decisions of the Morecambe Conference. The tone was tart, but no more. Doubtless it was the conjunction of this story and the one next to it which unloosed the storm. For in the next column appeared the irreverent headline: 'WHY THE "SIR", EVANS?', and underneath *Tribune* took severely to task Mr Lincoln Evans, general secretary of the Iron and Steel Trades Confedera-tion, for having accepted a New Year knighthood on the recom-mendation of the Churchill Government. The issue presented was not the general one of whether trade union leaders should accept honours, but whether Lincoln Evans should accept one just at the moment when the main measure of the Churchill Government in that particular session was to proceed with the denationalization of the steel industry, in defiance of the desires of Lincoln Evans's union members. Both the topics posed by *Tribune* may, at this date, appear proper for debate, but angry argument about them rumbled on for months. First, the General Council of the T.U.C. appealed for protection to the National Executive. Originally indeed, Vincent Tewson, general secretary of the Council, drafted a letter almost amounting to an ultimatum, suggesting that the whole collabora-tion between the T.U.C. and the Labour Party might be in jeopardy if the *Tribune* menace were not properly extirpated by the N.E.C. This had been softened in tone, but the demand for action was peremptory enough. Crossman reported the extraordinary scene in his diary: 'Morgan Phillips suddenly said that a message had just been received from the General Council of the T.U.C., which was meeting six floors below. He then read out the message, which was a protest against a short note in *Tribune* attacking Lincoln Evans for accepting a knighthood from a Government pledged to de-nationalize steel. The General Council requested the National Executive to do something about it. Suddenly the whole atmosphere changed and Nye, with his usual tactical acuteness, launched a tremendous attack on Will Lawther, Arthur Deakin, Tom Williamson and Lincoln Evans. All of them, he said, had attacked him personally and all of them had made speeches and written articles attacking the Morecambe decisions. *Tribune* was only replying to an attack. How could it be singled out for rebuke? There was then a dreary, bad-tempered debate, at the end of which the motion was passed, with only the six Bevanites voting against. At this point Harry Douglas said, "the next logical thing to do is to examine the *Tribune* Brains Trusts and see if they are a party within a party". This seemed to take Jim Griffiths and Attlee by surprise, but they raised no objections, whereupon Edith Summerskill burst out that they had been far too weak for too long in dealing with the danger. Stronger measures were required. Tom Driberg asked her what she meant by stronger measures, and she spat out, "I mean expelling those who are suspected of fellow travelling". This was said with her eyes fixed on Ian, who I think is the most hated of all the Bevanites. My impression is that Harry Douglas and Edith Summerskill were anticipating an action which had been planned for some weeks ahead. The debate made me so angry that I finally said that Edith and Harry were at least logical. First suppress the Left-wing press, then forbid us all to speak, and you will get the sort of monolithic Party which some people want. The motion was carried by 7 to 5, and Nye and I went across to the House to have lunch, with our entrails acid with anger. These meetings do really turn your stomach.'

On this particular occasion the Executive actually resolved to issue what the *Daily Herald* called 'a stinging rebuke' to *Tribune*. Then the *Daily Herald* denounced this latest 'explosion of Bevanite bile' and Sir William Lawther accused the Bevanites of attempting 'to undermine the leadership in the same way as Hitler and the Communists did. There is no difference whatever between them'. Then the National Executive deplored the outbursts of the *Daily Herald* and Lawther. Then Deakin weighed in with a defence of the *Daily Herald* and Lawther with the plain pronouncement: 'If people kick me in the shins, I am going to kick back whenever I can', and Low in the *Manchester Guardian* had a brilliant cartoon depicting Discipline at Attlee's Academy, with Arthur, a *Daily Herald* protecting his backside, appearing before headmaster Attlee: 'Fighting again, Deakin! If this does not stop, I shall have to send a doodle to your parents.' No one could say that the exchanges were especially edifying; but in the result *Tribune* came off best in the sense that the proposal to try to ban the *Tribune* Brains Trusts, which would infallibly have put *Tribune* out of business, was eventually dropped. The idea was condemned by John Strachey as 'utterly intolerable; what country is this, anyway – the birthplace of political liberty or some totalitarian state?' All the publicity helped to attract larger audiences, and both the General Council and the National Executive were compelled to watch enviously and impotently while Bevan himself and the miniature organizational machine run from the offices of Ian Mikardo and of *Tribune* attracted bigger crowds than anyone else. However, Bevan always continued to believe that a much more far-ranging offensive against the Bevanites had been prepared by Deakin and Co. and that Harry Douglas had ineptly and prematurely diverted the assault into the abortive inquiry about the *Tribune* Brains Trusts. The renewed attack might be expected at any time.

In the spring, he himself was able to make an escape from these infantile asperities and elephantine inquisitions, through a three-week trip to India, combined with brief excursions to Burma and Pakistan. He went originally on the invitation of the Indian President and the Indian Minister of Health, but the most important result of the trip was the consolidation of his old friendship with Jawaharlal Nehru. They had known each other since pre-1939 days when the campaign for Indian independence had been organized from the dingy India League offices at 165 Strand, across the road from *Tribune*'s office in Cliffords Inn, and when Bevan along with the other friends of Indian freedom had climbed to the top of those stairs to consult with the League's Secretary, Krishna Menon, who was in charge of Nehru's visits to England. Another particular friend who helped to fortify the intimacy was M. O. Mathai, Nehru's special assistant. But between Nehru and Bevan no inter-

mediaries or interpreters were necessary. By their different individual routes they mostly reached the same conclusions about the
world conflicts of the 1950s.

Especially at that moment Bevan appreciated the role India was
playing at the United Nations and elsewhere in seeking a peace in
Korea, and when he addressed a meeting of Indian Members of
Parliament in Delhi, his compliments in this sense were naturally
considered extremely eloquent. What in fact he did was to speak in
the very terms which could provoke against him in Britain outraged charges of anti-Americanism, but the Indian audience understood. 'Mr Bevan's very Bevanish speeches,' reported the
Manchester Guardian correspondent in Bombay, 'have on the whole
made an excellent impression.' At one point he was alleged to have
gone much further than the Indian Government would approve;
had he or had he not advocated a third bloc of nations holding the
balance of power between the two giants, America and Russia,
'hag-ridden by fear'? But in fact there was no divergence. Nehru
spoke of the need to secure as large as possible an area of countries
aligned to neither bloc, and that was Bevan's aim too, and he held
it to be desirable not only for the immediate diplomatic ends it
could serve. If the infant, independent nations were to fail, he
wrote on his return, it would mean 'an arid polarization between
the industrial power of the United States on the one hand and the
massed millions of the coloured people on the other. What we have
to do is to preserve the utmost variety of choice before mankind.
For after all, civilization is little more than the opportunity freely
to choose between a number of proffered alternatives . . . It is not
political democracy that is on trial in South East Asia. It is democracy as an instrument of revolutionary change.' All around him he
had seen how achingly desperate was the need for that change, and
how patronizingly misplaced could be lectures from Washington
or London on the infallible virtues of political democracy. 'The
great industries that we are so proud of, the great steelworks that
the Indians and Chinese have not got and which are responsible for
our high standard of life, were all built out of the wages which our
grandfathers went without.' Or again: 'We did not succeed in
revolutionizing our country by consent. Democracy came to us
after the Industrial Revolution, not before it. Our consent was not

asked, and we often did our best to withhold it, as the Luddites bear witness.' So Bevan drew different conclusions from most others from his visit to 'a part of the world where hunger thrusts even the fear of war from man's mind'. He could see Asian poverty through the eyes of his Marxist youth; and the explanation fitted the facts so much better than any comfortable liberal bromides.

He went sight-seeing in India, too, when he could; for instance to the Taj Mahal, reluctantly at first: 'so much had been claimed that I felt it could not conceivably live up to it all. I was wrong, quite wrong. There may be more beautiful buildings in the world. If so, I have not seen them. In the silver light of full moon it is a note of lovely music caught and held in exquisite masonry.' But much more deliberately he wanted to see the Himalayas, a desire which gradually changed into an irresistible resolve and which he traced to his Welsh longing for the mountains beyond Llangyndr in Wales. So he schemed to be taken from the show-piece state-farm at Terai northwards to Ranikhet, 7,500 feet up, where he was told he would see one of the best views of the Himalayan peaks. The news of his coming had gone ahead, and when his party reached Ranikhet they were welcomed by a large gathering of notables, and festooned with garlands – a charming custom, he said, but one which could have its drawbacks in the early morning when the flowers were wet and when he was required to retain his dignity and composure before a vast concourse of people, while the cameras clicked and the water trickled down his neck. 'But the sight of the Himalayas from the verandah of a mountain lodge above Ranikhet was all I could wish for and more. I was almost seduced from my allegiance to my favourite view of the Black Mountains and the Brecon Beacons above Tredegar. All the peaks of the Himalayas unfolded their chaste loveliness before us with the exception of Mount Everest, which was too far to the East. The mountains worked their old magic with me. They smoothed the fretfulness from my spirit like wrinkles from a worn garment. I went to my most refreshing sleep in India.'

For the biographer of Aneurin Bevan, India also displayed other treasures. For the reasons he explains, he hardly ever wrote letters to Jennie. But the few make one ache for more. They were scrawled

in the handwriting of his ungainly right hand which the Sirhowy
school tyrants of his boyhood had forced him to use.[1]

> Rashtrapeti Bhavan
> New Delhi
> *12 February 1953*

My darling,
   You will, I know, not expect a long and descriptive letter from
me. It would be as difficult for you to read as it would be tedious
for me to write.
   The air journey was a real trial and I found it quite impossible
to sleep. But now I am quite refreshed. The arm is much better.
The only addition I need is your presence. Now I come to
realize it this is the first holiday I have spent away from you and
I am not liking that part of it at all.
   This is just the place you would adore. The colours are fantastic and the weather divine.
   For the moment I am staying at Government House, and in
the grandest possible manner. The distance from my bed to my
private bathroom is almost a morning's walk. I am waited on by
a charming little man all dressed in scarlet and gold.
   But I must not attempt to describe it all here. It must wait
until I see you.
   There is only one thing which is causing me anxiety and this is
that you were not at all well when I left London, and I know you
will have no chance of complete recovery until the spring.
   Do please look after yourself as well as you can. You know I
love you so much, and can think of little else when I am away
from you. So please be a good girl and at least keep ticking over
as well as possible until we can have a holiday together in Porto
Fino.

> Love my darling,
> NI

Then again:

[1] See Volume I, p. 21.

President's House
6 March 1953

Darling,

It looks now as tho' I shall be home round about the 18th or 19th. The actual date I cannot be sure of because of plane arrangements.

I don't want to stay long in Pakistan but must not make it so short as to offend them.

To tell the truth I am now looking forward to being home again. The days are crowded with official engagements of various kinds and after a while they tend to pall. Also it is not so much fun when you are alone.

I am writing this at night before an open window which looks out on the golden Pagoda of Rangoon. It is very warm, at least for the natives, but for me it is grand.

Everybody has treated me with the utmost kindness and consideration. My mind is full of undigested impressions. I shall have to get them sorted out for the *Reynolds News* articles.

Tell Bill Richardson of *Reynolds* that he should aim at the first article for the Sunday after the meeting in Manchester. This will give him time for whatever adverts he may wish. I hope he doesn't splash too much. Lots of people have been to India and Burma so there isn't anything exciting to say.

I am putting this hurriedly into an envelope before the sight of the writing causes me to consign it with all the other unsent letters I have written.

Have just heard the news of Stalin, I am incapable of any reaction about it. He has been dead so long.

I do hope you are well. The Scottish tour sounded a grand tonic.

I am really longing to be home with you and look forward to a country visit with you in the spring.

Love,

NI

He returned to face the Deakins, the Morrisons, the Daltons, and, most remarkably, the consequences of the dead Stalin. While he was away, Dalton had written in his diary: 'I have, over the years, given him [Bevan] the benefit of many doubts. And he has many qualities and moods which attract me. But I'm afraid it is quite clear by now that both his temperament and his lack of judgment quite unfit him to lead the Party. He can't get on terms with his leading colleagues, and he won't be able to destroy enough of them to come out on top. And at Westminster his followers are mostly nobodies,[1] so that Bevanism is a one-man band. While he was away his followers were fairly quiet and quite uninfluential.'[2]

Dalton carries, and no doubt will continue to carry, much weight with the historians, since he was the only leading figure of the time who kept a regular diary, and diary extracts count powerfully against fading memories. But this extract and the immediate aftermath may assist in placing the proper qualifications on Dalton's verdicts. For the next internal Party debate in which Bevan found himself involved was of world-wide significance but receives no mention whatever by Dalton in his book or his diaries.

When he wrote to Jennie that Stalin had been dead for so long, Bevan was presumably referring to the Stalin who along with the other 'heroes' of the Soviet revolution or the valiant defenders of Moscow and Stalingrad had once possessed a romantic appeal for Socialists the world over. There was another sense in which the departure of one man did constitute a stupendous historic event. Right up to the time just before his death the Soviet world had been caught in the horrific, phantasmagoric climax of 'the doctors' plot' and the Slansky trials, scenes which could only be compared with the last days and nights at the court of Ivan the Terrible. But then, just after the tyrant's death, almost melodramatically, for the next few weeks and months, came one apparent sign after another that the Stalinite winter was making way for a long, refreshing, truly Russian thaw. It was natural that Bevan should greet the great moment expectantly and excitedly, for he had constantly prophesied that the Soviet dictatorship would eventually have to bow to the demands of some form of political participation from the new class of managers and skilled artisans. The chance of a

---

[1] Of Dalton's 'nobodies', one became Prime Minister, two Cabinet Ministers, one Ambassador to Washington, etc.

[2] *High Tide and After* by Hugh Dalton, p. 350.

détente, East and West, did appear, and it should surely be seized
with both hands, both for its own sake and for the further liberation
which it could bring across the Communist half of the planet. This
was the spirit in which Bevan would have welcomed the news anyhow, but his visit to India spurred his enthusiasm. It is not too
much to say that after all the dour cold war news since the late
forties, the British Left inside Parliament, and certainly outside,
was swept by a new exhilaration, and when first President Eisenhower and then his more articulate Secretary of State, John
Foster Dulles, seemed to watch developments with a surly scepticism, it was time for other voices to be heard. Dulles in particular
spoke a political language which grated on Bevan's ears. He attributed all signs of change in Soviet policies to American toughness;
so that was a recipe for more toughness. What hope could there be
of peace, if wisdom was always to be construed as weakness? This
was the theme which *Tribune* trumpeted week by week, with Bevan's
full backing; but amazingly it appeared that several of Labour's
leaders were dubious about showing too eager and uncritical a
response to the fresh Soviet attitudes. Some of them professed a
greater interest in the plans for the formation of a European
Defence Community which were then almost reaching fruition and
which a détente might set back for years. Perhaps that was the
Soviet idea; Stalin's death was just the last of his devilish tricks!
So, much to Bevan's fury and amid a rising resentment inside the
Parliamentary Party, arguments went unresolved in the Shadow
Cabinet, and the suggestion that Labour should take the initiative
by proposing high-level talks to test the new possibilities in Mos-
cow was subjected to endless dawdling – until Churchill stepped in
and took the same initiative himself.

It was the biggest haul in the art of stealing the Whigs' clothes
while they were bathing since Disraeli first invented the manœuvre.
For Churchill eagerly acknowledged the significance of the events
in the Soviet Union, brushed aside the idea implicit in the
Eisenhower-Dulles response that only a comprehensive settlement
must be sought ('It would be a mistake to assume that nothing can
be settled with Russia unless and until everything is settled'),
recognized that steps must be taken to allay Russia's fears for her
own security, and proposed 'a conference on the highest level

between the leading powers without delay'. The Churchillian proposition, delivered in his grandest manner, resounded round the
world. It was roughly the same proposition which had caused so
much haggling in the Shadow Cabinet. Once Churchill approved,
Labour approved too. It was natural that Bevan should watch the
sequel with a fascinated frustration, and remarkable too how much
he guessed – as is shown in his weekly articles – what was proceeding in the Tory Cabinet. He saw that Churchill had made the speech
without the prior consent of his Cabinet. He saw that Churchill
had used the fact that Anthony Eden was away ill at the time to
circumvent the Foreign Office. He saw that other members of the
Cabinet did not share Churchill's appreciation of the significance
of the moment in world history, even after he had spoken. And he
saw, what others could see too, that the Americans were stubbornly
blocking the whole idea, despite their acceptance of a proposal for
preliminary consultations between the leaders of the Western
powers at Bermuda. Then Churchill fell ill, and the Bermuda
meeting was postponed. What Bevan did not know was that there
was nothing 'diplomatic' about the severe stroke Churchill had
suffered. Rather he continued to protest against fresh delays.
'Apparently any full-scale effort to meet the Russian initiative,' he
wrote in *Reynolds* in June 'must await the recovery of Churchill. So
debauched is British public opinion by the excessive personalization of politics that this situation has been accepted as quite normal
and natural. The awful potentialities of a third world war are
dwarfed and scaled down to a charade of posturing personalities.
It seems to be assumed that the wheel of fate will pause in its
mighty revolution until an old gentleman of 79 years of age is able
to return to the stage.' Then he poured scorn on the inadequacy of
the members of Churchill's administration left to fill the gap.
There was talk of Mr Oliver Lyttelton – 'the lustre of his reputation is so dimmed that it is beginning to look like a smudge'. Mr
Butler was put up to show that British foreign policy is back on the
tramlines once more; 'Mr Churchill's joyous ramble is over.' Lord
Salisbury had been selected to speak for Britain in consultations in
Washington – 'great movements of opinion should be represented
by representative personalities. That is the proper relation between
the individual and the event. In that relationship the Marquess of

Salisbury is miscast.' And, much to Bevan's fury, the inadequate
Salisbury was permitted to depart on his mission without the
Labour Party even forcing a debate in the Commons to influence
his instructions. All through that summer and autumn – the hero-
ism and the hazards of the suppressed rising in East Germany on
17 June only added to the urgency – Bevan bewailed the 'Tory
betrayal of Churchill's peace initiative', and the curiosity is, as we
now know, that Churchill was doing the same.[1] It was the last great
exertion of his political life, and he made it amid scarcely concealed
derision from his sycophantic friends in Whitehall and Washington
but to the applause of his bitterest critic. Together the Foreign
Office and the State Department 'bitched things up', in Churchill's
phrase.[2] Bevan could not have put the point more pithily.

However, Bevan was not only concerned to secure an exploratory
top-level meeting; he wanted also to devise a new approach towards a general European settlement. He saw it was necessary to
relate the change in Russia to the immediate item on the Western
agenda, crudely described as 'German rearmament' and taking the
form at that time of the ratification of treaties establishing a European Defence Community. When Lord Salisbury attended the

[1] How little other members of Churchill's Government understood the
meaning of the death of Stalin is shown by Eden who wrote: 'I did not
share the optimism of those who saw in this event an easement of the
world's problems.' (*Full Circle* by Anthony Eden, Cassell 1960), p. 49.

Macmillan expressed his scepticism in his diary note for 6 March: 'I
cannot but remember the fable of the Sun and the Wind. The fake Sun of
the new geniality may (unless we are very careful) do more to hinder and
even stop rearmament than the icy blasts of the past few years.' (*Tides of
Fortune* by Harold Macmillan, p. 500.) And then later on 14 June: 'It
looks as if Europe was breaking up under Malenkov's sunshine. Stalin's
icy blasts kept it together.' (p. 513.)

[2] The phrase appears on p. 433 of Lord Moran's *Churchill* (Constable,
1966). Often it is necessary to accept Moran's report on political events
only with caution. But he has page after page on Churchill's fury about the
hold-up in his plans to meet the Russians. A year later, in a debate in the
House of Commons, Churchill intervened in a speech by Bevan to tell the
story of how his plans had been interfered with by his stroke. (See p. 460.)
But he unwittingly confirmed the fact that the Americans had blocked his
initiative while tacitly exonerating – most charitably but quite falsely – the
members of his Cabinet. So persistent are his diatribes and asides against
them in Moran's account that disbelief is here impossible.

conversations in Washington designed to concert the Western response to events in Russia, it became evident that neither the French nor indeed the Germans, for their different reasons, would be likely to ratify before a fresh attempt to have a conference with the Russians. A communiqué was issued on behalf of the British, French and American Governments, proposing a meeting of Foreign Secretaries with the Russians 'to discuss directly the first steps which should lead to a satisfactory solution of the German problem, namely the organization of free elections and the establishment of a free all-German Government'. No Government in Moscow would be likely to agree to meet on those terms alone; it would be tantamount to yielding in advance the main point at issue. And not only the Russians could see that 'the German problem' had other aspects. All the peoples of Europe were deeply involved and sharply committed on the subject, including the Labour Party and its leaders.

In view of the new Western orthodoxy on policy towards Germany, it is necessary to emphasize that, as recently as the spring of 1950, the British Government had been firmly and flatly opposed to German rearmament in any form whatever; both Attlee and Bevin at that time had rebuked Churchill when he had mooted the distant possibility in a Commons debate. When Bevin departed for America in the summer of 1950 for consultations about the war in Korea, the idea was still 'unthinkable', but several people had been thinking of it, notably the American military advisers in the Pentagon who reached the conclusion that without a German army Europe would be indefensible against the Russians. Henceforth the pressure was on, what Dalton called the 'bulldozing' operation.[1] The Pentagon persuaded President Truman and his Secretary of State, Dean Acheson. They in turn persuaded Attlee and Bevin to accept 'the principle' of a German contribution, but acceptance in practice was hedged around with many conditions about the need for arrangements which would forbid the revival of German militarism or about exploring afresh the possibilities of agreement with the Russians. One means of satisfying the first of these conditions was the proposal that the Germans should form part of an European Army, the so-called European Defence Community or

[1] See p. 305.

E.D.C. The idea had originated with the French, and Morrison had given support on behalf of the Labour Government on his visit to Washington in September 1951. But the project was inherently awkward and it offered opportunities for endless delay which those fundamentally opposed to 'the German contribution' in France, Britain and Germany itself could happily exploit. The E.D.C. debate had continued since 1951, but American patience, particularly when the new Republican regime took over in Washington, was becoming exhausted.

It was in this context that Bevan wrote for *Tribune* in July a major series of articles entitled 'In Place of the Cold War', in which he elaborated, in the light of the latest startling developments in the Soviet Union, the views he had expressed in *In Place of Fear*. A remarkable series of comments, prophecies, inspired guesses and constructive suggestions showed how little he derived his opinions from the ready-made conclusions of others and how much he relied on his own combined instinct and experience. Examining 'the compulsions at work in Soviet society', he foretold: 'in the short run or in the long run Russia will get her Reformation. It is for us to see that she is enabled to get it without fear of attack from the outside and to give her every reason to believe that her search for more urbane ways of life are watched with eager sympathy by hundreds of millions of people outside her frontiers.' Reasserting his long-standing opinion that in establishing her position so far westwards in Europe, the Soviet Union had injured her own security interests, he insisted, 'in coming so far to the West – particularly into Czechoslovakia – she overran her sociological frontiers. She could occupy but she had not been able to digest.' It should follow that the West must find the ways to encourage the loosening of the Soviet grip on the satellite states. If that process appeared to weaken the Soviet military position, it would be resisted. But other ways could be sought, and a further incitement to seek them was to be found in the divergent interests or stages of development in other Communist states – 'the life pulse of her potential allies does not beat in harmony with her own. In China the Soviet Union had gained an ally powerful enough to challenge her ascendancy in the Communist world and for that and other reasons China was not likely to increase Russia's military aggressiveness.' In the early

nineteen-fifties no other leading politician dared utter such out-
landish heresies or pleaded that they should actually form the basis
of policy. And sometimes, on much smaller issues, Bevan's premonitions could be uncanny. Discussing the likely developments in
the Communist Party leadership – long before Nikita Khrushchev
had emerged – Bevan guessed: 'The characteristic Communist
leader would be more bucolic in temperament and more amenable
to local values and pressures.'

However, the main purport of the series of articles was to discover a solution of the German problem, and they disprove any
accusation that in his 'anti-German rearmament' campaign Bevan
was content with crude slogans or actuated by demagogic anti-
German sentiment. He dodged none of the dilemmas and indeed
set them out with elaborate care. A solution, he wrote, must have
nine ingredients. '(1) The rearmament of Western Germany must
be avoided, for a divided Germany would try to re-unite itself
in war. (2) Germany must be enabled to re-unite under free
institutions and Russia must be brought to agree with this.
(3) Russia could not be expected to agree if a united Germany
would be free to add her strength to that of the West. (4) German arms must therefore be kept to a level which would not
enable her to be mistress of the West. (5) We could not acquiesce
in a Germany exempted from the competitive burden which
our arms impose on us. (6) Germany could not be permanently
neutralized, for this would not be consistent with national sovereignty. (7) General and progressive disarmament must therefore
be embarked upon. (8) This must be done by a method that
gets round the vexed question of mutual inspection. (9) Disarmament must be carried out in such a way that it avoids industrial
depression and mass unemployment.' After that, no one could
say that he had posed the challenge in deceptively easy terms: who
but some political Houdini could break loose from such bonds?
However, Bevan's answer was theoretically clear and practically
constructive. He elaborated and applied afresh the World Mutual
Aid Scheme he had adumbrated in *In Place of Fear*, showing how
reductions in the armaments sustained by the great powers should
go step by step with increases in their contributions to a world pool
for development programmes, with German participation in this

second operation. Perhaps the whole scheme sounds visionary and
grandiose. But even while lifting his head to the stars, Bevan could
also search for the next step; that was typical of his manner of
thinking, illustrated on this occasion by the proposal that, long
before the period set for carrying out the major operation, Russia
and Allied occupying forces in Germany should be withdrawn to
zones to be agreed. 'The further apart they are from each other, the
better. The nearer they are to each other, the more the number of
points of friction and the greater the danger of "incidents".' That
was the first published hint of a proposal for a plan for 'disengagement' in Europe, later to be associated in varying terms with the
names of Anthony Eden, Denis Healey, Hugh Gaitskell and
M. Adam Rapacki, Foreign Minister of Poland.

One other strand which should be noted ran through those articles on the cold war and all the frequent references to foreign affairs
which figured in Bevan's speeches in the country throughout that
year – his belief that 'Great Britain' could and should influence the
conduct of the greater powers; that a new independence in British
policy could influence the course of history. The biggest and most
hopeful event of 1953 was the armistice in the Korean war, and in
the estimation of Bevan and most other observers, the mediatory
role of India had made a considerable contribution to that achievement. Bevan constantly contrasted the brash, insensitive, restless
diplomacy of John Foster Dulles with that of Jawaharlal Nehru,
and undoubtedly he would have liked to see a British government
ranging itself more with the independent voices which rejected
'the polarization' of the world into two blocs, the very development
which Dulles encouraged.

He made a move of his own to help concert the actions of the
non-aligned nations. Following a second visit which he and Jennie
made to Yugoslavia that autumn, and further meetings with Tito,
he wrote in 'a personal, private and confidential' letter to Mathai at
the Prime Minister's House in Delhi:

We have a most cordial personal relationship with him [Tito]
and very intimate friendship with some of his chief ministers,
especially Milovan Djilas. I have reason to believe that President
Tito would be favourably inclined to an invitation to visit India

and I would like you to have a word with Nehru about it. Tito is a very considerable person. Indeed, I am convinced that if he were President of a bigger and more important country, he would be a world figure. There are very definite similarities between the situation in Yugoslavia and India. I mean economically, especially in respect of agriculture. The Yugoslavs are carrying out a most daring political experiment, and I am certain that Tito would be excited to learn at first hand what you are doing in India, especially in connection with village life . . . If my recommendations are of any weight, then I would urge Nehru to consider it sympathetically . . .

In training for the Party conference, the Labour movement conducted its normal summer and autumn manœuvres, but there were additions to the course. Some observers remarked upon Bevan's comparative quietness, but Bevanite undertones were never inaudible for long. Formally, controversy was expected to centre on the National Executive's policy document *Challenge to Britain* which was supposed to elucidate the instructions, particularly those on public ownership, given by the Party Conference at Morecambe. The outcome was a compromise. *Challenge to Britain* did contain proposals for the public ownership of the chemical industry, a radical outline of a plan for reshaping the engineering industry, the pledge to renationalize steel and road haulage, the promise to remove all charges on the Health Service, and other commendable items. It omitted several other major items for which the Bevanites had specifically argued on the Executive committees – in particular the nationalization of rented land, a National Investment Board, a capital gains tax, a clear statement on those hardy annuals, the future of the insurance companies and equal pay. But even the moderate programme which had won Executive approval was too daring for Arthur Deakin. At his own conference of the Transport and General Workers he attacked the public ownership proposals of the engineering unions. The incident had a significance somewhat different from that attributed to it by the Tory newspapers. Deakin and Co. had succeeded in blocking on the T.U.C. General Council the instructions about a new public ownership programme which they had been given at the 1952 Congress. But it was evident that there were growing forces in the trade union movement, no less than the constituency parties, who would not bow to his will.

Arthur Deakin was in fact at that moment tiptoeing towards the most notable of his behind-the-scenes manœuvres, and every fresh step rocked the whole stage and amphitheatre of the political world. Morecambe was burnt on his memory; not only those outrageous elections to the National Executive, but also the spectacle of Attlee doodling while he, Deakin, gave the necessary leadership. He and his friends had always resolved on revenge, and the idea they hit on was to get Herbert Morrison elected – *anointed* might be the better word – to the National Executive as Treasurer, an office for which the whole conference, and not just the constituencies, voted: in other words, the trade union vote was decisive. Deakin, Lawther and Williamson could guarantee two million of those votes for a start. The only trouble was that the office had been held for the past umpteen years by Arthur Greenwood. Aged and ailing he might be, but he was also venerated, almost loved, and when the first hint of the Deakin-Lawther-Williamson compact reached him, he had enough fighting spirit left to protest that he was not going to be 'bumrushed by that bugger Morrison'. Arthur had spent his life stepping backwards and forwards, according to what he considered to be the interests of the Party, but this time he saw a cabal at work. He refused to budge. Deakin became more determined than ever. Morrison dithered. And at the very last moment, caught in the predicament of having to move forward to stab Greenwood or to step back onto a Deakin dagger, he offered a way out through a compromise proposal whereby the Deputy Leader of the Party should ex-officio become a member of the National Executive. Deakin, it is said, never forgave Morrison for 'running away'; at the test he had shown himself another Attlee. 'I knew the little twister would wriggle out of it,' said a libellous Will Lawther to a receptive Crossman; 'if the political monkeys want to behave in that way, let 'em.' 'Morrison is finished,' confirmed Harry Douglas. 'When trade union allies choose an ally to go into battle, they don't expect him to pull out at five to twelve. We'll never trust him again.'[1] And they never did.

In the result, Margate was a restrained, inconclusive conference.

[1] Crossman's diaries.

Over the previous months, the Left had resolved not to open a new front against the Right, and, with the Morrison withdrawal, the Right were not pursuing their campaign of extermination against the Left. It was almost as if, having seen the chasm opened at their feet at Morecambe, no one from any section of the Party wished to tread near the edge. The six Bevanites were confirmed in their places on the Executive, each gaining more votes than in the previous year, Ian Mikardo, in the seventh place, having 637,000 against the runner-up Gaitskell's 533,000. On the other hand, the compromise *Challenge to Britain* was approved, with only minor amendments. The main Bevanite proposal, strongly approved by Bevan himself, for the public ownership of rented agricultural land was roundly turned down. Bevan was scheduled to speak for the Executive only once on the Thursday afternoon, on the subject of the National Health Service, including one resolution confirming the Party's determination to abolish all charges. 'I wish to say as little about this as possible. Let us put it behind us. We are all united now that these charges must go . . .'[1] Some might call that a magnanimous conclusion to the famous controversy, but truly at Margate all the combatants were watching one another too warily to afford time for courtesies. At the *Tribune* meeting the night before, the astringency had been more evident. Bryn Roberts, general secretary of the National Union of Public Employees and Bevan's old sparring partner from Rhymney, the neighbouring valley to Tredegar, gave a memorable account of how a handful of trade union leaders kept obedient colleagues like Tom O'Brien on the General Council of the T.U.C., and others – like himself – off. It was a deadly indictment, but delivered in un-Celtic, sepulchral tones. Bevan had to struggle to restore a semblance of good cheer.

Perhaps a verdict on Margate may be supplied in the private comments made soon after to three friends.

[1] He also said in protection of his Health Service: 'A great deal of evidence is now coming in from different parts of the country that patients who are well-to-do are able to buy their way to a hospital bed, frequently ahead of patients who are more seriously sick but have not got the means. It was never intended that such a situation should develop in the Health Service and any hospital management authority is violating the principles of the Service as well as offending against decent instincts if he keeps pay-beds idle when there are waiting lists at the hospitals.'

One was contained in the letter Jennie sent to her very good friend and long-standing admirer, Sir Charles Trevelyan, who had written, mystified, from Wallington. She wrote: 'There are more gains on the Left than at first appear. If we have a vigorous Labour Government it could do a great deal. The other side is that the trade union bureaucrats are becoming more bullying than ever, building up first Morrison, then Gaitskell as their political hench-men. But they are so obvious now that, at last, the reaction is beginning inside the trade union movement.'

The second comment was made to Alistair Forbes, a farmer friend of the other farmer friend, John Mackie, who had become in those years one of his and Jennie's closest companions. John Mackie, himself one of the best and most successful farmers in the country, had supplied much of the expert knowledge backing the case for land nationalization, and it was to John Mackie that Bevan naturally turned when he began to think of translating into reality his old dream of a country home. Anyhow, he wrote to Alistair on 15 October, thanking him for two smoked salmon. 'Margate was indeed a flop. I am still most unhappy about the situation inside the Labour Party . . . John will probably have told you that I have not yet become a farmer. The outlook for farming does not look so pretty. It would be just like me to plunge into farming when it was about to take a header.'

The third letter was to the Rev. Mervyn Stockwood, Vicar of St Matthew's, Bristol, an old friend dating back to the time when Jennie had fought the Bristol by-election in 1943. Bevan's fame was spreading far and wide; everyone wanted to meet him, including, wrote Mervyn who mentioned the name with some diffidence, Geoffrey Fisher. 'Of course,' replied Bevan, 'I should be delighted to meet the Archbishop of Canterbury. There is no reason why I should not bring about conversions in the highest places.'

Back at Westminster the same uncertain, contrary breezes of Margate seemed to be still blowing. Bevan stood against Morrison for the Deputy-Leadership, and received 76 votes against Mor-rison's 181, compared with 82 to 194 in the year before. 'This time I voted gloomily for Morrison,' wrote Dalton, 'because Bevan had been so impossible a colleague in the Shadow Cabinet, and so rude, so often, to Gaitskell and other friends of mine.' In the Shadow

Cabinet election, Bevan moved up three places and Wilson was
runner-up to number twelve, only one vote behind. No one, on this
occasion, attempted to alter the rules in the middle of the contest,
but the peace was short-lived. 'What goes on?' asked one of
J. P. W. Mallalieu's constituents in Huddersfield: 'how comes it
that the constituency parties at Conference vote virtually the
straight Bevanite ticket, while the constituency party representatives
in Parliament put Bevan three places from the bottom and exclude
all his associates? Or how was it that 136 Labour M.P.s with 12
votes each, could not give Bevan one? How was it that the Parliamentary Party was so unrepresentative?' It looks, replied Mallalieu
innocently in his 13 November article in *Tribune*, as if the majority
of Labour M.P.s are more to the Right than their management
committees; as if there are real differences of policy between one
and the other. But his constituent would not accept so placid an
explanation. 'It looks,' he replied, 'as though some of those chaps
say one thing in public in the country and another thing behind
closed doors in the Party meeting. Would it not be better if voting
lists were published after the Party meetings as they are published
after divisions in the House of Commons? After all,' he said, 'M.P.s
are representatives. We've a right to know how they do represent
us.' And at that the tempest broke round Mallalieu's unbowed
head. He had impugned the honour of his fellow M.P.s, he had
outraged the oldest of Party conventions, he had exposed the holy
of holies, the Party meeting, where hitherto Labour Members had
always been able to cluster for safety and comfort; where was
settled the Party line which they could always cling to when the
universe trembled.

The rage among the loyalists knew no bounds and within the
Shadow Cabinet Bevan found himself in his familiar role of defending one of his friends alone against all comers. He was particularly
incensed to discover that Mallalieu was being charged under the
resolution of a year before forbidding personal attacks. He could
produce a dossier of personal attacks on himself which both the
Shadow Cabinet and the Parliamentary Party seemed ready to
endure with unfailing equanimity. Almost every newspaper in the
kingdom attacked Bevan and Bevanism, except *Tribune*: so when
Tribune spoke, that must be suppressed too and a totalitarian

unanimity established. At one stage – according to Dalton – the clash was direct between Bevan and Gaitskell. Bevan 'says he has never been in favour of disciplinary measures and has never invoked them all the time he has been in the Party. He speaks of "the danger of discipline". When Gaitskell quite mildly refers to "the dangers of indiscipline", Bevan fixes him, straight across the table, with a glare of concentrated hatred and says "You're too young in the movement to know what you're talking about".'[1]

Dalton was never an unbiased reporter: his diaries can be exposed as highly selective and prejudiced. But no doubt the scene was fierce, and one reason why the Gaitskells, the Daltons, the Morrisons and the Attlees were so little qualified to comprehend the question of discipline and its relation to liberty was that they had spent so little of their parliamentary lives on the back benches. None of them had ever engaged in a Party revolt: only Dalton had sniffed the possibility from afar, years *after* 1931, when he admitted 'we should have kicked up much more fuss'. Bevan saw Parliament through such different eyes. None of them troubled even to consider how votes at a secret meeting could undermine the principle of public representation. None of them seemed to care about the rights of minorities to argue their case. None of them had shown any interest in recognizing how the rules of debate and voting in the House of Commons itself helped to protect freedom and responsible government, whereas at the Party meeting all such protections could be flagrantly violated. And nothing, no doubt, enraged Bevan more than the complacent face of Gaitskell who had never sat anywhere in Parliament, except for a few weeks, but on a well-upholstered front bench, with well-whipped Party cohorts at his back.

Fortunately, over the Mallalieu incident, the Party meeting came belatedly to its senses. After Attlee had severely suggested that the article offended against the resolution of the previous October forbidding 'personal attacks', Mallalieu refused to withdraw a single syllable in a deadly three-minute speech, concluding with the words: 'Freedom, you know, doesn't mean giving freedom to those you agree with, but to those you disagree with.' A few minutes later Attlee accepted a motion for next business and only 41

[1] *High Tide and After* by Hugh Dalton, p. 395.

intransigents (against 160) were left brandishing their hatchets. But the whole affair, whatever the rights and wrongs, added to the internal Party bitterness which grew sharper month by month.

For the Gaitskellites or the Deakinites, whichever they properly be designated, saw the issue of freedom in a different light. Crossman reported in his diary at this time:

3 December: I took Roy Jenkins home for a drink. I started the conversation by saying that I thought it was very depressing that the freedom of speech which we had in the first five years of Labour government within the Labour Party should be steadily constricted. Five years ago I was able to slosh Bevin about Palestine and he was able to slosh me, and nobody doubted the right of free speech. Roy replied, 'Well, they – I mean we – feel that every speech, every action must now be considered as part of the power fight within the Party. That's why we hate Bevanism. Before it began, one could have free speech. Now one can't afford to.' He repeated several times, 'We on the Right feel that every force of demagogy and every emotion is against us. In the constituency parties, which are now Opposition-minded, the Bevanites have it all their own way. I suppose one must wait for the tide to turn, as it slowly did in the 1930s, away from Opposition-mindedness of 1931, to constructive policies.' I asked him why it was so terribly important to defeat the Bevanites, and he said, 'The electorate is extremely conservative-minded and we can never win except with the kind of attitude represented by the Right-wing leadership.' He also repeatedly emphasized that, just because the Bevanites were so strong, Gaitskell was more and more forced to rely on forces such as Arthur Deakin which made him even further to the Right than he would naturally be.

Just at this same period Ian Mikardo had provoked a fresh scream of protest from the General Council of the T.U.C. by criticizing their attitude towards the Tory Government's action in suppressing the constitution of British Guiana. The respectable General Council and the slightly less respectable Party leadership frowned on two visitors from Georgetown, Dr Cheddi Jagan, the

deposed Prime Minister, and his colleague at that time, Mr Linden
Burnham, the deposed Minister of Education. Angered by the
Labour Party's inhospitable welcome to people struggling to be
free, Bevan promptly organized a deliberately publicized party at
Cliveden Place, where Jagan and Burnham could meet, among
others, Seretse Khama, an earlier victim of Labour's incorrigible
respectability. It is interesting to record that all three leading
guests at the Cliveden Place party for outcasts that night became
Prime Ministers of their countries.

But it must not be supposed that all Bevan's battles were with his
own leaders; he was still the main butt of Tory attack, and one of
the charges they thought would stick was that he had failed as a
housing minister where Macmillan was conspicuously succeeding.
Bevan's reply was threefold. First, he was quite prepared to argue
about the figures and to prove that, taking into account repairs,
more new accommodation was provided in 1948 than in 1953.[1]
Second, he suggested that Macmillan made his own performance
appear satisfactory by imposing restraints in other fields – 'You
hold back and it'll look as if I'm advancing' – and there was in truth
a genuine basis for the accusation. While, amid much trumpeting,
the figures of home building did appear to be moving upwards
speedily, industrial building was falling behind.[2] However, more
formidable and forward-looking was his counter-attack on the
other aspects of Conservative housing policy unveiled at the beginning of the 1953–54 session. Apart altogether from house-building
neither Party had discovered a successful way of dealing with the
rent and repairs of the great mass of house property owned by
private landlords. During his own period at the Ministry Bevan
had attempted no more than stop-gap measures; war-damage work
and new building made any other course impracticable, almost unthinkable. But more and more, the problems would clamour for
attention; indeed, as it proved, in the early 1950s more slums were
created each year by disrepair and dilapidation than were removed
by slum clearance. Bevan argued – in a Commons debate on 4
November 1953 – that the Labour Party would have to devise a new

[1] *Hansard* Vol. 520 Col. 229.
[2] See *The Age of Affluence* 1951–1964 edited by Vernon Bogdanor and
Robert Skidelsky (Macmillan, 1970), p. 63.

policy, and it was on this occasion that the first public expression
was given to the idea – it was a Bevan way of making policy – of
bringing all such rented property into municipal ownership. Only
thus could an escape be found from the unworkable system in
which neither the free market nor public control could operate
effectively. He was convinced that Macmillan's proposed palliative
measure, while offering the landlord a prize but not one sufficiently
enticing to do the job properly, would fail, and he expressed his
view more in contempt than condemnation. 'They started off this
Parliament by giving something to their friends, the brewers. They
went on to give something to the road haulage people, and then to
the steel barons and the bankers. Now they want to give something
to the landlords, and what they have given them is a mouldy old
turnip.'[1]

Amid such pleasantries, he was given sharp proof of how veno-
mous was the hatred he could arouse in some quarters. No judgment upon the controversies in which he was engaged in the early
fifties could be more foolish than that which suggests they were
conducted within the frontiers of parliamentary courtesy. When
some enemies saw the chance to 'get him', they struck. No doubt
one cause of the Tory anger on this particular occasion was that he
touched them on a nerve especially sensitive. Negotiations had
been continuing for months about the withdrawal of the 80,000
British troops who were kept in the Canal zone of Egypt at a cost
of £50 million a year. Even Churchill, who had once remarked that
he had not been appointed Her Majesty's First Minister in order to
preside over the liquidation of the British Empire, was hesitantly
preparing to do exactly that, in Egypt at least. But the approach to
the decision was being made grudgingly and with much spluttering
of rage against the Egyptians in general and their revolutionary
leader, General Neguib, in particular. Frustration was not confined
to the so-called 'Suez rebels' eager to show themselves more loyally
imperialist than Churchill; the more it looked inevitable, the more
the whole Tory Party hated the idea of withdrawal. Some Labour
leaders, notably Shinwell and Morrison, felt the same about it;
they desired, somewhat belatedly, to establish their pro-Israeli
sentiment. And the situation was made the more galling by the

[1] *Hansard* Vol. 520 Col. 241.

knowledge that the certainty of eventual evacuation had been long since foretold with exasperating assurance by the Bevanites, headed on this matter by Crossman.

Anyhow, one morning in December, blaring headlines across the whole front page of the *Daily Express* announced: 'BEVAN ARTICLES SHOCK. NEGUIB NEWSPAPER PRINTS THEM. Once a week column is launched alongside the "dancing major".' Thereafter every technical device was used to add fresh touches to the gruesome revelation. Bevan's picture appeared between that of the writers in neighbouring columns to his own, Vice Premier Gamal Nasser and the Propaganda Minister, Salah Salem, who as the 'dancing major' had for weeks past been portrayed as the ridiculous anti-British figure of the Egyptian regime. That afternoon the matter was raised in the House of Commons, without notice to Bevan, by Martin Lindsay, M.P. for Solihull (who, however, sent a letter asking for forgiveness for this discourtesy, to add to Bevan's now extensive collection of private apologies for public insults). Day after day most of the other newspapers and a few nondescript Lords joined the baiting. What exactly was the nature of Bevan's offence? Had he upset the negotiations at a supremely delicate moment? Had he brought comfort to the Queen's enemies? Had he broken his Privy Councillor's oath of allegiance to the Crown? He had chosen, wrote the *Evening Standard,* 'to denounce Britain's policy in terms which a soapbox orator in Hyde Park might envy, and in a place where few soapbox orators would wish to demean themselves by appearing; among the Britain-hating rabble of Cairo'. In the Commons debate a few days later Mr Lindsay returned to the attack: 'We in this country,' he said, 'are quite accustomed to his bombast and malice. But he is not yet so discredited in countries overseas. Overseas he has the high position of being an ex-member of the British Cabinet and a Privy Councillor. And in giving his sponsorship and encouragement to the revolutionary movement in Egypt, I think the right hon. Gentleman has done a dastardly thing and forfeited the respect of this House and his fellow citizens.' Next morning, Mr Lindsay, who never achieved parliamentary fame before or thereafter, found himself the hero of the *Daily Mirror* no less than the *Daily Express.*

So how heinous was the crime? In fact the article was one of the

syndicated series which Bevan had contracted to write week by
week;[1] it was not written specifically for Cairo; and it had been
published in New Delhi, Madras and Bombay without arousing
any scandal a month before it appeared in General Neguib's newspaper *El Gonmhouria*. Moreover, the article did not refer extensively to Egypt; it was more a philosophical comment on the nature of
imperialism, 'the death of the modern idea of Empire'. When the
debate came Bevan showed how inescapable were the doctrines he
had enumerated. 'The presence of the troops of another nation on
one's soil is a circumstance to be borne only when it is voluntarily
conceded'; but who would deny that? Or: 'a military base is useless
if it is surrounded by a hostile population'; and who would deny
that – except of course the Tory Suez rebels? So had he not been
stating the case of Government and Labour alike for the necessary
withdrawal? It was the fact which hurt, not his words. And if his
words were so offensive, could not one newspaper in Britain have
printed the article in full, as Bevan challenged them to do, before
they branded him as a near-traitor?[2] In fact no one did, until
Tribune appeared a week after the attack had been unleashed.

[1] Incidentally, these syndicated weekly articles provided the first real
regular income he had earned from journalism, and there was certainly
nothing secret or sinister in the way they were arranged. A few months
before he had met Pierre Mendès-France, the French leader who at that
time had a close connection with the Paris *L'Express*, and he had also become friendly with K. S. Karol, one of *L'Express*'s leading contributors.
It was arranged that Bevan should write weekly for *L'Express* who would
also establish connections with several of the other papers all over the
world who had been asking him for regular articles. Every Monday or
Tuesday, he dictated his pieces, in record time, to his Irish secretary,
Peggy Pain, and she typed them as he spoke. Not a single piece of paper
was thrown into the wastepaper basket or a single word altered. Jennie
then took over, not to intervene in the field of ideas where Nye needed no
assistance, but as a combined grammarian and security officer, with a
special eye on long sentences, split infinitives and possible unforeseen
political combustions. Nye had full confidence in what he teasingly
described as Jennie's pedantic Scots background.

[2] Lindsay claimed in the Commons debate that the article contained the
words: 'We shall evacuate Egypt whether we like it or not.' Bevan denied
the charge and the English text of the article upholds him. Lindsay
claimed that his version was based on Egyptian officials' translation of
what had actually appeared. But he never sustained the charge.

14

Today any reader must rub his eyes at the thought that the piece could have caused such a hubbub; it reads more like an anticipation of Macmillan's wind-of-change speech eight years later. Of course, an epoch intervened between the two, and Bevan had spoken much too plainly and too soon for Tory tastes. But these were not grounds for the denial of free speech, even in syndicated articles. No Privy Councillor had exercised that right more persistently and for larger fees than Winston Churchill. To be fair, Churchill did not join too vociferously in this particular anti-Bevan campaign; he left matters in the hands of his frustrated minions. Perhaps the reason was that he knew how soon he would be ordering the retreat from the useless hostile base.

A few days after the uproar in the Commons, Jennie and Nye turned up in Cairo, and for a breathless moment one or two of the newspapers thought there might be a fresh sinister twist to the 'traitor' story. But the trip was quite innocent and had been arranged months before. They stayed with an old friend, the Indian Ambassador, Sarda K. M. Pannikkar, and had the chance of some informal talks at the bedside of General Neguib, then recovering from flu. He struck them as a simple, warm, friendly man and a natural spokesman of the Egyptian passion for national independence: 'I cannot see anything but darkness and confusion for Egypt if Neguib should lose control of the situation,' reported Jennie. Neither was quite so impressed, at the first meeting, with some of the other revolutionary leaders, including Neguib's deputy, General Nasser; but the first glimpse of the new Egypt stirred hopes; they had seen men – and women – who wanted to lead the fight against the ancient evils of poverty and subjection. Then they crossed over to Amman and Jennie was brought up with a jolt at the Royal Palace when, while Aneurin was conducted to the King, she was escorted to the Queen's quarters; but there too, in Transjordan, they felt that change was in the air. He had been told that difficulties might occur in crossing from Transjordan to Israel, but when he arrived at the Mandelbaum Gate in Jerusalem, all went smoothly – except a new brush with the British press. A *Daily Express* reporter wrote in his paper on 5 January that 'under his arm Mr Bevan clutched a bottle of whisky – unopened'. In fact it was a bottle of perfumed rose water which had been given to Jennie

after she had admired the delicacy of the flavouring of the tea they
had drunk with leading Arab priests before crossing to Israel.
Prophetically Bevan had said to the reporters: 'My mind is a
blank, and I hope what you write on it will be interesting.'

Nothing he and Jennie saw in the Arab lands, however, could
compare with the impact of their first experience of Israel; the
meeting with a young friend, Yigal Allon, with whom they were to
become increasingly affectionate and intimate, on his kibbutz in
Upper Galilee; the whole stirring spectacle. 'For the Jew,' wrote
Bevan on his return, 'the immediacy of his remote past is an intimate reality. He is living among places whose names are enshrined
in his racial literature and they make sweet music to his ears. From
Dan to Beersheba, he can now make the journey – Nazareth,
Galilee, Jerusalem, all these and so many more belong to him in a
special sense, for they whisper in his blood, and evoke memories of
a time that was, before he was compelled to seek shelter in reluctant
lands. When therefore the Arab says that the Jew should find a
home anywhere except in Palestine he asks something the Jew cannot concede without mutilating his racial personality beyond en-
durance. It is no answer to say that many centuries have passed
into history since the Jew was at home in Palestine. If he had been
permitted the security of a safe home elsewhere, the answer might
do. But, as we know, it was not so.'

He was almost a Zionist. Certainly some of his very best friends
were Zionists, dating back to the pre-1939 days, when he had been
on intimate terms with Israel and Becky Sieff,[1] or the late 1940s
when Ernest Bevin had driven him near to resignation.[2] Friend-
ships could influence his outlook and it did possibly have an effect
that he had no friend among the Arabs to equal Yigal Allon. But his

[1] Israel Sieff's *Memoirs* (Weidenfeld & Nicolson, 1970), pp. 194–6,
contain one of the truest tributes ever written about Bevan and should be
read in their entirety: 'Wherever our proper realistic level in the modern
world lies,' he wrote, 'Nye would have seen it and could have led us there.
We would have gone there with eyes open, tails up, ready to make it not a
retreat but a triumph. Men must be led by men who above all can speak to
them. These are the prophets whose reason for being is to point the way
ahead, and make man able and willing to tread it.'

[2] See p. 89.

imagination was never checked. The Arab, he wrote at the same time, 'knows how much help Israel gets from the outside. It is essential that he should also be able to call on the resources of the more advanced nations or in his resentment, like a modern blind Samson, he will pull down the pillars of his society about his own ears – and about ours in the process.'

Soon after his return from Israel, news of another friend reached him. Milovan Djilas was dismissed from the Central Committee of the Yugoslav Communist Party, and further reports suggested that action might follow against Vladimir Dedijer who had spoken up for him at the Committee. Bevan's view is best revealed in the highly confidential exchange of letters which took place with President Tito at the time.

London, S.W.1.
1st February 1954

PRIVATE, PERSONAL AND CONFIDENTIAL

My dear President,

You will appreciate, I am sure, that I hesitated a great deal before deciding to write to you. Nevertheless, in my grief and anxiety I can delay no longer. You know that a strong affection exists between Vlado, Milovan and myself. The blow that has befallen them therefore affects me profoundly. Nothing that I saw or was told when I visited Yugoslavia in August prepared me for these calamitous events. On the contrary the relations between you and them and between them and their immediate colleagues were so cordial that I find it hard to believe what the press reports from Yugoslavia now compel me to accept.

Milovan, I gather, has been stripped of all his public offices and has now retired into private life; whilst apparently the same thing has happened to Vlado. I learn from a Paris report that Vlado is seriously ill. I am deeply concerned to know how he is doing and also about Veronica and the family.

In the circumstances I felt I dared not communicate with anyone but you. These terrible events have occurred so quickly that I am quite unable to form a correct judgment as to what is best to do. Some remarks which have fallen from people of high position in your country have suggested that I have had a bad influence on Milovan's political outlook, and that our friendship has had something to do with his recent attitude. This does little credit to Milovan's robust character and mental poise and I dismiss it as merely the rancour of political controversy. I am not going to enter into the merits of the controversy for two reasons. One because I do not wish to appear guilty of interfering with the domestic affairs of another country. Later on, when the personal side of the question has been softened by the passage of time it will be necessary for some of us to attempt an appraisal of what has happened. For you will appreciate that we have defended Yugoslavia against her detractors and are consequently involved in any major change which may have occurred in her policies.

The other reason is that only a confused picture has emerged to the world outside. This was all the more blurred because of the difficulties of translation, and the somewhat recondite employment of Hegelian language.

If I had written to anyone else under these conditions I felt that I might be putting them under suspicion, but you are above such consideration and our personal relations encourage me to hope that you might let me know concerning the personal welfare of Vlado and Milovan. In addition I would like to know whether there is any objection to me writing to them directly. If it would do them any harm then I would certainly not do so. You may rest assured that I would write about nothing but personal matters.

You may write to me in the strictest confidence either directly or through your Embassy here. I am concerned about nothing but the welfare of Vlado, Milovan and their families.

Please do not think I am unconscious of the private grief these events must have caused you.

Kindest regards,
Yours sincerely
ANEURIN BEVAN

Josip Broz Tito   Belgrade
                                                 February 22, 1954

PERSONAL AND CONFIDENTIAL

Dear Friend,

I am availing myself of Comrade Veljki Vlahovic's visit to London to answer your letter, which was full of concern for your two friends, Djilas and Dedijer. Comrade Vlahovic will tell you all about this unpleasant event in more detail, while I am going to deal with it only briefly.

First of all, your concern about the fate of Djilas is unnecessary, and you should feel even less concerned regarding Dedijer towards whom we have, in view of his old and known illness, adopted an attitude full of comradely attention and assistance.

This case has affected you owing to your personal and friendly relations with Dedijer and Djilas, but believe me that Djilas's case has hurt us twice as much, both as friends and collaborators of long standing in a revolutionary cause. All this has happened to the destructive character of his writing about our realities. However, he turned a deaf ear and went ahead so that we had to solve his problem in the only possible way; i.e. in the mildest and principled manner, in order to safeguard the unity of ranks of our League of Communists and the normal progress of our Socialist democracy, in other words all our development.

During this discussion your name was mentioned only on one occasion and I must say that we all regret that this received publicity, because we do not believe that you exercised any influence upon Djilas as regards the road upon which he had embarked, i.e. the road of anarchist conceptions, because we know you as a realistic political worker. Therefore, please do not take this tragically at all.

As far as the present fate of comrades Djilas and Dedijer is concerned, I think that a distinction should be drawn between them, because Dedijer was not in the course of the matter when he defended Djilas. I believe that he has already altered, to a certain extent, his opinions concerning Djilas's actions, in a sense positive to our general views. Comrade Djilas has been deprived of all his functions, but he was informed that he was entitled to material security as a high functionary and our collaborator of long standing. His personal liberty has not been affected and he remains a member of the League, with the possibility to think over and correct his erroneous conceptions, especially with regard to the harmfulness of factionist activity. This is the most that could be done for him: to offer him the possibility to work within the League of Communists for the welfare of our Socialist community, and now everything depends exclusively on him.

With kindest regards and best wishes to your wife and yourself.

Yours very sincerely,

PS. There is no obstacle whatever to your writing to either of the two comrades.

Comrade Aneurin Bevan

Writing in 1954, it was unbelievable to Bevan that he would never see his friend Milovan Djilas again, that the imprisonment would continue until beyond the time of his own death. Djilas dedicated his classic *Conversations with Stalin* (Methuen, 1962) to 'the memory of Aneurin Bevan', and his later book *The Unperfect Society* (Methuen, 1969) claimed that 'Bevan remained steadfast in his demands for my release'. He did indeed.

11

THE BEVANITES: III
1954

Recovering from a severe illness I sleep badly. The other night in my desultory reading, I met the following passage: 'He was thought to be dictatorial, irritable, impulsive and lacking in tact. He was often described as "the white elephant" – a liability to any government which he joined. On the other hand, his personality was magnetic; he might inspire love, or hate, but never indifference.' I rubbed my eyes (it was 4 a.m.). Good heavens, I thought, has Nye Bevan died? Is the *Manchester Guardian* splenetically pursuing him beyond the grave? But no; it was a description of Gladstone from the recent life by Philip Magnus.

Letter in Manchester Guardian October 1954

INDIA, ISRAEL, YUGOSLAVIA, and the new friend-ships made in each contributed to Aneurin Bevan's view of the international scene. It was never an unsophisticated synthesis he searched for, and, surveying the prospects for 1954, he could be forgiven some wry recollection of the prophecies of two or three years before. According to the military chiefs of the West, 1953 was to have been the year of destiny, the moment for which every resource must be mobilized. But the fatal hour had passed, with even a few signs of peace appearing. The clearest achievement of the year had been the Korean armistice; it showed how intractable crisis could make way for accommodation. Meantime, East and West, in the Soviet Union and the United States, there was talk of 'levelling off' the arms drive, and in Britain the highly contentious £4,700 million arms programme had been cut at least twice by such a firm upholder of 'negotiation from strength' as Churchill himself. It did seem to be true, as Bevan alone among leading Western politicians had unequivocally asserted, that a great march across Europe to the Channel ports had never been the aim of Soviet strategy. And if the alternative argument was propounded, that it was the protective measures of 1950 and 1951 which had produced the new equipoise, Bevan could embrace that deduction too. All the stronger was the case, particularly at a time when the intentions of the new Soviet leadership were still untested, for a period of cool, unhurried diplomacy.

Instead, it was the age of John Foster Dulles. On 12 January 1954, without the semblance of consultation with allies, he delivered the famous 'massive retaliation' speech; the decision of the United States National Security Council 'to depend primarily upon a great capacity to retaliate instantly, by means and at places of our own choosing'. Evidently he did not want the peace-making habit in Korea to spread to Indo-China where, as he believed, the essential resistance to global Communist aggression continued. And just a few weeks earlier, he had threatened his European allies with an 'agonising reappraisal' of policy in Washington, if the interminable debate about the European Defence Community (E.D.C.) was not speedily concluded. With the most devastating weapon mankind had ever seen at his disposal, Dulles preached an anti-Communist holy war, and for Bevan the performance was utterly repugnant as well as menacing. It justified and deepened the fears expressed in his resignation speech about where Britain and the world could be dragged behind American chariot wheels, and he became the more impatient to imbue the Labour Party with his scepticism and alarm.

But life in the Shadow Cabinet was still lonely, although on one issue he had a strong if embarrassing ally. 'No guns for the Huns' was Hugh Dalton's booming motto. Bevan reached the same conclusion without any xenophobic overtones. Against them Hugh Gaitskell and Herbert Morrison argued, with a touch of Dulles's own fervour, the case for the acceptance of a German contribution to Western defence, Gaitskell because of his overriding allegiance to the Anglo-American alliance and Morrison because he protested at the dangers of treating Germany as 'a pariah', as after 1918. For a while, throughout 1953, waverers could be rallied to the Dalton–Bevan line on the plea that, before the decisive step was taken, a fresh exertion must be made to see whether a general settlement of the German question with the Soviet Union was attainable. That had been one of the so-called Attlee conditions laid down ever since 1951 when, under pressure from America, he had accepted 'the principle' of German rearmament. It accorded with the anxieties which multitudes of Frenchmen could not suppress at the prospect of a rearmed Germany, however disguised or contained, anxieties they shared with many other good Europeans. Thus, the Margate Conference of the Labour Party, in the autumn of 1953, had approved the idea 'that there should be no German rearmament before further efforts have been made to secure the peaceful reunification of Germany'.[1] The tone contrasted with the hectoring demands of Foster Dulles.

However, in the early days of February 1954, a new conference with the Soviet Union did take place in Berlin. Neither the Soviet nor the Western negotiators moved from their previous entrenched positions and nothing remotely comparable with the Margate offer was advanced by Dulles or Eden. 'Mr Molotov,' wrote Bevan in his summary of the outcome in *Tribune* on 12 February, 'insisted that the Eastern German Government should rank in equal status with that of Western Germany. For their part the three Western allies made it clear that united Germany should be free to join any alliance it chose – which the Russians knew quite well would mean a German reinforcement of N.A.T.O. It passes comprehension that the Allies should believe the Russians would agree to that. What would they get in return? Precisely nothing. The Allies would get the integration of the whole of Germany into the Western bloc; German ascendancy would be firmly established in Western Europe and soon Russia would find herself defending her satellites against German claims for a revision of her frontiers . . . The Berlin Con-

---

[1] To overcome the difficulty that a spokesman of neither the Left nor the Right could speak readily for the whole Executive at Margate, the exceptional course was taken of entrusting the Executive case to the Party Secretary, Morgan Phillips. No question is possible about the specific delaying measure which he advanced: 'We can and should offer to halt the creation of the European Defence Community containing German armed forces until we have an opportunity of considering the question of unification. We can make this offer not only because we want to avoid German rearmament if it is at all possible, but also because if Germany is reunited the European Defence Community will no longer be relevant . . .' And then followed proposals for progress to a Peace Treaty – with Germany still disarmed.

ference was merely a formal procedure preliminary to the creation
of the twelve German military divisions upon which Dulles and
Eden have set their hearts.' That was the core of the German
question of the 1950s – the insensate demand of the West that the
Soviet leaders should contentedly watch the whole of a united Germany being incorporated into the Western military alliance. Anything less, according to the orthodox Western doctrine of the day,
would imply an infringement of the free choice, the rights of self-
determination of the German people. To counter these crudities
had been Bevan's principal contribution to the public debate for
months past, and he often spoke for those who would never tolerate
gibes about 'no guns for Huns'. The Western proposition presented
to the Berlin Conference was too naive to be worth making; that
was the last, almost the death-bed warning which came from Ernst
Reuter, the heroic Social Democrat Mayor of Berlin. He wanted to
see his country united and freedom for his people, in the East no
less than the West, but he foresaw that rearmament under Western
auspices could banish those legitimate claims for generations.

Dulles had no ear for men like Reuter; they were neutralists,
politicians with skins too thin to withstand the icy realities of the
cold war. Perhaps they lived too near to the brink to enjoy brinkmanship. But the British Labour Party should be more sensitive;
that was Bevan's hope. Instead, much to his astonishment and the
fury of Dalton, at that time absent from the meetings of the
Shadow Cabinet through illness, Morrison and Gaitskell insisted,
immediately after the Berlin Conference, that the Russians had
proved themselves irreconcilable, that the Attlee conditions had
been fulfilled, that the Party's outright support for E.D.C. could
no longer be withheld. A resolution to that effect was pushed
through the Shadow Cabinet and the idea was that it should be
presented to the meeting of the Parliamentary Party without delay.
Normally official backing from the Party leadership for a motion of
this character assured its passage by a substantial majority, but on
this occasion the plan misfired. At the most tense meeting which
the Party had known since the emotionally supercharged days of
1951, an amendment refusing to give support for German rearmament in the existing circumstances, moved by Harold Wilson, was
defeated by only two votes, by 111 to 109. At a meeting of the

National Executive a week later, the division was less narrow, but it was evident that the Party's final view could only be decided at the Party Conference later in the year. The Labour movement faced another long, hot spring, summer and autumn of argument. And at a meeting a few days later of the National Executive, Bevan gave notice that neither he nor the other leaders of the Party could be constrained by the conventional rules from expressing their opinions on an issue of such supreme importance: 'If a third world war breaks out and our cities are laid in ruins and somebody asks me why I did nothing to stop it, I cannot say: "Because it was against Standing Orders".'[1]

Sometimes these meetings of the Executive could suddenly collapse into frenetic horror, and some on the Right wing felt confirmed in the view that the issue could only be settled by expulsions. Discussion on German rearmament had usually been conducted with reasonable courtesy, since the lines of demarcation were not solely Bevanite versus anti-Bevanite. But there was another appalling incident when Ian Mikardo raised a complaint about a series of articles by Francis Williams which had appeared in the *People* alleging that Bevanite plots of one kind and another against Attlee, and in particular threats of resignation by Bevan himself, had been continuing since 1947. Francis Williams had once been Attlee's public relations officer at Downing Street and he was the author of a quasi-official history of the Labour Party. To place the matter on the Executive's agenda seemed to Mikardo a perfectly proper course in view of the series of complaints which had been made against *Tribune* at the Executive over previous months, even years. But the chairman adamantly ruled the matter out of order, despite the fact that Mikardo had given every proper form of notice. Bevan furiously protested against what he considered to be an act of anti-Bevanite discrimination by the chair. Eventually he shouted 'Point of Order' for several minutes on end and accused Attlee of being a liar. Attlee rose to his feet in turn and the altercation between the two proceeded furiously until Attlee at last conceded that he had only just read the Francis Williams articles and that he regarded them as completely false. No doubt Bevan would have been better advised to keep his temper, but the incident illustrated what he

[1] Speech in Stratford East, reported in the *Daily Express*, 5 March.

considered to be the absurd injustice of the whole situation. Any defence of his views in *Tribune* provoked demands for bans and censors; any attack upon himself, even when conducted by hench-men of other Executive members, was perfectly in order.

However, Labour's disputes about German rearmament or less momentous matters were soon interwoven with, or overcast by, the news which filtered through from the Pacific about the nature of the new weapons available for mankind's destruction. For the first time almost, the H-bomb and its hideous potentialities seemed to make an impact on world opinion. The Labour Opposition moved a resolution calling for an early summit meeting between the nuclear powers to consider the unprecedented perils of the moment and the need for a quite fresh impetus to be given to the work of disarmament. Attlee put the case in what everyone agreed was one of the most impressive speeches of his life. Bevan made no demur but, particularly in view of the controversies over the bomb which came later, it is necessary to note how his individual judgment was applied to the fresh evidence of the perils of nuclear annihilation. It was a waste of time, he said, to press for the bomb to be out-lawed; war itself had to be outlawed. The point was not original. But Bevan sought to relate the new intensity of alarm provoked by the H-bomb explosions to the immediate diplomatic crises which others sought to dodge. 'Peace diplomacy,' he wrote,[1] 'must dis-place war diplomacy. For example, when Mr Foster Dulles declares that the aim of the "Free World" is the defeat of Communism, he is using the language of the hydrogen bomb . . . When he demands that Chinese Communists should cease to be Communists before they are allowed into the United Nations, he is employing the diplomacy of totalitarianism. Its natural child is the hydrogen bomb. It means total submission or total destruction.' April 1954 he regarded as a supreme moment of danger.[2]

[1] In the *Daily Mirror* on 2 April 1954.
[2] One public statement of Dulles made at this time and quoted by Bevan in his *Daily Mirror* article of 9 April put the point with horrifying succinctness: 'The imposition on South East Asia of the political system of Communist Russia and its Chinese Communist ally by whatever means would be a grave threat to the whole free community. The United States feels that that possibility should not be passively accepted but should be met by united action.'

A few days later – on 13 April – following a visit by Dulles to London, Sir Anthony Eden reported to the House of Commons the results of 'the full exchange of views with reference to South East Asia' upon which the two Governments had been engaged. Both deplored 'the large-scale war' against the French which Communist forces were said to be intensifying, particularly on the eve of the projected conference at Geneva to deal with Far Eastern affairs which had been the one hopeful legacy of the abortive Berlin Conference. Both agreed that these activities threatened not only the countries directly involved, but 'a much wider area'. 'Accordingly we, that is the Governments of the United States and the United Kingdom, are ready to take part with the other countries concerned in an examination of the possibility of establishing a collective defence within the framework of the Charter of the United Nations to assure the peace, security and freedom of South East Asia and the Western Pacific.' The statement provoked some murmurs from the Labour backbenches, but Attlee appeared to subdue them. Would the Foreign Secretary realize, he asked, that in building up the forces of the free nations of Asia, he must call upon the Asiatic countries as well as those of European descent? Would the new organization be free for all to enter, thereby avoiding any misrepresentations about a defence of an obsolete colonialism? Eden was gratitude and accommodation itself. But then, a few seconds later, the House was startled to see a slightly breathless Bevan clambering his way to the Opposition despatch box. Since he was sitting at the far end of the front bench he had to push his way past a dozen pairs of knees and almost trample on his diffident leader to reach his destination. Then he asked, amid cheers from some of the Labour back benchers, released as if by a mechanical appliance: 'Is the right hon. Gentleman aware that the statement which he has made today will be deeply resented by the majority of people in Great Britain? Is he further aware that it will be universally regarded as a surrender to American pressure? Is he further aware that the interpretation that may be placed upon his statement, unless he clarifies it further, is that we shall assist in establishing a N.A.T.O. in South East Asia for the purpose of imposing European colonial rule upon certain people in that area, and will he realize that if that course is persisted in, it will estrange the Commonwealth members in that part of the world?'

Eden parried the accusations with surprising docility, but the House was scarcely interested in the answers. Bevan had made an open challenge to his leader, and he could hardly have done it more sharply and even rudely; that was the immediate charge against him in the parliamentary corridors and the rebuke was repeated more formally at the Shadow Cabinet. Next day, at the Party meeting itself, he announced his resignation from the Committee and in a statement professed himself 'deeply shocked' by the official leadership's response to the Eden proposals which must prejudice the hope of a negotiated settlement of the Indo-Chinese war at Geneva and assist American policy 'which was tantamount to the diplomatic and military encirclement of China'. So, not merely had he walked out; he seemed to have slammed the door, and the whole Labour Party edifice shivered at the impact.

Many observers at the time, including some of his closest friends, thought that Bevan's S.E.A.T.O. resignation was an act of impulsive folly which could ruin the whole Bevanite cause. The suggestion was that in the House of Commons he had acted on the prompting of the moment and that that night and next day he had struggled to rationalize his impetuosity. 'Has Bevan Encircled Himself?' was the title of an article in the *News Chronicle*, which described the affair as 'a masterpiece of bad timing'. At that precise moment Labour's fortunes in the country appeared to be improving. Two good by-election results had just been recorded and Attlee's prestige, thanks to his H-bomb speech, had rarely stood higher. The wounds and bruises of the earlier Bevanite quarrels were just starting to heal when Bevan had ripped them open again. 'Just when we were beginning to win the match,' Attlee himself was heard to mutter, 'our inside left has scored against his own side.' Several major parliamentary prophets shook their heads none too gravely, averring that once again, but this time for ever, he had wrecked his political career.

But against all the tides and protestations, Bevan was never more confident of the rightness of his decision. Normally he would have plenty of self-doubts about tactical choices, but he had few on this occasion. 'There is never a right time to make an awkward decision,' he would say, 'always the right course is supposed to be wrongly timed.' And whatever view may still be taken either about the moment chosen or the injury done to his own interest, it is impossible not to marvel at the way in which his political instinct had pierced through both Eden's sophistries and Attlee's muffled reaction, to touch the truth. For it was true that Dulles had pressed for a much more rigid and belligerent alliance than Eden described to the House of Commons. It was true that he proceeded at once to fashion this instrument according to his own design despite the protests from Britain on the effects on Commonwealth nations, notably India. It was true that he was urging, almost demanding, direct British participation in Indo-China. It was true that this immediate military action interlocked with the projected S.E.A.T.O. pact. It was true that Dulles cared not a straw that his policies would put in jeopardy the Geneva Conference: indeed that for him it was part of the appeal. To 'keep things on the boil in Indo-China,' he asserted, would be 'a very good thing'. He wanted armed intervention by the United States and Britain to prevent a French defeat, and the British answer was: 'what we were being asked to do was to assist in misleading Congress into approving a military operation, which would in itself be ineffective, and might well bring the world to the verge of a major war.'[1] That sounds like another quotation from Bevan; it was in fact Churchill's comment on the propositions put by Dulles to Eden. In other terms, April and May 1954 witnessed a series of British acts of independence *vis-à-vis* the United States, and the results were entirely beneficent; possibly they stopped the third world war. Possibly, too, it was an advantage that one leading figure in Britain was not content to wait until the memoirs were written before making the exposure of the Dulles doctrine overt and explicit. Certainly the exposure was welcomed in France where a then little-known French politician, Pierre Mendès-France, was preparing, by a French act of independence from the same ruinous policy, to save *his* country.

However, in the days after Bevan's resignation British interest seemed to concentrate on less lofty aspects of the affair. Where he

[1] *Full Circle: The Memoirs of Sir Anthony Eden*, p. 105. And the rest of the above description of Dulles's pressure is substantiated in the same pages.

was most open to criticism perhaps was that he had acted not merely at question time in the House of Commons but throughout the whole resignation episode without any consultation with his closest Bevanite associates, and these bruised feelings added piquancy to the sequel. Who would take Bevan's vacated seat on the Shadow Cabinet? That was the question. Would it be Harold Wilson, the runner-up in the previous year's voting? Could he take it, devoted Bevanite as he was? Could he take it, after he had avowed his support for Bevan's views about S.E.A.T.O.? Would he refuse it, if thereby he injured the already fragile unity of the Party? Would he? Could he? Since a short parliamentary recess interposed between Bevan's resignation and the next meeting of the Shadow Cabinet, several tantalizing days and nights were available for speculation and confabulation. Among the Bevanites themselves at first none thought that Wilson could and would take the vacant place. At least, that was the overwhelming opinion among several of them, according to Ian Mikardo's recollection, when they lunched a few days later. Would he take it? Impossible. However, the incredulous luncheon party did discover that he was seriously considering the impossible proposition, and that Dick Crossman, who had been one of those most shattered by the resignation and its aftermath, supported him. It was a cold lunch, and the Bevanites continued the argument among themselves.

Crossman then undertook the perilous mission of broaching the whole question with Bevan himself, on Wilson's behalf, as it were. He was left in no doubt about Bevan's reaction. Not merely did he oppose Wilson taking his place; he brutally prophesied that it would be the end of Wilson's political career if he did. And then, after a few ferocious comments on the nature of political animals, Bevan turned the conversation to the wider aspect of the perennial Party leadership problem, and it became growingly apparent that a divergence in attitude among the Bevanites – roughly between Crossman and Wilson on one side and Bevan and most of the others on the other – was now coming to the surface. How strongly could and should the assault on the Right wing be mounted; how much could be achieved by exploiting the fissures within the leadership itself, between Attlee on one side and Morrison and Gaitskell on the other? These tender themes could be debated with endless variations. But the immediate question remained. What did Harold intend? Crossman accompanied him on a visit to Cliveden Place where Wilson proposed that he should declare his support for Bevan's policy, but take his place on the Committee, making it clear that he was doing so with Bevan's approval. Bevan demurred, but the civilities were sustained. Decision was postponed to the usual Vincent Square lunch meeting next day which indeed had to be resumed throughout the whole afternoon to allow time for all the ramifications of the affair to be explored. Despite the opposition of almost all the others, perhaps because he differed with the others and agreed with Crossman on what should be the relationship sought with the Parliamentary Party, Wilson eventually decided to protest to Attlee his loyalty to Bevan's policies, to elaborate on his views on Party unity – and to take the vacant place. Attlee listened and made one comment, the single word: 'Quite'.

How tense relationships had momentarily become between old associates is indicated by this letter from John Freeman, despatched for the purpose of persuading Bevan not to retreat to his tent, instead of attending Crossman's lunch on the following Tuesday.

My dear Nye,

I know that you have not lacked advice, good and bad, in the last three weeks. I write now to add my word on one point only. I hope you will come to lunch at Dick's tomorrow. I don't mind what you say when you get there; but if you don't come, I fear it will mean that the inner circle of your following may be broken up – perhaps irreparably. This would be a great pity for the Party, and I think for yourself. Dick's folly and Harold's ambition have created a disastrous situation. Tomorrow we have to discuss – as comrades – how we can make the best of it. Such a discussion would be futile without you.

JOHN FREEMAN

The appeal worked, the comrades did discuss the situation, jagged egos were smoothed, and, quite genuinely, the common interest in the political and international scene reasserted its influence. Bevan never approved the decision Wilson had made, but the

Crossman lunches were resumed. None of the participants in those rhetorical orgies suffered from a poor appetite, and each, if need be, was ready to take on the rest. Far indeed from reality was the picture of 'the great man' surrounded by his tongue-tied sycophants. Crossman, in particular, would seize the initiative with a formidable new presentation of an argument and it might take long hours to tame the too headstrong logic. Between him and Bevan there had always been a wariness or suspicion which might break out into open irritation or anger, but then, one tragic summer, Dick was struck down by the sudden death of his wife, and he was embraced by the warmth of Bevan's personality, always especially sensitive and effective at such moments. He could win friends for life by a word and a look. He liked to talk to everyone as equals – except sometimes his benighted leaders – and those conspiratorial weekly meetings were truly more memorable for the zest and gaiety and the genuine argument than for any detailed plotting done. Sometimes when the political setbacks seemed most severe and the prospect of any Bevanite victory the more remote, a fresh current of political imagination would radiate through the place, and there was no doubt what was its source. Sir Robert Stopford, who commanded one of the ships with which Nelson chased to the West Indies a fleet nearly double in number, wrote home: 'We are half-starved and otherwise inconvenienced by being out of port, but our reward is that we are with Nelson.' And although they were never half-starved at Crossman's No. 9 Vincent Square, so it was with the Bevanites.

Certainly the contrast between the two public faces of the man had rarely been sharper than in the summer of 1954. One presented by Denis Healey in the *New Republic* described how Bevan had intervened in Eden's announcement on South East Asia 'red as a turkey-cock and in a voice shrill with emotion'; Healey assured his American audience how all but the wholly Bevanite M.P.s had decided he was 'impossible' as a colleague and that 'prompt and effective action' must be taken to shut him up.[1] Herbert Morrison,

---

[1] Healey's article added the footnote: 'Aneurin Bevan was fined in court last month for two offences which might well serve as his political epitaph – "dangerous driving and failure to stop after an accident".' This is the only instance I have come across where this incident was used directly

in an article in *Socialist Commentary*, revived the charge that the 'one word vermin' had cost Labour thirty to fifty seats in the 1951 election. A dozen other Right-wing polemicists took up the cry. He was the restless adventurer, the wanton destroyer of Party cohesion, a man scarcely in control of the demon within him. And yet at that very moment the world reflected the pattern which he described so much more imaginatively than the Morrisons, the Gaitskells and the Healeys. During that perilous summer 'the war party', as Mr Walter Lippmann called it, was at times in the ascendant in Washington and the world only escaped atomic calamity by, as Nehru said, a hair's breadth. At Geneva Britain was forced to perform the role of independent mediator, as Bevan had so often urged, while Dulles withdrew from the scene in surly desperation. How bitterly frustrating for Bevan to find his influence so circumscribed in his own Party just when his insight into the international scene seemed most piercing. It was all the fault, his critics would repeat, of his own temperament. Why did he not curb his tongue and bide his time and work with the team? But that was just what he had been doing in the early days of April 1954, when the Dulles journeyings and the Labour leadership's complacency in the face of them drove him to distraction. And how absurd it was – how vain it would be – to argue that it was his character which shaped the nature of his clashes with the Party. It was the nature of the Party which dictated its chronic timidity and lack of vision. At each of the National Executive meetings in the aftermath of his S.E.A.T.O. resignation, despite the ferment in the Party outside and despite the favourable shift in the international scene, he could make no dent on the sedate and solid Right-wing majority. In June, miraculously, they did decide to accept an official invitation to send a Labour Party delegation to China; that was a healthy sign of relaxation or at least curiosity. But for the rest, the six Bevanite

---

against Bevan for political purposes. He had indeed been fined £50 for these offences, and especially since the case came before the court just at the moment when the political crisis was at its height, it gave him much concern. Having had a smash – in which no one was hurt – he drove on for fear that his mother-in-law at home would be bombarded by press callers. Jennie was away at the time and the accident occurred some 20 miles out of London.

representatives from the constituency parties were voted down by the unbroken ranks of the trade union representatives. 'Can't I even be right once on the law of averages?' he asked a trade union representative who had voted on the other side on every opportunity. Every issue he raised became one of prestige between himself and the leadership. The obstacles across the path of change looked unbreakable.

Bevan had first been elected to the National Executive of the Labour Party in the constituency section in 1944; ever since 1945 he had headed the poll. This was a reflection, not only of his personal popularity, but also of the predominantly Left-wing temper of the constituency parties, a mood all the more strongly emphasized since the other Bevanite candidates had started ousting the Right wing in 1951. It was both significant and indisputable that the bulk of the active workers in the Party backed Bevan and his policies as consistently as the Parliamentary Party and the National Executive voted against them. However, over the same period and in the same degree, the bulk of the trade union votes had been enlisted to sustain the Right-wing leadership of the Party, and Bevan was convinced that this achievement of the trade union leaders was an illicit or, at least, an unrepresentative use of their power. After all, the rank-and-file within the constituency parties and within the unions – particularly, it might be said, in his own union, the miners – were not workers with conflicting interests; often they were the very same people. That so pronounced a swing to the Left in the constituency parties in the early 1950s was accompanied by so stolid a mobilization of trade union support on the Right seemed to prove that the exercise of power in the unions was more oligarchic than democratic. Of course, the process of election varied from union to union but in the two unions whose allegiance was firmly given to the Right – the Transport and General Workers' Union and the National Union of General and Municipal Workers – the authority of the central machine was enormous, and no one had supposed that such leaders as Bevin and Deakin or Dukes and Williamson had ever been squeamish in exercising it. But it was the vote of the miners which rankled most with Bevan. Lawther usually succeeded in joining forces with Deakin and Williamson. If that alliance could be broken, if the miners could be weaned back to their traditional Left-wing ties, the whole Right-wing posture of the Party might be loosened. In 1954, as it happened, there had been, following Lawther's retirement, an election for the presidency of the National Union of Mineworkers, and Bevan had seriously considered abandoning his membership of the House of Commons in order to enter the contest. Well-nigh unanimous opposition from his friends and his own second thoughts prevailed against the idea, but certainly he was driven more and more to examine how the structure of the Party prevented any effective breakthrough from the Left and what remedies must be sought.

Then, in June 1954, the same problem was presented in an unexpected form. Arthur Greenwood's death meant that the Treasurership of the Labour Party fell vacant and that a new candidate for the office would be elected at the forthcoming Party Conference in the autumn. Within a few days speculation in the press suggested that the most likely choice would be Hugh Gaitskell, and undoubtedly Deakin and his associates were resolved upon it. Deakin indeed, as we have seen, believed that the remedy for the Party's ills was the full-scale expulsion of Bevan, and his resignation from the Shadow Cabinet fed this determination anew; whether a compact in this sense was concluded with Gaitskell is unknown. But no time was lost in making it evident that, for the Treasurership, Gaitskell was Deakin's man – and Tom Williamson's and Jack Tanner's of the A.E.U. But what about the miners? Somehow a decision, tentative at least, had been reached there too. In the first few days after Greenwood's death, Bevan bumped into Sam Watson, the Durham miners' leader, and raised the question direct, asking whether he could count on the miners' vote. 'I had to tell him,' said Watson,[1] 'that the N.U.M. had already decided that its nominee for the succession was Hugh Gaitskell.' Bevan was very angry. 'How,' he asked, according to Watson's report, 'can you support a public schoolboy from Winchester against a man born in the back streets of Tredegar?' However, that sentence does not sound authentic. Bevan was fond of saying, and said again and again: 'What matters is not where you come from but where you are going.'

[1] Sam Watson's contribution to *Hugh Gaitskell* edited by W. T. Rodgers (Thames & Hudson, 1963), p. 110.

What was not in doubt was his anger that the miners' decision *had* been already made, even if it still had to be formally confirmed at the miners' conference. So Gaitskell was almost *elected* before he was even officially *nominated*! The arrangement struck Bevan as intolerable, and his own inclination to leave the constituency section and accept nomination for the Treasurership was fortified. Gaitskell had been defeated every time he had stood for the constituency section; for the trade unions to push him onto the Executive was both to flout the constituency parties and to illustrate how ineffective they were. However, the risks of Bevan's proposed action were all too clear. Certainly he would be defeated; in the same year he would have vacated, of his own volition, two positions of power within the Party leadership; and it might be that Gaitskell would be magnified rather than diminished by the challenge. Many of his closest friends, headed by Archie Lush on this issue, as well as the so-called moderate or middle-of-the-road sections of the Party, were opposed to his action; they pleaded and protested and warned. But he was adamant. He could see no better way of carrying the essential political argument into the trade unions; trade unionists would have to choose, as the constituency party workers had done. As for the consequences for himself, he acted with his eyes open. 'It will take us three years to win this particular fight,' he said to some of his originally sceptical supporters now won over or borne down by his conviction.

He had undertaken a considerable extra burden in persuading some of his friends in the country. Witness the reply he sent to Councillor J. M. Fagan of Barrow, the agent of another eager Bevanite, Walter Monslow:

My dear Jack, *July 12*

Many thanks for your letter and for the trouble you took to write it. However, I am afraid my position is being misunderstood. Perhaps that is inevitable.

It is absolutely essential that the forms of power should coincide with the appearance. It is no use saying that I am representative of the rank and file of the trade union movement through the medium of the constituency parties, if the policies of the Party are, in fact, determined by an irresponsible group of trade union bureaucrats. You should appreciate the fact that the block vote operates inside the Executive as well as at the Conference. We have actually reached the position where it would be true to say that the leaders of the Transport and General Workers' Union and the Municipal and General Workers' Union decide the policy of the Labour Party. The preponderance of votes they enjoy is such that no trade union representative can be elected to the Executive without their consent.

This power they have exercised ruthlessly and cynically. The decision to adopt Hugh Gaitskell for the Treasurership of the Party was taken by them as a direct consequence of his failure to be elected by the constituency section. As the Treasurer is elected both by the trade unions and the constituency party membership, I cannot conceivably allow it to be assumed that Gaitskell represents the whole movement, whereas I only represent the constituency parties.

Furthermore, it is essential that the movement should now be educated in the realities of the situation. The present reality is that the Party is now dominated by a bureaucracy. We all know that this was partly the case in the past through the instrumentality of the block vote. Today, however, the situation is infinitely worsened by the dominant position exercised by two general unions and by the subservience of the other unions to them.

This domination must be broken if democracy inside the Party is to have the chance to breathe.

The fight for the Treasurership is, therefore, part of the educational process.

Yours sincerely,
ANEURIN

He himself also wanted the chance to breathe, and that summer he was able to lead as exultant an exodus as any in recorded history. 23 Cliveden Place had been made into a beautiful home but nothing had ever reconciled Nye to the frenzy of London, and amid all its pressures and intrusions his deep homing instincts could never be fulfilled. He had always ached to find somewhere else and naturally he first looked to Wales and for some hideout within striking distance of the moorlands above Trefil, the Duffryn valley and the

Black Mountains, his favourite places on the whole planet. For a while he had a room with a great stone fireplace of local stone designed for him in his mother's house at 2 Queen's Square in Tredegar which had been taken over by his sister Arianwen. But when that arrangement did not work satisfactorily he was constantly looking for some place, conveniently situated between London and the constituency, like the Berkshire cottage he had surrendered at the beginning of the war. 'What about a wee farm?' said his farmer friend, John Mackie. Jennie scoffed at the idea. 'We will look marvellous,' she said, 'going to market to buy a pig and not knowing one end from the other.' Nye indignantly objected. He was passionately a countryman and eager to experiment. Anyhow, no suitable cottage seemed available. After much searching, they discovered a farm on the top of the Chilterns, with the farm-house in the centre of the fields, which seemed to offer the privacy they so ardently needed.

Alas, suddenly on arrival there, their hopes were overcast. At the cottage in Berkshire and at Cliveden Place, the light of their lives, Nye's no less than Jennie's, had been Ma Lee who had not only helped to infuse the home with so much physical well-being but was in a sense the spiritual fire which warmed the whole household. But suddenly, soon after their arrival at the farm, they were faced with the discovery that Ma Lee had breast cancer and would not be able to live long. In fact, carefully nursed, she lived happily for another eight years. But when the first news was broken to them by the local doctor, both were horrified and desolate. Nye caught hold of Jennie and she recalled always his first words: 'Life will never be the same again. Ma leaves too many gracious memories.'

Moreover, at that time Jennie was watching Nye and his health with some growing stabs of anxiety. His colds could constrict his chest appallingly; he retained from his mining days a touch of pneumoconiosis, and Jennie thought that he needed warmth and sun much more than the mists and mountains of Wales. What he truly needed, what he always cried out for, was a sabbatical year when he might escape from politics altogether for a period of renewal. How he envied his friend, Yigal Allon from Israel, who was permitted just such a dispensation at St Anthony's at Oxford.

Nye was never to be allowed, in Jennie's phrase, 'to get the halter off his neck'. Nonetheless, the release from London came as an inexpressible boon.

At last, with the assistance of a £6,000 mortgage, the move had become possible, and he purchased for £9,000 the 54-acre Asheridge Farm, Buckinghamshire, which was to be his pride and joy and well-stocked citadel against all political or newspaper invaders for the rest of his life. It was a lovely old Tudor farmhouse with the barns and outbuildings forming an agreeable square and offering plenty of room for Jennie's favourite roses and tobacco plants. The front door opened straight into a spacious white living room, a huge log-fire roared in the inglenook fireplace; the scents from the garden mingled with the burning wood. Jennie and her mother had been to work, Jennie ordering the demolition of walls and the liberation of windows and the provision of unobtrusive lights, and Ma Lee, then over seventy-five, having still insisted on doing the upholstery. There was nothing fake or plush or flamboyant about it; complete comfort combined with complete simplicity, and there was plenty of room for Nye to unleash his invective pacing up and down, or to dance his impression of Handel's 'Great Elopement' to set alongside Sir Thomas Beecham's. And there was room, too, for Ma Lee to have her own sitting room, for a dozen guests to sit comfortably in the dining room, for Ma Lee's Dickensian feasts to be acclaimed as they deserved. For some of us, an expedition to Asheridge could surpass even the enchantments of Cliveden Place.

First, on arrival, it was necessary to be instructed in the latest discoveries of modern agriculture. Originally, Nye had had the advice of John Mackie and Tony Harman, two of the best farmers in the land, but soon the education became a two-way affair, and whatever the financial accounts might prove, he was clearly born for the occupation. On their first night as they sat by the fire he informed Jennie that he had never exploited any man in his life and did not propose to start and that he would soon make Asheridge into a model place, a kind of Robert Owen settlement with the farm manager and his cowman embraced in a co-partnership scheme. But Jennie soon blunted these and other kindred expressions of his unworldly streak with inquiries about how losses and mortgage payments were to be shared with non-existent profits. She, after all, had to keep the accounts, deal with the facts, and instil some Scots reality into Welsh romanticism off the leash. He had strange notions of starting with an asparagus bed or launching an investment programme on the lavish scale which he always prescribed for the nation. And yet much that he proposed made eventual sense. His own total absorption could swathe through all obstacles: the same Bevan whose fits of impatience could shatter the Shadow Cabinet would sit up all night to tend a sick calf. And sometimes the arrogant, all-knowing agricultural expert would have to submit to irrepressible Welsh impudence. Archie Lush, on his first visit to Asheridge and being presented to the pedigree herd, was bold enough to say: 'Those are the most miserable lot of cows I ever saw in my life,' and Nye was naturally outraged and pressed for an explanation. It was all due, insisted Archie, to the system of artificial insemination, and perhaps his proper course was to get a decent bull.

Some protested that Asheridge wrenched Nye away from politics, but that was a misconception. He was always suspicious of the confinements metropolitan man had to endure and the injuries they might inflict; he felt these things within himself, almost a physical suffocation. Asheridge could renew him with great fresh draughts of freedom.

In August, 1954, he went via Stockholm and Moscow to China on the official Labour Party delegation – the other members of it were Attlee, Morgan Phillips, Edith Summerskill, Wilfred Burke – and the red carpets were laid out all the way. Sneers and jeers, from the British scarcely less than the American press,[1] accompanied these junketings, but post-Stalin Moscow and post-Geneva Conference Peking were clearly most avid to talk. It could have been a most fruitful moment in the post-war epoch. And, for the Bevan

[1] Lord Moran reports in his book on Churchill (p. 592): 10 September 1954: 'Winston was reading *The Times* when I called at Chartwell about ten o'clock. He picked up a page of the *Daily Mirror* which he had torn out, looked at it and passed it on to me. I saw a big picture of Aneurin Bevan standing at the foot of a gigantic statue of Lenin. "That might be useful to the Party Office as propaganda. It shows the fellow is a Communist," he said with great disgust.' But this, one feels, must have been one of the occasions when the doctor misunderstood his patient.

biographer, it appeared at first glance that a unique assistance
would be provided – an authentic scrap of a Bevan diary, the only
one he was ever self-conscious enough to keep. But, alas, the un-
filled old exercise book illustrates more the real nausea he would feel
for the actual act of handwriting. After some occasional decipherable
gleams and several scrawled-over pages, the Herculean labour was
abandoned. But several of the impressions which he noted then or
talked or wrote about later were strong and individual.

'In the evening,' stuttered the diary, 'we were taken to dinner
with Malenkov at his private house about 45 minutes in a fast car
from Moscow . . . As is usual on these occasions the toasts were
innumerable and tedious. Nothing seemed too trivial or banal to
serve as an excuse for a toast.' Malenkov was clearly Bevan's
favourite from the start, the other leaders present being Molotov,
Mikoyan, Khrushchev, Vyshinsky. None of them deferred to one
another; the stiffness of the Stalin era seemed to have abated and
real collective leadership to be taking its place. Malenkov showed a
lively, subtle, humorous mind; he was prepared more to argue than
assert. 'In the course of the dinner,' ran the diary, 'Khrushchev
made a very blunt speech. He said he realized there were differences in the Labour Party and even in the delegation. Although he
did not agree with everything in it, he did agree with the main proposals of the pamphlet I had just published [on German rearma-
ment][1] and he said he could not reconcile the delegation's good
wishes for the Soviet Union with the Labour Party's support for
the E.D.C. I could not of course allow this to develop because it
would have set me at loggerheads with my colleagues. In order to
make a diversion, I asked whether it would not be possible to meet
both Chinese and U.S.A. positions in stages. I asked them to consider both the possibilities and the attractiveness of putting
Nationalist China outside U.N.O. and taking Communist China in
but leaving her place on the Security Council vacant for the time
being. This seemed to take them aback. They protested that in no
circumstances could they support such a proposal because it would
be letting down their friend. "China is a great nation and is entitled
to full membership at once." This from Malenkov. Khrushchev

---

[1] The Bevanite pamphlet *It Need Not Happen* was published by *Tribune*
in early August.

went on repeating that I should ask the Chinese in Peking what they thought of it. I replied that I did not expect them to agree. They were bound to hold out for 100 per cent. Khrushchev seemed unable to grasp the argument. But Malenkov did. There is no doubt he is the ablest of them. Although Khrushchev is the Secretary General of the Party, I formed the impression that his appointment is an indication that the Party is destined to play a declining role in central administrative affairs. I suggested there were people outside who thought the Soviet Union was not averse to seeing China on the sidelines a little longer. This produced a sharp reaction from Malenkov who realized its full implications. He replied that he might be accused of wishing to humiliate China if he backed my proposal. "There is no profit in inviting the accusation," he retorted.' However, the next conversation concluded more profitably despite interruptions. 'Had long talk with Malenkov,' continued the diary. 'Would have been alone with him the whole time but E.S. [Edith Summerskill] kept barging in. Malenkov was at pains to point out the danger of rearming Western Germany. This was to be expected. But his line of argument was not so much the expected one that the balance of military power in Europe would be upset. This was no doubt in his mind, but what he chose to stress was the fear of the re-emergence in Western Germany of just those elements that proved so difficult before . . .' And with this and some further intrusions from Khrushchev ('He is an aggressive, forceful, and extrovert personality; he preached at us more forthrightly than the others. In doing so he explained jovially that he was free to do so because his office lay outside the Government'), Bevan felt that their previous views had been reinforced. He left Moscow freshly convinced, not only that the old Stalinite mould of Party leadership had been broken and not only that the new leaders genuinely desired a détente in Europe before German rearmament proceeded. He was also persuaded that an easement of Soviet domestic difficulties paved the way for more flexible Soviet diplomacy. 'It has always been my view,' he wrote in *Tribune* on 24 September, 'that the Soviet leaders were difficult to deal with after the war, not because they were strong but because of their overwhelming consciousness of weakness.' That had long been the essence of Bevan's individual interpretation of the Soviet-Western relationship, and the view was strengthened when he was the first Western leader to talk with Malenkov. Prior to the Labour Party delegation's arrival, the British Ambassador had never met Malenkov. Such was the puerile etiquette of the cold war.

Bevan did feel that he had reached the beginnings of an understanding with some of the Soviet leaders and, as it happened, the association with the rumbustious Khrushchev in particular was to ripen. Curiously perhaps the meetings with the Chinese leaders developed somewhat more stickily. He was impressed, almost charmed, like so many others before and since, by the outflowing, versatile, superlatively knowledgeable Chou En-lai. He was impressed still more, as who could not be, by Mao Tse-tung, his 'intuitive understanding of his own people', and the recollection of 'the superlative genius of his leadership in the civil war'. But he would not subdue his suspicions of the Chinese leaders' rigid allegiance to dogma, their unawareness of the outside world, their unMarxist contentment with their isolation and the errors of judgment into which it might lead them. Nothing could oppress Bevan's spirit more than political jargon, including Communist jargon, and in China he felt smothered by it. So he argued, sometimes furiously, with his hosts, much to the astonishment of some of his Labour Party colleagues who at home might fat-headedly sneer at him as a Communist fellow-traveller. No one could be more ready than Bevan to acknowledge the monumental achievements of the régime, in river and flood control, in vast irrigation schemes, in the opening up of undeveloped areas. But he pressed his question: how was the huge and rapidly increasing population to be fed? It was impossible, he said, to escape the conclusion that on this question of population versus food supply the Chinese Communists were evasive. They seemed unable to make up their minds whether they wanted less or more Chinese. The urban, educated Communist wanted a small family, but what was the policy for the rest? At the numerous lunches and dinners provided for the delegation he made his own test, going round the table asking how many children the fellow diners had. It rarely worked out at more than an average of two per family. Ministers, university professors and high-ranking Communist Party officials all practised family planning of one form or another. 'But when I pressed why they did not teach family planning to the peasants, I got a confused reply. Some said the peasants would resent it. Others that the peasants could not be taught effectively. Others again protested it would not be necessary because Marxist economic planning would ensure plenty for all.' And that, concluded Bevan, was the real reason: 'like their Russian counterparts they are trapped by their old-fashioned Marxist theology'. Marx had attacked Malthus and they must follow in his precise footsteps.[1]

He argued with the Chinese leaders in private and when he got the chance spoke out equally boldly in public. Called upon to give a formal reply on behalf of the delegation to the National Committee of the Chinese People's Consultative Conference, he refused to confine himself to co-existential courtesies. Instead he launched, in appropriately Marxist language, into a full-scale exposition of the nature of political democracy, parliamentary institutions and their revolutionary potentialities. He turned the ceremony into an old-fashioned Marxist study circle, for the benefit of the Chinese and Labour leaders alike. Not since Marco Polo probably had a phenomenon so strange alighted on those shores.

Of course, he never imagined that, within a few days and encumbered with all the officialdom of a Labour Party delegation, he had unravelled the secrets of the Orient. But no climate or company could inhibit him for long from unloosing his breathtaking generalizations. Everywhere and anywhere he was inclined to be made contra-suggestive by established orthodoxies, and Communist China was no place to abandon these good habits of a lifetime. China gave him a touch of claustrophobia, and, momentarily at least, he felt a sense of release when he and his colleagues found themselves exchanging ideas much more readily with Socialists in Japan.[2] And then, reporting these contrasts, he could expatiate on

---

[1] *Tribune* 8 October 1954.

[2] Some headlines in the British press suggested that Bevan had dropped another clanger in his speech in Tokyo. 'Bevan says "we in Britain have much to be ashamed of"' ran the headline in the *Evening Standard* on 3 September. But it was clear he had used his usual technique. For the report read: 'We believe the day of imperial power is over. We believe we in Britain have much to be ashamed of in our imperial past.' Adding, smiling: 'And you have much to be ashamed of in your imperial past.'

the advantages of island peoples, more especially if they were mountain people too, with their untameable spirit of innovation and enterprise and their eyes set on the open seas – all spoken like a true compatriot of Captain Harry Morgan.

He came back to face the climax of the national debate on German rearmament. After a series of extraordinary pressures and contortions, the E.D.C. proposal had been defeated in the French Assembly. It did seem possible that a fresh opportunity for a new four-power conference, along the lines urged by Bevan and the Bevanites, might be opened. Pierre Mendès-France, the French Premier, favoured it. So did Herr Ollenhauer, the German Social Democrat leader. And the explosions of anger from Dr Adenauer against France in general and Mendès-France in particular[1] might have been expected to add powerful assistance to the anti-German rearmament camp within the Labour Party. But the pro-rearmers had conducted, under the auspices of the official machine, a major campaign throughout the country, and the American and the British Governments seemed joined together to inflict revenge on Mendès-France. The determination to make him drink the poisoned cup of German rearmament presented a scene as bitter and painful as any in post-war history. At last a statesman had arisen in France. At Geneva he had saved his country from the worst consequences of the Indo-China calamity engineered by others. He was starting to offer the prospect of a similar escape from the cold war blind alley in Europe. But the old forces were mobilized to destroy him before he could work further miracles: Dulles, Adenauer, Churchill in his dotage and at the mercy of the Foreign Office – and the British Labour Party.

For, at the Scarborough Conference, the Right wing defeated the anti-rearmament campaign, after the most agile series of backstairs manœuvrings ever conducted. First, the anti-rearmers were landed, after the meeting to form a composite resolution, with a resolution

[1] In an interview in *The Times* (quoted in *Tribune* 10 September), Adenauer said: 'The French vote represents a second major diplomatic defeat the U.S. has recently suffered. The first was Geneva and now comes Paris.'

of a most extreme character. Next, the Executive of the Amalgamated Society of Woodworkers who had voted against rearmament at their own Conference and at the T.U.C., were persuaded
to switch their vote. 'We've fixed it,' cried Deakin, with unabashed
glee. 'Nye was done in by a coffin-maker' it was said. The first vote
showed a wafer-thin majority for the Executive's view of 3,270,000
to 3,022,000. It had not been a distinguished debate (Bevan and the
other leading Bevanites, of course, were, as members of the minority
on the Executive, prevented from speaking) and there had been
some ugly moments, one when the soft-spoken Ernest Jones, newly
elected President of the miners, suggested that the anti-German
rearmament campaign was Communist-inspired, and another when
the erstwhile Bevanite, Desmond Donnelly, sought to attract some
previously arranged publicity by pointing the finger of accusation
at Bevan himself, at which pandemonium broke loose in the hall.
It was betrayal in the cold light of morning. Few begrudged Donnelly his thirty pieces of silver, but it was somewhat provocative to
appear at the gates of Gethsemane to collect it. But possibly
Donnelly had adopted his manners from Deakin. When the votes
in the foregone election for the Treasurership were announced –
4,338,000 for Gaitskell against 2,032,000 for Bevan – Deakin looked
across to give Bevan the inverted V-sign. It did appear, despite the
thumping votes of support which the Bevanite candidates had still
secured in the constituency section, that the Left, with a momentous victory almost within their grasp, had seen it snatched from
them.

But that was not quite the end of Scarborough, for on the
Wednesday night the place was suddenly shaken by a detonation
of nuclear proportions. Two thousand delegates streamed into the
Floral Hall for the traditional *Tribune* meeting to hear Bevan with
'the muzzle off', and *The Times* Labour Correspondent reported:
'With all the varied gestures and wit and biting innuendo at his
command, he drew every ounce of drama from his situation, presenting a picture of himself as a lone figure striving to save the
Party from its leaders and by saving the Party saving the world.'
And no doubt, that was how many saw him, how they sought to
explain this phenomenon of a genius perpetually out of step with
his colleagues. But the portrait was false. Bevan had no taste for

15

self-dramatization and such notions offended his most deeply-held political convictions. But he did believe – as he expounded more forcibly than ever that night at Scarborough – that an irresponsible trade union bureaucracy was strangling the vitality out of the Labour movement and transforming it into a respectable, obedient handmaiden of capitalism; he did believe that all was not yet lost, that it could still be made 'the mighty instrument' which the nation and the century required; and he did believe that peace in the nuclear age might depend on the strivings of great masses of people the world over who might respond to what Great Britain and British Labour could say. 'What I am pleading for in foreign affairs,' he cried, raising his hands high, 'is time, time, time. Every year gone is a year away from catastrophe', and the peroration was infused with all his detestation of the Dulles prescriptions for mankind in that critical year. But these spacious themes required particular illustrations, and two which he gave especially seemed to have the power of a physical blow. At one moment, he had dealt with the Ernest Jones of the day before: 'We are not going to be intimidated by individual trade union leaders – just a handful of them – going to the rostrum and talking about fellow travellers and about Communists. I say frankly to my friend Ernest Jones: "Drop it. Drop it. We have enough of that from Will Lawther." I say furthermore to Ernest Jones: "In the vote you gave this week you did not represent the miners of Great Britain. He had better learn to behave himself. That is blunt".' And in other passages he commented on the plea to discard emotional responses with which Attlee had opened the German rearmament debate: 'I know that the right kind of leader for the Labour Party is a desiccated calculating machine who must not in any way permit himself to be swayed by indignation. If he sees suffering, privation or injustice he must not allow it to move him, for that would be evidence of the lack of proper education or of absence of self-control. He must speak in calm and objective accents and talk about a dying child in the same way as he would about the pieces inside an internal combustion engine.' And so the oblique essay in invective went on and the physical blows muffled within it retained their force even when the rest of the speech proceeded. And when the meeting was over and the shell-shocked delegates swayed back to their hotels, even

Bevan's friends trembled at his audacity. Could the Party long survive explosions such as these? And what would the miners do?
And whom did he mean: Gaitskell or Attlee or who? 'We'll have
him out within a year', was Deakin's comment when he heard the
report from the Floral Hall.

And away in Downing Street, according to Moran, Churchill
spoke of Bevan's performance with distaste. 'That fellow is a gold
mine to us,' he said cheerfully. 'Such a cad.' But Churchill also had
other weighty matters on his mind. The day before in Brussels at
the meeting of the Nine Powers, designed to refashion the plans for
German rearmament after the collapse of E.D.C., Eden promised
to keep British forces in Germany until the end of the century.
What did Churchill think of Anthony's pledge? 'It can be cancelled
at any time,' he went on with a mischievous smile. 'It does not
mean anything. All words. Of course I shall not say that,' he added
hastily.[1]

The great debate on German rearmament was finally transferred
to the House of Commons. Anthony Eden's solemn and expensive
pledge was presented for ratification. Mendès-France had been
forced to submit, but he still hoped, along with Bevan, that a fresh
conference with the Russians would be sought before the actual
rearmament was started. But indeed Dulles and Churchill and
Eden and Adenauer had exerted such pressures that the greatest
Frenchman of the epoch was soon to be forced out of office. The
Parliamentary Labour Party prepared for the final debate with some
exaggeratedly grotesque precautions. On the final vote, the Party
would abstain, a decision which would allow the Party to stay
united and the treaties to go through unopposed. But seven brave
spirits disobeyed the Whip and had it withdrawn from them at
another gruesome Party meeting in Westminster Hall. Bevan and
his closest Bevanite associates had decided not to follow the rebellious seven in disobeying the Party decree, since it was made clear
by the issue of a more doom-laden Whip than any issued in that
Whip-ridden Parliament that a vote against the Party meeting decision would have led to mass expulsions, to the final showdown
which the Deakinites were sternly advocating. Bevan's own speech
in the rearmament debate was one of his rare flops; he allowed

[1] *Churchill* by Lord Moran, p. 602.

himself to be led astray by interruptions into byways and never returned to the main road. He hated arguments which were exhausted and liked to look instead for fresh formulations.

But he had had another chance to learn what in fact he never learnt: how a phrase can linger in the political air longer than an argument. Such a phrase-monger as himself should have understood but, partly because so many of his were poured forth unpremeditatedly, he never did. The phrase 'desiccated calculating machine' was thereafter perpetually invoked as a fresh proof of his personal malice, but he always protested that he never intended to apply it to anybody specifically. He intended only to describe the composite figure which the bureaucratic processes of selection or election in the Labour Party would soon decree as the unalterable mould. Certainly he had no individual target in mind that night at Scarborough. 'Of course I wasn't referring to Hugh Gaitskell,' he himself said. 'For one thing Hugh is not desiccated – he's highly emotional. And (with a twinkle) you could hardly call him a calculating machine – because he was three hundred millions out!'[1]

[1] On 28 April 1959, Robin Day had a television interview with Bevan, in which he put to him the question: 'Do you still regard Mr Gaitskell as a desiccated calculating machine?' Bevan replied: 'I never called him that. I was applying my words to the synthetic figure, but the press took it up and it's never possible to catch up a canard like that, as you know.' After the interview was over, however, Day pressed the matter further, and Bevan replied with the words quoted above. He had often expressed the same view privately, if not so effectively.

After Bevan's death, Gaitskell, in a letter to Jennie Lee, said that he had looked up the reference and realized Bevan was *not* making a personal attack upon him.

12

THE ARCTIC VOLCANO

January 1955 – April 1955

Dullness is so much stronger than genius, because there is so much more of it, and it is better organized and more naturally cohesive inter se. So the Arctic volcano can do nothing against Arctic ice.—SAMUEL BUTLER

IN JANUARY 1955, on the first day of Parliament's recall after the Christmas recess, Bevan sought a private meeting with Attlee in his room at the House of Commons. It was not 'a peace mission', although there were undertones of appeasement. Some time in the year ahead, a general election was probable, and both men were concerned about the angry temper which had now become customary in the Parliamentary Party, and both could sense fresh dangers ahead. Throughout the autumn, ever since Scarborough, one event after another had increased the acrimony. Not merely had the Party had to endure the climax of the German rearmament debate and its aftermath of the withdrawal of the Whip from the seven offenders against Party meeting discipline; a more esoteric argument followed about how abject – or how cunning – the conscienceless leading Bevanites, headed by Bevan himself, had been in not following the example of the brave seven; how dare they cheat their executioners! Outside Parliament a different argument had contributed to the venom within. Forty thousand London dockers had come out on strike, led by the leaders of the diminutive National Association of Stevedores and Dockers, the so-called Blue Union, although clearly backing for the strike spread wide among the rest of the dockers, mostly members of the Transport and General Workers' Union. Arthur Deakin denounced the strike as Communist-inspired, although Dickie Barrett, general secretary of the Blue Union and a Roman Catholic, was the most notorious *non*-Communist east of Tower Bridge, whereupon *Tribune* denounced the Deakin outburst as 'A Slander on the Dockers', and the fat was in the fire, sizzling for weeks on end in exchanges between the General Council of the T.U.C., the National Executive of the Party and the three members of *Tribune*'s editorial board, who at that time happened to be Jennie Lee, J. P. W. Mallalieu and myself. Bevan himself was not directly implicated, which was probably why the outraged Deakinites did not move for the immediate expulsion of the three Tribunites, but he was as angered as any by the extraordinary demand which the National Executive put to them: *viz.*, 'How do you reconcile your attack on the leadership of the Transport and General Workers' Union with your membership of the Party?' The question smelt more of some ancient *auto-da-fé* than of a modern democracy.[1] During the dispute Bevan had taken the opportunity to warn Attlee that if the three were expelled, he would have to be expelled too. But he had not had so much success in persuading the other Bevanite members of the Executive, particularly Crossman and Wilson, to contemplate the same course. They did not relish the new controversy. 'Bevanism cannot do without Bevan,' said Wilson, 'but it could do without *Tribune*.'[2]

However, Bevan, at the meeting he sought with Attlee in Janu-

---

[1] *Tribune*'s reply to this inquiry ran to some 6,000 words and extended the debate from a discussion of the dock strike to the principles of free speech within the Party. It pointed out that the origin of the Transport and General Workers' Union itself was a revolt led by Ben Tillett, Tom Mann and others against an older trade union leadership which had become inadequate to meet the needs of a new age. 'Trade union leaders are not a special breed of humanity, always to be shielded from the rough breezes of democracy, rare birds to be protected by special game laws. They are there partly to be shot at – like all other elected persons who must run the risks of public life if they aspire to hold the prizes and the power.' This plea may sound strangely in ears attuned to the persistent newspaper vilification of men like Jack Jones or Hugh Scanlon, or, before them, of Frank Cousins. It takes a feat of the imagination to recall that a former general secretary of the Transport Union was the darling of the Tory press and the Labour leaders.

[2] Crossman diaries.

ary, looked more to the future; it was usually his way to see how deadlocks could be circumvented by unexpected detours, and the main features on the international landscape provided him with his opportunity. Renewed dangers appeared in the Far East, arising from the Chinese-American conflict over the off-shore islands of Quemoy and Matsu and the unqualified backing the United States gave to Chiang Kai-shek on Formosa. In Europe new, if still vague, proposals seemed to be forthcoming from the Soviet Union about a further approach to the German question. Above all, the world was starting to learn and to argue, freshly almost month by month, about the significance of the hydrogen bomb, and in Britain the interest was suddenly quickened by the revelation that this vulnerable island was engaged in manufacturing the bomb and was committed to the nuclear strategy. Imagination was still numbed by the immensity and complexity of the subject and few could claim that they did more at that first glance than see through a glass darkly. Bevan's proposition to Attlee was that these various strands could be gathered together to make possible the seizure of the initiative on the parliamentary and indeed the international stage. He recalled the resolution on the H-bomb and the need for a summit meeting of the great powers which Attlee himself had moved so impressively the year before, on 5 April 1954, and he recalled further that in the November debate on German rearmament Attlee had agreed that new talks with the Soviet leaders need not await the ratification of the treaties. Why could the Labour Party not unite in censuring the Government for failing to execute the 1954 resolution which the House had in fact carried unanimously and in demanding its implementation? It was a fair proposal, but the answer was deferred and dusty. Not so much Attlee but rather his Shadow Cabinet colleagues, headed by Morrison and Gaitskell, saw the Bevan proposal as yet another device to reopen the interminable German rearmament debate; at all costs he must be thwarted.

So Bevan turned, as the constitutional proprieties required him to do, to the Party meeting, and international events again strengthened his determination. Early in February came the news from France that the Mendès-France Government had fallen, and from Russia that Malenkov had been replaced by Bulganin as Soviet Premier; and the Formosa-Quemoy-Matsu crisis looked more menacing than ever. At the Party meeting on 10 February, Bevan moved a resolution reaffirming the Party leader's statement of November and instructing the Shadow Cabinet to place a resolution on the House of Commons Order Paper demanding that progress towards the high-level talks should be initiated forthwith. But since the proposition came from Bevan, rather than the Shadow Cabinet, it was rejected by 93 votes to 70; and thus the Parliamentary Party came near to renouncing itself. However, many who were certainly not Bevanites felt it absurd and churlish to reject a highly sensible proposition just because Bevan had moved it, and more than a hundred members of the Party, headed by John Strachey, Michael Stewart and Kenneth Robinson as well as Aneurin Bevan, Richard Crossman and myself, signed the resolution which he then placed on the Commons Order Paper condemning the failure of the Government to act on the April 1954 resolution 'as a contempt for the decision of the House of Commons' and 'a conspicuous failure to appreciate the gravity of the crisis in the affairs of mankind'. Two days later, while his own front bench sat glumly silent, he asked the Leader of the House when time would be allowed to debate the motion, inferring strongly enough that if the opportunity was not afforded it would have to be seized – from Bevan, the master of parliamentary procedure, no idle threat. The incident raised the internal Party temperature several degrees; was this not yet another attempt by Bevan to wrest the sceptre from Attlee? Moreover, that same afternoon the Government published its Defence White Paper indicating its decision to proceed with the manufacture of a British H-bomb. A week later the Parliamentary Labour Party held two meetings to grapple with the situation. At the one in the morning a general amendment for the defence debate was agreed and a reference to nuclear weapons was spatchcocked into the preamble. But at the evening meeting serious business was done. Bevan was formally rebuked by 132 votes to 72, although not even the most pedantic Party constitutionalist could define the offence. He had observed all the rules; it made his conduct the more insupportable. He offered to withdraw his resolution, if the Party would take it over, but Morrison pressed for the vote.

However, this initiative for high-level talks and its dissipation in the bogs and sands of internal Party manœuvre was only one aspect of the bitter arguments of those days. What *was* Bevan's view about the British manufacture of the hydrogen bomb and the newly expressed reliance of Britain on the nuclear strategy? Every Socialist could agree with his insistence on the paramount task of securing international détente and disarmament – Attlee, Morrison and Gaitskell all concurred when Bevan was not actually advocating it. Most people could agree also about the horrors of H-bomb tests, with their recently-revealed capacity to poison unborn generations; that made the need for high-level agreements the more imperative. All might dream of these most desirable objectives, but what was to be regarded as an acceptable defence policy in the meantime? How could reputable political leaders dodge that question? How could it be avoided when the House of Commons was within weeks of facing the first defence debate since the American explosions in the Pacific, since the news of the first Soviet explosions, since the revelation that Britain was following the same path and was interlinked with the same fate? Week by week the topic appeared high on the agenda of the Bevanite debates every Tuesday at Crossman's house, with Crossman taking the lead, until one week he produced a paper written by himself and George Wigg (not a member of the circle, but at that stage Crossman's aide-de-camp), setting out the case for accepting the reality of the nuclear deterrent and for recognizing thereafter how, once it was accepted, Socialists could make the case overwhelming for a big reduction in the arms programme and the abolition of conscription; alternatively, if the nuclear deterrent was to be jettisoned, how could the demand for more expenditure on conventional arms and longer conscription be resisted? Moreover, if the H-bomb was to be renounced, N.A.T.O. would have to be renounced with it, and would not such a step require, therefore, the acceptance of a full policy of neutrality? The paper and its implications provoked exhilarating, lacerating argument, but enough general interest and even assent to encourage Crossman and Wigg to publish it in the *New Statesman* under their own names. There it exploded with shattering reverberations, and all the pacifist or near-pacifist hackles of the Party and plenty of others besides were raised by so realistic a discussion of so horrifying subject. Indeed the Crossman–Wigg thesis was stated with

15*

such fierce assertiveness that neither of them was to remain wedded to that formulation in years to come. But, to be fair, no one, Right, Left or especially Centre, had a sure intellectual escape from the new dilemmas – no one except the out-and-out pacifists, and for them the questions were always easy since the bomb and the bow and arrow posed the same moral problem. But, in the first weeks and months of the H-bomb age, the rest of mankind, including the Bevanites, lurched forward from one insecure theoretical foothold to another, and on Wednesday 2 March the Bevanite leaders stumbled, still arguing, from a special recalled lunch in Crossman's house to the House of Commons, having reached no common view of their own and having agreed on no tactic to deal with the niceties of the defence debate. It was not, as some observers were soon to remark, the ever-headstrong Bevan who had dismayed even his closest political friends; it was the bomb itself. And Bevan had to speak in the debate and attempt to resolve a confusion in the public mind fully shared by his closest followers.

Churchill in opening the debate was sombre, eloquent and platitudinous ('the mediocrity of his thinking,' said Bevan later, 'is concealed by the majesty of his language'). John Strachey, on the second day, moved the official Opposition amendment which, in criticizing the competence of the Government, contained the indigestible preamble: 'While recognizing that thermonuclear weapons have effected a revolution in the character of warfare, and that until effective world disarmament has been achieved it is necessary as a deterrent to aggression to rely on the threat of using thermonuclear weapons . . .'[1] For many that was the hard core of the debate and upon it the two front benches were at one, always a danger signal. The real dispute, as so often, was *within* the Parties, and when Bevan rose to speak, the whole place crowded in to hear him,

[1] It may be asked why this resolution had not provoked a storm at the Party meeting at which it was moved and the answer is that it was moved, with no prior notice, at an ill-attended meeting which was expected to be asked solely to approve an amendment containing the inoffensive criticism of the Government. Even so, there should have been an outcry, but there wasn't. The hugger-mugger manner in which the amendment was pushed through is no doubt the reason why the Shadow Cabinet did not emphasize the point about the violation of a majority decision in the subsequent controversy.

all except the members of the Shadow Cabinet who at that moment were engaged in their weekly meeting; an unfortunate absence, since, contrary to anticipation and the suggestion implicit in subsequent analyses, three-quarters of Bevan's speech was devoted to an argument with Churchill on precisely the lines he had been recommending to Attlee since January. Everyone in his senses, he said, agreed that international agreement was the only final way to solve the problem: 'what we want to know is, when do the negotiations start? . . . We cannot discuss this White Paper as though what we are really doing is providing the instrument of policy alone – because, when the instrument which we are proposing to create is absolute, policy is intrinsically the instrument itself. We are discussing policy when we are discussing the hydrogen bomb. We are no longer discussing an instrument alone because, the weapon being absolute, it is also policy . . . Neither the scientists nor the military men have an answer to the problem of the world. The scientists have spoken. We have had enough science. It is now time to have a little more wisdom.' So why was the world waiting for the negotiations? At one moment Churchill had argued that the West must negotiate from strength, at the next that the Russians had not yet got the H-bomb effectively or the means to deliver it, and that power therefore rested with the West. So why were notes inviting negotiations not being sent from us to them, instead of the other way round? 'We are all displaying the posture of little men before big events.' Or could it be that Churchill wanted to meet the Russians but that the United States would not let him – 'a sombre thing to say, and a wicked thing to believe – that we have now reached the situation where Great Britain can, in a few short years, run the risk of the extinction of its civilization, and we cannot reach the potential enemy in an attempt to arrive at an accommodation with him because we are at the mercy of the United States'.

At which, the House, in a matter of seconds, found itself thrust into the most extraordinary last scene of Churchill's parliamentary career. The old man hauled himself up to the despatch box to make an intervention far more telling than his oration of the day before. No, it was wrong, he said, to talk of United States dictation. It was true that he had dearly wanted a top-level conference soon after

Malenkov took power, and had been ready to go to see Eisenhower to persuade the Americans. But then – and this was the first hint that the House or the country had had of the fact and it was emphasized when he displayed his left side with a sweep of the hand – 'I was struck down by a very sudden illness which paralysed me completely, physically'. Thereafter, it had not been possible to persuade Eisenhower to 'join the process'. But he had tried again. The Soviet Government's campaign against the ratification of E.D.C. had prevented the next moves, but the attempt to secure the high-level talks could be renewed. And thus, with apologies for the exceptional length of the intervention in Bevan's speech and with bows to all sides of the House and amid sympathetic murmurs, he resumed his seat. These, as it happened, were to be the last words spoken by Churchill in a major debate in the House of Commons, and the irony is that they amounted to a surrender, albeit conditional, to Bevan on the supreme issue of the time. It was the last parliamentary duel in the long combat between them which had started twenty-six years before when a brazen and impromptu maiden speaker dared to suggest that he had discovered the secret of Churchill's 'chameleon-like character in politics'; it was due to his 'temperamental disabilities which enabled him to fill all roles with such exceeding facility'.[1]

On this last occasion, Bevan garnered his victory gracefully. Normally he would have pounced, but he was content to underline that Churchill had indeed confirmed the charge that the Americans

[1] Volume I, p. 105. One other association between them which had occurred a few months earlier might be construed as Bevan's revenge for a parliamentary lifetime of insults were it not for the fact that the injury it did to Churchill was quite unintended by Bevan. When the House of Commons set up a committee to propose some all-Party method of honouring Churchill on his 80th birthday, it was Jennie Lee who proposed that a most appropriate course would be to arrange for Graham Sutherland to paint his portrait, and the committee acclaimed this happy suggestion. But Churchill could not abide the finished portrait. He managed to mute his fury on the day of the unveiling, but later and in private, according to Lord Moran, he described it as 'filthy' and 'malignant' and apparently arranged that the masterpiece should be concealed in some impenetrable cellar, where, I believe, it still rests today. It is not recorded that Churchill ever discovered that the artist had been selected on Jennie Lee's suggestion, or if he did, what he said.

had opposed his policy, and the Soviet opposition to E.D.C., since it had been a factor present throughout, afforded him no excuse. Churchill had offered trivial reasons for opposing such great projects.[1] 'We are not dealing with the possibilities of German rearmament. We are dealing with the preservation of the human race.' The case for the high-level talks, as stated in the now famous April Resolution of 1954, was reaffirmed, clinched indeed by Churchill himself.

However, the Bevan–Churchill exchange, enough to fill one parliamentary afternoon, was only the prologue. For Bevan turned to the specific commitments of the Defence White Paper and their implications for the Labour Party. According to the White Paper, aggression would be met by overwhelming nuclear retaliation and that was considered to be the surest guarantee that the aggression would never take place. Only by the use of nuclear weapons could the Western Powers counter the massive preponderance of the Soviet power in Europe. But did the words mean what they really said – that a conventional attack would draw a nuclear response, that the West would be the first to resort to the nuclear weapons which would infallibly bring general annihilation? Bevan put the question to the Government but he did not omit to put it also to his own front bench whose amendment with its clause about the necessity for the deterrent might carry the same inference. 'I want my right hon. Friends the leaders of the Opposition to answer me,' he insisted. 'Do they mean by that language what the Government mean by the White Paper? Do they mean that nuclear weapons will be used with the support of the British Labour movement against any sort of aggression? I want to know the answer. If my right hon. Friend, the Leader of the Opposition, says that that is the interpretation of that amendment, then I do not propose to vote for it this evening.' And then with the challenge delivered and the menace of Britain's commitment further underlined by quotations

[1] In an article in *Tribune*, two weeks later (11 March) Bevan was more severe: 'Let's not forget that what is under discussion is no less important than the future of the human race now threatened by the madness of nuclear weapons. Compared with the scale of the threat, the illness of one statesman, however regrettable it may be, is so trivial as to amount to imbecility. In venturing to put it forward seriously Sir Winston discloses a vanity so bottomless as to unfit him for his high office.'

from the experts, he knit the two sections of his argument together, and launched his final assault, part passion, part scorn, part mockery:

What policies are the Government developing to save us and the world? So far we have had none. All that the right hon. Gentleman has said is that he is postponing a discussion with the Soviet leaders in order to be able to get a German army, which now everybody knows is of no use . . . What is the German army to do? What will any of the armies do? What have they to do with it? All the generals are telling us that the armies will be no use. It is true to say that if such a war broke out the armies would be farther away from each other at the end of the war than at the beginning of it, because they would all have to march away from the radioactive centres they would create. They cannot march *into* the radioactive centres. So if you want to be safe, let us join the Army! The nation is watching and we want to know what policy the Government propose to pursue. The right hon. Gentleman said yesterday 'that he would meet the Soviet leaders and talk tough and then have supper'. The last supper, I presume. Because if those Soviet leaders can talk tough now, and he can talk tough, they can talk tougher then. If he meets them and they will not give in, what does he do? Does he pout and say that he is going to commit suicide? That is precisely where we have got. We have either to agree with our enemy or commit suicide. That is what we have come to. The world has already reached the point where either international difficulties are negotiated upon, or else mankind gives up. That is the point of no return. That is it. It is no use hon. Members arguing now that the situation is going to change. It will be no different – except worse; because the deterrents in the hands of the Soviet Union will be greater than they are now. If, therefore, we are to negotiate then, why not negotiate now? Why not find out if we can? That is the situation in which mankind is. It does not require experts to understand it. We do not require scientists to tell us. We do not need to employ expensive soldiers to advise us. They are out of date, they are outmoded; they are no longer of value. We are spending millions and millions of pounds on foolishness. The issue is simply this. Are we to conduct a peace policy or a war policy? We could do it. We could meet the Soviet representatives at once. I therefore beg the Government to measure up to the magnitude of this problem. Let the Prime Minister do deeds to match his great words; not attempt to delude the country by the majesty of his language but inspire it by the dedication of his behaviour. That is what we want from him. We want from my right hon. Friends the leaders of the Opposition an assurance that the language of their amendment, moved on our behalf, does not align the Labour movement behind that recklessness; because if we cannot have the lead from *them*, let us give the lead ourselves.

And those last words were delivered with some waving of the arms; every inflection and movement were to count in the subsequent days. 'That recklessness' signified the whole mixture of diplomatic immobility and nuclear dependence. 'No lead from them' was indicated by a sweeping of the hand along the Treasury bench, alighting on the half-noble, half-pathetic figure of Churchill. 'Let us give that lead ourselves' embraced his own Party which he sought to enlist, including the still absent front bench. That is what some of his audience heard and saw, but in the House of Commons others have their backs turned to a speaker from the back-benches, and *Hansard* offers no official report on the combined effect of accent and gesture. Within minutes, along the Westminster corridors, the whole speech, with the menacing challenge about the vote in the middle and the fierce tone of the peroration, had placed upon it a more sinister construction. Was not the whole affair an onslaught on Attlee rather than Churchill? And why should Attlee suffer such hectoring? How many abstainers would keep out of the lobbies on the Party's amendment? And, on second thoughts, could not those gestures mean that when he talked of no lead from *them*, that was just another stab at his own front bench and that, when he talked of *ourselves*, he was rallying his Bevanite claque and reviving afresh the old spectre of a party within a party? Throughout that evening, from 6.19 p.m. when Bevan resumed his seat to loud but apprehensive cheers on the back benches all round him, until 8.40 when Attlee rose to reply, the tension mounted.

How could the crisis be relieved? How would Bevan be answered?
How many *votes* might he muster? That is always the question.
But then, incredibly, as the minutes passed, it appeared that Attlee
intended to attempt no answer whatever. He ranged over the
generalities and the detail of the White Paper, but had little enough
to say about Churchill's disclosures of the afternoon, and nothing
at all about Bevan. It was either a determination to avoid the question or a calculated insult. Bevan waited until the very last available
moment, indeed when Attlee had actually sat down, and then interrupted as coldly as his leader: 'There is a matter on which hon.
Members on this side of the House would like to have some clarification. The amendment which has been moved by the Opposition speaks about the deterrent effect upon aggression of the threat
of using thermonuclear weapons. Paragraph 19 of the White Paper
says that we must rely upon this, and that "The knowledge that
aggression will be met by overwhelming nuclear retaliation is the
surest guarantee that it will not take place". It does not say
"nuclear aggression". but merely "aggression" of any sort. In the
meantime General Gruenther[1] has said that he has no choice but to
use atomic weapons, whether or not the enemy does so. What we
want to know is whether the use of the words to which I have
referred in our amendment associates us with the statement that
we should use thermonuclear weapons in circumstances of hostilities, although they were not used against us.' To which Attlee
replied: 'My right hon. Friend is asking me that question. I am
using this in the most general terms. I am not referring to anything
in the White Paper, but to the general thesis, with which I think
my right hon. Friend agrees, that deterrents, by the possession of
thermonuclear weapons, are the best way of preventing another
war.' To which Bevan was heard to mutter 'That's no answer,
that's no answer'. But that was all he was to get.

When the Labour Party's amendment was called at 10 p.m. that
Wednesday night Bevan stayed firmly in his seat and abstained
from voting and, as it was later discovered, sixty-two other Labour
M.P.s had followed his example. Some speculation was caused by
the fact that several leading Bevanites – Harold Wilson, Dick

[1] Bevan had quoted the full paragraph from General Gruenther,
Supreme Commander in Europe, earlier in his speech.

Crossman, John Freeman, Stephen Swingler, Leslie Hale and Hugh Delargy[1] – had voted with the Party majority, and there was some happy talk of 'a split within a split', but no one inside or outside the House of Commons doubted the dimensions of the new Party crisis. A special Party meeting was summoned the following Wednesday at which it was confidently prophesied that Bevan's expulsion would be called for, and at the weekend several backers of the official party line started to set the scene. 'We must clear up once and for all this question of the leadership of the Party,' said George Brown at Belper: 'we have seen the policy and Mr Attlee's leadership on it publicly repudiated in the most humiliating and damaging way by a man who seems determined never to accept a majority decision unless he makes it by himself. It is the denial of the essential basis of a democratic political society. If the Party tolerates this behaviour any longer it will connive at its own destruction.' And that same cry was taken up by many other ultra-loyalists, headed by Sir Hartley Shawcross. But when the Shadow Cabinet found itself locked in conclave on Monday night for two and a half hours it was by no means so clear that the expulsionists would carry the day. Indeed the first outcome of that confabulation which leaked to the outer world had its comic aspect; it was a decision to place a motion on the Commons Order Paper in the names of Attlee, Morrison, Noel-Baker and the Party officially, calling on the Government to seek high-level talks on the hydrogen bomb with the Governments of the United States and the Soviet Union – not precisely the motion Bevan had argued for since January but near

[1] Bevan had no more devoted follower than Hugh Delargy, and his vote on this occasion was proof of the general confusion. It also gave rise to a parody of an old American trade union song then popular in Bevanite circles:

> *Who will take care of you*
> *How'll you get by*
> *When you're too old to work*
> *And too young to die?*

After Delargy's temporary defection one parody ran:

> *Who will take care of you*
> *How'll you get by*
> *When you're too Left for Herbert*
> *And too Right for Nye?*

enough. ('Not only,' said one Tory commentator, 'do they throw him out into the snow, but they steal his trousers as well.') Some members of the 'Keep Calm' group professed to see here a concession to their efforts to still the weekend panic, but the reprieve was short-lived. The real decision had been kept secret only to afford time for Bevan to be informed. Prolonged discussion at the Shadow Cabinet had been inevitable since the issue could not be so easily resolved as the ultra-loyalists might suppose. For Bevan had not broken any of the Party's elaborate Standing Orders, unless it was also held that all the sixty-two abstainers had broken the rules too, and was a third of the party to be expelled along with him? Moreover, he had, most unhelpfully, not even offended against the amorphous edict forbidding personal attack. His words to Attlee, twist them as they might, could not be construed in that sense. The crime lay in his general purpose, demeanour and style, his undeclared intentions and maybe the strength of his following. Clearly action against him alone had its hazards too. But at last the Shadow Cabinet had staked all. By 9 votes to 4,[1] against the advice but not the vote of a hesitant Attlee but on the advocacy of Edith Summerskill, Frank Soskice, Chuter Ede and Herbert Morrison with Hugh Gaitskell and Jim Callaghan bringing up a powerful rearguard, it was decided to recommend to the Party meeting the withdrawal of the Whip from Bevan, and the clear inference followed that, once the matter was referred to the National Executive, he would be expelled from the Party altogether. The deed was to have been done that very week, but at the weekend Bevan had been struck down by flu. The great or fatal day had to be postponed for another week, and every other issue in British politics, even the brooding menace of the H-bomb now acknowledged in an official Labour Party resolution on the Order Paper, seemed suspended while the world awaited Bevan's execution. Osbert Lancaster's fav-

---

[1] Members of that Shadow Cabinet were as follows; Clement Attlee, Herbert Morrison, William Whiteley (Chief Whip), Hugh Gaitskell, Jim Griffiths, Sir Frank Soskice, Hugh Dalton, Edith Summerskill, Alfred Robens, Emanuel Shinwell, Philip Noel-Baker, Chuter Ede, James Callaghan, Glenvil Hall, Harold Wilson and three Labour peers, Earl Jowitt, Lord Shepherd and Lord Henderson. The four voting against the withdrawal of the Whip were: Wilson, Robens, Dalton and Griffiths. The three peers did not vote.

ourite peer, taking his wife into the Peers' Gallery in the Commons to gaze down on an entirely empty Chamber, expressed the mood: 'I'm afraid, darling, we've chosen rather a bad day – Winston in bed, Nye in bed, and most of the Opposition out looking for a nice comfortable fence!'

Kindly innuendoes were dropped in some quarters that Bevan's illness was 'diplomatic', but he was in fact propped up in bed and bombarded with advice from all sides. Statesmanlike rebukes for his conduct were administered by such widely-ranged wellwishers of the Labour Party as *The Times* and the *Daily Telegraph* and a special touch of virulence in the attack was noticeable in the *Manchester Guardian* and the *Daily Mirror*. *The Times* and the *Mirror* joined in the hint – made now for the first time, perhaps, except in the *obiter dicta* of Arthur Deakin – that the position of Attlee himself, 'the Archbishop of Compromise', might be involved if he drew back now from prosecuting the attack to its conclusion; only thus could he remove the stain of vacillation and weakness. Bevan himself, after receiving a bedside mission composed of Richard Crossman, Barbara Castle and Tony Greenwood, issued a statement insisting that his differences with Attlee were concerned with policy: 'What I have said or done is not a challenge to the personal authority of Mr Attlee as leader of the Party.' But scarcely a newspaper in the land would take that statement at its face value or speak a word in his favour. However the illness probably did assist. Thanks to the delay there was time for a mighty upsurge of protest to spread throughout the Labour movement. Party after party and union branch after union branch passed emergency resolutions calling on M.P.s to stop the expulsion. 'We understand,' said the *New Statesman*, 'that in the deliberations of the Shadow Cabinet Mr Attlee himself, as well as others, sought to dissuade his colleagues from a decision which would make electoral defeat a near certainty and might imperil the very life of the Labour Party . . . Those who think to restore the Labour Party to health by expelling Mr Bevan display astonishing ignorance of its rank-and-file, and unconsciously reveal the arrogance of which they so often accuse him. Do they seriously believe that once Mr Bevan is outside the Party, Butskellism will be joyfully accepted as a New Look substitute for Socialism?' But some did believe exactly that, and were prepared to say so. One was Arthur Deakin, another was Tom Williamson, and a third was Hugh Gaitskell who spoke out that weekend with a Stalybridgean bluntness and boldness which neither Deakin nor the *Daily Mirror* could surpass – except that the *Mirror* chose that delicate moment to condemn the doodling headmaster no less than the impossible, rebellious pupil. 'When Labour M.P.s meet on Wednesday,' said Gaitskell at Doncaster, 'they will not be concerned with questions of policy, but with standards of loyalty. In the House of Commons, Mr Attlee was subjected to a hostile interrogation in language which might have come from the leader of another party rather than from one of his own loyal supporters. There was even an implied threat that, if his answers were unsatisfactory, another lead would have to be provided. I do not see how this sort of thing can possibly be regarded as anything else but a direct challenge to the elected leader of our Party and therefore an affront to the Party which elected him.'

Oddly the man least affronted, seemingly, was Attlee himself. At the Shadow Cabinet meeting on the subject he had muttered his opposition to any move to expel. When the suggestion was made that the issue must be one of confidence, he demurred. When the pressures from different sides increased, he on one occasion snapped at Gaitskell: 'You wanted to expel him, I didn't. I was against it from the first, but you insisted, and now look at the mess we're in.' And on the eve of the Party meeting, when he was told that the National Executive incited by the Deakinites were eager to finish the job, he commented, 'Oh well, we'll have to deal with that if we come to it. I didn't want it to get into the hands of those people on the Executive and that's why I was against withdrawing the Whip, but the rest of them decided otherwise and now we'll have to do what we can to clear up the mess.'[1]

[1] This quotation, like some others noted, is taken from Leslie Hunter's book, *The Road to Brighton Pier* (Arthur Barker, 1959), p. 99. Despite its lack of cited authorities and its possibly too breezy reporting of conversations, it is in fact an indispensable source book for the period. The book's prejudices are anti-Bevan, anti-Attlee and pro-Morrison, and that may be taken into account. But Leslie Hunter was a qualified journalist; he had access to a background available to nobody else, and where his conversations are first-hand, as here, and not based on hearsay, as in most of his quotations from Bevan, they supply valuable evidence.

So – with the curious intrusion two days before of a debate in the
House itself on an official Labour Party motion demanding high-
level talks about the bomb – the Parliamentary Labour Party
assembled in Committee Room 14 on 16 March 1955. Only one
good sign could be detected by the augurers: at least the final rites
were not to be held in Westminster Hall. Over the years Bevan had
grown to detest appearances at the Party meeting beyond all other
tribulations and most of his friends came to share his touchiness
and tension, thereby adding to the anguish of the hours before.
Some of them might sometimes diffidently plead with him to use
the softness and the beguiling humour which he could summon at
will in most other assemblies, but it was idle and probably ill-
advised.[1] He seemed to believe that there was nothing to be done
with the Party meeting in one of its pathological spasms but to take
it by the scruff of the neck and shake till it screamed for mercy.
Certainly the increasing ill-temper of the series of meetings prior to
this one was not calculated to encourage a burst of tolerance. But
the strong swelling tide of opinion in Bevan's favour in the movement in the country and the assertion of moderate opinion in the
Parliamentary Party might put him on his best behaviour, or so
some of us achingly prayed as we squeezed into the execution yard.
But then, lo and behold, after a few minutes the prospective corpse
was on his feet unleashing an unlimited indictment against judge,
jury, prosecuting counsel, hangman, hatchetmen, and every other
conceivable opponent in sight or out of it. Attlee had opened the
meeting and moved the Shadow Cabinet's resolution calling for the
withdrawal of the Whip in his most clipped and dry manner. First
he made it clear that there would not be – as some hopeful Bevanites, looking round for a spanner to throw in the works, had suggested – a publication of how members voted at the meeting; that
would be quite contrary to custom. Next he made it clear that the

[1] On the night before the terrible day, a few of us (Jennie, Tom Driberg,
Hugh Delargy, my wife and myself) assembled to do what he loved to do –
to have a good dinner. We went to the Ivy where Nye and I had long
been friendly with the proprietor, Abel, a genial Italian with a good anti-
Fascist record. Next day a report of the scene appeared in William Hickey's
column in the *Express* where it was reported by the onlooker, accurately,
that Delargy was doing most of the talking. 'Delargy's definition of a
monologuist,' said Nye: 'Someone who interrrupts him.'

latest offence committed by Bevan in the debate was not the only one on the charge sheet; then he peremptorily recited the others. Next, he reminded the meeting how the Liberal Party had torn itself to pieces and finally he insisted: 'We have got to stop this.' And then he sat down like a man who believed the conclusion was foregone, and such was overwhelmingly the general belief. Attlee had not affirmed in so many words that the issue was one of confidence, that the Shadow Cabinet would all resign if the vote went against them. But that had been the formidable impression spread through the lobbies the night before; and that was the inference in Attlee's speech and his strongest card.

Bevan himself believed that the decision was pre-ordained, which was possibly another reason recommending to him the tactic of frontal counter-attack. Anyhow, no doubt was possible about his temper, despite the husky voice still recovering from the flu. Clem Attlee, he started, should have been the last man to move a resolution for his expulsion, for on notable if unpublicized occasions he (Bevan) had refused to join conspiracies against Attlee sponsored by some of his own chief accusers now. Let Attlee look along the platform and he would see some of the culprits, and he let his eye alight on George Brown who had been one of the loudest voices clamouring for expulsion in the last few days but who had led the anti-Attlee conspiracy in 1947. Indeed, a fresh conspiracy to remove Attlee from the leadership was afoot at that precise moment; anyone who doubted it had only to read the *Daily Mirror* of the day before.[1] But he (Bevan) had never been a party to any scheme to remove Attlee and if pursuit of his own ambition and the leadership was what he was after, he would surely have been an ass to go about it the way he had done; leaders climbed to the top on less rickety ladders. But let him turn to the indictment Attlee had made. It was altogether a strange trial; for until that precise moment he had not known what were the charges which would be levelled against him and now that he had heard them it was evident that they involved no exact breach of any Party rule, no offence against the Standing Orders readopted in 1952. If he had so offended

---

[1] See Chapter 5, p. 225. Of course, Bevan did not know at the time that George Brown was on the payroll of the *Daily Mirror*. See his book, *In My Way* (Gollancz), p. 61.

the point would not have been overlooked; but the awkward fact
was, he had not. However, judgment had been pronounced before
the trial began – by Gaitskell, for one, in his speech at Doncaster;
he had given his interpretation of what happened in the defence
debate, alleging that he (Bevan) had concluded his speech with a
threat to Attlee, although that was the inference drawn by only one
paper – Gaitskell 'must have known it was a lie'.[1] But Gaitskell
only echoed what had been said by others who had also pronounced judgment before the trial – by Arthur Deakin and Tom
Williamson. 'They have given their orders. They await the decision.' And they seemed to care nothing for Parliament and its
proceedings and pressures, for the arguments about policy, about
health charges, or German rearmament, or the hydrogen bomb
which had been dominant in his mind in all these disputes. *There*
was the real conspiracy, behind the backs of the Party and the
movement in the country, and it was one which now took the form
of trying to drive him out of political life altogether – 'Very well, I
am fifty-seven years of age. I have devoted myself exclusively to
this Party for forty-five years. My fundamental loyalties are with
this Party. Whatever you do now, I am not going out to form a new
party. But nothing can deny my right and the right of others to
help shape the future of the Party and make it the instrument we
want it to be.' Or that, since no verbatim reports of Party meetings
were kept, is the nearest approximation which can be pieced together of his final appeal. He had, as Attlee said at the end, shown
no evidence of regret for past conduct and offered no promise of
future loyalty. He had thrown the accusation back into the teeth
of his accusers. It was a defiant speech, but it was also something
else; he had also shown – displayed more than stated – to his fellow
members of the Labour movement that he was bone of their bone
and flesh of their flesh, and how to cut him out of their living body
might be an act of surgery beyond the Parliamentary Party's contrivance. And to illustrate the point came one ineffable moment in
the debate that followed. For the most part, after Bevan, it went
according to expectations. Anxious or eager supporters of the platform asked whether indeed the vote would constitute a vote of

[1] Gaitskell, it seems, had not troubled to check what happened. The
report in the *Daily Herald* – no friend of Bevan – is conclusive.

confidence, and the muffled answer seemed to be 'Yes'. Fred Lee proposed and Maurice Edelman seconded a moderate amendment designed to substitute censure in place of withdrawal of the Whip. George Brown anticipated, none too candidly, the section of his memoirs dealing with 1947. Percy Collick, whose voice was rarely heard at Party meetings, made a most moving straightforward appeal for Party unity and nobody knew which side he was coming down on until in the last second he said that no one conscientiously could vote for withdrawing the Whip without making electoral disaster certain. But the unforgettable moment, long treasured in Smoking Room reminiscences, was when Tom Fraser, M.P. for Hamilton, delivered what was presumed to be the last word of the ultra-loyalists. Yes, maybe, Bevan had served the Party in the days gone by, but the time had come for him to go now. 'So why,' interrupted Bevan, with his softness now restored, 'did you ask me to your constituency the other day?' 'Because,' replied the oblivious Tom Fraser, 'my local party people asked for you', and for a few seconds the meeting, for all its tensions, dissolved in happy jeers. No more apposite reminder could have been offered of how political feeling *outside* Parliament may penetrate even the medieval walls of the private Party meeting. And the sensational votes which followed drove the point home with a whack. For Fred Lee's amendment was defeated by only 14 votes, by 138 to 124, and Attlee's original motion was carried by only 29, by 141 to 112. Immediately after the meeting was over, I came down in the lift with Bevan from the committee floor of the Commons to the principal floor, making for the Smoking Room. Just as we got out, Attlee, also alone, approached from the opposite end of the corridor and what modern jargon calls a 'confrontation' was unavoidable. What happened was that Bevan wagged his finger at him and said: 'They'll be after you now!' And Attlee *scurried* – it is the only word – without reply, he scurried out of the corridor and down the stairs.

Such a narrow majority was not enough for a proper killing. Attlee, who knew the Labour Party, knew that, and perhaps he was secretly pleased at the discomfiture of his Shadow Cabinet colleagues, but there were plenty of advisers who did not share his detachment and instinct. Most observers were astonished by the smallness of the majority but most of the newspapers, *The Times*, the *Manchester Guardian*, the *News Chronicle*, clamoured all the more strenuously for the expulsion to proceed. 'To falter now in pushing the affair through to its logical conclusion,' wrote the *Economist* of 19 March, 'would be to concede the moral victory to Mr Bevan', and the *Economist* had no doubt how fearful that consequence might be. All these journals never wearied in exhorting the responsible leaders of the Party to exorcise not only Bevan but Bevanism, and their cries did not fall on unwilling ears. Whatever Attlee's qualms, others had none. The next stage in the procedure was the reference of the issue to the twenty-eight members of the National Executive, in which the trade union leaders wielded a much more direct influence than upon the Parliamentary Party. Few doubted what the outcome would be, and one man took precautions to make assurance double sure. Speaking publicly at Portsmouth at the weekend before the National Executive meeting, Arthur Deakin directed his remarks specifically to the man who was thought to be wavering: 'I do hope Mr Attlee will give a very, very clear lead, and make it perfectly clear that he is prepared to lead a united team and to put the people who won't play into the reserve.' Speaking privately at the St Ermin's Hotel on the Monday before the Executive to Hugh Gaitskell, the Party Treasurer, he made the matter plainer still. Since Attlee might be wavering, Gaitskell, it was said, might waver too. But Deakin soon extirpated any such weakness. If Bevan was not expelled, the unions would have to reconsider their relations with the Party. No mistake in the matter could be tolerated. Gaitskell's resolve was suitably or superfluously stiffened.[1] And the same treatment had to be applied in an

[1] Crossman's diary on the eve of the Executive meeting reported an astonishing interview with Gaitskell:

'That night, thanks to a one-minute telephone conversation I had had that morning, Hugh Gaitskell came secretly to a drink at Vincent Square. I had done this on George's [Wigg] advice to see what chances there were of weaning him from his lunatic advisers. What the interview told me was that there is none. Hugh is just as infatuated, if not more so, than Nye. I started by saying that I thought, from his point of view, withdrawal of the Whip was a grave mistake, since Nye had damaged himself much more in the defence debate than he had damaged the Right, and that there was now a Left Centre emerging which was not merely his stooge. I said that, from Nye's point of view, it might be better to be expelled but surely, from the Party's point of view, there was everything to be said now for keeping him

even stranger quarter. Jock Tiffin, the assistant general secretary of
the Transport and General Workers' Union and the union's member on the Labour Party's Executive, was nursing doubts about the
wisdom of expulsion, but Deakin quickly put them to rest. Tiffin
was soon to stand for election as Deakin's successor as the union's
general secretary and he was told that all Deakin's influence would
be thrown against him if, on the Bevan issue, he showed any
Attleeite squeamishness. Deakin took no chances; this was the hour
he had waited and worked for since the meeting in the St Nicholas
Hotel in October 1951. He examined all the figures, jerked the
necessary strings, and was confident that Bevan would be out by
16 votes to 11, or at least 14 to 13. And, of course, if the worst came

---

on good behaviour. To this Hugh replied that it was too late for all such
compromises. If my policy were carried at the Executive it would utterly
destroy the morale of the Right or, as he preferred to call it, the loyalists in
the Party, who had been going through hell in their constituencies owing to
the unfortunate accident of redistribution taking place. He also said we
must consider money, and many of our big backers were asking why we
hadn't acted three years ago. I then said we knew about his meeting at St
Ermin's Hotel, and he said, "Oh, that's a pure phoney, we've been having
regular meetings on the National Agency service and last Monday happened to be the last of them. But I don't deny that, in discussing the
money, this issue of Bevan has been not unimportant." I then said that he
should realize the role he seemed to be playing of merely being a stooge for
big forces outside. Was that really good for his political reputation? He
replied by a long speech about Bevanism. "Bevanism," he said, "is and
only is a conspiracy to seize the leadership for Aneurin Bevan. It is a
conspiracy because it has three essentials of conspiracy, a leader in Bevan,
an organization run by Mikardo, and a newspaper run by Foot." I
laughed and said, "You really believe in this talk about the Bevanite
organization of Mikardo?" He said, "Certainly. It's widespread in the
constituencies." I said, "How can you take the *Tribune* seriously, with
a genuine circulation of not more than 18,000?" He said, "It's read
everywhere in the constituencies. It's the single most important factor
which our people on the Right complain of." I tried to suggest that
Bevanism was also a protest against the totally inadequate leadership
of Morrison and himself and said that in my view Nye was only half
wanting to be Leader and that certainly there had been no serious conspiracy to replace Attlee with Nye. He then repeated the whole speech at
length and said, "It's got to be cleaned up. There are extraordinary
parallels between Nye and Adolf Hitler. They are demagogues of exactly
the same sort".'

to the worst, there was always the asset of the chairman's casting vote which that year rested with Dr Edith Summerskill, who would yield nothing to Deakin in indomitable anti-Bevanism. Always she had been Bevan's enemy; once he had wounded her at an Executive meeting as only he could wound; and in the previous week, just to prove that there can be a worse fury than a woman scorned on other grounds, she had lost the candidature in her redistributed constituency.

But by now the central feature of the affair was that Attlee had made up his mind; perhaps after his own peculiar fashion he had done so all along, and he had other guidance apart from Arthur Deakin's. He was deluged by a huge postbag at his home, Cherry Cottage, and in the House of Commons and at Transport House. Overwhelmingly and violently, the movement's opinion was against expulsion. Others came to call on him the night before the Executive meeting, among them Deakin himself. And Bevan came too and it was thought for a moment he had been there to offer some form of apology. But in fact he had called to ask Attlee to warn the Executive that if they tried to pass judgment on his conduct as a Member of Parliament and thereby to influence his future conduct, it might well constitute a breach of parliamentary privilege. Attlee was impressed. He consulted Labour's leading lawyers, Sir Hartley Shawcross and Sir Frank Soskice, and they were impressed too; the Speaker might agree that a *prima facie* case existed and the whole paraphernalia of the Privilege Committee might be trundled into action. Next morning, at an early stage in the proceedings, Attlee warned of these possibilities, but eventually the meeting proceeded undeterred. Percy Knight, of the Seamen's Union, proposed and Jack Cooper, of the General and Municipal Workers, seconded the blunt motion for Bevan's expulsion. Jim Haworth, of the Transport Salaried Staffs' Association, and the movement's most prominent disciple of Dr Frank Buchman, moved an elaborate 300-word amendment calling for undertakings, confessions and expressions of brotherly love, and Edwin Gooch, of the Agricultural Workers, seconded in more secular and earthy language. Then Attlee moved and Jim Griffiths seconded the stalling amendment proposing that a special committee should interview Bevan and seek assurances about his future conduct. 'There was,' as the official minutes record, 'a very long discussion at the close of which Mr Haworth, with the consent of Mr Gooch withdrew his amendment in favour of Mr Attlee's. Mr Attlee's amendment was then put to the meeting and there voted for 14 and against 13.' Something had gone wrong with Mr Deakin's plan, but what could it be? Since the prime expulsionists, Morrison, Gaitskell, Jock Tiffin, Sam Watson had all performed their allotted roles, what could have happened? One defector was Mrs Jean Mann, one of the five members on the women's section of the Executive, who had in fact been pushed onto the Executive by Deakinite influence to replace Mrs Eirene White who was pushed off once she was discovered to be unreliable. Mrs Mann, like Edith Summerskill, had been made an enemy for life by Bevan by a savage blow from his tongue at a Party meeting (fearfully provoked, he had turned on her with the words: 'Contain your bile, woman.') and when the rumour spread that she had helped to save him, hardened Lobby or Labour correspondents shook their heads, feeling that the planet was off its hinges, and when the news reached Deakin, he exclaimed, 'that's the end of that woman'. But Bevan – and the Party, as some thought – had been saved by one vote – by Jean Mann's aberration, by a last-minute Buchmanite embrace, by the secret wisdom of Attlee, by a series of accidents. And the ordeal was not yet over. He had still to face one of the most curious cross-examinations in Labour's inquisitorial history, which strayed, as inquisitions will, into uncharted dialectical territory. But fortunately for the Labour Party and its dignity, the nature of these inquiries was not deeply probed at the time. Two days after the National Executive meeting a newspaper strike closed down the main national newspapers for three weeks and by the time they reappeared there was much else to attract public attention – the replacement of Churchill by Eden at No. 10 Downing Street and the sheer survival of Bevan himself. But the workings of that unreported special sub-committee and the sequel at the subsequent meeting of the Executive prove once again how desperately near the expulsion was.

Soon after he had received the summons to appear at the special sub-committee, Bevan sought a meeting with Attlee. By now they were almost fellow conspirators against the Deakinites. Since Attlee had had the grace to acknowledge the surging demand for reconciliation from the rank-and-file of the Party, it would have been churlish and stupid if Bevan himself had seemed to discount it. One way or another, Bevan realized that he would have to offer some form of apology. Since he had never intended any personal insult to Attlee himself, the discharge of the necessary courtesy towards him presented no insuperable difficulty, however much Bevan disliked it. But very different was the thought of obeisance before the contemptible block-headed orthodoxies of the Deakins and the Morrisons. A decent compromise had to be designed between his loyalties and his pride. He must concede enough to Attlee to ensure that the leader was not rebuffed and yet insist on the rights of free debate within the Party and his own chance to exercise them. That is the formula[1] which they did devise and offer to the sub-committee at the outset of their proceedings, and Attlee doubtless hoped that it would be sufficient to conclude the business in the staccato manner he had made his own. But he was not in the chair; Edith Summerskill was, and it was soon apparent that she and other members of the committee[2] had come prepared for a much more widely-ranging investigation.

[1] The statement read as follows:
'Throughout this controversy it has been stated that no differences of policy are involved. Even if there were there seems no good reason why they should not be resolved within the Party, without personal recrimination and in a way that would leave the essential unity of the Party unimpaired. In a great Party such as ours there must always be argument about how to apply the principles of Socialism to a particular situation. The sense of democracy in a political party is to enable the argument to proceed while at the same time maintaining the effectiveness of the Party in action. It is not always easy to achieve this, but we must always strive for it and I shall do my best to make it possible. The charge is that in what I have done and also in the way I have done it I have created difficulties for Mr Attlee and caused him embarrassment in his position as the Leader of the Party. This was certainly never my intention. But if my action or speech could lend themselves to the interpretation that such was my motive, then I am sincerely sorry and I apologize to Mr Attlee for any pain I may have caused him. I ask for nothing more than the opportunity to serve our Party under his leadership. In doing so I claim no more privileges than, and accept all the obligations shared by, other members of the Party.'
[2] The members were: Summerskill, Attlee, Gaitskell, Griffiths, Castle, Knight, Haworth, Cooper, Morgan Phillips.

Led by Gaitskell who seemed to nominate himself as chief in-
quisitor, they wanted Bevan's explanations on three main aspects
of his alleged misdemeanours: (a) the constant attacks made upon
leaders of the Party and the leaders of the affiliated trade unions;
(b) the repeated refusal to accept majority decisions; and (c) the
existence of an organized group within the Party with its own
press. A lengthy exchange seemed foreshadowed, and Bevan at first
replied in his most patient, reflective mood. First of all, he
made it clear that any assurances for the future were contained in
his original statement; they were no more and no less restrictive
than the obligations undertaken by other members of the Party.
But he could not agree to include in any new statement a special
reference because that would, by implication, suggest that he
accepted the charges and this he strongly denied. As for the organized group and its press, he had no responsibility for *Tribune* or its
brains trusts, although he believed both were performing a useful
service to the movement. Neither was interested to pursue campaigns against the Party or its leadership, but that was often the
way in which the popular press, for its own purposes, sensational-
ized the issues. Argument within the Party was necessary and
unavoidable and healthy, provided it was carried on without acrimony. True, true, interrupted the members of the committee;
but did he not agree that finality in the argument must sometimes
be reached and the decisions honoured by all Party members? Yes,
indeed, the process of argument was continuous; the difficulty was
more theoretical than practical; all the time the Party was engaged
in the process of creating opinion, educating the people and formu-
lating policy. And then, amid further questions, he offered some
advice about how the Party's constitution might be reformed; how
the system of election to the Shadow Cabinet tended to produce an
unrepresentative leadership; how this in turn tended to create
groups within the Party; how, paradoxically, a Shadow Cabinet
reflecting different views in the Party was more readily achieved
when, as in 1945, the power and the responsibility of choice rested
with the leader rather than a distorting system of election. But this
was only one of the fascinating highways and byways of politics
which the dedicated Deakinites found themselves unwittingly exploring with philosophic curiosity. At one point they were brought

to a standstill when Gaitskell pressed the demand that Bevan should give assurances that he would not in future attack the leaders of affiliated unions like the Transport and General Workers' Union. Or, replied Bevan, like the Electrical Trades Union or his own union, the miners; was he to give an assurance never to attack union general secretaries who happened to be Communists or any future general secretary whoever he might be? And perhaps the best moment of all was when Gaitskell, slightly nettled by Bevan's stubbornness, asked simply: 'You do agree, don't you, that you *have* made mistakes in the past three years?' 'Certainly,' said Bevan, 'certainly,' and then leaning forward, 'Have you?' 'Naturally,' said Gaitskell with some testiness, 'In that case,' said Bevan, 'let's issue a joint statement.' Altogether, the ironies of the investigation were sufficient to make it impossible for the special sub-committee to make any recommendation whatever. The case was returned to the National Executive with little more than a page-long, slightly startled report to assist them in their approach to a decision.[1]

Several final twists in the drama occurred which are still difficult to unravel and which strike-bound Fleet Street never scrutinized closely. But the facts are indicated in the official minutes. First, Jim Griffiths moved and Attlee seconded a motion approving the withdrawal of the Whip from Bevan but accepting his apology and undertaking for the future. After the reiterated desire, indeed determination, of the leader of the Party, it might have been expected that this proposal would mark the end of the affair. But no: nothing so simple could be permitted. Jack Cooper moved and Harry Earnshaw seconded a tougher motion condemning Bevan and warning that the Executive 'will take drastic action against future violations of Party discipline', and Jim Haworth moved and Alice Horan seconded a tougher motion still: 'That Mr Bevan be expelled.' What shock to Mr Haworth's Buchmanite purity Bevan had dealt at the special sub-committee, history is left to guess, but suddenly the fact seemed to emerge that there might be a full Deakinite majority on the Executive after all. Haworth had switched against Bevan, Jock Tiffin, on the other hand, was absent from the

[1] The account of the sub-committee given here is based partly on the sketchy official record in the N.E.C. minutes, enlarged by talks with members of the committee at the time and since.

meeting altogether 'on union business'. The whole issue was still touch and go. But it was not so easy for the Cooperites to recover the abandoned position of full expulsion; that might move the votes away from their amendment back to Attlee's original resolution. And that would risk a plain victory – for Attlee. So first Haworth was persuaded to withdraw his expulsion amendment, then Cooper's amendment was carried against Attlee's motion by 15 votes to 10, with Attlee of course in the minority. Then a Wilson amendment to remove one essential part of the Cooper amendment, now the substantive motion, was defeated by 20 votes to 6 with Attlee in the majority. And then the Cooper substantive motion was carried, as the final decision of the Executive, with Attlee and Griffiths abstaining. So Attlee had blocked the expulsion but the Deakinites, assisted by Gaitskell and Morrison, had made it clear enough that he was certainly not master of his own Party. Across the road from Transport House at the 'Marquis of Granby' where the Labour correspondents would usually congregate but where in those strike-bound days the number of customers had fallen off, one National Executive member explained the voting accurately to Henry Fairlie, then the political correspondent of the *Spectator*. He had explained why the 16 to 7 majority *without* Attlee and the 15 to 10 majority *against* Attlee were more to be noted and cherished than the apparently more substantial vote of 20 to 6 against the Bevanites, or Wilsonites, with Attlee in the majority. Still, his chief lament was that the high hopes of dealing with Bevan once and for all had been dashed. 'We brought March in like a lion,' he said, 'and it's going to go out like a lamb – and the lamb will be led to the slaughter.'[1] And the lamb, of course, was not Bevan, but Attlee.

For Bevan himself the wretchedness of the affair was redeemed only by the strong currents of support which had come to him from all over the country and from nowhere more strongly than his own constituents. When the expulsion looked probable, the question was even mooted about who might be sent as the official Labour candidate for Ebbw Vale – some devotee of blood sports suggested the name of constituency-less Edith Summerskill. 'If the party bosses sent Attlee himself down,' said William Hacker, chairman of the Ebbw Vale Trades Council, 'the whole constituency

[1] Quoted in *Tribune* 8 April 1955.

would stand rock hard behind Bevan.' He was sustained from there throughout with something even more than a conventional loyalty, with a fierce, glowing Welsh combination of pride and a sophisticated interest in all the vagaries of politics. In a sense it was their fervent backing which made any formula of apology so hateful; to offer it went against every grain in his being and their outlook; but still they understood. At the weekend when it was over he spoke to one of the huge, throbbing, exultant audiences which always assembled on these occasions at the Palace Theatre, Ebbw Vale. There, he would even speak more considerately of his old enemy, the press. Having made the necessary attack on the *Western Mail* – 'I have always been puzzled to know why so great a country as Wales should be represented by so miserable a newspaper' – he offered a reprieve for the reporters; what eventually was printed in the headline and editorials was not their fault: 'The process is like the river Ebbw' – not famous as the most pellucid of streams – 'pure at the source, then somewhat muddied, and only actually stinking further down the valley'. Then he offered the elaborate, sophisticated statement of his case which was the best tribute he could pay them. 'It is foolish to imagine,' he said, 'that people are going to lose confidence in a party which is discussing the anxieties which they themselves share. They will turn away from a party which presents an immutable and stupid face to the rest of the world.' Minutes later when he added: 'I solemnly declare that I am not prepared to buy a successful public life at the cost of a shameful silence about things I think . . .', the end of the sentence was lost in cheers and applause. They loved him for saying it and perhaps also trembled lest he should say too much.

Ebbw Vale thus supplied the most agreeable epitaph on the whole affair. But others had not been ready or able to stand 'rock hard'. One was Dick Crossman who had fought with all his ingenuity on the Executive to oppose the expulsion but who disagreed on the nature of the H-bomb controversy and who said that and much else in his column in the *Sunday Pictorial* with which Bevan disagreed. They had a furious quarrel and at one moment the breach looked irreparable. Bevan was especially infuriated by a concluding sentence in a *New Statesman* editorial which pictured a new amity in the Party, with Attlee as the confirmed leader,

16

Gaitskell as the financial expert, and himself as – in his own words, not the *New Statesman*'s – a Jimmy Maxton, the inspirer of the Party's Socialist faith. 'In moments of crisis when the knives are out, equivocation is tantamount to treachery,' he said to Crossman, 'and Gaitskell is not a financial expert. Everybody knows that.' But, the explosion was beneficial; the misunderstanding receded; and the outcome was a letter (from Crossman to Bevan) incandescent with retrospective gleams of light on the intricacies of the previous few months. After the preamble referring to his journalism, he continued:

As you have often remarked, I am an intellectual, which means that, though I have warm personal feelings, my loyalty is primarily to ideas and to chasing ideas in argument, which is the only way I can think. This is why I was so angry with you when I thought you had been *intellectually* equivocal with regard to the H-bomb. You, on the other hand, are far less sensitive to intellectual equivocation, but much more sensitive to anything you regard as equivocation *in action*. There is the important difference between us.

So much for style of writing and temperament. Now for the most important things you discussed. You sketched out your strategy over the last twelve months and showed how, in your view, you had kept the long-term object firmly in view and how each of your actions had contributed towards achieving it. And then you rebuked me for thinking in weekly columns and in terms of trivial, tactical incidents.

What I think you sometimes forget is that, on the four critical occasions when we have discussed either strategy or tactics in the last twelve months, I have been in disagreement with you, and said so – first when you retired from the Parliamentary Committee, then when you decided to stand for the Treasurership, then your *Tribune* speech at Margate and, finally, this last Defence muddle. I believe your strategic aim is fantastically over-ambitious: my own is limited to trying to restore a proper balance between Right and Left in the Party by strengthening the Left. In so far as my 'piddling little aim', as you would no doubt call it, coincides with yours, we work happily together. But when your actions obviously militate against what I am trying to do, we disagree, and it's silly for either to charge the other with treachery and disloyalty. Inevitably, I regard some of your actions as wild and harmful to the cause. Inevitably, you regard my unenthusiastic comment on those actions as equivocal. Surely we can only work together satisfactorily if we both accept what you so often say – that we have a fundamental difference. One of the main reasons why I like working with you is because I don't always agree with you and because your mind works in a totally different way from mine, which is immensely refreshing. But it would be disloyal of me to disguise from you (and, to be fair, I never have) that in my view your general line in the last fourteen months has taken you further from effective power and nearer to the danger you mentioned of becoming a Jimmy Maxton. In the last three weeks this deterioration, as I regarded it, has been miraculously stopped by the over-confidence and stupidity of your enemies, and another superb opportunity has been presented.

Of course I know that you don't accept this analysis of what has happened and regard me as fundamentally wrong for doing so. Perhaps the main difference between us, which makes you a great politician and me a pretty good writer, is that I am sometimes sceptical about my own strategy as well as about yours, whereas you are only sceptical of mine. But I don't see why that difference of temperament should prevent collaboration, provided that we both keep to the rule you once told me years ago – that it's no good trying to change a person from what he is. I think this applies to your relations with me. I can be a friend and pretty useful to you provided that you do not demand of me that I should be false to myself. But that means that there will come occasions when we shall disagree publicly as well as privately. I do not see either how this can be avoided or that it will do any harm *if we continue to believe in each other's integrity*.

Of course, if we still had a group, with group policy and group decisions, the whole situation would be different. But, possibly correctly, you set your face against this – and as a result each of us on each occasion has to think and act for himself.

Love to Jennie,

DICK

Incidentally then, as the National Executive might have been interested to note, there was no group in any proper sense of the term and certainly not in the sense of the Bevanite group which had operated in 1951 and 1952. Here is the proof of a private letter. Perhaps Crossman was right and it would have been better if there had been. Others saw the whole affair in a different light, notably Attlee who said to Crossman when he was on one of his mediatory missions at the height of the crisis: 'Nye had the leadership on a plate. I always wanted him to have it. But, you know, he wants to be two things simultaneously, a rebel and an official leader, and you can't be both.'[1] But that was too abrupt and crude an explanation. The fact was that, leadership or no leadership, group or no group, Party or no Party, Standing Orders or no Standing Orders, Aneurin Bevan would not be *chained*. It was not perversity or ambition; it was his nature.

[1] Crossman diaries.

13

THE UNKNOWN FACTOR

1955–1956

Popularity is a Crime from the Moment it is sought; it is only a virtue
where Men have it whether they will or no.

GEORGE SAVILE, MARQUESS OF HALIFAX

AFTER THE TRAUMA of the abortive expulsion, the
general election of 1955 was seemingly drained of passion and any chance of an unexpected outcome. Every
pollster and tipster foretold a Tory victory, and the slight recovery
in Labour's rating in the polls in the early days of the contest did
little to alter the prospect. Sir Anthony Eden, the new Premier,
could present himself, following Geneva, as the man of peace; no
one expected to see *his* finger on any trigger. Mr R. A. Butler's
pre-election Budget gave the impression that the new age of polite
affluence was there to stay, and the phrase 'stop-go' had as yet no
economic connotation. As the campaign itself refused to catch fire,
Bevan suggested one explanation of the damp public mood. After
all the trials of the war and its aftermath, there was 'a sort of
spiritual exhaustion, a lethargy of the collective will' which inevitably reacted against the party seeking change. He himself went on
his normal general election tour, although on this occasion it was
not arranged by the Party machine, and inquirers at Transport
House were usually told that no information about his itinerary
could be supplied. But he was still the figure whom most of the
newspapers or the public who attended meetings, for their varying
purposes, found most interesting.

For a brief day or two some thought a new 'vermin' scare was in the making. 'A WORD TO THE "SWINE" ' ran the headline in the *Daily Mail* on 25 April, and thereunder the text: 'Good morning, vermin! Oh, we beg your pardon. What a thing to say! And how absurdly old-fashioned. For you are "swine" now – all 14,000,000 who vote Tory. Gadarene swine. Mr Bevan says so, and he ought to know about livestock, for he's a farmer.' But all Bevan had said, in much the same words as many other politicians before him, was that, unlike the intelligent, inquisitive even quarrelsome Labour Party, the Conservatives showed the dangerous monolithic tendencies of the Gadarene swine. No one could make much of that for long. 'I am not allowed to use these time-honoured allegories,' he complained at Oldham. 'I have to be exceedingly careful. Even if I say that they follow their leaders like sheep, I am told that I am calling them sheep. But now I have been joined by an illustrious colleague or should I say potential fellow-victim – the editor of the *Manchester Guardian*. He said yesterday that the Government was trying to swindle Lancashire. So has he called Eden a swindler? And will he now be rebuked for bad language by the other newspapers, as he and the others have so often rebuked me? It is the same logic. But nothing will happen; dog does not eat dog. But there, I've done it again.' And so they persistently said he had but without too much conviction. 'BEVAN BRINGS RELIGION INTO IT – Toryism and Christianity inconsistent,' said some *Daily Express* headlines, but that did not run long either, particularly after he had been given qualified absolution by his closest Christian colleague, Donald Soper. Then too, nearer polling day, he found himself in a quarrel with Churchill who, doubtless lamenting the more robust times of Limehouse or Eatanswill, branded Bevan as 'a voluble careerist'. 'That from Churchill,' replied Bevan, '. . . when he was a Conservative he wasn't very mealy-mouthed about what he said about the Liberals. Then he changed and became a Liberal and the things he said about the Tories were nobody's business. Then he became a Tory again – and that man talks about careerists! I have been in the same party all the time – I admit, precariously, now and again.'

But the recollection of these outbursts of good humour, frequent enough, leaves a false emphasis. Passion was seldom absent from the huge stifling meetings he drew wherever he went and where he

searched for the weak places in the Conservative electoral shield –
much to Tory fury, he prophesied a big increase in rents if the
Tories were returned[1] – or he turned back persistently to the great
themes of the new weapons and of foreign policy which he believed
must dominate the new Parliament even more than they had done
the last. *Tribune* tried to make the stopping of H-bomb tests and
the H-bomb itself the main issue of the election and succeeded
sufficiently to stir an exchange with Churchill on the subject.
Bevan was never inclined to adopt anyone else's formulation on
this subject or most others. He never lost sight of his spacious
Marxist vision, and would eagerly clamber back to it from the
darkest corners of politics, even in the pedestrian campaign of
1955. As with Churchill – although for the two of them the
message was so different – the storms of the century were never for
long silent in his ears.

The Tories won the election, increasing their parliamentary
majority over Labour from 17 to 59, even though the total Tory
vote fell by 400,000. However, Labour's total vote had fallen by no
less than 1,500,000. There, staring everyone in the face, was the
proximate cause of Labour's defeat, and most observers pounced
to explain the disaster according to previously expressed prejudice.
The *Daily Mirror* called it 'THE COST OF BEVAN' and denounced 'the
wayward Welshman who has torn the Party in two by one public
brawl after another with the official leadership', and shrieked in all
the varieties of type available: 'IS BEVAN – AT FIFTY-SEVEN – WORTH
ONE-AND-A-HALF MILLION VOTES?'; and yet did not omit to infer,
slightly less boldly, that, of course, Attlee must go too. 'I ACCUSE
BEVAN. He was worth a million votes to the Tories,' wrote Woodrow
Wyatt in the *Sunday Express*. Several other casualties of Party
meetings, headed by Edith Summerskill, Bessie Braddock, Jean
Mann and Emanuel Shinwell, raised a similar cry. Hugh Gaitskell
asked and answered his own question: 'Can anyone honestly say
that if the Labour Party had chosen a policy which reflected more
or less the line of the Communist Party, we should have achieved
a larger vote? Do we really think the marginal voters who failed to
go to the poll were skulking at home because the Labour Party is not
revolutionary enough? I do not believe for a moment that anyone

[1] This was Bevan's anticipation of the 1957 Rent Act.

could be led into believing any such thing.' But that was not a satisfactory analysis. No one had proposed that the Labour Party should follow the Communist Party line – except the Communist Party – and the case of the skulking voter called for more detailed examination. Bevan, like the rest, found that his verdict accorded with his previous warnings, but he also touched another note. Those engaged in the Labour Party's post-mortem, he said, should remember that it was 'a living body' they were examining. He was bitterly downcast by the 1955 result, particularly because some of his closest friends had been individually defeated; a drop of 2,300 in the Ebbw Vale majority, although no more or less than the national average, added to the gloom. He was more than ever persuaded that the movement was being moulded into shapes which could rob it of its historic purpose. But the body was still living and must be treated all the more tenderly at its moments of weakness. This was the part of him his enemies never saw, never dreamed existed, but it was rarely more evident than in the aftermath of the 1955 defeat.

It was the mood in which he went to the first Party meeting after the election – the Whip had been quietly restored to him in the last days of April – when, according to custom, the election of the leader may be the first business on the agenda. Attlee said that he was ready and willing to accept nomination for a further period but that in view of considerable public speculation on the matter, he must make it clear that he was entirely in the Party's hands and would do whatever they desired. Amid cries of 'carry on', Bevan rose to urge that not merely should Attlee stay but that he should set no time limit on the term for which he would serve, and, amid universal outward acclaim, the happy suggestion was approved. The ceremony perhaps was not quite so formal as it might appear; Attlee had confronted the Party meeting with the issue before any alternative arrangement had been prepared and had done the same with the Shadow Cabinet the night before. No Deakinite breathed a word of dissent and indeed Arthur Deakin had died at the beginning of the election campaign, still vowing to the last that he would have his revenge on Bevan and Attlee. No doubt if he had lived, the leadership issue would have been forced to the front that June, for there was a plan afoot, 'among the extreme anti-Bevanites' as the

Manchester Guardian called them, to push Attlee out and Morrison in without too much delay. But the seventy-two-year-old Attlee moved with astonishing agility and found himself the hero of a thunderous ovation, led by the man whose removal from the Parliamentary Party he had proposed no more than nine weeks before. Bevan at the same meeting indicated that he would not be contesting the Deputy Leadership against Morrison, a decision taken however only after much havering through the previous days and nights. Time was needed for the Party to heal its wounds.

Most developments on the international scene helped his good intentions. Despite the departure of Malenkov from the Soviet Premiership, the Russian thaw continued; a State Treaty with Austria was signed, Khrushchev was received in Belgrade, Adenauer visited Moscow and a renewed four-party meeting at Geneva offered some fresh prospect of a settlement in the Far East; military operations in the Formosan straits ceased, and, at a conference in Bandong, many of the new states of Afro-Asia appeared to devise a far-seeing strategy of their own. Bevan, in the syndicated weekly articles he wrote for international distribution, naturally welcomed the trend, urging constantly that the West must show themselves more eager, more adventurous in seizing the opportunity.

In the House of Commons, he was unwontedly quiet, only breaking his 'oratorical fast', as one newspaper called it, to join a debate initiated by Ian Mikardo, protesting at the curtailment of the activities of the Remploy factories for the disabled in which Bevan had shown a special interest during his short spell as Minister of Labour. However, the Minister of Labour at the time was Sir Walter Monckton, for whom Bevan confessed such 'feelings of personal friendship' that he found it difficult 'to knock him about: I have to choose between this unusually benevolent feeling on my part and the adjuration which I have just received in the form of a letter from a handicapped person. He is 50 per cent handicapped and has been trained, but he cannot obtain a job at Remploy and is being kept by his wife, who is a nurse. He writes: "I will close hoping that you will knock hell out of those complacent Tories and all those who draw fat pay packets pretending to look after the cripples' welfare. Yours to a cinder." ' Bevan did not by his own

standards knock hell out of Monckton, but he did use the opportunity to renew an old quarrel with an old enemy, never allowed
to escape too long from his thoughts. He pictured the scene between
the Chancellor of the Exchequer and the Minister: 'Look here,
Walter, I want to have a reduction in this cost. I am asking everybody else to make his contribution. What are you going to make?'
and then he continued himself: 'In my experience Chancellors act
as though there is a democracy of facts and that everybody ought to
make a contribution when sacrifices are needed, including the
cripples.' But by what sort of accountancy were these conclusions
reached? 'For example, the Minister of Labour can form no estimate at all of the cost to the social services by reason of the fact that
these handicapped people are not being rehabilitated. When they
are left to their own resources, they decline; they become depressed; they become introspective; they very often develop all
sorts of mental disorders and become permanent charges on the
other social services. That figure is not on the balance sheet at all.
That is the myopic way in which the Treasury always reasons. If it
cannot give a precise figure, then of course, the figure does not
exist at all . . .' Bevan, like the author of the Proverbs, did not
believe that a politician's eye should be fixed on the ends of the
earth. Politics on the domestic hearth should never be neglected
for long.

He believed too that, at its Conference at Margate in the autumn,
the Labour Party should be brought back to face its unfinished
business. Despite every form of pressure and cajolery from different quarters, he had once again accepted nomination for the
Treasurership, and long before the delegates assembled his defeat
was certain, but that in a sense only further fortified his case, and he
spelt it out again, in an article in *Tribune* (7 October), just before
the Conference opened. Labour's defeat in the election, he argued,
had been due to the failure to offer 'an arresting alternative', but the
excuse for this attitude often was that people, even the rank-and-
file Labour supporters, did not want fundamental changes. If that
were true, it would make the case for more Socialist education, not
for muting the challenge. But was it true that 'the Socialist impulse
beat more feebly' than it formerly did among Labour supporters?
He did not believe it; on the contrary he was convinced that the

great bulk of the trade union membership was as ready for a new thrust forward as the constituency parties. The obstacle was to be found in the structure of the Party, the fact that the thrust could not find expression in the upper reaches of the Party, and the key to this failure must be looked for in the way the constitution worked. When the rough-and-ready system of the block vote was combined with the dominance of the general unions and their absolute determination to act together, the result was a travesty of democracy; it meant that overwhelmingly the places on the Party's Executive were 'in the gift of the leaders of the general unions'. If leaders manipulating such power had pressed for Socialist policies, they would long since have been pilloried by the Tory newspapers. But their immunity was a tribute to their lack of militancy. And then he recalled his own recent clashes with these leaders; their anger when he sought to invoke parliamentary privilege which was in fact devised as a shield against those who would prevent Members of Parliament speaking freely; their demand to him at their special sub-committee that he would give assurances never to attack trade union leaders. 'So I accepted nomination for the Treasurership knowing that when I did so I would be inviting implacable hostility from the most powerful persons in the Party. Before and since I have been accused of unbounded ambition. It is a curious charge. I would have thought that ambition consisted in coming to terms with the powerful and not in challenging them at the very centre of their power. I knew that, at least for some years, my defeat was practically certain. But it seemed to me then as it seems to me now that the Party will never regain its health until the stranglehold of the bureaucracy is broken . . . I am aware of the deep desire for unity within the Party, especially against the background of our recent electoral defeat. But unity must be achieved on the basis of policies which will inspire the Party to fight and not by slurring over the issues that divide us. The Labour Party must have as its aim the establishment of a Socialist society. Otherwise it will have no significance in the life of the nation.'

On the Tuesday of the Conference itself the result of the contest for Treasurership was announced, and Bevan must have been shaken by the crushing nature of it – Gaitskell had 5,475,000 votes against his own 1,225,000, an increase in the majority by more than

two million since the previous year.[1] But that afternoon he celebrated the event with a speech at the private session, when the
Conference was supposed to be discussing the report of a committee headed by Harold Wilson on the Party's organization, a
criticism of the Party's 'penny-farthing' way of organizing elections. In the brief speech allowed to an ordinary delegate, Bevan
brushed aside the topic under discussion and brought the Party
back to the question of whether it wanted to be a fighting Socialist
Party or not. Delegates thumped out their enthusiasm so violently
that the reporters who thought they might have had an afternoon
off came running back to discover what explosion had shaken the
Margate pavilion. Blaring headlines suggested next morning that
he had split the Party once more; but the rumour was falser than
ever. That night at the *Tribune* rally he deliberately lowered the
temperature by a few degrees, and next day, in the Conference
itself, he proved that he could walk a tight-rope with more impudence than anyone. During the course of a debate on the three-year
programme for reshaping Party policy which the Executive had
announced, he came to the rostrum, as the constituency representative from Ebbw Vale, to move a motion about the future of the
National Insurance scheme, his proposition being, first, that the
earnings rule regarding retirement pensions should be abolished
and all pensions should be related to the cost of living and, second-
ly, that the whole scheme should be financed through the Exchequer
and on the principle of equal benefits. The first of these proposals
was not supposed to be controversial although, alas, they have not
been carried fully into operation nearly twenty years later, but
the second was more delicate. It involved a direct clash with some

---

[1] Improperly realized at the time was the fact that one cause of the
increased anti-Bevan vote was the huge increase in the numbers upon
which the two big unions, Deakin's Transport Workers, and Williamson's
General and Municipal Workers, and some other unions, affiliated to the
Party between the election of 1954 and 1955. The total increase was 470,000,
of which the two big unions accounted for 350,000. It seems that Deakin
and Williamson were not fully satisfied with the anti-Bevan majority in
1954, and wanted to leave nothing to chance in 1955. However, it was
also the fact that some unions and considerable numbers of constituency
parties had transferred their votes to Gaitskell. See Martin Harrison,
Trade Unions and the Labour Party (Allen & Unwin, 1960), p. 65.

of the experts of the T.U.C. General Council who were still wedded to the insurance principle, although Bevan had on his side his own union, the miners, and growing sections of the Parliamentary Party who were becoming more and more restive under the continued increase in insurance contributions and the T.U.C.'s apparent acceptance of it. The situation suited exactly his desire, without offending any rule, to remind his audience that trade union leaders were not infallible; indeed on this occasion he showed how an omelette can miraculously be made without breaking any eggs. And the issue itself was one on which he had long held his own individual view. The use of the term insurance, he believed, was a misnomer; when everybody was in, when insurance was universal and compulsory, the system was no longer based upon the insurance principle; it involved a poll tax. So the money ought to be raised by taxation. Of course, the T.U.C. and the Labour Party had always clung to the old system for fear that the abandonment of the insurance principle would mean that people would not get their benefits as of right and that there would be a danger of a fresh means test. But did not the T.U.C. insist, and rightly, that unemployed persons should continue to draw benefits whatever contributions had been paid? So that was an abandonment of the insurance principle, and the time had come to get rid of many comparable anomalies. 'To say that a man is debarred because he is just one contribution short,' said Bevan, 'is a lot of nonsense, you know. The amount of money which the State spends in order to find out how much we are short of contributions is far more than it would cost the State to pay the benefit without bothering.' Then, warming to the task, he concluded with almost a friendly pat on the head for the platform. 'People say, "It is necessary for us to defend the fund. We must keep the fund on an actuarial basis." Comrades, that is a lot of nonsense. There ain't no fund. It is absolute nonsense. Gaitskell knows it better than any of us. Once you raise money on such a scale as this you have got to invest it. When we had this discussion before in the Cabinet, some of my comrades suggested that we might meet the increased cost of a National Health Service by making a contribution from the insurance fund which had then grown to enormous proportions. Of course, the Treasury had to tell us, "There is no fund." It is just an actuarial fiction. The so-called fund was invested in the pits, in the power stations, in the new towns, in the houses, in the factories, in the refineries. *There ain't no fund.*' The speech drew another rapturous reception, even if the appeal not to worship 'these old actuarial gods' fell then, as it falls still, on deaf or too reverent ears.

However, neither Bevan's two speeches nor a brilliant one from Barbara Castle on the opening day, nor a marvellously canny one from Morrison nor a superbly delivered peroration from Gaitskell – calculated perhaps, but certainly not desiccated – provided the theme of Margate. That came from the steady undercurrent of rumour about Attlee's imminent retirement which merged, as the Conference ended, into a flood in the newspapers, not merely of speculation but of peremptory demand. George Brinham of the Woodworkers, acting on behalf of the leaderless Deakinites among the trade unions, had mooted the question at the eve-of-Conference rally. Barbara Castle approached it on behalf of the Bevanites with a fulsome invitation to Attlee to stay as long as he wished or could. ('It's no use having young leaders and elderly policies.') Morrison, Gaitskell and Bevan too, of course, were all portrayed as rivals engaged in a desperate scramble for the crown. But one man remained ethereally immune. After the Conference was over and a few days before Parliament reassembled Attlee gave an official interview to the *Daily Herald*: 'I have no intention whatsoever,' he said, 'of resigning at the present time. There is nothing on the agenda of the Parliamentary Party meeting about it. I have heard of no one who intends to raise the subject. There was no such suggestion at Margate either in the Conference or behind the scenes.' Nothing could be sharper.

Six weeks later, on 8 December, he was sharper still. At a meeting of the Parliamentary Labour Party, he announced his enforced resignation in language which left no doubt about his feelings: 'Before proceeding to the main business for which you have been called, I wish to make a personal statement. After the last general election, I intimated that I would continue as chairman of the Party. It is regrettable, however, that since that date there has scarcely been a week pass without one prominent member of the Party or another talking about my resignation. That certainly does not help the Party. I desire to intimate that I am resigning from the leadership of the Party, and this resignation takes place from now.'

So who were the 'prominent' members of the Party who had engaged in this 'regrettable' campaign? A considerable number of names are available for the historian to choose from. One was Percy Knight of the National Union of Seamen and a member of the National Executive, and another was George Brinham of the Amalgamated Society of Woodworkers and also a member of the National Executive, both of whom had raised the matter at Margate. A third was James Crawford, general secretary of the National Union of Boot and Shoe Operatives and a well-liked member of the T.U.C. General Council. Attlee could be excused for supposing that these members of the Party did speak on behalf of a larger group of union leaders, since he had seen all these operating cohesively as a group at the time of the attempted Bevan expulsion. Then there were others: Alfred Robens M.P. had actually announced the date of Attlee's departure, inaccurately as it turned out, and he had made the embarrassing guessing game the more respectable for the smaller fry. But 'the loudest bagpipe in the squeaking train' was the *Daily Mirror* which also made clear that it insisted upon Hugh Gaitskell as Attlee's successor. Persistently the campaign was sustained. 'Lord Limpet' was their nickname for Attlee, until his position became intolerable. Bevan characterized the whole business as 'an unworthy conspiracy'; the Labour Party, he wrote,[1] 'will come to rue the day it permitted the least reputable among newspapers to fill the role of kingmaker'. He was especially shocked because he had been given the clearest proof of how unwilling Attlee was to go. After the Party Conference and before the resignation both had been members of the delegation visiting Malta, and in the course of lengthy talks – or, at least, lengthy by Attlee's time-scale – he had given plentiful evidence of his detestation of the influences to which, in the end, he felt forced to submit.

By the time Attlee made his announcement, few members in the Parliamentary Party doubted that Gaitskell would be his successor. Support for Morrison had been seeping away for some weeks, partly owing to his performance in the House at the time and partly through the assiduous work of Dalton on behalf of his younger

[1] *Tribune* 16 December.

protégé; chiefly no doubt through the growing evidence of Gaitskell's capacity and determination. But among the others who were
horrified at the speed with which the Gaitskell bandwagon gathered
momentum was Bevan himself, and he was ready to use every
means to block it. Therefore when, after he and Morrison had been
nominated for the vacancy, he was approached with a feasible plan,
he approved it without hesitation. The idea came from Shinwell;
it was backed by nine more of the most respected members of the
Party, headed by D. R. Grenfell, Charles Key, Tom Williams,
R. R. Stokes, Sam Viant and a few others, and it was that both
Gaitskell and Bevan should withdraw to give Morrison an uncon-
tested succession to the leadership. The move had been sponsored
primarily by some of Morrison's friends who felt that he was about
to suffer the worst humiliation of his life, but clearly also Bevan
would be the gainer. He and Gaitskell would be left to contest the
issue later in circumstances which could hardly fail to be more
propitious for Bevan than they were that December. For this
reason, the whole notion was dismissed as another squalid or
devilish Bevan contrivance. But it was what its originators intended,
a lifebelt for Morrison. Despite all the manifold occasions on which
he had flayed Morrison, Bevan would rather stomach him than
Gaitskell. And it was certainly not surprising that the Gaitskellites
refused to relinquish the victory so nearly within their grasp. When
the figures were announced, Gaitskell had 157 votes to Bevan's 70
and Morrison's 40. Morrison's cup of bitterness was indeed overflowing, and doubtless the taste was made all the more acrid by the
legitimate suspicion that Attlee had been content to see the whole
situation arranged to his disadvantage. Gaitskell's victory was far
more overwhelming than most observers had thought possible even
a few weeks before. Bevan had been outmanœuvred by the man who
had the big unions and the big newspapers behind him – a man,
moreover, whom he thought quite incapable of leading the Labour
Party to victory. It was a galling moment.

He retired to the farm at Asheridge for that Christmas, to brood,
to give time for his intuitive juices to circulate – and to direct the
next stage in the agricultural revolution. Visitors could not fail
to admire the extensive reclamation he had set in hand and to note

how vast was his recently acquired countryman's proficiency and knowledge. It was, for him, no mere pose or hobby; it was another life into which he plunged with total absorption. But in the evenings and late into the night, after Ma Lee had provided another of her feasts, he would reflect and debate with himself, with Jennie or with his guests, about the future of his infuriating Labour Party, and Christmas 1955 gave a twist of tragedy and desperation to the argument. Just after his retirement, he had written a graceful tribute to Attlee[1] and the quality which, in Bevan's assessment, had redeemed his leadership from so many timidities and failures; he defined it as an intuitive sense whereby Attlee shared his decisions with the rank-and-file and could make them feel that he was acting as they would act, and he added: 'that is not something to be acquired by study or by intellectual training. It is the subtle deposit of experience working through the imagination.' However Attlee's mental mechanism may have worked, this was certainly Bevan's method, the deposit, of course, sometimes becoming explosive. With Attlee and his intuition, Bevan knew that he could reach eventual accommodations, however painful their achievement and however inadequate the compromise might be – the expulsion crisis of 1955 had merely been the classic, compressed example of how political understanding between the two men could be first ruptured and then repaired. But Gaitskell and Gaitskellism offended against everything in his spirit and vision.

His talent for invective was enhanced that Christmas by the contribution of Dick Crossman to the leadership controversy. Crossman, in a sudden explosion of anger, had written a column in the *Daily Mirror* explaining how he thought Bevan had 'thrown away the leadership' by supporting the manœuvre to withdraw in favour of Morrison and why he would back Gaitskell against Morrison, the inference also being that he would now back Gaitskell against Bevan. The absurd charge looked more like a rationalization by Crossman of his own vote, but it was also part of a larger supposition, repeated by others then and frequently thereafter, that the prize would have been Bevan's if only he had shown a better tactical sense, if only he had kept quiet at the right moments, if only he had displayed his assiduity at the correct committee meetings

[1] In *Tribune* 14 December.

instead of flouncing off to his cronies in the House of Commons Smoking Room. Perhaps there was a streak of truth in the estimate that could make him angrier still. 'What do you want me to be, a political gigolo?' he would retort when someone proposed that he should cultivate friends in the Tea Room or ask some wavering trade union leader to dinner.

But the response was not always so mild. Are we to keep quiet, he would ask, in one of those near-all-night sessions at Asheridge, in the face of each fresh retreat, while obstacle after obstacle is placed across the path of achieving Socialism – such as the latest plan proposed by the Executive at Margate for conducting a whole series of individual inquiries into which industries might be brought into public ownership, the project commended by Gaitskell in the very same speech in which he had been acclaimed for the avowal of his Socialist faith? 'Sheer demagogy,' Bevan was heard to mutter at the time the speech was being delivered, and the charge from him against the misnamed calculating machine could provoke mockery; but Bevan meant it seriously and would frequently reaffirm it. Too clever intellectuals could be the worst demagogues – by which he meant that they were ready to rouse emotions they had small intention of ever satisfying. Gaitskell had won the cheers by talking like a man who wanted to change society while he was happily discarding the weapons to make the change possible. Gaitskellism had to be attacked and defeated in the open; real political victories could not be won by sleight-of-hand. Indeed with so much of the press ranged against him, it was necessary to shout to be heard. To keep silent, content to whisper only in those suffocating committees, was a crime; that way, not only the opportunities of advance, but the very meaning of Socialism would be eroded.

Labour's rank-and-file must perpetually be given the right to choose the better course, to select people who would genuinely *represent* them, who would be truly *representative* figures. For Bevan the word had a full, pulsating significance. How could the working class be properly led by leaders without a drop of working-class blood in their collective veins? What would happen to the Labour Party if lawyers and accountants and university dons not only ousted trade unionists from parliamentary seats, but now moved in to monopolize the leadership? Where would the Labour

Party be led by these regiments of public school intellectuals like Gaitskell and Crossman? 'Or like Attlee,' I might sometimes bravely interpolate at this point when the anti-middle-class intellectual pressure seemed to be becoming too hot to tolerate. But exceptions to disprove his rule he would brush aside and it was hard to contest his main presentiment. He certainly had no wish or interest to be sentimental about working-class M.P.s; he himself had abundant experience of how the dead-weight of the trade union group in the House could be thrown into the scales to favour the Right wing of the Party. Yet the will and the power to change society implicit in the British working class remained the central truth of his political heritage. He still felt those forces could be made explicit and effective only through the Labour Party but that they were perpetually tamed by the bureaucratic middle-class leadership. Gaitskell's victory once more revealed the dilemma and put the stamp of a kind of bogus historical approval upon it.

One of his characteristic gestures, unsuspected by those who didn't know him, was the shrug of cheerful resignation with which he could accept such situations and turn to face them, instead of yielding to the sulkiness or fury which his enemies so constantly attributed to him. That Christmas he made some plans or confirmed some he had already embarked upon. Gaitskell or no Gaitskell, he could not cut himself off from the Parliamentary Party. He was already back in the Shadow Cabinet, having been re-elected the previous June at the elections just after the general election.[1] He had to consider what he should do if, as was expected, Jim Griffiths was nominated for the Deputy Leadership. It was not an easy choice, since a refusal to stand might be interpreted as a promise of complete non-co-operation with the new leadership. He decided to fight,[2] though he would be inviting yet another defeat which the newspapers would use to taunt him. He also decided to enter the lists with an announcement at an early stage for that year's election for the Treasurership, so that every union in the land

[1] The votes had been Griffiths 186, Gaitskell 184, Callaghan 148, Robens 148, Wilson 147, Summerskill 133, Bevan 118, Brown 101, Noel-Baker 100, Greenwood 95, Stokes 77, Mitchison 76.

[2] In the contest, at the end of January, Griffiths got 141 votes against Bevan's 111.

would be forced to declare itself. And he decided further to undertake the labours of a heavy new independent campaign in the country. *Tribune* had been suffering from one of its regular financial crises. Bevan not merely made prodigious private exertions to secure fresh doses of capital but agreed to address a series of *Tribune* mass meetings at which all concerned, headed by the leadership, could be instructed that the struggle to make the Labour Party into an instrument of Socialism was not to be abandoned. The first of these was scheduled to take place at the Albert Hall, Manchester, on 4 February, and others besides those in charge of *Tribune*'s diminutive organization were nervous. It came in the same week just after the vote for the Deputy Leadership in which Bevan had made an advance on his vote against Morrison; a total of 111 for a man who had had the Whip withdrawn less than twelve months before was considered a remarkable result. And it was the first Bevan speech since the Gaitskell victory.

Manchester was indeed the kind of meeting which those present were never likely to forget. It was jammed, boiling, red-hot, packed with rank-and-file trade unionists as well as constituency workers and the clearest proof that the Left in the Party was recovering some of its militancy. Bevan responded with one of the great platform speeches of his life. He took as his text, in the Methodist hall where he was speaking, the *Manchester Guardian*'s stricture of a few days before that he might have been the leader of the Party if he had learnt to play in the team: 'I want to say this to the editor of the *Guardian*, that I am not interested in being the leader of any party, merely for the sake of being leader. If the Labour Party is not going to be a Socialist Party, I don't want to lead it. I don't believe you can measure the progress of society by individual careers. I know of so many people who imagine a society has succeeded because they have succeeded in it.' As for playing in a team, what game was it to be? 'When you join a team in the expectation that you are going to play rugger, you can't be expected to be enthusiastic if you are asked to play tiddlywinks.' It had always been understood that one of the premises of the movement was to transform society from institutions based on private property and private exploitation into institutions based on public service. 'If it is not that, I am not interested in it. It loses its appeal when some people go about saying we are going to investigate industries, one by one, to see whether they qualify for nationalization. I regard that as a retrograde step. The National Health Service would never have been established in 1948 in the mood of the movement in 1956.' And then, interlaced with his reassertion of the Socialist principles of public ownership went the reiteration of the democratic principles of how the aims could be achieved, how in practice the surge from below was blocked by all manner of bureaucratic distortions of democracy; 'You elect a Labour M.P. to represent you. In the secrecy of a Party meeting he plays in the team, keeps a straight bat and a stiff upper lip and then reaches decisions. You don't know about them. He is not allowed to say. That is a travesty of democracy; a representative of the people has no right to secrecy. At our meetings "upstairs" in the House of Commons, we arrive at our secret decisions and come to the floor of the House and make speeches, and if those speeches do not accord with what has been decided "upstairs" we are threatened with expulsion, although you do not know how your representative voted "upstairs". Is that democracy? It is a conspiracy. If it goes on, it will be the end of parliamentary institutions.' At which, a woman's voice from the back shouted: 'Why didn't you tell us all this before?' And he replied, 'I have, I have told you for the past ten years, but the trouble is you haven't been listening.' And something much the same, he insisted, was happening in local government: the council chamber was being reduced to a farce and the caucus was getting more powerful than the electors. And then he concluded that he knew such words might get him into trouble and not merely in one quarter. 'But I am not a Communist. I am a democratic Socialist. We must keep democratic institutions healthy and active. But the trouble in our movement and outside it is that decisions are being reached on top and imposed on the bottom.' And after he had spoken, the rank-and-file of the conference itself took charge and voiced its criticisms, protests and proposals for the future. After some fallow years, there was a new rising temper on the Left, reflected only with frightening pallor in the Parliamentary Labour Party.

When the Manchester speech provoked widespread press comment that once again Bevan had split the Party from top to bottom,

Gaitskell and his advisers did not react in quite the way the head-line writers might have wished: they stared stolidly in the opposite direction. Undoubtedly some voices were raised on the Right urging that the new leader would be wise to tackle the matter in his first months of power, but one awkward fact was that Bevan had broken no specific Party rule, and undoubtedly any move against him would have pushed the issue of 'free speech' within the Party to the forefront of the political arena. Possibly caution was also induced by the fact that the speech had stirred slumbering memories of freedom in the offices of the *Manchester Guardian*; almost for the first time in those years the leading article in that journal gave a grudging admission to Bevan's case about secret meetings and caucuses without adding the usual savage attack on his sincerity. So perhaps, it was authoritatively whispered at Westminster, the Manchester speech was just another Nye outburst, not to be treated too seriously or likely to be repeated. One problem was, what front-bench responsibility to offer him; the most obvious was the position of spokesman on colonial affairs which Jim Griffiths as Deputy Leader had just vacated: it was duly offered and accepted. Not even a hint was dropped that he had committed some misdemeanour at Manchester. In any case, he was resolved to carry through his campaign without inhibitions. Its centrepiece was a renewal of the demand that there must be a big new thrust in the extension of public ownership so that 'the community should own the commanding positions in the economy'. He went to another *Tribune* meeting in Birmingham to put the case, coupling it with a special warning that 'some of our comrades are suggesting that an alternative to public ownership is to become shareholders in private concerns'. He went to Cardiff and urged that 'the new thrust forward' must be accompanied by an attempt to make the old nationalized industries more accountable to the public through Parliament; 'we should not have put between the Government and the industry a bastion like the Coal Board. We put the Board into an administrative cul-de-sac. They are doing their best with it. But you know what you get in a cul-de-sac? You get appendicitis.' And he went to Merthyr, next door to his own home territory, where Keir Hardie had been elected in the year 1896, to join in the Labour Party's fiftieth anniversary demonstration. Jim Griffiths spoke emotionally and recalled that in the old days it was not quite polite to be a Socialist, and Bevan reflected: 'Yes and now we have almost reached the position where we have to be polite to remain a Socialist.' Everywhere he went he put the case against the expulsions and proscriptions which were taking place in so many local parties or the talk of fresh discipline against himself – and for a new birth of freedom in the Party. For him, this whole question of Party freedom was never secondary, but he did not want people to suppose that he was just whining about his own fate. Some blows were inseparable from the course he had chosen. 'Damn it all,' he said at one of these meetings, 'you can't have the crown of thorns *and* the thirty pieces of silver'. Immediately the more pious sections of Fleet Street, especially that area owned by Lord Kemsley, convicted him of an unforgivable blasphemy.

He even provoked a cry of secular anguish from Attlee who wrote an article repudiating some of his views directly, and insisting in particular that the private Party meeting was necessary to concert tactics against the Tory enemy. Of course, replied Bevan, no one could doubt it; but the votes at the Party meeting, 'the instrument of decision', as Attlee himself called it, moved from tactics to policy, and yet Attlee defended the system of 'democratic secrecy' on policy matters too. Parliament under the system Attlee approved could become 'a mere register in public of decisions privately arrived at. I can conceive of no more effective way of undermining Parliament than that. It amounts to the right of Members of Parliament privately to contract out of obligations that they are publicly committed to support . . . It is implicit in democracy that public representatives must be publicly accountable for the exercise of the power conferred upon them. By no means can those who have elected them hold them to account, or form a judgment on their suitability to continue to represent them. This I regard as cardinal. Any Party rule or Standing Order that says otherwise is an offence against the letter as well as the spirit of democracy.'[1] He had become, more than ever, the defender of Parliament against the reductions in its power which M.P.s themselves connived at, and he set the argument in the context of the individual entrammelled and subdued by the organization

[1] *Tribune* 2 March 1956.

supposed to serve him. A decade or more before the word 'participation' became fashionable, Bevan was probing the problem,
insisting that the scale of modern organization altered the nature
of the problem itself.

Then, in 1956, as if the heavens had suddenly opened, the hopes
for freedom everywhere on the planet were raised by an event
which no one had foreseen. Khrushchev's denunciation of the
crimes of Stalin at the Twentieth Congress of the Soviet Communist Party opened up new vistas for the Russian people, for
Europe, for the whole course of world politics, and Bevan was
naturally fascinated. His renewed fear was that the response of the
Western leaders would be too blinkered and cautious – that had
been the melancholy story through most of 1953 and 1954 and
1955; while Khrushchev had been preparing his secret speech
Dulles had been preaching new sermons about 'brinkmanship'.
However, Bevan was not uncritical or starry-eyed about the motives
of those who had made the Twentieth Congress revelations. As
befitted a Socialist who grew to political manhood at the time of the
October Revolution, he had never ceased to argue about the nature
of Soviet Communism, and he did so as eagerly now. The absolute
rejection of Stalinism, he said, was on the same level as the absolute
acceptance; the infallible leader was now loaded with all the guilt.
But the Communists should be required to answer what institutions
they would devise to protect society, including Communist society,
from the horrors of evil men. 'Why was Stalin able to make a
mockery of Soviet democracy unless the Soviet constitution gave
him the opportunity? He became the tyrant because he was all-
powerful and not all-powerful because he was by nature a tyrant.
He grew into tyranny because the character of the Soviet constitution enabled him to do it.' So what protections did the Communists
propose for the future? In the decadent Western democracies, the
protections were provided by the independent judiciary and the
existence of more than one political party. No doubt these methods
worked inadequately and slowly. But they also 'enshrine many of
the most cherished achievements of the human race'.[1]

It was questions of freedom which partly caused the explosion
when, during the visit of Khrushchev and Bulganin to London in

[1] *Tribune* 23 March 1956.

April, they were invited by the Labour Party National Executive to a dinner in the House of Commons and the ceremony ended in uproar. The *Daily Worker* reported that Gaitskell and Bevan had turned the affair into 'a cold war propaganda stunt' and that Khrushchev had burst out: 'I have not met people like you for thirty or forty years!' And no doubt that was true. It was a novelty to meet people who called themselves Socialists, talked about freedom and dared to argue with him. But Bevan indeed had sought with no great success to reduce tempers after a clash between Khrushchev and George Brown had made them boil over, and after Gaitskell had presented him with a list of social democrats still held in prison in the satellite states. During the course of his reply Khrushchev said that, in the so-called satellite states, for which he was not responsible, or in the territories for which he was, it was sometimes necessary to take action against 'enemies of the people', whereupon Bevan asked how 'the enemies of the people' could be defined and how their guilt was established. And these old-fashioned liberal questions did not find favour with the Soviet leader. However, Bevan was not inclined to take too tragically, as some commentators did, the fiasco of the dinner. He believed that Khrushchev's fury might subside as quickly as it rose, and when they met on the next occasion an understanding between them was immediately established. Soviet and Western leaders were talking to one another; the Twentieth Congress had greatly widened the arena of debate; these were developments of supreme importance in the nuclear age. 'It may be,' he wrote at the time of the Khrushchev-Bulganin visit, 'that the Russians are seeking to win their ends by diplomacy, other methods not being open to them any more than they are to us. If so, this is a cause for rejoicing. It is a duel for which our long history well fits us. In any case, it is not a disagreeable thought that in an age when Britain can no longer compete with her former power, power itself is no longer the final arbiter.'[1] The spring and summer of 1956 did seem to offer a prospect of a new age. Upsets at a dinner table counted for little against the signs that the Russian thaw, the great event of the time, was continuing, and Bevan greedily welcomed every one of them – the dissolution of the Cominform which had helped to make every

[1] *Daily Express* 2 April 1956.

Communist Party outside Russia the puppet of Moscow, the removal of the old hard-line Stalinite Rakosi from the leadership of
the Hungarian Communist Party, the liberation of Gomulka from
prison in Poland, and the burgeoning hope, a promise for others
besides the long-suffering Poles, that there might be a Polish road
to Socialism.

It did truly appear that there might be a chance of breaking up
the old cold-war pattern of world politics which Bevan found so
oppressive and futile. The thought made it all the sadder to have to
confront daily a Tory House of Commons oblivious or resentful of
the new world-wide opportunities and a Tory Prime Minister,
Anthony Eden, who was losing command over his followers and
who might be all the more tempted to embark upon outmoded
Tory policies to win it back. They thought he was weak; so there
was always the added danger that he would wish to take the stage
as a strong man. They demanded, in the words of the famous *Daily
Telegraph* article of the time, 'the smack of firm government', and
on one occasion in March they thought they had got it when the
Colonial Secretary announced that, following the breakdown in
negotiations with leaders in Cyprus, Archbishop Makarios was to
be deported to the Seychelles. Bevan had had a special interest in
Cyprus since he had intervened from the back benches in the
original debate on the matter, initiated by his friend, Tom Driberg,
in July 1954, when the Minister in charge had spoken the fatal word
'never' – never would the British Government be able to accept the
idea of independence for Cyprus, since the base there was essential
to the maintenance of N.A.T.O.'s strategic position in the Eastern
Mediterranean. Since then, the violence, the killings, the ineffectual
suppression of what the British Government refused to acknowledge as a genuine independence movement continued predictably
until the breakdown of negotiations with Makarios. The Tory
benches cheered as if, said Bevan, 'we had just heard news of a new
battle of Trafalgar', and how dangerous those cheers were, since
they seemed to show the Government had learnt nothing from the
history of Ireland, of India, of the new African states. 'Why,' said
Bevan in the censure debate which he opened officially on behalf
of the Labour Party, 'does the Tory Party keep on deceiving itself
that it can take an original line in these matters?' Why had they

never made up their minds on whether they wanted 'Cyprus as a base or a base in Cyprus'? They could have had the second if they had not insisted on the first. Why could they not understand that the people they called 'terrorists', their fellow-nationals called 'patriots'? Why could they not appreciate the futility of establishing a military base in the midst of a hostile civil population? It appeared that the Tory Party had not adjusted themselves at all to the contemporary world – they suffered from 'a sort of truculent nostalgia'. Then he almost pleaded with the Anthony Eden he had known all his parliamentary life. Let him not be affected by the propaganda of the Tory newspapers which would turn him into 'a man of iron'; he had enough political experience to know that the results of that kind of resort might be 'diabolical'. This speech had started in the tone of a fierce vote of censure, but in the end he roared as gently as a sucking dove. It was almost like a private conversation between him and Eden, and the raucous Tory backbenchers found themselves eavesdropping. Just a little earlier he had reflected, in quite uncensorious terms, on the necessities of the Middle Eastern situation which, presumably, had made the Tories so sensitive and inflexible about Cyprus. The Russians had been told and understood that access to Middle Eastern oil was essential for Western society. So must the Americans be told that, and more particularly, their oil lobby could not be allowed to ride roughshod over British interests, and perhaps Britain and the United States would be better able to think in commercial rather than military terms – 'it may be that military operations will risk us the oil, but military operations will never win us the oil'.

Even if the predominantly Tory House of Commons would find unpalatable this last unmilitaristic moral, the linked word of warning to the Russians and the Americans had its appeal. It was perhaps the first time that particular Parliament – each new Parliament has to fashion its own judgments – began to appreciate how Bevan could pick his own path through a crisis; how he could not be neglectful of what others might call 'British interests' even though he would define them in different terms. It was in part, if you wish, a display of the debater's device to win the ear of his opponents; but how much more effective could it be when the sympathy was not feigned. It was a feat indeed to have the Tory backbenchers catching themselves unconsciously nodding, in the same censure debate in which he convicted them of having damaged the name of Great Britain all over the world, of having achieved, by contrast with 1940, 'an ignoble loneliness'.

A few days later they were nodding again. In the debate on the report of the Malta Round Table Conference, of which he had been a member, he put more imaginatively and less ambiguously than the Minister himself the case for the 'integration' of Malta with Britain – the solution favoured by the Conference and tentatively by the Government. It was objected, mostly from the Tory benches, that the proposed amalgamation might be dismissed as 'a constitutional fiction'. But, said Bevan, there was much to be said for fiction in the making of constitutions. A famous book by a German had once explained how much mankind owed to the use of fictions.[1] A fiction could grow to a tangible fact. Thus Bevan instructed the Tories in 1956 in truths which Edmund Burke could have applauded, but not with sufficient effect, alas, to prevent them, by their coolness and their failure to seize the moment, from impairing whatever chance there might be of establishing a new and original relationship between Britain and Malta.[2]

To teach Tories about freedom, however, was not a mission casually to be undertaken, either at home or abroad. In July 1956, following a flagrant case of improper inquiry against a civil servant on political grounds, a Committee for the Limitation of Secret Police Powers was set up on the initiative of two of Bevan's closest friends, Will Griffiths M.P. and Benn Levy, and Bevan spoke at the inaugural meeting. 'It is always known,' he said, 'that the security police are used against the enemies not of the nation but

---

[1] One of his favourite books which Bevan had borrowed from the Tredegar Workmen's Institute library and which he constantly quoted thereafter was *The Philosophy of 'As If'* by H. Vaihinger (Kegan Paul, 1924).

[2] Bevan had gone to Malta as a member of the Round Table Conference delegation in November 1955 and while there was alleged to have said at the Governor's cocktail party: 'You Maltese breed like rabbits and this must be stopped. Your Archbishop is a bigot and a medieval tyrant'. Meetings of parish priests were held at which protests were made and demonstrations carried banners with the sign: 'Don't trust Bevan, the atheist.'

of the Establishment . . .' and he recalled his meeting with M.I.5 or their equivalent in the war: 'a stupider lot I have never met. They were not spying on Hitler – they were spying on me.'[1] Precious man-hours had been lost at the height of the nation's crisis recording conspiratorially the seditious opinions he was freely expressing in the House of Commons. However, the traditions of free speech in that assembly had protected him against both the secret police and the totalitarians within his own Party. It was hard to resist an old-fashioned respect for the place.

All through the spring, summer and autumn of 1956 trade union executives, national committees, branches and lodges found the question of Bevan and the Labour Party Treasurership cropping up on their agendas, and many a general secretary cursed the intrusion. The fellow did succeed in his unseemly aim of introducing politics into industrial affairs, but the hardiest anti-Bevanite campaigners resolved at the outset that he should be made to suffer for it. However, there were obstacles across the path. Gaitskell, as the Party leader, would no longer be the candidate and a valiant substitute must be discovered. When, late in February, the news leaked out that the 140,000-strong Yorkshire miners had decided, in the teeth of the advice of their President, Ernest Jones, to vote for Bevan, the danger signals were clear. Yorkshire along with Durham had always been looked upon as the Right-wing bulwark within the union, and Yorkshire might have been expected to forget less easily than others the alleged insults which Bevan had heaped on Ernest Jones less than two years before. With the Yorkshire vote switched, the whole union might plump for Bevan, giving him a flying 600,000 figure start in the race. However, all was not lost. Owing to a bizarre provision of the N.U.M.'s constitution, they voted in 1956 for the way they would cast their vote for the Party offices in 1957, and the union was already committed to vote for Gaitskell in 1956; so that provision could still offer plentiful opportunity for manoeuvre, if only another worthy candidate, preferably a miner, could be found. The obvious man was Sam Watson, the highly respected commander-in-chief of the Durham Miners' Union; he would have been ideal for other agents of the

[1] Volume I, p. 338.

general unions looking for candidates no less than for the Will Lawtherite miners' leaders. But he rejected the approach almost before it was offered, and several others followed his discreet example, Jack Cooper of the General and Municipal Workers, Alfred Robens of the Shopworkers, Harold Wilson and some others. Another possibility was George Brown, but Tom William-son of the General and Municipal Workers, who had undertaken the work of recruitment, could not at first persuade his fellow general secretaries that the bet was sufficiently sure. 'They don't want to back a losing horse,' he said to Leslie Hunter.[1] 'Bevan has a lot of support among the rank and file, and it would make dif-ficulties for some of them if they backed someone against him who got beaten.' After all, the old Deakinite tradition dealt in certain-ties. Never once since 1945 had the combined vote of the general unions been rebuffed, once their general secretaries had applied their minds to the matter in hand.[2]

Meanwhile, Bevan's candidature was already stirring a hornet's nest of constitutional niceties. Who was actually entitled to cast the vote for the Treasurer? Different unions had different rules and in the Amalgamated Engineering Union there was a long-standing dispute about whether the decision rested with the Executive or the delegation at the Party Conference. Twice in previous years the Executive – guided by a master of guile, more a medieval cardinal than a modern trade union leader, Brother W. J. (later Lord) Carron – had arrogated to itself the right to vote for Gaitskell while the members of the delegation were insisting on their right to vote for Bevan, and twice the union's Final Appeals Court had upheld the delegation's claim. Moreover, the Standing Orders of the Labour Party itself laid down indisputably that the votes of the unions should be cast *by the delegations*, but while the Right-wing majority on the Executive was so impregnable, this point was never likely to be invoked or at least pressed to a successful issue. Such controversies, centring chiefly round the A.E.U., had been as regular a feature of Party Conferences as the smiling photographs of notables on the seashore. But now other unions were becoming

---

[1] *The Road to Brighton Pier* by Leslie Hunter, p. 189.
[2] See *Trade Unions and the Labour Party* by Martin Harrison, p. 317. This is the indispensable book in discussing the relations between the

infected. Members of the Union of Shop, Distributive and Allied Workers and branches of the National Union of Railwaymen started asking why their votes had been previously given to Gaitskell and how they could now make sure they voted for Bevan, and at the U.S.D.A.W. Easter Conference the direct demand for a clear pro-Bevan vote was only warded off by a device of the general secretary, Alan Birch; he carried by 148,236 to 88,876 a resolution declaring that the election for Treasurer should not be made 'a cockpit of ideological strife', thus leaving to the delegation the critical question of where the union's 325,000 votes should be placed.

Meantime, the search for a Right-wing standard-bearer continued. Since a certain winner had not immediately come to mind, it was even momentarily suggested that perhaps the best solution might be to give Bevan a free passage to the office without a contest at all; but Tom Williamson swept the idea aside with proper contempt. His thoughts were returning to George Brown, when an event unforeseen and undesigned by the Williamson coterie changed the prospect and, as many of them believed, immensely for the better. For a move had been made by the A.E.U. whose 600,000 votes, it had been thought, might go to Bevan, if the Executive were not able once again to override their delegation. The idea was that the A.E.U. should nominate one of their own members, Charles Pannell M.P., thereby sidestepping the awkward constitutional question of whether the A.E.U. Executive should finally accept the Appeals Court ruling and ensuring at the same time that those 600,000 A.E.U. votes would be withheld from Bevan. And who knows, might not the general unions go further and rally to

---

unions and the Party, especially during the Bevanite period. However, part of the author's contention is that both Bevanites and anti-Bevanites saw the picture mistakenly, since they were inclined to imagine that overwhelmingly the constituency parties were on one side and the unions always overwhelmingly on the other. Certainly it is true that the idea of a straight unions-versus-local parties clash was always a myth, and Mr Harrison has the grace to quote *Tribune* saying exactly that on 3 September 1954. But his detailed figures also prove (on p. 249) how many of the crucial votes in the whole period were dependent on the votes of the three unions, the Transport and General Workers, the General and Municipal Workers, and the Miners.

Pannell? There had been nothing quite like it since Sir Andrew Aguecheek and Sir Toby Belch (any couple of trade union knights could fill these roles) put their heads together to flatter the ambitions of Malvolio. Let Pannell once put on the yellow stockings of nomination for the Treasurership and the maiden's heart and hand – the soul of the Labour Party – would be his for the asking. Everywhere the cry was heard 'Malvolio for Treasurer': 'Go to, Charlie, thou art made, if thou desirest to be so; if not, let me see thee a steward still, the fellow of servants, and not worthy to touch Fortune's fingers.'

But if these ambitions did ever soar so high, they were shockingly disappointed when, before Pannell could make his candidature official by a public declaration, George Brown announced from Belper that his constituency party had sent in his nomination, and it quickly became apparent that the two general unions – together wielding some 1,600,000 votes – would be voting for him and that he would therefore be the real contender against Bevan. From that moment forward both Pannell and a fourth candidate, D. Rhydderch, treasurer of the Clerical and Administrative Workers, who was nominated against Bevan by a vote within his union, were classed as outsiders. Expectations swayed back and forth. 'ODDS ON BROWN NOW – NOT BEVAN' said a headline in the *Daily Express* at the beginning of May when the General and Municipal Workers declared solidly for Brown. 'BEVAN IS FAVOURITE', said the same paper later in the same month. And then in June came the sweetest news of all, from the miners. Derbyshire, Kent, Lancashire, the Midlands, North Wales, South Wales, Nottingham, Scotland and Yorkshire all came out for Bevan, with only South Derbyshire for Brown. Next, a strong pro-Bevan vote was recorded at the National Union of Railwaymen's conference, with a scolding added for the way the Executive had switched the vote against him in Gaitskell's favour the year before. By the time the Party Conference agenda was published in September, everyone was confused. Assuming, as most people did, that the bulk of the 1,165,000 constituency party votes would go to Bevan, it seemed that the final result would rest with U.S.D.A.W. who had already had trouble enough over the complaints about their conduct the year before. Their Executive had decided to leave the decision to the delegates who would assemble at Blackpool, but they were outraged to be told – in the columns of the official *Daily Herald* which made it worse – that they were likely to give the vote to Brown in return for backing from the general unions for a new nominee of theirs, Walter Padley, for the Party's Executive. The imputation that 'horse-trading' might influence so solemn an affair as the election of Labour's National Executive was fiercely repudiated. The thirty union delegates and eight M.P.s assembled at Blackpool on the Sunday in October to make the decision and, after a final appeal from the union's general secretary that they should vote for neither Bevan nor Brown but for Rhydderch, the angry delegates made the vote for Bevan clear and irreversible. But still the outcome was in doubt. U.S.D.A.W.'s 324,000 votes were partly offset by the 130,000 Amalgamated Society of Woodworkers' votes destined for Brown although that in turn would have been more than offset if several members of the A.E.U. delegation had been able to make good their right to decide the issue. But Brother Carron would have none of it, even though twenty-five out of the twenty-six elected delegates protested to the Party's Conference Arrangements Committee that their rights were being violated. Threatening disciplinary action against any member who divulged the proceedings to the press, Carron insisted that their vote would go to Pannell. On the night before the election Brown was estimated to be ahead by 650,000 in votes committed by the unions. Everything would still hinge on how the 1,165,000 constituency party votes would be shared. Morgan Phillips made the calculation that same night that Bevan would need over 90 per cent of the constituency votes to have a chance. One fact was sure: never in the history of the Labour Party before had so clear a democratic wind blown through the cobwebs and entanglements of the Party's electoral processes. It was not the thorough reform of the constitution which Bevan had long advocated, but it was a start.

Despite all the great matters to be considered at Blackpool that year – in particular the rising alarm about the Government's policy towards Egypt – it was the election for the Treasurership which gripped the Conference until the figures were announced on the Tuesday morning. When the Treasurership category was reached and the name 'Bevan A' was read out, a great roar of rejoicing

17

almost struck the roof off the Empress Hall.[1] Then the whole place dissolved in excitement, gaiety and a demonstration such as no one could recall: what the *Evening Standard* reporter described as 'the most remarkable ovation of any post-war Socialist Conference'. Gaitskell on the platform, reported *The Times*, smiled enigmatically until some delegates called to him through the din 'Cheer up! Cheer up!' It was the face, said someone else, of a Hamlet who almost swooned as he saw the ghost appear on the battlements of Elsinore. But the vast majority of delegates had no time for these sideglances; they wanted to celebrate what *Tribune* called 'the most significant shift in British politics since 1951'. As Bevan mounted the platform at the *Tribune* meeting the following night, Barbara Castle gave him a friendly tug on the arm and an admonition: 'Nye, do be careful!' And in one sense, he was. 'I don't want to be too reminiscent tonight,' he said, but he did not lose his astringency. He reiterated the case which he had been making throughout the country, all through that campaigning year, for a reform in the Party's structure,[2] for a move of the whole Party leftwards, for the elevation once more of the principle of public ownership to its central place in the Party's thinking. And at Blackpool, as Bevan was most eager to acknowledge, another powerful voice was raised, speaking of public ownership and Socialism without apology: the speech of Frank Cousins, the newly-elected general secretary of the Transport and General Workers' Union, offered an entirely fresh prospect of the relationship between the Party and the unions. Yet the vote of the Transport Union that year had gone to Brown, not Bevan, so difficult was it for even a powerful union leader like Cousins to escape from the entanglements of the past.

[1] These were the figures:

Bevan, A.	3,029,000
Brown, G.	2,755,000
Pannell, C.	644,000
Rhydderch, D.	44,000

[2] Asked at the press conference on the night of his election what he thought of the block vote now he replied: 'I think it has adjusted itself to some extent to the point of view of the rank and file. I don't think the structure of the Party is as democratic as it should be. The apparatus is not satisfactory to me just because it happens to favour me.' *Daily Express* 3 October.

'Always look for the unknown factor,' was one of Bevan's favourite mottoes, sometimes used to comfort his friends in moments of despondency. Who would have dared prophesy the Blackpool victory a bare eighteen months after the attempt to expel him from the Party altogether, and who could have foretold that among the first to congratulate him would be the general secretary of the Transport Workers' Union? No longer were Labour politics set in an unbreakable mould. No more could the Labour Establishment rely on predictable conquests. Never again would a few trade union leaders meeting in private behind the backs of the rest of the Party be able to distribute offices and determine policy according to their whim. Henceforth trade union leaders would increasingly appear not as a praetorian guard shielding the leader, but as independent forces whose allegiance and enthusiasm and votes must be enlisted precisely because they themselves had become responsive to their own rank-and-file: a development most healthy for democracy. The fight for the Treasurership was only one element in those changes, but it came at a critical moment; it helped to save the Party from atrophy.

However, no one could stay long to analyse the effects of Blackpool on the Labour Party. Soon Bevan and everyone else were caught up in the supreme crisis of the 1950s.

14

SUEZ

1956–1957

But if the cause be not good, the King himself hath a heavy reckoning to make; when all those legs, and arms, and heads, chopped off in a battle, shall join together at the latter day, and cry all – We died at such a place; some swearing; some, crying for a surgeon; some, upon their wives left poor behind them; some, upon the debts they owe; some, upon their children rawly left. I am afeard there are few die well that die in a battle; for how can they charitably dispose of any thing when blood is their argument?—MICHAEL WILLIAMS, speaking to the King on the eve of Agincourt in *Henry V*. Quoted by Aneurin Bevan in the House of Commons on 16 May 1957

ANEURIN BEVAN'S attitude to the concurrent crises of Suez and Hungary differed from that of Hugh Gaitskell, and, scarcely less, from that of many of his friends on the Left wing of the Labour Party. Outwardly, the difference was no more than one of emphasis, enabling opponents to make mild taunts about his 'statesmanship' compared with Gaitskell's 'pure hysteria', or to suggest, in the gibe of the House of Commons corridors, quoted by R. A. Butler in one of the debates, *anything Hugh can do, Nye can do better*. This contrast was concerned with no more than the small change of parliamentary tactics and it did nothing to impair the effectiveness of the Labour attack. Indeed, the speeches of Gaitskell and Bevan throughout the crisis – the combination of Gaitskell's relentless, passionate marshalling of the whole legal and moral case against the Government's expedition to Suez and Bevan's sardonic and reflective commentary upon it – complemented one another and constitute together the most brilliant display of opposition in recent parliamentary history. Bevan was also newly impressed, as who could not be, by the revelation of the iron in Gaitskell's character; somehow what formerly looked like obduracy was transmuted to a shining courage. But inwardly he had doubts and qualifications about the manner and the meaning of Labour's opposition, a desire to set the international scene in a different and larger perspective. These criticisms could only be made fully explicit in private, for he could not, even if he had wished, have provided ammunition for the Party's enemy in such a conflict without destroying himself and his capacity to influence anybody. But in all his speeches and writings during that period of the most ferocious party strife Britain had known for generations he did strive to transform the national argument into one which, on his own estimate, could help save the H-bomb-ridden world from destruction.

Partly his view was shaped by his strong sympathies for Israel; what he had seen and felt there of their inescapable necessities was never absent from his reckoning. Partly it was shaped by the imperfect accord he had established with President Nasser; for all his acceptance of much of the nationalist case, Arab nationalism never had for him the tug which his understanding of Israeli emotions could exercise. But these were more the obvious than the truest explanations of his individual judgment; they were shared by many in the Labour Party leadership, including Gaitskell himself. More important, and much less appreciated as a dominant factor in his mind, was his unabated suspicion throughout of American intervention and motives. When he expressed his sympathy for those who had to submit to Dulles's sermons, men who had been blackguarding him almost as a traitor for his so-called anti-American diatribes in years gone by now pricked up their ears and found his continued scorn for the Dulles diplomacy most soothing. But they did not comprehend. Bevan's 'anti-Americanism' was never designed to ease the pride and envy of British nationalists who could not endure the altered relationship between the two countries, although he would not object if that proved to be one of the side-effects, since he could never agree that Tories should be allowed the best patriotic tunes. No: the driving force with him was a deep conviction that the policies of the most powerful nation the world

had ever seen were set along the wrong course, in Europe and Asia,
and that they were as little adapted to suit British interests as those
of many other countries squeezed between the giant powers. How
could those policies be diverted into wiser channels; how could
British influence be used to promote genuine world-wide negotiation – these were the objectives he kept before him, and it was on
this account that he sometimes found the Gaitskell statement of the
case so deeply at odds with his own kind of politics. For not only
was Gaitskell gratified to find his criticism of the British Government coinciding so closely with that which came from Washington
– indeed it was probably the injury to the Anglo-American alliance
which gave the spur to his passion – he was also inclined, and brilliantly equipped, to deliver the indictment in legalistic and moralis-
tic terms. But Bevan, the old Marxist, did not believe that reality
could be described predominantly in terms of law and morals;
interests counted more. The interests of the various nations involved
– British interests included – must be recognized if the crisis was
to be guided into less dangerous courses, and, above all, the new
requirements of the nuclear age must take precedence over all other
demands and pressures. Thus Bevan assimilated the new events
into his previous thinking; he would not become overnight anti-
Israeli, pro-Nasser, pro-Dulles, opposed to a settlement with the
Russians in Europe; rather, the incalculable nature of the peril
facing mankind was proved all the more. On that last test, Suez
might be secondary in significance to what happened in Budapest.
Within the Labour Party, Suez and Budapest stirred the deepest
moral ferment. Bevan understood the emotion and helped to
express it, but he was not overwhelmed. The faculty within him
most affected, the one which forbad him to analyse the conflict
between nations as criminal conspiracies or holy wars, was his
unsleeping imagination.

When Nasser suddenly nationalized the Suez Canal in July 1956,
British opinion, as it first found expression, was almost unanimously
hostile. In the House of Commons Anthony Eden won general
assent for his unqualified condemnation; Gaitskell said: 'it is all
very familiar. It is exactly the same as that we encountered from
Mussolini and Hitler in those years before the war'; and only one
or two voices on the extreme Left were able to dent the bone of

front-bench consensus. All the national newspapers – with the two
exceptions of the *Manchester Guardian* and the *Daily Worker* –
backed Eden. A third was *Tribune* which shrieked on 3 August:
'Labour must not let Britain be hustled into a shooting war. STOP
THIS SUEZ MADNESS!'

In his own article in that same issue of *Tribune*, Bevan adopted a
different tone. He indulged in none of the totalitarian comparisons
so popular in newspapers like the *Daily Mirror* and the *Daily
Herald* no less than *The Times* or the *Telegraph*, but he refused to
accept Nasser's claims uncritically. First of all, he sought to analyse
the nature of the movement Nasser led, concluding that it did not
as yet add up to a social revolution or anything like it; from its first
days its driving power had been strongly nationalistic, with social
and economic objectives playing a secondary role. The two aims
need not have become antagonistic; nationalist resurgence could
have been canalized for social and economic purposes, but instead
some of Nasser's actions, the attempt to keep the pot of nationalist
passions boiling, injured his other legitimate aims, for example the
building of the Aswan Dam. 'Having tasted the heady wine of
nationalist success, Nasser wanted more and more draughts of the
same stimulant' – as the leader of the Arabs against Britain and
against Israel. Such attitudes and the actions which followed from
them could hardly commend themselves to Socialists. Rather 'the
Socialist reply . . . is to internationalize all these waterways through
which the commerce of the world is articulated. And this goes for
those in British possession as well as those in the control and possession of others. If Nasser's action has brought this on to the world
agenda, it is all to the good.' A world authority to control these
waterways, superseding national sovereignties, was what the world
community required. Meantime, Nasser had done great harm by
his action to the cause of helping underdeveloped countries. He
was acclaimed as the champion of his country, a proud title; it
would be prouder still to be his country's saviour. That was Bevan's
first response to Nasser's actions, and a week later – in *Tribune* of
10 August – he still directed his main argument to the same quarter.
True, Nasser's right to nationalize the Canal Company could not
be contested; true, any condemnation of the brusqueness with
which he had done it must embrace the way the Western Powers

had withdrawn the finance for the Aswan Dam. But the claims of the world community were 'equally incontestable', and could not be abandoned just because they appeared to be entangled with the musty legalities of the Suez Canal Company. It was no real service to Egypt just to advise her to stand solidly on her national rights. 'If we rule out force – and it should be ruled out' – there were two other considerations which, in Egypt's own interest, could not be pushed aside. First, the extreme assertion of nationalist rights would not assist Egypt in securing the economic aid she needed; it might condemn her people to a much longer economic servitude. And Europe, with its reliance on Middle Eastern oil, would not permit its commerce to depend on the discrimination of one nation, and, ruling out force, it would seek other trade routes. Therefore, 'Egypt's ascendancy, should she insist upon it, is likely to be short-lived. She can separate herself from Europe by hostility or she can bind herself by conciliation and friendship'.

Wise counsels no doubt, and the long agony of unrelieved poverty for the bulk of the Egyptian people which he foresaw did indeed come to pass; but in those first weeks more peremptory warnings in other quarters were surely required. For it was true – unbelievable though it first appeared to both Gaitskell and Bevan and most others – that the British Cabinet was contemplating a resort to force, in defiance, if need be, of the United Nations and its Charter and several other treaties besides. Hysteria was in command in Downing Street much more than in Cairo, but, for once, Bevan's antennae had not immediately diagnosed the symptoms. Both Gaitskell and he acted swiftly when they did begin to recognize how Eden was misinterpreting the original near-unanimity of the House of Commons. Nothing he had said, wrote Gaitskell to Eden early in August, justified the idea of Labour support for the use of force except with United Nations' approval. A few days later, the Shadow Cabinet underlined Labour's absolute commitment to the search for a settlement by negotiation, and when Eden made a bellicose broadcast in neo-Churchillian accents, pillorying Nasser as the arch-enemy, Bevan characterized it as 'one of the biggest blunders of modern times'.[1] The British Government had on its side a good case, a strong bargaining position and widespread international

[1] *Tribune* 17 August.

support. All this could be mobilized to secure a settlement fair to Egypt and fair to the world; but all could be cast away by bombastic speeches and spectacular troop movements threatening Egypt with measures which it was never intended to execute. Or did Eden intend to impose a solution by force; was that the explanation? Bevan posed the question but he still found it inconceivable. As the weeks of August and September passed, and maritime conferences came and went, and representations were made to Nasser (when Parliament was recalled the voice of Labour, backed by several Conservatives, was able to speak out against precipitate action), and Eden squandered his advantageous position, Bevan came to believe that the most dramatic side-effect in the affair might be the removal of Eden himself. A decent interval would be interposed between the thought and the deed. 'A cushion of time will be allowed to permit the amenities of political assassination. Even a minor Caesar is entitled to be despatched with due decorum.'[1]

Those words were written just before the Labour Party Conference of that autumn and Bevan returned to London thereafter, greatly invigorated by the Blackpool victories and ready to lend any expert assistance he could offer to the assassins' work. But within a few days great events, dwarfing anything at Blackpool or Westminster, even the Suez Canal commotion, swept across the horizons. From Poland came reports of a trial of men and women – and children – who had allegedly staged reactionary riots a few months before at Poznan, but instead of grim sentences imposed behind closed doors, the reports told how one defendant or witness after another had turned the attack against their accusers; then came confirmation of swift changes in the leadership of the Polish Communist Party; then rumours of the sudden descent by Khrushchev and other Soviet leaders on Warsaw; then of the movement of Russian tanks towards the capital; then the indisputable evidence of a startling new voice on the Warsaw radio: 'Blood would not have flowed in Poznan if the Party, that is to say, its leaders, had told the truth.' It was the voice of Wladyslaw Gomulka, released

---

[1] *Tribune* 28 September. It cannot be said that all his prophecies in this article were equally perceptive. Talking of Eden's successor, he wrote: 'Time favours Mr Butler. It does not smile on Mr Macmillan . . . As for the dark horses I can call to mind, they are not only dark, but spavined.'

17*

from one of Stalin's gaols a few months before and now appointed
general secretary of the Polish Communist Party, despite Khrushchev's protests. No one welcomed this news more excitedly than
Bevan; he did not believe that the Soviet leaders would dare to use
the force at their command to crush the Polish 'spring in October';
he hailed it as a fresh proof of the new Communist awakening he
had long dreamed of and prophesied. And while he wrote came the
reports of even more turbulent events in Budapest. The whole
Continent was shaking. It was the most hopeful hour for European
freedom since 1945, yet the most heartrending and perilous.

But the political earthquake in Eastern Europe did not make the
British Government pause; they barely acknowledged the tremor
except with an occasional hypocritical tribute to Hungarian hero-
ism. On the afternoon of 30 October, having given the Opposition
no more than a few minutes' notice, Eden made his sensational
announcement to the House of Commons. Five days earlier news
had been received that the Israeli Government were taking certain
measures of mobilization, whereupon the British Ambassador in
Tel Aviv had urged restraint and President Eisenhower had called
for tripartite discussions in Washington between the representatives of the United Kingdom, France and the United States. But
the night before, news had been received that Israeli forces had
crossed the frontier and penetrated deep into Egyptian territory.
'Very grave issues' were at stake, said Eden, and accordingly the
French and British Governments had agreed that 'everything possible should be done to bring hostilities to an end as soon as
possible'. To that end a meeting of the Security Council had been
called in New York, but meantime the British and French Governments had addressed urgent communications to Egypt and Israel
calling upon them, again in Eden's words, 'to stop all warlike
actions by land, sea and air forthwith and to withdraw their military
forces to a distance of ten miles from the Canal. Further, in order to
separate the belligerents and to guarantee the freedom of transit
through the Canal by the ships of all nations, we have asked the
Egyptian Government to agree that Anglo-French forces should
move temporarily – I repeat, temporarily – into key positions at
Port Said, Ismailia and Suez.' Both countries were given twelve
hours to comply, and it was made clear that if compliance was not

forthcoming British and French forces would act to secure it. And next day, slightly later than the schedule, the threat started to be executed. Two hundred Canberras, Venoms and Valiants, backed by forty French Thunderstreaks, operating from aircraft carriers from Malta and from Cyprus, opened the attack on Egyptian airfields, and Nasser, who had found it almost as difficult as Gaitskell or Bevan to believe that Eden would use the sword he had brandished, found himself faced with the astonishing truth – that Britain had gone to war in breach of her treaties, in defiance of the United Nations' Charter, without consulting the Americans, without consulting the official Opposition, without even consulting the British Ambassador in Cairo. And the ultimatum which was the instrument of the action was one of the most curious documents in all history: for the victim of aggression was required to conduct a major retreat within its own territory whereas the aggressor, while at first encouraged to advance on all fronts, was invited to comply under the threat that failure to do so would mean the penalty of a further fresh attack upon its enemy.

Eden's declaration – 'Eden's war', as the *Daily Mirror* called it – plunged the House of Commons and the country into a more furious contention between the major parties in the state over an issue of foreign policy than anything known in British history. Opposition by smaller groups in Britain to the Boer War, the Crimean War or the French Revolutionary wars provides no exact parallel, but there was a flavour of those previous clashes in November 1956, and it should not be forgotten. A British Government under the leadership of a Prime Minister previously most famous for his peacemaking policies was turning to military action; it was hard for patriotic people to believe that there was not some good cause, perhaps one which could not be fully disclosed, why resort had been made to these extreme remedies. British troops were going into action: would not those who raised doubts be guilty of stabbing them in the back? The charge of treachery stirred immediately in the minds and hearts of Tory back-benchers in the House of Commons, even if the rules of order forbad them to utter it explicitly. On the other hand, the Labour Opposition did feel, in those early days when no one knew how long the conflict might last, that they might have to face a stinging backlash of jingoistic sentiment, but from the first moment they did not draw back. Rather, every fresh development, every contradictory excuse for the action, offered by Ministers, fed their detestation and their resolve to resist. The question seemed to be posed whether Parliament itself could contain such conflicting passions, and on 1 November, on the third day of well-nigh continuous debate, the uproar was so uncontrollable that the Speaker felt forced to suspend the sitting. Bevan was on his feet protesting when the action was taken; he had picked up a point in a statement by the Minister of Defence, astutely pounced upon by Sydney Silverman. According to the Government's fiction it was an 'armed conflict', not a war, in which British troops were engaged; no declaration of war against Egypt had been delivered; so what was the status of British troops engaged in these operations and what protection could be afforded them? What could the House of Commons do to ensure, as Silverman put it, 'that those who have taken an oath of allegiance to Her Majesty are not required by that oath to commit murder all over the world?' The Minister had no answer. The Speaker had no answer. The learned clerks had no answer. And the House of Commons erupted into a cacophony of ignorant rage.

Later that night Bevan made his first great speech of the Suez crisis, concluding the Labour Opposition's case for its censure motion, and it might have been expected that the storms would rise even higher. Certainly he did nothing to relax the direct attack on Ministers. He talked of the distraught mind of the Prime Minister: 'there is something the matter with him'; he compared the ultimatum to Egypt with that of the Kaiser to Belgium in 1914 or of Hitler to Norway in 1940; he mocked the failure to consult allies – 'one cannot stab a man effectively if he is given too long notice beforehand' – and he posed the question of the Government's expectations: 'Do they really imagine that, if they overrun Egypt, that is the end of the story? Are they going to bleed Britain to death in Egypt as France is bleeding herself to death in Algeria?' And he spoke too of the dishonour of it all, how the action stained the reputation of the country in a way that could never be wiped clean. So Bevan conceded nothing to Tory chauvinism; but there was another note running through the speech which stilled the passions of the afternoon – never, he said, had he seen feelings run

so high, yet uneasiness and private anxieties to be so general – and
reduced the place to silence. When he said that he spoke with 'a
deep sense of sorrow', with 'the sense of humility which every
public man should have in face of these intractable problems', they
did not jeer. They listened to a new Bevan – although some of us
believed he had been there to be heard all our political lives. Two
major developments, he said, had cancelled 'all the finesse and
sophistications of conventional diplomacy'. Due to the advent of
the hydrogen bomb, 'the great Powers are stalemated by their own
power', but they had not yet properly sought the means to settle
their disputes by methods other than war. And, by a token not so
different, the Soviet Union was discovering that 'it could not hold
down whole populations merely by terror and police action'. That
was the background which he painted at the beginning of his speech
and to which he returned at the end: 'How do we answer now,
when we drop bombs on helpless people? [*Hon. Members*: Oh]
Yes, when we drop bombs. How do we answer now at whatever
judgment seat any hon. Member likes to mention? A nation more
powerful than we may drop even worse bombs on British cities.
How answer that? With bombs? Bombs with bombs? That is the
bankruptcy of statesmanship. The world has travelled that way in
my own lifetime twice. We dare not travel that way again, because
this time there will be no return.' And the House still listened when
he pleaded with the Government to retrace their own steps. It was
more than an indictment; it was an attempt to mobilize for his
cause the fears and the prayers of the anxious world. 'Having found
that their best friends do not sustain them in this action, that their
allies are themselves dismayed by it, that the world is shocked, it
would be an act of statesmanship for the Government now to say,
"We halt at this point. We are not going to lead mankind over this
road any further".'

It was not easy to speak such elevating words in the angriest
House of Commons of modern times, harder still to speak them in
Trafalgar Square. Yet that is what he did that Sunday when the
Labour Party organized a great 'Law not War' rally. Long before
the meeting began, the open space round Nelson's column was
filled, and marching columns and trade union banners arrived from
all directions. Then the surrounding pavements and the steps of

St Martin's-in-the-Fields and the National Gallery filled up until
thirty thousand or more people crowded in to hear the speakers.
Since the great hunger march demonstrations of the thirties – since
Bevan himself had spoken at the last of them in 1936[1] – London
had seen nothing like it. And as the meeting proceeded, fresh
rumours ran through the crowd, rumours from Budapest, rumours
that Russian tanks were returning to exterminate the Hungarian
revolution, rumours of world war. And while the proof was offered
of how the peoples of so many lands seemed to be connected by
electrical and revolutionary currents, Bevan from the platform
reiterated that if Britain dropped bombs, others could do the same
and that the lessons to be learnt from Hungary and Suez were not
so vastly different. It was not the speech of a man looking for easy
things to say: 'I am not saying that the United States is blameless.
I have been spending the last five years blaming them for a number
of things. I am not saying – and let us get this right – that because
Eden is wrong, Nasser is right. I am not saying for a single moment
that the Israelis did not have the utmost provocation. What we are
saying is, that it is not possible to create peace in the Middle East
by jeopardizing the peace of the world . . . We are stronger than
Egypt, but there are other countries stronger than us. Are we prepared to accept for ourselves the logic we are applying to Egypt?
If nations more powerful than ourselves accept this anarchistic
attitude and launch bombs on London, what answer have we got?'[2]
The only immediate response available to many thousands that
dark November afternoon was to storm down Whitehall towards
Downing Street, where a police cordon almost broke and where, if
the massed mounted police had tried to scatter them, a bloody clash
would have been inevitable. The crowd did not disperse until they
had marched through the streets of London late into the night. It
was a huge near-spontaneous movement, led by the Labour Party
but commanding support far outside its ranks. And a few days
later in the House of Commons, M.P.s were still engaged in clearing up some of the political debris left by that demonstration.
Bevan commented on the way mounted police could be used to
overawe crowds, how they could sometimes turn a lawful into an

[1] Volume 1, p. 239.
[2] *Daily Express* 5 November 1956.

unlawful assembly: 'I have taken part in demonstrations and when I see a policeman on horseback nudging the haunches of his horse against women in the crowd, my natural instinct is to pull him off the horse [*Ministerial cries of dissent*] and that is the natural instinct of any ordinary Englishman. I ask hon. Members opposite to have more regard for these things, for the maintenance of law and order, and pay less attention to bullying the public like they are trying to bully the Egyptians.' [*Loud Opposition cheers*]

The great upsurge of British radical opinion was one reason why the Egyptian war was brought to a sudden halt; Eden's temperament and perhaps his ill-health was another; a third, conceivably, was provided by the threats of retaliatory action from the Soviet Union; a fourth, the revulsion of the Commonwealth, led by Canada; a fifth, the instructions from the United Nations, led by the United States; and sixth and most powerful of all, the direct pressure from the U.S. Government and the threat to the pound. How these various factors weighed with the Cabinet can only be guessed, but the conclusion which stared them in the face was clearly an ignominious defeat. Or rather, and most curiously, it was not so clear at the time. So agreeable had it been in many ears to hear the jingoistic drums beating, so glamorous had been Eden's past reputation, so strong were the cohesive forces of the Conservative Party, that reality was blurred. Instead of opening the Canal, it was blocked; instead of saving British lives and property, they had been put at Nasser's mercy; instead of toppling Nasser, he was enthroned; instead of keeping the oil flowing, it was soon to be rationed; instead of winning friends, we had lost them. Thus on one count after another it may appear that the expedition had achieved the exact opposite of the Government's declared intention. But there were counter-arguments: a war had been stopped; the combatants had been kept separate; other nations, less prompt in discharging their duties than Britain and France, had been compelled to take notice; a United Nations' force was being introduced to assume the tasks of the British and French forces in Egypt soon to be withdrawn. That case too, in the mood of the time, was plausible, and it was sufficient to preserve the Conservative majority in the series of critical Commons votes. But just suppose the sequence of events had been contrived between Britain, France and

Israel; suppose there had been *collusion*; that would bring the whole case tumbling down in ruins and infamy. The word was mentioned in the first debate and the idea dismissed by Selwyn Lloyd, the Foreign Secretary. As for the Israeli action, he said, 'there was no prior agreement between us about it'.[1]

During the ensuing weeks, Bevan along with his colleagues sought to unravel these mysteries, to distinguish in ministerial policies, as he said, which is 'the mask and which is the reality', why 'the speeches from the front bench are so blurred; there is something going on inside their minds, quite different from what they are saying'. And yet another aspect of the affair continually fascinated him more: the inter-connection between Hungary and Suez; the hideous possibility that the re-entry of Russian troops into Buda-pest had been partly prompted, as it had certainly been shielded from the world's condemnation, by the British action in Suez; that this action might have been the last touch tipping the scales in the Kremlin where clearly there had been contending arguments about the wisdom of intervention. In the midst of the crisis, Imre Nagy, the leader hoisted into the saddle in the Budapest revolution, had appealed for assistance to the United Nations Security Council; not for the deadly succour of armed intervention but for far-ranging negotiation proposals to be presented to Moscow by the West. But his cry was smothered by the Suez bombardment as well as by Soviet tanks. The only hope for Hungary in that extremity would have been a political offer from the West for a neutralized Central Europe, with troops withdrawn East and West. But the British Government was in no condition to contemplate a diplomatic initiative; it had itself gone to war instead. However, Bevan was not content to see the betrayal of Hungary pass with no more notice accorded than the hypocritical denunciation of Soviet aggression in the British Parliament or at the United Nations. If the world relapsed into the old postures of the cold war, other nations would suffer the fate of Hungary, and the Hungarians would be condemned to an endless night of despotism. 'It is time,' he insisted, 'to write a new chapter in our relations with Russia and Europe. I believe that in this way we can best help heroic Hungary.'[2] A

[1] *Hansard* Vol. 558 Col. 1569.
[2] *Tribune* 16 November.

week later he was even more insistent. The Soviet Government had made fresh proposals for disarmament and Khrushchev talked of the possibility of the withdrawal of Soviet armies in the East if comparable moves could be envisaged by the West. Amid the frightened stupor of the Budapest-Suez aftermath, these notions were brushed aside as a propaganda stunt. Bevan was appalled. If stunt it was, such a response could only bestow upon it an unwarranted effectiveness. But it was worse, 'yet another example of the blunderings of Western diplomacy'. Ever since 1950 the Western powers had grossly overestimated Soviet strength and they vainly strove to fit Hungarian events into their unimaginative, preconceived pattern. It would be wiser to accept that the whole structure of alliances was crumbling – 'The Baghdad Pact is dead; the Warsaw Pact is nearing the same end; S.E.A.T.O. never came alive, and N.A.T.O. just manages to maintain a tepid existence. What are we to put in their place? More alliances? Or are we going to try to discover an approach which corresponds more closely to contemporary realities?'[1]

Constantly during those weeks, Bevan tried to turn the nation's mind to these ideas, but he, like everybody else, was always dragged back to Suez, and on 5 December the House of Commons had the first of a long series of inquests. Bevan was by now the official spokesman of the Party on foreign affairs, his replacement of Robens in that post having gone through so smoothly that it seemed almost a decree of nature; indeed in those traumatic Suez times even the earth-shaking elections for the Shadow Cabinet were conducted by the Parliamentary Labour Party without any sign of turmoil, without a bitter word.[2] The unity was genuine, even if the emphasis in the argument varied, and in his speech on 5 December – regarded by many who heard it as the greatest of his life – Bevan welded the scattered indictment into a single glittering synthesis; the wit merged with the wisdom and the wisdom with the wit, like two edges of the same sword. One after another he dismissed the earlier conflicting reasons which Ministers had offered for their

[1] *Tribune* 23 November.
[2] The votes, in fact, were as follows: Wilson 185, Robens 149, Bevan 148, Mitchison 146, Callaghan 140, Greenwood 137, Soskice 137, Noel-Baker 133, Summerskill 112, Brown 110, Younger 106, Fraser 98.

action and then turned with relish to the new ones; for example, Eden's claim that the action had been necessary to get the United Nations force into the Canal Zone. 'It is, of course, exactly the same claim which might have been made, if they had thought about it in time, by Mussolini and Hitler, that they made war on the world in order to call the United Nations into being. If it was possible for bacteria to argue with each other, they would be able to say that their chief justification was the advancement of medical science.' And then, gravely and gaily, he turned to the talk of collusion, 'the most serious of all the charges', and one which, if sustained, could demolish the complete fabric of the Government's case. So he fingered and massaged the possibility from its manifold aspects. Selwyn Lloyd, the Foreign Secretary, had touched on the matter in opening the debate, but his repeated protestations that Ministers had not 'conspired' with France and Israel did not dispose of the accusation. Did they *know* about the Israeli attack? Did they give warnings? Apparently they warned against an Israeli attack on Jordan but with no reference to one directed against Egypt. 'If we apprehend trouble of these dimensions – we are not dealing with small matters – if we apprehend that the opening phases of a third world war might start or turn upon an attack by Israel on anyone, why did we not make it clear to Israel that we would take the same view of an attack on Egypt as we took of an attack on Jordan?' In fact, all the elaborate tales of long telephone conversations and conferences between M. Guy Mollet, M. Pineau and the Prime Minister were only intelligible on the assumption that 'something was being cooked up'. Did the French know? Did they tell the British Government? Did M. Guy Mollet, on 16 October, tell the British Government that he expected an attack on Egypt? Every circumstantial fact pointed to that conclusion – the comings and goings, Ben-Gurion's remarks in the Israeli Parliament about Egypt being the real enemy, his claim that Israel had at last found a reliable friend. And then, with the Conservative benches in front of him as riveted as the Labour ones behind, he whispered: 'What happened? Did Marianne take John Bull to an unknown rendezvous? Did Marianne say to John Bull that there was a forest fire going to start, and did John Bull then say, "We ought to put it out," but Marianne said, "No, let us warm our hands by it. It is a nice fire"? Did Marianne deceive John Bull – or seduce him?'

These questions were to hover in the political atmosphere for hours, for months, for years. The direct official answer – by the two men chiefly concerned, Eden and Selwyn Lloyd – has never been forthcoming from that day to this;[1] but in a sense nothing could be more deadly than the unanswered questions themselves and what happened when they were first asked – the dissolution of the whole House of Commons in laughter on 5 December 1956. Poetic truth may provide the most lasting impeachment.

After the seduction scene, it took what seemed long, delicious minutes for the House to recover. But, oh yes, continued Bevan, there was still another clinching reason for the Government's course of action. After their long voyage, getting almost wrecked several times, they had come to safe harbour. 'It was a red peril all the time. It was Russia all the time.' It was the unmasking of the massive supply of arms to Egypt by the Russians which was the final vindication of the Government's action – this had figured in the peroration of another of the Ministers a few days before. But, again, the Ministers had contradicted themselves. They knew about the Russian supply of arms before the aggression was ever organized and they had protested all the while that the balance of

[1] Of course, there have been a whole series of unofficial attempts to discover the answer, perhaps the most notable being Anthony Nutting's *No End of a Lesson* (Constable) and Hugh Thomas's *The Suez Affair* (Weidenfeld & Nicolson, 1960). Nutting offers the most elaborate first-hand evidence of collusion. Thomas spells it out more directly. Of Thomas's book, *The Times Literary Supplement* on 27 April 1967, wrote: 'If the historians who repeat each other are right, then senior Ministers lied to the House of Commons at the end of 1956. Professor Thomas in fact makes the accusation in so many words with reference to Selwyn Lloyd's statement on 31 October 1956 that "there was no prior agreement" with Israel and to Eden's statement on 20 December that "there was not fore-knowledge that Israel would attack Egypt". Each of these statements, according to Professor Thomas, "appears in the light of evidence summarized here, to be a straightforward lie". A few generations ago, such an accusation would have led to a duel. Today there are other legal remedies . . . It is a question of whether two eminent public men are prepared to rebut explicitly a serious and sober historian's allegations. If they are not, is there any alternative but to assume that the allegations are true?'

arms between Israel and Egypt was not so disproportionate. No: the Russian arms story was an irrelevant afterthought – not that Bevan justified the supplies by the Russians – 'it was a wicked thing to do' – or their purchase by Nasser – 'his hands are not clean by any means . . . We have never taken the position that in the exercise of sovereign rights Egypt has the right to inflict a mortal wound upon the commerce of the world'. However, all legitimate aims could have been secured by negotiation, and in any case the objectives of the Government had been unrealizable by the means they had adopted. As shocking as the immorality of their action was its imbecility. 'The social furniture of modern society is so complicated and fragile that it cannot support the jackboot. We cannot run the processes of modern society by attempting to impose our will upon nations by armed force. If we have not learned that, we have learned nothing.' And from all these strands together he wove, not a peroration – since his speeches could often end more quietly, more severely, than the polemical climax in the middle – but rather some additions to the tapestry which he had unfurled as the background to all these debates: some bitter words on the unconcern about the killing of innocent men and women in Port Said, an appeal that men and women living in great capital cities like London should apply their imagination to the questions posed by 'the barbarism of modern weaponry', an outburst against how conscript boys had been sent out upon the exploit with 'epic weapons used for squalid and trivial ends', and finally an attack on the Ministers most directly responsible. What did he call them? It was a curious, almost nonchalant aside; in any other speaker, an impossible transition – a gesture not of hate, not of fury, but of inordinate derision. They were *synthetic villains*. Not even real ones; for they had only set off on a villainous course and they could not even master the language of villainy.

That speech won an acclaim, both inside the House of Commons and outside, quite beyond the flattering courtesies which M.P.s may exchange with one another. Chuter Ede, a connoisseur of parliamentary skills but no bosom friend of Bevan, wrote to offer congratulations on 'the great speech . . . it will rank for all who heard it as the greatest parliamentary utterance to which they have listened'. Megan Lloyd George, no academic judge of oratory,

called it 'a brilliant and withering speech. You can judge of its
revolutionary character and effect by the fact that it brought Violet
Bonham Carter and me together in almost glowing unity in the
gallery. A thousand congratulations!' And Horace King, later to be
Speaker and another no mean judge: 'Yesterday's speech was one
of the finest you have ever made and made those of us who have
felt great sadness about the rifts inside the leadership in the past
few years tremendously happy. It is now clear that under what B
and K call "collective leadership" British social democracy can
save Britain and give again the moral leadership that Europe and
the world need'.[1] And away from the Commons, in Fleet Street,
some of his old enemies began to scratch their heads and think
again. The new Bevan, said the *Daily Mirror*, was the obvious man
to be the next Foreign Secretary. He had staged, said the *News
Chronicle*, 'a remarkable recovery, the third or fourth of his political
career, but by far the most spectacular'. And Henry Fairlie, neither
an old enemy nor a new disciple, noted the development more
perceptively: 'Once again one is faced with the enigma of this immeasurable man', and he put his finger on one of Bevan's distin-
guishing assets which no one else had described so well. 'He is not
bemused by the size, strength or wealth of the two big powers.
Faced by the evidence of Russian and American power, most Conservative and Labour politicians are reduced to a state of intellectual
and physical paralysis. Mr Bevan is not, and it was because he
sensed the comfortable coma into which the Labour Party was
drifting when faced by American disapproval over Suez that he
struck, in his first speech in the House of Commons, a note of
independence which could have come only from him.'

He struck it again in the debate on 19 December when the House
discussed the Hungarian tragedy and the Government spokesmen
had nothing to offer but the old un-Celtic sermons, preached all the
more ineffectually by evangelists with the blood of Suez on their

---

[1] T. W. Jones, M.P. for Merioneth at the time and now Lord Maelor,
went to offer his congratulations and told him that it was worthy of the
giants of the Welsh pulpit. Nye was very fond of T.W. and blushed with
pleasure, until Delargy, the Catholic, protested that that was nothing of a
compliment. 'None of that,' said Nye with the utmost scorn, 'I know what
T.W. means. He has paid me the highest compliment of all.'

hands. Bevan was still captivated by the question which no one would answer; whether in fact the British decision to go into Suez had spurred the Russians to re-enter Budapest, and sometimes the attempt of Ministers to escape from the implications of that charge impaled them on one even worse. They knew Soviet tanks were moving westwards, across the borders from Russia, from Rumania, back into Hungary; British intelligence supplied the evidence. And yet they had struck at Suez and released the Russians from their moral isolation, and this from those who contended that the only lever left to use in the hopeless Hungarian situation was to express the international odium the Russians had brought upon themselves. But Bevan himself would not preach sermons, even though on this occasion he and the Labour Party had not robbed themselves of the title to do so. It was not a style that suited him. He searched instead for a political escape from the new European deadlock, and he elaborated, in the new context, 'the policy of disinvolvement, the policy of disengaging', the attempt to establish 'cool areas' between the great powers, and this in turn, he argued, must involve the readiness to imagine that Soviet policy, even in Hungary, was perhaps not actuated by a cold malignancy, but by a failure to comprehend the Hungarian situation – 'whenever I meet Russian representatives the thing that impresses me is not their infallibility, but their sheer ignorance'; it must involve an understanding that the world was not engaged in an apocalyptic struggle between the angels of light and the angels of darkness. And in the midst of the argument, he would seem almost content to bandage the wounded vanities of his countrymen generally, not excluding his Tory opponents in the House, with the necessary medicament. 'Hon. Members opposite,' he said, 'have inclined to be very defeatist these last few weeks. They think they have come to the end of their glory. They say "England is now a second-class nation. We have demonstrated to the world, by the futility of our conduct in Egypt, that the flame has passed from us and been taken up by someone else, but now we have to consider ourselves as a second-class power and shelter under a higher wall than our own." I do not take that view. I do not take the view that Great Britain is a second-class power. On the contrary, I take the view that this country is a depository of probably more concentrated experience

and skill than any other country in the world. I may be wrong; it
may be that I am looking at the facts slightly askew, but I do not
see that what is called the extinction of the British Empire is necessarily followed by the rise of another empire, that we are a second-
class power and now have to defer to first-class powers, because the
fact is there are no great powers – there are only frustrated powers.
We are not in a situation where great empires are quarrelling about
the spoil and inheriting the corpses of those they have extinguished.
It is not true. It is not correct. The great powers of the world today,
as they look at the armaments they have built up, find themselves
hopelessly frustrated. If that be the case, what is the use of speaking
about first-class, second-class and third-class powers? That is
surely the wrong language to use. It does not comply with contemporary reality. What we have to seek are new ways of inspiring and
igniting the minds of mankind. We can do so.' That was Bevan
seeking to cool the House of Commons, as he would wish to subdue
the fevers of central Europe. In private conversation, it was said, he
could make what in literal terms was a curse feel like a caress, and
in public debate, he could summon the pride of patriotism to
excoriate outdated militaristic sentiments.

Early in the New Year of 1957, Anthony Eden retired from the
Premiership and his place was taken by Harold Macmillan, much
to Bevan's astonishment. He continued to expect right up till the
last minute before the official announcement from Buckingham
Palace that R. A. Butler, despite all his Suez prevarications, would
have the succession. I can remember the morning in *Tribune* office
when he was still shaking his head over Randolph Churchill's
exclusive story in the *Evening Standard* that it was to be Macmillan, and how when I told him over the telephone in the afternoon that the report was confirmed, he could only gasp, 'Good
God'. Of the three Tory leaders of his own generation with whom
he had spent so much of his parliamentary life in enforced intimacy,
it was Butler whom he regarded as the most formidable adversary,
and he did not like to see merit spurned. But no time was lost in
lamentations, and in by-election meetings at the time, he would
happily explain how the transition had occurred. 'The Tory tribe
got together and decided that a sacrifice must be made. Only liba-
tions of blood upon the altar would suffice. In such circumstances,

after so monstrous a crime and so deep a guilt, no old ram would do
– only the most precious lamb in the flock. And so the Prime Minister was sacrificed. But don't imagine that the lamb was dragged
willingly to the sacrificial stone. He had to be hauled there.'[1] And
so, in point of fact, he had had to be, and Bevan for the most part
was ready to let him depart without pursuit. He waged war on a
collective enemy, most of whom were still present on the battlefield,
and he knew how direct was Macmillan's responsibility in the Suez
affair. He preferred to address him than the Foreign Secretary. As
he said in one debate a little later: 'If we complain about the tune,
there is no reason to attack the monkey when the organ grinder is
present.'[2]

He was happy to escape from these preoccupations for a few days
to his beloved Italy, to Venice and to Rome, although the trip was
an official one undertaken on behalf of the Labour Party's International sub-committee. In Venice, the Italian Socialist Party,
under the long-standing leadership of Pietro Nenni, was engaged in
the task of extricating itself from its post-war association with the
Communist Party, and the hope, certainly shared by Bevan, was
that this might lead to a strengthening of democratic Socialism in
Italy, a possible re-alliance between Nenni's Socialist Party and the
Social Democratic Party led by Signor Saragat, and the emergence
of stronger representation within the Socialist International. All
went well at Venice; Nenni led his Party towards the new course
with the skill of an old master; Nenni and Bevan found they had
much in common, despite the different routes they had travelled to
reach their present resting place. Both were critical of Soviet
policy and American policy; both favoured the disengagement of
the great powers in central Europe and the Middle East. It was a
happy reunion of two Socialists who could trace their anti-Fascist
antecedents back to the days of the Spanish civil war, and it was
natural that Bevan spoke hopefully of the Italian Socialist Party's
reassociation with the International. Then with the business done –
despite murmurs of doubt or dissent from Signor Saragat which

---

[1] *Sunday Express* 1 March 1957.
[2] *Hansard* Vol. 570 Col. 680.

were quickly put right on the visit to Rome a few days later[1] – he and a selected few of his friends and enemies among the journalists adjourned to the Grand Canal where Bevan actually helped to serenade his unlikely companions in his silvery Welsh baritone. The immortal city, beloved of Rossini and Hazlitt and Stendhal and Casanova, suited him exactly. He revelled in the rich, expansive, bright-coloured, secular, lion-hearted, adventurous Serenissima, and was not altogether surprised to be told (some years later) that Hugh Gaitskell could not stand the place; at that, he would just shrug his shoulders and smile a serene smile worthy of San Marco himself.

On that particular occasion, he himself was landed, much against his will, in an adventure with the press, the one and only libel action he ever took against a newspaper, despite his extensive experience of defamation. On 1 March, an article about the Congress appeared in the *Spectator* entitled 'Death in Venice'; it included the words: 'And there was the occasional appearance of Messrs Bevan, Morgan Phillips and Richard Crossman who puzzled the Italians by their capacity to fill themselves like tanks with whisky and coffee, while they (because of their livers and also because they are abstemious by nature) were keeping going on mineral water and an occasional coffee. Although the Italians were never sure if the British delegation was sober, they always attributed to them an immense political acumen.'

It was a libel, as the courts established when the matter came before them later that year, and certainly in Bevan's case a most improbable one, as anybody might discover who inquired about his habits from those who knew him. No one could ever call him abstemious, but hardly anyone ever saw him drunk. He rarely 'drank' when he was working, never when he had to make a speech. He had an extremely strong head which seemed unaffected by the quantities of liquor that might upset others. And to return to the libel, and the incident (rudely referred to sometimes by his friends as 'the Venetian blind') it was, among other oddities, highly improbable that he would be drinking whisky when so

[1] Alas, there were still strong objections to the fusion to be overcome from sections of Nenni's party.

well-situated to call upon the immobile delights of Soave and Valpolicella.[1]

But back to London and Suez and a Britain with her foreign policy in ruins; however, in the immediate post-Suez period it was not so much British policy – Britain, alas, had forfeited the power to influence anybody – which disturbed him. The United States stepped tentatively along the same path where Britain had strutted so disastrously, and few critical voices were raised to hold her in

---

[1] Bevan, with Dick Crossman and Morgan Phillips, took a libel action against the *Spectator*, and when, after the failure of the *Spectator* to publish a satisfactory apology, the issue was brought to court, each of the three defendants was awarded £2,500 damages. However, a wretched sequel to the affair came in 1963 – three years after Bevan's death – with the publication of a book, *The Old Fox: A Life of Gilbert Beyfus* (Frederick Muller) by Iain Adamson. Beyfus was Bevan's counsel in the case. The book contained extraordinary sentences which, of course, could not have been published with impunity in Bevan's lifetime: 'Bevan was committing perjury. He had been drunk. He was also eager to sue. "I've been libelled too often. I can get them on this," he told a companion ". . . Beyfus did not know that Bevan was lying." ' It might have been expected that accusations so serious would not have been made without the publication of full supporting evidence, even though the death of the man defamed removed any risk from the assailant. But neither in his book nor in the newspaper correspondence in which he subsequently engaged did Mr Adamson produce a tittle of evidence. He merely reiterated, without explanation: 'there are obvious reasons why I do not want to comment on my sources of information, but there is no doubt that Aneurin Bevan did commit perjury in the witness box'. Even more deplorable, however, was an article which appeared in the *Western Mail* of 9 July 1963 by the 'Junior Member for Treorchy' which was the pseudonym for a former Cardiff Conservative M.P., Sir David Llewellyn. The article was entitled 'Was Nye a perjurer?' It talked of Mr Adamson's 'powerfully argued case', although he had confined himself to bare assertion without any argument whatever. To lend substance to the charge where so much was needed, he added the claim: 'What makes the charge of perjury even more damaging is that Iain Adamson has had access to the papers of Gilbert Beyfus who appeared for Bevan in the case.' This seemed to offer a clue to where the missing evidence might be sought. So I consulted at the time the very experienced junior counsel who had appeared with Beyfus, and he confirmed to me – and authorized me to state and publish – that nothing in the papers lent a shred of support to this wicked libel.

check. 'If the imperial mantle slips from the shoulders of John Bull,' Bevan wrote, 'it fits snugly on Uncle Sam. This is the simple formula which has governed the diplomatic strategy of the Western powers since the Berlin airlift. It is the Big Brother concept, or as Marshal Tito has described it, the idea of "the leading nation".' Early in the year, the United States administration enunciated as applicable to the Middle East what later became known as the Eisenhower doctrine. Bevan was suspicious from the start. It was, first of all, an exclusively American policy; it was, like Suez, a policy declared without consulting allies. It was, like Suez, a policy which could envisage the by-passing of the United Nations, since it talked of action by the United States to protect countries which became the subject of 'overt armed aggression from any nation controlled by international Communism'. It was, in the words of the original declaration, a proposal to 'give economic and military assistance to all countries or groups of countries in that region wishing to benefit from it, it being understood that this assistance could include the use of American forces'. Apart even from the military reference, the proposed method of offering economic aid offended Bevan's deepest instincts about how international investment should be channelled, if it was to do its work. Only by such investment on a huge scale could the developing countries be saved from the kind of slavery to the future to which the Russian people had been subjected; and only thus could India, for example, be enabled to sustain her democratic institutions; and yet the new nations would not, could not, accept this assistance from a paternalistic Big Brother. The proper agency to conduct the whole operation was the United Nations. Tirelessly Bevan had argued this thesis ever since the pamphlet *One Way Only* was published in 1951 and he returned to it with renewed force when confronted with the Eisenhower doctrine. Nasser called it 'a corollary of the Franco-British policy of aggression', and Bevan was inclined to agree. And he was naturally displeased when his leader, Hugh Gaitskell, on a visit to the United States at the time of the Eisenhower declaration, responded in different terms (and without any attempt at consultation), calling it 'a valuable contribution to peace', and thereby seemed to award a quite gratuitous victory to the post-Suez Government.[1] Could the political reflexes of the two men ever be harmonized? By the one, declarations from Washington must be given the benefit of all doubts. For the other, they were the source of many of the world's ills, not of its likely salvation. And by a similar reckoning, he was not prepared to dismiss out of hand all proposals that came from Moscow. As it happened, in February of that year, in response to the Eisenhower doctrine, the Soviet Union put forward their own proposals for a Middle Eastern settlement, for the removal of foreign troops, an arms embargo, and the neutralization of the area. Since it echoed so much that he had been saying for weeks – ever since the effective collapse of the Baghdad Pact – Bevan was bound to give it a qualified welcome.

But for all the Suez upheaval, Bevan had not altered his view about Nasser and Nasser's methods. ('If the sending of one's police and soldiers into the darkness of the night to seize somebody else's property is nationalization, then Ali Baba used the wrong terminology.') And Nasser having won his victory, and being sustained for a period at least by it in the eyes of the Arab peoples, Bevan was all the more eager to exploit the moment for a genuine Middle Eastern settlement and to secure the recognition of what he considered to be the legitimate claims of Israel. He was anxious about the pressure exerted by the United Nations, with full American and British backing, to secure a seemingly unconditional Israeli withdrawal from the Gulf of Akaba and the Gaza strip. Of course, the principle that no nation should profit by an act of aggression was unquestionable, but it was necessary also that nations should be able to live and trade and conduct their commerce through the Gulf of Akaba and the Suez Canal itself; what became of *that* principle? It was a part of the United Nations' responsibility to ensure that the state of affairs which helped to provoke the war should not be reconstituted. And when, after much agonizing debate on the issue among

---

[1] In the Commons debate later in May, the announcement of the Eisenhower doctrine was hailed by Macmillan as one of the successful outcomes of the Suez expedition and the division between Gaitskell and Bevan on the subject helped to secure for Macmillan what he considered a parliamentary triumph. (See *Riding the Storm* by Harold Macmillan, p. 238.)

the Israeli leaders and, as Bevan believed, full and proper consideration for Nasser's susceptibility, the withdrawal was made, he underlined how disastrous it would be for the reputation of the United Nations if the expectations founded on the withdrawal were betrayed. He was back to his pre-Suez theme, and he believed he had proved his consistent allegiance to it throughout; it was *not*, he repeated, the function of the United Nations to preserve national sovereignties as though they were something inviolable. The very opposite was the case; one of the purposes of the United Nations was to secure the voluntary and collective limitation of national rights in the interests of peace.[1] And it was these sober themes which he drew together in another major speech in the House on the Middle East, once he had quietened some Suez group interruptions. ('It does not come well from guilty people to misbehave in the dock.') It was the United Nations, he said, which had secured the protection of Egypt's rights and it was the United Nations which had the duty to secure the protection of Israel's rights. It would be appalling if 'Israel's act of courageous faith' went unrequited, and it would be 'unforgivable' if shipping were to be interfered with in the Gulf of Akaba, and the same understanding would have to apply, after a reasonable interval perhaps, to the Suez Canal itself. But what would happen, went the interruptions, what would he propose, if these expectations were unfulfilled? 'There is nothing more foolish in public life,' he replied, 'than to imagine all the various alternatives that may happen and then try to find an answer to each of them. We cannot go into negotiations with anybody with a shillelagh in one hand and an olive branch in the other. They cancel each other out.' The proper course was to negotiate in the hope of success and continuously to seek to provide the conditions of success – 'otherwise we shall live with calamity three times – once in anticipation, once in realization, and once in recollection'. And the primary condition of success was to find new policies entirely different from those which had blocked the oil supplies, inflamed the fervent nationalism, and failed to relieve the grinding poverty of the area. It would not be done by substituting American patronage for British patronage, for

[1] *Tribune* 15 March. The argument about the Israeli withdrawal was followed up in detail over previous weeks and in the House on 14 March.

that would still require nations to accept the subordinate status against which they were revolting, and it could not be done by preaching homilies to the Russians. But was it not the right approach to look for the common interests between the great states themselves and the smaller ones, by devising at last the international system whereby the rich nations could help the poor without insulting their nationhood and their dignity? And when, in particular, the Russians said they were ready to discuss the provision of economic aid, should we not have jumped at it? Instead they had been brushed aside with something like diplomatic contempt.

But some other particular messages from the Soviet Union had been treated with equal scorn, and as the strange story leaked out, Bevan read it with amazement: amazement that so many of his contemporaries did not read them with the seriousness he did, since they seemed, in his opinion, to add a new dimension to the Suez crisis. They were the private letters which Marshal Bulganin had addressed to Anthony Eden and Guy Mollet during September and October of 1956, and of course the fact that they had clearly not been written originally for propaganda purposes added to their significance. But eventually – in April 1957 – the Russians did decide to publish the documents, and the Foreign Office, by a brilliant coup, just got in first. But it was not these capers which interested Bevan. He took the opportunity of the next debate on the Middle East[1] to underline the significance of this 'very remarkable correspondence'. One was a letter from Bulganin to Eden, dated 11 September 1956. It was written in a friendly tone; it took account of 'the interests of Britain and France as maritime powers'; but it spelt out what would be the consequences of the attempt to seize the Canal by force, and 'how it might end'. It would cause tremendous destruction on the Canal itself. It would cause the destruction of the oilfields nearby and the pipelines running through the Middle Eastern countries; it could end only in failure. And so, concluded Bulganin, 'I must declare to you, Mr Prime Minister, that the Soviet Union, as a great power which is interested in the maintenance of peace, cannot stand aside from the question'. And here, said Bevan in the debate, 'Her Majesty's Government are

[1] *Hansard* Vol. 570 Col. 683 16 May 1957.

told by a great power that the action we took might result in a third world war – *yet they took it* . . . In face of that correspondence, and of the warnings and premonitions of the Soviet Union, the action of Her Majesty's Government in declaring war on Egypt last November can only be described as an *act of criminal, frivolous lunacy*'. But that was not all. There was another letter – sent on 23 October, a significant date, only seven days before the Suez ultimatum – giving the Soviet view on the proposals then before the Security Council for solving the crisis and indicating that the Soviet Government were satisfied that an agreed decision had been reached with the British representative among others, welcoming the step forward and the prospect of further negotiations. Here, said Bevan, in private correspondence, was the indication of a significant advance in the negotiations 'only a few days before we launched the attack upon Egypt. *Only a few days*'. Often during the Suez controversies, it was assumed by the expert commentators that the attitude of the Soviet leaders was a presumption or an irrelevance, both their warnings and their threats. Their own hands were to become so deeply stained in Hungary and their capacity for cynicism was so unplumbable and, as it happened, their dire warnings were never executed – so why, the argument ran, should any interest or credence be attached to their rantings? But Bevan could not listen patiently to such protestations, particularly when it appeared that the Government were more interested in fostering anti-Soviet animosity than in understanding Soviet aims.[1] He was too concerned to consider whether the people of Hungary could have been saved if the folly of Suez had never been perpetrated; too eager to discover how a common interest between East and West could be extracted from their perpetually jarring antagonisms;

[1] Macmillan noted in his diary, as recorded in *Riding the Storm* (p. 237). 'His speech (Bevan's) which was to have been absolutely devastating, failed completely. He spoke for 45 minutes – was rather dull and made a great error in resting too much of his case on the Bulganin letters to Eden. (Even the Socialists, after Hungary, don't much like Bulganin's Pecksniffian lectures.) It was rather like my speech yesterday, though (I think) worse. He had two good jokes, and that was all.' Most other observers did not agree about the failure of Bevan's speech, but it is interesting to note afresh how little significance, either in the privacy of his diary or later in 1971, Macmillan attached to the Bulganin correspondence.

too determined to see how fresh Budapest or Suez tragedies could be avoided. And the truth was there to be read in the Bulganin letters, private letters not written for their propaganda effect; letters written not, be it noted, in a minatory, grandiloquent tone, but written surely to stop a war. More than ever he himself wanted to talk to the Soviet leaders, to argue with them, to search for the bedrock of common interest on which peace could be constructed.

However, it was not in parliamentary debate in Britain that Bevan achieved his most spectacular victory in the post-Suez period. In April he went on his second visit to India and he arrived in New Delhi when official relations between Britain and India were more strained than at any time since the Indian Independence Act of 1947. India had been deeply affronted not only by the Suez policy itself but by the insensitivity shown by the British Government in refusing to consider or consult Indian interests, and this attitude had naturally intensified all the irritations arising from British wariness over the years in accepting Nehru's policies for Korea, Indo-China and the Far East generally. But in April 1957, a fresh and even more potent cause of division was added to the others: Britain at the United Nations – it looked like a tit-for-tat against Nehru for his Suez strictures – had taken the lead in criticizing Indian policy in Kashmir. Altogether, the issue of the continued membership of the Commonwealth had come starkly to the forefront, and for a few days Nehru and his Foreign Minister, Krishna Menon, seemed to be fighting a losing battle to keep the Commonwealth connection. Immediately on his arrival Bevan sat through a foreign affairs debate in the distinguished visitors' gallery of the Indian Parliament and could measure for himself the scale of the storm. Nehru was compelled to say that the question of membership of the Commonwealth might 'some time or other require further consideration', and next day Bevan addressed both Houses of the Indian Parliament. He spoke soothing words about Kashmir, fierce words about the dangers of the Eisenhower doctrine and any other such patronizing displays of a new imperialism, complimentary words about the role India had played in world affairs – but these might be expected, since his voice had reached them from afar before. But then he offered a history lesson in strictly Bevanite style. He told how Edmund Burke and Charles James Fox had advocated American independence as ardently as George Washington; how it was one of the glories of British freedom that rebel voices in Britain could reach out to find an alliance with rebels in other countries; how the Opposition in British Parliaments had the right to be heard in distant lands, since they might later become the Government; how wrong it would be for Indians to despair of British policy; 'how the Churchills and the Cecils were in Parliament for many centuries before the Bevans arrived and brought a certain civilizing influence'. By the time he had reached the core of his appeal, he had won the title to speak bluntly. He said that Indians who exercised the right to criticise British policy must not complain if British people returned the compliment – even on Kashmir. He argued that the Commonwealth was only held together, for the good of nations East and West, by this readiness to disagree and yet not to quarrel irremediably, and he insisted that for India to leave the Commonwealth would be an act of folly, a profound blunder, just at the moment indeed when the institution was transforming itself into the kind of body which the new nations required in their own interest: stronger language than Nehru himself could employ. 'Mr Bevan's epic speech,' wrote 'Darem', the political correspondent of the *Times of India*, was 'a major factor in stemming the tide of public opinion.' 'Using all the Celtic magic at his command,' wrote Elisabeth Partridge, Indian correspondent of the *News Chronicle*, 'he has revived India's respect for Britain and the Commonwealth. It has been a miracle. And it has confirmed Mr Bevan as among the most accomplished Welsh wizards since Merlin.'

A day or two later, at a press conference, he was caught in another mood. Of course, many of his replies found favour: on Suez, on American policy, on much else, but nothing could stop him expressing his views on Israel and Nasser and all the tender topics which he might have sidestepped. Indian opinion, he suggested, was 'getting more instructed' on these questions; Indian opinion should exert its influence to inform Nasser that 'it was not only the duty of other nations to live at peace with him – it is his duty to live at peace with them'. Indian leaders had agreed that the Arab states must recognize the existence of the state of Israel, and

18

that fact of life should be accepted along with the others his audience had been cheering a few minutes before.

So India listened to this soft-spoken rabble-rouser who rarely left a press conference without having said, in language they could somehow not find offensive, the awkward home truths they had most wanted not to hear. On his contrary way home he called at Karachi without suppressing his unpopular views about Kashmir; at Baghdad and Teheran where, alas, his deep distaste for the blacker side of Moslem customs went unrecorded, but not, it may be suspected, unhinted at; at Istanbul where he did make a powerful plea for the right of Archbishop Makarios, as the spokesman for the majority of Cypriots, to be heard; at Tel Aviv where, to the amazement of officials, he arrived without a visa. 'So you come to Israel as an illegal immigrant?' 'Yes,' he replied, 'and I'm certainly not the first.' But his abiding friendship for Israel would not dissuade him from offering awkward advice there too. 'No settlement of Middle East problems,' he said, 'will be possible without the participation of the Soviet Union. Russia is here and should be recognized and reconciled with.' Few other Eastern travellers have dared use the same technique. Once upon a time Napoleon said: 'It was by becoming a Catholic that I ended the Vendée war. It was by becoming a Mussulman that I established myself in Egypt, by becoming an ultramontane that I gained the priests of Italy. If I governed a nation of Jews, I should re-establish the Temple of Solomon.' Bevan somehow achieved his triumphs by an exactly opposite method; whenever he saw the old gods exercising their malign magic on the human spirit or, worse still, new ones being erected, he could not resist the temptation to knock them down, and never was the taste more startlingly displayed than on that iconoclastic odyssey of April 1957.

And that tour offers three other treasures; three more of the rare letters to Jennie; the first reveals what he truly felt about Pakistan; the second gave a hint of Labour Party struggles to come; and the third was for Jennie alone:

Tomorrow, I am off to Pakistan where I propose to stay three days as a guest of the Government. I am not looking forward to it in the least. With my departure from India the most pleasant part of my tour is at an end. From now on I shall be, if not among enemies, at the best in a cold area. The collective psychology of the Moslem states is definitely repulsive to me. It is so morbid and wildly irrational that I am conscious of an abiding sense of unease when I am in one of them. Forty per cent of the Budget of Pakistan is now provided by money from the U.S.A., although it is clear that as a nation Pakistan is falling apart. In the meantime the rearming of Pakistan is frightening India into diverting too much of her resources to the provision of defence. If the advisers of the U.S.A. were drawn from the Kremlin, the result could not be more harmful to democratic institutions in South East Asia.

Travelling is good but home is better. I shall take a good deal of persuading to leave you and the farm once I get back.

The second letter referred to reports just received about arguments concerning H-bomb tests – to be treated in the next chapter – and the political implications:

April 11.

It sounds as though you have been having an exciting time at the P.L.P. meetings. From what I can learn in the press Crossman has been doing his usual turnabout. He is reported as saying in Germany that he favours us making the bomb tests. Brown was merely saying what he knows Gaitskell supports. The more I reflect on Gaitskell the more gloomy I become, and the more I dread the ordeal before me if ever he becomes Prime Minister. With that power and authority in his possession it will be difficult to brake his reactionary impulses and compel him to make concessions early enough. Even the thought of the effort needed to influence him to the right courses makes my spirit sink.

It is true that Gaitskell will give in in the last resort but only after the Party suffers damage and leaving the leaders exhausted by wholly unnecessary private exertions.

I am delighted to learn that you intervened to such good effect. It is so hard in those awful meetings not to be strident and over-strained. I can never recall any occasion, after all these years, when I can look back with any feeling other than distaste on a speech of mine made at a Party meeting.

And finally, before departing on the tour which he would not omit, remembering his previous visit:

I shall pay my respects to the Taj and whisper your name to myself in the moonlight.

15

THE BOMB

1957[1]

Get the advice of everybody whose advice is worth having – they are very few – and then do what you think best yourself.

—CHARLES STEWART PARNELL[2]

DURING THE early months of 1957 men and women of the nuclear age began to perceive in clearer outline than before fresh aspects of its obscenity and horror. Not only were they equipped with instruments which could exterminate whole cities at a single blow and wreak unimaginable human tortures thereafter; not only had war between the great states become a calculation of total absurdity; but the mere testing of these weapons might condemn unknown numbers of children to be born crippled, deformed or imbecile. Whatever varying political remedies might be thought proper for this new plight of the human race, every civilized person must at first feel aghast and humble in the presence of it, and this was the sense which Aneurin Bevan had expressed even amid the ferocities of the Suez debates. All the strongest features in his personal psychology and political philosophy, and the two could not be separated, prompted him to

[1] Throughout most of this book I have sought to indicate my own personal relations with Aneurin Bevan in impersonal terms. I have thought this wise both for reasons of reporting and for the reasons of my own hero-worshipping attitude to him indicated in the footnote which appears on p. 164 of Volume I. But in this chapter, and at some other points in the rest of the book, I have sometimes found such personal reflections unavoidable if particular moments and scenes were to be illustrated.

[2] Quoted in Conor Cruise O'Brien's *Parnell*, p. 145.

believe that the approach to the unprecedented problem must be questioning, diffident, sceptical. Instead the world was offered the shrieking certainties of the Kremlin and the Pentagon, the trumpets of the holy war from both camps. One reason for Bevan's alleged 'anti-Americanism', adding to his inveterate suspicions of American capitalism, was that, according to the orthodoxy of the 1950s – approved by many in his own Party, headed by Gaitskell – America's dogmatism must be accepted as the cool light of democratic wisdom.

Suddenly these great matters became transmuted into the minutiae of Parliamentary Labour Party politics, and the process was not to be despised. Often, of course, disputes within the Party were influenced by personal rivalries or ambitions, and thus they were commonly represented in the newspapers; but more frequently they were dictated by the circumstance that politicians who wished to keep their parties together for effective action still could not help approaching new problems with clashing temperaments and principles. The narrowly averted H-bomb test split of April 1957 was a classic example. No Bevanite plotters were looking for a new crisis – in any case the arch-plotter was away in India, helping to hold the Commonwealth together. Every section of the Party, both inside and outside Parliament, was hoping that the effective unity displayed by the leadership in the Suez debates would lead to a revival in electoral prospects and the removal of the Government from office long before it had reached the limit of its allotted span. But the bomb was no respecter of Party requirements. Suddenly it disrupted the routine of Parliamentary business.

At a meeting in Bermuda at the end of March, the British Prime Minister and the United States President agreed that, in the absence of any general disarmament settlement with the Soviet Union, they should continue with the testing of nuclear weapons, and for Britain this meant that the final orders would soon be given for the explosion of the first British H-bomb near Christmas Island in the Pacific. 'Independent scientific organizations,' said the Bermuda communiqué, although their names were not specified in it, 'had agreed that no dangers to health were involved in the experiments,' and in the last week in March an official note was despatched to the Japanese Government reaffirming that Britain would not be de-

terred by the protests of those living in the area. All the official
announcements and all the answers in the House of Commons
were made with the same bland assurance. But the fact that the
deed was actually to be done in Britain's name shook the Parliamentary Labour Party, and on a Thursday night, at one of the
regular Party meetings, a commotion resulted in an understanding
that the leadership would attempt to clarify the Party's attitude at a
special meeting arranged for the following week. Formally, it might
be held that the Party's view was still governed by the support for
the manufacture of nuclear weapons contained in the official Opposition amendment proposed in March 1955 – the same which had
so nearly resulted in Bevan's expulsion. No one had dared to
attempt to dismantle that delicate piece of mechanism, lest he
should detonate a new explosion. On the other hand the conference
in 1956 had carried, with Executive approval, a resolution opposing
the continuing of nuclear explosions, and when many in the Party
pressed the view that Britain should propose 'an immediate cessation of H-bomb tests', this implied that Britain's bomb should
never be tested at all. Evidently, there was much confusion to be
dispersed, but neither vision nor tempers were improved when, at
the weekend, before the Party had the chance to conduct its review,
George Brown, the official spokesman on defence, intervened with
a Party broadcast in which he claimed that the tests must be
regarded as quite proper and inevitable. At the specially called
meeting a few days later, the Shadow Cabinet sought to pacify
ruffled feelings with a proposal urging a British initiative to secure
international agreement to stop the tests. But it was not enough.
Led partly by Jennie Lee, the meeting persuaded the Shadow
Cabinet not to proceed with its own resolution but to consider the
demand pressed from the floor that the British tests should be
suspended pending the attempt to secure the international agreement. The meeting was adjourned to give time for the processes of
parliamentary democracy to operate and at the re-convened meeting in the evening, Gaitskell, Brown and their colleagues bowed to
the will of the back-benches. Aneurin Bevan in India, as we have
seen,[1] read the news with a wry discernment and approval, and he
also gave his view on the subject of the H-bomb tests themselves in

[1] See p. 547.

terms which carried the issue wider. He was reported as saying: 'I wish to heaven that Britain would rise to her moral stature by surrendering her hydrogen-bomb experiment. I can see no good purpose at all in Britain also arming herself with that useless weapon.'

But those were words taken from their context; not wrenched or maliciously distorted, but without the ruminating accompaniment Bevan normally used in discussing the weapons themselves. For he would rarely talk about the weapons without referring in the same breath, if he could, to the policies, the strategies, the diplomacy, of which they were supposed to be the instrument and where the procedures for their abolition must be sought. The same man who knew that politicians must shout to be heard and simplify to be understood, would also insist that some truths could only be stated with the aid of conditional clauses.

No doubt is possible about how persistent and pervasive was the impact of the bomb on his thinking at the time. On the day of his return from India he said at a press conference that the proposed execution of the British test was 'immoral' and that any excuse about it being only a single test, necessary to establish that the British bomb would work, could not be sustained, since, presumably, we, like the Russians and Americans, would soon be insisting that further tests were needed to keep the weapons in trim. He was quickly engaged in angry scenes on the subject in the House of Commons with Macmillan,[1] Butler and other Ministers, and week

[1] How grotesquely a supposedly astute observer like Macmillan could misread Bevan's character and his approach to the issue raised by the bomb is indicated in Macmillan's memoirs. On p. 298 of *Riding the Storm*, he records that on 4 June 1957 he wrote in his diary: 'A flaring row, started by Gaitskell, continued by Bevan, and directed at me about the H-bomb; this is the first time that Bevan has really declared himself. He was away when we had the big debate. It's clear to me that he thinks the H-bomb can be an electoral winner for the Socialists and worked up into a sort of Peace Ballot Campaign. I fear that he is right.'

Next day Macmillan also sent a message to Charles Hill, in charge of publicity: 'I have been meditating during the last day or two about the by-elections and the swing of opinion from us. It is the fashion to say that it is the revolt of the middle class against the cost of living, coupled with the fear of the Rent Act . . . I wonder . . . whether all this propaganda about the bomb has really gone deeper than we are apt to think. This, combined with Suez, has drawn away from us that wavering vote with

after week he returned to the same subject in the country. Other nations, he said, might invoke the reasoning which Macmillan and the British Government used to defend their actions; 'we now have the H-bomb and can commit suicide like the rest. Before this reckless race ends, before this macabre logic works itself out, most nations in the world will want to possess the means of wiping out the rest of the world and themselves included'.[1] Furthermore, the discussion could not proceed without pondering the insidious effects of the weapon on our political institutions: 'The hydrogen bomb is essentially a weapon of surprise . . . by its very nature it withdraws from the people all rights of control over the issues of peace and war. It is essentially a weapon of dictatorship . . . there is only one way of continuing democratic institutions in this or any other country and that is by disarmament which involves the destruction of the hydrogen bomb.'[2] And sometimes he pointed to what he considered to be the most direct action a British Government could take: 'If Britain had the moral stature she could say: "we can make the H-bomb, but we are not going to make it. We believe that what the human race needs is leadership in the opposite direction, and we are going to give it. We are going to prove that there are influences and principles in the world that rise superior

---

vague Liberal and nonconformist traditions which plays such an important role because it is still the no-man's land between the great entrenched Parties on either side. I was very much struck by Bevan's intervention yesterday – clearly much to Gaitskell's disgust. He has obviously thought a lot about this. He was away in India when we had the debate in the House on the bomb and therefore is, up to now, uncommitted. He has obviously decided to go violently anti-bomb . . . and out-manœuvre Gaitskell, who still has some . . . qualms of conscience and is forced by intellectual pride, if for no other reason, to take a reasonably middle position. Bevan is by nature a Radical rather than a Socialist and not at all in sympathy with the intellectual Socialists. He is an old-fashioned Radical, who 50 years ago would have been Lib/Lab-anti-Church, anti-landlord, anti-Royalty and anti-militarist. I believe that he senses all this and thinks that the bomb will be the great grappling point. After all, it presents many features useful to the agitator. It has an appeal for the mother, the prospective mother, the grandmother and all the rest, and every kind of exaggeration or misstatement is permissible.'

[1] Speech at Eastbourne 14 June.
[2] Speech at Belle Vue, Manchester 24 June.

to those that attach still to the story of barbarism." I believe that if
we could say that, tens of millions of people all over the world
would once more lift their eyes to Britain. A nation like Britain,
with all its experience, all its sophistication, all its remaining
idealism, despite the fact that in the traditional sense it is no longer
as powerful as it was, nevertheless can still become the leader
throughout the world if it has the courage and the vision.'[1] And
occasionally, as at the miners' gala at Cardiff in June, he would urge
that if the Government would not act, the case required to be backed
by demonstrations on the streets.

Sometimes, too, he turned to argue with the defenders of the
bomb – with Lord Cherwell, for example, who attempted to assuage fears that large numbers of people would be given bone cancer
by the higher levels of radioactivity, and who insisted that the
price was small to pay for the nation's safety. Bevan disputed 'this
morality of numbers', insisted that other nations would also be con-
tributing to the macabre total, and therefore posed the question:
'what proportion of innocent people should be condemned to die
in this way before it would constitute an offence under the moral
code?' Or he turned, again, from the scientists to the soldiers; for
example, to Lieutenant-General Sir Frederick Morgan who had
written of 'all those nice-minded people who will say that we must
not be the first to use the bomb . . . even though if we are not the
first to use it, we shall never use it'. In other words, replied Bevan,
the temptation to strike first might become overpowering; so 'bearing in mind all these facts, the only conclusion that a calm appraisal
justifies is that the existence of nuclear weapons can no longer be
regarded as a deterrent to war, but as making war a certainty. In any
major crisis between the great powers the mounting tension will
tend to become unbearable . . . Decisions about life or death, about
the future of the human race, have passed out of the control of
civil political institutions so long as weapons of this character are in
the possession of governments . . . If the people are to recover
control . . . then we must apply our minds to the destruction of
nuclear weapons before they have the chance to destroy us'.[2]

[1] Speech at Reading 5 May.
[2] *Tribune* 24 May – the first comment by him after the Christmas
Island explosion.

Perhaps some of these utterances might be regarded as rhetorical. Certainly they were influenced by the mood he discovered or helped to elicit among the great audiences he was addressing up and down the country. He would not regard that as a criticism; it was his method of public speech and political activity. Ordinary people, he said, when the House of Commons had a debate on disarmament generally in July, were becoming impatient with the whole tenor of the debate. 'It just makes no sense,' he said; the politicians have evolved 'means that no longer serve the ends that all of us cherish.' Who could believe that weapons of mutual suicide were still weapons of national defence? And then he pictured the great masses of people outside escaping, as he had been tempted to escape with them, from the plodding next step of the political leaders at Westminster. But he could not, however much he wished, make the escape complete himself. He had to engage in detailed discussions and interminable committee meetings with other members of the Shadow Cabinet, with Gaitskell, George Brown, Philip Noel-Baker and the others, to shape their attitude towards the international disarmament discussions then proceeding at Geneva and to relate these in turn to the other opportunities for political settlement in Europe, and sometimes a shift or advance in one sphere might entail the acceptance of a retreat in another, and the essential compromise – essential for the purpose of winning *any* advance – would not be easily understood by or explained to the audiences justly obsessed with the overriding peril. So it was in that summer of 1957. Notable advances, in Bevan's estimate, had been made in Labour's official attitude, and especially in its outlook on European policy, from the period only a few years before when some had talked of the need to fill every 'vacuum' in Europe with armies and guns and cold war pronunciamentos. 'Disengagement' was now accepted by the Opposition, although not by the Government, and it enabled Bevan to speak on behalf of the Party in accents and in concrete terms quite different from those the Party leaders had employed only a year or two before.

Why, he would ask, did the British Government not respond directly to the repeated suggestions from the Russians that they might be ready to consider a new European security system, one in which the Russian armies could be withdrawn from the satellite states? Why did the Government not try to find out whether the Khrushchev offers were genuine? Why did they not seek a special prior agreement about stopping H-bomb tests? Macmillan seemed to argue that progress towards disarmament must depend upon reaching a political settlement, which in turn meant an agreement about Germany, which meant in turn again giving Dr Adenauer a veto over all progress towards a European settlement. An election was soon to take place in the Federal German Republic and the Western leaders seemed more interested in assisting his victory over his Social Democratic opponents than in seeking any détente with the Russians.[1] Macmillan had replied to the Russians officially 'that all Western proposals for European security are contingent on a unified Germany with a freely elected all-German Government, free to choose its own foreign policy'.[2] Such are the ironic convolutions in which statesmen may find themselves unconsciously trapped – to accord, without a blink of historical reflection, the highest of all priorities to the achievement of a Germany 'free to choose its own foreign policy'. Not so many years before, that apparition had been the cause of most of Europe's troubles. Bevan could not turn his back on this part of the argument even if he had wished. He knew how much the German problem bulked in the minds of the Soviet leaders; how could it not do so? He knew how they feared the rise of another Hitler; were not the same kind of social forces being assembled there? These political questions jostled for settlement with the disarmament questions. In that same July speech Bevan recalled the old inter-war debate about which should come first, the reduction of the arms or the settlement of the quarrel. He had some sympathy with the French view of that period that men would not throw away their arms while they were still afraid, while the cause of the quarrel still festered. But now the nature of the weapons themselves meant 'the duplication of the old primordial fears'. Often in a speech he would argue with himself. Sometimes this was a dialectical trap for an opponent, but sometimes he would be feeling his own way towards a synthesis. And sometimes the synthesis might not be reached; always he ran the risk of exposing himself to the misinterpretation which

[1] *Tribune* 2 August.
[2] Quoted in *Tribune* 21 June.

might be placed upon some uncompleted, tentative judgment he had made in the course of his search. But this was the way his mind worked; the risks were the price to be paid for his originality.

Another controversy on a different subject altogether intertwined with the Party's disputes about the H-bomb and contributed to the awareness of many of the participants that the new-found unity of the Party, following the Blackpool Conference, was still fragile. At once an old question presented itself in the new context: did the controversies create the suspicions or the suspicions the controversies? It was often hard to determine; in the main the Left adhered to the first contention, the Right to the second, the Left arguing that there was a fundamental, relentless exertion by the Right to wean the Party away from its commitment to public ownership as a central feature of Labour Party policy, while the Right might retort that the lines could not be drawn with this exactitude, that a more pragmatic approach could, without any departure from principle, help to remove the danger of superfluous or factitious quarrels. Some of these ancient arguments were stirred anew when the National Executive published in July a policy document called *Industry and Society* on which a sub-committee had been working intensively for several months. Bevan had been one of the fourteen members of the sub-committee and was fully committed to its recommendations. But, thanks partly to his Indian and Middle Eastern tour, he had not been a diligent participant in the sub-committee's work. He had tended to sit on the sidelines and await the outcome.

Industry and Society – it was drafted by Peter Shore, then in the Labour Party research department – contained the most powerful, up-to-date statement of the case for public ownership issued officially by the Labour Party since 1945. It described how private industry in Britain was concentrated as never before in the hands of some five hundred big companies in which the shareholders had ceased to perform the functions once supposed to justify their existence, such as the provision of capital or the taking of risks. They performed no national purpose whatever; the good old Socialist word of abuse, 'the parasites', had become an exact definition. Jubilantly *Tribune* pointed out that official blessing was now given to the aphorism of one of Bevan's mentors, the great Thorsten Veblen: 'The ordinary investor is, in effect, an anonymous pensioner on the enterprise; and his share in the conduct of the industry is much like the share which the Old Man of the Sea had in the promenades of Sinbad.' And the fact that so much of the nation's wealth went to those who played no part in creating it helped to distort the economy, to encourage inflation, to forbid planning, and to sustain a gross inequality between different classes in the community. The first thirty-odd pages of the document might be regarded as a manifesto directed against MacDonaldism, Morrisonism, Deakinism and Butskellism, but in the middle the tone changed abruptly. Clearly the conclusion had been mangled in committee, or at least compromise had been reached by a resort to ambiguity. Apart from the firm commitment to renationalize the iron and steel and road haulage industries denationalized by the Tories, and a confirmation of the established Party policy to bring privately owned rented houses into municipal ownership, no guarantee was offered of a major extension of public ownership. Instead, the State would consider taking shareholdings in some of the five hundred companies. But what proportion of the shares and for what purposes and in how many industries? All these and many other questions were left open, and within a few days of the publication of the document a whole series of different interpretations were placed upon it by everyone who commented, including members of the sub-committee itself. Gaitskell gave the impression at a press conference that the Party's intention was to nationalize very little, that the commitment was only to take over, after investigation, inefficient firms, and that the private owners of the efficient firms would be left to reap their unearned profits. Crossman, who had never been an enthusiastic nationalizer, concurred in that judgment. Harold Wilson wrote an article for *Tribune*'s rival, *Forward*, in which he stated the possibilities in terms somewhat less restrictive than Gaitskell's. Ian Mikardo, on the other hand, who had been an active member of the sub-committee, explained in *Tribune* how the document could be used, by a Labour Government which had the will, for a far more ambitious programme of extended public ownership than anything the Party had put before the electorate in the previous three elections; in short, the conclusions of the document *could* be made to follow logically from its devastating premises. Literally that claim was incontestable, but in the ensuing controversy it soon became submerged. The share-takeover plan was paraded in the press as a substitute, welcome or sinister according to taste, for full-scale nationalization. 'Has the lion got any claws?' asked *Tribune*, contrasting the roar in the opening pages of *Industry and Society* and the reprieve which seemed to follow. Such rough debate among the old Bevanites offered much amusement and instruction for onlookers.

One person who fully participated in the exchanges was Jennie Lee. 'Too pink, too blue, too yellow,' was her unequivocal verdict on the conclusions of the document itself, but who could ever have expected a Right-wing Executive to bring forth a Left-wing manifesto, and why must it be assumed that the only way ahead for the Party was for the Left on the Executive to resign or threaten to resign when the Right blocked the path of advance? It was necessary for the movement itself to exert its powers and to realize that the chance was available to do so as never before, now that the Party was no longer weighed down by the old rigid system whereby Left-wing constituency parties confronted a solid Right-wing trade union leadership in unbroken, unbreakable conflict. It so happened, by deliberate decision, that Jennie Lee that year became a candidate for the women's section of the National Executive. She knew she was certain to be defeated, and in any case had no desire whatever to add all the hazards and labours of Executive membership to her other occupations of looking after Nye, looking after her mother, looking after her own constituency, and her own parliamentary duties. Moreover she had always been strongly opposed to the women's section on grounds of feminist principle. But it was essential to move the Executive to the Left, and the capture of two or three places out of the five in the women's section was the only way whereby this could be ensured. Jennie felt she was forced to undertake the task, even though she dreaded it more than any other political duty which had befallen her since 1945. Her aims accorded with the course of developments which Bevan's own decision to stand for the Treasurership had started three years before. But immediately also, in the debate over *Industry and Society*, Jennie welcomed the strange sensation of seeing Nye outside the direct firing line; too heavy a burden, she believed, *could* be placed on those shoulders.

At the particular moment when she made her final choice about the Executive, he was away in Scotland for a few days staying with the Mackies in Laurencekirk, and some misapprehension occurred in their telephone conversation. Two days later she received this letter:

Darling Jennie,

You sounded very depressed last night on the phone, and you left me very anxious about you. I do hope nothing more serious upset you than a passing mood. I went to bed full of conjectures and worries about you. I realize that your vitality is low now, particularly when you need it most.

But cheer up. It will soon be over, and you must keep in mind that the outcome, whatever it may be, will be right for us.

You announced the arrival of the new car as though it is a calamity. A new car always excites me and I am looking forward to driving it – that is if you will allow me. I am delighted that you have a car more suited to you than the other.

Darling I love you very much and I am always upset when I think you are worried or unwell. So please buck up and remember we have a whole summer ahead of us to spend at the farm. You must hug the thought of our secret happiness and not let public duties weigh on you too heavily.

But what did he think himself of the public ownership issue which had come so much to the fore again? Any notion that his interest had abated, that he had become engrossed solely in the great matters of foreign affairs, momentous as they were, was untrue. He never believed that people would prove themselves good Socialists abroad who were bad Socialists at home. That was a form of escapism – evident at that particular time in connection with talk about the Socialist content of the Common Market – in which he was never likely to indulge.[1] Nothing had altered in his view

---

[1] In *Tribune* of 30 August 1957 he wrote: 'In European political circles, the argument about the Common Market is hotting up. If Conservatives get their way we shall soon be talking about nothing else . . . Tariffs, proscriptions in trade and restrictions of various kinds imposed by a congerie of sovereign Parliaments are vexatious and may constrict

about the role which public ownership must play in any policy worthy of the name Socialist,[1] and he was determined to use his newly-gained influence in the hierarchy of the Party to that end. But the crucial questions were: when, and how, and what might be lost if he exerted that influence too soon? Ian Mikardo's interpretation of the document and Jennie Lee's exhortation both suited his purpose, and *Tribune*'s carefree invective on the subject he greeted with a laugh and a special celebration at Fleet Street's El Vino's, once his haunt in the years of his own exultant editorship. He had never been exclusively a journalist and his distaste for Fleet Street had grown inordinately with the years, but he knew enough to agree that newspapers should not be edited by statesmen. And what made anyone think that politics should be conducted by them either, he would cheerfully ask? He wanted poets and philosophers to take over and a curse on all committees!

However, a crucial weakness of the Bevanites in those times was the scattering of anything which resembled the old group. The one in the House of Commons had been effectively destroyed by the Party meeting's decree of 1952, and the Crossman lunches had

---

production forces. But in the absence of a wider sovereignty, all the conception of a common market does is to elevate the market place to the status now enjoyed by the various European parliaments. It is at this point that Socialists become suspicious of what is intended. Is it the disenfranchisement of the people and the enfranchisement of market forces? Are we now expected to go back almost a century, reject Socialism and clasp free trade to our bosom as though it were the one solution of our social evils? ... The conception of the Common Market ... is the result of a political malaise following upon the failure of Socialists to use the sovereign power of their parliaments to plan their economic life. It is an escapist conception in which the play of market forces will take the place of political responsibility ... Socialists cannot at one and the same time call for economic planning and accept the verdict of free competition, no matter how extensive the area it covers. The jungle is not made more acceptable just because it is almost limitless.'

[1] In his main comment at the time *Industry and Society* was published, in an article in the *News of the World* of 21 July, he wrote: 'It is essential if we are to live in a stable society that the community should take charge of the commanding heights of industry. It is not necessary for public ownership to be universal. It is, however, essential that it should be sufficiently extensive to prevent the whole economy running amok.'

been poisoned by the H-bomb. *Tribune*'s Monday editorial meetings, with Bevan in highly exhilarating attendance every two or
three weeks, were not a satisfactory substitute. Some of us outside
the Commons were largely cut off from those cloistered within,
and how prodigiously different the world looked from the vantage
point of far-away Fleet Street than from those suffocating
hermetically-sealed Westminster corridors! One July night at the
end of that parliamentary session we sought to repair the failures of
communication with a dinner for a dozen of the old group at
Leoni's in Soho, the restaurant in the house where Karl Marx had
once found sanctuary. At the beginning of the proceedings we
drank a toast to the great man's memory and there was no sign then
– or at any other time, for that matter, in my knowledge of him –
that Bevan wished to disown his debt to Marxism, so long, of
course, as the doctrine was undogmatically interpreted. However,
Marx himself had once posed the question whether he was a
Marxist, and some people had asked whether Bevan was a Bevanite.
And, whatever these disputes over nomenclature might entail, I
recall that we spent so long that evening arguing about public
ownership and the tactical permutations which might arise at the
forthcoming Brighton Conference about *Industry and Society* that
no more than a few minutes were left to talk about the bomb. In any
case, M.P.s in late July are not usually in a fit condition to save the
universe; they are more like seasick voyagers who have narrowly
escaped shipwreck and cannot wait to get back to port and totter
down the gangplank.

During that summer Bevan undertook three journeys abroad in
his capacity as Labour spokesman on foreign affairs or as a member
of the Party's National Executive. He went to Toulouse as fraternal
delegate to the French Socialist Party Congress and was greeted
satirically as 'Citizen Bevan', doubtless come to deliver instructions
on anti-colonialism, by Max Lejeune, a Minister in Guy Mollet's
Government responsible for French policy in Suez and Algeria.
Bevan, unmoved by the jeer, sat silent while Mollet received a
standing ovation, and was horrified by the burst of strident chauvinism which seemed to punctuate the Congress and stifle effective
criticism. It was a terrifying exhibition of how all semblance of
Socialism could be drained away from a Socialist organization, how

a Party which abandoned the hard task of challenging capitalist power at home could become corrupted in its foreign aims too. Fortunately, on his return via Paris, he was able to renew his acquaintance with Mendès-France, and renew too his respect for French statesmanship. And he went, a little later, to Vienna, to the meeting of the Socialist International, and reopened the debate of Toulouse on more advantageous territory. Nobody there – except the embarrassed French delegate – would dare defend the French Socialist denial of Algerian independence, and everybody there was heartened by Bevan's robust defence of both the democracy and the Socialism in which democratic Socialists believed. He came away feeling that the Socialist International, so long sunk in a kind of 'twilight sleep', might be revived to help give Socialists the internationalist faith of which they had long been starved. He also went to Warsaw, via Bonn and Berlin, and talked with Gomulka and elaborated the Labour policy for disengagement in Europe, recently approved in Vienna, which might be expected to be popular in the city so often the victim of Russo-German engagement. But he did not omit to expatiate on the virtues of a free press, a much freer one than that contemplated by the recently-liberated Gomulka.

These were no more than skirmishes; even though, thanks to his contra-suggestiveness, Bevan's trips abroad were never likely to resemble the conventional exchanges of leading politicians. Much more significant was his journey, with Jennie, to Moscow and then down to the Crimea for a few days of intimate discussion with a genial and apparently confident Khrushchev. They talked long enough to be able to laugh and exchange reminiscences as ex-miners, and to discuss when – if ever, according to Khrushchev's taunt – the British steel industry would be nationalized in a manner ensuring that no one could denationalize it. Bevan quickly counter-attacked with some audacious criticism of Khrushchev's agricultural plan and the supposition underlying it that a vast investment in machines could solve the problem in the absence of the trained manpower to keep the machines operating. Of course, Soviet pride in their technological prowess was a topic that had to be treated tenderly but by the end of their talks Bevan could joke about this too. A huge jeroboam of Russian champagne adorned the lunch table. After others had failed to open it with a corkscrew Khrushchev, as unconventional a host as Bevan was a guest, challenged Bevan to show his prowess. So he picked up the bottle, crossed to the heavy mahogany door of the room where they were sitting and used the door to manipulate the cork, remarking with a broad grin, 'Western technique.'

But most of all they discussed the prospects of the H-bomb-ridden planet, starting with the Middle East but not stopping until they had discussed Karl Marx's locomotive of history. 'Why is it,' asked Khrushchev, 'that your diplomats are making so many mistakes these days? And why it is that we in the Soviet Union are having so many successes? You are more experienced than we are, you have centuries of diplomatic training behind you and much more knowledge of international affairs. Look at the Middle East, consider your failure in Jordan, your blunder over Egypt and now' – looking as he spoke across the Black Sea in the direction of Turkey – 'consider Syria. I will tell you why. It is not because you have lost your skill but because your line is not correct, and ours is.' And then he went on to spell it out. 'In the Middle East your Government and that of the United States are on the side of im-perialism against the Arab masses. We are on the side of the people against imperialist exploitation. The Arab people know that we have no interest to serve in the Middle East. We have got all the oil we need, but without Middle East oil you could not live.' And at this point Bevan interrupted. 'Yes, and it is just this dependence on Britain and the whole of Western Europe on oil that you must keep in mind in all your policies in that area. What may seem to you to be a mere diplomatic game is for us a very serious affair.' To which Khrushchev replied: 'We in the Soviet Union have always realized that fact. We have no wish to cut off the people of Europe from their oil supplies but you should get them on commercial terms and under conditions which maintain the independence of the Arab peoples and their right to choose what government they desire.' And while Bevan, as he said in reporting the exchange, suppressed the temptation to mention Hungary and Poland, Khrushchev continued: 'Take Syria. We have loaned her credits, and we have supplied her with weapons for defence at her request. This has been described, especially in America, as evidence of

Soviet aggressive intentions, and was an act of provocation. When you and the United States provide weapons to members of the Baghdad Pact and especially to Saudi Arabia and to Jordan, it's all right. But when the Soviet Union does the same with Egypt and Syria, it is an act of provocation.' And to that, said Bevan, he could see no effective reply, and Khrushchev pressed the point home. 'We offered some time ago to stop the supply of arms to the Middle East if you and the Americans would do the same. But you had committed yourself to the Baghdad Pact which was aimed at us. What did you expect us to do?' And then he suggested that the Turks and the Americans were engaged in an elaborate scheme to stage a counter-revolution in Syria, like enough to what might happen to be seriously considered. 'And as I came away from that conversation,' wrote Bevan in *Tribune* on 16 October, 'my conviction grew that the line taken by the Labour Party is even more true today than when we first promulgated it many months ago. It is that no arrangement for a Middle East settlement will have any validity unless it is negotiated with and agreed to by the Soviet Union. Time is not on our side. But it does no harm to the Soviet leaders. The trumps are assembled in their hands but they also are aware that if they play them too strongly, and too brutally, they themselves would be involved in the holocaust that would follow.'

Altogether, he came away from the talks convinced that an arms embargo leading to a Middle East settlement *was* possible, if only the West would undertake an intelligent initiative; convinced too that the Labour Party's official policy about the tests – the cessation of nuclear tests without conditions – could start the world on the road to disarmament; convinced that the gulf in understanding between East and West was not so wide that it could not be bridged; that there was a common appreciation of the threat overhanging all mankind. War had once been the locomotive of history, and the Russian revolution emerged from one world war and the Chinese revolution from another, but, said Bevan, he and Khrushchev had discussed the outcomes of a third world war: 'it would not enlarge the area of revolution, it would contract the area of mankind'. And the British bomb and its manufacture? It was not on the agenda, and Bevan had seen no reason for putting it there. It was not that he was ever afraid to raise awkward topics, although clearly there were several which he knew were scarcely suitable for a Khrushchevian Crimean holiday. But between questions of the British bomb and the large possibilities of a world settlement there seemed to be a lack of proportion.[1]

He returned to face a Britain and a Brighton in which the political consequences of the bomb for the Labour Party and for himself – not overlooked before, but never properly explored – were at last coming to be appreciated. While he had been on his travels, the agenda for the Party Conference had been published, and 120 resolutions on the bomb, almost all of them calling for unilateral repudiation in one form or another, showed that this topic would push all others, including even the furious controversy over *Industry and Society*, into a quite subordinate place. A body known as the H-bomb Campaign Committee had attracted 5,000 people to a meeting in Trafalgar Square, addressed, among others, by Bevan's three close associates on the National Executive, Barbara Castle, Ian Mikardo and Anthony Greenwood. More and more it did appear – due chiefly no doubt to the Christmas Island explosions earlier in the year – that the strange numbness which seemed to afflict the national consciousness on the subject was being removed, and Bevan himself had played a principal part in the achievement. He had the ear of the nation on these and all inter-allied subjects of peace probably more than any other politician in the land, certainly more than anyone else in the Labour Party, and he was aware of the likely dilemmas which would confront him at the Conference. He knew that, as Labour's Shadow spokesman on foreign affairs, he might be called on to make the main speech on the subject, but since he was not the chairman of the Party's International sub-committee that was by no means certain. But neither he nor his

---

[1] Those talks were mutually educative. Tom Driberg recalls two long private interviews with Khrushchev, one before Suez, one after the holiday with Bevan. On the former occasion, he had to spend the first hour of the discussion defending the Labour Party – and even its leadership! – from Khrushchev's assumption that it was a mere appendage of the Tory Party. On the latter occasion Khrushchev's opinion of the Labour Party had entirely changed: one reason was that Labour had led the opposition to the Suez aggression; the other, Khrushchev conceded, was his encounter with Bevan.

closest friends had seen the implications of these dilemmas in all their sharpness, and most of the discussions on the subject, like the dinner at Leoni's in July, had ended in a desultory indecision, a vague assumption that some formula might be found to push the Party further Leftwards – as had happened on the issue of the H-bomb tests – without provoking a rupture. I believed, and I think he believed, that however awkward the corner to be turned, he would be able to do it in a major speech covering the whole perspective of foreign policy and setting the issue of the British bomb in its proper place within it. I spoke to him just after his return from Moscow, particularly to remind him that the *Tribune* meeting, normally held on the Wednesday of Conference, was this time to be held on the Tuesday. Both of us were scheduled to speak at it and we might need some prior consultation which I wanted to fix in advance since, being engaged in the production of *Tribune*, I would not be arriving till Tuesday. 'See you next week at Brighton, boy,' he said cheerfully enough and not at all like a man on the way to a crucifixion.

The next scene in the drama, concealed from public knowledge and unreported at the time, took place on the eighth floor at Transport House when the Party Executive met for its usual pre-conference meeting. At an earlier meeting of the International sub-committee of the Executive, before Bevan's return, Gaitskell had insisted that a document on defence and disarmament policy should be drafted for presentation to clear up the general ambiguities in the Party's policy which had existed ever since the previous April when agreement had been reached to oppose H-bomb tests without defining the consequences. But several other members of the committee had objected to this course and for varying reasons; Sydney Silverman and Barbara Castle because they were outright 'unilateralists', Crossman because he now argued that a repudiation of the nuclear dependence was required for the development of a coherent defence policy, and Sam Watson, the chairman of the International committee because he wanted to avoid a crisis within the Executive. However, Gaitskell had committed himself to the idea of a new declaration and it was his proposed draft, refashioned in the interval by Morgan Phillips and Dick Crossman, which formed the first basis of discussion at the full Executive meeting;

it reflected the compromise of the previous April, offered no concession to the demand for a unilateral cessation of the manufacture
of the bomb, and in effect excluded the real issue of the British
H-bomb altogether. For a moment it seemed that this pallid and
ineffectual compromise might carry the day, and recollections and
reports now differ on the question of how and why the Executive
was launched into the next part of the proceedings. But within a
minute or two Bevan was making an elaborate statement ranging
over his talks with Khrushchev, the general issues of the defence
dilemma and the precise dilemma facing the Executive and the
Party. He believed that if the Party adhered strongly to its commitment to stop the tests Russia would follow suit and the United
States would, therefore, be compelled to follow suit also, and he did
not seek to escape the logic that if tests were stopped manufacture
would have to stop also. But he did not like and could not support
the Gaitskell-Morgan Phillips draft. It raised, implicitly at least, all
the questions about whether Britain would ever use the bomb first,
a question particularly delicate for him in view of the 1955 controversies; it made insufficient concessions to his point of view to
enable him to speak on it. If the Executive pressed it, he would
have to sit silent while someone else replied. And he had his alternative suggestion. Why not substitute for the draft the resolution of
the Socialist International at Vienna which had already been approved by so many Socialist Parties in Europe and which, as
Bevan could testify, found considerable favour with the Russians.
It was an elaborate well-considered proposition which had the
special merit of emphasizing that the suspension of H-bomb tests
should not be made dependent on securing prior agreement on the
whole of the rest of a disarmament programme or on the kind of
political settlements upon which the Western powers officially
were insisting. And then, according to the bare words of the official
N.E.C. minutes, Bevan added: 'There should be an addendum to
the resolution stating the Party's case for stopping unilaterally the
manufacture of all nuclear weapons.' In fact, Sydney Silverman
and Barbara Castle had pressed the point that the Vienna resolution
did not meet the immediate question about the manufacture of the
British bomb and Bevan had immediately agreed that the addition
was necessary. Thereafter the meeting was plunged deeper and

deeper into the dilemma previously sidestepped. The debate 'on the question of unilateral disarmament', again in the words of the official minutes, looked as if it could continue all night, until everyone suddenly agreed that the matter must be postponed until the next day while the rest of the business was transacted. But on the next day Bevan and Gaitskell were at one at least in the view that the decision should be postponed again. He suggested and Gaitskell seconded that the matter should be deferred until the Sunday when the nature of the composite resolution agreed by the delegates on the Saturday would be available and when a new draft statement could be presented. But why not, asked Sydney Silverman, have an immediate discussion to help in the preparation of the draft? He wanted to renew the debate of the day before when Bevan had been able to use his leverage in refusing to speak, if no statement satisfactory to him was devised. But that motion was defeated by eighteen votes to six, with Bevan in the majority. It was no more than a procedural resolution, but the pressures upon him were already being strongly applied. If he used his sanction of refusing to speak it would appear, certainly several of the newspapers would do their best to make it appear, that the Party was heading for another 'split' – provoked by Bevan.

Next day he went to the meeting of delegates where resolutions on the bomb and all its ramifications were to be 'composited' into the single critical resolution for the debate, but any idea, if he had such, of moderating its terms was vain. The resolution to be moved by Vivienne Mendelson of Norwood and seconded by Harold Davies, M.P. – the Norwood resolution or No. 24 resolution, as it came to be called – was a fair representation of the will of the delegates concerned; it was a direct, comprehensive resolution calling on Britain and the Labour Party to renounce the testing or manufacture of nuclear weapons in any form whatsoever. Hanging in a fortnight can concentrate the mind no more wonderfully than a Labour Party Conference 'composite' resolution. No escape from the direct test was now available. Bevan spent the rest of that day arguing with Sam Watson, with Ian Mikardo, with Hugh Delargy and others, and above all, with Jennie and with himself. It was a mental process he was sometimes ready to do on his feet; but not this time. Next day he would have to give his answer to the Executive, and some time that night he made his decision. At the Sunday meeting, Mikardo proposed and Silverman seconded that the Norwood resolution should be accepted, and Bevan, in reply, set out the general form of response he proposed making on behalf of the Executive and why he believed – to quote the official minutes – 'the full implication of accepting this resolution would mean the dismantling of international alliances and commitments, dismaying the Commonwealth and reducing Britain to complete negation in the councils of the world. The policy set out in the resolution on disarmament carried by the Socialist Congress in Vienna should be accepted as Party policy'. And then after a lengthy discussion, Mikardo's motion was defeated by eighteen votes to five. Barbara Castle attempted a last-minute rescue operation with a proposal that Norwood should be invited to remit the resolution on the basis that the question of renunciation would be left open for the Executive to decide later. She was defeated by seventeen votes to eight. And finally: 'Mr Watson said that in view of the excellent statement made by Mr Bevan and the way in which he had outlined the policy, he did not think there was need for a second National Executive Committee speaker in the debate and he wished to withdraw. This was agreed to.'

Next morning no news of this last momentous confluence leaked to the newspapers, although portentous whispers had been percolating since the Saturday afternoon. On the Tuesday morning a report in the *Daily Express* said that Bevan had shocked the old Bevanites on the Executive and left them 'mystified, hurt and angry', and when I saw him at his hotel he gave me the account of the line he had developed to the Executive, and since he made it clear that his choice was irrevocable, there was not much to be said. I urged him to consider saying at some stage in his speech that the decision now would not exclude unilateral action about the bomb later and he said that he would, but this implied no real qualification of his main case. Then we defined a few frontiers for observation at the *Tribune* meeting that night, where I would be reiterating the *Tribune* policy of renouncing the bomb and where he would be specifically avoiding the issues of the conference debate on Wednesday about *Industry and Society* and any reference whatever to the bomb debate fixed for Thursday. Then we also agreed, come hell or high-water, to have a good dinner at English's on the Wednesday night. And that evening a vast queue of delegates swarmed outside the Corn Exchange long before the doors were opened and then poured in to fill every stifling inch of it. They laughed when I said, referring to *Industry and Society*, that the Executive had been acting on a principle hitherto unknown to science – spontaneous unity combined with simultaneous leakage. They cheered when I said that the way to peace was for Britain to renounce the bomb. But both the laughter and the cheers were subdued and apprehensive. Nothing else mattered for that audience except what Bevan would say, nothing in the political world for most of them for years had counted much beside that. But that night, as he explained, he could say little and that week he could not speak in the 'uninhibited' manner which he envied. He talked of Germany and 'the sharp defeat' suffered in the return of Adenauer; he talked of America and the hazards of Dullesism; and he talked of his visit to Russia and his hopes and his fears; and his voice dropped: 'I have the deep conviction that we have not very much time left. There are forces abroad in the world that could bring us to disaster.' And he talked, too, of making the Labour Party effective in action, of the importance of our new-found unity, and yet he could add in the next breath and no one could challenge him: 'I do not regard loyalty to parties as the first of all loyalties. There are other supreme loyalties.' It was a masterly and moving performance, accurately assessed by one Conservative journalist who had come to jeer at the carousals supposed to be enacted at *Tribune* meetings. 'For the first time in my life,' he wrote, 'I heard an audience break into puzzled cheers. They had come to see a rowdy can-can – and they had been fobbed off with King Lear.'[1]

They streamed out into the Brighton pubs and cafés, sensing for sure now that terrible events were in the making but not able to estimate their scale and nature. And that was my feeling too. I believed he had made a deep error; I dearly wished he had followed his first instinct not to speak in the H-bomb debate or that he had accepted Barbara Castle's later escape route. But I believed still, more than ever after Tuesday and the dinner on Wednesday, that much would be salvaged by the way he would speak. Besides, there

[1] Charles Curran in the *Evening News* 2 October.

was work to be done and *Tribune* to be edited and the most awkward headline of the year to be devised; and a paper to be put to bed on the Wednesday afternoon in a manner which would not look too inappropriate on Thursday and Friday. All through that Wednesday the Conference debated *Industry and Society* and at the end the critical amendment moved by Jim Campbell of the National Union of Railwaymen and strongly supported, among others, by Jennie Lee, was defeated by 5,383,000 to 1,442,000. No one could disguise the size of the Left-wing defeat, and it was hard to find that headline for *Tribune*. Then I suggested: 'WE'LL KEEP THE RED FLAG FLYING HERE' – with the HERE heavily underlined. A few days later I heard that Nye thought the barb was aimed at him. But it never was.

As I sat in the gallery the next day, none of the other speakers gripped my attention, and most of the rest of that assembly, I suspect, tingled with the same expectancy. But it was a fine debate. Vivienne Mendelson from Norwood put her case with considerable force, not omitting to recall that 'one of the most prominent members of our Party' had been calling for marches through the streets against the bomb not so many months before. Harold Davies seconded with his own rich flow of Welsh exuberance. Then, scarcely less eloquent, followed Wedgwood Benn, Judith Hart, Philip Noel-Baker, John Strachey, and Frank Cousins, speaking with the kind of emotion no Labour Conference had heard from a general secretary of the Transport and General Workers for many generations. His speech against the bomb and the final appeal from one of the Party's greatest natural orators, David Pitt, produced the effect of a mounting, ominous thunder. And then Bevan was on his feet, speaking so quietly after the storm, and I still hoped against hope that a miracle was possible. He was saying that to state the argument as though it was one between those who support the hydrogen bomb and those who were against was to falsify the issue. If the Executive had asked him to come to the platform and support the bomb, of course he would have refused; he had made more speeches to more people condemning it than anybody in the Conference. But composite resolutions could be clumsy instruments; they could contain unintended or unexplained implications. And let the Conference be clear too about the policies to which the

Party was committed; the far-reaching programme for disarmament accepted by the Socialist International at Vienna and the Labour Party's notable addition – that a Socialist Government would take the initiative in suspending all tests, first to give a lead, as the Conference had urged, and second because it was immoral for a nation to make tests which would poison not only its own people but other peoples besides. And suspending the tests could mean suspending the production of the weapons, and in the interval made possible by the suspension, it would be hoped to move to the further stages in the disarmament; there too the Labour Party and the Socialist International were trying to remove the obstacles blocking the path to settlement, such as the insistence of the British Government that all moves to disarmament must be made contingent on political settlements. So far, so good; then he turned to the Norwood resolution. 'The great difficulty is that what it will mean does not appear on the surface. I do not believe this Conference ought to resolve all fundamental issues of British international relationships and British foreign policy as an incidental by-product of a resolution. Let me explain what I mean. You may decide in this country unilaterally that you will have nothing to do with experiments, nor with manufacture, nor with use. With none of these sentiments do I disagree, none of them at all. But you can't, can you, if you don't want to be guilty, appear to be benefiting by the products of somebody else's guilt? Let me put that more concretely. You will have to say at once – immediately, remember, not presently – that all the international commitments, all the international arrangements, all the international facilities afforded to your friends and allies must be immediately destroyed. [Cries of 'Why not?']. If you say "Why not", then say it in the resolution. It is not said there. It has not been said. [A cry of 'It is implied.'] Yes, it is implied, but nobody said it. Everybody argued about the horror that the hydrogen bomb is in reality, but what this Conference ought not to do, and I beg them not to do it now, is to decide upon the dismantling of the whole fabric of British international relationships without putting anything in its place, as a by-product of a resolution in which that was never stated at all.' And that indeed was the essence of his case and a powerful one, and the interruptions which had so far come from the floor were no more than developments of the debate. But then – and he was nearly halfway through his speech – something stirred his animosities and awakened his belligerence, and he turned to crush his opponents as I had heard him do a hundred times before. How much the deed was premeditated no one will ever know; the theme, yes, of course; but the actual words, the lash laid about our backs: who could tell whether that was intended?

'I saw in the newspapers the other day,' he continued, with a cold hate which we also knew, and perhaps indeed it was some cynical commentator who had unleashed the assault, 'that some of my actions could be explained only on the basis that I was anxious to become Foreign Secretary. [And there were, shamefully, some faint cries of 'Hear, hear.'] I am bound to say that it is a pretty bitter one to say to me. If I thought for one single moment that the consideration prevented the intelligent appreciation of this problem, I would take unilateral action myself, now. Is it necessary to recall to those who said "Hear, hear," that I myself threw up office a few years ago? And I will not take office under any circumstances to do anything that I do not believe I should do.' And he above all other politicians in the land had indeed the right to say that, but the diversion, if such it was, led him on: 'But if you carry this resolution and follow out all its implications and do not run away from it you will send a Foreign Secretary, whoever he may be, naked into the conference chamber.' And at that murmurs started in the body of the hall which never quite subsided the whole time he spoke, a low rumble of protest, just occasionally breaking out into open protest but more often confined to an 'Oh, no', and 'Don't say it, Nye'. Occasionally he would offer a gesture of appeasement to the interrupters but more often he drove on to a fiercer assault. He was still picturing that naked Foreign Secretary: 'Able to preach sermons, of course; he could make good sermons. But action of that sort is not necessarily the way in which you can take away the menace of the bomb from the world. It might be action of that sort will still be available to us if our other actions fail. It is something you can always do. You can always, if the influence you have upon your allies and upon your opponents is not yielding any fruits, take unilateral action of that sort.' And perhaps that was a concession designed to meet our talk on the Tuesday morning, but, alas, it only availed to prompt another deadly diversion. For those words provoked from the audience louder cries of 'Do it now! Do it now!', and his scorn was off the leash. ' "Do it now", you say. "Do it now." This is the answer I give from the platform. Do it now at a Labour Party Conference? You cannot do it now. It is not in your hands to do it. All you can do is to pass a resolution. What you are saying is that a British Foreign Secretary gets up in the United Nations without consultation – mark this; this is a responsible attitude! – without telling any members of the Commonwealth, without concerting with them, that the British Labour movement decides unilaterally that this country contracts out of all its commitments and obligations entered into with other countries and members of the Commonwealth – without consultation at all. And you call that statesmanship. I call it an emotional spasm.' At that moment, as the words indicate, he was caught in a frontal clash with a great section of the audience, and if many had not been nearer to tears, the whole place might have broken into uproar.

But then, miraculously, he was soft once again, and he stuttered and he argued. He was pleading for a British Foreign Secretary to have the opportunity to exercise some leverage on the policies of the Soviet Union and the United States. 'Do not disarm him diplomatically, intellectually and in every other way before he has a chance to turn round.' Within a few minutes he was paying tribute to the complete sincerity of those who had backed the Norwood resolution. 'But I am sure that in your secret hearts you will admit that you have not fully thought out the implications. You have not realized that the consequence of passing that resolution would be to drive Great Britain into diplomatic purdah.' Then he gave some examples and the arguments with the floor were renewed. 'I am endeavouring to face you with the fact that the most important feature of this problem is not what we are doing in this country, because that lies within our control. What we have to discuss is the consequences of the action upon other nations with far more deadly weapons than we have. I do beg and pray the Conference to reconsider its mood in this matter, and to try and provide us with a workable policy.' But now the murmurs were beginning to decline, and he had almost succeeded in regaining his mastery.

Then he paused and surveyed the most tremulous, heartbroken

audience he had ever addressed in his life, and he would not relent.
'I have thought about this very anxiously,' he said, 'I knew this
morning that I was going to make a speech that would offend and
even hurt many of my friends.' Then the voices of protest broke
out again, and he stopped and cried: 'Of course. But do you think
I am afraid?' The question rang out like a bell through the hall and
not a single soul dared answer, and his courage drove him on,
remorselessly once more: 'I shall say what I believe, and I will give
the guidance that I think is the true guidance, and I do not care
what happens. But I will tell you this, that, in my opinion, in carrying out resolution 24, with all the implications I have pointed out,
you will do more to precipitate incidents that might easily lead to a
third world war' – but he could not complete the sentence; it was
deluged in the shouts of 'rubbish' and 'shame' and it was seconds
before he could continue: 'Just listen. Just consider for a moment
all the little nations running one here, and one there, one running
to Russia, the other rushing to the U.S.A., all once more clustering
under the castle wall, this castle wall, or the other castle wall, because in that situation before anything else would have happened,
the world would have been polarized between the Soviet Union on
the one side and the U.S.A. on the other side. It is against that
dangerous negative polarization that we have been fighting for
years. We want to have the opportunity of interposing between
these two giants modifying, moderating, and mitigating influence.'
He was back on his great theme, but it was too late. He could be
possessed by Lloyd George's terrible urge to claw down an enemy
and on this occasion the enemy was his friends. 'I am convinced,'
he said, near his conclusion, 'profoundly convinced, that nothing
could give more anxiety to many people who do not share our
political beliefs than if the British nation disengaged itself from its
obligations and prevented itself from influencing the course of
international affairs. I know that you are deeply convinced that the
action you suggest is the most effective way of influencing international affairs. I am deeply convinced that you are wrong. It is
therefore not a question of who is in favour of the hydrogen bomb,
but a question of what is the most effective way of getting the damn
thing destroyed . . . It is the most difficult of all problems facing
mankind. It can be resolved, I agree, only by a combination of

resolution and of intellectual belief. I have reached my conclusion after a lot of agonized thinking, and I am convinced deeply of this, that if resolution 24 is adopted with all the implications that I have pointed out, it will very greatly embarrass a Socialist Government and may have disastrous consequences throughout the world.'

That was Brighton 1957. Nothing that happened there thereafter counted for much, not even the huge vote of 5,836,000 to 781,000 recorded against the Norwood resolution nor the novel democratic spectacle of the general secretary of the Transport and General Workers' Union asking for time to consult his delegation and finding himself outvoted by 16 votes to 14. Nothing mattered, for the Bevanites certainly, but the feeling that they had been clubbed into insensibility, and others who had never distantly called themselves Bevanites gave evidence that they understood. 'When Bevan sat down,' wrote one of the old Right-wing M.P.s,[1] 'I had to get up and go away. I couldn't stand any more. I felt as if I had been present at a murder – the murder of the enthusiasm that has built the Labour movement.' During the rest of that evening, during the rest of that weekend, multitudes of delegates and more multitudes up and down the country shared that impulse 'to get up and go away'. Or at Brighton they gathered in clusters and waylaid Ian Mikardo, Barbara Castle, myself and the others and asked over and over and over again: 'Why has he done it? Why, why, why?' And the only answer was to point to the speech itself. But that was no balm for wounds such as these, and indeed there was no balm to be offered.

I myself never asked him why: it would have been an insult. The speech was a deed, not a word, and I knew he would never withdraw or qualify a single particle of it. But no doubt was possible about how deeply he was hurt, by the upsurge in the Conference Hall, by the strictures and laments of his friends, and worst of all, perhaps, by the bouquets of his enemies. Every Conservative newspaper in the land revelled in it. 'BEVAN INTO BEVIN,' gloated the *Daily Telegraph* editorial – 'not since the days of Ernest Bevin have Socialist misconceptions about the place of force in foreign policy been so scathingly exposed.' The comparison was highly popular; not since Ernest Bevin had disembowelled George Lansbury at

---

[1] As reported in the *Daily Herald* Friday 5 October.

19

another Brighton Conference in 1935 had the Tories thought they
had witnessed such a rout of the woolly-minded idealism of the
Left, and swiftly in the process the actual words he had used became outrageously distorted and vulgarized. 'Naked into the conference chamber' was transformed from what it clearly was in its
context, a reference to the relationship between Britain and her
allies, into an outright defence of the most ancient gospel of
tooth-and-claw politics. He had resorted, it was suggested, to the
weary orthodox argument that the British bomb helped to constitute a deterrent against potential Soviet aggression or blackmail
when in fact one of the fascinating features of the speech was that
he had done nothing of the kind.[1] But the vacuous Tory press had

[1] This letter was typical of many which he wrote at the time to old
friends, questioning or disturbed:

Mr. Huw T. Edwards,
Crud Yr Awel,
Sychtyn,
Nr Mold, Flints.   *23rd October 1957*
My dear Huw,
     Many thanks for writing to me.
     I am afraid that my Brighton speech has been misunderstood but I
suppose I must accept most of the responsibility.
     I do not regard the possession of the hydrogen bomb by Great
Britain as making the slightest contribution to peace or to our security,
so the argument is not for, or against, Britain possessing the hydrogen
bomb. My case is a little different. It rests upon the argument that if we
unilaterally reject the bomb, then we are at the same time rejecting all
the alliances and obligations in which this country has become involved,
either rightly or wrongly. We could not keep an alliance with countries
possessing the bomb and yet repudiate it ourselves. When I spoke of
Britain going naked into conference, I was not thinking of the bomb at
all. I had in mind the fact that without substituting anything for them in
the meantime we should have made a shambles of all our treaties,
commitments, obligations and rejected our friends, and this without
consulting them and especially without consulting members of the
Commonwealth.
     In my opinion, such a position would precipitate an international crisis
of the first order, and this might bring about the very thing that we hope
to avoid. I am convinced that we must so conduct our affairs as to bring
about the abolition, not only of the British bomb, but the American and
the Russian as well, and it is from those bombs and the policies behind

no interest in such niceties; Hugh Gaitskell and his close friends rejoiced more demurely; there were few open gesticulations of triumph, yet they had good reason to congratulate themselves. The Left of the Party looked for a moment as if it had exterminated itself. Without its incomparable leader it was unlikely to regather strength for years. And all these reckonings were calculated to make Bevan smart more than the criticisms of his friends.

The weekend after the event was no moment to attempt to disentangle all these elements in the new political world which Brighton had created. But, some urgent business had to be transacted: what was *Tribune* to say? On the Monday morning we all assembled at the offices at 222 Strand, and something of the tumultuous atmosphere of Brighton seemed to have been brought with us. Our planet was rocking and just to add to the sense of disorderly motion the Russians had chosen that week to send their sputnik round the earth and plunge the American continent into fresh screams of panic. I proposed writing an article in which I would try to reply to the Brighton speech while disowning the scandalous misrepresentations of it, but, to my astonishment, Bevan suggested that *Tribune* should carry no comment at all for a week or two; report

---

them that catastrophe could come. If we could not modify American policy, then repudiation is always available to use in the last resort. It is not something with which we should bargain, but something with which we should end if no other course is left open to us.

Also, I think it is as well to keep in mind that if the Brighton Conference had decided to adopt Resolution 24, we could say goodbye to any Labour Government being elected again in Britain. The Tories would not have attacked us for repudiating the bomb, but for taking Great Britain into an international purdah, turning her back on the rest of the world and indulging in exhibitionism, and not taking her proper position.

You will have seen that this did not apply to tests, because I consider that we have no right to poison the air for other people, as well as for ourselves, by carrying out the tests, so we should unilaterally suspend the tests and hope other nations would follow our example.

I write this to you very hurriedly on the eve of my departure for the United States.

I appreciate your writing to me, and I always have.

Yours affectionately,

ANEURIN BEVAN

the proceedings, let readers write, and let the dust settle. It was the first of several awkward editorial arguments which were to engage us in the subsequent weeks. Theoretically, Jennie Lee and Howard Samuel, the two other directors of the paper with myself, could out-vote me, but we had never dreamt of conducting our business on that basis. And I was the editor in possession, convinced, apart from other evidence, by the huge anti-H-bomb deluge pouring in from readers that a failure to state our case against Bevan's Brighton line would destroy the paper altogether. Besides, I disagreed with him. And yet, despite the disagreement, I could not help marvelling at the sheer, clean audacity of the man, and there was still plenty of his superabundant supply of that quality in brazen evidence on that coldest of Monday mornings. So we argued and he eventually accepted a compromise, but with a continual ill-grace and no sign whatever of the bursts of gaiety with which he had settled all pre-vious disputes with *Tribune* editors dating back to 1937. I would write my precious article about the bomb; Jennie would help clear up the mess, if need be, in the following week, and he himself would write about the Russians and their rocket. What amazed me most about that conversation, the first I had had with him since the Conference, was that he did truly seem to underestimate the nature of the wrench which had occurred with so many of his fol-lowers. But perhaps that was just my misapprehension. It was always a mistake, in any field, to underestimate the range and delicacy of his sensitivities.

So why *did* he do it? Why had he risked so much and for what gain? During the days and weeks that followed, every kind of com-bination of answers was pieced together. Some reports said that his conversations with Khrushchev had tipped the balance, that the Russian leader had stressed how eager he was for Britain to keep the bomb or how contemptuous he would be if we abandoned it. Clearly, the visit to the Soviet Union and the dangers he saw on the whole international scene had influenced him, but it is not neces-sary to accept the paradox that Mr Khrushchev had backed Britain having the bomb because he wanted Britain to be suitably equipped to deter Mr Khrushchev. This was a bowdlerization of his Khrush-chev talks and the deductions he had drawn from them. And in any case, those talks came before the National Executive meeting on

Thursday 27 September, when he had supported unilateral action to stop the manufacture of the weapons as well as the tests. So the search for clues must move to the Friday and Saturday. Was it true, as another explanation suggested, that Sam Watson and Hugh Gaitskell together had persuaded him? Was it true that Sam Watson in particular had taken him to a high mountain and shown him all the kingdoms of the earth, the offices and influence in the Labour Party which would be his, if only he would defend the Executive's position on the bomb? Was it true – in the allegation of the *New Statesman*[1] – that he had made a cynical, comprehensive compact with Gaitskell and the Right wing of the Party covering the whole field of domestic and foreign policy? This was the stinging falsehood which Bevan resented more than any other accusation during those days, and perhaps his resentment was prompted by the knowledge that it did contain a half-truth. Of course, it was true that Party considerations influenced his conduct, and why not? During that Friday and Saturday he saw more clearly than ever before the divisions which might occur if he refused to speak, if a new split developed. He saw the chasm opening at his feet, he saw the renewal of the old battles as the months went by, he saw the destruction of any hope for a new Labour Government, he saw the accusations of his opponents – and perhaps of history – that he could have forestalled the catastrophe but that he had preferred the ease of his own conscience and the comfort of his friends. He saw the long trek back for the Bevanites and himself into the wilderness and the endless sojourn there, and he never had the taste, despite all the taunts, for martyrdom, for the locusts and wild honey. He was interested in power to achieve great objectives and never more so than in that autumn of 1957 when Suez and the bomb and the litanies of the holy war intoned from East and West oppressed his spirit, and he perpetually searched for remedies, and sometimes the remedies varied. It was true that in the spring in India he had seen the renunciation of nuclear weapons in one light, and in the autumn and in Britain in another, but he was not to be frightened

---

[1] It would be necessary to quote the whole anonymous article on 'The End of Bevanism' in the *New Statesman* on 12 October to expose its viciousness and malice. One sentence indicates the tone: 'Has Bevan, one is bound to ask after Brighton, sold himself too cheap?'

by the hobgoblin of being told he had changed his mind; although, as the record faithfully produced above without any calculated suppressions proves, there was also a deep consistency. Amid all the uproar of Brighton, it was too easily forgotten that many of the policies he had argued for for years – disengagement in Europe, a Middle Eastern settlement with the Soviet Union invited as a party, the retreat from S.E.A.T.O., the unilateral abandonment of tests – were now officially backed and would form part of the garb which a Labour Foreign Secretary could wear into the conference chamber. And these necessary judgments about immediate policy mingled with the spirit of the age, and the revelation of man's lunacy in having discovered the means to destroy human life altogether. Often Bevan himself would say that it was easy to re-state the external facts of previous periods in history, but much more difficult or impossible to recapture the emotions of those times. The arrival of the bomb had created an explosive emotional climate in which the forms of policy looked irrelevant or indecent. Bevan was haunted by what he considered to be the narrow balance between hope and total destruction, by the vastly enhanced dangers of the polarization between East and West, by the duty which rested on himself to steer the mood of the Labour movement into practical channels. During the course of these Brighton dis-cussions he said to some of his friends: 'I think I can just about save this Party, but I shall destroy myself in doing it.' These were words he used to Hugh Delargy, and he had said much the same to Jennie alone quietly by their own fireside. When he used them to her he doubtless had in mind the strains which would be imposed, if he became Foreign Secretary under Gaitskell – witness the letter he had sent to Jennie earlier in the year. But he had agreed to bend his proud head to this distasteful yoke because of his obsession about the most perilous brink upon which mankind was lodged. His fears for the world and for his Party interwove. It was in such a mood that he made up his mind on that last Sunday evening.

The core of his case was truly the one he made from the plat-form, there were no secret clauses. Could he then have done it less brutally? Yes indeed again; he could have spared us the naked entry, the diplomatic purdah, above all, the emotional spasm with its ironic reminder of the Conference at Scarborough no more than three years earlier where he had defended *his* right to emotion against his desiccated accusers. But could he? Once he was on his feet and once he was challenged from the floor, he had to fight to win; it was the habit of a lifetime and the source of the whole rich avalanche of invective which had been unleashed from Charles Street, Tredegar. Once in spate no one could check it. Any suggestion that at Brighton he had suddenly transformed himself into the calculating machine which so many politicians become – the precise item on the *New Statesman* charge sheet – would be the indictment of a fool, whatever the other motives. The whole performance belied it. He might have kept quiet; he might have struggled to impose unfamiliar restraints; he might, in the term he used about others, have spoken with a twisted tongue. But: 'Do you think I am afraid?' he had cried out at Brighton. It was the sentence in the speech which in my mind echoed most persistently.

There was no doubt about the torment which his courage had invited. At his meetings in the country he had often to face a quite new kind of hostility, from a new quarter, and he hated the letters in *Tribune* reflecting these sometimes savage criticisms which we insisted on publishing; it was *Tribune*'s oldest boast that we did not censor our readers, and how could we start now? But the stabs were hard for him to bear in the columns of the paper he had been associated with for twenty years from the day of its birth. Even in his own constituency he could not count on the overwhelming tide of support which had swelled up in previous crises, and at the management committee meeting angry exchanges broke out and were not easily stilled. 'He veered,' said Archie Lush, more as a description of what had occurred than a criticism, but Ebbw Vale was a Left-wing constituency and would normally have sided with the three-quarters of the constituency parties which, it was estimated, had voted for the Norwood resolution. Perhaps the note of criticism which he encountered in his own constituency was the sharpest cut of all. For it came from those who had learnt every item in their Socialist religion from him, and it was often the expression of a turmoil of heart and mind almost as poignant as his own. Overwhelmingly he could still command the support which had been his in previous trials, but it was mingled with questioning and harsh words. As the days passed, it became evident that his relationship with the Left of the Party and therefore with the Party itself was profoundly altered. That had never been part of his intention; nothing had been further from his purpose than to assist the Right at the expense of the Left. But this was the outward appearance and all the mythology of pitiless Socialist sectarianism was invoked in many quarters to sustain the charge. 'You must defend Nye's honour,' Jennie would say to me, and she had every right to say it, the more so since she knew better than anyone how lonely he had been in his ultimate decision; for she too had been against him on the issue itself. But it was difficult to say to her and impossible to say to him that some of us thought we were doing so – in ceaseless arguments with those who went on asking, 'Why did he do it?' – even if the defence did not take the form he wanted. Our assistance and comradeship were inadequate. Everybody who knows anything knows that politics can be cruel, but no man ever felt that cruelty more than Aneurin Bevan in the autumn of 1957.

16

THE MERETRICIOUS SOCIETY
1958–1960

The characteristic trait of irrepressible restlessness is not always an indication of exuberance and strength. When nonconformity to present conditions and an aspiration to new and better things are not determined rationally nor translated into constant resolute action, they will be a devouring fever, not a life-giving warmth. Sterile turbulence, like a sluggish somnolence, is a disease of the will.

—JOSÉ RODO, *The Motives of Proteus*

ANEURIN BEVAN'S idea of Socialism, true to his Marxism, involved an interplay between the pressures of domestic and foreign politics. His prophecies of the likely conduct of the Soviet Union in international affairs derived from his interpretation of the internal stresses and relaxations which Soviet leaders had to cope with, and his sceptical attitude towards American statesmanship was traceable to his analysis of the unresolved strains in American society itself. It was this same refusal to confine different aspects of politics into closed compartments which gave him his sympathetic comprehension of the problem facing so-called backward countries, whether in the Communist bloc or outside it; he saw these countries engaged in the process of industrialization which Britain had accomplished in the nineteenth century only at the cost of a savage exploitation of the working class, his own ancestors among them. How futile and bitter to lecture the men engaged in these revolutionary tasks on the virtues of Western parliamentary democracy and their allotted role in the world-wide crusade against Communism! The only hope was to

help to provide them, on dignified terms, with the economic surplus in which democracy could take root. And yet all too often the
rich nations bestowed aid on the poor nations, withholding the
money for the Aswan Dam or granting it to a military junta in
Pakistan, in a manner intolerable to national pride or leaving behind red-hot resentments; it was an old habit of the ruling classes.
Thus Aneurin Bevan would apply his Socialist thinking to the
problems of foreign policy, but by the same reckoning, he never
saw the stage of international diplomacy as an escape from the
sordid or mundane choices of domestic and party warfare. He
thought the world might blow itself to bits; he thought statesmen
were faced with problems of unprecedented magnitude, unforeseen
in any Marxist textbook; he thought he himself might play an
important role in helping to find the impalpable solutions. But it
was certainly not true that he saw himself, as many at the time
alleged, as the indispensable, Messiah-like Foreign Secretary, alone
able to divert the course of world history by the delicacy of his
sensibilities and accent. Not merely would such megalomaniac
notions conflict with the first principles of his Marxism, they
splintered on other less momentous facts concerning the way the
British Cabinet system worked and the way British elections were
won – matters not to be despised at all, at least by those politicians
who wished to avoid the charge of dilettantism. Possibly Bevan did
think it would be his best course to accept the post of Foreign
Secretary; certainly he talked in these terms to some; and certainly,
if he had so desired, Gaitskell would, after Brighton, have been
virtually compelled to make the offer to him. But he also talked of
what might be another advisable course altogether; he could decide
to take another post, such as Leader of the House of Commons,
which would mean that he would be always there, at the essential
meetings of the Cabinet, where the decisions would be taken –
decisions about the steel industry, the planning of the nation's
economy, the future of Socialism in Britain which would in turn
help to shape Britain's influence in world affairs. So, on that count
for a start, the Bevan of Brighton, 1957, was not turning his back on
Britain's domestic politics, as so many of the political commentators
foolishly suggested. It was collective power, not personal power,
he sought, and there was the other obstinate fact: the election had

still to be won. Bevan firmly believed, like many others at the time, that there might soon be a general election which Labour could win; he freely confessed that he could not describe the exact process whereby the issue might be forced; but so humiliating had been the Suez fiasco, so low was the morale of the Tory benches, so dramatically fitting was it that what he called 'the squalid Parliament' should meet its deserts, that he did believe the early expulsion of the Tories from office would happen. This was part of his calculation at Brighton. But he agreed also with those who held it almost as an axiom of British politics that a British election could not be fought and won on an issue of foreign policy alone. The direct interests, the just grievances, the radical tradition of the British working class must be enlisted for the battle; that was Bevan's conviction. It made him suspicious of those on the so-called Left of the Party who might suddenly elevate an issue of foreign policy into a position of *exclusive* attention; and it made him furious with those on the Right who degraded the broad conceptions of public ownership and collective action into secondary instruments, to be scorned or sneered at. All these ideas were in his mind and often expressed in fierce terms, as some of us learnt in those argumentative days after Brighton. Nothing could be further from reality than the portrait of 'the new Nye' or 'the reformed Bevan' which some observers chose to present: the weary Socialist Titan who had lost his vitality, abandoned his old friends, and was offering his benign services to assist in upholding the Labour Establishment, with even a helping spare hand occasionally to be offered from Her Majesty's loyal Opposition front bench for Harold Macmillan's affluent society.

Two weeks after Brighton he went on a nineteen-day trip to the United States, partly to engage, in his capacity as Shadow Foreign Secretary, in discussion with President Eisenhower and John Foster Dulles and partly to fulfil a series of speaking engagements. Much speculation naturally arose whether 'the new Bevan' would soon have his hosts swooning before his charm or whether 'the old Bevan' would provoke his old enemies, particularly since the whole country was smarting from the news about the way the Russians had just put their sputnik in orbit. But the expedition fitted into no pre-conceived pattern; possibly there had been nothing quite like it since Oscar Wilde executed his coast-to-coast conquest of the outraged continent in 1882.

On arrival in New York he was mellowness itself. Asked what he thought of the sputnik, he strove to cool jagged nerves; it did not fundamentally alter the diplomatic and military situation; nothing was changed 'except that American cities are now in the front line – where ours have been for the last six years'. Asked what he thought of another item of news from Russia concerning the removal from his post of Marshal Zhukov, he replied: 'I hadn't heard. I suspect that all generals of the last war ought now to be relieved', and while the sweetness of his smile could prove that the barb against Eisenhower was half intended as a joke, fierce headlines were soon convicting him of the grossest ill-manners. Or what did he think of the arms race generally? 'It doesn't make much difference if the blocs slaughter each other in a month or a week.' And finally, when he had pronounced the recent Eisenhower-Macmillan talks in Washington 'sterile' and had called for a proper Summit meeting with the impossible Khrushchev, one nettled correspondent who could stand the display of unpatriotic candour no longer asked what he thought 'as an Englishman' of Her Majesty the Queen's reception in the United States. 'I'm not an Englishman,' he replied. 'I'm a Welshman. But I'm naturally delighted at the success here of anyone descended, however remotely, from our House of Tudor.' In that same tone he repudiated the accusation of anti-Americanism: 'On the contrary, I've always had a certain proprietorial attitude towards the American people. I remember on one occasion I had to visit Ireland in order to meet the Prime Minister, Mr De Valera, on a semi-diplomatic mission. In the course of our discussion, he in a moment of excitement pointed across the room and said, "There is my political bible", and I walked across to see what it was. It was a facsimile of the American Declaration of Independence. And I said to him, "Do you see how many Welsh names are on it? Do you realize it was written by a Welshman?" So my attitude to the United States has always been somewhat proprietorial. We, as it were, started you off.' Who could resist that?

Then he crossed to the West coast, pleading in accents of cajolery rather than reproof for four major changes in American policy which he hoped closer co-operation with a Labour Britain – the term itself was scarcely spoken – might bring: recognition of Communist China and her admission to the United Nations; an agreed policy for the Middle East, based partly on an understanding of the right of the Soviet Union to participate in the settlement; a full-scale Summit Conference with the Russians; and an attempt to secure a settlement in Central Europe in which a reunited Germany would be neutralized and denied access to nuclear weapons. Somehow these propositions, so scandalous in the ears of 1957 America, were advanced in such an inoffensive manner that his audiences failed to grasp them at the moment of utterance. But after he had departed to the next town, editors stiffened in their editorial chairs and sought to warn the nation, as if some scurvy deceit had been practised upon them, that, to quote one, 'the man who will run British foreign policy if the Socialists return to power disagrees with practically everything the U.S. is doing in the world'.[1] Distant tempers not subject to the lecturer's personal mastery were not improved when he compared Mao Tse-tung with George Washington, elaborated on the revolutionary character of the American War of Independence, and chose to present his most needling criticisms of current American lapses in the field of civil rights in the language of his favourite Welsh-American, Thomas Jefferson. Reports of what the Hearst press dismissed as his 'ill-will campaign' seeped back to England; Macmillan lamented in the House of Commons his 'relapse into demagogy' now that he had gone abroad, whilst others more fiercely protested that he was breaking all conventions about what a politician on his travels might properly say. 'Ridiculously juvenile,' commented Bevan; 'I cannot say one thing at home and then tells lies over here just to be courteous,' and he continued undeterred with his questioning, in the White House, in the State Department, and elsewhere. Why should the American leaders fear public discussions about disarmament with the Russians on the grounds that the Russians were solely interested in propaganda; 'why should their propaganda be better than ours?' Why should negotiations with the Russians be postponed until the United

[1] *U.S. News and World Report* quoted in *Bevan, the Cautious Rebel* by Mark M. Krug (Yoseloff, New York, 1961), p. 261.

States could produce some new gadget to make them equal with the Russians? That race could be endless. Why – when he was asked again by inquisitive bankers about Marshal Zhukov – 'why all this solicitude for the Marshal. I don't particularly care for the man, do you?' And, as for Khrushchev, about whom they questioned him eagerly, he was 'a simple sort of chap' who ought to get on well enough with the President he had just met. 'I shook hands this evening,' he told the New York Economic Club, haven of the financial élite, 'with a number of people, some of whom looked exactly like Khrushchev . . . We know he is ruthless. But I shook hands with a number of persons tonight who I also thought were ruthless.' Khrushchev had some of the characteristics of 'many high-ranking executives I have met in the United States'. And let it not be forgotten that worse than anything Khrushchev could inflict on the Western world, more serious than the sending of a few satellites into outer space, would be the effect of an American recession. Britain was bound to be concerned with the United States' 'high displacement power' in the world; 'it was like sleeping with an economic giant; if the giant turns over to scratch his leg, he may kick you out of bed'. And serious too, he thought, and did not forbear from mentioning before he departed, was the intellectual climate he had breathed all around him – 'your group behaviour is too primitive for the modern world'. He thought it less healthy than that which he had experienced on his last American journey in 1934, felt it to be too conformist, too stereotyped, too little questioning on the great issues, too afraid, particularly in the universities, of the 'intellectual recklessness' so sorely needed to help in the construction of the good Jeffersonian society. Perhaps it was not altogether surprising that some Americans found the prospect of Bevan becoming Foreign Secretary even more alarming than the sputnik. But one who did not wrote to him: 'I am most disappointed that I missed you. I look forward to an early opportunity to remedy that. I believe I can report with fair accuracy that your visit here was an unqualified success. I gather that it may even have been helpful in Washington! – Adlai Stevenson.'

He saved his strongest verdicts until he had returned home, and for months thereafter he could not escape the impressions his talks with Eisenhower and Dulles had left upon him and indeed the atmosphere of the whole country. Dulles, he said, appeared to be unable to think in any other terms but the most fanatical anti-Communism, and Eisenhower's leadership was a source of disappointment and dismay throughout the world. But the leaders of the Democrats – if Dean Acheson's statements were taken as an indication – offered no better hope. Both Republicans and Democrats seemed to have sunk so much of their capital in anti-Communism that they had become the playthings of their own propaganda.[1] Everywhere in official Washington he found the attitude that it was no use trusting the Russians, meeting the Russians, negotiating with the Russians; 'in other words, an attitude of complete hopelessness. I found it everywhere there. In fact, I did not find inspiration so much as obsession. They were just obsessed with the whole Communist idea. When on top of that there came the sputniks, there was a state of mind in the United States which, I am bound to say frankly, frightened me.'[2]

And mingled with his immediate horror at the spectacle of the most powerful nation on earth caught in the grip of a near-religious fanaticism went confirmation of his previous conviction about a society which, stuffed with material prosperity, would not question, or think it possible to question, its basic assumptions. Perhaps these might be called his Socialist prejudices but there is no doubt how deeply embedded they were in Bevan's mind. 'North American life seems . . . to proceed in that vicious circle which Pascal described as the course of the pursuit of well-being which has no end outside itself. Its titanic energy of material aggrandisement produces a singular impression of insufficiency and vacuity.' Those were the words Havelock Ellis had written in introducing Bevan's revered José D. Rodo.[3] It would be idle to contest the charge that Bevan, who certainly did not know the United States with any intimacy at all, allowed his reading and his Socialist theory to colour the judgment he passed on the America of Eisenhower and Acheson. But did not Rodo remain amazingly apt? Both on account of its domestic and its foreign policies, Bevan had not the slightest confidence in American leadership; he remained stolidly unimpressed by its

[1] *Tribune* 17 January 1958.
[2] *Hansard* Vol. 580 Col. 754.
[3] See Volume I p. 466.

technological triumphs when most of Western mankind was being bidden to bow down and worship them. He believed that the United States of the 1950s had lost its Rooseveltian role and found John Bull's, and that its leading liberal intellectuals seemed incapable of noting the difference.

For many months after the Brighton Conference, indeed for the next two years, Bevan found himself arguing on the inextricably associated subjects of foreign policy and nuclear weapons at three different levels and with varying allies. His principal task, as he saw it, was to use his influence and the Labour Party's to alter the sense of direction within the N.A.T.O. alliance, and possibly its nature, in order to move towards settlements with the Soviet Union. Most of his major speeches in the House of Commons and in the country or on his visits abroad – he went to Berlin and Bonn soon after his return from America – were directed to this end. Next, he was involved, in the Shadow Cabinet and on the National Executive, in a constant attempt to push the Party's official declarations along the lines he desired. Mostly these new statements of policy, by the time they were published, had at least the stamp of familiarity; but the minutes of the National Executive, particularly during this period, show that the wear and tear required for the achievement of these accommodations was considerable. But most painful and arduous of all were the renewed and quite novel clashes in which he found himself engaged with the ferment outside Parliament; with angry supporters of the newly established Campaign for Nuclear Disarmament, with the Left of the Labour Party inside and outside the House of Commons and in his own constituency, and with some of his oldest friends, such as myself. The agony of the period can be appreciated only when it is seen – as some of us saw so inadequately at the time – how the three levels of argument interacted.

During the course of his Brighton speech, while arguing that the Norwood resolution about the bomb should not be accepted partly because it would rupture – unwittingly, as it were – the country's international relationships, he had referred to 'a variety of treaties and alliances most of which I do not like . . .' The aside had attracted no attention at the time, but it did express one of his constant preoccupations. To both the Baghdad Pact and S.E.A.T.O., he had been opposed from the start; pretending to unite the nations or areas concerned, in fact they proved a potent cause of division. But N.A.T.O. was in a different category altogether. Bevan had been a member of the Government which gave British support to its establishment as a defensive alliance in the first place and he had never questioned the right of the nations concerned to come together for the purposes stated. But the passage of time, the invention of nuclear weapons, the decision to incorporate a rearmed Western Germany into the alliance, the changes in United States strategy, had altered the nature of the alliance itself, and Bevan had persistently argued that the British Government, while recognizing the need to sustain the alliance, had the paramount interest to secure transformations in its aims and methods. Paradoxically, the man who had elevated to the first place at Brighton the case for not abruptly rupturing the nation's alliances was eager to revolutionize the way those alliances worked; and, to secure the change, the allies themselves had to be persuaded. After Brighton, as it happened, he thought the moment might be especially favourable for an initiative in this desirable direction. For one thing, the Russians had renewed their offers to stop H-bomb tests and to call a Summit conference, and for another, a fresh alarm had been provoked by the revelation that bombing planes loaded with hydrogen bombs were patrolling the skies in Western Europe incessantly throughout the twenty-four hours and the fact that answers given in Parliament about the control of these flights were hesitant and equivocal. Bevan was as much shaken as any nuclear disarmer by these disclosures. Apart from all the other considerations, he believed that the transfer of controlling powers over life and death into some ill-defined part of the alliance apparatus touched questions of democracy. 'If sovereign powers,' he wrote,[1] 'are to take flight from the parliaments of the Western world where is it that they are proposed to alight? . . . We should refuse to surrender the ability to act independently, except in a cause which promises wider and more beneficial consequences than are likely to be obtained by adherence to our traditional powers.' The round-the-clock flights, undertaken without any parliamentary sanction, showed how the supposed needs of

[1] *Tribune* 13 December 1957.

defence were wresting the essential controls from civilian hands. It was, as he said in a debate a few days later, 'a state of mobilization only one step short of war'.[1] Did the international situation justify preparations of that character, such reliance on what he described as 'a weapon of instantaneous action, not a weapon of reflection'. In that speech he deplored the 'entirely arid' policy of the Government about the stopping of H-bomb tests, the moves towards a Summit conference, the chances of securing areas of disengagement in Europe and the Middle East. Instead they preferred to concentrate on making additions or refinements to the armaments of the West, although no addition could make any real difference: 'You cannot be deader than dead.' At which a Tory voice interrupted with the single word: 'Dishonoured', and Bevan replied: 'All those terms are ceasing to be meaningful in this relationship – [*Hon. Members:* No] – because honour implies a relation between a man and his social code, but if society is itself destroyed, nothing either honourable or dishonourable will be left . . . We are profoundly depressed when representative after representative of the Government gets up and repeats over and over again this liturgy of hate, injecting into the international situation no element of buoyancy or optimism at all, having no advice to give to the nation except to pile one more tier of ridiculous armaments on the useless pile already created'.[2]

That was Bevan conducting the argument on one level, and he could truly claim that some of the policies he now advocated officially on behalf of the Party bore a striking resemblance to those he had campaigned for, with the assistance only of his derided Bevanites, a few years before. Notably that claim applied to the proposal for an area of disengagement in central Europe, to be guaranteed by the Soviet Union and the Western powers, and Bevan had been gratified to discover widespread support for the idea on his visit to Germany. At a reception at Bad Godesberg, he had been asked whether he agreed with the idea recently advanced by George Kennan for the withdrawal of troops, East and West. He replied enthusiastically: 'Of course I agree with it. I first proposed it five years ago.' He then gave the old Bevanite policy a new

[1] *Hansard* Vol. 580 Col. 756.
[2] *Hansard* Vol. 580, Col. 762.

formulation. He called it a policy of 'detachment' for Germany. It would mean that Germany would stay detached from nuclear weapons and might become detached from her present alliances, and that in turn could prepare the path to German unity although it would mean an infringement of German sovereignty. 'But do you,' he had asked the Germans, 'regard this as an affront against your sovereignty?' and they had laughed and said, 'We would rather be limited and alive than free and dead'. And there indeed on this first visit to Germany he had revived the core of the argument about German rearmament. A few months later similar proposals, first for establishing a nuclear-free zone in central Europe to be followed later by the withdrawal of conventional forces, were put forward by M. Rapacki, the Foreign Minister of the new Polish Government, and Bevan naturally responded even more eagerly on behalf of the official Opposition. Taken in conjunction with the proposal first for the suspension and then the stopping of H-bomb tests, the Labour Party had a body of proposals which could form the basis for a new initiative, and Bevan had played his part in shaping them.

A glimpse of how long and testing those debates behind the scenes within the Party leadership might be is given in the reports of the meetings which took place in March 1958 between representatives of the National Executive and the T.U.C. General Council.[1] Twelve N.E.C. members confronted eleven General Council members, but the discussion was predominantly triangular between Gaitskell, Bevan and Frank Cousins – with Bevan and Cousins, backed by Barbara Castle, ranged against Gaitskell with a fairly secure majority at his back. Bevan wanted a clear declaration, repudiating the Government's White Paper of 1957 which set down a doctrine of massive nuclear retaliation, and making it plain that Britain under a Labour Government would never use nuclear weapons first. It was, of course, the old undertaking he had asked from Attlee in 1955 but the intervening years had made the point more respectable even in military circles, and in any case he believed that commonsense, no less than audiences in the country,

[1] N.E.C. Minutes. Summary report of meeting between International Committee of the Labour Party National Executive Committee and the T.U.C. General Council at Transport House on Thursday 6 March.

would demand an answer to the question: 'If the Russians attack with conventional weapons, would you counter with the ultimate weapon?' He pleaded that the Party should give a plain 'No' to the question, and the report of his elaboration of the argument continued: it was said that because the Russians have an over-whelming preponderance of conventional forces, they will feel free to attack the West. He considered that a phantasmagoria. There is no possibility of the Russians attacking. They have offered a declaration that they too would not be the first to use nuclear weapons. Did the committee really think the Soviet leaders would have such faith in the West that they would start a major war because the West had given their word not to use these weapons first? He would rather lose a conventional war than win a nuclear war, but he did not believe there was any fear of the Russians in fact launching a conventional war. Why deprive ourselves of a statement that links with the contemporary mood of people every-where over what is a dialectical trap? If we did not make such a statement we would be in a very different situation . . . The deter-rent has never been a means of winning a war. How can you say we would leave ourselves defenceless by declaring we would not use a weapon the use of which would lead to our destruction? . . . He was convinced that it was not possible to combat an evil with an evil which is greater than that which is being combated. He would prefer to be overrun by the Communists than have civiliza-tion extinguished . . . He asked the meeting to imagine a Russian attack. They attack and we chuck atom weapons at them, that is at the Russian troops who are all mixed up with the European population; having burnt out the centre of Europe, we then decide to chuck nuclear weapons at them. Do we believe that the people of central Europe will not repudiate all of us and our way of defending them by making the centre of Europe a red-hot cinder and perhaps this country too a radioactive desert?

Thus Bevan pounded at the question from one side and another but neither he nor Frank Cousins nor Barbara Castle could make any impression on an adamant Gaitskell resolutely repeating the proposition that neither he nor the Party could declare that if the Russians attacked with overwhelming force we would prefer to be overrun rather than use nuclear weapons. 'If we say we will never be the first to use nuclear weapons, we must mean just that, we cannot hedge or qualify the declaration. Therefore we would have to concede the argument as soon as the question was put "Do you prefer occupation by the Russians to the use of nuclear weapons?" The reason why we cannot make such a declaration is that if the Russians believe us, and this will be a public declaration which we must assume they will take seriously, the power of the deterrent is removed.'

The argument, and it was a real one, continued for hours, until Jean Mann intervened with the obstinate drawl which could drive Bevan to frenzy. What was she to say on public platforms? 'Was she to say that we do not want a Labour Foreign Secretary to go naked into the conference chamber and therefore wish to retain this weapon until we can get agreement, but at the same time, say we will in no circumstances ever use it?' Whereupon it is not recorded that Bevan exploded. Somehow he kept his temper and replied that 'it was agreed at Brighton to reject a proposal not to produce, use or test nuclear weapons. He had said that the consequence of such a declaration would be to make it impossible for a Labour Government to have any leverage in international affairs and would destroy alliances, including Commonwealth defence pacts etc. We were now discussing something different. The nuclear bomb would remain as a deterrent, and the Russians would realize that if they chucked the bomb at us first it would be an act of suicide because we would retaliate. But the deterrent had never been regarded as a means of defence. It had always been regarded as a last desperate way of stopping a war. This was the nub of the difference between us. The Russians have a superiority in conventional weapons which the West has countered by the development of nuclear weapons. You say, if they try to defeat us in a conventional war, we will chuck H-bombs at them. You say, the British must be told this. He would say that the British public understands that you cannot regard as a means of defence weapons which if we used them first would result in mass destruction for us or mutual suicide.' But still the argument continued, and Gaitskell was still more adamant, and his majority held. Bevan and Cousins felt forced to concede for the moment on the understanding that the discussion would be reopened another day, and the Executive, limp and weary after one of the longest arguments ever recorded, agreed to launch 'a national campaign' in favour of their policy documents *Disengagement and Nuclear War* and *Disengagement in Europe.*

And parallel with these Executive-T.U.C. discussions others on the same topics proceeded within the Parliamentary Party and the Shadow Cabinet. At one extreme of the argument stood John Strachey and George Brown, usually backed by or reflecting the ideas of Gaitskell himself; they advocated a nuclear strategy indistinguishable in the main from that of the Government White Paper. At the other extreme stood the nuclear disarmers, represented on the Executive by Ian Mikardo, Barbara Castle and Tony Greenwood. But in between the two and exercising a considerable influence in the Parliamentary Party an independent or middle-of-the-road policy was sedulously and skilfully advanced by Dick Crossman and George Wigg; they wanted to see a practical and conceivably more expensive defence policy based on conventional rather than nuclear weapons. Bevan had no power to impose a policy on all these various jarring groups and individuals: indeed, apart from the simplistic policy of the nuclear disarmers there was no simple policy available to be imposed. He found himself tugged and torn between these factions in a manner which drove him to distraction, and his temper was not improved when superimposed on all the other quarrels he found himself at the Executive one morning involved in a dispute over the establishment of the 'Victory for Socialism' organization which several of the old Bevanites, headed by Ian Mikardo, had initiated in an attempt to revive Socialist and anti-H-bomb activity in the country. Hugh Gaitskell in his worst Torquemada manner at once sniffed indiscipline; Ian Mikardo roused old hackles with the pertinacity of his defence. In the Smoking Room afterwards, as reported in his diary, Crossman expressed his anger to Bevan about Mikardo: 'How right you were to say of a friend of ours that he has the antennae of an elephant.' Then the diary continues: 'Bevan heartily agreed and said, "Yes, throughout the whole meeting he showed himself absolutely impervious, making enemy after enemy," and I only discovered he had been talking about Gaitskell when he added after five or six minutes, "and Ian is nearly as bad".'

But the national campaign promised by the Labour National Executive had been anticipated by others. In February 1958 the Campaign for Nuclear Disarmament was launched at a meeting in the Central Hall, Westminster, when huge crowds, far exceeding those expected by the newspapers or the organizers, gave the first proof of many which were to follow that a new phenomenon had appeared in the political life of the nation, particularly among the young. A few weeks later even larger crowds massed in Trafalgar Square on Good Friday to give a send-off to the marchers on the road to the nuclear weapons plant at Aldermaston. Suddenly, the horror of nuclear weapons seemed to provoke an adequate response, although the inexplicable curiosity is how slow the awakening had been in coming. One immediate cause of the Campaign's electric appeal was undoubtedly the 'massive retaliation' boasts in the Government White Paper; another, within the Labour Party, was the aftermath of Brighton. Ostensibly the Campaign was the Norwood resolution carried to the country; without question, it was the emphasis on 'unilateralism', that Britain could do something here and now to check the race to nuclear catastrophe, which gave the movement its bite. Somehow the polemic suited a part of the national mood, or that mood produced the polemic. For C.N.D. seemed to roll all the moral, military, diplomatic and political arguments against the bomb into one ball, to be hurled at the head of the Establishment, Conservative or Labour. The 1950s had not been an estimable or adventurous decade, particularly in a timorous, Conservative Britain which seemed content to take instructions about how to live and how to comport itself in world affairs from across the Atlantic. Suddenly, in C.N.D., national pride and disgruntlement, scarcely less than intelligent alarm about the bomb, found notable expression – in the limpid beauty of Bertrand Russell's English, in the humanity of J. B. Priestley, in the invective of John Osborne, in the release which many of the young described as 'a new kind of politics'.

One immediate result was that the campaign organized by the Labour Party's National Executive was quite overshadowed. True enough, when official demonstrations took place in April, Trafalgar Square looked jammed, 'Aldermaston' banners floated in the breeze alongside those of several great trade unions, and one mighty cheer went up when the chairman, Tom Driberg, said that the meeting was not the end of a rally but the beginning of a campaign, and another when Aneurin Bevan stressed the Party's rooted opposition to the supply of nuclear weapons to Western Germany. The hearing for the Party's leaders was respectful, even warm. But some of Bevan's words attracted critical attention. 'The time has come,' he said, 'when all the elements, diverse elements, sometimes even apparently contradictory elements, that go to make up the Labour movement must agree, at the most critical point in our history, to close our ranks and accomplish what can be done in the immediate circumstances facing us. I have every sympathy with those who engage in educational propaganda, whose eyes may be fixed on more distant horizons – I have spent some time at that myself – but the time comes when the harvest has to be gathered in . . . The time has come for the Labour movement to be united. No more discordant voices. I do not ask for abrogation of thinking. I ask that action should not be frustrated by theoretical differences.'[1] And that was a view which many of us had heard him express before, in the periods just prior to a general election. It was not part of some sinister compact made at Brighton; he always argued that the debate inside the Party must at times be muted or postponed in order to make successful the encounter with the Tory enemy. But in April 1958 the appeal jarred hopelessly with the spirit of Aldermaston; it was useless to tell those discordant voices to be stilled when they had just discovered their resonance, and among those who would undertake no Trappist vow was *Tribune* which for several weeks had carried on its front page the banner headline: 'THE PAPER THAT LEADS THE ANTI-H-BOMB CAMPAIGN'.

Soon the respectful response of Trafalgar Square changed to something fiercer, and at one of the regional conferences for Labour and trade union delegates held in the St Pancras Town Hall, Bevan found himself catching the full impact of it. He expounded the Party's new policy statement, claimed that it marked a considerable advance on any previous pronouncement on the subject, but continued, in the face of protests and interruptions: 'We have been told that what we have decided is not enough. We have been engaged for some months past in reaching agreement with repre-

[1] *The Times* 14 April 1958.

sentatives of the trade unions. This movement of ours has to move forward on a broad front.' Then, when he also added that some members of the Party believed that more could be achieved by unilateral action, the conference broke into prolonged applause, and he continued: 'You are perfectly entitled to believe that', but was stopped again by shouts of 'And we are the majority' from different parts of the hall. He went on: 'We are perfectly entitled to believe otherwise. There is no ethical difference between us.' There were shouts of disapproval, and he flung out an arm and said: 'There you are! There are the moralists. These are the pure saints. You see how these comrades like to polarize the movement.' And after more loud shouts of protest: 'Do not let us destroy this movement by charges of insincerity from one side or the other.' Then he appealed to the conference to face the issues he had put at Brighton; to recognize that the problem was how to get rid of not only our hydrogen bomb but the other hydrogen bombs as well; how if as a nation we decided to repudiate the bomb on ethical grounds, we would have to repudiate all the alliances based upon the possession of nuclear weapons by all the other allies; how he deeply believed in the possibility of a settlement with the Soviet Union: 'But I know this. If we, as a consequence of a decision of that sort, destroyed all the alliances in which we are at present involved they would laugh at us and have no respect at all for us.' And when that stirred violent cries of 'Nonsense', he raised his voice to a shout and went on: 'Those who desire that Great Britain should have no allies, and only Russia should have allies, are enemies of the working-class movement. We are only able to have an influence on the rest of the world if we have friends in the rest of the world'. But the breach between him and sections of the Left wing of the Party could not be healed in such public confrontations.

Sometimes the private confrontations of those times ended just as fiercely and sadly. I recall one terrible evening in July when I met him and Jennie accidentally at the Polish Embassy and they both returned to our house to drink a few reconciling nightcaps. Delicately for a few minutes we tiptoed round the explosive issue of the bomb only to stumble into some other too sensitive territory connected with one of the periodic campaigns of expulsion from the Party which the Organization sub-committee of the National

Executive was then engaged in on a near-Stalinite scale. Who was the aggressor in the argument, I cannot recall. Either I suggested that he had not done enough to stop the expulsion of a well-known St Pancras rebel, John Lawrence, or he made some too sweeping allegation against the protesters at some of his public meetings. Perhaps it was the mere mention of St Pancras which started it. One way or another, the questions of Party discipline, liberal priggery, the crassness of the Party leadership or the impotent self-righteousness of the rank-and-file, and all the other ramifications of the bomb debate were thrown like faggots onto a blazing bonfire of a row, with much ill-considered obstinacy from me and some more eloquent and even four-lettered responses – I had never heard him use them before – about my 'sterility', until he picked up a Sheraton chair and smacked it to the ground, as if he almost wanted to throw that too on the polemical flames. It was an horrific occasion, never to be re-enacted. Next day, on a telephone call from my wife, he came round, in my absence, and made his peace. To her surprise he wanted to pursue the debate about the bomb, to persuade her of the correctness of his view. Such was his respect for the authority argument. Eventually he yielded to her persuasion that, whatever else happened, we could not part on this note of uncomprehending stridency, and his anger subsided.

But our friendship remained prickly and painful and requiring much circumspection to avoid renewed outbreaks. He still continued writing for *Tribune*, but hated our slogan, 'The Paper that Leads the Anti-H-Bomb Campaign', as a calculated affront to himself. Some of those who shared the full tension of the times with him believed that he treated us on *Tribune* much too leniently. Jennie in particular was outraged, the more so since she now concurred with the general political judgment he had reached at Brighton. She knew how *Tribune* had often depended for its survival on subventions from people who gave the money solely because of their friendship with Nye – Howard Samuel, Jack Hylton were the two who contributed most liberally but there were others besides. Howard Samuel was, with Jennie, also a director of the paper – which doubtless made it the more galling to be confronted with the third director and the editor, myself, obstinately and absolutely insisting on the editor's right to decide the policy of the paper. 'I would have been bloody-minded,' says Jennie, 'and the others would have been too. It was Nye who restrained us despite the heartbreak he felt from *Tribune*'s attitude.'

However, it was not any individual pinpricks which made him bleed. It was the general rupture with so many of his closest friends, with the newly-stirred rebels in his constituency, with the saints at public meetings who would parade their spotless purity in such loud-mouthed chorus. And let no one suppose that his hot temper was due to any sense that he had committed a great error. Rather, the more he pondered, the more he was convinced he was right. The irony was unbearable. No politician in the land had done so much to shake the smug orthodoxy of the 1950s, but, once broken, it had exploded in his face.

Possibly an additional source of irritation was that he so frequently found himself reacting to a political situation differently from the leader with whom he was accused of having reached a cynical compact. Emphasis and tone were always likely to vary even when they had agreed on the course of action to be followed. One example that session was the Life Peerages Bill which Gaitskell was quite ready to oppose on the grounds that it left the overwhelmingly hereditary character of the House of Lords and its powers unimpaired, but which Bevan saw in a somewhat more sinister light. He believed that the actual new measures set in train by the Conservative administration would help to enhance the respectability and therefore the authority of the Lords, and he wanted a root-and-branch opposition. 'The proposal to make life peers,' he said at the end of his speech, 'is, in my opinion, the unimportant part of these proposals. That is the façade. The important part is that it is now intended . . . that there should be remuneration for the peers . . . Pelf for the peers. It is now being said that it is fair not only that noble Lords should inherit powers from their parents, but that we should confer an honorarium on them. That is the intention. Already there is a beginning. Already they are paid, I think, three guineas a day expenses. It is not much, but it will go up. It is certain to go up. The fact is that it is now intended to pay the House of Lords, but it is of course a big step to pay 867 people, and an ingenious method is therefore being devised by which some of their noble Lordships can have leave of absence from the Crown. They can have absence from attendance. That will leave, we do not know how many but a small number, perhaps two hundred or three hundred, who will still attend. Then some life peers will be made – how many we do not know – and they will go to the House of Lords and a nice honorarium will alight on all of them. And here, the House of Commons, which has not yet given its own Members pensions, will give pensions for life to the Lords. That is exactly it. Never was a slimier trick played . . . [*A voice*: 'Give them a "bob for the job"] Yes, jobs for the boys . . . I would not have invented so vulgar a phrase myself, but of course it is true that outside this Palace not very much interest is taken in this measure. For us here, at present, it is a matter merely between ourselves. But Milton warned us about this. He said: "Consider Liberty, and do not bind her when she sleeps".'[1]

His own brand of belief in parliamentary institutions led him into another more overt dispute. When, in May 1958, General de Gaulle was hoisted back into power in France by military rebellion-cum-political conspiracy in Algiers and Paris, and behind the backs of the French Parliament, Bevan saw no reason to be reticent in his comment. He was deeply antipathetic to the grandiloquent language in which the new Napoleon III talked of 'assuming the power of the Republic' and dismissing 'the régime of parties', and he could not stomach the excuses offered by the Mollet section of the French Socialist Party for the connivance they had given to the operation. 'No doubt,' wrote Bevan,[2] 'it is a painful dilemma for the French Socialist Party. Nevertheless, it is not enough to plead that because you cannot prevent a crime you are justified in becoming an accessory to it. If a period of dictatorship is inevitable in France, then let it appear in its own garb. Let it show its own face and not mask itself behind what it is not. A dictatorship established by parliamentary authority is not the alternative to civil war. On the contrary, by depriving the French people of the possibility of democratic solutions, it will leave them nothing but the alternative of revolution.' But these pronouncements naturally angered Mollet; he protested to Gaitskell, who had in fact resolutely suc-

[1] *Hansard* Vol. 582 Cols. 692–3.
[2] *News of the World* 1 June.

ceeded in saying nothing worth noticing on the subject of the convulsion in France. Mollet's protest was passed on to Bevan but he was not inclined to yield to the man whose disservices to the cause of European Socialism had already reached monumental proportions. So when in June, at the meeting of the International in Brussels, the Mollet representatives tried to secure a retrospective blessing for their role in the May crisis, Bevan blocked the resolution and was able to plead the blessed verdict of a majority decision for his attitude; had not the French Socialist Deputies in the end voted 49 to 42 *against* de Gaulle's investiture, and should not respectable British parliamentarians respect that decision too?

Much more serious, at least at the first impact, were the divisions between the two men which arose over the proposed treatment by the Western powers of the new ferment in the Middle East. A revolution in Iraq involving the overthrow and murder of the British-backed Nuri-e-Said threatened, or was alleged to threaten, further revolutionary action in neighbouring countries, notably the Lebanon and Jordan, and in one hectic week in July American troops landed in the Lebanon, in response to the appeal of the Lebanese President Chaumon, and British troops were despatched two days later to sustain King Hussein in Jordan. It looked for a moment as if the perils of Suez were being courted again in a new setting, and some bloodcurdling warnings from Moscow helped to fortify the impression. But even apart from these grave aspects of the situation, Bevan believed that the response of the Western Governments was ill-advised and unworkable. He thought that, once again, London and Washington were making the mistake of thinking they could play off one Arab state against another; they should have learnt the hopelessness of that policy from the collapse of the Baghdad Pact, 'the silliest creation in the history of diplomacy'. They still did not seem to realize the indigenous character of Middle Eastern nationalism, and Washington in particular, he believed, seemed to regard any disturbance anywhere as just 'one more piece of evidence of a universal Soviet plot. We believe that that is mere obsessionism.' So he hoped, as he told the House of Commons, that the British Government would tell the American President urgently that he would have no backing from Britain for

Middle Eastern adventures. That was the plea he made to Macmillan on the first day's debate during the crisis – after the landing
in the Lebanon, but before the news about Jordan – but in fact it
was addressed more to his own colleagues. For, with Gaitskell and
George Brown, the Party's Defence spokesman, ranged against
him, Bevan had been outvoted in the Shadow Cabinet on the proposal to divide the House against the British support for the
American action, and Gaitskell's attitude was strongly upheld at a
Party meeting. Twenty-four hours later, however, when the news
burst that, after a hasty Cabinet meeting, British troops were to be
sent to Jordan, the tables were turned, and the whole Labour Party
– with the exception of an ostentatious absentee from the Shadow
Cabinet, George Brown, and one or two others – backed in the
voting lobbies the Bevan view that it was not the duty of the British
Government to uphold tottering governments or ancient thrones
against revolutionary action by the people. But even though united
in the lobbies, the difference in tone between Gaitskell and Bevan
in their speeches was striking, and the contortions of the Parliamentary Labour Party had achieved the eccentric result of making
the Party more ready to back action by the Americans than by the
British.

However, the worst fears of July 1958 went unrealized, thanks to
the coolness and caution of no statesman in the West; the award on
that occasion must go to Khrushchev. After the first denunciation
of the Western action, he did not respond, as he might have done,
by sending troops to Iraq, but preferred to reopen diplomatic
channels, and within days the extraordinary announcement followed that he would soon be visiting the United States to engage in
pre-Summit meeting conversations about the Middle East and
other problems. The crisis subsided almost as swiftly as it had
arisen, and several bold commentators shook their heads, averring
that 'a firm stand' had produced its proper reward, and that those
who had shown the most alarm during the hot days of crisis –
Bevan at the head – now deserved censure. But he was unabashed
by such misconceived attacks, especially since the immediate crisis
was terminated when the authority of the United Nations was interposed between the giant powers. In the last debate of the series, he
regained any mastery he had allegedly lost with a spacious reitera-

tion of the constructive principles which should underlie a Middle Eastern settlement and which must be urgently applied, if there were to be no new Middle Eastern war. Without any departure from his long-established support for the State of Israel, he surveyed more intricately and sympathetically than before the prospect of Arab nationalism,[1] and he was able to return once again to his constant insistence. Of course the Soviet Union must be a party to the settlement; it was that possibility which gave new hope. Of course, both East and West would have to consider changes in attitude – 'if the Russians have made the mistake of sticking too rigidly to Karl Marx, hon. Members opposite have stuck too rigidly to G. A. Henty'. It was time they understood that oil supplies could not be assured by military adventures, British or American. But clearly this remonstrance was not directed solely towards the Tories. A chief interest of the episode was the way in which, in treating a new event, Bevan and Gaitskell found themselves at odds, emotionally and intellectually. Once more at the

[1] A little earlier that year he had received a letter from his firm friend Yigal Allon, asking him to attend the Congress of Allon's Party Ahdut Ha'avodah and contribute to the Party's journal on the tenth anniversary of the establishment of the State of Israel, and he had replied:

My Dear Yigal,

Your letter occasions me a little embarrassment. My attitude to the State of Israel is, I hope, well known to the people of Israel, at least to those who take an interest in these matters.

It is also known to the leaders of the Arab States. In fact my capacity to be of service in improving the relations between Israel and her neighbours has been to some extent weakened by this knowledge by the Arabs of my friendship with Israel.

It seems to me that, at this time, the best course I can pursue is to try to adopt a posture that will enable me to have more influence with Arab opinion. Not that I propose to weaken in my support of Israel in the slightest degree, but rather to avoid public expressions of opinion which might make it impossible for the Arab ears to be ready to listen to what I have to say.

I hope this does not sound too pompous, but I am most anxious to extend some influence from British Labour to nascent Socialist groups in the Arab world.

As for a message to your Conference, you must know that in my position as Treasurer of the Labour Party, I should subject myself to the most embarrassing trouble with Mapai. The leaders of that Party would be on the telephone at once to Morgan Phillips . . .

test, it was revealed how sharply contrasted was the allegiance of the two top men to the American alliance; for one, it was an instrument which, although not to be discarded, needed to be dramatically reshaped; for the other, it sometimes appeared as the Ark of the Covenant carried aloft to inspire. Never had Labour's rank-and-file been summoned to follow a stranger device.

Nothing in the United States's conduct of foreign affairs made Bevan relent in response to Gaitskell's persuasions; indeed they soon found themselves thrust into solid alliance against the latest American excursion in foreign policy – much to the benefit, ironically, of Gaitskell. First, in preparation for the forthcoming meeting of the United Nations, Dulles issued a highly provocative statement reiterating the American determination to keep Communist China out of the United Nations, and, a few weeks later, renewed bombardments of the islands of Quemoy and Matsu off the Chinese coast led to such a furious intensification of the Far Eastern crisis that it did appear conceivable that the American forces might carry their backing for Chiang Kai-shek on Formosa into much more open intervention on the Chinese mainland itself. Against the first proposition Bevan was foremost in raising violent protest: 'If Mr Dulles was a secret Communist agent, he could not be more successful . . . Communication is the very essence of civilized ways of living. It is a most monstrous offence against this principle that the most populous nation on earth should be cut off from communication with so many nations merely because the vision of the leaders of the United States falls so lamentably short of the material power they command . . . If they persist in their present policies, then the smaller powers should concert among themselves to defy a leadership so myopic, so smugly self-satisfied, so dangerous and so unequal to the imperious needs of the time.'[1] That was as extreme a statement of his 'anti-American' attitude as he had ever uttered; but before any reproof could come, events seemed to justify the most violent protests. The whole Party, Gaitskell included, joined in condemning American policy over the offshore islands and Chinese representation at the U.N., and the complaisance of the British Government on both subjects. When the Party Conference met at Scarborough in October, with the madness of a Far Eastern

[1] *Tribune* 15 August.

war still threatening, other business made way on the Monday morning for an emergency resolution, moved by Gaitskell, condemning American policy and demanding that Britain's voice should be raised against it. Bevanite language had become the only one suitable.

Some lesser business also was transacted the night before. Had it not been for the overshadowing international crisis, the atmosphere of dejection in the Party might have found more overt expression. For 1958 had been a year of setbacks and irritation and querulousness. The Left of the Party had not recovered from the near-mortal wounds of Brighton; the Right had displayed no gift for exhilarating leadership; the co-operation between Gaitskell and Bevan had been stiff and embarrassing. Macmillan seemed to be escaping from his post-Suez impasse – the most spectacular escape since Alfred Hinds, said *Tribune*. The much-hoped-for general election of 1958, expected by Bevan among others, had been successfully warded off by the adept Macmillan but a contest in 1959 was well-nigh certain. No one wanted to upset the prospect; but many criticisms of the leadership were heard. ('Does the Labour Party still exist?' asked *Tribune*, at its rudest, in August.) The assurance of a Labour victory was slipping. Bevan was aware of all the rumours and anxieties when he spoke at the eve-of-Conference demonstration on the Sunday, and he started with a few comments on the publicity methods being used to build up Macmillan, with glances at appropriate moments to Gaitskell on the platform beside him. 'If you have a leader you either have to make a hero of him or assassinate him . . . It is quite impossible to have an unpopular leader for long . . . If you haven't got a policy then you have to give the impression that you have a leader . . . This is one of the essential principles of leaderology, though it is not so important in our Party as in the Conservative Party . . . The movement should realize that the leadership of the Party has been settled and the gossip should stop. Hugh Gaitskell is there, elected by the Party, and he commands the loyalty of us all.'

Scarborough confirmed the unspoken and unwritten compact made at Brighton, but, in Bevan's understanding, it never took the form which his old enemies on the Right of the Party claimed or some of his old friends on the Left feared. Gaitskell was assured of

20

the leadership; that was certain; it was never possible to 'half-assassinate' a leader. Bevan was established as the second figure in the Party hierarchy; when he received an ovation at the end of an hour-long speech on foreign affairs at the Conference, Gaitskell walked across the platform, slightly too effusively, to clap him on the back, and when Parliament resumed, he was elected at the head of the poll for the Shadow Cabinet, a transformation from the twelfth place accorded to him five years before. During that same Conference speech, Bevan repeated his case on the H-bomb, but scarcely a whispered rebuke came from the floor. He re-emphasized too his general approach to the international scene, a far remove from the cold war aridities preached officially from the Conference platform in the early 1950s, and the night before, at the *Tribune* rally, he repeated that one supreme purpose of winning victory at the election was 'to change the face of Britain, to ensure that the commanding heights of the economy are publicly owned'. That too, he believed, was part of the compact; by much tugging and heaving a shift Leftwards in the Party had been secured. That *Tribune* meeting might have ended in catastrophe; a few shouts, a few jibes from the floor might have seemed an inevitable consequence of Brighton and the stridencies of the intervening year. But he drew upon the wealth of affection and allegiance in his audience. 'I am not going to permit the differences that have arisen between us to destroy more than thirty or forty years of work for Socialism in Great Britain. Neither am I going to permit myself to become sour if some things are said which are often hurtful . . . If you dedicate yourselves to the cause of Socialism, I believe we can win the next election. But having won, I am certain that victory will be dead ashes unless it is supported by a reinvigorated Socialist movement in this country.' That was part of the compact too; the restless pressure of the rank-and-file on the leadership would continue. If Labour in power lost its will to change society, a languor in democratic feeling would ensue and upon it would supervene a kind of neo-Fascism.

But the strongest strain which burst through at the moments of emotional climax in his speeches at Scarborough was his feeling that time was running out, time to stop the arms race getting out of control altogether, time to achieve sanity at the Summit before universal darkness buried all. And perhaps it was inevitable that some political observers should link these references to an unfolding tragic drama with his own age – he was just turning sixty –or the suggestion, then gaining wider acceptance, that the Labour Party might well lose the coming election and be condemned to another dreary period in opposition. It would have been impossible if no such personal calculations ever crossed Bevan's mind and perhaps they reinforced his sense of passionate urgency. But since he would never pose, there is no need to doubt what he himself said. It was not that he felt, like Chatham, that 'I can save this country and nobody else can', but he did feel – had, in one sense, felt ever since 1945 – that if democratic Socialism failed, democracy itself would not survive, and he did feel that he could give expression to that spirit in a way no one else could, and that it was the temper of democratic Socialism which was required on the world stage to rescue the peace. At Scarborough, all these considerations came to the surface, and at the *Tribune* rally, so *The Times* political correspondent reported, he had made 'a speech (to use a Bevanish phrase) of *inspissated* despair', and truly enough that was the kind of word he liked to twist round his recalcitrant tongue. He was in fact fighting off a fierce bout of influenza and some other undecipherable pain. Usually when he was under great strain, it was revealed in a swelling in the neck which his friend and physiotherapist, Jack Buchan, would treat with great skill. Jack came racing to Scarborough and to his distress could not find the usual curable symptoms.

Savagely, a headline in *The Times* a few months later reported, or purported to report: 'NO LONGER THE HOTSPUR OF PARLIAMENTARY DEBATE. Puzzle of Mr Bevan's Lost Buoyancy.' Bevan would throw the paper aside with contempt; everyone could make bad speeches; only political commentators were fools enough not to understand that. The effectiveness of every Bevan speech had always trembled on a knife-edge; for him, the price of success was to risk failure. But undoubtedly, apart even from his presentiments about world affairs, he did feel that he carried a special burden; he did feel that over the years the guidance which the Labour Party had given the nation and the world had been pitifully timid and inadequate – indeed he felt this even more about domestic than about foreign policy – and none of the accommodations or compacts he had reached could banish the awareness from his mind. 'What leadership! What leadership!' he would say. Yet the times when these sombre thoughts took command must not be painted in colours too black. Even at inspissated Scarborough his wit pierced through. He gave his own pithy definition of the Establishment: 'I mean those people who have arrived – and don't want to depart.' He described how the mass media were manipulated: 'A Tory majority puts a megaphone in the mouth of property and a gag in the mouths of the people.' He gave his verdict of the expedition to Jordan: 'This Ivor Novello conception of modern politics just won't do. In any case, if we just want to save King Hussein, why don't we give him a house in Surrey? It would be much cheaper.' And he spoke of Harold Macmillan and the famous book outlining his liberal professions he had written in the 1930s called *The Middle Way*: 'I once had a talk with Harold Macmillan about his book. It was very brief. I said that if the middle was a point equidistant between the two extremes then you didn't know where you are until the others had taken up their positions. He still doesn't know where he is. He and all his middle-of-the-roaders are the parasites of politics.' When, back in the House of Commons, Macmillan pitched his defence of the Jordan expedition on the highest grounds of morality and honour, Bevan complained that he was inclined to overstate his case: 'He reminds me of some writings of my friend Milovan Djilas. He describes another highlander, a Montenegrin, as one who held a high line of talk as though he was always on horseback.' To appreciate the analogy to the full, it was necessary to have been subjected extensively to Macmillan's stilted vein of eloquence. Similarly, some of Bevan's most unforgettable flights of humour derived from the way he saw familiar sights with new eyes. One Tory backbencher, especially obtuse and objectionable, as we thought, appeared to have no neck, his head being seemingly screwed directly into his body. Bevan looked across at him and muttered, to us but not to the benches opposite: 'The hangman's puzzle.'

The Labour Party's doubts and anxieties at Scarborough did not disappear; in the House of Commons they seemed imperceptibly and inexplicably to take a firmer grip. That Parliament, the most wretched Bevan had ever sat in, had received a mortal wound in 1956 and should have been allowed to die at the polls at an early date thereafter. Instead, it had been kept in being solely for the convenience of the Conservative Party. His name for it, 'the squalid Parliament', was primarily due to the lingering stench of Suez about the place. Ministers had been charged with misconduct on a scale which in early centuries would have brought impeachment. More recent precedents suggested that at least there should have been a Select Committee to examine how the fiasco had happened and whether the House of Commons had been properly treated in the information presented to it; after all, after the failure of the Dardanelles expedition in 1915 such a Committee was established even in wartime. But over Suez, Macmillan and his fellow Ministers resisted all demands for an inquiry and the Opposition did not seem to pursue the matter as relentlessly as they might have done. The charges of collusion – a most serious one according to the Oxford English Dictionary definition: 'a secret agreement or undertaking for the purposes of trickery or fraud; underhand scheming or working with another; deceit, fraud, trickery' – were flung across the Chamber without stirring the response which questions of a Minister's probity might normally arouse.[1] In one debate in March, Bevan himself said: 'It is, of course, believed all over the world – and privately believed on those benches opposite – that there was collusion. I have not spoken to anybody of any informed opinion in any part of the world who does not take the same view.' But even that indictment spelt out so plainly did not reawaken the fury of the Suez debate. A jaded, smirking cynicism had descended on the Treasury bench and it was found to be a safer shield than any punctilious sensitivity about charges of dishonour.

Somehow the atmosphere of Suez – the feeling or supposition

[1] For example, in one Suez debate on 15 December 1958, Leslie Hale, M.P. [backed by Bevan] put the question thus: 'In view of the fact that these articles [by Mr Randolph Churchill] make a specific allegation against the Government, that of planning an aggressive war – for which fifteen criminals were hanged at Nuremberg – do you feel you are upholding the reputation and dignity of the British Government by saying that you are not even concerned to say that you and your colleagues are not guilty of a capital offence?' But there was still no answer.

that the reports given to the House were being deliberately befud-
dled – seeped into the other discussions of the times; on the settlement in Cyprus, on the killings at the Hola camp in Kenya, on the
discovery of a murder plot in Nyasaland, on the lack of progress
towards a ban on H-bomb tests. Bevan spoke for the Party on all
these subjects (except Hola) and by all normal standards the
speeches were excellent. They lacked only the attribute of his
greatest attacks; the supreme quality of *deadliness*. Inevitably, some
observers suggested that he was succumbing to the conventional
disease of ageing Left-wing politicians, the loss of zest for the fight,
the shuffle Rightwards, a growing taste for the urbanities of the
House of Commons. But in Bevan's case the explanation was
different. Partly the decline in vitality was sheerly physical – during
that spring and summer he had several recurrences of the con-
gestion which had struck him at Scarborough and Jennie wondered, with a sudden stab of alarm, whether he was stricken with
latent pneumoconiosis, the disease from which his father had died.
But partly also it was a revulsion against the odours of 'the squalid
Parliament'; he was genuinely shocked that such accusations of
collusion produced no serious attempt at defence from those he
assailed. And partly he suffered from a sense of political isolation
within his own Party, finding himself out of sympathy with so
many of his old friends on the Left but not having overcome his
lack of sympathy with his old enemies on the Right. For all this
variety of reasons, he was, in 1959, not 'a new Bevan' but rather
one who found it difficult to act in the old style in the new circumstances. There was aptness as well as wit in Macmillan's description of him and his front-bench colleagues, in one of those debates,
as 'a shorn Samson, surrounded there by a bevy of prim and ageing Delilahs'. But Samson's locks, be it not forgotten, could grow
again.

One other cause of his irritation, although it figured infrequently
in his parliamentary speeches, since it was outside his direct front-
bench responsibility, was his ever persistent belief that the Labour
Party lamentably failed to present the Socialist case on domestic
affairs in proper terms. This, he believed, was the profound reason
why Macmillan and Co. were able to escape from the consequences
of their crimes and blunders abroad. The more the defenders of

capitalism paraded the virtues and benefits of the so-called affluent society, the more it was necessary for Socialists to make their condemnation of it in terms which would survive short-term changes, and it was thus that his comments were phrased in language no other politician was inclined to choose. 'Private economic adventure – miscalled "private enterprise" '– he wrote[1] – 'insists upon mystery. If the behaviour of market forces could be predicted, capitalism could not survive. It depends for its survival on the deliberate cultivation of unpredictability. It is wholly opposed to the scientific spirit of the age which strives to understand and control what is happening around us.' And then he put his own gloss on the phenomenon of the loss of wealth due to the under-employment of resources. 'The old Marxist thesis stated that a time would be reached in the development of capitalist society when property relations would limit the expansion of the productive forces. That analysis was too severe. The position today is not that capitalist society is plunged into an epic economic crisis. Instead the economy functions but in an enfeebled condition, like a patient with a persistent low fever. We are not in the old phase of boom or bust. There is never a real boom or a real bust. There is only a persistent sabotage of productive potentialities.' Indeed, the main reason why the swing of the economic pendulum was not as violent as previously was to be found in the quasi-Socialist principles inserted into the economy, the leverage offered by the publicly-owned sector of the economy, where investment could be controlled. But how long would these quite inadequate controls be sufficient? 'Western Europe and the United States,' he also wrote,[2] 'are floundering about, forced to make purely empirical choices among a number of alternatives at a very low common pattern that can be said to emerge from a myriad of unrelated decisions. The result is a total absence of design, and without design the human soul itself feels adrift.' Thus always, in 1959, as in 1949 or 1929, Bevan saw the relationship between his case for public ownership and, on the one hand, the immediate economic controversies of the day and, on the other, the larger philosophical Socialist case and its conformity with the deepest human instincts.

[1] *Tribune* 7 November 1958.
[2] *Tribune* 9 January 1959.

One weekend that spring, on the initiative of his friend, K. S. Karol, of *L'Express*, a meeting was arranged at his Asheridge farm between him and Pierre Mendès-France and Pietro Nenni, at which they discussed these themes, and on this aspect in particular (although also on the others) Bevan did most of the talking: Why was the Left all over Europe – so the question was posed – in a state of discouragement? To which Bevan jumped in with the answer that it was the Right more than the Left which *ought* to be discouraged; it was the policies of the Right which were so signally failing to achieve the aim of economic expansion without inflation. 'Orthodox economists in the Socialist sense of the term,' he said, 'have been pointing out for some time that it is not possible to get the American economic machine running at full speed, unless American capitalism adopts what we regard in Britain as the apparatus of the Welfare State. That is to say, social spending on a vast scale. Were it not that the arms programme had taken the place of a vast public works programme, the economic crisis in Western countries would be almost as great as it was in the thirties.' And then having dismissed such 'gimmicks' as the Common Market, he stressed the importance that 'the Left – and I use the term as a generic term, I would prefer to say Socialists – should present to the people an analysis so clear that it is never over-whelmed by contemporary circumstances. But it is because our continental friends, and I hope I am not appearing superior in this matter, appear to me to allow themselves to make the immediate psychological situation the object of their strategy, that they give the appearance of being permanently empirical.' And of course, that was also his fear for the British Labour Party: that it would become as *permanently empirical* as the Social Democratic parties of the Continent which had come near to abandoning their Socialism altogether.

However, it is not the political discussions at the time of the Nenni and Mendès-France visit which Jennie most graphically recalls. She saw Nye's face framed in the window and had a fresh stab of fear about his health. And after they had gone, she remembers him stepping outside the front door with a wine glass in his hand, and looking at a favourite cherry tree which had been cruelly and senselessly pruned. He called it Lavinia and grieved for it as if it had been a living human being (or his beloved Health Service) and never forgave the insensible hands that had butchered it. Holding up the glass, Jennie heard him say: 'Not many more springs.' The next moment he was his usual smiling self. Jennie pretended not to have heard, and led him back, as she always tried to do at such moments, when the Welsh mists looked like descending, to the immediate things of the warm sensual world which he loved so much and with such tender discrimination.

During that spring and summer of 1959, Bevan found himself involved in renewed altercations with Aldermaston marchers; renewed arguments on the Labour Party's National Executive on the devising of a Party disarmament policy; renewed disagreement with Macmillan and the Government about their movements towards a détente. Although there were still fierce arguments over the proposal for a non-nuclear club, which was the outcome of the Labour Party discussions, some of the bitterest pains and dissensions within the Party showed signs of subsiding. Bevan himself sought to make a virtue of the Labour Party's debate and to contrast it with the monolithic infertility of his opponents. A conference on nuclear tests had been convened at Geneva; that was a welcome start. Macmillan himself had been to Moscow ('one of the most highly publicized Odysseys since the Greeks,' said Bevan, and alas, despite his own claim, he had not brought back the golden fleece), although the major result seemed to be a dispute about what he had promised in the field of disengagement. Early in the autumn it was arranged that the Labour leaders should follow in Macmillan's footsteps. Bevan was dubious whether the time was the best chosen, but he had spoken so often on the need for the world's leaders to talk to one another that he could not have declined the invitation even if he had wished.

Moscow in September 1959 could not offer the same interest and illumination which he had experienced on his visit to the Soviet Union two years before. For one thing, he was part of an official Party delegation, a form of excursion which, ever since his visit to China in 1954, in the company of Attlee and Edith Summerskill, he had learnt to regard as one of the most subtle of political tortures. 'In Italy,' wrote Stendhal, 'the women watch the men; in France,

20*

they watch the other women'; comparably on political delegations abroad, politicians thrust into painful intimacy with travelling colleagues not of their own choosing may find themselves morbidly fascinated by their companions rather than their hosts, and in Bevan's case, on the journey to Moscow, this distraction operated with a peculiar force. He and Gaitskell had never engaged in any private relaxation together; almost exclusively their contacts had been official and concerned with political business. Inevitably on the Moscow trip they – and Dora Gaitskell who was a member of the party – were thrown together at meals and continuously on other occasions, and Gaitskell happily recorded later that it was at this time he had had his first chance to appreciate the warmth and gaiety of Bevan's companionship. Doubtless there were many genuinely convivial moments. But the whole affair had also an element of pathetic farce. Gaitskell had not consulted Nye about the composition of the delegation, and Jennie had no wish to travel 'in the baggage van' with the group of 'wives'. So she and Nye, horror-struck at the thought of the hours of beleaguerment he might be called upon to endure, had the brilliant idea of inviting his journalist friend, K. S. Karol, to accompany him as a kind of personal interpreter and adviser. But would the Soviet authorities see the point as swiftly and accommodatingly as they should? The last time Karol had been in Moscow was in 1945 when he had been returning from Siberia to his native Poland; since then he had become a stateless person and a leading Socialist authority on Communist affairs, but these were not exactly qualifications guaranteed to supply him overnight with the necessary Soviet visa. Bevan pooh-poohed all objections, said he would fix everything with Malik, the Soviet Ambassador in London, and miraculously he did, and, on arrival in Moscow, he also fixed, in defiance of all protocol, that Karol should not be despatched to the scheduled quarters reserved for the other journalists but should stay at his side, in the same apartment, and never wander. Karol soon discovered that his principal duty, apart from providing the safety-valve for Nye's explosions, was to discover ways and means, by the use of his expert Russian, to find relief from the oppressive proximity of the rest of the delegation. It was not such an easy task in the Moscow diplomatic world; but they did escape to the Indian

Embassy and to the Polish Embassy, and all the while Nye sighed for other escapades like a would-be truant schoolboy.

The evidence of imperfect sympathy between the two leaders of the Labour Party accumulated to such a degree that it almost obscured, in Karol's reckoning, the discussions with the Soviet leaders in the Kremlin and elsewhere. In any case, Khrushchev was on the very eve of departing for his highly-publicized visit to the United States, and was clearly in no mood to embark on serious discussion with leaders of the Labour Party soon to be involved in an election which most experts foretold they were unlikely to win. So Bevan sought, obliquely almost, to infiltrate areas of discussion which might offer advantages for the future and which might retain some value after Khrushchev's obsession with his United States visit had subsided. This is what he sought to do by arguing with Khrushchev at the Polish Embassy, in Gaitskell's absence, about the role a Labour Government could still play. But on other occasions Gaitskell, in Bevan's and Karol's estimate, tended to make discussion too sharp or provocative in circumstances where no compensation in clarity could be hoped for – at one moment, for example, he stumbled into an argument on the unpopular subject of the Nazi-Soviet Pact of 1939. Sometimes Gaitskell seemed less interested in what he actually told the Russians than in what he could tell the British journalists he had told them. For Bevan, this exhibition was faintly indecent, and yet he could not altogether withhold a meed, not of admiration but at least of fascination, at the success of the operation. Gaitskell was good at getting himself a good press. But sometimes also Bevan was driven near to open protest at the general Gaitskellite style, the nearest being the incident in Leningrad at a grand reception given by the Mayor. Gaitskell and Bevan would take it in turns to reply to the endless toasts, but it soon became noticeable that Bevan had the better head for vodka, and on the Leningrad occasion he sought to cut loose from the usual banalities and dared to talk of the common working-class ancestry which Communists in Russia and Socialists in Britain shared and which one day might help to refashion a new Socialist internationalism. The Russians were puzzled, but a few of them cheered until Dora launched into a wild invective directed against all this 'working-class nonsense' and most obviously against

Nye. The Russians became even more puzzled, the British were embarrassed and Nye could only remark to Karol later how fortunate it was that Jennie had not been present. Otherwise Leningrad might have witnessed scenes unmatched since the last days of St Petersburg.

Another strange incident arose from Bevan's ineradicable taste for philosophical discussion. Somehow the name of Joseph Dietzgen cropped up; the old Marxist philosopher, author of *The Positive Outcome of Philosophy*, a volume much pored over in the Tredegar Workmen's Institute. Bevan was delighted, particularly because one of the arguments in which he tended to become implicated with his Russian hosts concerned their excessive puritanism. But perhaps Dietzgen could make him respectable. Did they know Dietzgen had written a poem? Would they like him to recite it? He then treated the assembled company to the lines called 'Hard Times' which he had known since his first acquaintance with Dietzgen.

> *Pretty maiden, bright and bonnie*
> *Winsome, charming, blithe and wry!*
> *If I only had the money*
> *For a homestead snug and cosy*
> *You would be my bride, my honey!*
> *But alas! Though Cupid's craving*
> *Is as wild and strong as ever,*
> *Yet in vain is all my raving*
> *Never shall I hold you, never!*
> *Woe is me! The tide has turned.*

But suddenly the whole slightly purposeless, slightly claustrophobic, too official, too alcoholic expedition to Moscow was interrupted by news from London. Harold Macmillan announced the date for the general election – 8 October – a bare five weeks ahead. Some similar announcement had been expected but not quite so soon. Bevan started packing; the news obviously meant that their proposed stop at Warsaw on the way home would have to be cancelled; Karol was instructed to forget his diplomatic diversions. But where was Gaitskell, the leader of the Party? The newspaper correspondents he had fostered so amiably were eager for an interview. They had to be content with a few austere words from the *bon viveur* Bevan, since the Gaitskell whom he had never called desiccated had made a miscalculation about the vodka. Not a word of his condition was reported back to Britain; and Bevan could not help thinking that if the same ill-timed misfortune had befallen himself the reporters might not have been so reticent. Not a word also escaped of Gaitskell's final suggestion, once the news had penetrated, that the Warsaw visit should proceed undisturbed; he was soon persuaded to have second and soberer thoughts about that too. So the two men returned to face the British electorate. Gaitskell, it seems, was obliviously well-satisfied with the relationship fraternally established while Bevan felt himself handcuffed, for ever it might be, to this most incongruous of comrades. To get back as speedily as possible to England, to Asheridge, was the only conceivable remedy.

Throughout the election of 1959, Bevan undertook a full tour, addressing four or five meetings a day, a programme he detested at any time. He much preferred a single meeting where he could spread himself and develop his thoughts, but the exigencies of the election campaign had to be met. Despite his ill health, he fulfilled almost the entire programme, until he came to the last engagement away from Ebbw Vale, which happened to be in my constituency of Devonport. His meeting there had been the climax of all our election campaigns since 1945. However, on that Friday morning, 2 October, he woke up with a high temperature and low spirits, and even though he did make the effort to get to the station, he had to turn back, and get a special message sent through that he could not come. Two days later he managed to reach Tredegar, although the illness was clearly not thrown off. In fact, he should never have taken part in the election at all; he was already deeply sick.

The campaign was different in many respects from any he had fought before. Despite the tension which always seized him at such times, he was usually buoyed up by the meetings themselves, and once they were over, he would argue late into the night, sustaining the spirits of all around him. But even while it was on, and even more afterwards, he characterized the 1959 election as the worst he had ever fought. In his own speeches he concentrated, largely but not entirely, on foreign affairs, the scandals of Suez, Nyasaland,

Hola and Cyprus, partly because he would scarcely trust himself to speculate on the Labour Party's domestic commitments. He had little faith that a Gaitskell Government *would* attempt to do what he thought was essential in that field, and he feared that a few unguarded words from himself might re-open the old battles. And these thoughts mingled with other and deeper anxieties. However, for the biographer, there is available one authentic indication of what he was thinking and feeling about that election in contrast with all the others he had ever fought since the first contest in 1929. All through his 1959 tour, Bevan was accompanied by Geoffrey Goodman, at that time the Industrial Correspondent of the *Daily Herald*, with whom he had formed one of his rare friendships and relationships of trust with a working journalist. Geoffrey went everywhere with him through the last weeks of September and the beginning of October, and sat up with him, night after night, when the meetings were over. Then, since he found it even more difficult to sleep than Bevan himself, he would stay up a little longer and make a few notes of what they had talked about. He gives a unique flavour of Bevan's moods at the time – not, it may be emphasized, the fully considered verdicts which he would have given to the world, but the tentative ideas and conclusions which circumstances, and perhaps his sickness, pressed upon him. They met first in London to discuss the way in which the campaign might be covered, but thenceforward some brief extracts from Geoffrey's night-by-night reports reveal more than any of Bevan's 1959 campaign speeches:

18 September, London: He looks tired and weary. Oppressed by the scale of the problems inside the Labour movement and outside in the wider political arena. Still bitterly critical of Gaitskell whom he regards as 'sincere enough in his own beliefs – but no Socialist'. He had just returned from a visit to the U.S.S.R. with Gaitskell and Denis Healey. No doubt Khrushchev faces serious problems both at home and abroad. This colours his perspective on his own difficulties, if he were to go to the Foreign Office – 'It won't be an easy time, many problems are only capable of being solved by time and patient negotiation.' That is one reason why he is against Britain renouncing the bomb in advance of any international agreement. His long-term aim is to try to establish

a wider Commonwealth association in which Britain would co-
operate both politically and economically with some of the
emerging countries; cites India, Ghana, Australia and New
Zealand – joint development. Britain on her own a limited influence. But combined with these other groups she could have a
very powerful influence. He recognizes already that his position
in the Cabinet will be a very difficult one. 'Gaitskell is constantly
interfering. He will never leave you alone to carry on the job.'
Gaitskell has a meticulous mind for detail and administration,
but no capacity for imaginative leadership. 'The pure economist's
mind,' says Bevan. The most that Bevan seems to expect to do is to
influence the trend of Cabinet discussion. He is gloomy about
anything more decisive. 'The Left is very weak,' he believes:
'No more than about fifty M.P.s [about one-fifth] are Socialists,'
he says. This is the problem, since it is the Parliamentary Party
which elects the Party leader, not the Labour movement as a
whole. The whole state of Parliament is now in a parlous condition. Its most important decisions are now taken by committees, meeting in secret and beyond the sanction of their local
parties. This reduces the role of the ordinary M.P. to an insignificant status and made most parliamentary debates of little
importance. The standard of debate has fallen and the impact of
parliamentary institutions in the life of the nation was becoming
less. The dignity of Members was affected. He quotes his own
case – a leading member of the Opposition, with responsibilities and tasks covering a wide and complex field. Yet he is
paid exactly the same as a back-bencher; he has no proper room
to work in in the Commons, library facilities are poor, the general
amenities of the House altogether low. It made the burden of
public life incredibly hard, and led to men of ability turning
away from Parliament as an attractive prospect. The institution
in fact reflected the period before the Labour Party came into its
ascendancy. It was then a Tory club; a place for a few top political leaders and a mass of part-timers, time-servers, in the pay of
the administration. Liberals too were basically no different. Then
came the influx of working men. But the institution had not been
changed in any way to accommodate the social transformation in
the composition of Parliament. All this reflected Bevan's overall

gloom and depression about British political life today. He
lamented that if the Tories won the election and a period of continued economic prosperity followed, there would be a further
degeneration of Socialist spirit in the Labour Party. He saw no
obvious chance of a revolt against the leadership of Gaitskell and
'the clique of statisticians'. He still regarded it as an immense
tragedy that Gaitskell was ever elected the leader – 'but I can't
see what can be done about it now'. He still believes Morrison
would have been a better choice – 'though I disliked him intensely over some of his policies. Nevertheless, he was more in the
tradition of the Labour Party.' He reflected much on the past and
was more and more reluctant to predict the future. As one gets
older, 'the past becomes nearer and the present more and more
difficult to remember'. He recognizes his age. He reflected sadly
that another defeat would mean another five years in the wilderness, by which time he would be approaching 70.

22 September: Nye said he told Khrushchev that he was no
longer the only great power – soon there would be others. It
could be that small nations would soon be able to inflict as much
damage as large ones. Khrushchev didn't like this. Bevan said to
Khrushchev that he mustn't try to split the American people
from their President. Khrushchev said he couldn't talk to them
as he talked to the British Labour Party. Bevan doesn't think
that Khrushchev is genuine in his offer to 'scrap the lot' – that is,
the bomb. Not because he is being deliberately dishonest, but
because he does not realize what this really means. It can't be
achieved this way. Even the non-nuclear club is only a step. It
must lead to wider agreement. Ending N.A.T.O. and the Warsaw Pact. Khrushchev regarded the non-nuclear club as being
unreal because it still left N.A.T.O. bases in Britain. 'You have
bases too,' said Bevan. We must win this election, it is vital. A
great deal hangs on it.

24 September, Llangollen: He speaks of doubting whether he
will stand the Foreign Office for more than a year. He became
defeatist about the immensity of the task and the complexity of
the problem. He regards Gaitskell as a great obstacle. He asked
me what I thought would happen if Labour lost. I told him that
that would let loose a period of dejection, followed by searching

for leadership by the Left. It would then be open to the Left for
them to take advantage of it. He did not disagree with this
analysis. But he thought there would have to be a fundamental
transformation in the Parliamentary Party before there could be
any change at the top and any new political direction. He says: 'I
am heartily sickened by the Parliamentary Labour Party. It is
rotten through and through: corrupt, full of patronage, and seeking after patronage; unprincipled.' He reflected that the leaders
could at any time, in government, find anything up to a hundred
jobs. That completely dominated the relationship in the Parliamentary Party. He would change the system so that there were
no more secret meetings, etc., where decisions were taken later
and M.P.s hid under the cloak of the privacy of the private
meeting. He would compel each M.P. to account for his actions
and votes in the Parliamentary Party by a discussion on which
issues he supported or opposed, and whom he supported or
opposed. This would then be seen by his local party. It could
make M.P.s much more responsive to pressure from local parties
and he believes help to revive Socialist activity in the Labour
Party. On the Labour Party as the instrument: 'Well, what other
instrument is there? Though I know that, sometimes I didn't
know how I could stay in the Labour Party. It isn't really a
Socialist Party at all.'

26 September, Coventry: He was in one of the strangest moods.
Tired, obviously quite fatigued by the whole business. His eyes a
curious green/blue and ablaze in a strange half madness, which
seemed to sear through you in anguished contempt. He was
angry; frustrated; like a fenced tiger. I had not before seen him
in this mood. He spoke with immense irritation about everything.
The meetings were plainly becoming burdensome. One could
see why he evoked such enmity as well as devotion. He can snap
and bite. Turn like a wounded tiger and snarl. We were talking
about the meeting he is to have in Coventry tomorrow night. He
kept saying that he wasn't looking forward to it. 'It will be a good
meeting,' I comforted. He didn't reply. 'What are your worried
about – the bomb?' I asked. 'The bomb – what do you mean?'
he asked scathingly. I explained about the C.N.D. 'No, no, no,
no – sometimes you are very stupid. Have you ever spoken at a

meeting?' 'What's the analogy?', I threw back 'One is bound to
be frightened of what one might say,' he went on; 'a large meeting has its dangers. You are sometimes tempted to say things you
shouldn't say. That is what I am worried about.' He explained
he had been forcing himself to exercise tremendous restraint in
his meetings so far. This plainly was the clue to his temperamental outbursts; his obvious frustration; his curious quietness
at times. In all his meetings so far he had been extremely
restrained – meetings dealing particularly with the Suez affair
and pointing out that because of this the Tories were incapable
of representing Britain at the Summit. But obviously he would
have liked to have had a great outburst on Socialist policies. He
is resentful of the self-imposed restraint. But he knows that if he
let off the brakes he would do immense damage and could lose
the election... Foreign Office – he reflects about the burden which
Foreign Secretaryship would bring. He rejects the convention
of attending on the Queen when he is about to go abroad, he
says, 'I want none of that.' He will cut out most of the dinners
and receptions. He will battle against the foreign service interests in the F.O. who are so fearful, at the present, of his coming.
His hopes centre on 'creating a habit of talking together', in
order to bridge the gap between East and West. But he is not that
hopeful. Somehow he has moments of great doubt about the
amount of influence that can now be wielded. This is linked with
his attitude about the bomb. He clings to it as a buoy. To throw it
away in advance would be 'an act of sheer folly'. We must first
try to get agreement on tests, inspection. Then see how things
are. Part of the trouble will be to break down the suspicions of
ourselves which are only reflections and in themselves reflect the
other fears and suspicions. 'You know that the fellow across the
table is suspicious of your motives because you know, in your
heart, that you are suspicious of his. This is the great problem
facing us. Sometimes I am not sure that we will be able to overcome this. We can try.' On the British working class: It may no
longer be so important. History gave them the chance – and they
didn't take it. Now it is probably too late. The great changes in
the world will take place in spite of them. They will be carried
forward with the momentum. But as far as stirring the British

working class into pioneering action – it's not so much that it
may not be possible as that it no longer matters all that much.
'Why is it that the mood matters so much on this island? It is
small you know.' Defeatism: that the problems and complexities are so great as to rule out the chances of achievement. But
man cannot accept this as the final guide to his own actions.
'There is always the unknown factor. You must carry on on that,
if there is the chance of winning or at least doing something. If
you forget that, you might as well commit suicide.'

4 October – By car from farm to Ebbw Vale / Tredegar: . . .
getting rid of Gaitskell will not be an easy task. If we lose, there
will be a rallying around and a protection society will be formed
round Gaitskell. Even if Bevan stood for leadership against
Gaitskell, they (P.L.P.) would calculate that it would be no use
electing him because of his age – 62 now, 67 at the time of the
next election. 'No,' he says, 'we must transform the character of
the P.L.P. to make it more answerable to the constituency parties; 'every vote taken by M.P.s should be recorded on a ballot
paper so that the rank-and-file can know how they voted. At the
moment they are answerable to no one and while that lasts the
P.L.P. will not be transformed into a Socialist force. At least half
the present P.L.P. is interested in perpetuating their own positions and the status quo. This is Gaitskell's strength. If we are
defeated we must decide the next stage not so much within the
parliamentary machine, but outside, with those trade unions and
other forces which can be brought together. He mentioned
Cousins in this respect. Even if Labour wins, Bevan would be far
from a happy man. He recognizes that Gaitskell is round his neck
all the time. 'He is a stubborn man, always interfering, will never
let me alone. I don't know how long I will be able to stand it.'

7 October, *Ebbw Vale*, *Eve of Poll:* Bevan is in bed with a head-
ache, 'looking green' as his nephew Robert Norris reported to
me. I am not surprised. He stayed up talking last night very late.
We got in front of the coal fire in his sister's house in Tredegar.
He reflecting on the enormous strain imposed by public life
today. I had been commenting on the low performance of the
Prime Minister [Harold Macmillan] on TV in the final Conservative broadcast. He defended not so much Macmillan as the

burden which statesmen like him carry in a modern election campaign. Paraded up and down the country on tour, mouthing phrases in which one can only half believe, even if they are true. (This is a free translation of his comments.) Growing more and more tired, weary and helpless. Thrust forward by the forces of mass communication; then at the end having to appear before millions on a TV screen, only able to repeat the same shibboleth. 'Public life now is becoming an intolerable burden with few redeeming features. If it goes on we shall all degenerate into pure salesmen – like the American politicians.' He constantly says: 'I am no politician.' He is resentful at having to parade with the phraseology of electioneering. He hates slogans; is conscious all the time of the need to educate (not sloganize), but the impossibility of doing this indicates the limitations of the election campaign. Of course he is resentful of Gaitskell all the time, regards him as 'a complete gimmick man'. Now only concerned with the trappings of power – not with any intentions of transforming society. 'Gaitskell wants to make capitalism work better – but with controls. That's what makes him so dangerous. He wants capitalism to go on existing – but without the prizes which capitalism earns for itself. Of course this is impossible. It cannot work.' So he is deeply puzzled and anxious about the future, win or lose. Win: It could still be bad. Can you imagine me playing flunkey to the Palace when I am at the F.O. I won't do it. And I shall make my position clear straight away. Then comes the question about the Summit. 'There will be a long, difficult road. But I think we can get something by agreement on the limitations of arms spending. But it won't be easy.' And lose; Well, there will have to be a showdown. 'I will quarrel with Gaitskell straight away. I refuse to belong to a Party unless that Party is the vehicle of principles in which I believe – Socialist principles.' He is tired of course. He is 62, but still has amazing vitality on the platform. Last night, just recovering from flu, psychological flu perhaps, he was vigorous, effective, passionate, alive. He quickly becomes despondent afterwards. He is frequently anxious and querulous both before and after meetings, particularly larger ones. Anxious, especially on this occasion, lest he allows to slip some phrase which could expose his inner conflict.

When he heard the news, late at night or rather early in the morning of 9 October, in his own committee rooms in Ebbw Vale, that Gaitskell with the television cameras on him in the Leeds City Hall, had 'conceded' defeat. Bevan gave way to a symbolic display of rage. 'I would never concede,' his supporters remember him saying, 'I would wait until the last vote was properly counted.' It was a sign of his bottomless disappointment, but a sign too of how much he despised the whole paraphernalia of psephologists' forecasts, public opinion polls, television campaigning, and the presentation of so-called party 'images'. He preferred his own political instinct to any course of action recommended by these new-fangled instruments. He believed that they debased the art of politics since they were all contrivances tending to increase the politicians' reliance on careful calculation and diminish his faith in political ideas and his courage in stating them. Just as he regarded the 1955–59 Parliament as the most wretched he had ever sat in, so the 1959 election had for him no redeeming feature. The end of an election campaign can leave even victors drained of all vitality, and Bevan had all the additional anxieties of his own illness. He limped back to Asheridge as soon as he decently could and was not at all exhilarated to have Gaitskell on the line, asking for an early meeting. Arrangements were made for him to come to Asheridge for lunch and, after the natural lamentations about the result, the main business was evident: assuming Jim Griffiths's withdrawal as the Party's Deputy Leader, would he be prepared to stand for the office? Bevan said 'Yes'. And, apart from some consideration of the thorny question about the Speakership which came at the beginning of most Parliaments, no other business was transacted.

That was always Bevan's attitude at the acrid moments of the Party's defeat – it had been the same in 1955 and 1951. He believed that a little time should be given for wounds to heal, before new battles could be envisaged. And immediately he took special care to bind up the particular fresh wounds which I had received at Devonport; no prodigal son was ever welcomed with such a feast as my wife and I had at Asheridge that gloomy weekend. He told us of the conversations with Gaitskell the day before; why he had agreed to accept the Deputy Leadership; why (apart from his ill-health) he had found the campaign so dispiriting, all the more so in a sense

because of the obvious enthusiasm of the rank-and-file, straining
with such ardour for daring leadership. And he remarked, too, not
with any pent-up venom but more as a clinical verdict, that Gaitskell was a Jonah; the Party would never win with him. The sentence was certainly not pronounced with the idea of starting some
plot. Rather the drift of his discourse pointed in a quite different
direction. The Party, like himself, required time for reflection;
time to consider how the masks of the so-called affluent society
could be stripped aside, how its indecencies and vulgarities could
be exposed, how the idea of Socialism could regain the radiant
appeal which it had lost. It is hard to recall that particular weekend
of conversation without making him sound sanctimonious which
he never was in any sense whatever, and, moreover, his mockery or
derision of political enemies and friends, mixed with his more
philosophical utterances, ensured that the dish never lacked garlic.
We had, I remember also, on that occasion, a long diversion on the
comparative demerits of Attlee and Gaitskell as Party leaders, with
myself stoutly and vainly sustaining the pro-Gaitskell corner. But it
was still true that in private, no less than in his public professions,
he hated, to use his own horrible word, 'the personalization' of
politics. He truly thought in impersonal terms and believed that a
new Socialist thrust could emerge from the post-election debate.

But others drew different and sharper deductions from the 1959
defeat, and some of them assembled at Gaitskell's house on Sunday
11 October. How detailed a plan of action was devised there; how
much Gaitskell himself led or approved the individual steps proposed; how consciously 'the party within a party' set out to transform the Party itself are not matters which a Bevanite biographer
can expect to determine. But it is indisputable that a bold initiative
was set in motion by the Right wing of the Party, and it does appear
that the lever which helped to let it loose was pulled at that Sunday
night meeting in Frognal Gardens, quite unpublicized, of course,
at the time. However, the course of shock treatment for the Party
prescribed by the Gaitskellites sometimes became intermingled
with the deluge of speculation about the future of British politics
generally unleashed by the 1959 results and the apparent, supposed
evidence which it offered that Labour was condemned to a role of
permanent opposition, if not chronic debility. For the Party to lose

three elections in a row, to see its total vote reduced by a further 200,000 after the stay-at-home losses of 1,500,000 in 1955, to see the electoral pendulum broken beyond repair, did seem to indicate that British politics had taken a decisive turn Rightwards. Immediately, large sections of the Conservative press claimed that the real significance of the victory was that it meant the end of Socialism, and Bevan, in his first published comment on the result, was at pains to point out that this deduction could only have been true if 'the Party had held aloft the banner of Socialism in the course of the election and before it'. But it did no such thing; Labour had in fact fought on a programme which might be better defined as 'pre-1914 Liberalism brought up to date', and those who interpreted the result as the collapse of British Socialism were 'engaged in a subtle and persistent effort to convert the Labour movement into a faceless nonenity'. They suggested that what we should do is to 'find out why a majority of the electorate voted Conservative and then adjust our policies accordingly'.[1] But if Bevan's contribution was intended as a barrier to check the tide of speculation, it was immediately swamped. Next day in the *Evening Standard*, Paul Johnson, purporting to describe what had happened at Socialist gatherings 'all over London (but chiefly Hampstead)', said that an alliance with Grimond's Liberal Party was one favoured item on the agenda, the abandonment of public ownership another, and a change in the name of the Party from 'Socialist' to 'Radical' was a third. Only the Socialist Adullamites, he said, would object, and they, like Bevan himself, were negligible factors in the new world opened by the catastrophic election results.

Mr Johnson had not been a frequent visitor at Frognal Gardens; but Douglas Jay, M.P., of course, had, and it was his article on the following Friday in the semi-official *Forward* which gave a semi-official stamp to the post-election revisionist démarche. He proposed also that the Party should change its name and place a complete ban on further measures of nationalization in general and steel nationalization in particular, adding, to guard against any hazard of a future Left-wing relapse, proposals which would transform the Party's Executive into a federal body in which the Parliamentary Party's influence would be increased and the influence of

[1] *News of the World* 11 October 1959.

the Party Conference and the trade unions correspondingly diminished. The idea was to erase the working-class 'image' of the Party, to remove the 'danger of fighting under a label of a class that no longer exists'; to seize the moment to carry forward the revisionist ideas of recent years no longer solely by relentless pressure but by a *coup d'état*. That without doubt was the mood among the Gaitskellites in those first days. 'From the moment of his [Gaitskell's] return to London', wrote Roy Jenkins, not always to be viewed as Douglas Jay's *alter ego*, 'Gaitskell was active in the search for the causes of the setback. Perhaps mistakenly, he allowed himself no period of recuperation. Without doubt, he and those of us who were close to him made serious tactical mistakes during the ensuing weeks. We over-estimated the rationality of political movements.'[1] Jenkins, like Jay, it seems, was intimately acquainted with post-election Gaitskellite manœuvres.

But to Bevan who was not engaged in any tactical manœuvres at all after the election – unless the acceptance of the Deputy Leadership must be seen as such – it was not only the weakness, even cowardice, involved in the proposed misnamed 'Radical' re-orientation of the Party which offended him; it was not only his fear that such a departure from Socialist ideas at such a moment could spread demoralization far and wide in the rank-and-file; it was the sheer banality of the so-called new thinking; what sort of new thoughts could they be, for example, on the subject of public ownership, which might find their place in a *Daily Telegraph* leading article?

But practice was better than precept: what *should* the Labour leadership say to the country and the Party in that period of defeat? Bevan offered one part of his answer in his contribution to the Queen's Speech debate a few days later. To speak in a new Parliament, from the Opposition benches, is a particular ordeal. The place has suddenly altered its character; those who had its ear a few weeks before may unaccountably speak in accents which jar; a raucous and ugly bunch of intruders infest the back benches opposite, imagining that their victorious election campaign is not yet concluded; and the jeers and taunts of the wretched night of

[1] *Hugh Gaitskell* by Roy Jenkins, edited by W. T. Rodgers (Thames and Hudson), p. 126.

electoral defeat are seldom beyond earshot. Bevan professed to approach the debate in a non-controversial spirit. 'I recall,' he said, 'an incident in the life of Abraham Lincoln, when somebody made charges against him of being concerned in some army contract scandals and an officer serving under him asked leave to surrender his commission in order to allow him to give evidence before a Congressional committee. Abraham Lincoln replied in character-itsic manner, "My dear young friend, if the mercy of Almighty God falls upon our banners and we are victorious, I shall require nothing but that to defend me; but if, on the other hand, He frowns upon us, and, in His infinite providence, we are defeated, ten thousand angels pleading for me will not suffice".' And then Bevan continued: 'There has been no evidence of any angels rushing to our defence on this occasion. On the contrary, there has been an enthusiastic rush forward of a number of little devils turning us around on a spit to make quite sure that we are done well on every side.' And perhaps even the little devils were made to blush, and the way was prepared for the jauntiest of attacks, a little while later, on the newly-appointed Minister of Science in the new Govern-ment, Lord Hailsham, who had just distinguished himself as the bell-ringing Conservative chairman in the election:

The expansion of the Communist world is proceeding forward dramatically and we have to ask ourselves how the Government propose to meet the challenge. We have had one instance today. I am quite certain that when Mr Khrushchev heard that Lord Hailsham has been made responsible for the British answer to the Russian scientific challenge, a chill ran right through the Kremlin. Here at last we have found the answer. The Prime Minister's choice fell upon the obvious person – a man of detached judgment, of objective thinking, with his emotions under control all the time, able to appraise in a mood of cold austerity the claims of science. We are not quite certain what he is going to do. We are not quite certain who he is going to do it to. If I may be allowed a colloquialism, the Prime Minister's suggestion for the organization of science in this country reads like a dog's dinner. I never heard of such a muddle. I understand why – because he is not really serious. The Prime Minister has an absolute genius for putting flamboyant labels on empty baggage. Of course, we are able to guess what is in his mind. He had to do something with Lord Hailsham. He had to do something with him during the election. What was he to do with him afterwards? . . . I warn Lord Hailsham of the fate reserved for him, because he is a man without a department, a man without precise responsibilities who will be flickering from department to department, interfering with everybody, making an enemy of every Minister in every department in turn, and, when he has covered himself with sufficient unpopularity, will either resign, or the Prime Minister will remove him as a piece of useless ministerial rubbish. Such is the malignity of Prime Ministers.

But it was not the banter which made that speech so memorable. It was the way in which he helped to restore the self-respect of his political friends and sow doubts among self-satisfied enemies by the same process of revealing his brooding conclusions on what truly was happening in 'never-had-it-so-good' Britain. So little did he think in the slogans attributed to him and so unwilling was he to accept the crude categories of the pollsters about people being 'for' or 'against' or 'middle class' and 'working class'. Human nature and political nature was ten thousand-fold more complicated than that, and it needed to be unravelled by artists, not statisticians. Modern society had confused in the worker's mind his clashing interest as producer and consumer, as voter and striker, as one who naturally wanted his just share of the new affluence but might gird at the restraints needed to secure it. In one sense, Bevan detested the expressions of the casino society of the Macmillan age more than most other politicians; he hated all forms of gambling (particularly in steel shares on the Stock Exchange) – it was the one remnant of his Welsh puritanism; he felt that the rickety edifice of hire-purchase and the 'never-never' made the worker conservative in instinct, afraid of change, unready for the communal restraints without which the move towards a Socialist society would be impossible. These developments did pose real problems for Socialists – as Bevan was quite prepared to say to his fellow members of the Parliamentary Labour Party in the series of discussions they held about the election – but the challenge to the new Tory Government could not be dodged either, and he put it in terms which reduced them, not to silence, but at least to less raucous rejoicing. How were they going to solve what he called 'the central problem falling upon representative governments in the Western world' – how to persuade people to forego immediate satisfactions in order to build up the economic resources of the country? How were they to restrict the pressure for consumption sufficiently to secure the necessary capital equipment on which future devlopments would depend? The Labour Government had failed to solve the problem because, while making the necessary provisions for the future, it had sacrificed its parliamentary majority. The Macmillan Government made the opposite choice; it sacrificed future industrial resources to keep political popularity. How were they to prevent a repetition of that failure in the future? How were they to prevent all expansion being eaten up in immediate personal consumption? And how could any proper planning of the nation's resources be undertaken without the control of the commanding heights of the economy? There was no answer forthcoming in that debate on 3 November 1959, and the questions still echoed throughout the length of the 1960s. What Bevan did in that debate was to inter-weave the questions with the Marxist and democratic strands in his creed. He believed that, seeing the prospect of advance blocked in the field of politics, the militant working class might turn, as it had so often before, to industrial action, and then might learn only after painful experience that a return to the political battlefield would be necessary to win substantial victories. He was filled, as he had been since 1929, with a sense of the fragility of democratic institutions. He longed to see Parliament rooted in the affections of the people; that was the great theme of English history since the Levellers, and his speech in the House of Commons on 3 November sustained the tradition.

Of course the survival of parliamentary democracy depended on whether it could command and eliminate the economic conflicts in society. But Bevan did not scorn what many might consider quite minor steps forward to assist the purpose. One of his first acts as Deputy Leader was to propose that the Parliamentary Party's Standing Orders which he had always found so repugnant should be abandoned and that the Party should return to the situation which had prevailed between 1945 and 1952 when business had been satisfactorily conducted without any such cut-and-dried disciplinary code. Resistance from the Right wing and from Gaitskell himself was strong, but eventually Bevan had the better of the compromise solution presented by the Shadow Cabinet to the Party and overwhelmingly endorsed. Standing Orders were abolished and a code of conduct was substituted for them. Bevan still found distasteful the odour of Boy Scout morality which the code seemed to exude; but he had secured a fundamental change in the way the Party would conduct its affairs: a true enlargement of freedom.[1]

The second of his proposals for early reform in the conduct of Parliament – made in the same 3 November speech – was that the House of Commons should be televised or at least that the technical problems should be examined to see how feasible the proposition was. The idea derived from his belief that the gulf between Parliament and the people was growing wider, just at the moment when such a development was so dangerous for democracy itself. The reporting of Parliament in most of the newspapers, he claimed, had become a travesty, and on television and radio a highly invidious system had arisen whereby the broadcasting authorities could select the M.P.s they wished to favour as well-known public performers. 'The British Parliament had become almost incommunicado', and it was the duty of M.P.s to find the remedy. A decision to televise the proceedings and thereby end the new secrecy could be as significant as the famous Wilkesite victories which led to the reporting of Parliament in the 1770s. But, of course, the proposal, as Bevan expected, brought a shudder of disapproval from M.P.s who objected that so revolutionary an idea should have been mooted from Labour's front bench without previously having

[1] The significance of his victory was not immediately apparent, since, soon after his death, both the spirit and the letter of the idea of abandoning Standing Orders were broken by Gaitskell, Brown and other leaders of the Party. However, in the 1964 and 1966 Parliaments, a reversion to the Bevan methods was carried through by Dick Crossman and John Silkin with Harold Wilson's general approval, and later sustained by Douglas Houghton and Robert Mellish, with the result that the parliamentary inquisitions, burnings and *auto-da-fés* of the Gaitskell era now seem almost as distant as the Spanish Inquisition itself.

received the blessing of the appropriate Party committees. But Bevan had anticipated that objection too. 'I have not,' he said, 'consulted my right hon. Friend the Leader of the Opposition about it at all – for one good reason that when one makes a suggestion, either here or there, it passes through the interstices of the Party machine so slowly that by the time it emerges it has only a meagre resemblance to its former self.' Never did he reconcile himself to the pre-digestive processes of the Parliamentary Labour Party. They could mean that all debate would lose its savour, and that an additional reason would be added to the several others blunting the essential asperity of the national argument.

However, it was not on the parliamentary stage that the final drama was to be enacted. A special two-day conference of the Party had been fixed to take place at Blackpool in the last week of November, and Gaitskell had imposed on himself an undertaking to reserve his own comments on the general election and the deductions for the future until that occasion. Some of his close friends thought this an error, particularly because he had received an ovation at the first meeting of the Parliamentary Party. One of them at least urged that he should seize the initiative, make known his ideas for the reform of the Party to the Parliamentary Party, and give time for the wisdom of the leadership to percolate downwards. But Gaitskell was adamant; he owed his first speech to the whole Party. So little had the doctrine of the subordination of the Party Conference to the Party in Parliament, steadfastly described by Professor Robert Mackenzie, been accepted in the Party hierarchy. Gaitskell did not accept it in 1959. But Gaitskell was no less adamant ('He was obstinate as only Hugh knew how,' said the same informant) in rejecting advice from those who overheard whispers of what he proposed to say and were alarmed. 'Promise me one thing,' said Charles Pannell to him in his room on the Thursday before the Conference started: 'Show your speech to Nye Bevan before you make it.' He said that he would.[1] What ensued belongs to a later part of the story. For the rest, Gaitskell's scrupulous deference to the authority of the Conference did indeed add to the tension with which his speech was awaited. How far did he go with his friend Douglas Jay and the notorious *Forward*

[1] Charles Pannell, M.P., in conversation with the author.

article, described by another friend Lord Pakenham[1] as 'one of the most epoch-making events in the Party's history', ensuring that 'things can never be the same again'?[2]

But the setting at Blackpool, one suspects, was not quite what Gaitskell had foreseen. True, the kites had been flown; true, some of the reactions had been gauged; true, his own standing in the Party had, in a sense, never seemed more secure, thanks to the enthusiasm aroused in the election. But already the strongest Socialist elements in the Party had been alerted, and Barbara Castle, as that year's Chairman, gave expression to them in the most telling chairman's address ever delivered at a Party Conference. Normally the chairman's opening speech is little more than a convention, but suddenly, on the Saturday morning, the startled delegates discovered that they were being offered the Socialist answer to the affluent election; an answer as deep in Labour Party tradition as the writings of R. H. Tawney, as up-to-date as the hovercraft. Public ownership in one form or another (and the Conference was appositely reminded that nationalized industries accountable to neither workers, consumers nor Parliament had never been part of the Left wing's idea of Socialism) must bulk so large in so many aspects of policy that no one could push it aside, and the inference was that no one had better try. But Gaitskell's speech was already drafted to the last comma, and ready for distribution to the press; such are the straitjackets which modern politicians have tailored for themselves. It did not purport to be the reply to Barbara Castle's case. What it did purport to do was to examine the influences 'more fundamental' than programme, organization or the conduct of the campaign itself which had led to Labour's defeat; to analyse the 'significant change in the economic and social background of politics' resulting from all the manifestations of the so-called affluent society; to reassert the Party's will to power and yet to express its ideals in modern terms: 'It is no use waving the banners of a bygone age.' And yet the more precise purpose of the speech was surely indicated when, a little more than half way through, he said: 'Now I turn to public ownership and nationalization,' and thereafter he returned by one route after

[1] Now Lord Longford.
[2] Article in the *Daily Telegraph* 21 October.

another, to this gnawing obsession. It was not that he repeated Douglas Jay's specific call for a ban on nationalization, especially steel nationalization;[1] those pitfalls were carefully circumvented, just as he had emphatically repudiated the other proposals to change the Party's name, weaken the connections with the unions and alter the relations between Conference and the Parliamentary Party. So many of the Jay ideas had been abandoned that it did appear a genuine Party compromise had been attempted. And yet again, had he appreciated how the Conference would interpret his reference to the Party's Constitution itself?

I do think that we should clear our minds on these fundamental issues and then try to express in the most simple and comprehensible fashion what we stand for in the world today. The only official document which embodies such an attempt is the Party Constitution written over forty years ago. It seems to me that this needs to be brought up to date. For instance, can we really be satisfied today with a statement of fundamentals which makes no mention at all of colonial freedom, race relations, disarmament, full employment or planning? The only specific reference to our objectives at home is the well-known phrase: 'To secure for the workers by hand or by brain the full fruits of their industry and the most equitable distribution thereof that may be possible, upon the basis of the common ownership of the means of production, distribution and exchange . . .' Standing on its own, this cannot possibly be regarded as adequate. It lays us open to continual misrepresentation. It implies that common ownership is an end, whereas in fact it is a means. It implies that the only precise object we have is nationalization, whereas we have in fact many other Socialist objectives. It implies that we propose to nationalize everything, but do we? Everything? – the whole of light industry, the whole of agriculture, all the shops – every little pub and garage? Of course not. We have long ago come to accept, we know very well, for the foreseeable future, at least in some form, a mixed economy; in which case, if this is our view – as

[1] Crossman in his diary entry for 18 February 1958 reports a private conversation with Gaitskell in which he had stressed his desire to play down steel nationalization.

I believe it to be of 90 per cent of the Labour Party – had we not better say so instead of going out of our way to court mis-representation?[1]

But, as he asked these questions, the murmurs started and a curious restiveness, mixed with a few open cries of protest, continued to the end. He sat down to prolonged applause, and yet everyone knew that the ferment within the Conference could not be long contained. It rippled and then roared all that afternoon and the next morning, with speeches from a series of pro- and anti-Gaitskellites, including one from myself in which I had asked with others: where are we going, where is Gaitskell leading us? And that evening I bumped into Nye and he took me off for a drink with the most genial of greetings and congratulations on my speech, in words more precious than rubies. 'I agree with the verbs if not the nouns,' he said, and I made the obvious reply: 'And you have always told me that it is the verbs, not the nouns, which count.' What did *he* think of the Gaitskell speech? As far as I can recall, he threw back his head with an unspoken gesture of dismissal. Had he seen and approved it in advance? I never asked him then or later, but my belief is (based partly on Jennie's understanding and the similar understanding of two others who saw him that day) that Gaitskell had given him a general outline of what he proposed to say at a stage too late for fundamental amendments to be possible.[2] In any case, Gaitskell had his own case to make, and must put it in his own style. Bevan did not propose that Gaitskell should design *his* speech and the tolerance must be reciprocated. And the next day he not only answered Gaitskell and Denis Healey and Frank Pakenham and many more; and not only did he define, with much political delicacy but, also, with a touch of blasphemy, as his Chris-

[1] Gaitskell omitted to mention the highly relevant ensuing words from the Constitution which pledged Labour to secure 'the best obtainable system of popular administration and control of each industry or service'; and of course he also omitted to refer to Clauses VI and VII of the Constitution, less famous than Clause IV, which do refer to colonial territories, the promotion of world peace, and the raising of living standards throughout the world.

[2] Charles Pannell says that Gaitskell assured him that he had shown the speech to Bevan and that Bevan had said he could not fault it in any way.

tian critics averred, his place in 'the trinity' between Barbara Castle and Gaitskell. He reopened the Socialist argument, and yet preserved the unity of the Party; he spoke from the platform of the revisionist Establishment and yet kept alive the fundamental attack on modern capitalism, the meretricious society. It was the classic Bevan speech shaped to secure an immediate end and yet elevating the Party debate to the realm of political philosophy. He had, momentarily, overcome his sickness and the weaknesses of the previous months. Samson's locks had grown again but he used his strength not to destroy but to sustain.

It was to be his last speech, but it must be counted among the three or four greatest he ever delivered:

I should first of all like to start what I have to say as the Treasurer of the Party by expressing my very grateful thanks on behalf of the Executive for the generous response that we received to the appeal I made at the last Conference. I want particularly to thank the trade unions for the way in which they sent in their cheques. I am not quite satisfied with what they did, of course, and I shall be coming to them again very soon. They gave me more than they have given anybody else, as a general act of repentance, but they have not won their way completely back into favour. So I shall soon be sending out to them for more money, because I hope that one of the results of this Conference will be that we are not going to wait for four to five years before we start winning the next election.

Elections are not won in three weeks. We lost the election last time before it began and we have to be very careful to see it does not happen again. So I want a lot of money. In fact, we shall have to consider raising money not only by generous contributions from the trade unions but by some other schemes of getting it from the constituency parties as well. We shall need an awful lot of money, not because money alone will count but because even innocence requires guile.

My position in this debate is rather an anomalous one. It is like taking part in what we hope will be a symphony the score of which has not yet been published. In fact, I am reminded of the old jest of the man who played the triangle in the orchestra. He

21

went up to the conductor and asked to be allowed to get his part over first because his wife was at home ill.

Hugh Gaitskell said yesterday that he was speaking for himself; Barbara, the chairman, talked for herself. I am talking for myself. Of course you would imagine that from such a combination as that only discord could be produced, and there has been some suggestion in the newspapers – amongst our comrades there [pointing down to the press table] – that the result of this Conference is going to be the disintegration of the Socialist Party. They are not very perspicacious; they do not seem to be able to see below the surface of things. They do not seem to realize that the speech of Hugh Gaitskell yesterday and the speech of Barbara before did in fact contain a very important ingredient of unity.

I used to be taught as a boy, not at university but even in the Board school, one of Euclid's deductions: if two things are equal to a third thing, they are equal to each other. Yesterday Barbara quoted from a speech which I made some years ago, and she said that I believed that Socialism in the context of modern society meant the conquest of the commanding heights of the economy. Hugh Gaitskell quoted the same thing. So Barbara and Hugh quoted me. If Euclid's deduction is correct they are both equal to me and therefore must be equal to each other.

So we have a kind of trinity – I am not going to lay myself open to a charge of blasphemy by trying to describe our different roles. I am not certain in which capacity I am speaking, whether as the father, the son or the holy ghost. But you will have seen that, despite the attempts which are made to exploit differences of opinion, so as to inflict mortal wounds upon the Party, those differences are not really fundamental differences of a character that should divide this movement permanently.

That is not to say that there are not differences. Of course there are! Hugh Gaitskell and Barbara Castle and myself would not be doing a service to this movement if we did not make our individual contributions to its variety, but making the contributions to its variety and to its diversity without mortally injuring its unity.

One of the reasons why we have got into trouble in the last few weeks, I think, was because one or two people rushed too early into print in order to try and alter in their minds the programme we put before the country at the last election. That was a mistake. It was a mistake tactically, it was a mistake psychologically, and it was a profound error philosophically. You cannot really go before a country with a programme and tell the country that you thought the programme was good for the country and, immediately the country rejected it, say you would like to alter it. It won't work; it is not right. It is almost like saying you put before the country a false prospectus. The programme we put before the country we believed in. We are very sorry that the electorate rejected it. We think the electorate is going to be sorry for having rejected it. In the course of time, as the years go by, and as circumstances change and the issues are altered, we may find it necessary to change some part of the programme; that will not be because we thought the programme was wrong, but just because we think it might be re-adjusted to changing conditions. You know, comrades, to change programmes is not an admission of error, otherwise all history would be a series of confessionals.

I am told by some of my comrades that one of the reasons why we lost the election was because nationalization was unpopular. Hugh said – and I think he was right – that from the information we can get, a lot of people said that one of the reasons why they did not vote for us was because they did not believe in nationalization. I think it is correct that they did say this; but what does it amount to when they have said it? Are we really now to believe that the reasons that people give for their actions are the causes of their actions? Such a naive belief in the rational conduct of human beings would wipe out the whole of modern psychology. Of course many of them said they did not like nationalization, and therefore they did not vote for us. Is it suggested that because of that we should drop it? After all, comrades, we start off pretty well, don't we? We may not have hung nationalization around our own necks, but our opponents did it for us. It was not our own propaganda that made us the champions of public enterprise, because a great deal of our propaganda kept that very much in the background. It was our enemies that fastened public ownership around our necks, and I am extremely grateful to them for doing it.

What does it prove? If it is said that we lost the election because of our belief in public ownership, then 12,250,000 people voted for us because they believed in public ownership. It is not a bad start-off, is it? Now you may say: 'Ah, but they did not vote for you because they believed in public ownership.' Well, you cannot have it both ways, can you? Or even suppose you were allowed to have it both ways, then you must conclude that 12,250,000 people did vote for us despite their distaste for public ownership. That is the biggest single vote ever given for public ownership in any country in the whole world. Then why the hell this defeatism? Why all this talk that we have actually gone back? Of course it is true that in the present-day affluent society a very large number of people are not as discontented as they were, and because we are a Party that stands for the redress of discontent and the wrongs caused by discontent, the absence of so much discontent therefore has reduced our popularity. But you know, comrades, I have been in this movement now for many years. I was in this movement in between the war years when there were two million unemployed, and still the Tories got a majority. You would have thought that there was some spontaneous generation of Socialist conviction; but we lost before the war years. Even the unemployed voted against us. Even in the areas where there was as much as 20 per cent and 30 per cent of unemployment we lost seats. Should we not therefore have voted in favour of unemployment?

The fact is – and that is accepted, and derive your lessons from it – that a very considerable number of young men and women in the course of the last five or ten years have had their material conditions improved and their status has been raised in consequence and their discontents have been reduced, so that temporarily their personalities are satisfied with the framework in which they live. They are not conscious of constriction; they are not conscious of frustration or of limitation as formerly they were, in exactly the same way as even before the war large numbers of workers were not sufficiently conscious of frustration and of limitation, even on unemployment benefit, to vote against the Tories.

What is the lesson for us? It is that we must enlarge and expand those personalities, so that they can become again conscious of limitation and constriction. The problem is one of education, not of surrender! This so-called affluent society is an ugly society still. It is a vulgar society. It is a meretricious society. It is a society in which priorities have gone all wrong. I once said – and I do not want to quote myself too frequently – that the language of priorities was the religion of Socialism, and there is nothing wrong with that statement either, but you can only get your priorities right if you have the power to put them right, and the argument, comrades, is about power in society. If we managed to get a majority in Great Britain by the clever exploitation of contemporary psychology, and we did not get the commanding heights of the economy in our power, then we did not get the priorities right. The argument is about power and only about power, because only by the possession of power can you get the priorities correct.

Therefore I agree with Barbara, I agree with Hugh and I agree with myself, that the chief argument for us is not how we can change our policy so as to make it attractive to the electorate. That is not the purpose of this Conference. The purpose is to try, having decided what our policy should be, to put it as attractively as possible to the population; not to adjust our policy opportunistically to the contemporary mood, but to cling to our policy and alter its presentation in order to win the suffrage of the population. That is our job, and I hope that is exactly what is going to emerge from this Conference.

I would also like to remind our comrades of another thing. There is a very precious responsibility resting upon us. I mentioned it in the House of Commons the other day. I am not despondent; it is the Tories who are in trouble, not us. They have not won. We may have lost, but they have not won. The prize still dodges them. There they are now in the House of Commons, with a majority of a hundred, and they just do not know what to do. They are still in difficulty. The price level has remained constant, at a time when, according to all the orthodox capitalist economists, the price level ought to have fallen, and as soon as the production begins to expand you will find the price level going up again. The fact of the matter is: modern capitalism has not succeeded; it has failed. Even from its own mouth it has failed. We are asked in 1959 to believe that if we are only patient, if we only work hard, we will double the standard of living in twenty-five years. That is the same rate of progress as before the war. With all the techniques of modern production, with automation, with electronics, with all the new industrial techniques, the capitalists of Great Britain can promise us exactly the same rate of progress as before the war.

The challenge which is going to take place in the next ten years is not going to come from Harold Macmillan. He cannot challenge anything! One of the most disgraceful exhibitions in public life has been Harold Macmillan in the course of the last few years. He has been lying to the population. I say lying, because he lied in the election in the most disgraceful fashion when he said that in a few days the Summit date would be fixed. He lied! But the fact is, they are beaten. The challenge is not going to come from them. The challenge is going to come from Russia. The challenge is not going to come from the United States. The challenge is not going to come from Western Germany nor from France. The challenge is going to come from those nations who, however wrong they may be -- and I think they are wrong in many fundamental respects -- nevertheless are at long last being able to reap the material fruits of economic planning and of public ownership. That is where the challenge is coming from, and I want to meet it, because I am not a Communist, I am a Social Democrat. I believe that it is possible for a modern intelligent community to organize its economic life rationally, with decent orders of priority, and it is not necessary to resort to dictatorship in order to do it. I believe that it is possible. That is why I am a Socialist. If I did not believe that, I would be a Communist; I would not be a capitalist! I believe that this country of ours and this movement of ours, despite our setbacks, nevertheless is being looked upon by the rest of the world as the custodian of democratic representative government. But, comrades, if we are going to be its custodian, we must at the same time realize what the job is. The job is that we must try and organize our economic life intelligently and rationally in accordance with some order of priorities and a representative government; but we must not abandon our main case. Our main case is and must remain that in modern complex society it is impossible to get rational order by leaving things to private economic adventure. Therefore I am a Socialist. I believe in public ownership. But I agreed with Hugh Gaitskell yesterday: I do not believe in a monolithic society. I do not believe that public ownership should reach down into every piece of economic activity, because that would be asking for a monolithic society. In fact, it would be asking for something that does not even exist in China or Russia. But what I do insist upon is this, and as a movement we must insist upon it. We will never be able to get the economic resources of this nation fully exploited unless we have a planned economy in which the nation itself can determine its own priorities.

I said they are in trouble; they are in serious trouble. Their intention was two or three years ago to produce about 10 per cent or 15 per cent of unemployment in Great Britain. That was the intention, because only unemployment on that scale could enable them to achieve what they wanted to do. But the general election overtook them, and they had to retreat from their policy of mass unemployment before they had achieved it. The idea was to get the unemployment, and to get the disciplines following in their minds from mass unemployment, and then on the falling unemployment figures go to the country; but they never got the degree of unemployment that they expected, and the result is that they had once more to start the engines of production going before the unemployment was as high as they wanted it to go. The Chancellor of the Exchequer makes speeches in which he says there must be a reduction in prices. Of course he said it before, but the poor man is in an awful jam, because they have not got what they wanted to get. They need to have a period of deflation in order to cut out the dead wood from private enterprise in Great Britain. But they have not got it. They have got the plateau and the dead wood. The result is that we start off from this plateau to a new spiral, and before very long they will be in trouble again. The only way in which they can meet their trouble is the Keynesian way, that is to say, by reducing the total volume of purchasing power and keeping down the total volume of production in order to prevent prices from rising again. In other words, Western capitalism has got itself into a situation where it has permanently to sabotage the factors of production in order to prevent a permanent economic crisis.

Therefore, the challenge I have to meet is not from them. I despise them! They are neither intelligent nor moral. Why on earth we should have an inferiority complex about them, I do not know. Frank Pakenham made a speech here yesterday in which he said that his beliefs were derived from his religion. I do not claim to be a very religious man; I never have. But I must remind Frank Pakenham that Christ drove the money-changers from the Temple. He did not open the doors wide for them to enter. He drove them away. If we go on to apply the principles of Christianity to contemporary British society, they have been done elsewhere rather better than they have been done here. I think there is something evil, something abominable, something disgraceful in a country that can turn its back on Hola, that can turn its back on the old age pensioners, that can starve the Health Service, and reap £1,500 million from the Stock Exchange boom immediately after the election is over.

What are we going to say, comrades? Are we going to accept the defeat? Are we going to say to India, where Socialism has been adopted as the official policy despite all the difficulties facing the Indian community, that the British Labour movement has dropped Socialism here? What are we going to say to the rest of the world? Are we going to send a message from this great Labour movement, which is the father and mother of modern democracy and modern Socialism, that we in Blackpool in 1959 have turned our backs on our principles because of a temporary unpopularity in a temporarily affluent society?

Let me give you a personal confession of faith. I have found in my life that the burdens of public life are too great to be borne for trivial ends. The sacrifices are too much, unless we have something really serious in mind; and therefore, I hope we are going to send from this Conference a message of hope, a message of encouragement, to the youth and to the rest of the world that is listening very carefully to what we are saying.

I was rather depressed by what Denis Healey said. I have a lot of respect for him; but you know, Denis, you are not going to be able to help the Africans if the levers of power are left in the hands of their enemies in Britain. You cannot do it! Nor can you inject the principles of ethical Socialism into an economy based upon private greed. You cannot do it! You cannot mix them, and therefore I beg and pray that we should wind this Conference up this time on a message of hope, and we should say to India and we should say to Africa and Indonesia, and not only to them, but we should say to China and we should say to Russia, that the principles of democratic Socialism have not been extinguished by a temporary defeat at the hands of the Tories a few weeks ago!

You know, comrades, parliamentary institutions have not been destroyed because the Left was too vigorous; they have been destroyed because the Left was too inert. You cannot give me a single illustration in the Western world where Fascism conquered because Socialism was too violent. You cannot give me a single illustration where representative government has been undermined because the representatives of the people asked for too much. But I can give you instance after instance we are faced with today where representative government has been rendered helpless because the representatives of the people did not ask enough. We have never suffered from too much vitality; we have suffered from too little. That is why I say that we are going to go from this Conference a united Party. We are going to go back to the House of Commons, and we are going to fight the Tories. But we are not only going to fight them there; we are going to fight them in the constituencies and inside the trade unions. And we are going to get the youth! Let them start. Do not let them wait for the Executive, for God's sake! Start getting your youth clubs, go in and start now! Go back home and start them, and we will give all the help and encouragement that we can.

I have enough faith in my fellow creatures in Great Britain to believe that when they have got over the delirium of the television, when they realize that their new homes that they have been put into are mortgaged to the hilt, when they realize that the moneylender has been elevated to the highest position in the land, when they realize that the refinements for which they should look are not there, that it is a vulgar society of which no decent person could be proud, when they realize all those things, when the years go by and they see the challenge of modern society not being met by the Tories who can consolidate their political powers only on the basis of national mediocrity, who are unable to exploit the resources of their scientists because they are prevented by the greed of their capitalism from doing so, when they realize that the flower of our youth goes abroad today because they are not being given opportunities of using their skill and their knowledge properly at home, when they realize that all the tides of history are flowing in our direction, that we are not beaten, that we represent the future: then, when we say it and mean it, then we shall lead our people to where they deserve to be led!

Vicky provided one verdict on Blackpool: he showed a nervous Gaitskell and a vigilant Bevan riding their tandem towards Blackpool tower on the journey there and an even more alert Bevan and even more nervous Gaitskell, with their positions reversed, returning home. Certainly Bevan had grown in political stature. Some said he had saved Gaitskell from the worst consequences of the Clause Four gaffe. Others – and not only the interested Conservative press – suggested that a new disturbance within the Party could not be long postponed. No doubt is possible too about the serious mood in which he returned to London; a first hint was given in the article he wrote for *Tribune*:

The present controversy in the Labour Party has been described as a division between the pragmatists and the fundamentalists. This is a false description. Those described as fundamentalists are people who believe that there are certain principles that have held good and are likely to hold good so long as British society is based in the main on the institutions of private ownership. They take the view that if the Labour Party was to abandon its main thesis of public ownership it would not differ in any important respect from the Tory Party. The only conflict would be about nuances, about semi-tones and half-tints ... If the Labour Party decided to adjust its policy in accordance with these ideas, it would be practically certain to wreck itself. The Party has been nurtured in the belief that its *raison d'être* is a transformation of society . . . The controversy is between those who want the mainsprings of economic power transferred to the community and those who believe that private enterprise should still remain supreme but that its worst characteristics should be modified by liberal ideas of justice and equality. It is a classic conflict. It has been going on in Western European society right throughout the first half of the twentieth century. It is hardly likely to be settled in the Labour Party by an absolute victory on one side or the other, but what is quite certain is that the overwhelming majority of the Labour Party will not acquiesce in the jettisoning of the concept of progressive public ownership.

That was Bevan's only published verdict on Blackpool and it gives no indication that a comfortable accommodation had been reached within the top leadership. In private, he was even fiercer and more aggrieved. What he had seen and heard and felt and smelt at Blackpool convinced him that the Clause Four controversy marked a deliberate design to alter the nature of the Labour Party, and the project had been set in hand without any consultation with the newly-elected Deputy Leader of the Party. 'We are living in the presence of a conspiracy,' he said when a few of us met in the week after the Conference. The phrase may sound melodramatic, but undoubtedly it represented his belief at the time and most of the facts subsequently revealed vindicate his suspicion. The occasion was a meeting of the *Tribune* Board to discuss many of the delicate topics which had often gone undiscussed in the two years of anguish since Brighton, and the business was transacted in a private room at the Café Royal. A good meal and the reconciliations of Blackpool helped to ease the H-bomb conflicts; not to remove them but to ensure at least a less acrimonious *modus vivendi*. And, in any case, that item was not reached until late in the afternoon. The discussion before had tended to concentrate on 'the conspiracy' which Bevan believed he had done something to block at Blackpool but which was obviously not broken. There was no disguise in what he described; no relish and little malice but plenty of bitter invective. He saw Gaitskell and Gaitskellism as more of a threat than ever to the kind of Socialism he had dreamed of and fought for all his life, and he said that great upheavals would have to be faced if the Party was not to be twisted into a caricature of what a Socialist Party should be.

He told us, too, that he would soon, just after Christmas, be going into hospital for an operation, but that he hoped soon to be back to join whatever political festivities the New Year might hold. A few days later, one Monday morning, I had a call from Jennie. 'Nye,' she said, 'is in the Royal Free in Grays Inn Road. He's going to be operated upon tomorrow. Go in and see him now. Take a few books. Have a good rough argument; make him feel that everything's normal.' So I went and for half an hour or more talked with a man who showed little sign of weakness; indeed he was clearly at the peak of his powers, if he had wished to exert them. But he did not want to just at that moment; most of the post-Blackpool melancholy seemed to have vanished or perhaps he just disguised it. And we had no disagreements – except a most mild one about what he had always called my 'quixotry' in insisting in standing again for my native Devonport where he had assured me long before I would be certain to be defeated. 'Now you'd better look properly for another seat,' he said, '– perhaps you needn't look further than Ebbw Vale.' I told him, of course, not to talk such rubbish and muttered some bromide about how his operation would no doubt turn out for the best, just the thing needed to remove the traces of illness he had had through the previous year. Then he shrieked with laughter: 'Oh I dare say it'll all turn out for the best. That's what Charlie Edwards used to say. My neighbour, the Member for Bedwellty and my Whip, poor fellow. Whenever we were faced with some more than usually int-int-tractable mess in the Party, he would say "maybe it'll all turn out for the best".' And then in the course of our talk that followed and as we ranged over the gossip about the state of the Party, he did that famous shrug of the shoulders I knew so well and gave me a genial dissertation, half-warning, half-lament, on how nothing could be achieved outside the Party: 'never underestimate the passion for unity and don't forget it's the decent instinct of people who want to do something'. And then we talked of the books at his bedside, J. B. Priestley's *Literature and Western Man* and H. L. Mencken's

Treatise on the Gods. I hadn't argued but everything else was back to normal between us.

Two days later when I saw him again after a four-hour operation for malignant cancer, he had all the tubes and paraphernalia stuck in his sides and could not speak or give any real sign of recognition. He was like a great tree hacked down, wantonly, in full leaf.

17

1960

The same man who decreed that one should be oneself also said that
everything should be related to the common people.
—JEAN GUÉBENNO, in his book *Jean-Jacques Rousseau*

The oratorical gift is not great in itself – it is great as an aptitude
subordinated to the supreme art of action, which supplies it not only
with its transitory utility but also with its perennial and peculiar beauty.
—JOSÉ RODO. *The Motives of Proteus*

ANEURIN BEVAN often contended that when the cause
of cancer was eventually discovered it would be found to
be inextricably connected with mental distress and frustration. It seems almost certain that the political agonies he had
endured contributed to his physical destruction. Moreover, it is
hard to imagine that, with his extensive and instinctive interest in
medical matters, he was not entirely aware of what his own
operation must mean. But, on this personal aspect, the reality was
different.

Sir Daniel Davies, his physician, was his close personal friend;
they had arrived in London together in the 1930s and had never
lost touch or a common pride in their Welsh upbringing. Sir Dan
might give the outward impression of the boy from a poor Welsh
home who had risen to the topmost heights in Harley Street, a
figure parodied almost on the hero of A. J. Cronin's *The Citadel*,
but there was no falsity in the friendship between the two of them.
Sir Dan resolved to hide the truth about the operation from his
patient; and to have any hope of success he must hide it from Jennie
too. So the verdict was sedulously spread that the cancer was not
malignant; no one could tell how long he might have to live; it

might be months or years, several years. Apparently, the recovery started well, and after six weeks of fight and excruciating pain at the Royal Free Hospital he was able to return to Asheridge. But, just before the move, Dan took Jennie back to his home from the hospital, and 'pronounced the death sentence' – in Jennie's words. 'Why didn't you tell me before?' she asked, and the answer was: 'He would have read it in your eyes, and would have lost the will to pull through.' So Jennie had to face the decision of how to deal with the Nye who had been led to believe that the ulcer was benign and that he might recover completely. She resolved to do everything that human contrivance and love could to sustain the illusion and the hope; and Dan had made it clear that it might be a short time or several years left to him. A few of his closest personal friends – John Buchan, Trudy Zahler, aided by Archie Lush and Jack Norris on occasional visits from Tredegar – were recruited to assist Jennie with the round-the-clock nursing vigil. The doctors came from London almost every day. Ma Lee was still well enough to bestow her peculiar grace on her beloved Nye. The illusion seemed to succeed. Jennie wrote a little later: 'He questioned and cross-questioned his doctors, John Buchan and me, but we managed to deceive him and I am proud of that and take what comfort I can from it. He was spared at least the final sorrow of knowing that he would never complete his job, that he was beaten by illness. He was more optimistic than before his illness, enjoyed the praise and love that flowed into him; he was ready to start all over again.'

Towards the end of March he was fit enough to give an interview to a group of correspondents from the newspapers which had been clamouring for authentic news. His only condition was that he would not talk about politics. One newspaper had printed the rumour that he was writing his memoirs, and he was eager to repudiate the indictment. 'There is no basis in it at all,' he said, 'I strongly disapprove of people in active public life writing their memoirs. They do nothing but mischief. If they tell the truth it is hurtful, but usually they don't tell the truth.' The questions then strayed over his recent reading, his television-watching, and what he considered the abysmal nature of the programmes, apart from his matchless Tony Hancock. He still preferred the written word, notably, in those last weeks, J. B. Priestley's *Literature and Western Man*, and then he added, proof surely of successful convalescence: 'I understand that Mr Macmillan reads political biographies. I have never been able to achieve that level of credulity. My experience of public life has taught me to know that most of them are entirely unreliable. I would rather take my fiction straight.' Then he added, proving that his sense of timing had lost little of its acuteness: 'Newspapers of course, I read avidly. It is my one form of *continuous* fiction.'

He was already making preparations for the rest of the year. He would go to Brighton to stay with his friend Lewis Cohen for a few days, return to Asheridge for Easter, and then go to the south of France – to be painted by Graham Sutherland; Alfred Hecht, who had first introduced him to Sutherland and who had become one of his most treasured friends of the last years, was making the arrangements. Then he would return, fit for the autumn and whatever renewed ordeal the Labour Party might have to offer, starting at Scarborough, notable in Labour history for its scrapheap of desiccated calculating machinery. 'I want to live because their are one or two things I want *to do*,' he said to Archie Lush at this time, exactly reflecting the tone in which they had discussed the same questions in the 1920s. He surveyed the prospect ahead and Jennie bought some gay summer dresses to encourage the illusion that they would soon be on the way to the south of France. But the Brighton expedition was the only part of the programme he was able to fulfil. Back at Asheridge he was freshly afflicted by an attack of thrombo-phlebitis. A few, but very few, more visitors were able to call – one of them, Jawaharlal Nehru, then attending a Commonwealth Conference. But he was sinking again. Dan Davies talked of bringing him back to London but he would have none of it; he would not become 'a surgeon's plaything'. And in truth there was no remedy to be found in London or anywhere else; nothing could be done except to surround him with warmth and love and every available protection against pain, and on 6 July 1960, gently in his sleep, he died.

Next day Jennie wrote to me in these terms:

Ni is asleep next door. Later today he will be taken home to

Wales. Tomorrow he will be cremated in keeping with his known views. It will be near Tredegar, a small family gathering. Later in the week a memorial service will be held in Tredegar to give a chance to his own people to ease their sore hearts, later still a suitable memorial and place in the hills will be found.

I wrote to Donald Soper and to Mervyn Stockwood two days ago. Here is essentially what I said to them: 'Ni was never a hypocrite. No falsity must touch him once he is no longer able to defend his views. He was not a cold-blooded rationalist. He was no calculating machine. He was a great humanist whose religion lay in loving his fellow men and trying to serve them. He could kneel reverently in chapel, synagogue, Eastern mosque, Catholic cathedral on occasions when friends called him there for marriage or dedication or burial services. He knelt reverently in respect to a friend or a friend's faith, but he never pretended to be other than he was, a humanist. Often in the last few years he talked of "the mystery that lies at the heart of things", nothing more definite than that.'

His particular insight into 'the heart of things' derived partly perhaps from what his old preceptor José Rodo had written on the subject but he took no judgment ready-made from anybody and accepted no doctrine without transforming it into his individual expression. He had no use especially for the ascetic aspects of Christianity and would still quote the Swinburne he had relished in his youth on 'the pale Galilean', or, faced with the latest evidence of the unspeakable cruelties heaped upon humanity, he would sigh, 'God is love'. He would prefer to put his view on mortal or immortal matters mockingly. 'Mankind,' he would say, 'has only been able to survive by the help of sex, drugs and fairy stories' and the fairy stories included all the gods and devils religious men had created. Often he would protest furiously: 'O God why did you make the world so beautiful and the life of man so short?' But he would also say, with Nietzsche, 'this is my truth, now tell me yours', thus invoking his special gift of imaginative tolerance. Just as he would apply it to the political circumstances of others, so he could apply it to their religious convictions. He could still be captivated by the music of the Welsh valleys, the best of it religious,

and would gladly, as Jennie had indicated, honour his friends and
their faiths in the place of their choosing. He had always searched
himself, in the new conditions of his own experience, for the complicated syntheses between tragedy and hope, struggle and reflection, which both Marx and Rodo had looked for by their different
mountain roads. His faith too was always an essay in words and
deeds, never one without the other. What he thought about the
heart of things must be seen not in what he said and wrote but in
his life and death. And it was for sure most fitting that his ashes
should be scattered high on the mountain above the Duffryn valley
underneath the mountain ash and where the bluebells grew; that
was the wild place which, from his youth, he had loved most of all.

From the time of his illness a mood of affection and sympathy
towards him, swelling at the moment of his death to something
deeper still, swept across the country. Nothing quite comparable
was evoked by the death of any other political figure in the post-
war world or indeed in this century. Churchill and Lloyd George
received, in their different ways, great and proper honour as
acknowledged leaders of the nation in times of supreme peril, and
several lesser figures have their meed of tribute too. But Aneurin
Bevan held office for a period of only six years out of his thirty-one
in Parliament, and during that period especially he never ceased
to be the target of calumny and libel; he was the squalid nuisance,
the Minister of Disease, the revolutionary Caliban. Frequently his
political enemies and his nominal friends had been eager or content
to see him broken and driven from public life altogether – that had
been the aim of the Gaitskellites a bare five years before. Yet with
his illness and death came a great tidal flood of national and international sentiment which seemed to wash away so much that had
gone before. It was as if he were suddenly revealed as a prophet
denied his true honour or as if the scales were struck from the
nation's eyes and the history of the previous decades were given an
entirely new complexion. The Establishment, Tory, Liberal and
Labour, assembled in Westminster Abbey to acclaim the man they
had reviled, and to hear his friend Mervyn Stockwood, Bishop of
Southwark, preach a sermon which faithfully enshrined Jennie's
strict instructions. But even this was not the most ironic scene nor
the ceremony on Waunpound in his constituency where he had

addressed his eve-of-poll rallies and where his own people were
joined by dozens of his parliamentary colleagues, including a
nameless few who had voted for his expulsion. Shoals of letters
poured into Jennie from every section of the community, from all
classes, from all countries, from legions of friends, from the
enemies of yesterday; and this too might not be unprecedented,
although the avalanche was truly vast. Most remarkable of all was
the way such multitudes shared the same emotion. While he lived,
everyone seemed to stop to hear the latest bulletins. The newspapers, with whom he had never called a truce, devoted endless
space to the one event by which their readers were entranced.
When he died, no formal or forced note was heard. The nation
expressed its sense of loss unfeignedly, spontaneously, without
restraint. What could be the meaning of it all?

Some answer, I hope, has been given in the preceding pages. For
Socialists, for those of us who heard him speak and talk and argue
and who shared his political aspirations, he was the man who did
more than any other of his age to keep alive the idea of democratic
Socialism. With him, it never lost its power as a revolutionary
creed. Others might define it as well or serve it as faithfully. But no
one else, for most of us, could give it a vibrant and audacious
quality and make it the most ambitious and intelligent and civilized
of modern doctrines. He was, as the Speaker of the Indian Parliament had said in introducing him to its members during his visit of
1957, a man of passion and compassion; but only his closest friends
could know that to the full. The feeling which surged towards him
in those months of 1960 cannot be thus explained. For it was not
confined to his political friends or his own Party; it burst all banks
and frontiers. It was, maybe, a sense of national guilt; a belief that
he had been cheated of his destiny, that some part of his greatness
had been shamefully thrown away; an awareness that he had had
much to say to our perplexed, polluted world, and that we had
listened only fitfully. What the nation mourned was the tragedy
which mixed with the brilliance and the genius, and what it did in
expiation was to acknowledge his unique place in our history.

INDEX

Abel, Lawrence, 166
Abel, Signor, 469(n)
Acheson, Dean, 305, 403, 591
Adamson, Iain, 538(n)
Addison, Lord, 25, 325
Adenauer, Dr Konrad, 448, 451, 489, 556, 571
Africa, 344, 506, 649
Airey House, 81
Alexander, Viscount, 363
Allon, Yigal, 419, 441
Amalgamated Engineering Union, 354, 375, 438, 510–11, 513
Amalgamated Society of Woodworkers, 449, 494, 513
American bases in Britain, 229, 345
Analgesia in Childbirth Bill, 253(n)
Archbishop of Canterbury, Dr Fisher, 127, 264, 410
Ashcroft, Peggy, 298
Asheridge Farm, 441–3, 496–7, 498, 547, 560, 616, 629, 655, 656
Ashworth, Herbert, 86(n)
Assheton, Ralph, 254
Aswan Dam, 519, 520, 586
Atlantic Pact, 229
Attlee, C. R. (Lord): and Bevan 20; the new Prime Minister 24; forms his Government, 24–5; Bevan's opinion of, 25–30; 241–242; his personality and policies, 25–7, 29; Bevin's influence, 26, 32, 349(n); and the Labour Party, 26, 28; compared to Churchill, 29; on himself and his colleagues 29–30; dinner jacket episode 30–1; and Morrison, 37; on Cripps and Bevan, 38, 290; on cancellation of Lead-Lease, 53; and Loan negotiations, 54, 58; shortage of

building workers, 84; 1947 fuel and financial crisis, 88–9; supports Bevin, in particular his Palestine policy, 89; hesitant leadership, 91, 224–5; plot to remove him, 92–4; and steel nationalization, 222–3, 224; suggests change of office to Bevan, 226; letter from Bevan on Bevin and Germany, 231–3; broadcast on N.H.S., 237; letter to Bevan on vermin speech, 241; in devaluation debate, 270; pressed by Bevan for an election – decides against, 275; announces cuts, 276–7; letter from Bevan, 276–7; rumours of Bevan putsch, 284, 290; refuses to lead, 289; letter from Bevan on N.H.S. finance, 292; and possible Government reshuffle, 297–8; on Gaitskell's appointment, 300–301; offers Bevan Ministry of Labour, 301, 310; and American alliance, 302; flies to Washington, 304, 308–10; on rearmament programme, 308, 312; results of Washington meeting, 310; sees Gaitskell, 314; Bevan's resignation warning, 318; Bevin's ill-health 319; in hospital, 319; visited by Bevan, Wilson, Gaitskell, 323–324; considers election date, 323, 328; hopes for a compromise, 324; writes to Bevan, 329–31; shown *Tribune* article, 331; Bevan resigns – exchange of letters, and comments, 332–3, 341; announces election date, 349; Tory Defence White Paper, 363–4; his resolution at Party meeting,

365–6; reprimand to Bevan, 376–7; angers Deakin, 383, 408; 'party within a party' issue, 384, 386, 390; N.E.C. argument about *Tribune*, 393–4; German rearmament, 403, 425–6, 427, 455; Mallalieu's *Tribune* article, 412–13; Francis Williams's articles, 428; H-bomb speech, 429, 431; on S.E.A.T.O., 430–2; response to Wilson, 434; on Party delegation to Russia and China, 443; Bevan seeks meeting, 453–5; on the H-bomb, 457; challenged by Bevan, 461, 466; no reply, 463–4; motion for high-level talks, 465; against expulsion, 466, 467, 468, 475–6; P.L.P. meeting, 469–72; first N.E.C. meeting, 475–6; Bevan apologizes, 477; member of sub-committee, 477–9; second N.E.C. meeting, 479–80; *New Statesman* article, 481; on Bevan, 484; campaign to remove him, 487, 488–9; continues as leader, 488, 489; rumours of retirement – denied by him, 494; resigns, 494, 496; campaign against him, 495; on the privacy of party meetings, 503; compared with Gaitskell, 630; mentioned, 36, 40, 60, 61, 71, 294, 296, 299, 315, 319(n), 322, 324, 433, 450, 473, 499, 595, 617

Attlee, Mrs., 31
Australia, 161, 349, 623
Austria, 489
Ayerst, David, 384(n)

Bagehot, Walter, 246, 275
Baghdad, 546
Baghdad Pact, 529, 540, 565, 593, 605
Baillieu, Sir Clive, 94
Baldwin, Stanley, 37, 42, 145(n)

Ball, John, 264
Balogh, Thomas (Lord), 391
Barber, Frank, 312(n), 341(n), 349(n)
Barrett, Dickie, 454
Barrington-Ward, Sir Lancelot, 211
Barton, Derek, 63(n), 85(n), 87(n)
Beecham, Sir Thomas, 442
Beer, Samuel H., 371(n)
Belgrade, 229, 347, 489
Belloc, Hilaire, 178
Ben-Gurion, David, 530
Berlin, 229–30, 563, 592; conference, 426–7, 430
Bermuda, 401, 550
Bevan, Aneurin: verdict on 1945 election, 18; the new House of Commons, 19; youngest member of Cabinet, 20, 25; his political faith, 20–4, 34, 283–6; on the Tories, 21; champion of Parliament, 22–4; relationship with Attlee, and opinion of, 25–30, 241–2, 630; dinner jacket episode, 30–1 and Bevin, 31–3, 35, 89, 232–4; and foreign affairs, 33–4, 585–6, 592–4; on the Soviet Union, 33–4, 283–5, 305–7, 404–405, 504–6; and America, 34, 302, 550, 587–92; Bevin's Palestine policy, 35, 89; and Dalton, 35–6, 92, 226; and Morrison, 36–7, 287–9; and Cripps, 38–9; other Cabinet colleagues, 39; entry to Ministry of Health and relations with officials, 40–3; daily routine transformed, 44; and Jennie, 45–6; his individualism, 46–9; ties with the Labour Party, 49–50, 388, 488, 497–9, 500–1, 611–612, 625, 650–2; American Loan Agreement, 52–3, 55–9; speech in housing debate, 60–1; Churchill's antagonism, 61–3,

83, 242–3, 250, 251; housing policy, 66–83; on demobilization plans, 70–1; local authorities and housing, 72–3; his insistence on quality and aesthetic standards, 77–80, 81–2; prefabrication, 81; the 'squatters', 82–3; achievement in housing, 84–7; heads N.E.C. constituency section, 91, 236; defeated on tied cottages, 91, 236; opposed to plot to replace Attlee, 93–4, 225–6; cuts in housing programme, 94–7; brings in N.H.S. Bill and National Assistance Bill, 97–9; and Local Government Bill, 99–100; and the B.M.A., 102–6, 118–23, 128, 138–45, 148–52, 160, 164–95, 202–9, 211, 213, 338; as a diagnostician, 104; impression made on doctors' leaders, 119–21; on Dr Dain, 122; and the Royal Colleges, 123–5; Lord Moran's opinion, 125–6; and Dr Cockshut, 126, 151; National Health Service Bill, 128–38; plan for hospitals, 131–5, 146, 153–4; fight in Cabinet, 134–5; plan for general practitioners, 135–6, 154–5, 159, 168, 180–7, 201; private practice and specialists, 137, 152–3, 188; presents his proposals to B.M.A., 139–40; Bill's Second Reading, 145–8; Committee stages – changes to Bill, 154–5; Third Reading, 156–8; responds to Royal College Presidents' initiative, 163–4; two meetings with Negotiating Committee, 168–70; further debate on N.H.S. – and the B.M.A., 174–93; reports to House on B.M.A. discussions, 176–81; and their objections, 181–9; no plans for improvised service or postponement, 193,

211–12; speeches about the N.H.S., 195, 198, 212; private talks with Moran and others, 199–200; statement in the House, 200–201; meets B.M.A. leaders, 202; meeting with Regional Hospital Boards, 212; N.H.S. inaugurated, 213, 237–8; assessments of service, 216–18; tribute from *B.M.J.*, 216–17; and from Dr Hill, 217; on steel nationalization, 219–28, 235, 238; Ebbw Vale's experience, 220–1; resignation threat – wins Cabinet victory, 224–7; on Germany and Berlin blockade, 229–34; letter to Attlee and note about Bevin, 231–3; at 1948 Conference, 234–236; 'vermin' speech, 237–8; repercussions, 239–43, 249–50, 252, 278, 280, 436; letter from Attlee, 241; at Durham Miners' Gala, 243; on Churchill, 243–4, 245, 267–8, 271–5, 279–80, 486; on the art of speaking, 244–6; the orator, 246–9; newspaper irresponsibility and intrusion, 248, 250–1; housing debate, 252; and on N.H.S. Supplementary Estimates, 253–6; policy debates in N.E.C., 257–62; his views on nationalization, 258–60, 370–2, 560–1, 615; industrial assurance, 261–2; at 1949 Conference, 262–264; views of Labour's policy – disagreement with colleagues, 265–7; considers resignation, 266–7; devaluation debate, 270–275; presses for election, 275; fight over cuts – letter to Attlee, 276; 1950 election, 277–82; Devonport meeting, 279–80; Election Address, 280–1; shocked by result, 282; fights for N.H.S. and housing, 289–90; votes of censure, 290–2; Cabinet disagreements – letter to Attlee, 292; prescription charge, 276–7, 293–5, 290, 292, 293–7; and Gaitskell, 294–5, 312, 315, 342, 347, 412, 497–9, 547, 604–8, 609, 619, 622–4, 627, 628, 630, 651–2; attends Cripps's weekly dinners, 294; gives them up, 296–7; urges reconstruction of Government, 297–8; weekend relaxation at Stratford, 298–9; impact of Korean war, 299, 305–6, 308–9; objection to Gaitskell's appointment as Chancellor, 299–301; offered Ministry of Labour, 301, 310; accepts, 311–12; rearmament, 307–8, 312–13; 'brand China' manœuvre, 313–15; speech on arms programme, 315–16; at Ministry of Labour – dock strike, 317–18; resignation threat, 318, 320; on German rearmament, 319, 404–6, 425–8, 448, 451, 461, 594–5; opposes charges on teeth and spectacles, 319–20, 333, 341; talks to Dalton about Gaitskell, 322; near resignation, 322–3; visits Attlee in hospital, 323, 324; letters from colleagues, 324–7; and from Jennie, 327; P.L.P. meeting – resignation agony, 327, 328–30; resigns – exchange of letters – resignation speech – Party meeting, 331–41; colleagues' comments, 342–3; *One Way Only*, 344–6; meetings throughout country, 346; holiday in Yugoslavia – working on book, 347–8; election announcement, 349; and campaign, 351–2; at 1951 Conference, 351–4; Deakin's hostility, 353; Churchill: 'right by accident', 355–6; on Churchill and economic planning, 357–8; and the Bevanites, 358–9, 373–6, 385,

435; vote of the 57 against Defence White Paper, 364; aftermath, 364–7; his personal ambition, 367, 611; *In Place of Fear*, published, 367–71; on the P.L.P. and the Commons, 375–6; clash with Attlee, 376–7; attacks on him from the Right, 377–9; 1952 Conference, 380–2; his anger at attacks, 384–6; stands as Deputy Leader and for Shadow Cabinet, 386–7, 410–11; B.B.C. broadcast, *This I Believe*, 389–90; attends *Tribune* editorial meetings, 390, 562; at Crossman lunches, 390–1; *Tribune*, the N.E.C., and the T.U.C., 393–4, 453–4; visits India – letters to Jennie, 394–8; on death of Stalin, 398, 399–400; on Churchill's proposed, and postponed, Summit Conference, 400–2; 'In Place of the Cold War' articles, 404–6; letter about Nehru and Tito, 406–7; at 1953 Conference, 409; defends Mallalieu's article – 'personal attacks', 411–13; hospitality to Jagan and Burnham, 414; Macmillan's housing record, 414–15; attacked for articles in Egyptian paper, 416–18; visits Egypt, Transjordan, Israel, 418–20; correspondence with Tito about Djilas and Dedijer, 420–3; on the H-bomb, 429, 547, 551–7, 565, 568–77; S.E.A.T.O. resignation, and aftermath, 430–6; Wilson takes his place on Shadow Cabinet, 433–5; motoring offence, 435–6(n); constituency support in N.E.C. elections, 437; decides to stand for Treasurer, 438–40; the move to Asheridge Farm, 440–3; Jennie's concern over his health, 441; on delegation to Russia and China, 443–8;

1954 Conference – defeated for Treasurership, 448–9; *Tribune* meeting – 'desiccated calculating machine', 450–2; suggests to Attlee call for high-level talks, 453–5; P.L.P. rejects his appeal, 455–6; H-bomb debate – exchange with Attlee – abstains, 458–65; Shadow Cabinet decision to recommend Whip is withdrawn, 466; issues statement from sickbed, 467; his loathing of P.L.P. meetings, 469, 547–8; his speech at P.L.P., 470–472; parliamentary privilege invoked, 475; form of apology to Attlee – called before sub-committee, 476–80; support in the country, 481; quarrel with Crossman, 481–4, 497–8; 1955 election, 485–7; Right-wing verdict – and Bevan's, 487–8; supports Attlee as leader, 488; Remploy debate, 489–90; 1955 Conference – defeated for Treasurer, 490–4; condemns campaign to get rid of Attlee, 495; visits Malta, 495; stands for leader – defeated, 496; tribute to Attlee, 497; stands for Deputy Leader, 499–500; *Tribune* mass meetings, 500–1, 502; spokesman on colonial affairs, 502; on Party freedom and obligations, 503–4; Khrushchev-Bulganin dinner, 504–6; on Cyprus, 504–7; and Malta, 508; Treasurership campaign, 509–513; wins, 513–15; on Suez, 516–521, 524–7, 529; and Hungary, 518, 533–5; and Poland, 522; spokesman on foreign affairs, 529; speech on collusion, 529–532; visits Italy, 536–8; *Spectator* libel action, 537–8; on Eisenhower doctrine and the Middle

East, 539–42; on Government reaction to Bulganin's letters, 542–4; second visit to India and Pakistan, 544–8; and Israel, 546; and disarmament, 555–7; *Industry and Society*, 557, 560–1; on the Common Market, 560 and (n); delegate to French Socialist Party Congress, 562–3; Socialist International, 563; visits Gomulka, 563; visits Russia with Jennie – discussions with Khrushchev, 563–6; at N.E.C. pre-conference meetings, 568–9, 570; Norwood resolution, 569–570, 572–7; speech at *Tribune* meeting, 571; conference speech, 572–7; aftermath – situation at *Tribune*, 577–80, 583–4; conjectures and reasons, 580–3; a future policy for the party, 586–7, 592; visits U.S.A., 587–90; nuclear policy arguments on N.E.C., P.L.P.; Shadow Cabinet, 595–8; speaks at N.E.C. campaign meetings, 599–601; private quarrel with author, 601–3; on Life Peerages Bill, 603–4; and Mollet, 604–5; and Middle East crisis, 605–8; and Far East, 608–9; has flu, his ill-health, 611, 614, 616–17, 621, 628, 629, 641; the 'squalid Parliament', 612–14; on capitalism and Socialism, 614–15; meeting with Mendès-France and Nenni, 616; on delegation to Soviet Union, 617–621; 1959 election – Goodman's diary, 621–9; on Parliament and the P.L.P., 623, 624; on Khrushchev, 624; on Foreign Office, 622, 624, 626, 628; stands for and gets Deputy Leadership, 629, 632, 635, 651; on future of the Party, 632; speech in new Parliament, 632–5; proposes abolition of Standing Orders, 635–6; in favour of televising of Parliament, 636–7; Gaitskell's speech at two-day Conference, 640; Bevan's speech, 640–50; on the election and Party programme, 642–5, 648–9; on the Tories, 645–6, 647–8; 'why I am a Socialist', 646–7; Vicky cartoon, 650; verdict on Blackpool, 650–1; 'a conspiracy', 651; operation for cancer, 652–3; returns to farm, 655; newspaper interview, 655–6; plans ahead, 656; death, 656–7; his humanism and religious views, 657–8; public affection during illness, 658; universal sense of loss, 658–9; his democratic Socialism and place in history, 659.

Speeches quoted:
N.H.S. Bill Second Reading, 145–6; N.H.S. debate, February 1948, 176–91; 1948 Conference, 235–6; N.H.S. finances debate, 253–6; 1949 Conference, 262–4; devaluation debate, 271–74; on arms programme, 315–16; resignation speech, 333–9; on economic planning, 357–8; Churchill's American policy, 361–2; 1952 Conference, *Tribune* rally, 382; 1954 Conference, *Tribune* rally, 449–50; nuclear weapons debate, 458–63; 1955 Conference, 492–4; *Tribune* Manchester meeting, 500–1; Suez debate in Commons, 524–5, 526–7; in Trafalgar Square, 525–526; in Commons on collusion, 529–32; 1955 Conference, H-bomb debate, 572–7; contribution to Queen's Speech, 632–5; at two-day Conference, 640–50

Quotations from writings:
In Place of Fear, 23, 100, 105, 117–18, 133–4, 214(n), 220, 259, 317(n), 368(n), 369–70; *Why Not Trust the Tories?*, 281; in *Tribune*, see under *Tribune*; *Relations with author*, see under Foot

Bevanites: term first used, 343; popularity with Party workers, 352–3, 380, 437; Deakin's hostility, 354; organization and meetings, 358–9, 385; tactics, 360, 375; on Tory Defence White Paper, 363–4; vote of the 57 and P.L.P. action, 364–7; on public ownership, 370–2; and Bevan, 373–6, 435, 562, 581; and unions, 375; German rearmament, 375, 428, 448–9, 451; 'party within a party', 378–9, 384–6; disbanded, 386, 483–4; Roy Jenkins on, 413; reaction to Bevan's S.E.A.T.O. resignation, 433–5; propose high-level talks, 456; and the H-bomb, 457–8; Gaitskell on, 474(n); support Attlee, 494; scattered, 561–2; H-bomb issue and Bevan, 570, 577; 'Victory for Socialism', 598; mentioned, 550, 594

Beveridge, Sir William (Lord), 102, 109, 121, 262

Beveridge Report, 98, 102, 110, 112, 206, 207

Bevin, Ernest: becomes Foreign Secretary, 24; influence on Attlee, 26, 27, 29, 32; and Bevan, 31–3, 35; his foreign policy, 32–4, 89–90, 265; and Palestine, 35, 89–90, 413; on Keynes, 53; housing promises, 63; demobilization scheme, 70–1; attacks his critics at Party Conference, 91; plot that he should replace Attlee, 92–4; Marshall Aid, 93; on steel nationalization, 221; German policy, 230–4; conversation with Bevan on

Germany, 232–3; blocks defence cuts, 265; and American alliance, 302; recognizes China, 304–5, 306; and German rearmament, 305, 345, 403; away ill, 314; failing health, 319; agrees to teeth and spectacles charges, 319; intervenes with Attlee, 323; death, 329; and Deakin, 353; power over his union, 437; mentioned, 267, 277, 366(n), 382, 577

Beyfus, Gilbert, 538(n)
Bing, Geoffrey, 90(n), 375
Birch, Alan, 511
Birch, Nigel, 270, 364
Birmingham Gazette, 278
Births and Deaths Registration Bill, 100
Blake, William, 102
Blatchford, Robert, 385
Blenkinsop, Arthur, 325
Boardman, Harry, 384(n)
Bogdanor, Vernon, 414(n)
Bonham Carter, Lady Violet, 533
Bonn, 563, 592
Boothby, Robert, (Lord), 270, 272–273
Bourdet, Claude, 391(n)
Braddock, Bessie (and Jack), 318(n), 487
Bradlaugh, Charles, 243
Bradley, General, 304
Bretton Woods Agreements, 54
Bridges, Sir Edward, 54
Bright, John, 278
Brinham, George, 494, 495
British Guiana, 413–14
British Hospitals Association, 107
British Iron and Steel Federation, 222
British Medical Association (including B.M.A. Council, Representative Body and Divisions): pleasure at Beveridge's defeat, 102; and Bevan, 102–6, 118–21;

doctor-patient relationship, 103; fear of state medicine, 103, 104–105; early proposals and Draft Interim Report, 106, 107–10; opposition to Willink White Paper, 111–12; on 'the 100 per cent' issue, 112–13; its structure, 114–18; 'Seven Principles', 128; Bevan presents his proposals, 139–40; meeting to consider them, 140–1; opinions on the Bill, 140–5; opposition after Second Reading, 148–52; on weak ground over hospitals, 150; from protest to action – referendum, 156, 160–3; result–'no mandate to negotiate', 162–3; anger at Royal College Presidents, 164–5; agrees to meet Minister, 164; talks with Ministry officials, 166; misapprehensions over negotiating terms, 167; two meetings with Minister, 168–70; gets Bevan's reply in writing, 170; public protest and new plebiscite, 172–174; meetings and objections discussed by Bevan, 176–89; defying an Act of Parliament, 190–1; result of plebiscite, 193; Council's recommendations to Representative Body and response, 195, 196–7; mood changing – new plebiscite, 202–203, 207–8; plebiscite results, 205; bewilderment, 209; general practitioners join Service, 210; personal relations with Bevan restored, 213; appoints Porritt Committee, 217–18; mentioned in resignation speech, 338; see also General Practitioners, Hospitals, Local Executive Councils, Negotiating Committee
British Medical Journal: on Beveridge's defeat, 102; protest

on Beveridge Report, 110; and Willink White Paper, 111; editorial freedom, 116; on Bevan, 118–19, 120, 126; doctors being 'gagged', 139; correspondence on the Bill, 142; reports Bevan's speech to medical students association, 160; on the referendum, 161(n), 162; action of Royal College Presidents condemned, 165 and (n); reports Annual Representative Meetings, 166, 196; reports meetings with Bevan, 169; on Bevan and N.H.S. Act, 171; appeals to the consultants, 173; calls for adverse vote in plebiscite, 173–4; four main issues of disagreement, 181–9; welcomes plebiscite result, 194; reflects confusion of leadership, 202; Council meeting not reported, 202; changes its attitude, 205, 206; protest letters, 206–7, 211; editorial on 'what we have gained', 207–8; on Dr Cox – his letter to *B.M.J.*, 208; wrongly prophesies confusion, 213; on Bevan and the N.H.S., 216–17, 218; mentioned, 163, 200, 204

British Medical Students' Association, 160

British Orthopaedic Association, 159

British Standards Institution, 76

British Steel House, 81, 223, 279

Brittan, Samuel, 356(n)

Brook, Sir Norman, 308

Brown, Ernest, 110, 112, 121, 178, 179, 182, 207

Brown, George (Lord George-Brown): supports Attlee, 225; attacked by Bevan, 375, 470; attacks Bevan, 377, 378, 465; and conference, 380; in Shadow Cabinet, 499(n), 529(n), 555;

Khrushchev-Bulganin dinner, 505; stands for Treasurer, 510–514; favours nuclear strategy, 598; and Jordan, 606; and Standing Orders, 636(n); mentioned, 472, 547, 551

Bruce, Donald, 43, 90(n)

Brussels, 229, 451, 605

Buchan, John: asks Sir William Douglas about Bevan, 42–3; treats Bevan's illness, 611; visits Bevan, 655

Buchanan, George, 45, 336

Budapest, 518, 522, 526, 528, 534

Bulganin, Nicolai: becomes Soviet Premier, 455; visits London with Khrushchev, 504–5; letters to Eden, 542–4

Bulman, Rev. Irving, 207

Bunyan, John, 264

Burke, Edmund, 508, 545

Burke, Wilfred, 443

Burma, 394, 398

Burn, Duncan, 219(n)

Burnham, Linden, 414

Butler, R. A., (Lord): in N.H.S. debate 187, 191–2, 194; announces permanent N.H.S. charges, 359–60; pre-1955 election Budget, 485; Bevan tips him as Eden's successor, 521(n), 535; mentioned, 250, 401, 516, 552

Butler, Samuel, 453

Café Royal, 123, 651

Callaghan, James: writes to Bevan over resignation, 325, 328; supports withdrawal of whip, 466; in Shadow Cabinet, 499(n), 529(n)

Campaign for Nuclear Disarmament, 592, 599, 617, 625

Campbell, Jim, 572

Carlyle, Thomas, 23

Carron, W. J., (Lord), 510, 513

Casanova, 537

Castle, Barbara: 'brand China'

letter 313(n); elected to N.E.C.,
352, 380; and Bevan, 374, 514;
at Crossman lunches, 390–1; on
special sub-committee, 477 (n);
Conference speech, 494; N.E.C.
H-bomb debates, 567–70, 571,
595–6, 598; chairman's address
to Conference, 638; Bevan's
response, 641–2, 645; mentioned,
365, 467, 577
Central Medical Board, 111
Challenge to Britain, 407, 409
Chamberlain, Neville, 25, 220
Charter for Nurses, 128(n) and
129(n)
Chartered Society of Physiothera-
pists, 126–7
Chaumon, President, 605
Cherwell, Lord, 554
Chesterton, G. K., 178
Chiang Kai-shek, 303, 304, 305,
345, 455, 608
China, 303, 304, 305, 306, 309, 310,
311, 313–14, 345, 361, 404, 431,
444–5, 589, 608, 649; Labour
Party delegation to, 436, 443,
446–8, 617
Chou En-lai, 446
Christian Scientists, 127
Churchill, Randolph, 535, 613(n)
Churchill, Sir Winston: 1945 election defeat, 17–18; compared
with Attlee, 29; on Britain's post-
war bankruptcy, 50; attacks
Bevan as squalid nuisance, 61,
62, 63; aims to destroy his
reputation, 62; and demobilization, 70; again attacks Bevan, 83;
on Bevan and the doctors, 102–3,
138; in N.H.S. debates, 156;
attacked by Bevan, 157, 238,
271–5; 'responsible for N.H.S.',
214; calls Bevan 'Minister of
Disease', 242; Bevan's reply,
243–4; Bevan on his oratory,
245; Bevan, the arch-aggressor,

250–1; on N.H.S. finances, 253–
254; never attacks Bevan on
health and housing in the House,
254, 270; propagating a lie,
267–8; devaluation debate, 269–
272; and 1950 election, 277;
Bevan on, 279–80, 388, 486;
after the election, 286; on
Bevan's rearmament speech, 316;
after 1951 election, 350; Bevan
'right by accident', 355–6; visits
Washington, 361; advice from
Bevan, 376; Vicky cartoon, 378;
proposes Summit Conference,
400–1; falls ill – conference
postponed, 401–2; withdrawal of
British troops from Egypt, 415–
416, 418; cuts arms programme,
424; comment on S.E.A.T.O.,
432; comments on Bevan, 443(n),
451; on Eden's pledge, 451;
in H-bomb debate, 458–64;
illness prevented Summit, 460;
on Sutherland portrait, 460(n);
retires, 476; mentioned, 20, 25,
33, 38, 40, 43, 45, 64, 65, 66, 67,
68, 69, 71, 73, 84, 91, 95, 118,
240, 262, 265, 269, 302, 316, 448,
487, 658
The Citadel, 654
Clarion, 385
Clayton, W., 51–2, 53
Clerical and Administrative
Workers' Union, 512
Cliveden Place, 42, 44, 45, 240,
250, 275, 328–9, 331, 359, 414,
434, 440, 441, 442
Coalition Government, 21, 32, 63,
70, 102–3, 114, 182, 218, 221,
252
Cobden, Richard, 279
Cocks, Seymour: on Dalton, 35;
on Cabinet, 84; on Bevan as
Minister of Health, 213
Cockshut, Dr Roland: on Bevan,
119–20, 126(n), 151; on his pro-

posals, 140; 'slaughters' Moran, 141; opposition to Bill, 148–149; calls for further victories, 161; condemns Royal College Presidents, 164; on reopening of negotiations, 166; addresses mass meeting of doctors, 172; letter to *Times*, 173; declares service will not start, 193–4; declares it is time to give up fight, 209; mentioned, 212

Cohen, Lewis, 656

Collado, E. G., 51–2, 53

Collick, Percy, 472

Committee for the Limitation of Secret Police Powers, 508

Common Market, 560 and (n), 616

Communist Manifesto, 251

Communism, Bevan's attitude to, 22, 504

Conservative Central Office, 214

Conservative Party: Bevan on, 21, 272–4, 609, 612, 645–6, 647–8; attacks Bevan, 84–5, 138; and the N.H.S. Bill, 157, 214, 255; and 'vermin' speech, 238, 240; on the Labour Government, 265; and Suez, 415, 527; and Cyprus, 506–7

Conversations with Stalin, 423

Cook, A. J., 243

Cooper, Jack, 475, 477, 479–80, 510

Co-operative Party, 261

Corbet, Freda, 376

Cornish unit house, 81

Cousins, Frank: on public ownership and Socialism, 514–15; anti-H-bomb speech, 572; consults delegation, 577; on N.E.C., 595–7; mentioned, 454(n), 627

Cox, Dr Alfred, 142, 208–9

Crawford, James, 495

Crawley, Aidan, 378

Cripps, Lady, 93

Cripps, Sir Stafford: President of the Board of Trade, 24; and

Attlee, 27, 29; and Morrison, 37; and Bevan, 38–9; housing promises, 63, 95; blames Shinwell for fuel crisis, 88; proposals for beating crisis, 90; plots to remove Attlee, 92–4, 225–6; becomes Chancellor, 93; austerity measures, 96, 97; on steel nationalization, 221, 224; conflict with Bevan, 265–6, 267, 290; devaluation, 269–70; in N.H.S. vote of censure debate, 291–2; Cabinet disagreements, 292; on N.H.S. charges, 293–4; Wilson acts as go-between, 294; weekly dinners and Bevan, 294–297; Strachey's comment, 295; resigns, 299; Bevan's resignation warning, 318; mentioned, 61, 81, 145(n), 272, 277, 317, 377, 382

Cromwell, Oliver, 36, 181, 165, 228, 281

Cronin, A. J., 654

Crookshank, Captain Harry, 84

Crosland, Anthony, 366(n)

Crossman, R. H. S.: criticises Bevin's foreign policy, 90; in devaluation debate, 270; 'brand China' letter, 313(n); opposed to resignation, 343; moves Bevanite amendment in Defence debate, 363–4; aftermath of vote, 365; on P.L.P. vote, 366(n); and Bevan group, 373–4, 378; and Bevan, 375–6, 435; *Sunday Pictorial* and Morrison, 379(n); wins N.E.C. place, 380; on organization of Right, 387; weekly lunches, 390–1; N.E.C. discussion about *Tribune*, 392–3; Morrison and Treasurer issue, 408; conversation with Roy Jenkins, 413; on withdrawal of troops from Egypt, 416; Bevan's resignation and Wilson as replacement, 433–5; *Tribune–*

Deakin dispute, 454; Commons resolution, 456; on the H-bomb, 457–8, 567, 598; votes with majority, 465; interview with Gaitskell, 473–4(n); quarrel with Bevan and letter, 481–4, 497–8; on leadership controversy backs Gaitskell, 497–8; Bevan on, 499, 547; *Spectator* libel, 537–8; on *Industry and Society*, 558; Standing Orders, 636(n); mentioned, 467, 561

Extracts from diaries: 366(n), 373–4, 375–6, 379(n), 387, 392–393, 408, 413, 454, 473, 598, 639(n)

Cudlipp, Hugh, 378

Cullingworth, J. B., 85(n)

Cummings, A. J., 377, 378

Curran, Charles, 571(n)

Cyprus, 506–7, 523, 546, 614, 621

Czechoslovakia, 404

Daily Express, 141, 142(n), 239, 240, 288, 339, 359, 416, 418, 428(n), 469(n), 486, 512, 514(n), 526(n), 570

Daily Graphic, 199

Daily Herald, 364, 368, 378, 385, 393–4, 471(n), 494, 513, 519, 577(n), 622

Daily Mail, 141, 278, 362, 486

Daily Mirror, 237, 333, 380, 383, 384(n), 385, 416, 429(n), 443(n), 467, 468, 470, 487, 495, 497, 519, 523, 533

Daily Sketch, 142(n), 194, 339

Daily Telegraph, 86, 218, 327, 339, 377, 467, 506, 519, 577, 632, 638(n)

Daily Worker, 383, 505, 519

Dain, Dr Guy: on the '100 per cent' issue, 113; chairman of B.M.A. Council, 114; long experience with B.M.A., 115; on Bevan, 119, 121–2; on N.H.S. proposals, 141–2, 144, 148; in no hurry, 151; militant appeal, 151; 'no mandate to negotiate', 162–3; reports on decision to negotiate, 166–7; stormy meetings with Bevan, 168–9; tells doctors' meeting to oppose Act, 172–3; referred to by Bevan in House, 176; resolution following plebiscite, 195; says Act is unworkable, 197; repudiates Moran's compromise, 200, 202; painful decision, 201; new plebiscite – meets Bevan, 202; reverses plebiscite judgment, 202–3; successfully challenged by Hill, 203; in fighting mood, 203–4; forced to retreat – letter to *B.M.J.*, 204–5; suggests postponement, 205; examines situation, 209–10; accepts Service and pledges support, 211; mentioned, 123, 143, 162, 206, 207, 210, 212

Dalton, Hugh: becomes Chancellor, 24; and Attlee, 27, 29; and Bevan, 35–6, 89, 92, 399; and Morrison, 36–7; on Land-Lease cancellation, 52; and Loan negotiations, 54, 58; finance for housing, 75–6; accepts lower housing standards, 80; blames Shinwell for fuel crisis, 88; warns about financial crisis, 88–89; Bevin's Palestine policy, 89; proposals for beating crisis, 90–1, 92; architect of disaster, 92; resigns, 92; plots to remove Attlee, 92–4, 225–6; on Bevan and N.H.S., 134; strong support for N.H.S., 137–8; on steel nationalization, 221, 224; plan to put Bevan at Ministry of Supply, 226; his intrigues, 226; against nationalization of industrial assurance, 261; presses for defence cuts, 265; on Government reshuffle, 297; supports Gaitskell, 301; on Korea, 306; on Bevan and Gaitskell, 312, 410–11, 412; on German rearmament, 319, 425, 427; on health charges issue, 319–20; Bevan's resignation threat, 320; talk with Gaitskell, 321–2; talks to Bevan, 322; visits Attlee in hospital, 330; 1951 conference – election manifesto – votes, 351, 352; and Bevanite proceedings, 358; loses seat on Executive, 380; on Gaitskell, 384; on Shadow Cabinet elections, 387; supports Gaitskell for leader, 495; mentioned, 19, 61, 374, 403, 466(n)

Quotations from memoirs and unpublished diaries: 266, 297, 301, 305, 309(n), 314, 316, 319, 320, 321, 323, 324, 330, 331, 380, 384, 399

Davies, Sir Daniel, 654–5, 656

Davies, Harold (Lord), 90(n), 569, 572

Davitt, Michael, 243

Day, Robin, 452(n)

Deakin, Arthur: 'Stop Bevan' ringleader, 353–4, 438; on Bevanites, 359, 364, 365–6; Morecambe conference, 379–80, 381, 382; turns from Attlee to Gaitskell, 383, 408; *Tribune* on, 392; Bevan attacks him, 393; *Tribune* and N.E.C., 393–4; attacks N.E.C. programme, 407; on nationalization, 407; 'Morrison for Treasurer' plot, 408; Roy Jenkins's comment, 413; power over his union, 437; supports Gaitskell for Treasurer, 438–40, 492(n); 'fixes' Bevan, 449, 451; and Blue Union – *Tribune*

article, 453–4; favours and works for Bevan's expulsion, 468, 471, 473–5; death, 488; mentioned, 467

Dedijer, Vladimir: close friendship with Bevan, 348; dismissed by Tito – Bevan's letter, 420–3

Defence White Paper, 363–4

Delargy, Hugh: friendship with Bevan, 238–9; on vermin speech, 238–9; on resignation, 327; votes with majority, 465; dinner at Ivy, 469(n), mentioned, 533(n), 569, 582

Demobilization, 67–8, 70, 90, 91

Democratic Socialism, Bevan's attitude to, 20–1, 338–9, 563, 646–7, 659; description in *In Place of Fear*, 369–70

Deutscher, Isaac, 49(n), 257, 388(n)

De Valera, Eamon, 588

Devaluation, 267, 269–76, 291

Devonport, 278, 279–80, 621, 629, 652

Dietzgen, Joseph, 620

Disengagement, 406, 555, 563, 582, 594, 617

Disengagement and Nuclear War, 598

Disengagement in Europe, 598

Disraeli, Benjamin, 29, 400

Djilas, Milovan: close friendship with Bevan, 347–8; dismissed by Tito – Bevan's letter, 420–3; mentioned, 257, 283, 406, 612

Dock Strike, 317–18

Docker, Sir Bernard, 150

Donnelly, Desmond, 358(n), 449

Donnison, D. V., 65(n)

Douglas, Harry, 393, 394, 408

Douglas, Sir William, 42–3, 121, 394

Driberg, Tom: elected to N.E.C., 352, 380; at Crossman lunches, 390; N.E.C. meeting, 393;

dinner at Ivy, 469(n); initiates Cyprus debate, 506; on Bevan and Khrushchev, 566(n); Labour Party chairman, 600; mentioned, 327(n)

Dryden, John, 17

Dudley, Earl of, 80

Dugdale, John, 349(n)

Dukes, Charles, 437

Dulles, John Foster: anti-Communist policy, 361–2, 608; foreign policy, 400, 406, 425–7, 448, 450–1; 'massive retaliation' speech, 425; Bevan on, 429, 608; visits London – S.E.A.T.O., 430, 432; his 'brinkmanship' policy, 504, Bevan's talks with, 587, 590–1; mentioned, 391, 436, 517, 518

Duncan, Sir Andrew, 222, 225

Durham Miners, 339, 438, 509; Gala, 243–4

Earnshaw, Harry, 479

Ebbw Vale: steel industry, 220–1, 268; 1950 election and Bevan's election address, 280–1; Bevan's speech following resignation, 346; 1951 election results, 351–2; backs Bevan, 364–5, 480–1; 1955 drop in vote, 488; Bevan as conference delegate, 492; H-bomb issue, 583; 1959 election, 621, 627, 629; mentioned, 119, 652; Ebbw Vale Trades Council, 480

Eccles, David (Lord), 177, 192, 193, 270

Eckstein, Harry, 115(n), 117(n)

Economist, 94, 207, 227, 473

Ede, Chuter: praises Bevan's speech, 316, 532; visits Attlee in hospital, 330; attacks Bevan, 340; favours withdrawal of Whip, 466

Edelman, Maurice, 472

Eden, Sir Anthony (Lord Avon): Churchill uses his illness, 401–

402(n); Berlin Conference, 426–7; S.E.A.T.O., 430–2; German rearmament, 451; becomes Prime Minister, 476; 1955 election, 485; Cyprus and the Middle East, 506–7; Suez, 518, 521–7, 529–31; retires, 535–6; letter from Bulganin, 542–3; mentioned, 406, 435

Edwards, Charlie, 652

Edwards, Huw T., 578(n)

Egypt, withdrawal of troops, Bevan's articles, visit, 415–18; Suez crisis, 513, 520–7, 530–2, 534, 543, 546

Eisenhower, President: and the Soviet Union, 400; and Churchill, 460; and Suez, 522; Bermuda conference, 550; Bevan's visit, 587, 588, 590–1; Eisenhower doctrine, 539, 540, 544

Electrical Trades Union, 479

El Gonmhouria, 417

Elizabeth II, 588, 626, 628

Elliott, Captain Walter, 84, 101, 291

Ellis, Havelock, 591

El Vino's, 561

Emergency Medical Scheme, 107

Empire News, 198

Ethiopia, 274

European Coal and Steel Community, 233

European Defence Community, 400, 402, 403, 404, 425, 426(n), 427, 451, 460, 461

Evans, Lincoln (Sir), 392–3

Evans, Stanley, 342

Evening News, 571(n)

Evening Standard, 142(n), 162, 228, 348, 416, 447(n), 514, 535, 631

L'Express, 417(n), 616

Fagan, J. M., 439–44

Fairlie, Henry, 480, 533

Family Allowances Scheme, 103
Faringdon, Lord, 294
Federation of British Industries, 94, 175
Firth, Sir William, 220–1
Fleming, D. F., 314(n)
Foot, Jill: Stratford weekend, 298–299; meal at the Ivy, 469(n); makes peace, 602; visit to Asheridge, 629–30
Foot, Michael: member of 'Keep Left' group, 90(n); elected to N.E.C., 261(n); 'brand China' letter, 313(n); *Tribune* article, 342; on Attlee, 349(n); at Crossman lunches, 391; *Tribune* attack on Deakin, 454; resolution on high-level talks, 456; Gaitskell on, 474(n)
Relations with Bevan: Bevan helps cure his eczema, 104(n); 1950 Devonport election meeting, 279–80; Stratford weekend, 298–9; meal at the Ivy, 469(n); encounter with Attlee, 472; argues about the Labour Party, 499; personal reflection, 549(n); dinner at Leoni's, 562; pre-conference discussion, 567; *Tribune* meeting, 570–1; on Bevan and the H-bomb, 571–2, 583; listens to debate, 572–7; aftermath of speech, 577–9; *Tribune's* policy, 579–80; Jennie Lee's feelings, 583–4; personal clashes, 592, 601–3; Bevan cancels Devonport meeting, 621; visit to Asheridge, 629–30; Bevan comments on his speech, 640; visits Bevan in hospital, 652–3
Forbes, Alistair, 410
Foreign Office, 33, 231, 234, 314, 401, 402, 448, 542, 622, 624, 626, 628
Formosa, 303, 305, 314, 345, 455, 608

Forward, 558, 631
Fox, Charles James, 545
France: Berlin blockade, 229; E.D.C., 403, 404, 448; and Indo-China, 432; Suez, 522, 524, 527, 530, 542; de Gaulle returns to power, 604–5
Fraser, Tom, 472, 529(n)
Freeman, John: letter to Bevan, 326–7, 329; he and Wilson visit Bevan, resigns, 331; advice to Bevan, 365, 434; at Crossman lunches, 391; votes with majority, 465; mentioned, 387
French Socialist Party, 391(n), 562–3, 604–5; Congress, 562–3

Gaitskell, Dora (Lady), 618, 619
Gaitskell, Hugh: Cabinet disagreements, 292; and Bevan, 294, 312, 315, 342, 347, 412, 497–9, 547, 603, 607–8, 609, 610, 619, 622–4; 627, 628, 630, 651–2; presses health charges argument, 294–5, 296, 317; appointed Chancellor, 299; supported by Dalton, 301; supports 'brand China' move, 314; and rearmament, 316; Bevan's resignation warning, 318; on German rearmament, 319, 425, 427–8, 455; proposes charges for teeth and spectacles, 319; on Bevan's resignation threat, 321; threatens to resign, 323; visits Attlee in hospital, 323, 330; presents Budget, 324; compared to Snowdon in *Tribune*, 331; in Bevan's resignation speech, 334, 336, 337–8; no concessions, 341; Washington visit and *Tribune's* taunts, 355; replies in *Tribune*, 356; fails to win N.E.C. place, 380, 409; Stalybridge speech, 382–3; and *Spectator* article, 384; attitude to *Tribune*, 384,

385; 'disengagement', 406; clash
with Bevan, 412; Roy Jenkins's
comment, 413; stands for
Treasurer – union support, 438–
440; wins, 449; on the H-bomb,
457; favours withdrawal of Whip
and expulsion, 466, 468, 471,
476; Deakin speaks to, 473; talks
to Crossman, 473–4(n); on
Bevanism, 474(n); member of
sub-committee, 477–9; N.E.C.
meeting on expulsion, 480; in
New Statesman article, 482; on
1955 election, 487–8; elected
Treasurer, 491–2; speech, 494,
498; rival to Attlee, 494, 495,
497; elected leader, 495–6, 500;
Shadow Cabinet, 499(n); Bevan's
Manchester speech, 502;
Khrushchev-Bulganin dinner,
505; no longer eligible for
Treasurer, 509; Bevan as
Treasurer, 514; Suez crisis, 516–
518, 520, 523; disliked Venice,
537; Eisenhower doctrine, 539–
540; pro-American, 550; and the
H-bomb, 551, 552(n); disarmament, 555; on Industry and
Society, 558; on defence document, 567–8, 569; on Bevan's
H-bomb speech, 579, 581; after
Brighton, 586; on nuclear retaliation, 595–7, 598; and Mollet,
604–5; Middle East crisis, 605–8;
and Far East threat, 609; leads
delegation to Soviet Union, 617–
621; concedes election defeat,
629; visits Bevan, 629; Right-
wing plan of action, 630–2;
opposed to abolition of Standing
Orders, 636; deference to Party
Conference, 637–8; speech at
conference, 638–40; in Bevan's
speech, 642–3, 645, 647; Vicky
cartoon, 650; mentioned, 410,
433, 493, 510, 598
22*

Gallup Poll, on N.H..S, 195
Gammans, Captain, 240
De Gaulle, General, 604–5
Geddes, Charles, 354
General Elections: (1945), 17–19,
281; (1950), 214, 277–82; (1951),
214, 342, 349, 350, 351–2;
(1955), 485; (1959), 621–9, 632,
637, 641
General Practitioners: pre-N.H.S.,
108–9; in Willink White Paper,
110; predominant in B.M.A.,
114; Bevan on, 126, 160; among
B.M.A.'s 'Seven Principles', 128;
plans for in N.H.S. Bill, 135–6,
154–5; and private practice, 137,
152–3, 188; full time salaried
service, 152, 154, 182–3, 199,
201; revised terms, 159; vote in
referendum, 162; B.M.A.'s demands for, 162; clarification of
position in N.H.S., 164; discussed at Negotiating Committee
meeting, 168; asked by B.M.A.
if they will accept service, 173–4;
discussed in special N.H.S.
debate, 180; local executive
councils and appeals machinery,
185–7; voting in plebiscite, 193;
bare majority still opposed, 206;
Dr Cox's letter, 208; majority
join service, 210, 213; debate on
N.H.S. finances, 254
Geneva, 436, 448, 489, 617
George VI, 349 and (n)
Germany, 33, 50, 229–30, 231–3,
274, 426–7, 547, 556, 570, 589,
593, 594–5, 646
German elections, 233–4, 556;
industry, 231–4; problem, 403,
556; rearmament, 305, 319, 345,
375, 402–4, 405–6, 425–9, 448–
452, 461, 471, 595, 600; East
German rising, 402
Ghana, 623
Gielgud, John, 298

Gilliatt, William, 163-5, 199, 201, 202
Gladstone, W. E., 23, 278, 424
Glasgow Herald, 194
Giving Our Way?, 349, 352, 354
Gomulka, Wladyslaw, 506, 521, 563
Gooch, Edwin, 475-6
Goodman, Geoffrey, election diary, 622-8
Goodman, Dr, 166
Gordon Walker, Patrick, 225, 366(n), 378
Graham-Little, Sir Ernest, 192
Gray, Dr F., 195
Greece, 89
Greenwood, Anthony, 467, 499(n), 529(n), 566, 598
Greenwood, Arthur, survey of social services, 39; on housing, 63; Chairman of Cabinet Committee, 137; letter to Bevan, 325-6; Treasurer of Party, 408, death, 438
Gregg, Dr, 198
Grenfell, D. R., 496
Griffin, Cardinal, 127
Griffiths, James: introduces National Insurance Act, 97; industrial assurance, 261-2; teeth and spectacles charges, 319; elected to N.E.C., 352, 380; N.E.C. meeting on *Tribune*, 393; on Shadow Cabinet, 466(n), 499(n); expulsion issue, 475, 477, 479-80; Deputy Leader, 502, 629; at demonstration at Merthyr, 503
Griffiths, Will, 508
Grimond, Jo, 631
Gruenther, General, 464
Guillebaud, Professor, 215
Guillebaud Committee Report, 215, 291(n)
Gulf of Akaba, 540, 541

Hacker, William, 480

Hailsham, Lord, see Quintin Hogg
Hale, Leslie, 90(n), 465, 613(n)
Hale-White, Dr Reginald, 211
Halifax, Lord, 55
Hall, Glenvil, 466(n)
Hancock, Tony, 655
Handel, 442
Hardie, Keir, 243, 264, 502
Harman, Tony, 442
Harris, Wilson, 180
Harrison, Martin, 492(n), 510-1(n)
Harrod, R. F., 53(n), 54(n), 55(n)
Hart, Judith, 572
Hastings, Dr Somerville, 293
Haworth, Jim, 475-6, 477, 479-80
Hawton, Sir John, 41, 43, 131
Hazlitt, William, 28, 29, 237, 537
H-bomb: 429, 455, 456-9, 471, 481-2, 525, 564, 565-6, 568, 572-7, 578(n), 581-2, 610, 622, 625-6; tests: 457, 487, 550-7, 568, 573, 581, 582, 593, 594, 617; and the Labour Party, P.L.P., 465-6, 469, 550-7, 565-577, 595, 597, 600-1; nuclear retaliation, 595-7; round-the-clock bombers, 593
H-bomb Campaign Committee, 566
Heald, Lionel, K. C., 240
Healey, Denis, 'disengagement', 406; on Bevan and S.E.A.T.O. debate, 435 and 436(n); on delegation to Soviet Union, 622; Bevan on, 648-9; mentioned, 380, 640
Health, Ministry of, 40-4, 66, 73, 87(n), 121, 135, 198, 208, 265, 298, 301
Health centres, 110-11, 136, 171, 214
Health Service charges: prescription, 276-7, 290, 292, 293-7, 318; teeth and spectacles, 319, 321, 324, 333, 341, 347; Tory permanent charges: 359, 360,

375; Labour's promise to remove, 407, 409
Hecht, Alfred, 656
Henderson, Lord, 232–3, 466(n)
Henry V, 516
Henty, G. A., 607
Hill, Dr Charles, (Lord): B.M.A.'s Draft Interior Report, 109, 113; Secretary of B.M.A., 114; long experience with B.M.A., 115; on its structure, 117; on Bevan, 122 and (n), 138; on N.H.S. proposals, 141–2, 143–4; in no hurry, 151; on the referendum, 161; approached by Webb-Johnson, 163; stormy meetings with Bevan, 168–9; addresses mass meeting of doctors, 172; listens to debate in House, 193; on the fighting fund, 198(n); meets Bevan, 202; challenges Dain over plebiscite, 203; on Bevan and the N.H.S., 217; and Macmillan, 552(n); mentioned, 123, 128, 143, 200, 207
Himalayas, 396
Hinds, Alfred, 609
Hitler, Adolf, 119, 274, 307, 393, 474(n), 508, 518, 524, 530
Hogg, Quinton (Lord Hailsham), 270, 633–4
Hola camp, 614, 621, 648
Holland, Eardley, 123, 124, 158, 163
Horan, Alice, 479
Horder, Lord: against any form of health service, 124; on Bevan's proposals, 139; repudiates Moran, 144; in House of Lords debate, 159; appeals to consultants, 173; no yielding, 196, 207; appeals to doctors and public, 204; censures B.M.A.'s conduct, 211
Hospitals: pre-N.H.S., 107, 108; in Willink White Paper, 110;

B.M.A.'s plans for, 128; N.H.S. Bill's proposals, 131–5, 146; discussed in Second Reading, 147; B.M.A. opposition to State ownership, 148, 162; parliamentary opposition, 150; in Committee Stage, 153–4; in Third Reading, 157–8; discussed at Negotiating Committee meeting, 168; *Lancet* – problem solved, 171; proposals secretly approved, 171; in special N.H.S. debate, 180, 188; Hill's comments, 217; Willink's comments, 218
Houghton, Douglas, 636(n)
House of Lords, 23, 58, 157, 158, 223, 226–7, 238, 240, 603–4
Housewives League, 320(n)
Housing: debate, 60–4, 67, 252; Bevan's first speech on, 60–1; shortages, 62–3; pre-war situation and Coalition's plans, 63–6, 67; building force, 65; 1939 numbers, 65; and post-war estimates, 66; prefabricated houses, 67, 81; short-term palliatives, 68–9; long-term measures, 69; local authorities' responsibility for, 69, 72–4; demobilization of building workers, 71; finance for, 74–6; Housing Bill presented, 75; standards and materials, 76–82; 'the squatters', 82–3; assessment of Bevan's policy, 84–7; housing figures, 86, 252; programme cut, 87, 94–7, 276–7, 289–90; Tory vote of censure, 291; Macmillan's record – Commons debate, 414–15
Housing (Financial and Miscellaneous Provisions) Bill, 75
Howard, Anthony, 19(n)
Hudson, R. S., 84
Hughes, Emrys, 386
Hungary: Soviet thaw, 506; and

Suez, 518, 526, 528; Soviet repression, 522, 543, 564; discussed in House, 533, 534; mentioned, 516
Hunter, Leslie, 288(n), 468, 510
Hussein, King, 605, 612
Hylton, Jack, 602
Hyson, Dorothy, 298

Imperial Chemical Industries, 260
'In Place of the Cold War', 404
In Place of Fear, 23, 347–8, 367–71, 404–5
India, Britain's debt to, 57; independence, 89; and Bevin, 305; and Korea, 311, 406; famine, 346; Bevan visits, 394–8, 400; and Yugoslavia, 406–7; influence on Bevan, 424; Bevan's second visit, 544–8, 550, 551, 581; mentioned, 344, 345, 432, 506, 539, 623, 648, 649
India League, 394
Indo-China, 394, 425, 431, 432, 448, 544
Indonesia, 649
Industrial assurance, 261–2, 266
Industrial Injuries Act, 97, 103
Industry and Society, 557–9, 562, 566, 570–1, 572
Institute of Almoners, 195
Iraq, 605, 606
Ireland, 506
Iron and Steel Board, 222, 223
Iron and Steel Trades Confederation, 392
Israel, Bevan visits, 418–20, 546; influence on Bevan, 424, 517; Suez crisis, 518, 519, 522, 526, 528, 530–2, 540–1, 545; mentioned, 415, 607
Istanbul, 546
Italy, 274, 536, 546
It Need Not Happen, 444
Ivy, 469(n)

Jagan, Dr Cheddi, 414
Jameson, Sir Wilson, 41
Japan, 52, 68, 447, 550; Peace Treaty, 345, 349
Jay, Douglas, XYZ Club, 359; votes to expel Bevan, 366(n); *Forward* article, 631–2, 637–8, 639
Jefferson, Thomas, 298, 589
Jeger, Dr Santo, 293
Jenkins, Roy, 366(n), 380, 632; on Bevanism, 413
Jervis, Professor Johnstone, 158
Johnson, Paul, 631
Jones, Ernest, 449, 450, 509
Jones, Jack, 454(n)
Jones, Dr Thomas, 42
Jones, T. W. (Lord Maelor), 533(n)
Jordan, 530, 564, 565, 605, 606, 612
Jowitt, Earl, 466(n)

Karachi, 546
Kardelj, Edvard, 347
Karol, K. S.: contributor to *L'Express*, 417(n); arranges Bevan - Mendès - France - Nenni Meeting, 616; accompanies Bevan to Soviet Union, 618–20
Kashmir, 544, 545, 546
'Keep Left' group (and pamphlet), 90–1, 343, 358, 359
Kemsley, Lord, 60, 61, 198, 240, 503
Kennan, George, 594
Kenya, 614
Key, Charles, 43, 75, 496
Keynes, Lord: Anglo-American economic concordat, 51, London conference, 51; Loan Agreement negotiations, 52–5, 58; Bevan's view of, 56, 57
Khama, Seretse, 414
Khrushchev, Nikita: Bevan on delegation to Soviet Union, 444–446; goes to Belgrade, 489; visits London with Bulganin, 504–5;

and Poland, 521–2; on disarmament, 529, 556; Bevan on private visit to Soviet Union, 563–6; Bevan on his talks, 568, 580; and Middle East crisis, 606; obsessed with visit to U.S.A., 619; Bevan's views on Khrushchev, 622, 624; mentioned, 405, 588, 590, 633

Kidrik, Boris, 347

King, Horace (Lord Mabray-King), 533

Knight, Percy, 475, 477, 495

Korea, 299, 301, 302–4, 308–11, 356(n), 361, 403, 406, 424, 454

Kropotkin, Prince, 243

Krug, Mark M., 589(n)

Labour, Ministry of, 70, 289, 103, 310, 311, 317

Labour Party (see also National Executive Committee, Parliamentary Labour Party and Shadow Cabinet): 1945 election victory, 17–19; too deferential, 21; and Attlee, 26, 28; Bevan's attitude to 49–50, 268, 388, 497, 498–9, 500–1, 611–12, 616, 625, 650–2; in favour of payment for councillors, 99; policy in fifties and sixties, 257; Bevan, the future leader of, 264; and Churchill, 273; after 1950 election, 286–7; and the Bevanites, 352–3, 373; on German rearmament, 426–8, 448; policy decided by leaders of big unions, 437, 440; policy for 1955 election, 487–8; policy on National Insurance, 493–4; Treasurership and electoral processes, 513–14; Suez and Hungary, 518, 525–6, 533, 534; the H-bomb, and tests, 551–7, 565, 568; disarmament, 555–7; and the Middle East, 565; Khrushchev on,

566(n), 624; new policy proposals, 595; fails to present Socialist case, 614–15; after 1959 election, 630–2; Gaitskell on its Constitution, 639–40; mentioned, 20, 140, 171, 557, 571, 656

Labour Party Conferences: (1944), 222; (pre-1945 election,) 19, 114, 133; (1947), 91; (1948), 234–6, 258; (1949), 259, 262, 263–4; (1950), 299; (1951), 351–4; (1952), 378, 379–82, 392, 407; (1953), 408–10, 426; (1954), 448–51; (1955), 490–4; (1956), 513–14, 521, 551, 557; (1957), 562, 566–77, 586, 592, 597, 599, 600, 601; (1958), 608–11, 612; (1959), 637–651

Lancaster, Osbert, 466

Lancet: on doctor-patient relationship, 130; on Bevan, 131, 155, 170–1; on the discussions, 151; on Royal Colleges' attitude, 156; blames B.M.A. leaders, 162; questions to Bevan, 174; calls for conciliation, 204

Lansbury, George, 145(n), 337, 577

Laski, Harold, 249, 278

Latham, Lord, 134

Law Richard (Lord Coleraine), 146–8, 192

Lawrence, John, 602

Lawther, William (Sir): on Bevan and Bevanites, 353, 366, 393–4; Morecambe Conference, 379, 380, 382, 383(n); Bevan attacks, 393; Treasurership issue, 408; Mineworkers' vote, 437–8; mentioned, 392, 450

League of Nations, 274

Lebanon, 605, 606

Lee, Fred, 90(n), 325, 472

Lee, Jennie: dinner jacket episode, 30–1; changes in her life, 44–6; elected as Labour M.P. for Cannock, 45; relationship of her

career to Bevan's, 45–6; at
Cripps's tea party, 93; foul
letters and press harassment,
250–1; Nye discusses resignation, 266; on Nye and the
Cabinet, 294; weekend at Stratford, 298–9; Nye to Ministry of
Labour, 311, 312; protests at
health charges, 324; on resignation, 327, 328–9; and *Tribune*
article, 342; holiday in Yugoslavia, 347–8; helps Nye with
book, 347–8, 368; at Crossman
lunches, 391; Nye's letters from
India, 397–8, 546–8; Nye on
Stalin's death, 398, 399; second
visit to Yugoslavia, 406; verdict
on Margate Conference, 410;
visits Egypt, Transjordan, Israel,
418–20; the move to Asheridge
Farm, 441–3; watches Nye's
health, 441, 614, 616–17; *Tribune*
attack on Deakin, 454; meal at
the Ivy, 469(n); on H-bomb
tests, 547, 551; on *Industry and
Society*, 559, 561; letter from
Nye, 560; visits Russia, 563–6;
H-bomb issue, 569, 579–80;
candidate for N.E.C., 559;
defeated, 572; 'defend Nye's
honour', 583–4; and author –
Tribune, 601–3; Nye's operation and cancer, 652, 655, 656;
letter to author, 656–7; Nye's
beliefs 657–8; funeral arrangements, 657–9; letters of sympathy, 659; mentioned, 47, 284,
436, 483, 497, 582, 618, 620, 640
Lee, Mr, 45, 359
Lee, Mrs, 45, 312, 436(n), 441–2,
497, 559, 655
Lee, Peter, 243
Left Book Club, 385
Lejeune, Max, 562
Land-Lease Agreement, 50, 52,
68, 302

Lenin, V. I., 210, 443
Leningrad, 619–20
Leoni's Quo Vadis, 562, 567
Let Us Face the Future, 19, 219, 260
Levy, Benn W., 90(n), 508
Liberal Party, 470, 631
Life Peerages Bill, 603
Lincoln, Abraham, 369, 633
Lindsay, Dr Almont, 216
Lindsay, Martin, 416–17
Linwald, Dr, 149
Lippmann, Walter, 314, 436
Lipson, D. L., 183
Lipton, Marcus, 313(n)
Literature and Western Man, 652,
656
Liverpool Philharmonic Orchestra,
100
Llewellyn, Sir David, 538(n)
Lloyd, Selwyn, 528, 530, 531
Lloyd George, David (Earl), 42, 60,
106, 109, 139, 178, 249, 273,
274, 316, 321, 576, 658
Lloyd George, Megan, 532–3
Loan Agreement, 52–5, 56, 57–8,
88, 90, 92
Local Executive Councils, 135,
154, 185
Local authorities: championed by
Morrison, 37; and housing, 69,
72–4, 80–1, 82, 84, 86, 95;
Local Government Bill, 99–100;
their health services, 107; in
Willink White Papers, 110–11,
131; and N.H.S. Bill, 131, 133,
136, 146(n); duty to provide
health centres, 136; Bevan's
plan for reform, 266(n)
Local Government Bill, 99–100,
101
London: Bevan's attitude to, 440–1
London, Jack, 298
London County Council, 133, 134
London News, 343
Low, David, 394
Lush, Archie (Sir): appointment

of Sir William Douglas, 42; on Bevan's resignation, 329; Tom Proctor's story, 340; on election for Treasurer, 439; at Asheridge, 443; on H-bomb speech, 583; last visits, 655, 656; mentioned, 20, 48
Lyttelton, Oliver, 401

MacArthur, General, 302–4, 308, 309, 310, 327, 330, 343
Macartney, Wilfred, 329
McCarthy, Senator Joe, 303, 346, 383
MacColl, Ewan, 239
McKay, John, 386
Mackay, R. W. G., 90(n)
Mackenzie, Robert, 637
Mackie, John, Bevan stays with, 378, 560; advises Bevan on buying a farm, 410, 441–2
Macleod, Iain, 214, 360(n)
Macmillan, Harold: housing, 85–7, 414–15; on death of Stalin, 402(n); Bevan's surprise that he becomes Prime Minister, 521(n), 535–6; on Eisenhower doctrine, 540(n); Bulganin correspondence, 543(n); Bermuda Conference, 550; British H-bomb tests, 552–3, 556; on Bevan's demagogy, 589; Middle East crisis, 606; Bevan on, 609, 612, 614, 627–8, 633–4, 646, 656; defends Jordan expedition, 612; refuses Suez inquiry, 613; visits Moscow, 617; announces general election, 620; mentioned, 418, 587, 588
McNeil, Hector, 319 and 319(n)
Makarios, Archbishop, 506, 546
Malenkov, G. M., 402(n), 444–6, 455, 460, 489
Malik, Y. A., 618
Mallalieu, J. P. W.: 'Keep Left' group, 90(n); comment on

Bevan's speech, 274–5; at Crossman lunches, 391; his *Tribune* article and the N.E.C., 411–13; *Tribune* article attacking Deakin, 454
Malta, 495, 508, 523
Manchester Guardian, 83(n), 94, 145, 191, 193, 199, 227, 237, 239, 384, 385, 394, 395, 424, 467, 473, 486, 489, 500, 502, 519
Mann, Jean, 476, 487, 597
Mann, Tom, 243, 454(n)
Mao Tse-tung, 306, 446, 589
Marquand, Hilary, 319
Marshall, General, 93, 97
Marshall Aid, 56, 93, 97, 235, 302
Marx, Karl, 562, 564, 607, 658
Marxism: Bevan's attitude to, 20–2, 24, 49, 258, 396, 447, 487, 562, 585–6, 615, 635
Mathai, M. O., 394, 406–7
Maxton, James, 45, 482, 483
Maxwell Fyfe, David (Lord Kilmuir), 84
Mayhew, Christopher, 375, 380
Medical Planning Commission, 107, 108, 109, 110, 113, 136
Medical Practices Committee, 136
Medical Services Review Committee (Porritt Committee), 217–18
Medical Women's Federation, 115(n)
Mellish, Robert, 320(n), 636(n)
Mencken, H. L., 652
Mendelson, John, 381
Mendelson, Vivienne, 569, 572
Mendès-France, Pierre; meets Bevan, 417(n), 563, 616–17; and Indo-China, 432; favours four-power conference, 448; and German rearmament, 451; his Government falls, 455
Menon, Krishna, 394, 544
Menzies, Sir Frederick, 211
Messer, Sir Frederick, 155

Michelangelo, 100

Middle East, 265, 344, 507, 520, 526, 536, 539–42, 546, 564–5, 582, 589, 605–8

The Middle Way, 612

Middlesex Hospital, 240

Mikardo, Ian: 'Keep Left' group 90(n); moves nationalization resolution, 222; 'brand China' letter, 313(n); elected to N.E.C., 352, 380, 409; and Bevanites, 358, 373, 386, 394; angry with Bevan, 374; at Crossman lunches, 390; most hated Bevanite, 393; criticises T.U.C. over British Guiana, 413–14; complains about Francis Williams's articles, 428; Gaitskell on, 474(n); Remploy debate, 489; on *Industry and Society*, 558, 561; Bevan and the H-bomb, 566, 569, 570, 577, 598; mentioned, 270, 433

Mikoyan, A. I., 444

Millington, Ernest, 90(n)

Mitchell, Joan, 357(n)

Mitchison, G. R. (Lord), 499(n), 529(n)

Mollet, Guy, 530, 542, 562, 604–5

Molotov, V. M., 426

Monckton, Sir Walter, 392, 489–90

Monmouthshire County Council, 242

Monslow, Walter, 439

Montaigne, 47, 48

Moran, Lord: on doctor-patient relationship, 103–4; President of the Royal College of Physicians, 124; on Bevan, 124–6; discussion with Bevan on hospitals, 132; welcomes Bevan's proposals, 140, 144, 150; furious with Hill, 141; in House of Lords debate, 159; tries to break deadlock, 163; move towards a compromise, 199–201, 202; on Churchill, 402(n); re-

ports Churchill's comment on Bevan, 443(n), 451; Churchill's comment on Sutherland portrait, 460(n); mentioned, 164, 165, 167

Morgan, Lt-General Sir Frederick, 554

Morris, Claud, 333(n)

Morris-Jones, Sir Henry, 145

Morrison, Herbert (Lord): Leader of the House, 19 and (n); 24, 37; and Attlee, 27, 28, 29, 288, 301; Bevan and Dalton on, 36–7; his personality, 37–8; champion of local authorities, 37, 134; on Cripps and Bevan, 38–9, 290; proposes suspension of Standing Orders, 45; in housing debate, 63–4; 1947 fuel crisis – falls ill, 88; at 1947 Conference, 91; plot to remove Attlee, 92–4; on Health Service Bill and Willink White Paper, 129, 148; opposed to transfer of hospitals, 134; in favour of piecemeal introduction of N.H.S., 134, 138; his discretion, 168; opposed to steel nationalization, 222–4; talks with Sir Duncan Forbes, 222–3; and Dalton, 226; on 'vermin' speech, 249, 436; on N.H.S. finances, 253, 293; v. Bevan on policy, 257–66, 267, 287–8; on nationalization, 258–62, 266; his chairmanships, 259; 1950 election, 277; post-election 'consolidation' policy, 287–9, 371; Cabinet disagreements, 292; on Bevan as Minister of Health, 297; teeth and spectacles charges, 319, 324; interprets Attlee's views, 319, 323; on sacking of MacArthur, 327; visits Attlee in hospital, 330; and Bevan's resignation, 333, 341, 343; and election announcement, 349; 1951 conference vote, 352; fails in attack on Churchill,

361, 362; Tory Defence White Paper, 363; loses seat on Executive, 380–1; 'party within a party' issue, 386; elected Deputy Leader, 386, 410; on German rearmament, 404, 425, 427–8, 455; turns down Deakin's Treasurership proposal, 408–9; on withdrawal of troops from Egypt, 415; on the H-bomb, 457; motion for high-level talks, 465; in favour of withdrawal of whip and expulsion, 466, 476; at N.E.C. meeting on expulsion, 480; plot to make him leader, 489; speech at Conference, 494; rival to Attlee, 494; stands for leader – defeated, 495–6, 497; Bevan on, 624; mentioned, 31(n), 61, 90, 219, 277, 299, 318, 374, 375, 410, 433, 456, 474(n), 500

Moscow, 443, 489, 563, 617, 618, 620

Mumford, Lewis, 60, 298

The Municipal Journal, 214(n), 266(n)

The Municipal Workers Journal, 383

Mussolini, Benito, 307, 518, 530

Nagy, Imre, 528

Napoleon, 546

Nasser, General Gamal: episode of Bevan article, 416; Bevan's opinion of, 418, 517, 526, 532, 540, 545; nationalizes Suez Canal, 518–21; Suez crisis, 523, 527, 540–1; on the Eisenhower doctrine, 539

National Assistance Bill, 97–9, 103

National Association of Maternity and Child Welfare Centres, 212

National Association of Stevedores and Dockers, 453–4

National Association of Theatre and Kiné Employees, 354

National Executive of the Labour Party: 1947 Conference, Bevan heads constituency section, 91; 1948, again heads poll, 236; Bevan urges offensive policy, 251–2; policy debates, 257–62; nationalization discussions, 258–62; industrial assurance, 261–2, 266; post-election discussions, 287–9; weekend policy meeting, 288–9; Attlee's leadership of, 289; conflicts with Cabinet, 298; trade union votes, 352; 1951, Bevanite successes, 352–3; publishes Our First Duty – Peace, 354; on Bevanite revolt, 366; German rearmament, 375, 428; 1952, Bevanite successes, 380–1; Gaitskell appeals to, 383; document on nationalization, 391; the T.U.C. and 'menace' of Tribune, 392–4; Challenge to Britain, 407; 1953, Bevanite successes, 409; and Francis Williams's articles, 428–9; S.E.A.T.O. issue, 436; Bevanites on, 437; delegation to Russia and China, 443–8; considers Tribune attack on Deakin, 454; considers expulsion of Bevan, 468, 473, 475–6; votes 14 to 13 for stalling amendment, 476; second meeting, 479–80; Krushchev-Bulganin dinner, 505; Industry and Society, 557–9; pre-Conference meetings, 567–9; and the H-bomb and tests, 568; Bevan on, 592; meeting with T.U.C. General Council, 595–8; national campaign against H-bomb, 599; expulsion campaigns, 601–2; disarmament policy, 617; delegation to Soviet Union, 617–621; Jay's proposals for, 631; mentioned, 362, 370, 495, 513, 562, 580; see also Labour

Party Conferences, Treasurer of the Labour Party

National Health Service: plans for, 128; Bill introduced, 129–30; proposals for, 130–7; hospitals in, 131–5; general practitioners in, 135–6; health centres, 136; private practice and fee-paying hospital patients, 137; financial arrangements, 137–8; proposals to interested bodies, 139; stages of Bill, 145–8, 152–5, 156–8, 160; special debate on, 174–93; starting date, 5 July, 1948, 174–5, 191, 213, 237; run-up to starting date, 198; finances, 214; 'brain-child of Churchill', 214; Guillebaud Report, 215; Dr Lindsay's report, 216; Porritt Committee Report, 217–18; Churchill on, 242; huge success of and Supplementary Estimates, 252–6; and midwifery services, 253(n); proposals for prescription charges, 276, 289–90, 293–7; vote of censure in Supplementary Estimates, 291–2; proposals for teeth and spectacles charge, 319; Bevan's resignation speech, 336–338; in *One Way Only*, 346; Labour Party reasserts free principle, 383; Bevan speaks at conference, 409, 493; mentioned 502, 648

National Health Service Bill: introduced, 97, 129–30; first clause, 130; Second Reading, 145–8, 152, 157, 214; Committee Stage, 152–5, 156; Third Reading, 155, 156–8, 214; receives Royal Assent, 160; starting date, 5 July 1948, 174, 175, 191, 213; special debate, 174–93

National Health Service Bill, Amending Act discussed, 170,

184, 197, 199, 203, 206, 208, 210, 294

National Health Insurance, 106, 107, 132, 135, 144, 155, 174, 185, 492

A National Health Service, see Willink White Paper

National Institute of the Deaf, 239

National Insurance Act, 97, 103

National Union of Agricultural Workers, 475

National Union of Boot and Shoe Operatives, 495

National Union of General and Municipal Workers, 353, 437, 440, 475, 492(n), 510, 511(n), 512

National Union of Mineworkers, 353, 385(n), 437–8, 449, 479, 493, 509, 511(n)

National Union of Public Employees, 409

National Union of Quarrymen, 223

National Union of Railwaymen, 375, 511, 512, 572

National Union of Seamen, 476, 495

Nationalization, public ownership: 258–63, 265, 288, 391, 498, 587, 631, 639, 651; industrial assurance, 261–2, 266; Bevan's views on, 235, 238, 370–2, 501, 502, 560–1, 615, 643–4, 647; in *Industry and Society*, 557–9; Gaitskell's speech on Clause IV, 638–40; see also under Steel

Nazi-Soviet Pact, 619

Negotiating Committee (for National Health Service), 115, 123, 151, 156, 165, 166, 167–70, 179–180, 188, 208(n), 212

Neguib, General, 415–18

Nehru, Jawaharlal: on Korea, 303, 311, 406; famine in India, 346; Bevan visits, 394–6, 544–5; close friendship, 394–5; and

Tito, 407; Kashmir, 544–5; mentioned, 436

Nelson, Lord, 435

Nenni, Pietro, 536, 537(n), 616–17

New Republic, 435

New Statesman, 374, 391, 457, 467, 481–2, 581, 583

New Zealand, 623

News Chronicle, 189, 312(n), 320, 341(n), 349(n), 377, 431, 473, 533, 545

News of the World, 60, 561(n), 604(n), 631(n)

Nicolson, Harold, 61

Nietzsche, 46, 657

Noel-Baker, Philip, 465, 466(n), 499(n), 529(n), 555, 572

Norris, Arianwen (sister), 441, 627

Norris, Jack (brother-in-law), 655

Norris, Robert (nephew), 627

North Atlantic Treaty Organization, 305, 306, 307, 426, 457, 506, 529, 592, 593, 624

Norway, 234

Norwood Resolution, 569, 570, 572–7, 579(n), 583, 592, 599

Nuri-e-Said, 605

Nutting, Anthony, 531(n)

Nyasaland, 614, 621

O'Brien, Conor Cruise, 549(n)

O'Brien, Tom (Sir), 354, 366, 409

Observer, 194, 240

Ollenhauer, Erich, 448

One Way Only, 344–6, 349, 352, 539

Order 1305, 317, 320

Osborne, John, 599

The Other Animals, 239

Our First Duty – Peace, 354

Padley, Walter, 513

Paget, Reginald, 187

Pain, Peggy, 417(n)

Paine, Thomas, 17

Pakenham, Frank (Lord Longford). 324, 638, 640, 648

Pakistan, 394, 398, 546–7, 586

Palestine, 35, 89–90, 413, 419

Paling, Wilfrid, 385(n)

Pannell, Charles, 372–3, 511–14, 637, 640(n)

Pannikkar, Sarda K. M., 418

Parliamentary Labour Party: pre-1945, 20; sense of purpose, 40; suspends Standing Orders, 45; meeting after Gaitskell Budget, 327–8; meeting after Bevan's resignation, 340–1; on the Bevanites, 358, 385, 437; attitude to arms programme and Bevanite revolt, 363–6; reimposes Standing Orders, 365, 372, 375; votes to disband Bevanite group, 386; Mallalieu's *Tribune* article, 411–13; resolution against German rearmament, 427–8; German rearmament debate, 451; in angry temper, 453; arguments on high-level talks, 455–6; the H-bomb, 456, 550–1; expulsion meeting, 469–72; Attlee resigns, 494; his successor, 495–6; and the constituencies, 50; elections, 529; nuclear weapons argument, 598; Middle East crisis, 606; Bevan on, 623, 625, 627, 637; Jay's proposals for, 631; post-election discussions, 634–6; Standing Orders abolished, 635–636; ovation for Gaitskell, 637; mentioned, 224, 236, 249, 356, 364, 400, 488, 493, 499, 547, 639

Pannell Charles Stewart, 549

Partridge, Elisabeth, 545

Pascal, 591

Payne, Reginald T., 165(n)

Peake, Osbert, 292

Peking, 304, 306, 445

Pelling, Henry, 86(n)

People, 428

Persia, 344

Philippines, 314

Phillips, Morgan: against Morrison, 289; drafts election manifesto, 351; on Bevanites, 383; *Tribune* and N.E.C., 392–3; on German rearmament, 426(n); on delegation to Russia and China, 443; member of sub-committee, 477; on votes for Treasurership, 513; *Spectator* libel, 537–8; mentioned, 287, 289, 391(n), 567

Pigott, Alderman, 339

Pijade, Moshe, 347

Pineau, M., 530

Pitt, David, 572

Pitt, William, 28–9

Poland: Prudential investments, 261; Soviet thaw, 506; 'spring in October', 521–2, 565; Rapacki proposals, 406, 595; Karol's birthplace, 618

Porritt, Sir Arthur, 217–18

Port Said, 522, 532

Portal, Lord, 43, 67, 279

The Positive Outcome of Philosophy, 620

Poznan, 521

Prague, 229

Priestley, J. B., 599, 652

Proctor, Tom, 340–1

Prudential Assurance Company, 261

Quayle, Anthony, 298

Que'benno, Jean, 654

Quemoy and Matsu, 455, 608

Raglan, Lord, 242

Rainborough, Thomas, 228, 281

Rakosi, Matyas, 506

Rankovic, Aleksander, 347

Rapacki, Adam, 406, 595

Reading, Lord, 240

Rearmament, arms programme: 305, 307, 310, 312–13, 317, 319, 346, 347, 351, 362, 381, 424; Bevan's views on, 307, 329, 332, 341; in resignation speech, 334–338; Churchill's 'Bevan right by accident' speech, 354–6; Bevan's disagreement with Attlee, 376–7

Regional Hospital Boards, 132, 134, 153, 212

Remploy factories, 489

Rent Act, 69

Resignation: not contemplated by Bevan over Loan Agreement, 58; contemplated and rejected over Palestine, 89; and housing acts, 95; Bevan threatens it if steel nationalization abandoned, 224–225; he discusses the possibility, 266–7; threatens over health charges, 294, 296, 317, 322–30; resigns, 331–4; reasons for, 341–342; aftermath, 346–7, 351

Restrictive Practices Commission, 262

Reuter, Ernst, 427

Reynolds News, 391, 398, 401

Rhydderch, D., 512–14

Ribar, Ivan, 347

Richardson, Bill, 398

Robens, Alfred (Lord), 325, 466(n), 495, 499(n), 510, 529 and (n)

Roberts, Bryn, 409

Roberts, Goronwy, 343

Robinson, Kenneth, 456

Rodgers, W. T., 438(n), 632(n)

Rodo, José, 47, 585, 591, 654, 657, 658

Rogers, Dr Talbot, 208(n), 212

Rogov, A. A., 227(n)

Rome, 536–7

Rosebery, Lord, 350

Ross, George W., 221(n)

Rossini, 537

Royal College of Obstetricians, 114, 115(n), 123, 124, 147, 156, 158, 163–5, 199, 217

Royal College of Physicians, 114, 115(n), 123, 124, 137, 141, 147, 156, 159, 160, 163–5, 199, 200, 201, 202, 217

Royal College of Surgeons, 114, 115(n), 123, 137, 147, 156, 160, 163–5, 165(n), 217

Royal Free Hospital, 652, 655

Royal Medico-Psychological Association, 118

Royal Scottish Medical Corporation, 115(n)

Royal Society of Medicine, 208(n), 212(n)

Rumania, 534

Russell, Bertrand, 599

Sabatino, Richard A., 95(n)

St Pancras Town Hall meeting, 600, 602

Salem, Major Salah, 416

Salisbury, Lord, 401–2

Samuel, Howard, 580, 602

Sandys, Duncan, 43

Saragat, Signor, 536

Saunders, Sir Alan, 42

Saudi Arabia, 565

Scanlon, Hugh, 454(n)

Schacht, Dr, 55

Schumacher, Dr Kurt, 233

The Scotsman, 142(n)

Shadow Cabinet: attacks Churchill's pro-American policy, 361; on the Tory Defence White Paper, 362–4; on Bevanite revolt, 365; elections for, 386–7, 529; Bevan's position in, 388, 425; discusses high-level talks, 400–1; Mallalieu's *Tribune* article, 411–412; pro-E.D.C. resolution, 427; Bevan resigns from, 431–3; Wilson replaces him, 433–5; turns down Bevan's proposal for high-level talks, 455; members absent from H-bomb debate, 459; recommends withdrawal of

Whip on abstentions, 465–6, 467, 470; Bevan's views on, 478, 592; Bevan elected to, 499; on Suez, 520; and the H-bomb, 551, 598; on disarmament, 555; on Middle East crisis, 606; Bevan heads poll, 610; accepts abolition of Standing Orders, 636; mentioned, 482, 488

Shawcross, Hartley (Lord), 19, 318(n), 342, 465, 475

Shepherd, Lord, 466(n)

Shinwell, Emanuel (Lord): and Attlee, 27; and Bevin, 31(n); and Bevan, 39–40, 328; on Loan Agreement, 52–3, 55; 1947 fuel crisis, 88; 'tinker's cuss', 192; and Dalton, 226; on Soviet military strength, 305; and election announcement, 349; loses seat on Executive, 352; on withdrawal of British troops from Egypt, 415; supports Morrison for leader, 496; mentioned, 277, 363, 374, 466(n), 487

Shore, Peter, 227(n), 557

Sieff, Israel and Becky, 419

Silkin, John, 636(n)

Silkin, Lewis, 77

Silverman, Sydney: Suez crisis, 524; on the H-bomb, 567–70; mentioned, 270

Simon, Sir John, 213, 246

Skidelsky, Robert, 414(n)

Smillie, Bob, 243

Smith, Norman, 386

Snowden, Philip, 331, 340

Socialist Commentary, 436

Socialist International, 536, 563, 568, 570, 573, 605

Socialist Medical Association, 107, 114, 133, 149, 293

Society of Apothecaries, 115(n)

Society of Medical Officers of Health, 115(n), 158

Soper, Donald (Lord), 486, 657

Soskice, Sir Frank, 466, 475, 529(n)

South East Asia, 430; South East Asia Treaty Organization, 430–3, 435, 529, 582

South Wales, 47, 99, 107, 246, 262, 268, 440, 481, 593

South Wales Voice, 333

Souttar, Henry, 144, 161

Soviet Union: Bevin's attitude to, 32; Bevan's attitude to, 265, 284–285, 306–7, 315–16, 395, 404–5, 585; steel production in, 228, 230, 307; German problem, 229–231, 426–7, 556; and Korea, 303, 305; military strength, 305, 306, 345, 424–5; and Yugoslavia, 311; Stalin's death – West's reactions, 399–403; Labour Party delegation, 443–6; Summit meeting proposals, 459–61; Twentieth Congress and thaw, 504; and the Middle East, 507, 540, 542–544, 546, 607; and Hungary, 521–2, 525, 526, 527, 528, 529, 534, 543; and the H-bomb, 550, 552, 560, 587(n), 596–7, 624; and disarmament 555–6, 592; Bevan-Khrushchev discussions, 563–6; launches sputnik, 579, 580, 587; Labour delegation to, 617–21, 622; mentioned, 571, 575, 576, 601, 646, 649

Spectator, 288(n), 384, 480, 537–8

Spens, Sir William, 159

Sputnik, 579, 587–8, 591

Squatters, 82–3

Stalin, Joseph, 33, 303, 306, 346, 444, 522; death of, 398, 402(n); and Bevan's reactions, 398, 399–400; Khrushchev's denunciation of, 504

Standing Orders, of the P.L.P.: suspended in 1945, 45; reinposition and use, 365, 372, 375, 428, 466, 470, 484, 503, 510; abolished, 635–6

Stanley, Oliver, 270

Steel: industry, 220–3; Bevan on, 228, 236, 279; nationalization, 219, 221, 223, 224–5, 227, 260; Bevan's commitment to, 219, 223–4, 227–8, 586; Khrushchev on, 563; Tories denationalize, 392; Labour's renationalization pledge, 407; Bill, 221–2, 226–7, 265, 266–7, 318

Stendhal, 298, 537, 617

Stevenson, Adlai, 590

Stewart, Michael, 325, 456

Stockwood, Mervyn, 410, 657, 658

Stokes, R. R., 326, 378, 496, 499(n)

Stopford, Sir Robert, 435

Strabolgi, Lord, 386

Strachey, John: and Attlee, 27; on Bevan and Gaitskell, 295; on possibility of war, 316; considers resigning, 321; against Bevan's resignation, 329; mediatory amendment, 365; review of *In Place of Fear*, 368; on *Tribune*, 394; Defence debate, 456, 458; and the H-bomb, 572, 598; mentioned, 386

Strauss, George, 38, 226, 365, 386

Suez, Suez Canal, 516, 518–36, 538–45, 549, 552(n), 562, 566(n), 581, 587, 613–4, 621, 626

Summerskill, Edith: in favour of teeth and spectacles charges, 319; attacks *Tribune* and fellow-travellers, 393; on delegation to Russia and China, 443, 445, 617; in favour of withdrawal of Whip, 466; chairman of N.E.C. for expulsion meetings, 475–7, 480; on Shadow Cabinet, 499(n), 529(n); mentioned, 487

Sunday Chronicle, 142(n)

Sunday Dispatch, 240

Sunday Express, 359, 487, 536(n)

Sunday Pictorial, 378, 382, 481

Sunday Times, 60, 240; *Weekly Review*, 295(n)

Supply, Ministry of, 222, 327(n)

Sutherland, Graham, 460(n), 656

Swaffer, Hamer, 61

Swift, Jonathan, 299

Swinburne, Algernon, 657

Swingler, Stephen, 90(n), 465

Syria, 564, 565

Taj Mahal, 396, 548

Tanner, Jack, 354, 438

Tawney, R. H., 638

Teheran, 546

Tel Aviv, 522, 546

Tewson, Vincent, 392

Thailand, 314

This I Believe (B.B.C. programme), 389–90

Thomas, Hugh, 531(n)

Thorneycroft, Peter, 253(n)

Tied cottages, 91, 236

Tiffin, Jock, 474, 476, 479

Tillett, Ben, 454(n)

The Times, 94, 143, 149, 162, 170, 173, 176, 200, 201, 211, 227, 239, 291, 339, 362(n), 377, 383(n), 443(n), 448(n), 449, 467, 472, 514, 519, 600(n), 611

Times Literary Supplement, 531(n)

Times of India, 545

Tito, President: Bevan's visit to, 347–8; subject of letter to Mathai, 406–7; correspondence with Bevan about Djilas and Dedijer, 470–3; mentioned, 229, 306, 311, 539

Tokyo, 447(n)

Tolpuddle martyrs, 264

Tomlinson, George, 323

Town and Country Planning, Ministry of, 77

Trades Union Congress, General Council: on nationalization, 372, 381, 407; on a free N.H.S., 381; takes *Tribune* issue to the N.E.C.,

392–4, 454; Right-wing bias, 409; on British Guiana, 413; views on insurance scheme, 493; joint meetings with N.E.C., 595; mentioned, 495

Trafalgar Square meetings: Suez, 525; H-bomb, 566, 599, 600

Transjordan, 418

Transport and General Workers Union, 353, 407, 437, 440, 453, 454, 474, 479, 492(n), 511(n), 514–15, 572, 577

Transport House, 73, 277–8, 287, 352, 390, 475, 480, 485, 567

Transport Salaried Staffs Association, 475

Treasury, 50, 53, 54, 75–6, 81, 87(n), 91, 92, 94, 95, 97, 137–8, 253, 265–6, 269, 275, 290, 293, 308, 317, 320, 322, 336, 347, 356, 358, 490, 493

Treatise on the Gods, 653

Tredegar, 20, 106, 251, 268, 276, 280, 329, 366, 384(n), 387, 396, 409, 438, 441, 582, 621, 627, 655, 656–7; Tredegar Iron and Coal Company, 69; Tredegar Workmen's Institute, 508(n), 620

Trevelyan, Sir Charles, 410

Tribune: on the Civil Service, 275; on Gaitskell's Budget, 331, 340, 342; on rearmament figures, 355, 356; and Deakin, 359, 381, 454; and Defence White Paper, 363; conference rallies, 382, 409, 449–450, 492, 514, 570–1, 610–11; Gaitskell on, 383, 384; and the T.U.C., 392, 454; reported to N.E.C., 392–4, 454; Mallalieu's article, 411–13; Bevan's syndicated articles, 417; and the N.E.C., 428–9; its 'organization', 478; and the H-bomb, 487; mass meetings, 500, 502; on Suez crisis, 519; on *Industry and Society*, 557–9, 561; during 1957

Conference, 567, 572; and after Bevan's speech, 579–80, 583, 600, 602–3; attacks the leadership, 609; Board meeting, 651–2; Brains Trusts, 385, 390, 393–4, 478; editorial meetings, 390, 562; pamphlets, *One Way Only*, 344–6, 349, 352; *Going Our Way?*, 349, 352, 354; mentioned, 270(n), 444(n), 448(n), 482, 511(n), 535, 565, 567, 650

Bevan's articles quoted: 18, 284–286, 317(n), 371, 385, 426, 445, 447, 461(n), 490, 497, 503, 504, 519, 521, 528, 529, 554, 556, 565, 591, 593, 608, 615, 650; 'In Place of the Cold War' series, 404–6

Trotsky, Leon, 48–9, 388

Truman, President Harry: cancels Land-Lease, 52–3, 55; on American demobilization, 70; opposes North Koreans, 302; Attlee's visit on Korea, 309–10; sacks MacArthur, 327; on German rearmament, 403

Turkey, 89, 564, 565

Union of Post Office Workers, 354

Union of Shop, Distributive and Allied Workers, 375, 381, 510, 511, 512, 513

United Nations, 302, 303, 304, 311, 313–14, 395, 429, 430, 520, 522, 523, 527, 528, 530, 539, 540, 541, 543, 544, 575, 589, 606, 608

United States of America: postwar isolationism, 34; Lend-Lease Agreement, 50–1; cancelled, 52; Loan Agreement negotiations, 52–5; Marshall Aid, 56, 93; steel consumption, 220; and the Soviet Union, 229–31, 424–5; and Germany, 231–2; attacks Socialist Britain, 268–9; and Korea, 301–4, 308–10; rearmament programme, 308, 312; 'brand China' demand, 313–14; and Europe, 345; Churchill and, 361–2; view of Bevanism, 373; Bevan's attitude to, 395, 585, 615, 616; and S.E.A.T.O., 430, 432; and Summit meeting, 459, 589; and the Middle East, 507; and Suez, 518, 522, 523, 526, 527; Eisenhower doctrine, 538–539; and Pakistan, 547; and the H-bomb, 550, 552, 568, 578(n); Khrushchev on, 564–5; reaction to Russian sputnik, 579, 587–8, 589–90, 591; invades Lebanon, 605–6; and the Far East, 608–9; mentioned, 24, 571, 575, 576, 593, 656

The Unperfect Society, 257, 283, 423

Vaihinger, H., 508(n)

Veblen, Thorsten, 558

Venice, 536, 537

'Vermin' speech and repercussions, 238–44, 249–50, 252, 278, 280, 287, 333, 436, 485–6

Viant, Sam, 496

Vicky, 377, 650

Victory for Socialism, 598

Da Vinci, Leonardo, 100

Vlahovic, Veljki, 422

Vyshinsky, Andrei, 444

Wadsworth, A. P., 384(n)

Walker-Smith, Derek, 84

Wand, Dr Solomon, 142, 168

Warburg, James P., 345(n)

Warsaw, 521, 563, 620, 621

Warsaw Pact, 529, 624

Washington, George, 545, 589

Watson, Sam; against Morrison, 289; on Bevan's resignation, 339; drafts election manifesto, 351; miners' vote for Treasurer, 438–9; in favour of expulsion,

476; refuses Treasurership nomination, 509–10; N.E.C. discussions on H-bomb debate, 567, 569, 570; his part in Bevan's H-bomb stand, 581

Waunpound, 280, 658–9

Webb, Maurice, 342

Webb, Sidney and Beatrice, 115

Webbe, Sir Harold, 133, 134

Webb-Johnson, Sir Alfred (Lord), 123–4, 156, 161, 163–5, 169, 199, 201, 202

Wedgwood Benn, Anthony, 572

Wells, H. G., 48, 298

Western Mail, 278, 481, 538(n)

Western Morning News, 278

Westminster Abbey, 658

White, Eirene (Lady), 476

Whiteley, William, 330, 363, 466(n)

Wigg, George, 90(n), 457, 473(n), 598

Wilde, Oscar, 37, 123

Wilkinson, Ellen, 39

Williams, Francis (Lord Francis-Williams), 32(n), 53(n), 58(n), 71(n), 92(n), 428–9

Williams, Tom, 313(n), 496

Williamson, Tom (Lord); on Bevan and Bevanites, 353, 366, 383, 468, 471; Bevan attacks, 393; Treasurership issue, 408, 510, 511; power over his union, 437; supports Gaitskell for Treasurer, 438, 492(n); mentioned, 392

Willink, Henry (Lord): speaks on housing, 84; Minister of Health, 110; produces White Paper, *A National Health Service*, 110–12; discussions with B.M.A., 112, 118; on nationalization of hospitals, 133; speaks in Second Reading debate, 146–8; Committee Stage, 152; and the B.M.A., 178, 179; doctors' appeal machinery, 185; *B.M.J.*'s comment on, 207–58; Seymour

Cocks's quip, 213; reviews Porritt Committee Report, 218

Willink White Paper: proposals and implications, 110–14; in Bevan's view unworkable, 118, 128; Morrison's comment, 129, 148; ambiguities, 130, 131, 132, 136; general practitioners and health centres, 136; Tories accuse Bevan of abandoning it, 147; Bevan's break with, over hospitals, 150, 153

Willis, Robert, 354

Wilmot, John, 222, 226

Wilson, Harold: asks about Morrison, 63; speaks in devaluation debate, 270; acts as go-between, 294; on Gaitskell, 294–5; opposes rearmament programme, 313, 317; opposes teeth and spectacles charges, 319; Bevan's resignation threat, 320; Gaitskell on, 321; visits Attlee in hospital, 323, 324; Bevan's resignation and his own, 331; 1951 conference vote, 352; first chairman of Bevanites, 358; after Defence White Paper vote, 365; wins N.E.C. place, 380; stands for Shadow Cabinet, 387, 411; at Crossman lunches, 390; on nationalization, 391; resolution against German rearmament, 427–8; takes Bevan's place on Shadow Cabinet, 433–5; *Tribune*-Deakin dispute, 454; votes with majority, 464; N.E.C. meeting on expulsion, 480; report on Party organization, 492; Shadow Cabinet, 499(n), 529(n); refuses nomination for Treasurership, 510; on *Industry and Society*, 558; Standing Orders, 636(n); mentioned, 466(n)

Winterton, Lord, 64

Women's Public Health Officers' Association, 198

Woolton, Lord, 94, 238, 242, 250

Works, Ministry of, 43–4, 67, 72–3

Wrigley, Sir John, 41, 43, 76, 95–6

Wyatt, Woodrow, 90(n), 366(n), 487

XYZ Club, 359, 390

Yorkshire Miners' Union, 509, 512

Younger, Kenneth, 365, 529(n)

Yugoslavia: Bevan's visit to, 347–8; and India, 406–7; Djilas and Dedijer, 420–3; mentioned, 229, 306, 311, 345, 368, 424

Zahler, Trudy, 655

Zhukov, Marshal, 588, 590